Proceedings of the 2009 International Conference on

Computer and Network Technology

ICCNT 2009

Proceedings of the 2009 International Conference on

Computer and Network Technology

Chennai, India 24 – 26 July 2009

ICCNT 2009

editors

V. Mahadevan

Swinburne University of Technology, Australia

J. Zhou

Sichuan University, China

World Scientific

NEW JERSEY • LONDON • SINGAPORE • BEIJING • SHANGHAI • HONG KONG • TAIPEI • CHENNAI

Published by

World Scientific Publishing Co. Pte. Ltd.
5 Toh Tuck Link, Singapore 596224
USA office: 27 Warren Street, Suite 401-402, Hackensack, NJ 07601
UK office: 57 Shelton Street, Covent Garden, London WC2H 9HE

British Library Cataloguing-in-Publication Data
A catalogue record for this book is available from the British Library.

Proceedings of the 2009 International Conference on
COMPUTER AND NETWORK TECHNOLOGY (ICCNT 2009)

ISBN-13 978-981-4289-67-2 (pbk)
ISBN-10 981-4289-67-1 (pbk)

Printed in Singapore by World Scientific Printers

IACSIT
WWW.IACSIT.ORG

Honor Chairs

Prof. Ce Zhu, Nanyang Technological University, Singapore

Prof. Kaninda Musumbu, LaBRI – Université Bordeaux 1, France

HOD, Prof. B. B. Biswal, National Institute of Technology, India

Conference General Chairs

Prof. Venkatesh Mahadevan, Swinburne University of Technology, Australia

Dr. Jianhong Zhou, Sichuan University, China

Program Committee Chairs

Dr. Srinivasan Alavandar, Indian Institute of Technology, India

Dr. K. S. Cheung, University of Hong Kong, Hong Kong

Prof. Ashwani Kush, IIT Kanpur and Kurukshetra University, India

Publication Chairs

Dr. Xiaoxiao Zhou, Nanyang Technological University, Singapore

HOD, Prof. Sekhar Ranjan Bhadra Chaudhuri, Bengal Engineering & Science University, India

Dean, Prof. Shishir K. Shandilya, Rukmani Devi Institute of Science and Technology, India

Dr. Yi Xie, Cagayan State University, Philippines

Publicity Chairs

Dean, Prof. G. Selvakumar, School of Electrical Sciences, V.M.K.V. Engineering College, India

Prof. Xuesong Zhang, Claremont Graduate University, USA

Dr. Sun Yung-Chien, McGill University, Canada

Technical Committee

Preface

Dear Distinguished Delegates and Guests,

The Organizing Committee of ICCNT 2009 warmly welcomes you to the 2009 International Conference on Computer and Network Technology (ICCNT 2009), held on July 24–26, 2009 in Chennai, India. ICCNT 2009 is sponsored by International Association of Computer Science and Information Technology (IACSIT), and the conference proceedings are published by World Scientific Publishing.

If you have attended the conferences sponsored by IACSIT before, you should know that the conferences together report the results of research efforts in a broad range of computer science and information technology. The conference is aimed at discussing with all of you the wide range of problems encountered in present and future high technologies. The ICCNT 2009 is organized to gather members of our international community of Computer and Network Technology scientists so that researchers from around the world can present their leading-edge work, expanding our community's knowledge and insight into the significant challenges currently being addressed in that research. The conference Program Committee is itself quite diverse and truly international, with membership from the Americas, Europe, Asia, Africa and Oceania.

This proceeding records the fully refereed papers presented at the conference. The main conference themes and tracks are Computer and Network Technology. The conference aims to bring together researchers, scientists, engineers, and practitioners to exchange and share their experiences, new ideas, and research results about all aspects of the main conference themes and tracks and discuss the practical challenges encountered and the solutions adopted. The main goal of the event is to provide international scientific forums for exchange of new ideas in a number of fields that interact in-depth through discussions with their peers from around the world. Both inward research; core areas of Computer and Network Technology and outward research; multi-disciplinary, inter-disciplinary, and applications will be covered during the event.

The conference has solicited and gathered technical research submissions related to all aspects of major conference themes and tracks. All the submitted papers in the proceeding have been peer reviewed by the reviewers drawn from the scientific committee, external reviewers and editorial board depending on the subject matter of the paper. Reviewing and initial selection were undertaken electronically. After the rigorous peer-review process, the submitted papers were selected on the basis of originality, significance, and clarity for the purpose of the conference. The selected papers and additional late-breaking contributions to be presented as lectures will make an exciting technical program. The conference program is extremely rich, featuring high-impact presentations.

The high quality of the program — guaranteed by the presence of an unparalleled number of internationally recognized top experts — can be assessed when reading the contents of the program. The conference will therefore be a unique event, where attendees will be able to appreciate the latest results in their field of expertise, and to acquire additional knowledge in other fields. Attendees arriving as specialist experts will thus have the opportunity to leave the conference as enriched scientists, be they from academia or industry. The program has been structured to favor interactions among attendees coming from many diverse horizons, scientifically, geographically, from academia and from industry. Included in this will to favor interactions are social events at prestigious sites.

We would like to thank the program chairs, organization staff, and the members of the program committees for their work. Thanks also go to the editors of World Scientific Publishing, for their wonderful editorial service to this proceeding.

We are grateful to all those who have contributed to the success of ICCNT 2009. We hope that all participants and other interested readers benefit scientifically from the proceedings and also find it stimulating in the process. Finally, we would like to wish you success in your technical presentations and social networking.

We hope you have a unique, rewarding and enjoyable week at ICCNT 2009 in Chennai, India.

With our warmest regards,

ICCNT 2009 Organizing Committees
24–26 July 2009 in Chennai, India

Contents

Session 3

Session 4

Session 5

Session 6

Session 7

Session 8

Session 1

ANALYSIS OF A MATHEMATICAL MODEL FOR WORM VIRUS PROPAGATION

WANG SHAO-JIE

Department of Mathematics, Shijiazhuang Mechanical Engineering College
Shijiazhuang 050003, China

CHEN LIANG

Department of Science and Research, Shijiazhuang Mechanical Engineering College
Shijiazhuang 050003, China

LIU QI-MING

Department of Mathematics, Shijiazhuang Mechanical Engineering College
Shijiazhuang 050003, China

In recent years, the two-factor model has been improved in many papers. In this paper, we consider two new factors and build a new consider SIQR model for Internet worm virus propagation. By using theory of differential equations, the dynamical property of the model is analyzed and the regularity of Internet worm virus propagation is gained. In the end, the numerical simulation is presented.

1. Introduction

With the popularity of the network, the state of information security is subjected to unprecedented threats .Almost all countries have taken measures to protect their own information security. Recently, computer worms remain a significant threat to networks. Computer viruses have caused millions of dollars of damage and untold aggravation. It is a focus for the scholars to discuss how worms spread, and how we can monitor and defend against the propagation of worms effectively. Many people have studied the computer virus [1-3] by using differential theory. To understand the characteristics of the spread of Code Red worm, Zoo C C Builds a Two-factor model [4].But this model has not considered two things: (1) Because some users can reinstall their computer system for some especial reasons, the removed hosts can become the susceptible hosts. (2) Lacking the network knowledge, some computer users have not known how can protect their computers against worms. But if many users around them have taken measures to protect their hosts before being infected, they can study from them. So the number of the hosts which is removed from to is not only related to the number of and but also related to the number of. We will consider the two probabilities in this paper and build an improved Two-factor model. By using the theory of differential equations, the stability of equilibrium point is analyzed and the regularity of internet worm virus propagation is gained. By using MATLAB, the numerical simulation is presented.

2. Mathematical Modeling

The early stage of the outbreak of the worm, every system in the Internet is susceptible to the outbreak if they posses exploitable vulnerability, and network worms propagates at a startling speed. We let $S(t)$ is the number of susceptible hosts at time t, $I(t)$ is the number of infected hosts at time t and β is the initial infection rate. So the differential equation model is

$$\begin{cases} \dfrac{dI}{dt} = \beta I \\ S + I = N \end{cases} \tag{1}$$

Theorem 1. The system (1) has a unique globally asymptotically stable equilibrium $(0, N)$.

From Theorem 1, we can get that $I(t)$ must satisfy $\lim_{t\to\infty} I(t) = N$. But in fact hardly any worm can infect all the hosts. Thus the system (1) can not fit the worm propagation in the later. In order to describe the behavior of worm propagation in the later, we give some appropriate assumptions as follows:

(1) $R(t)$ is the number of removed hosts from infected hosts at time t., and $Q(t)$ is the number of removed hosts from susceptible hosts at time t.

(2)Let $\mu > 0, k > 0, \lambda > 0$ denote removal rate from $S(t)$ to $Q(t)$, from $Q(t)$ and $R(t)$ to $S(t)$ and from $I(t)$ to $R(t)$ respectively.

(3)The exponent $\theta > 1$ is used to adjust the infection rate sensitivity to the number of infectious hosts.

(4)The number of the hosts which is removed from $S(t)$ to $Q(t)$ is not only related to the number of $I(t)$ and $R(t)$ but also related to the number of $Q(t)$.Because the more the hosts have taken action and their computers have been immune from the worm, the more the rest hosts can get the technique to protect their computers .In the same time this can build up user' confidence to immune their computers. So the number of the hosts which are removed from $S(t)$ to $Q(t)$ can be $\mu S(I+R+Q)$

Based on the above hypotheses, we now propose the following differential equation model:

$$\begin{cases} \frac{dS}{dt} = -\beta\,(1-\frac{I}{N})^{\theta} SI - \mu S(I+R+Q) + k(R+Q) \\ \frac{dI}{dt} = \beta\,(1-\frac{I}{N})^{\theta} SI - \lambda I \\ \frac{dR}{dt} = \lambda I - kR \\ \frac{dQ}{dt} = \mu S(I+R+Q) - kQ \end{cases} \qquad (2)$$

Theorem 2 Given system (2),

(1) If $R_1 \le 1$, the equilibrium $P_0(N,0,0,0)$ of system (2) is globally asymptotically stable.

(2) If $R_1 > 1$, the equilibrium $P_0(N,0,0,0)$ of system is unstable, and there exists positive equilibrium $P_1(S^*,I^*,R^*,Q^*)$ of system (2), which is local asymptotically stable provided that $\beta\theta N > (\theta+1)(k+\lambda)$. On this basis, the equilibrium $P_1(S^*,I^*,R^*,Q^*)$ is global asymptotically stable if satisfies $\mu N < k$ .Where $R_1 = \beta N/\lambda$, I^* is a unique positive solution of the equation

$$\mu\lambda N - k\beta\lambda = (k\beta N - k\beta I - \lambda\beta I)\beta(1-\frac{I}{N})^{\theta} + \frac{\mu\lambda^2}{\beta(1-\frac{I}{N})^{\theta}}$$

Proof: It is obvious that there always exists equilibrium $P_0(N,0,0,0)$ of system (2), and there may be is a possible equilibriums $P_1(S^*,I^*,R^*,Q^*)$ of system (2) in the non-negative cone $T=\{(S,I,R,Q)\in R_+^4 : S+I+R+Q\le N\}$ with $R^* = \frac{\lambda}{k} I^*$ and $S^* = \frac{\lambda}{\beta(1-\frac{I^*}{N})^{\theta}}$. Let

$$F(I) = \mu\lambda N - k\beta\lambda,$$

$$G(I) = (k\beta N - k\beta I - \lambda\beta I)\beta(1-\frac{I}{N})^{\theta} + \frac{\mu\lambda^2}{\beta(1-\frac{I}{N})^{\theta}},$$

we can get that

$$G'(I) = \beta(1-\frac{I}{N})^{\theta-1}\left[\frac{(\theta+1)I\beta}{N}(k+\lambda) - (\theta k + k + \lambda)\beta\right]$$

$G(0) = k\beta^2 N + \frac{\mu\lambda^2}{\beta}$ and $G(N) = +\infty$ .If $R_1 > 1$, together with $\mu\lambda N - k\beta\lambda > k\beta^2 N + \frac{\mu\lambda^2}{\beta}$, leads to $F(0) > G(0)$, consequently, there is a unique positive point of intersection in the curves $F(I)$ and $G(I)$, which implies that the equation $\mu\lambda N - k\beta\lambda = (k\beta N - k\beta I - \lambda\beta I)\beta(1-\frac{I}{N})^{\theta} + \frac{\mu\lambda^2}{\beta(1-\frac{I}{N})^{\theta}}$ has unique positive solution . So we can get equilibrium $P_1(S^*,I^*,R^*,Q^*)$.

(I)Let $E = R+Q$, then $S = N - I - E$, the system (2) can be reduced to

$$\begin{cases} \frac{dI}{dt} = \beta\,(1-\frac{I}{N})^{\theta}(N-I-E)I - \lambda I, \\ \frac{dE}{dt} = \mu(N-I-E)(I+E) + \lambda I - kE. \end{cases} \qquad (3)$$

Constructing Lyapunov functional $V(I,R,Q) = I$ and calculating the derivative of V along the system (3), we can obtain

$$\left.\frac{dV}{dt}\right|_{(3)} = [\beta(1-\frac{I}{N})^{\theta} S - \lambda]I \le [\beta(1-\frac{I}{N})^{\theta}(N-I) - \lambda]I$$

$$\le [\beta N - \lambda - \beta I]I \le -\beta I^2 \le 0$$

Hence we can get $T = \{(I,R,Q)\in D \,|\, V'(t) = 0\} = \{I = 0\}$. Thus the equilibrium P_0 is globally asymptotically stable by the LaSalle invariant principle and the theory of the limitation.

(II) The Jacobi matrix of the system (3) about (0,0) is given by

$$J_0 = \begin{pmatrix} \beta N - \lambda & 0 \\ \mu N + \lambda & \mu N - k \end{pmatrix}.$$

Then the characteristic equation of liberalized equations corresponding to system read $(r+\lambda-\beta N)(r+k-\mu N)=0$. If $R_1>1$, the characteristic root $r=\beta N-\lambda>0$, equilibrium $(0,0)$ is not stable.

(III)The Jacobi Matrix of the system (3) about $P_1(I^*,E^*)$ is given by

$$J_1=\begin{pmatrix}-a_1-a_2 & -a_2\\ a_3+\lambda & a_3-k\end{pmatrix}$$

Where

$$a_1=\frac{\lambda\theta I^*}{N-I^*},$$

$$a_2=\frac{\lambda I^*}{N-I^*-E^*},$$

$$a_3=\mu\left(N-2I^*-2E^*\right).$$

If $\beta\theta N>(\theta+1)(k+\lambda)$, we can get

$p=a_1+a_2-a_3+k>0$,

$q=|J_1|=ka_1+ka_2-a_3+\theta a_2+\lambda a_2>0$

Thus the equilibrium P_1 is locally asymptotically stable. Let $D(I,E)=\frac{1}{I}$. Note that $\frac{\partial(PD)}{\partial I}+\frac{\partial(QD)}{\partial E}<0$ dues to $\mu N<k$. The Bendixson-Dulac criterion holds and thus the equilibrium (I^*,E^*) of system (3) is globally asymptotically stable.

3. Simulation

(1) Let $N=500000, I_0=100, \beta=0.00002$, $\theta=2$, $k=0.2, \mu=0.0000003, \lambda=0.2$, where $R_1>1$. We can see the result in Fig. 1..

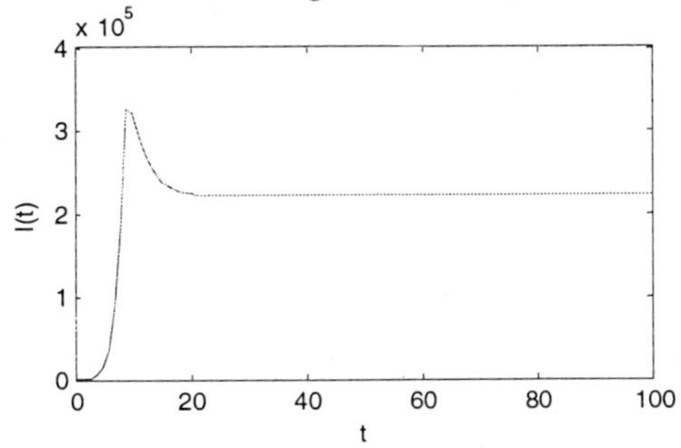

Fig.1. the number of infected when $R_1>1$

From our recorded data in Fig.1, we know that the worms have spread freely at the early stages of a worm incident, so the worm was spreading very fast. When the users have woken up to the harm of the worm and effective countermeasures have been taken, the number of infected hosts reduces. Due to $R_1>1$, the number of infected hosts $I(t)$ tends to a certain value.

(2) Let $N=500000, I_0=100, \beta=0.00002$, $\theta=2, k=0.2, \mu=0.0003, \lambda=0.2$, and we have $R_1<1$. The result of numerical simulation is presented in Fig. 2.

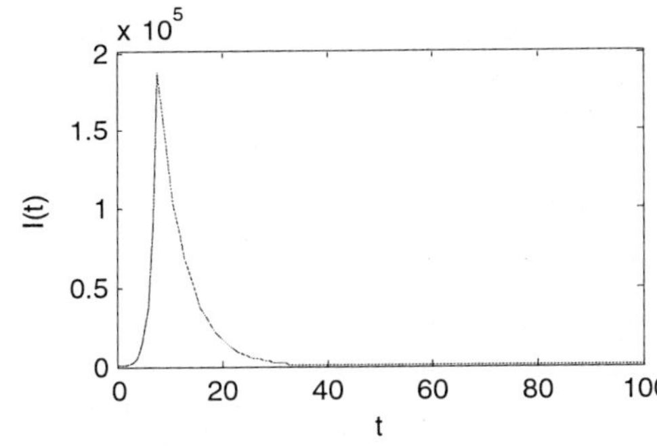

Fig.2. the number of infected when $R_1<1$

From Fig.2, we can see that the worm will eventually disappear if $R_1<1$, This is in line with the conclusions of Theorem 2.

(3) Let $N=500000, I_0=100, \beta=0.000002$, $\theta=2$, $k=0.2, \mu=0.0000003, \lambda=0.2$, let us see the result in Fig. 3.

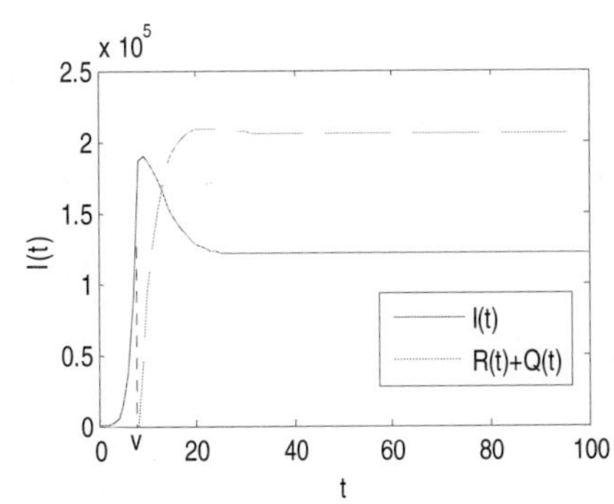

Fig.3. Influence of the number of infected hosts when β is Changed

(4) Let $N=500000, I_0=100, \beta=0.000002$, $\theta=2$, $k=0.6, \mu=0.0000003, \lambda=0.5$, let us see the result in Fig. 4.

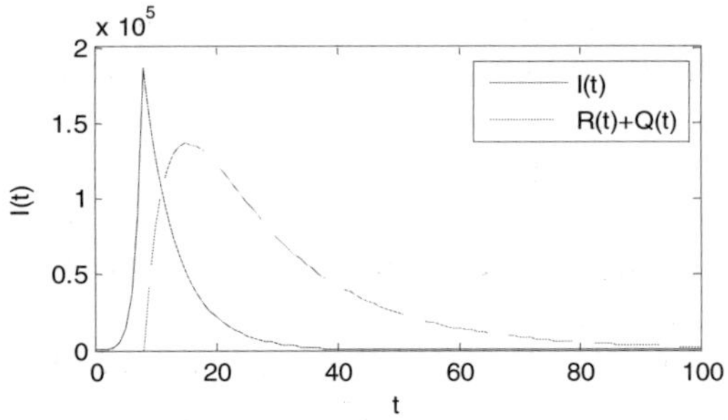

Fig.4. I(t) and E(t) when $R_1 < 1$

We describe I(t) and E(t)when $R_1 > 1$ and $R_1 < 1$ respectively in figure 3 and 4, and simulation results illustrates the theorem is correct.

4. Conclusion

In this paper, we build an improved Two-Factor model. By analyzing the model, we get the conditions for the disappearance of the worm. We can find that if the sample population N is certain, the disappearance of the worm is closely related to β and λ. According to Theorem 2, it is necessary to take some effective measures to reduce β and to increase λ. Thus we can provide some theoretical basis to prevention and treatment of worms.

References

1. J. O. Kephart. S. R. White. Directed Graph epidemiological Model of Computer Viruses [A] .Proc. of the 1991 IEEE Symposium on security and Privacy [C]. 1991:343~359.
2. Wang Y, Wang CX. Modeling the effects of timing parameters on virus propagation [EB/OL]. http://xys.ccert.edu.cn/reference/Worms/Worm2003/p61-wang.pdf.
3. Jonghyun Kim, Radhakrishnan S., Dhall S.K.. Measurement and analysis of worm propagation on Internet network topology [C] .13th International Conference on Computer Communications and Networks, 2004:495~500.
4. Zou CC, Gong W, Towsley D. Code Red worm propagation modeling and analysis. In: Proc. Of the 9th ACM Symp. on Computer and Communication Security. Washington, 2002. 138-147.

SABAD: SELF ASSURED BLACK-HOLE ATTACK DETECTION ON AODV PROTOCOL IN MANET

KUMAR SIDHARTH CHOUDHARY

ABV-Indian Institute of Information Technology and Management Gwalior, India
Email: sidharth@iiitm.ac.in

SOMANATH TRIPATHY

Indian Institute of Technology Patna, India
Email: som@.iitp.ac.in

KARM VEER ARYA

ABV-Indian Institute of Information Technology and Management Gwalior, India
Email: kvarya@iiitm.ac.in

Designing of a secure routing protocol is a challenging issue in mobile ad-hoc network (MANET) because of the lack of trusted centralized authority, easy eavesdropping, dynamic network topology and limited resources. The false alarm raised during malicious node detection prevents the genuine nodes, from their normal activities. If an adversary could succeed on generating false alarm and therefore isolates a number of nodes from the network which leads to a DoS attack. This paper proposes a defense mechanism called SABAD, against black-hole attacks on AODV protocol in MANET. SABAD considers all the major factors contributing for packet dropping to reduce false-alarm during black-hole node detection.

1. Introduction

The desire to be connected anytime, anywhere, anyhow has led to the development of wireless networks. A wireless or mobile ad hoc network (MANETs) [1] is formed by a group of wireless nodes which agree to forward packets for each other. They have many potential applications, especially in military information system of battle field, civil emergency search and rescue operations (e.g. flooded area) and also it is suitable for areas where it is not possible to setup a fixed infrastructure. Each node in a mobile ad hoc network can act as a host or a router or both in the network. Since the nodes communicate with each other without having infrastructure, they provide the connectivity by forwarding packets over themselves. To support this connectivity, nodes use some routing protocols like Ad-hoc On Demand Vector Routing (AODV) [2], Dynamic Source Routing (DSR) [3] and Destination- Sequenced Distance Vector (DSDV) [4].

Wireless ad-hoc networks are vulnerable to variety of security attacks. Black hole attack is one of the most generous attacks in which malicious node absorbs and drops all data packets in AODV protocol. In this, Black hole node always responds positively with a Route Reply (RREP) message to every Route Request (RREQ), even though it does not really have a valid route to the destination node. Since malicious node does not have to check its routing table, it is the first to respond to the RREQ in most cases. Once the data packets are reaching at the black hole node, it drops all these packets instead of forwarding them to the destination node.

A lot of research works [1][5][8][9][10] has been done to identify the malicious black hole nodes in AODV protocol in MANET. The first solution to the problem of misbehaving nodes in an ad hoc network was proposed by Marti, Giuli, Lai and Baker [5]. Their solution uses the watchdog to monitor the data forwarding activity of the neighboring node. They use a component called pathrater that prevent paths containing misbehaving nodes. The chance of reduction in network capacity and wastage of energy because of the watchdogs are one of the major problems incurred in this scheme. Secondly the scheme relies only on overhearing transmissions in promiscuous mode but do not check other factors such as mobility as addressed in [6].

A cooperative distributed intrusion detection system (IDS) was proposed by Zhang and Lee [7]. Here, every node that participates in MANET analyzes the locally available data for anomalies. Intrusion-attempts are detected by employing a distributed cooperative mechanism in which all participating nodes cast their votes according to the data they have previously analyzed. The authors avoid the reliance on known attack patterns, using an anomaly detection model. Unfortunately, this IDS models suffer from performance penalties and arises high false alarm rates.

The proposed simple solutions in [9] [15] address the black hole attack by using ROUTE REPLY packet. These solutions cross check the legitimacy of the ROUTE REPLY from intermediate node by verifying the existence of the route between intermediate node and destination. If the intermediate node has a valid route to the destination, it sends ROUTE-REPLY along with its next hop information. The source then verifies the route (between the intermediate node and destination) by initiating Further-Request to the next hop node. To avoid recursion, only the next hop node is permitted to respond via Further-Reply with the check result field containing the result of the query. If the response confirms that the next hop node lies in between the intermediate node and the destination, then the route through the intermediate node would be chosen. If the response informs that next hop node is not in-between the intermediate node and the destination but has a valid route to the destination, then the ROUTE-REPLY from the next hop would be chosen. If neither of the above two possibilities are successful, then the source initiates a new route discovery. Buchegger et al. [10] also proposed a similar approach called CONFIDANT.

Venkatesan and Vijay have studied the "packet drop attack" in [11]. After analyzing both the class of secure routing protocols (the protocols that deploy cryptographic techniques and the protocols that deploy monitoring techniques); the authors in [11] demonstrated their inability to achieve complete secure routing. From the detailed examination of the packet drop events and the study of secure routing protocols, they proposed an efficient defense-in-depth strategy to secure mobile ad-hoc networks through the integration of three layers: prevention layer (based on cryptographic techniques), detection-reaction layer (based on monitoring technique) and enforcement layer (based on obligations) but their method is too complex and can increase significant overhead.

Majority of the above protocols have not considered the selfish node which silently drops packets to save battery power and/ or bandwidth. At the same time, most of the existing defense mechanisms identify the malicious nodes considering the packet loss results in false alarm. False alarm marks the good node as malicious and isolates that node from the network. There are many factors such as mobility of node, low battery power, weak signal strength causes packet drops and increases the false alarm rate. Unfortunately to our knowledge none of the existing algorithms considered all these factors to reduce the rate of false alarm.

In this paper, we propose a mechanism called SABAD (Self assured Black-hole attack detection). SABAD takes the account of all the major factors those contribute in packet-loss so as to reduce the false alarm.

The rest of the paper is organized as follows. Section 2 describes about the network assumptions. The proposed mechanism SABAD is discussed in Section 3. Section 4 describes about the parameter prediction and discussion is given in Section 5.We conclude the paper in section 6.

2. Network Assumption

We consider MANET that consists of similar types of nodes. Each node may freely roam, or remain stationary in a location for an arbitrary period of time. In addition, each node may join or leave the network, or fail at any time. We assume that the nodes communicate using a single shared bi-directional wireless channel. All the nodes operate in promiscuous mode, and the network may contain heterogeneous nodes with different energy levels and different computational powers. It is assumed that each node has a unique nonzero ID. We refer the nodes that are one hop away is neighbor, and the node's transmission range is the nodes environment. We also assume that every data packet and acknowledgement packet is hashed to protect the integrity of the message.

3. SABAD: The proposed mechanism

SABAD (Self Assured Black-hole Attack Detection), uses AODV protocol for route discovery while detecting a malicious node. The proposed scheme includes following two major objectives.

1.Detecting the black hole node

2.Distinguishing secure path from insecure path.

We define the secure path as "*the path that starts from source to destination touching all the intermediate nodes whose trust value is equal to 1*". On the other way the path is said to be insecure, "*if at least one of the intermediate node has trust value 0*". SABAD identifies black hole attack by co-operative detection of the nodes in the network. Once a node is detected to be malicious it alarms to all other non malicious nodes for isolating and disallowing the malicious node for further participation in the network.

Execution of SABAD comprises of following five steps, are discussed in subsequent sections.

Algorithm-SABAD

1. ***Neighborhood data collection*:** Collect data from the neighbors. Store and maintain in the Data Routing Information (DRI) table.

2. ***Trust Value calculation*:** Estimate the trust value of each intermediate node considering the parameters impacting on packet drop.

3. ***Route discovery*:** Execute the Route discovery phase and detect the malicious node if any.

4. ***Alarm Phase*:** If any node is found to be malicious during the route discovery phase, notify others for isolating that node.

5. ***Route Maintenance*:** If link would be broken after isolating that malicious node find an alternate route.

3.1. *Neighborhood data collection*

Each node collects the (data-forwarding) information of its neighborhood and stores it in an additional Data Routing Information (DRI)Table (as depicted in Table 1 with reference to the topology in Figure 1). The 'From' and 'Through' columns in the DRI table hold value '1' (True) or '0' (False). While trust value column, holds '1' if $\eta \geq \eta_{threshold}$ and holds '0' otherwise. As an example as showed in Table- 1, sample of the database maintained by node 2. The entry (1 0 1) for node 1 implies that node 2 has routed data packets from node 1 but has not routed any data packet through node 1 (before node 1 moved away from node 2) and 1 in Trust value says that its trust value is higher than the threshold trust, so we can consider it for sending packets. The entry (1 1 1) for node 3 implies that, node 2 has successfully routed data packets from and through node 3 and 1 in Trust value implies that its expected trust value is greater than threshold trust so we can also considered 3 for sending packets. The entry 1 1 0 for node 4 implies that, node 2 has successfully routed data packets from and through node 4 but 0 in trust value field implies that its trust value is less than threshold trust, so node 4 will not be considered for sending packets.

Table 1. DRI table maintained by node 2

Node	From	Through	Trust value
1	1	0	1
3	1	1	1
5	0	0	0
4	1	1	0

In this way, each node constructs and maintains its DRI table. After a certain time interval (depending on the mobility of the network) each node identifies its neighbors with which it has not interacted, and invokes subsequent detection procedures to probe them further.

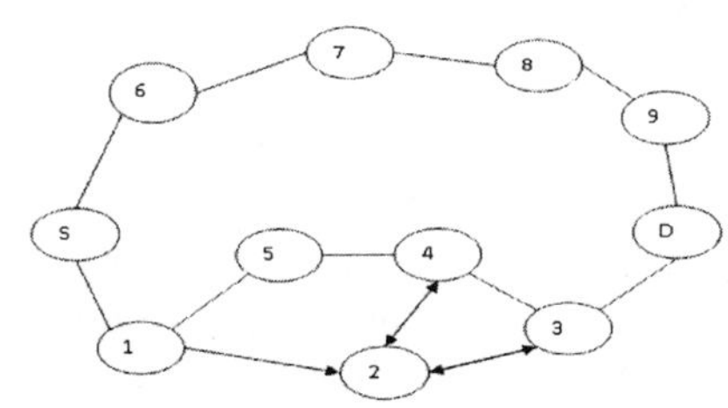

Figure 1.Topology of MANET

This identification is done on the basis of the nodes that have '0' entries both in the 'From' and 'Through' columns in the DRI table. For example, as shown in Table-1, node 2 has not communicated to node 5, so the node 2 will send a hello message to node 5 and then node 5 will send its data to node 2. Based on the data, node 2 calculates the trust value.

3.2. *Trust Value calculation*

Trust value of the intermediate nodes is calculated from the packet loss and three parameters (mobility, signal strength and battery power) those have impact on packet drop.

SABAD relies on trusted nodes (nodes whose trust value is 1) to transfer data packets. The trust value of any node is calculated as follows:

$$\eta = [(\alpha + \beta) + (3p + m)] \quad (1)$$

$$\begin{cases} \eta = 1 \text{ if } \eta \geq \eta_{threshold} \\ \quad = 0 \text{ otherwise} \end{cases} \quad (2)$$

where η, α, β, p and m respectively represent the trust value, battery power, signal strength, percentage of packet loss and mobility of intermediate node. The procedures to estimate these factors (α, β, p, m) are discussed in Section 4.

3.3. *Route discovery*

SABAD uses a modified AODV protocol for route discovery to detect a malicious node. The mechanism is illustrated in Figure 2. The Source Node (SN) broadcasts a Route Request (RREQ) message to discover a secure route to the destination node. After broadcasting the route request, SN waits for some fixed time to receive the acknowledgements. During this period, the data packets to be transmitted are stored in a buffer. The Intermediate Node (IN) generating the Route reply (RREP) provides its Next Hop Node (NHN) and DRI entry for the NHN. Upon receiving RREP message from the INs, SN checks its own DRI table for choosing the reliable IN (node is reliable only when trust value of that node is 1). Two different cases may arise there. First case would be that none of the intermediate nodes is trusted. In this case source has to retransmit the route request. The second case would be the existence of multiple trusted nodes. In such case SN will randomly picks any of the IN and then check for its NHN. Then that NHN will be chosen whose trust value is 1. If none of the NHN is found to be trusted then source will go for other IN. The algorithm described for route discovery is as follows.

Algorithm (Route discovery):

The abbreviations used in this algorithm are:

SN: Source Node, **IN**: Intermediate Node, **DN**: Destination Node, **NHN**: Next hop Node, **FRq**: Further Request, **FRp**: Further Reply, **Reliable Node**: The node whose trust value is 1, **Malicious Node**: The node whose trust value is unknown or whose trust value is 0, **ID**: Identity of Node, **DRI**: Data Routing Information

1.SN broadcasts RREQ and waits for some time to receive RREP.
2.IF (RREP is from DN)
{Route the data packets (route is assured to be secure route).
}
3.Else
{for each IN whose trust value is 1
{for each NHN {
if the trust value of NHN=1
{Current IN = NHN, continue for another NHN}
else {
NHN is assumed to be malicious.
(IF many nodes confirm about it, then it will be discarded from the network);
}
Continue for another NHN.
} }
}
4.Repeat Steps from 3 until we find the complete trusted route.

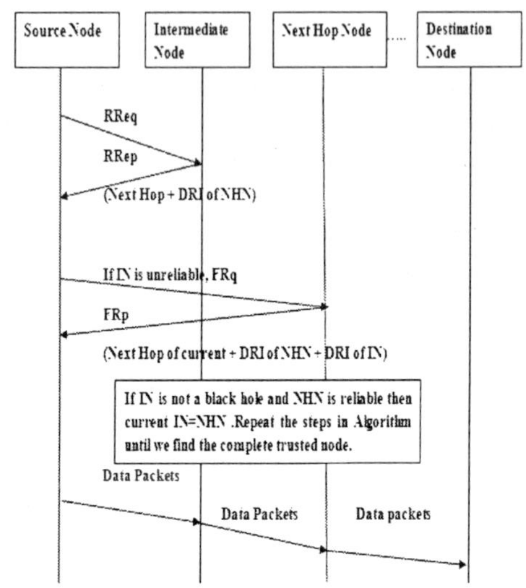

Figure 2. SABAD-Route discovery

3.4. *Alarm Phase*

This phase (alarm) is invoked if a black-hole is detected during the previous phase (route discovery). Objective of this phase is to notify others for isolating the detected malicious node. The detection and isolation mechanism of malicious nodes may raise the security issues in which a group of malicious nodes can launch a bad mouthing attack by falsely accusing a good node to isolate the victim from the network. To prevent this, we borrowed the idea used in [14]. Once a node is identified as malicious, the detector node generates a k-digitally signed alarm message, which would be constructed by *k*-different nodes. The malicious node ID is be entered into a global list of malicious nodes called 'faulty list'. The faulty list is periodically flooded in the network, as and when an update is made into it. In order to reduce the overhead, we propose two alternative methods of propagation of faulty list. The faulty list may be piggybacked with the normal routing messages (RREQ and RREP messages) so that it does not cause any extra overhead. Alternatively, each node may maintain a partial list of faulty nodes which are in its immediate neighborhood. This partial list is updated as and when the neighborhood of the node changes.

This mechanism will be particularly suitable for routing protocols like AODV, as nodes need to know the information regarding their neighboring nodes for routing.

3.5. *Route Maintenance*

After selecting the route between the source and the destination, if trust value of any node participating in the route becomes 0, a link break is detected. The corresponding node then determines an alternate route by searching its cache (finds only those node whose trust value is 1) to reach the destination. If any route has fond, it sends data through that new route. Otherwise, it creates a 'Route Error' packet and sends it to the source node to indicate the failure of the link. When forwarding the route error packet, the intermediate nodes remove the cache entries corresponding to the node which is moved and then forward the packet. On receiving the error packet, the source node also removes the entries corresponding to that node and tries to find another route to the destination in its cache.

4. Parameter Prediction

In this section we discuss the way to predict the factors has an impact of packet loss. This is to isolate the genuine node from the malicious one and hence, reduces the false alarm.

4.1 *Estimation of Battery Energy*

Each node estimates its battery lifetime base on the past activity. For this purpose, once node i send a data packet, it keeps track of residual energy value (α_r), and the corresponding time instance (t). This information is recorded and stored in the node. After n packets sent, node i gets the time instance (t') when nth packet is sent the corresponding residual energy value would be ($\alpha_r(t')$). The intermediate node sends the energy value α calculating from equation (3), along with acknowledgement packet.

$$\alpha = \frac{\alpha_r(t')}{\alpha_{max} - \alpha_{min}} \quad (3)$$

where α_{max} is the maximum power that is required and α_{min} is the minimum power that is required for transmitting the packet.

4.2. *Prediction of Signal Strength*

Our approach uses only the receiving node's computing power to measure the signal strength of receiver node. There are two choices available for collecting the signal strength information; first by active route and second by inactive route [13]. Active route is deduced from the received packets if data traffic is available. In inactive routes, we will create traffic between neighbors so that the nodes can get their information. We will use the latter case and introduce hello messages, which are already used in the AODV protocol. The signal power strength at the receiver is

$$\chi = \frac{P_t \cdot G_t \cdot G_r.(h_t^2.h_r^2)}{d^4} \quad (4)$$

Where P_t is signal strength at the transmitter. G_t is unity gain of the omni directional transmitting antenna. G_r is unity gain of Omni directional receiving antenna, h_t is height of transmitting antenna, h_r is height of receiving antenna and d is the distance between transmitter and receiver. Furthermore, the following assumptions are made in our paper: (a) P_t is constant at all nodes in the network. (b) The heights (h_t and h_r) of the antennas are assumed to be constants for every node (receiver and transmitter). Therefore,

$$\beta = \frac{\chi}{\chi_{max} - \chi_{min}} \quad (5)$$

where χ_{max} is the maximum signal strength that is required and χ_{min} is the minimum signal strength that is required for transmitting the packet.

4.3. *Estimation of Packet Loss*

P_o is calculated by using number of packets sent and number of packet received by destination.

$$\%P = \frac{P_o}{P_{min} - P_{max}} \quad (6)$$

where P_o is the percentage of packet loss occurred during transferring the last message, P_{min} is the minimum percentage that a node can lose packet and P_{max} is the maximum percentage that a node can lost packet.

4.4. *Prediction of Node Mobility*

The proposed mobility prediction technique is based on the signal strength which is already used in [13]. Our algorithm deduces the distance between the receiving and the transmitting nodes by the received signal strength which we have calculated earlier. Based on several distance related information within a certain time span, the distance change metric is calculated. On this metric the node decides whether intermediate node is mobile or not.

The distance between the transmitter and receiver is calculated as follows using Eq. (4)

$$d = \sqrt[4]{c.(\frac{P_t}{\chi})}$$

where $c = G_t \cdot G_r \cdot (h_t^2 \cdot h_r^2)$

In our algorithm, we introduce distance change $\dot{d}$. This metric is calculated based on the reception of the last two packets from the same transmitting node within a certain time.

$$\dot{d} = \frac{d(t_n) - d(t_{n-1})}{t_n - t_{n-1}} \tag{7}$$

where $t_n - t_{n-1} < t_h$ (certain threshold time) and t_n respectively t_{n-1} is the nth respectively $n\text{-}1^{th}$ packet, which the node received from the same transmitter. If a node doesn't hear from the neighbor within this time, the node assumes that the neighbor left the transmission range. After a possible reentry in the transmission range the older distance information is not used anymore. So here mobility (m) of any node is 1when $\dot{d}$ will be large and 0 when $\dot{d}$ will be small.

$$\left\{\begin{array}{l} \text{m} = 1 \text{ when } \dot{\text{d}} \text{ will be large.} \\ \quad = 0 \text{ when } \dot{\text{d}} \text{ will be small} \end{array}\right\} \tag{8}$$

5. *Discussion*

Raising false alarm may prevent the genuine nodes from their rights and leads to denial of service (DoS) attacks. Therefore, reducing false alarm is a critical issue. The proposed mechanism SABAD determines the trust value using Eq. (1) that considers the parameters such as mobility, battery power, signal strength which is responsible for packet drops. The weight of packet drop is heightened to 3 multiples because three different parameters have considered. SABAD claims that the false alarm would be reduced while detecting the malicious nodes i.e. assures the detected node would be malicious one as the major factors those cause packet drops are considered in the trust value calculation.

If an adversary targets to isolate a victim node by capturing few nodes, he fails to form a group signature. Thus SABAD is resistant against node capturing attack.

6. *Conclusion*

In this paper, we have proposed a mechanism called Self Assured Black-hole Attack Detection (SABAD) to defend against black-hole attacks in MANET. SABAD considers mobility, battery power, signal strength and packet loss from genuine node, to reduce the false alarm.

References

1. Y. Hu, A. Perrig, and D. Johnson, "Ariadne: A secure on-demand routing protocol for ad-hoc networks." In Proc. of the ACM International Conference on Mobile Computing and Networking (MobiCom'02), pp: 12-23, Atlanta, 2002.
2. C. Perkins, E. Belding-Royer, and S. Das, "Ad hoc on-demand distance vector (AODV) routing." Internet Engineering Task Force (IETF) draft, July 2003.
3. D. B. Johnson, and D. A. Maltz, "Dynamic Source Routing in Ad Hoc Wireless Networks." Mobile Computing, Chapter 5, pp: 153-181, (Kluwer Academic Pub.) 1996.
4. C. E. Perkins and P. Bhagwat, "Highly Dynamic Destination-Sequenced Distance-Vector Routing (DSDV) for Mobile Computers." Computer Communications Review, pp: 234-244, October 1994.
5. S. Marti, T. Guili, K. Lai, and M. Baker, "Mitigating routing misbehavior in mobile ad hoc networks." In Proc. of MOBICOM 2000, pp: 255-265, 2000.
6. W. Yu, Y. Sun, and K. J. Liu: HADOF: "defense against routing disruptions in mobile ad hoc networks." INFOCOM 2005, pp: 1252-1261, 2005.
7. Y. Zhang and W. Lee. "Intrusion detection in wireless ad-hoc networks." Mobile Computing and Networking, pp: 275–283, 2000.
8. B. Awerbuch, D. Holmer, C. Nita-Rotaru, and H. Rubens. "An On-Demand Secure Routing Protocol Resilient to Byzantine Failures." In proc. Of ACM Workshop on Wireless Security (WiSe), pp: 21-30, September 2002.
9. H. Deng, W. Li, and D. P. Agrawal, "Routing Security in Wireless Ad Hoc Networks." IEEE Communications Magazine, 40(10), pp: 70-75, Oct 2002.
10. S. Buchegger and J.Y. Le Boudec, "Performance Analysis of the CONFIDANT Protocol." in Proc. of the 3rd ACM intl. symposium on Mobile ad hoc networking & computing (MOBIHOC'02), Switzerland, pp: 226-236, June 2002
11. V. Balakrishnan, V.Varadharajan and Tupakula, "Fellowship: Defense against Flooding and Packet Drop Attacks in MANET." in proc. Of Network Operations and Management Symposium, NOMS 2006. pp: 1 – 4, 2006.
12. K.Kowalik, B.Keegan and M. Davis. "Making OLSR Aware of Resources." in Wireless Communications, Networking and Mobile Computing, WiCom 2007. pp: 1488-1493, 2007.
13. R. Pomplun, A. Datta: "A Study of Long Distance Traffic Using the AODV Protocol in a Vehicular Ad Hoc Network." VTC Fall 2007, pp: 2154-2158, 2007.
14. J. Sen Et.al: "A Mechanism for detection of Gray hole attack in Mobile ad Hoc Network." Information, Communications & Signal Processing, 2007, pp: 1-5, 2007.
15. V. Balakrishnan, V. Varadharajan, "Packet Drop Attack: A Serious Threat to Operational Mobile Ad hoc Networks." Proceedings of the International Conference on NCS 2005, Krabi, Thailand April, pp: 89-95, 2005.

LIC-BASED FAST FORWARDING TOWARDS SCALABILITY, SIMPLICITY, FLEXIBILITY AND SECURITY

KE XIONG, ZHENG-DING QIU, YU ZHANG
Institute of Information Science, Beijing Jiaotong University, Beijing, 100044, China

YU-CHUN GUO, HONG-KE ZHANG
School of Electronics and Information Engineering, Beijing Jiaotong University, Beijing, 100044, China

To reduce the cost of routing devices and to improve network performances for both wired and wireless packet networks, this paper proposes the Link Interface Code (LIC) based forwarding, which can achieve fast flexible switching with scalability, simplicity, security and enhancement of the network QoS ability. LIC-based forwarding uses the LIC to route and forward the data packet in each router. It executes like the explicit route by establishing the connection-oriented LIC path in advance and it can run on existing routing protocols. We design two types of codes for the LIC-based forwarding, the One-way connection-based LIC (OLIC) and the Two-way connection-based LIC (TLIC). The OLIC just contains route information from a send to its receiver and the TLIC contains both the route information from the send to its receiver and the route information from the receiver to its sender. Compared with OLIC, TLIC is more suitable for interactive real-time applications. Experiment result shows that LIC-based forwarding achieves lower end-to-end delay than MPLS does and it can provide flexible fast forwarding.

1. Introduction

Today's computer network accounts for 80% of information exchange in people's life and it is expected to be a multi-service network containing heterogeneous networks with increasing traffic [1]. The ever-growing Internet multimedia applications, such as VOIP and IPTV, demand networks to transmit more and more packets per second and to provide flexible forwarding to meet their Quality of Service (QoS) requirements. Moreover, good communication security is often required.

As packet forwarding is a primary function of routing devices, it has great influences on network performances and the forwarding cost exerts critical influence on the lives of energy-limited networks, including MANETs and WSNs.

However, the Longest Prefix Matching (LPM) routing lookup and the Destination-based Hop-by-hop Forwarding (DHF) mode make it difficult to achieve fast flexible forwarding with less cost in current networks. Firstly, LPM requires routers to search variable-length address prefixes in order to find the longest matching prefix of destination IP address and retrieve the corresponding forwarding information for each packet traversing the router. Latest statistic shows that BGP routing tables have approximate 10,451,000 entries and the active ones are in excess of 285,200 [2]. To find the output link for each packet in such a huge routing table costs too much to improve the speed and the performance of forwarding. Although some effective techniques are applied to speed up routing inquiry, ongoing growth routing table and increasing transmitting speed push the routing lookup to the bottleneck in high-performance routers and high-speed networks yet. Especially in IPv6 network, such problem becomes more serious due to the 128-bit IP address which incurs increasing memory requirement and time cost [3]. Secondly, under the mode of DHF, each router forwards a packet according to the destination IP in the packer's header, without knowing the whole delivering path. Thus, DHF is unlikely to provide flexible forwarding to implement all forwarding policies [4].

To achieves fast flexible forwarding, we proposed the TNPOSS [5] forwarding previously, which has good scalability, simplicity, security and QoS ability. However, TNPOSS was only designed for IP networks. In this paper, we extend the TNPOSS to Link Interface Code (LIC) based forwarding, which can be used in any packet network, no matter wired or wireless ones.

Section 2 gives the related work. Section 3 proposes two LICs, the one-way connection-based LIC (OLIC) and the two-way connection-based LIC (TLIC), where the OLIC uses the output link interface ID as the code, which is the extension of TNPOSS, and the TLIC uses input-output link pair identification as the code, which fits the real-time interactive applications better. In Section 4, we analyze the merits of LIC-based forwarding. Section 5 implements it on a test work with experiments and Section 6 summarizes this paper.

2. Related Work

There are two kinds of fast flexible forwarding approaches in current packet networks. The one is IP tunnel-based and the other is label-based.

IP-in-IP tunnel [4] is an effective IP tunnel-based method, which uses the encapsulation of IP packets to carry all IP addresses of the routers along the transmission path. Although it can achieve flexibility, the overhead of the IP addresses in each packet header leads to very low transmission efficiency, which makes IP-in-IP tunnel inapplicable. Moreover, IP-in-IP tunnel is unable to achieve fast forwarding because of the LPM IP routing lookup.

As to the label-based ones, MPLS [6] [7] is though to be the most excellent method. MPLS encapsulates IP frames in MPLS packets to operate Fixed-Length Matching (FLM) label switching. Compare with LPM IP switching, it is able to achieve fast forwarding. By transmitting packets along Label Switch Paths (LSPs), MPLS can implement explicit routing and traffic engineering very effectively. However, MPLS has two big problems difficult to be solved [8-10]. Firstly, MPLS needs the label switch router (LSR) to preserve the Label Switch Table (LST) which is growing with the increasing of network flows. The more LSPs a LSR supports, the more memory are needed [8] [9]. With the rapid growing of network size and the number of flows, the scalability problem of MPLS is becoming more and more severe. Secondly, MPLS is too complex. In order to set up LSPs, MPLS has to run label switch protocol (LDP) which is so complex that makes the control plane of MPLS be considerably challengeable. What's more, running MPLS in current IP networks demands both the software and the hardware of all deployed routers to be upgrade [10].

Recently, Ref. [11] proposed the global domain identifier (GDI) to perform label forwarding to simplify MPLS. In their scheme, GDI is used to identify a flow uniquely in a domain. As GDI-based forwarding belongs to FLM label switching, it can achieve fast forwarding. However, it requires routers to maintain LSTs, which grow with the increasing of flows. Thus, GDI-based forwarding has the scalability problem, too.

3. LIC-based Forwarding

To achieve fast flexible switching with scalability, simplicity and enhancement of network QoS ability, we propose the LIC-based forwarding method in this paper.

As is known, the forwarding function of a routing device is to forward a packet to its output link according to the destination address in the packet's header and the aim of routing lookup is to find the correct output link corresponding to LPM entries in the forwarding table for the packet. Hence, the forwarding table actually indicates which of the router's link interfaces the packet should be forwarded. From this perspective, the link interface in fact contains real routing information, which can be carried in the packet header to indicate the output link directly without looking up the route tables.

A routing device, no matter what kind of network it belongs to, usually has multiple link interfaces, which are known as the ports in IP routers. Generally, the number of the link interfaces of a router is fixed and often ranges from tens to hundreds. Thus, a router can identify each of its interfaces by a certain code with a few bits on its own. As the code is local unique within the router, the length of the code must be much shorter than the globally unique IP address.

In this paper, we fully consider the role of the link interface and the routing information contained by it, and two kinds of link interface codes, the OLIC and the TLIC are proposed for the LIC-based forwarding.

3.1. *OLIC-based Forwarding*

In OLIC, we use a set of binary codes to identify the link interfaces of a router. Such code can be seen as the ID of the corresponding link interface. If a router has m link interfaces, $\lceil \log_2 m \rceil$ bits are required for its OLIC. For example, consider the network shown in Figure 1, S and R are the terminal devices. a , b , c , d and e represent the routing devices. The solid lines between any two nodes are the communication links. The binary code near each node is the OLIC of the corresponding link interface. Suppose $S \to a \to b \to d \to c \to e \to R$ is the selected path to delivery the packets from S to R , the path can be represented by the OLIC 10 11 11

100 01 which consists of the OLIC of the output link at each hop on the path.

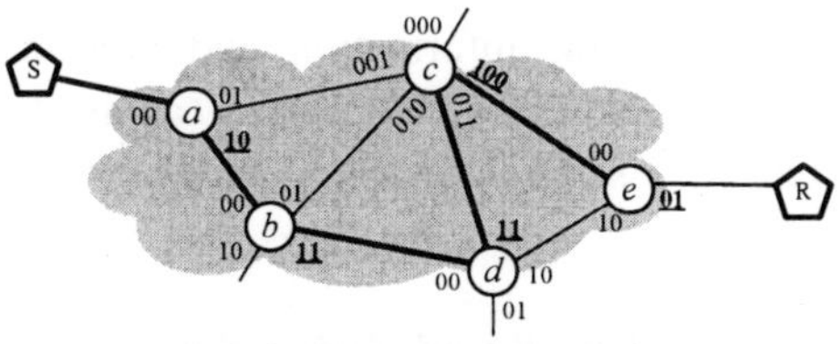

Figure 1. The OLIC of routers

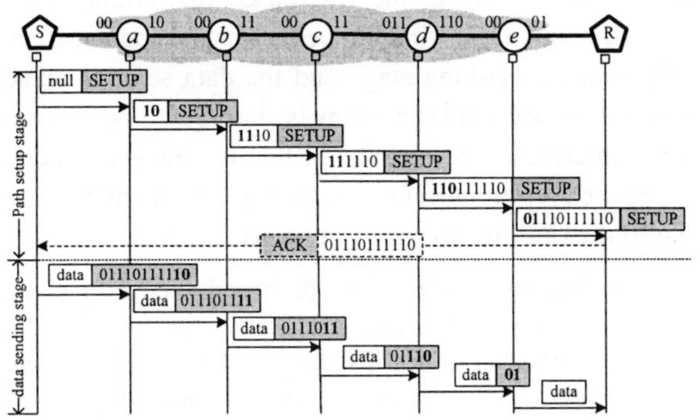

Figure 2. The work process of LIC-based forwarding

The work process of LIC-based forwarding can be illustrated by Figure 2, which contains two steps. The first step is responsible for establishing LIC path and the second step is the data delivering via the LIC. In Figure 2, the OLIC is used. Before sending data to R, S sends the SETUP message to the network to request to establish an OLIC path. When the router receives the SETUP message, it will find the output link interface from its forwarding table according to the destination address in the packet header, putting the OLIC of the output link interface into the SETUP message, and then send the updated SETUP message to its downstream node. All routers on the transmission path do the same operations above in turn. When the SETUP message arrives at R, the OLIC of the transmission path will be obtained. Then, R returns the OLIC via the ACK message. Once S receives the ACK message, it begins to send data to R with the OLIC which in fact indicate the transmission path from S to R. When each router receives the data packet, it extracts the certain bits of the OLIC from the packet header according to the length of its own OLIC. The value of the extracted bits is just the OLIC which indicates the output link interface for the packet. Thus, the router is able to forwarding the packet to the next hop without looking up its routing table any more. The detailed information can be understood easily by referring Ref. [5].

3.2. *TLIC-based forwarding*

Recently, real-time interactive services, including Internet phone and video conference, are becoming more and more popular. The communication terminals in these applications simultaneously play the roles of both senders and receivers. The data packets sent by such terminals are often expected to be delivered on the same route to obtain similar delay and jitter and the communication sessions are expected to be established as soon as possible.

However, if using OLIC, it needs to establish OLIC paths twice (One is from S to R, the other is from R to S). The reason is that OLIC only indicates the direction from upstream node to its downstream node. Thus, the OLIC of the transmission path only carries the routing information from S to R. If R wants to send data to S, R has to send the SETUP message to request an OLIC of the path from itself to S.

To meet the requirements of real-time interactive applications, we propose another type of LIC, the two-way connection-based LIC (TLIC) which does not identify the link interface ID but the input-output link interface pair. In TLIC, it is required to establish LIC path only once, both the sender and the receiver can delivering their packet to each other by LIC-based forwarding.

Consider a router with m link interfaces, group any two of them l_i and l_k into a pair $\langle l_i, l_o \rangle$ with $i \neq o$ and $i, o \in [1, \ldots, m]$, where l_i denotes the input link interface and l_o denotes the output one. Each $\langle l_i, l_o \rangle$ is called a pair of link interface mapping. Thus, the router with m link interfaces has totally P_m^2 pairs of mappings, where P_m^2 represents the number of permutations of m things taken 2 at a time which can be calculated by:

$$P_m^2 = \frac{m!}{(m-2)!} = m(m-1). \tag{1}$$

For example, a router with 3 link interfaces has 6 mappings, which are $\langle 1,2 \rangle$, $\langle 2,1 \rangle$, $\langle 1,3 \rangle$, $\langle 3,1 \rangle$, $\langle 2,3 \rangle$ and $\langle 3,2 \rangle$. We assign a set of binary code to identify each of them and the code is called TLIC.

Definition 1. (SM: Symmetric Mapping). Let l_i and l_k be two link interfaces within a router with $i \neq k$, $\langle l_i, l_k \rangle$ and $\langle l_k, l_i \rangle$ are a pair of symmetric mappings.

Definition 2. (SP: Symmetric Path). Let P and P' denote two paths, where P is from the source S to the destination R and P' is from R to S, if P' consists of the same nodes and revered links of P, P and P' are called a pair of symmetric paths.

Definition 3. (SC: Symmetric Code). Let A and A' denote two sets of binary code, where $A = a_1 a_2 ... a_m$ with $a_i \in \{0,1\}$ and $1 \leq i \leq m$, if $A' = a_m a_{m-1} ... a_i ... a_1$, A' and A are called a pair of symmetric codes.

For example, the SM of $\langle 1,2 \rangle$ is $\langle 2,1 \rangle$. The SP of path $S \to a \to b \to d \to c \to e \to R$ is its reversed path $R \to e \to c \to d \to b \to a \to S$. The symmetric code of 00 is itself and the symmetric code of 0010 is 0100.

Property 1. Suppose path P and its TLIC is $TLIC(P)$, if P' is the SP of P, $TLIC(P')$ must be the SC of $TLIC(P)$.

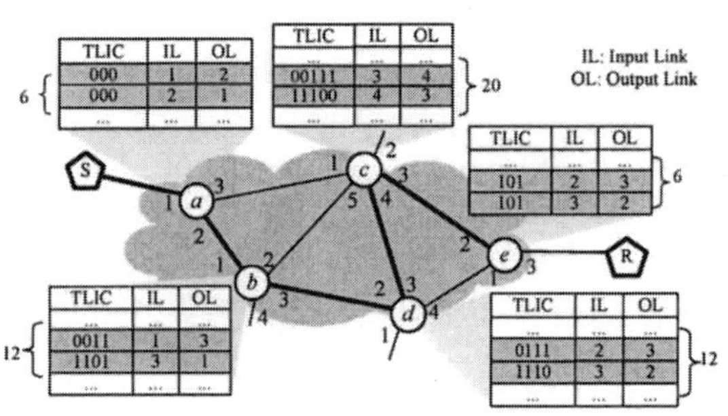

Figure 3. The TLIC of the routers

In TLIC, we use a pair of symmetric codes to mark a pair of symmetric link interface mappings. Thus, the length of TLIC of the router with m link interfaces is $\lceil \log_2 m(m-1) \rceil$. If using TLIC, the coding tables of the routers in Figure 1 can be illustrated by Figure 3 and the TLIC of path $P = S \to a \to b \to d \to c \to e \to R$ is 000 0011 0111 11100 101. When R receives the SETUP message from S, it knows the TLIC of P. As the SC of $TLIC(P)$ 101 00111 1110 1100 000 is just the TLIC of path $P' = R \to e \to c \to d \to b \to a \to S$, R need not to establish a new LIC path to S. It can use the SC of $TLIC(P)$ directly to send its data to S.

From the explanation above, we can state that a TLIC is an identification of a directional link interface pair. Since a pair of SMs is coded by a pair of SCs, the TLIC of a pair of SPs are also coded by a pair of SCs. Given the TLIC of path P, its SC $TLIC(P')$ can be known easily. Thus, a TLIC actually contains bidirectional routing information and can make the flows of the real-time interactive applications be transferred on a same path by establishing a LIC path only once.

4. Analysis of LIC-Based Forwarding

Both OLIC-based forwarding and TLIC-based forwarding belong to the LIC-based forwarding. They have the same working procedure which contains the LIC path establishing stage and the data sending stage. The difference between them is that OLIC is one-way link interface code and TLIC is two-way code. Compared with current forwarding mechanism, LIC-based forwarding has following merits:

1. ❖ *Fast forwarding.* In LIC-based forwarding, just during the path establishing stage, the routing table has to be accessed. During the data sending stage, each packet is forwarded directly according to the path LIC in the packet's header, so the cost of routing lookup is greatly reduced. Thus, the LIC-based forwarding can achieve fast switching.
2. ❖ *Good scalability.* In LIC-based forwarding, no additional table, such as the LST of MPLS, is required to be preserved and maintained. If any, only a small TLIC coding table is needed to be stored in TLIC-based forwarding. For all that, the size of TLIC coding table never grows with the increasing of either network size or the number of flows. Therefore, no matter how large the network scale is, the LIC-based forwarding is able to reduce and release the overhead of storage and memory greatly. Furthermore, each router codes its own link interfaces independently, so new routers can join in the network easily and freely. Therefore, LIC-based forwarding has very good scalability.
3. ❖ *Simplicity.* LIC-based forwarding is not responsible for route computing and it runs over the current or future routing protocols, including RIP, OSPF, BGP, DSR, and AODV. No complex management and signaling are needed, so it can be deployed easily in any kind of packet networks.
4. ❖ *Flexibility and Enhancement of TE and QoS ability.* LIC-based forwarding works in the mode of explicit routing and transmits data packets on LIC paths. If the routing protocols provides multi-path route, LIC-based forwarding can support multi-path

delivery by establish multiple LIC paths in advance. If the routing protocol provides QoS routing, LIC-based forwarding can transmit the packets on the QoS-supported paths. Despite providing no QoS tools, LIC-based forwarding deliveries the packets of a flow on the specified connection-based path, so it can enhance and improve the network QoS ability. Because of the good flexibility and the explicit routing working mode, it tends to support TE well obviously. Moreover, since the working procedure of LIC-based forwarding is similar to that of the Resource Reservation Protocol (RSVP) in IntServ model, it can be combined with IntServ easily by a tiny extension of RSVP. Besides, it also can be combined with DiffServ and other models and propocols easily due to its flexibility.

5. ❖ *Security*. First, during the data transmission stage of LIC-based forwarding, both the source and the destination IP addresses are not used, so the IP address information of the packet can be encrypted and hidden. Second, since the LIC in the packet header changes hop by hop during the data transmission, if an eavesdropper captures the data packet from the network, he can know neither the sender nor the receiver of the packet. Third, routers do the coding on themselves independently, so it is not easy to find out the information of a specific code outside the routers. Therefore, LIC-based forwarding can make data packets' routing and forwarding information more secret. Thus, it can enhance network security significantly.
6. ❖ *Lower header overhead comparing with IP-in-IP tunnel*. The measurements show that the average hop count in internet is about 14 to 16. We choose the hop count as 15 to do comparison. Suppose each router has 256 link interfaces, the results of Figure 4 show that the packet header of OLIC and TLIC are much lower than that of IPv4 and IPv6. It is deserved to be stressed that 256 in fact is a very large number for the link interface count in a routing device, so the real packet header overheads of TLIC and OLIC should be lower than those shown in Figure 4. Thus, LIC-based forwarding makes it practical to implement scalable explicit routing in IP networks.
7. ❖ *Low energy consumption*. During the data transmission procedure of LIC-based forwarding, no computational routing lookup is required, so LIC-based forwarding consumes less energy compared with current forwarding techniques. It tends to save the power and prolong the lives of the routing nodes in energy-limited networks such as WSNs and MANETs.

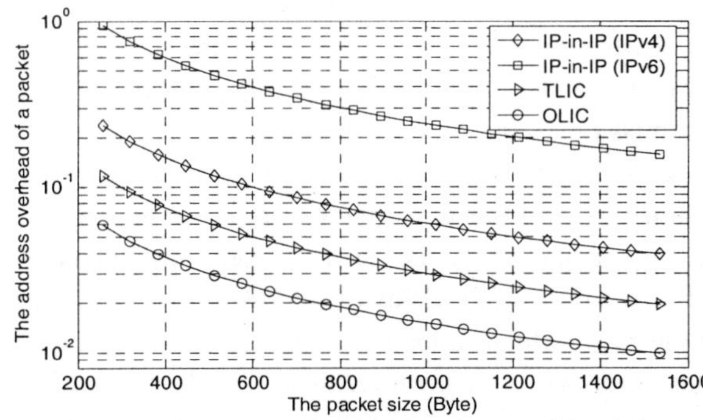

Figure 4. Comparison of packet header overhead

5. Experiment Results

We implement the LIC-based forwarding on the test network of our Lab. The topology of the test network is shown in Figure 5. T1, T2 are terminal devices. R1, R2, R3, R4, R5 and R6 are the routers.

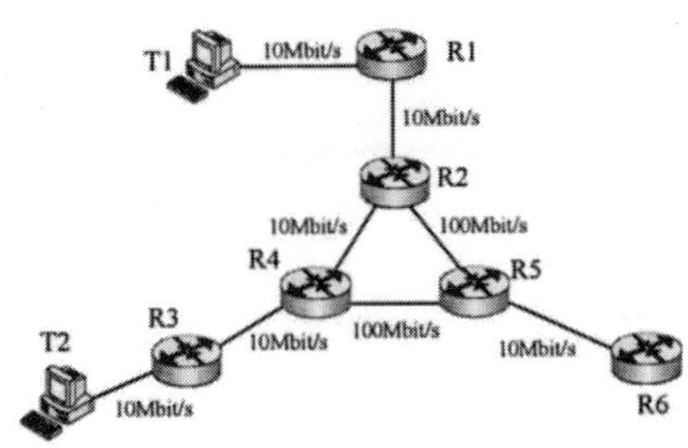

Figure 5. The test network topology

In the experiments, we set T1 as the sender and T4 as the receiver. The static route was used to set up the route T1→R1→R2→R5→R4→R3→T4. First, let T1 send data packet to T4 by MPLS. After this, start up the LIC-based forwarding by establishing the LIC path on route T1→R1→R2→R5→R4→R3→T4 in advance. Then, deliver the packets from T1 to T4 according to the LIC. All data packets sent by T1 belong to UDP traffic and the packet length is 500 Bytes. Figure 6 gives the comparison of the end to end (E2E) delay of MPLS and our scheme.

As is known, the E2E delay is composed of the total processing delay d_{proc}, the total queuing delay d_{queue}, the total transmission delay d_{tran} of the nodes and the total propagation delay d_{pro} of the links on the path, which can be denote as the equation (2)

$$d_{e2e} = \sum_{i=1}^{n}(d^{i}_{proc} + d^{i}_{trans} + d^{i}_{queue} + d^{i}_{pro}) . \quad (2)$$

Where n denotes the hops from the sender to its receiver, and i denotes the *ith* router on the transmission path. Since the same packets, the same devices, the same topology and the same transmission path are used in our experiments, d_{tran} , d_{pro} and d_{queue} of the two methods can be seen as the same. Thus, the difference of the E2E delay of the two method is caused by the d_{proc} , which reflects routing lookup cost actually. Therefore, the experiment result in fact shows that LIC-based forwarding achieves the lower routing lookup cost and the faster flexible forwarding than MPLS. We emphasize that, with the increasing of the network size, the difference of the E2E delay of these two methods will be more obvious than Figure 6 shows.

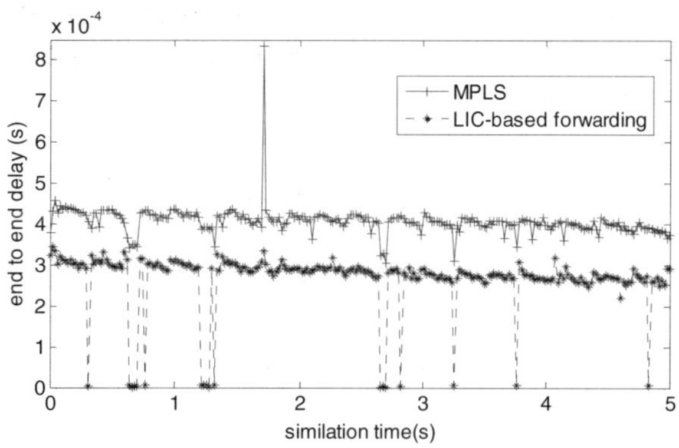

Figure 6. Comparison of end to end delay

6. Conclusion

This paper proposed the LIC-based forwarding which uses the link interface code to indicate the output link for the packet and can be deployed easily. Two codes, the OLIC and TLIC were designed for LIC-based forwarding. The analysis and the experiments result shows that our approach can achieve fast flexible forwarding with scalability, simplicity, security and enhancement of network QoS ability.

Acknowledgments

This paper is supported partially by the National Basic Research Program of China ("973 program") under contract No. 2007CB307101 and 2007CB307106, partially by the National High-Tech Research and Development Plan of China under Grant No. 2007AA01Z202, partially by the Program of Introducing Talents of Discipline to Universities ("111 Project") under contract No. B08002, partially by the Cultivation Fund of the Key Scientific and Technical Innovation Project, Ministry of Education of China under contract No. 706005, and partially by the National Natural Science Funds under grant No. 60772043.

References

1. J. Feng, A special issue on advances in new generation Internet architecture research, *Science in China Series F: Information Sciences*, Public release date: Oct. 22 (2008).
2. BGP Routing Table Analysis Reports, http://bgp.potaroo.net/as2.0/bgp-active.html, 12, Nov. (2008).
3. Z. Q. Li, et al., Tree, Segment Table, and Route Bucket: A Multi-Stage Algorithm for IPv6 Routing Table Lookup, *The 26th IEEE Conference on Computer Communications, INFOCOM 2007*, pp. 2426 -2430, May (2007).
4. J. Y. He and J. Rexford, Toward internet-wide multipath routing, *IEEE Network*, vol. 22, no.2, pp. 16-21, (2008).
5. K. Xiong, et al., A Scalable Fast Forwarding Approach for IP Networks, *International Journal of Internet Protocol Technology*, vol. 3, no. 2, pp. 119-127, (2008).
6. B. Davie, et al., MPLS using LDP and ATM VC Switching, *RFC 3035*, Jan. (2001).
7. M. Smith and T. Howes, Lightweight Directory Access Protocol (LDAP): Uniform Resource Locator, *RFC 4516*, June (2006).
8. S. Fernando, et al., Full Label Space Reduction in MPLS Networks: Asymmetric Merged Tunneling, *IEEE Communications Letters*, vol. 9, no. 11, pp. 1021-1023, (2005).
9. I. Minei, P. R. Marques, Scalability considerations in BGP/MPLS IP VPNs, *IEEE Communications Maga[illegible]*, vol. 45, no.4, pp.26-31, (2007).
10. C. Me[illegible], et al., Beyond MPLS … Less Is More, *IEEE Internet Computing*, vol. 11, no. 5, pp. 72-76, (2007).
11. E. B. Fgee, et al., Comparison between a Proposed QoS Mathematical Model and other IP QoS Models, *Communication Networks and Services Research Conference*, pp. 595-599, May (2008).

PUSH TECHNOLOGY WITH LOCATION TRACKING & DATA FILTERING FOR WIRELESS*

CH.PRADEEP REDDY
Department Of Telecommunication Engineering, Srm University, CHENNAI, India

K. PRAKHYA
School of Computing Sciences, VIT University, Vellore, TN, India

T. RAMA RAO
Department of Telecommunication Engineering, SRM University, CHENNAI, India

In the context of modern man constantly moving from place to place there is a need for a mechanism which gives mobile user the necessary information about the new location. The scope of the present work is to simulate the use of "Push Technology" for the purposes of efficient location-oriented data transfer to the user. Push technology stems from a very simple idea. Rather than requiring system to explicitly request (i.e., "pull") the information that they need, data can be sent to users without having them specifically ask for it. The advantages of 'push' are straightforward. The traditional 'pull' approach requires that users know a priori where and when to look for data or that they spend an inordinate amount of time polling known sites for updates and/or hunting on the network for relevant sites. Push relieves the user of these burdens. The paper also proposes a location tracking method which predicts the users futures movement based on the information of the past movements of the user. This prediction system can allocate the resources to the most probable cell with the instead of allocating excessive resources blindly to the neighboring cells of the user. Further, the paper recommends a filtering mechanism, which avoids the unwanted data to be sent to the user by the server. Agent based mechanism is used in this paper to do the necessary filtering of data.

I. INTRODUCTION

Popular Internet information systems like the World-wide Web still require the user to actively locate and retrieve information which is a time-consuming and monotonous task. Push systems [1] try to remedy this by reversing the communication pattern: information is actively disseminated to users. It's been an evolving concept and being used in almost each and every area of research. With push systems the user is required to state his/her preferences explicitly and register for the services required for him one time as an initialization process. In mobile networks and wireless data transfers, filtering of data [2] is another major issue because in wireless networks all the resources are highly used and there is a scarcity of abundant resources for every node and also the mobile and wireless gateways. Push systems tailors the data to users' profiles, decreasing the heavy traffic considerably. Additionally, an appropriate transport infrastructure like use of repeaters can further cut down on network bandwidth. Location Management techniques like AOO (angle of origin) identify and locate the user in a wireless network [3]. Mobility management in mobile computing environments covers updating and sorting of location information of the mobile users served in a system [3]. Mobility prediction, a hot topic in mobility management research, can be defined as the prediction of a mobile user's next movement between the cells of a PCS or 2GSM network [4, 5]. This enables the system to effectively allocate resources to the most probable-to-move cells instead of a blind allocation of excessive resources in the cell-neighborhood of a mobile user [6], improving resource utilization and reducing the latency in accessing the resources [7]. Predicted mobility patterns [8, 9], also benefits the broadcast program generation, since the data items can be broadcast to user-moving- cells. Accurate prediction of location information is also crucial in processing location-dependent queries of mobile users [10, 11]. Effective prediction of location can possibly answer the queries in application areas like health care, bioscience, hotel management, and the military basing on the current location and the possible future position of the user [12]. A prediction module in the paper is proposed which predicts the future movement of the user, for an effective sharing of limited wireless resources.

II. ELATED WORK

Sun et. al [1] proposed a method for developing the application of network and the network integration techniques for the implementation of push technology. The construction of communications interface between field control network and Internet, the accomplishment of the information exchange between web database and field control network, and the technique of real-time alarm system on Web are discussed. Venkata Krishna [2] proposed a filtering technique for extracting necessary data based on the location of user and to transform the data across the wireless link and the wired gateway. The goal of this filtering technique information is to reduce bandwidth demands of the network. The authors [4] presented an overview of mobility management in heterogeneous wireless networks and introduces a scheme which improves location management efficiency in terms of total signaling costs and intersystem paging delay. Artur

* This work is supported by SRM UNIVERSITY.

Ziviani et. al [5] presented two distinct phases for the location management proposal in mobile networks. The, two distinct phases are: i. the location query of the position of a destination node and ii. the transmission of a flow toward the destination node. This TCP-tailored approach can be applied to previous proposals in location management with minor changes in their particular features. Kyandoghere Kyamakya et. al [6] compared the different location management techniques available before this. And also presents results of a related extensive performance comparison of the most important paradigms for location management in cellular networks.

C.K. Ng et. al [7] proposed a model which explains, how distance based method can be effectively used for location management using the cell co ordinates. This approach is advantageous as it is independent of the size, shape, and distribution of cells. This paper gives the analysis of accuracy in using cell coordinates instead of actual location for distance comparison. Yang Xiao et. al [8] explained the location management technique in two ways dynamic movement-based scheme (DYNAMIC-3G) and a static scheme (STATIC-3G) for third generation networks where home location registers, gateway location registers (GLRs), and visitor location registers form a three-level hierarchical mobility database structure. It also gives the performance schemes with the proposed model to the models in 2G. Samir K. Shah et. al [9] proposed a location update algorithm which gives the location updates of the mobile terminal which is critical in uninterrupted communication. Previously proposed location update algorithm is implemented in one-to-one basis, which is costly in terms of traffic between MT [mobile terminal] and base station. Riky Subrata et. al [10] paper examined the use of cellular automata (CA) combined with genetic algorithms to create an evolving parallel reporting cells planning algorithm. In the reporting cell location management scheme, some cells in the network are designated as reporting cells; mobile terminals update their positions (location update) upon entering one of these reporting cells. Jie Li et. al [11] proposed dynamic location management methods to improve the system performance of PCS networks. The available architectures do not provide effective results because of the complexity and difficulty of the problem. This paper uses two mechanisms for location updating mechanism. The movement-based location update scheme and the existing static location update scheme. Karunaharan Rattan et. al [12] illustrated an efficient fault tolerant distributed location management protocol for personal communication service networks. The benefits of this approach are low connection establishment delay and low overall cost when compared to other protocols (under specific conditions). This approach solves the problem of triangular rounding in traditional mobile networks.

III. DESIGN METHODOLOGY

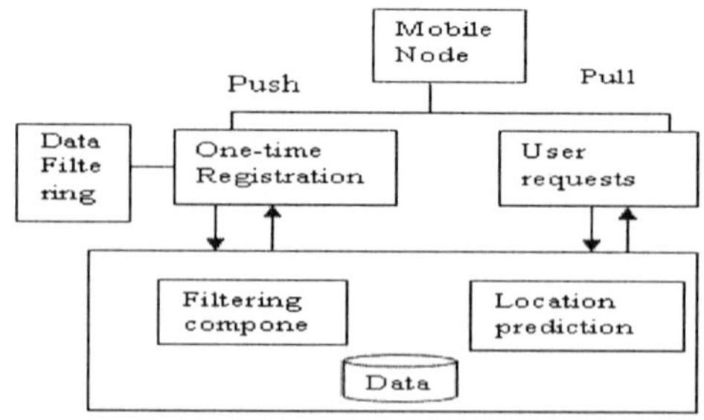

Fig. 1: Overall System Design

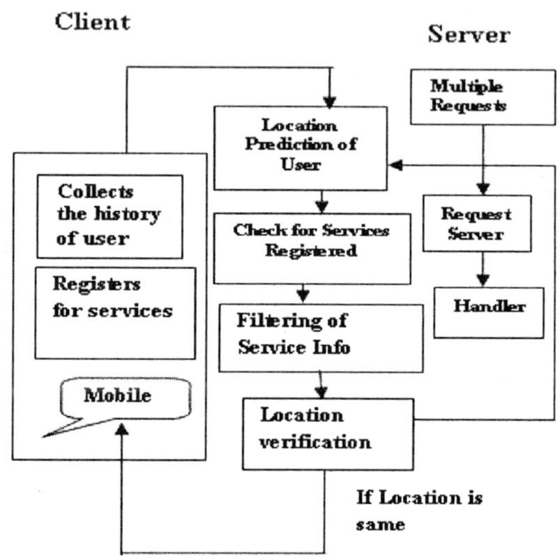

Fig. 2: Client-Server architecture using push model

Push technology

The overall system is as shown in figure-1. Whenever a mobile user moves into a different location, the need for continuous and region-based information is necessary for the user's support while traveling. So, presently there are two mechanisms where the user can get services from the Service Provider. One is Push Service fig-2 where the service provider automatically sends region-based data to the user on the change of user's location. The user has to subscribe for the services before it with the service provider, so as to get the region-based information. The other one is pull service where the user needs no registration and whenever feels the need of this region-based information, he sends a request to the server so as to get the information pertaining to that particular location. The proposed paper shows the push service and the major scope of the paper is getting accurate location information from the mobile node and implementing filtering of data, so as to clear unnecessary information that is not needed for the user. Also a queuing model has to be developed to serve the need of multiple users and multiple requests.

IV. IMPLEMENTATION

The proposed system consists of three modules

- Using Push technology
- Trajectory Prediction
- Data Filtering.

Algorithm 1: # Push System Methodology
Input: user's current location
Output: required information for the registered services
Step1: user registers for the required services
Step2: The server collects all the past history of that particular user
Step3: The collected information is given to the Prediction phase for location updating
Step4: After getting the location of the user server checks for the registered services
Step5: Once the services are ready to deliver it goes to the Filtering module
Step6: the server again verifies for the users location as the user is moving
Step7: If the location is same as the previous location the server sends the data
Step8: if the user changes his location before delivering the information it again goes to Step3

Trajectory prediction Module

In our work, we collect the movement trajectories of a user in the form of T = h(id1, t1), (id2, t2), . . ., (idk, tk)i. Here id1 denotes the ID number of the cell to which the user enters at time t1. It is evident from the record that two consecutive ID numbers should be the id numbers of two neighboring cells in the network. During the course of the movement of the user his history in the format is collected in predefined time intervals, this record is partitioned into subsequences. This procedure is accomplished as follows: If the mobile user stays in a cell idi more than a threshold value, before moving to another one idi+1 at ti+1, we assume that his trajectory up until now <id1, . . ., idi> ends here, and at idi+1 a new trajectory is started. So the initial subsequence is <id1, . . ., idi>. Continuation in this way enables partitioning of record into subsequences which are recorded to be used in our algorithm. The trajectories thus obtained by the above procedure are named as user actual paths (UAPs). The UAPs are considered as a valuable source of information because the mobility of the users contains both regular and random patterns. Hence use of the UAPs enables us to extract regular patterns for use in predictions. It is assumed that the UAPs we have, have the form U = {c1, c2, . . ., cn}. In this notation, each ck denotes the ID number of the kth cell in the coverage region. We generalized the pattern mining method to find the trajectories, used frequently by the user. The intention of the method presented in this work for mining the UAPs from web logs is used for effective caching and pre-fetching by using these access patterns. The frequently followed trajectories are named as user mobility patterns (UMPs). Mobility rules are generated by mining these UMPs. Prediction of the next inter-cell movement of the user is done by a consideration of the mobility rules and trajectories of the user.

PHASE 1
UMP Mining Algorithm

Input: All the UAPs in the database D.
Minimum value for support, supp-min
Coverage region graph, G
Output: User Mobility Patterns (UMPs), L
Step1: Take the patterns with length-1 C1-> L1 patterns
Step2: k=1
Step3: Initially the large patterns are empty L= { }.
Step4: while Ck != { } (While Loop Started)
Step5: for each UAP a in D
Step6: if s is a subset of a and belongs to Ck then
Step7: s.count = s.count + $s.supp_{min}$
Step8: choose the candidates which have more support than $supp_{min}$ and add to large
Patterns L= L U Lk, where Lk is the last generated large pattern.
Step9: generation of next length candidates
Ck+1< --- candidate generation (Lk,G)
Step10: K=K+1 (End While Loop)
step11: return L

The support assigned to a candidate by an UAP ia calculated using the formula

$Supp_{incr}$ = 1/ 1+ totDist

if pattern B is contained by UAP A, 0 Otherwise

We can define the totDist value by means of the notion of string alignment. Gusfield illustrates methods of determining the similarities between two strings, where a string is a sequence of characters, by finding the optimal alignment between them. Assume for instance the two strings are ''xzyzsy'' and ''zxsys''. The two strings can be aligned where the special character ''-'' represents the insertion of a space.

x z - - y z s y
\- z x s y - s –

If x and y are each single character or space, then D(x,y) denotes the score of aligning x and y. In our case, the scoring function is defined as follows:
D(x,y)= 0 if x=y , D(x,y)=1 otherwise

PHASE 2

Generation of Mobility Rules: In the second phase of our movement prediction algorithm, the mobility rules which will be used in the next phase (i.e., the prediction phase) are generated. Subsequent to the mining UMPs in the previous phase, the set of mobility rules from these UMPs can now be produced. For instance take a UMP C = <c_1, c_2, . . ., c_k>, where k > 1. The various possible mobility rules derivable from such a pattern are:

$<c_1>$---$\rightarrow$ $<c_2; \ldots ; c_k>$
$<c_1; c_2>$---$\rightarrow$$<c_3 \ldots ; c_k>$ $<c_1; c_2; \ldots ; c_k>$---$\rightarrow$ $<c_k>$

For a mobility rule, the part of the rule before the arrow is called the head of the rule, and the part after the arrow the tail of the rule. Consequently a confidence value is calculated for each rule basing on the generated rules.

For mobility rules R: $<c_1; c_2 \ldots c_{i-1}>$---$\rightarrow$$<c_{i+1}, c_{i+2} \ldots ; c_k>$ the confidence is determined by using the following formula:

Confidence R= $<c_{i+1}, c_{i+2} \ldots ; c_k>$ .count / $<c_1; c_2 \ldots c_{i-1}>$.count * supp $Supp_{min}/2 * 100$

PHASE 3
Mobility Prediction ( )
Input: current trajectory of the user
Set of mobility rules
Maximum predictions made each time
Output: set of predicted cells
Step1: let the predicted cells be empty first.
Pcells = { }:
Step2: for each rule r find the matching rule and add them to matching rule set.
Finding the matching rule ()
If $<a_1,a_2,\ldots\ldots a_i>$ is contained by P= $<c_1,c_2,\ldots\ldots c_{i+1}>$ and $a_i= c_{i+1}$ then
the rule is said to be matching rule.
Step3: keep them in a tuple array order with the factors conf R and support value
Step4: now sort the tuple array with respect to the factors in it.
Step5: Add the sorted tuple array index to the predicted cells set
Pcells-$\rightarrow$ Pcells U Tuple Array index
Step6: return Pcells

Filtering Module
This module plays a vital role in the proposed system. Since the information available in the server is very huge the mobile user is not accomplished with sufficient amount of memory and another disadvantage of not using filtering technique is unnecessary transmission of data in the network which leads to the network overhead and degradation of system performance. The proposed system follows two approaches for the filtering of data. The two approaches are 1.Traditional approach, 2. Agent Based approach. The algorithms for the above mentioned two approaches were explained below.

Algorithm 1: # Traditional approach #
Input: location information predicted in the prediction module.
Output: Filtering the information before delivering to user.
Step1: Server receives the location information of the user.
Step2: Server processes the registered requests and receives information from internet.
Step3: Server sends all the information to the user.
Step4: User filters the data received and takes the required information.

Algorithm 2: # Agent Based Approach#
Input: location information predicted in the prediction module.
Output: Filtering the information before delivering to user.
Step1: User launches a mobile agent using IP address.
Step2: User sends a proxy agent to the server to launch its code.
Step3: Server receives the location information of the user.
Step4: Server processes the registered requests and receives information from internet.
Step5: The proxy agent installed in the server filters the information at the server.
Step6: server now sends the filtered information to the user.

V. RESULTS & ANALYSIS

Location tracking
For simulation we used NS2 simulator. In simulation we showed how a mobile user moves from one location to other and also shows how the server keeps track of the user movement and sends the data from the server to the MSC and from there to the mobile user. It also gives the various snap shots of NS2 NAM files. The first graph (Fig 3) shows that the mobile user node7 receives the data from the server as soon as it enters to the coverage region of Base station-4. Similarly in the next graph we show how the system keeps track of the location of user and sends data to the particular base stations as shown in (Fig 4).

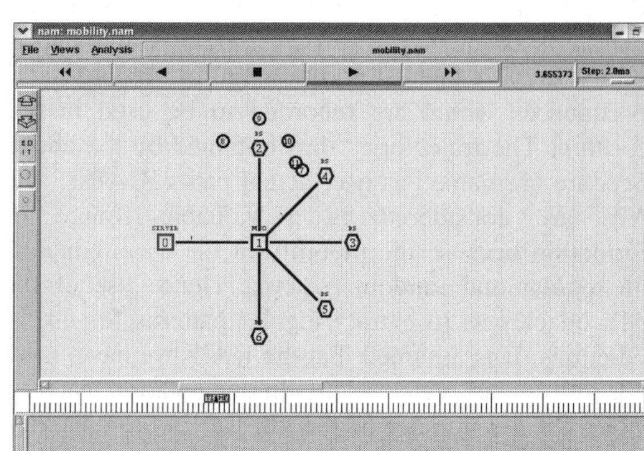

Fig. 3: Data Movement from server to BSC 4

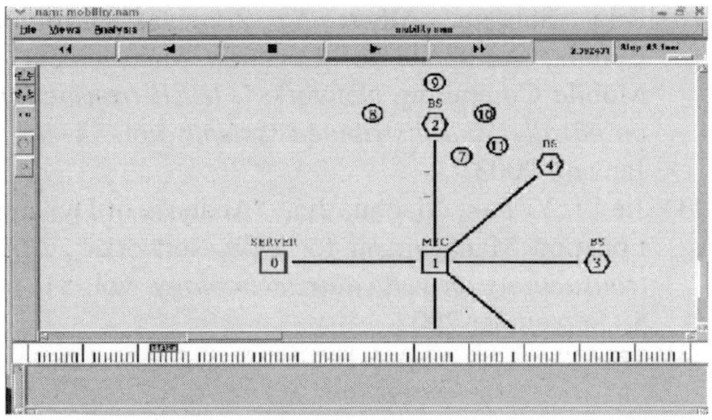

Fig. 4: Data Movement from server to BSC 2

In this phase mobile agents are used for filtering the data at the server. The agent installation and discovery are done as shown in the design methodology. The graph below shows, how the system performs with the filtering technique and with out the filtering technique. Fig: 6 give the performance analysis of the filtering technique taking the prediction factor as a basic criterion. The system with prediction phase executed before performs efficiently as it knows in advance what to filter.

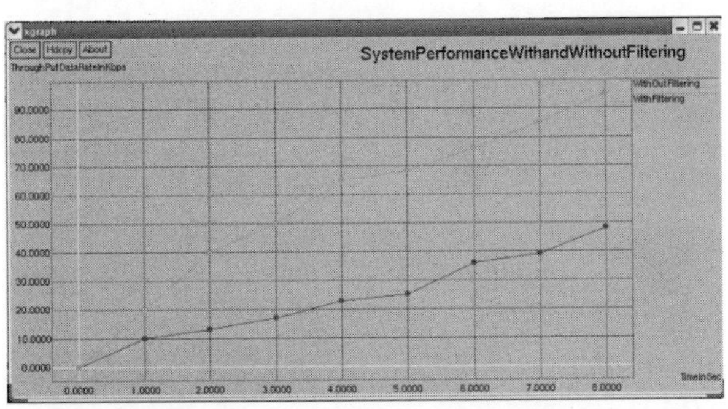

Fig. 5: Throughput of the system with and without filtering

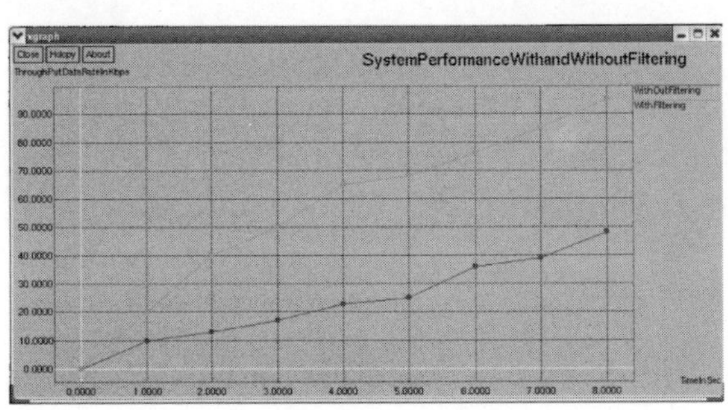

Fig. 6: Throughput of System with prediction and without prediction.

VI. CONCLUSIONS

A 'Push' application is designed to simplify and enhance the distribution of corporate data to mobile employees. Users do not have to request or download the data, because the push application delivers the information as it becomes available. Through accurate prediction of mobile user movements, the system will allocate resources to users in an efficient manner, thus leading to an improvement in resource utilization and a reduction in the latency in accessing the resources. Another benefit of our paper is the use of filtering techniques which delivers effective small amount of data for mobile users when the location is changed. Though the model performs better still it lacks a queuing model to be developed. The queuing model is needed for the efficient request-reply handling between the server and the mobile users. Also, QOS parameters have to be taken to see whether the system sustains various quality standards, also the system should continuously support these quality attributes for a better performance.

ACKNOWLEDGEMENT

The authors wish to acknowledge the support of the SRM University, Chennai to carry out this research work.

REFERENCES

1) Sun, Junman Fang, Huajing Wang, Ganyi He, Zhendong "Information Push Technology and Its Application in Network Control System", *Computer Science and Software Engineering, 2008 International Conference,* Wuhan, China, vol.no*:2* (198-201) Dec. 2008. ISBN: 978-0-7695-3336-0.
2) Venkata Krishna P, "A Model for Filtering Data Streams on Location Prediction Systems", Proceedings of ICSCI - International Conference on Systemics, Cybernetics, Informatics, Vellore, India, 2006.
3) Samir K. Shah, Sirin Tekinay, Cem Sarayadar, "Co-operative Location Update Algorithm For Mobiles In Next Generation Cellular Networks", *IEEE Communications Magazine,* April 2004.
4) IEEE. 802.21, "Draft IEEE Standard for Local and Metropolitan Area Networks: Media Independant Handover Services, IEEE P802.21/D02.00," September 2006, http://www.ieee802.org/21/.
5) Abdoul Djalil Assouma, Ronald Beaubrun," Mobility Management in Heterogeneous Wireless Networks", *IEEE Jrn. on selected areas in communications*, vol. 24, no. 3, March 2006.
6) Artur Ziviani, Serge Fdida, Jos´e F. de Rezende and Otto Carlos M. B. Duarte, "A TCP-Tailored Approach to Location Management in Mobile Ad Hoc Networks", *IEEE communications letters*, vol. 9, no. 12, December 2005.
7) Kyandoghere Kyamakya and Klaus Jobmann, "Location Management in Cellular Networks: Classification of the Most Important Paradigms, Realistic Simulation Framework, and Relative Performance Analysis", *IEEE Trans on VT*, vol. 54, no. 2, March 2005.

8) C.K. Ng and H.W. Chan, "Enhanced Distance-Based Location Management of Mobile Communication Systems Using a Cell Coordinates Approach ", *IEEE transactions on mobile computing,* vol. 4, no. 1, January/February 2005.
9) Yang Xiao, Yi Pan, Jie Li, "Design and Analysis of Location Management for 3G Cellular Networks", *IEEE Trans. on parallel and distributed systems,* vol.15, no. 4, Apr 2004.
10) Riky Subrata, Albert Y. Zomaya, "Evolving Cellular Automata for Location Management in Mobile Computing Networks", *IEEE transactions on parallel and distributed systems,* vol. 14, no. 1, January 2003.
11) Jie Li, Yi Pan, Xiaohua Jia, "Analysis of Dynamic Location Management for PCS Networks", *IEEE transactions on vehicular technology*, vol. 51, no. 5, September 2002.

DYNAMIC SPEED RESPONSE OF THE INTERNAL MODEL CONTROLLER WITH DITHER INJECTION*

N. AMUTHAN[1]

[1] *PET Engineering College/Department of Electrical and Electronics Engineering, Valioor, Tamil Nadu, India*

R. MOHAN[2]

[2] *PET Engineering College/Department of Electrical and Electronics Engineering, Valioor, Tamil Nadu, India*

N. SIVAKUMAR[3]

[3] *SUN College of Engineering and Technology/Department of Mechanical Engineering, Nagercovil, Tamil Nadu, India*

Abstract—This paper investigates the speed response characteristics of the internal model controller. Speed response parameter of the internal model controller is adjusted from low value to high value. The different value speed response is plotted using Matlab/Simulink. Chirp noise is added in the plant and the dynamic behavior is studied, sinusoidal dither signal is injected and the suppression of limit cycle oscillation is proof read and the performance is presented.

Index Terms—IMC, Speed Response, parameter tuning, sinusoidal dither.

1. Introduction

In the modern control system less maintenance and cost effective controllers are gaining importance throughout the world. Internal model controller is robust controller getting popular in the recent years from the small gadgets to high power industries because of its less maintenance and effective utilization.

Computer is one of the main areas where internal model controller is widely used [1] [2].Immanence work is in progress on in the internal model controller application and the performance improvement [3] [4] [5] [6].Direct model reference internal model controller is proposed in [7].

Parameter tuning is one of the main areas identified in all control system. Improvements in gain scheduling and tuning are the commonly accepted research area till date. Settling time of the parameter depends on the speed response parameter. If the settling time is high the controller performance is increased, also it is act as an energy saving controller. So speed response parameter is considered as an important parameter. The response of IMC is sluggish although it does not have any overshoot [8] and integral action of this controller is used to eliminate offset.

In this paper speed response parameter of the internal model controller is presented. Controller is tuned from small value to the large value and the dynamic response is observed using SIMULINK.To the best of authors' knowledge, this investigation is done first time in Internal Model Controller.

2. Internal model controller

2.1. *Controller design*

The IMC controller design method is prescribed in [9] for first order system.

First order Plant model $$G_p = \frac{K_P(S-a)}{(S+b)} \tag{1}$$

Internal model $$G_{inv} = \frac{S+b}{S-a} \tag{2}$$

Low pass filter F is used to avoid model mismatch

$$F = \frac{1}{(1+\phi s)^n} \tag{3}$$

ϕ =speed response tuning parameter, n =order of low pass filter

$$H = FG_{inv} = \frac{S+b}{(S-a)(1+\phi S)^n} \tag{4}$$

* N. Amuthan, E.Mail:amuthannadar@gmail.com.

The controller is

$$G_{imc} = \frac{H}{1-HG_{inv}} = \frac{(S+b)(S-a)}{(1+\phi S)^n (S-a)^2 - (S+b)^2} \quad (5)$$

Fig.1 shows the general diagram of IMC principle; IMC is stable in low frequencies because of the low pass filter. .

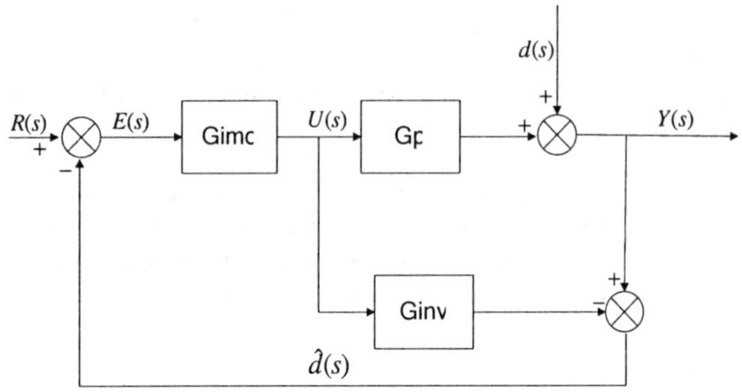

Fig. 1. General IMC diagram

The transfer function of the IMC is

$$Y(s) = \frac{G_{imc}(s)G_p(s)R(s) + [1 - G_{imc}(s)G_{inv}(s)]d(s)}{1 + [Gp(s) - G_{inv}(s)]G_{imc}(s)} \quad (6)$$

3. Dynamic speed response

To obtain the dynamic speed characteristics,

Consider $n = 1$, a=1, b=1

For high speed response large values are used

$\phi \rightarrow \infty$

Fig. 2 shows the dynamic response of the controller for different values of ϕ. ϕ=1, 10, 100, 1000

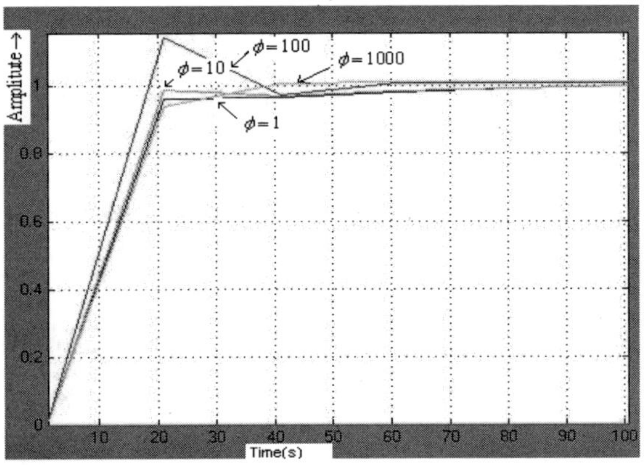

Fig. 2. Dynnamic speed response of IMC

In the Fig.3 chirp signal noise is introduced to introduce the oscillation in the output of the signal

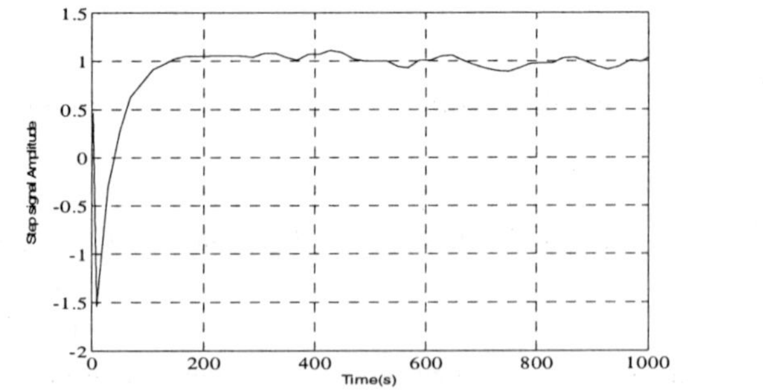

Fig. 3. Speed response with chirp signal noise in the plant at $\phi = 1$

4. Dither injection

The dither signal application is explained in the ref [9].Triangular signal dither is excellently used to improve the Direct torque control [11].Fig.4 shows the sinusoidal dither injection in internal model controller and shows the removal of limit cycle oscillation in the output without tuning integral action like PI controller.

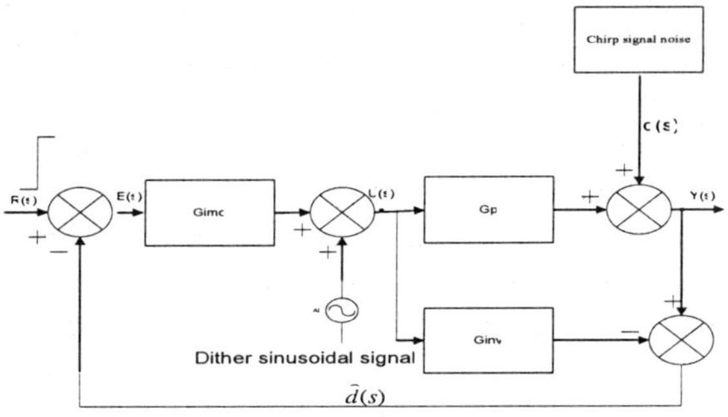

Fig. 4. Internal model Controller with dither injection

Fig.5 shows the output of the sinusoidal dither injected signal. The frequency of the sinusoidal dither signal is adjusted closely to reduce the dip in the signal.

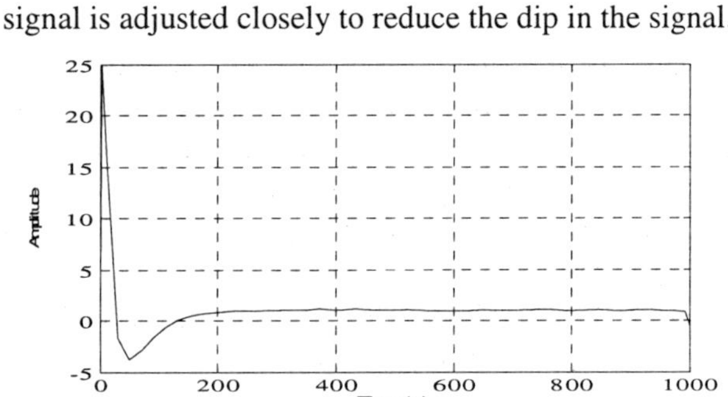

Fig. 5. Dither injected signal without limit cycle oscillation

5. Conclusion

From this investigation, it is concluded that if the speed response parameter is less than plant gain, the internal model controller yield better results. The dither signal is added in the controller side of the Internal Model Controller and the performance is improved. Further research work is going on for the different types of internal model controller.

Acknowledgments

The authors greatly acknowledge for the support given by PET Engineering College, Vallioor, Tamil Nadu.

References

1. David Anders Tingdahi,"Implementation of an adaptive internal model Controller for systems with large time delay," Master's thesis, Lulea University of Technology. October (2007).
2. QingWei Jia and Shinobu Yoshida,"Design of HDD Servo Controller with Adaptive IMC Structure," Proceeding of IEEE International Conference on Mechatronics and Automation, pp. 1280 -1285, June25-28, (2006).
3. Hu Jia-bing, He Yi-kang, Zhu Jian Guo,"The Internal Model Current Control for Wind Turbine Driven Doubly-Fed Induction Generator, "Industry Application Conference, 41st IAS Annual meeting, vol: 1, pp. 209-215, Oct.(2006).
4. A.Petersson." Analysis, modeling and control of doubly fed induction generators for wind turbines," Ph.d.thesis, Champers University of Technology, Sweden, (2005).
5. Lenart Harnefors and Hans-Peter Nee,"Robust current control of AC machines using the internal model control method," ©IEEE Industry Application Conference, 1995.30th IAS Annual Meeting, vol.1, pp. 303 – 309, 8-12 Oct. (1995).
6. Bogdan Marinescu,"A robust coordinated control of the doubly-fed induction machine for wind turbines: a state-space based Approach," Proceeding of the American Control Conference, vol.1, and pp.174-179, (2004).
7. N.Amuthan and S.N.Singh,"Direct Model Reference Adaptive Internal Model Controller using Perrin equation adjustment mechanism for DFIG Wind Farms", IEEE-ICIIS (2008), DEC 8-10, IITKGP.
8. Yongji Wang, M.Schinkel, and Ken J.Hunt,"PID and PID-like controller Design by pole assignment within D-stable regions," Asian Journal of Control, pp. 1-28, (2002).
9. Ching-Yaw Tzeng,"An internal model control approach to the design of yaw-rate-Control ship-steering autopilot," IEEE Journal of Oceanic Engineering, vol .24, No.4, pp.507-513, October (1999).
10. Astom K and B.Wittenmark,"Adaptive Control",©(1995) by Addison-Wesley,2nd Edu.pp.387.
11. R.K.Behera and S.P.Das,"Improved Direct torque control of Induction Motor with dither injection", Sadhana, Vol.33, Part 5, October (2008), pp.551-564.

Biographies

N. Amuthan, Presently Senior Lecturer in the Department of Electrical Electronics Engineering. PET Engineering College, Valioor, Tamil Nadu, India. He received his Master degree from the "University of Madras". His research interests include Power Electronics in Energy Management, Power Electronics in Energy Conservation, Power Electronics in Energy Compensation, Impact of Electricity Markets Pricing policy in Environment and adaptive control systems. He was a co-convener of National Conference on "Power Electronics in Energy Conservation" IEEE-PEECON 2004, held on Feb-19, 2004.He is a member of IACSIT (80331919) and IAENG (102137).

R. Mohan, Presently 3rd year B.E (EEE) Student in the Department of Electrical Electronics Engineering. PET Engineering College, Valioor, Tamil Nadu, India. His research interests include Power Electronics in Energy Conservation, Power Electronics and Drives, control system and power system. He is a member of ACEEE (7000443), and IACSIT (80332270).

N. Sivakumar received M.E (Engineering design) from Government College of Technology, Coimbature. Presently, he is working as a Lecturer in the Department of Mechanical Engineering at SUN College of Engineering and Technology, Erachakulam, Nagercovil, Tamil nadu, India. His research interest includes Finite Element Method, adaptive control system, Dynamics of Mechanics. He is a Member of IAENG (102142).

AN OWNERSHIP SHARING PROTOCOL FOR RFID WITHOUT A TRUSTED THIRD PARTY

GAURAV KAPOOR, SELWYN PIRAMUTHU

Information Systems and Operations Management, University of Florida
Gainesville, Florida 32611-7169, USA

Ready and secure communication between multitude of devices (tags, tag-readers, databases) employing RFID networks is paramount to increase RFID adoption. In addition, the ability to change (and even share) ownership of these devices is equally important, keeping in mind privacy issues. Given the low level of technology available in tags, it is necessary to keep these communications simple and lightweight, yet have the necessary cryptography built in. In this paper, we propose a light-weight protocol that meets these requirements, and use it for sharing ownership. This protocol does not rely on a Trusted Third Party, does not involve any key transfers between owners, and uses lightweight cryptographic techniques. Thus it is easily implementable, even in the most basic tags. We also perform necessary security analysis to ensure that this protocol is accurate, maintains confidentiality and provides forward security.

1. Introduction

RFID tags are increasingly being used in disparate domains to identify, track, and to sense ambient conditions of tagged objects. A majority of these applications dictate that these RFID-tagged objects be owned by different entities at different points in time. This necessitates the existence of a mechanism for seamless ownership transfer of tagged objects as they change ownership. Ownership transfer can occur at many different junctures. For example, in a supply chain, change of ownership of a tagged object can occur when a distributor delivers this item to a retailer.

Strictly speaking, when ownership transfer occurs the previous owner should not be allowed or be able to access the tagged object while the new owner is allowed complete access to the tagged object. While this constraint is perfectly enforceable without their presence, it is not trivial when RFID tags are present. Since RFID tags broadcast the identity and other information about the tagged object, a previous owner of this tagged object potentially has access to communication from and to this tagged object. This information leakage naturally leads to related privacy and security concerns. Several researchers have attempted to address this issue through cryptographic means, however a majority of these have vulnerabilities (e.g., Kapoor and Piramuthu 2008 and the references therein).

Given the importance of security and privacy in RFID networks and the technology constraints associated with RFID tags, it is necessary to keep communications simple or lightweight, yet have the necessary cryptography built in. We propose a light-weight protocol (details in Section 2) that meets the security requirements of RFID devices, and use it for ownership transfer. Strictly speaking, this is only an ownership sharing protocol since all resourceful previous owners may continue to maintain RF access to the tag. The proposed protocol does not rely on a trusted third party (TTP), does not involve any key transfer between owners and uses only lightweight cryptographic techniques, thereby being easily implementable, even in the most basic RFID tag. We perform security analysis (in Section 3) to ensure that this protocol is accurate, confidential and provides forward security.

2. The Proposed Ownership Sharing Protocol

2.1. *Notation*

Following is a list of nomenclature for entities used in ownership transfer protocols, and a few assumptions:

N'_T, N_T, N_{R1}: random l-bit vectors
s_1, s_2: shared keys
H_k: keyed (k) hash function - $\{0,1\}^* \rightarrow \{0,1\}^l$
f_k: keyed (with key k) encryption function

We consider the simplest case involving the following parties, namely Tag, previous owner R_1 and new owner R_2. Once the request for transfer of ownership has been invoked and approved, the procedure for the actual transfer of ownership works as follows:

Step 1: Upon receiving a OT request, R_1 generates a fresh random nonce N_{R1}, XORs the key shared with the tag (s_1) with this nonce and sends it to both the tag as an encrypted message and to R_2 via a secure channel. This is the "initialization" phase as depicted in Figure 1. The tag responds to R_1 with an acknowledgement. R_1 waits for a pre-determined amount of time to receive this acknowledgement, which when not received, triggers R_1 to repeat the process with another freshly generated random nonce. This message sent to the tag acts as a trigger for the tag to initiate the steps that follow. These are depicted in Figure 2.

Step 2.1: Upon receiving N_{R1} XOR s_1 from R_1, the tag generates a fresh random nonce N_T, and sends the nonce XORed with the key s_1 to R_2. Now both T and R_2 know N, (where N = N_{R1} XOR N_T). As another measure or layer to preserve forward security, R_2 is not allowed to know s_1.

Step 2.2: The tag now randomly flips one bit in N and creates a vector N' and creates another fresh random nonce N'_T. It then sends N'_T, an encrypted function containing N' XOR N'_T, using N' XOR N'_T as the key and a similarly keyed Hash function with the same values to R_2.

Step 3.1: Knowing N, R_2 uses a brute force technique to determine N' so as to decrypt the value sent in f. Since R_2 knows that N' is really just N with only one flipped bit, this process is feasible and R_2 is assumed to possess the necessary computational resources to accomplish this very quickly. R_2 verifies the solution obtained using the hashed value.

Step 3.2: The new owner R_2 now generates and sends a new key s_2 to the tag by XORing with N' and encrypting it with a function that uses N' as the key. This step is repeated after a pre-determined time period until Step 4 successfully happens.

Step 4: Finally, the tag acknowledges receipt of new key using a hash function, keyed with the new key s_2 XORed with a newly generated nonce. R_2 acknowledges receipt of this message. The tag repeats the steps in Figure 2 until it receives the final acknowledgement from R_2.

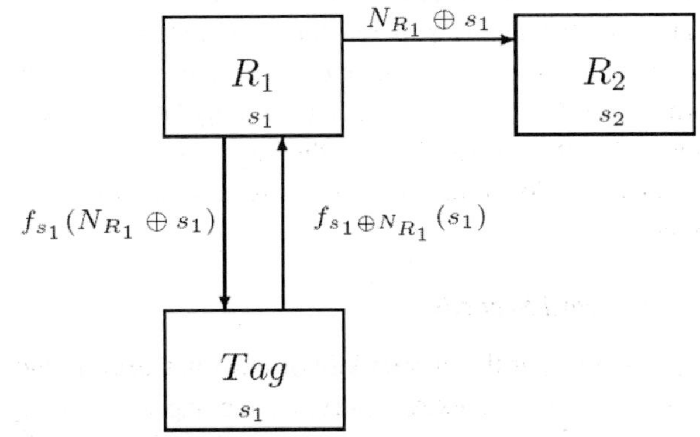

Figure 1. Ownership Transfer Protocol without TTP: Initialization.

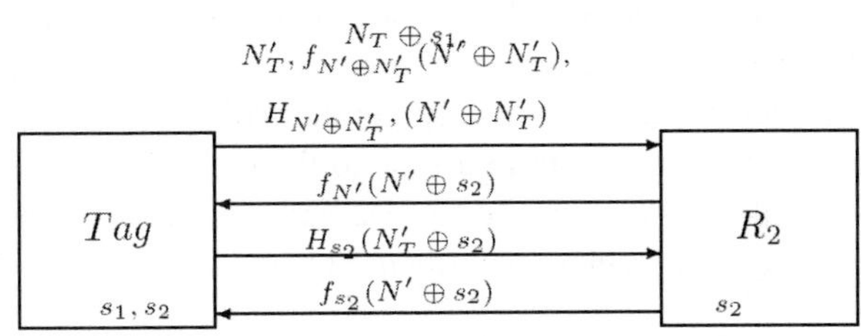

Figure 2. Ownership Transfer Protocol without TTP: Key change.

3. Security Analysis

The security design of the protocol should not impede normal operations, and should prevent a malicious adversary from getting any information. We consider the following measures:

3.1. *Secrecy/Authentication*

The cryptographic methods used (for example the keyed Hash function H_{si}) reasonably guarantee the secrecy of the message. Using key based cryptographic function ensembles (H_{si}, f_{si} etc.), we assure the recipient that the messages originates from valid sources.

3.2. *DoS/Synchronization problem*

Assume that an adversary intercepted the initial communique from R_1 to the tag. R_1 waits for a pre-determined amount of time to receive an acknowledgement message from the tag. If this acknowledgement is not received, R_1 repeats the steps given in Figure 1. R_2 always receives the message from R_1 since it is sent through a secure channel. Next, if the adversary blocks the first message from tag to R_2 during the "Key change" phase, R_2 may contact R_1 and have the process initialized again. At this juncture, while messages can be blocked, no key change has taken place, so the tag is still reachable. Only after R_2 has received the acknowledgement of the change (by processing the last message, namely $H_{s2}(N'_T \text{ XOR } s_2)$), does he attempt to contact the tag with operational commands. So at no point is there a synchronization issue.

3.3. *Forward Security*

This means that the current key of a tag has been found, and can be used to extract previous messages (assuming that *all* its past conversations are recorded). Let's say the adversary somehow finds s_2. The tag always communicates using a keyed hash function. The adversary cannot use the key to decode any of the tag's messages because the one-way hash function H is considered computationally un-invertible. In other words, he needs to have access to the hash digest table for lookups. Also, he cannot decipher/recreate any past messages sent with previously used keys.

3.4. *Passive Replay/Tracking*

The nonces are used to create an element of randomness in the protocol. Let's say an adversary wants to replay any messages, say the first message from the new owner R_2 to the tag. This message is $f_{N'}(N' \text{ XOR } s_2)$. The tag generates a new nonce N" *each time* and therefore the hashed message it returns is different, and so an adversary cannot track the tag or gain any advantage by replaying this message. A similar analysis can be described for all messages in the system.

4. Discussion

Adoption of new technology is facilitated by its operation being transparent to the end user, while its operational benefits are clearly visible. As we have seen in this paper, most attempts to provide a secure protocol (that ensures privacy), either for authentication or Ownership Transfer have been vulnerable to attacks. Addressing this problem is now crucial to inspire more confidence in the end users of this technology.

Although it is not easy to accomplish ownership transfer even in the presence of a TTP, achieving the same without a TTP is rather challenging. Moreover, unlike key distribution in computer networks where asymmetric cryptography is commonly used, resource constraints dictate use of symmetric cryptography in RFID systems. The high proportion of RFID ownership transfer protocols with TTP compared to those without TTP attest to this difficulty. The proposed protocol is not strictly for ownership transfer in the sense that it relies on the benevolence of the previous owners to not listen in on the messages between new owners and tags. All previous owners are able to know the content of these messages if they so desire, since they are privy to all the initial secret information. However, the protocol is relatively secure under most circumstances because a malicious adversary cannot listen to the entire set of initial messages, and so is unable to decipher the new key.

References

1. G. Kapoor and S. Piramuthu, “Protocols for Objects with Multiple RFID Tags," *Proceedings of the Sixteenth International Conference on Advanced Computing and Communications (ADCOM08)*, IEEE Computer Society (2008).

QUEUING ANALYSIS OF IEEE 802.11 WLAN

OMPRASAD BHAT[1], VENKATARAMANIAH K[3]

Department of Physics, Sri Sathya Sai University, Prasanthi Nilayam
Puttaparthi 515134, Andhra Pradesh, India

SAI SHANKAR N[2]

Bluetooth Engineering Department, Broadcom Corporation, San Diego
92127, CA, USA

IEEE 802.11 WLANs (Wireless Local Area Networks) have become synonymous as one of the main access technologies to the internet almost everywhere including business, office and home. This paper develops a simple queuing model to analyze the performance of IEEE 802.11 WLANs. We model a single IEEE 802.11 Wireless Station (WSTA) by means of a single server queue with infinite buffer wherein the service time is a function of backoff process which is function of number of stations trying to compete in the medium along with retry limit. We first derive the mean and second moment of backoff time of a WSTA using the Markov Chain Model outlined in [2]. Then the service time distribution is obtained. Then different distributions for the arrival process - Poisson, deterministic, normal and Pareto, are considered to model traffic realistically and analyze the waiting time and the queue length in the GI/G/1 queues for different network sizes.

1. Introduction

Recent advances in IEEE 802.11 based wireless local area networks (WLANs) have begun to successfully replace wired networks for the Internet access, owing to their high mobility, ease of installation, and low costs. The latest version of the IEEE 802.11 standard [1], provides detailed medium access control (MAC) and physical layer (PHY) specifications for WLANs. Due to the wide acceptance and fast – paced deployment of wireless LANs, different analytical models have been elaborated in the last few years to analyze the IEEE 802.11 MAC performance. The 802.11 MAC layer uses the carrier sense multiple access collision avoidance (CSMA/CA) mechanism with binary exponential backoff to control access to the shared wireless medium.

Bianchi [2] assumes that every Wireless Station (WSTA) has infinite buffer and always has packets waiting to be transmitted. With this assumption, if we consider the performance of a single WSTA, it is similar to the performance of other WSTAs. In this paper, we provide a queuing model that considers a WSTA's CSMA/CA as a server and obtain the delay seen by an application before it accesses the medium (queue waiting time) and also the average number of packets waiting in the queue to be transmitted after undergoing backoff (queue length). Each WSTA is assumed to be modeled by a single server queue with infinite buffer. The service time is modeled as following general distribution whose mean and second moments are derived from the Markov chain model [2]. Each packet that arrives at the IEEE 802.11 Medium Access Control (MAC) queue has to perform backoff using CSMA/CA protocol before the packet is transmitted by the 802.11 radio over the air. We first assume that the arrivals to this MAC queue follow a Poisson distribution and hence model the queue as M/G/1 queue. Then we extend the model to GI/G/1 queue wherein the arrivals can be from any general distribution with a constraint that the arrival of one packet does not trigger the arrival of the next packet. This is less generic than the G/G/1 queue but is representative of most of the traffic that arrives in Internet. The distributions considered for arrival processes are deterministic, normal and Pareto distributions. We thus analyze the performance of IEEE 802.11 WLAN by obtaining the waiting time and queue length results for different packet arrival rates in all cases.

The rest of the paper is outlined as follows. In section 2 we introduce the mathematical model of backoff process and solve for mean and second moments of backoff time. In section 3 we provide a generalized queuing model for each WSTA. Numerical results of waiting times and queue lengths are given in section 4. Concluding remarks are given section 5.

2. Mathematical Model of Backoff Process

The mathematical analysis of backoff process makes use of the same assumptions as in [2], in order to analyze and study the performance of the IEEE 802.11 WLAN. We assume that the network consists of a finite number of n contending stations operating in saturation conditions, i.e., every station always has a packet waiting to be transmitted (its transmission queue is assumed to be always non – empty), immediately after every successful packet transmission. We also consider ideal channel conditions (no hidden terminals and capture). The key approximation in our model is that the conditional collision probability p (probability of a collision seen by a packet being transmitted on the channel) is constant and independent of the number of retransmissions that the packet has suffered.

The backoff time counter behavior for a given WSTA can be modeled as a stochastic process given by $b(t)$. As in [2], a discrete time scale is adopted: t and t + 1 correspond to the beginning of two consecutive slot times, and the backoff time counter of each station decrements at the beginning of each slot time. Let $s(t)$ be the stochastic process representing the backoff stage $(0,\ldots,m)$ of the WSTA at slot time t. We let the pair of indices (i,k) represent the two – dimensional state of the bi – dimensional process $\{s(t),b(t)\}$, where $i \in (0,m)$ is the backoff stage and k, is the backoff counter time slot. Thus, i starts at 0 at the first attempt to transmit a packet and is increased by 1 every time a transmission attempt results in a collision, up to a maximum value m after which its value remains fixed at m. The backoff counter, k is initially chosen uniformly between $[0, W_i - 1]$, where typically $W_i = 2^i W$ is the range of the counter and W is the 802.11 parameter CW_{min}. While the medium is idle, the counter is decremented. Transmission is attempted only when $k = 0$. After each successful transmission, the backoff stage, i is reset to 0 and k is chosen uniformly in the range $[0, W_0 - 1]$. If the medium is sensed busy when the counter is decrementing, the WSTA freezes its backoff counter and resumes decrementing from this point once the medium is sensed idle again after DIFS.

As in [2], we denote the stationary distribution of the bi – dimensional Markov chain as $b_{i,k} = \lim_{t\to\infty} P\{s(t)=i, b(t)=k\}, i \in (0,m), k \in (0, W_i - 1)$. The probability τ that a station transmits a packet in a randomly chosen slot time is given by:

$$\tau = \frac{2(1-2p)}{(1-2p)(W+1)+pW(1-(2p)^m)}, \tag{1}$$

and the conditional collision probability p that a transmitted packet encounters collision when at least one of the remaining (n – 1) WSTAs transmit is given by:

$$p = 1-(1-\tau)^{(n-1)}. \tag{2}$$

Equations (1) and (2) represent a nonlinear system in the two unknowns, τ and p, which can be solved using numerical techniques. We use the *Newton's method* to solve this nonlinear system of equations and obtain values of τ and p for different network sizes (no. of contending WSTAs, n).

In order to model the IEEE 802.11 WSTA as a single server queue we need to obtain the mean service time of the queue. To take into account the nonlinearities that arise in backoff process, we model the service time of the queue as general distribution. In order to study this queue we need to determine the first and second moments of the service time. The service time is a function of backoff time and packet transmission time. To determine the service time of the queue we first determine the mean and second moment of the backoff time using these values of τ and p. The mean of the backoff time is given as:

$$E[b_{i,k}] = \left[\sum_{i=0}^{m}\sum_{k=0}^{W_i-1} ikb_{i,k}\right]T_{slot}, \tag{3}$$

where T_{slot} is the average length of a slot time. The second moment of the backoff time is given by:

$$E[b_{i,k}{}^2] = \left[\sum_{i=0}^{m}\sum_{k=0}^{W_i-1} i^2k^2b_{i,k}\right]T_{slot}^2. \tag{4}$$

On simplification (3) and (4) yield:

$$E[b_{i,k}] = \frac{b_{0,0}}{6}\left[W^2\left\{\frac{4p}{(1-4p)^2}\left(1-(m+1)(4p)^m+m(4p)^{(m+1)}\right)\right\} - \frac{p}{(1-p)^2}\left\{1-(m+1)p^m+mp^{(m+1)}\right\}\right]T_{slot}, \tag{5}$$

$$E[b_{i,k}^2] = \frac{b_{0,0}}{12}W\left[W^2\left\{\frac{-(m+1)^2(8p)^{m+1}}{(1-8p)}+\frac{\left(8p-(2m+3)(8p)^{m+2}\right)}{(1-8p)^2} +2\frac{\left((8p)^2-(8p)^{m+3}\right)}{(1-8p)^3}\right\}+\frac{(m+1)^2(2p)^{m+1}}{(1-2p)}-\frac{\left(2p-(2m+3)(2p)^{m+2}\right)}{(1-2p)^2} -2\frac{\left((2p)^2-(2p)^{m+3}\right)}{(1-2p)^3}\right]T_{slot}^2. \tag{6}$$

The service time is defined as the sum of packet service time and the time taken by a station to perform the backoff process before transmitting a packet. Thus the overall mean service time is the time taken by a packet to get dequeued from the WSTA's buffer and is given by:

$$E[S] = E[b_{i,k}] + \frac{E[P]}{PHY\ rate}, \qquad (7)$$

where $E[b_{i,k}]$ is given by (5), $E[P]$ is the average packet length and PHY rate is the transmission rate supported by the PHY layer. The second moment of the service time is obtained by using the second moment of backoff time given by (6) as follows:

$$E[S^2] = E[b_{i,k}^2] + \left[\frac{E[P]}{PHY\ rate}\right]^2. \qquad (8)$$

We use the system parameters of OFDM (Orthogonal Frequency Division Multiplexing) PHY specifications which are summarized in Table 1, to obtain the values of the mean and the standard deviation of the backoff time.

Table 1. IEEE 802.11 System Parameters

OFDM PHY parameters				
Packet size	***Channel bit rate***	***Slot time***	***CWmin***	***m***
1024 bytes	6 Mbps	9μs	16	6

With increase in network size, there is more competition to access the medium and there is an increased probability of collision, whenever an attempt is made to transmit the arbitrary packet. Hence, the network size plays an important role in deciding the backoff time in the exponential backoff process. Thus the backoff time increases exponentially with increase in the number of contending stations as shown in Figs. 1 and 2.

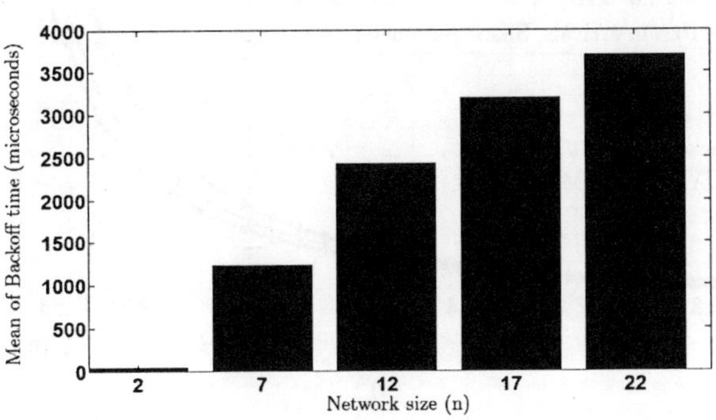

Figure 1. Variation of mean of backoff time with network size, n

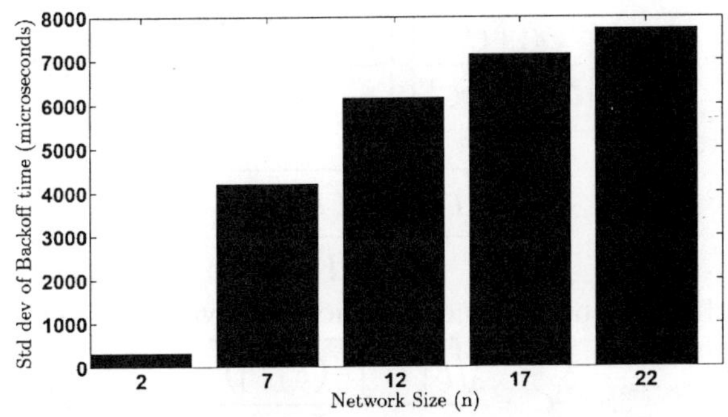

Figure 2. Variation of standard deviation of backoff time with network size, n

3. Queuing Model for Individual WSTA

Many applications are sensitive to queue characteristics such as waiting time and average queue length. Thus it is important to analyze the queuing model for wireless LANs to obtain such performance metrics. In order to analyze the queue realistically we assume that the packet arrivals to this queue follow different distributions like Poisson, deterministic, normal and Pareto with average arrival rate λ. Since the performance of this particular WSTA under consideration is similar to other WSTAs in the network, we can obtain the average queue length and other statistics of this single WSTA to design MAC buffer practically.

We first assume that the arrivals to this MAC queue follow a Poisson distribution and hence model the queue as M/G/1 queue. Under the M/G/1 assumption, the expected queue waiting time is given by the Pollaczek – Khinchin formula [3], [4]:

$$E[W]_{M/G/1} = \frac{\lambda E[S^2]}{2(1-\lambda E[S])}, \qquad (9)$$

where we use general distribution for service time whose mean and second moment are given by (7) and (8) respectively.

The queue length is then obtained using the Little's formula which is given by [3]:

$$L = \lambda E[W], \qquad (10)$$

We now extend the model to the GI/G/1 queue wherein arrival process can follow any general distribution with a constraint that the arrival of each packet is independent of each other. This is less generic than the G/G/1 queue but is representative of most of the traffic that arrives in the Internet. For the GI/G/1 queue, the expected waiting time is given by [4]:

$$E[W]_{GI/G/1} \approx \left\{ \frac{\rho(1+C_s^2)}{2-\rho+\rho C_s^2} \right\} \left\{ \frac{\rho(2-\rho)C_a^2+\rho^2 C_s^2}{2\lambda(1-\rho)} \right\}, \quad (11)$$

where,

$$C_s = \frac{\sqrt{E[S^2]-(E[S])^2}}{E[S]}, \quad (12)$$

is called the coefficient of variation of service time $E[S]$,

$$C_a = \frac{\sqrt{E[T^2]-(E[T])^2}}{E[T]} \quad (13)$$

is called the coefficient of variation of interarrival time $E[T]$, and

$$\rho = \frac{E[S]}{E[T]} \quad (14)$$

is called the utilization factor. Equation (11) holds when $1 < C_a^2 < 2$. If $C_a^2 \leq 1$, the best approximation for waiting time for GI/G/1 queue is given by [4]:

$$E[W]_{GI/G/1} \approx \left[\frac{\rho C_a^2\left(1-(1-\rho)C_a^2\right)+\rho^2 C_s^2}{2\lambda(1-\rho)} \right] \quad (15)$$

The distributions considered for arrival processes in GI/G/1 queue are deterministic, normal and Pareto distributions.

For deterministic arrivals, since the interarrival times don't deviate from their mean values, we note that $C_a = 0$ and hence the formula in (15) simplifies to:

$$E[W]_{deterministic} = \left[\frac{\rho^2 C_s^2}{2\lambda(1-\rho)} \right] \quad (16)$$

When we consider normal arrivals, there are two parameters, the mean (interarrival time) and its standard deviation (SD) that need to be defined. Thus the queue waiting time for normal arrivals follows the same expression as in (15). In our model we assume only those values of standard deviation of interarrival times that obey $C_a^2 \leq 1$.

For Pareto arrivals, we define two quantities called scale x_m and shape k. For such arrivals C_a is independent of the scale parameter x_m and depends only on the shape parameter k and is given as:

$$C_a = \frac{1}{\sqrt{k(k-2)}} \quad (17)$$

Again the waiting time is given by (15) where C_a is given by (17) for Pareto arrivals.

In all these cases the packet arrival rates can be varied and the waiting times can be calculated. The queue lengths for the different arrival distributions can be calculated using (10) by multiplying the respective queue waiting time with the arrival rate.

4. Numerical Results

In this section, we present some numerical results to show the behavior of MAC layer packet waiting time and queue length for different arrival distributions as discussed earlier. We use the system parameters of OFDM (Orthogonal Frequency Division Multiplexing) PHY specifications which are summarized in Table 1. Fig. 3 compares the waiting times and queue lengths for M/G/1 and GI/G/1 queues for a fixed network size of 12 stations.

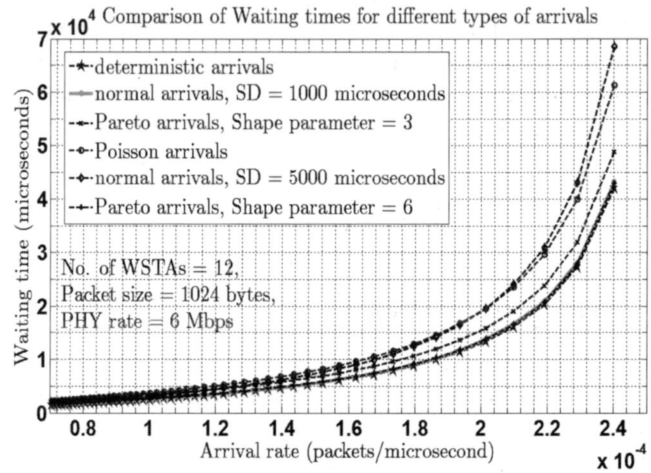

(a)

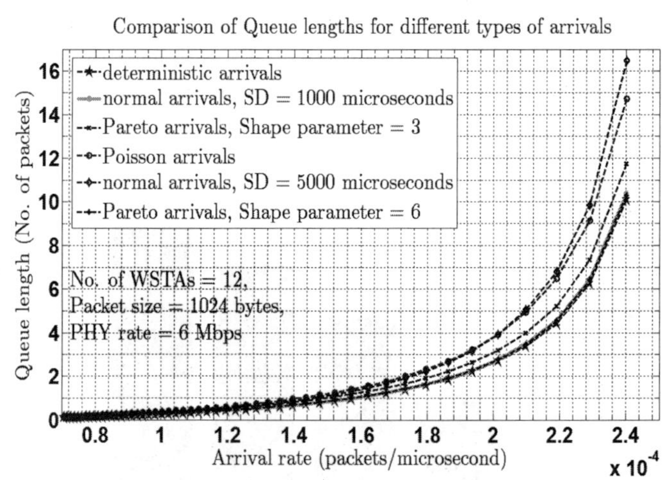

(b)

Figure 3. Performance for different types of arrivals for a fixed network size : (a) Waiting times (b) Queue lengths

From Fig. 3, it is evident that for Poisson arrivals (M/G/1 queues), the waiting time and queue length performance is only marginally better than normal arrivals (standard deviation, SD = 5000 microseconds). For Pareto arrivals with an assumed shape parameter of 3, we observe improved performance compared to the 2 previous cases. It is clear from Fig. 3 that the performance is the best when we consider deterministic packet arrivals at a station. When we decrease the SD value of interarrival times for normal arrivals to a value of 1000 microseconds, or increase the shape parameter value of Pareto arrivals to 6, we observe that the performance almost matches that of deterministic arrivals. It is clear that larger standard deviation in the arrival process has significant impact on waiting time and hence the delay in delivering the packet.

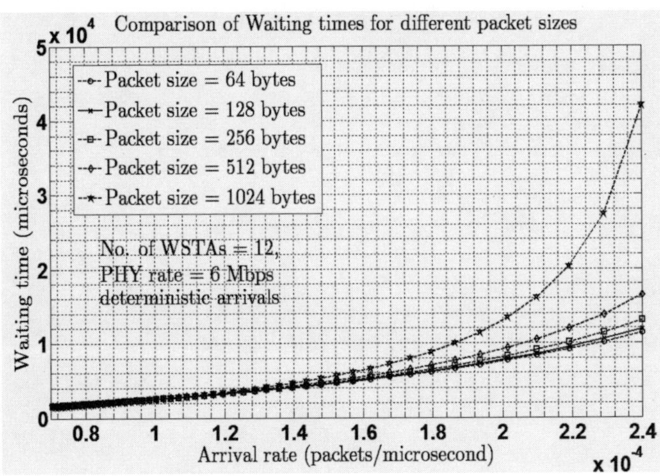

(a)

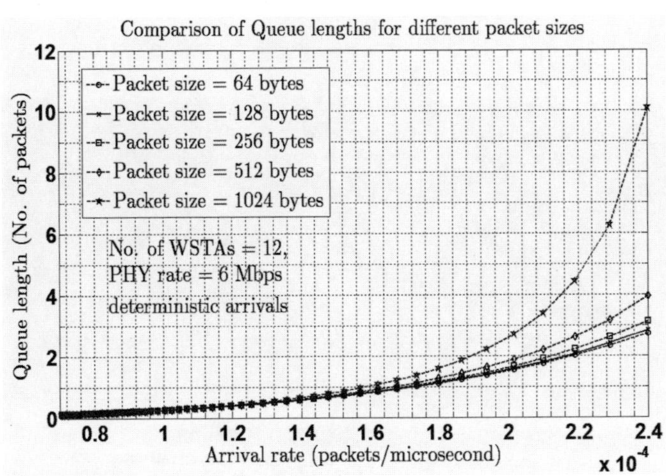

(b)

Figure 4. Performance for different packet sizes for deterministic arrivals for a fixed network size : (a) Waiting times (b) Queue lengths

We now show the comparison of waiting time and queue length performances for different packet sizes for deterministic arrivals considering that the network size is 12.

A larger packet involves greater packet transmission time and thus the service time which is modeled as a function of backoff time and packet transmission time increases with increase in packet size. Thus, Fig. 4 shows that with increase in packet size, the waiting time and the queue length in GI/G/1 queues also increase.

Fig. 5 shows the waiting times and the queue lengths in GI/G/1 queues considering deterministic arrivals for different network sizes. We observe that the waiting times and the queue lengths increase with increase in network size for deterministic arrivals.

This happens primarily due to the increase in the backoff time when the number of contending WSTAs in the network increases. As a result of increased competition to access the medium for attempting a transmission, the probability of collision of packets increases. Due to this, the WSTA under consideration increases its backoff time after following the exponential backoff rules that govern the CSMA/CA protocol. We can generalize this result and claim that for different types of arrivals also, the same behavior holds.

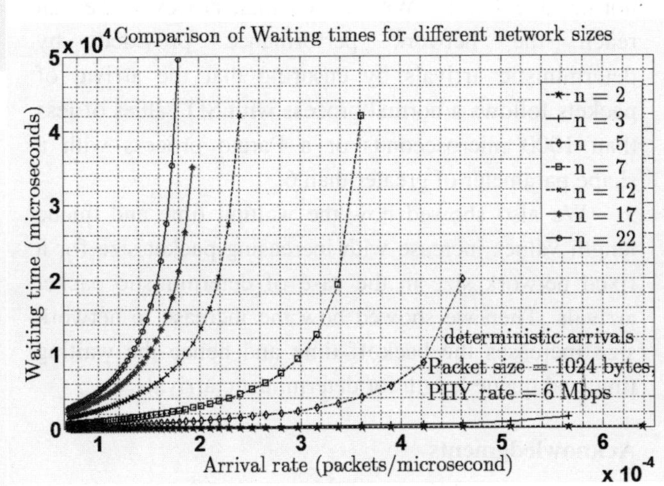

(a)

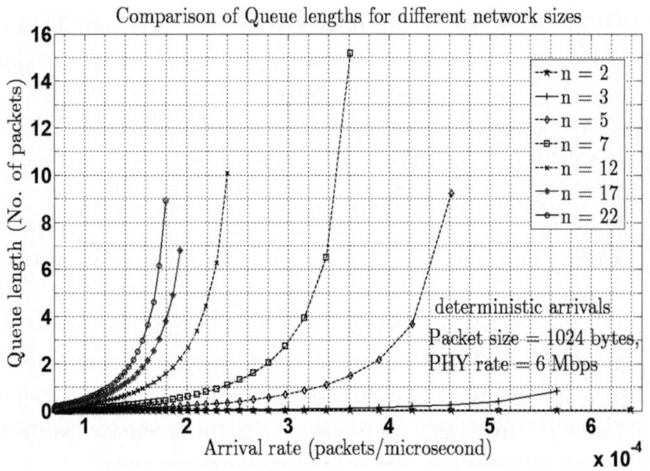

(b)

Figure 5. Performance for deterministic arrivals for different network sizes : (a) Waiting times (b) Queue lengths

5. Conclusions

This paper modeled the IEEE 802.11 WLAN STA by a single server queue and studied its performance for different types of arrivals. We arrived at the result that deterministic packet arrivals enhance the network performance in terms of packet waiting time and queue length compared to other types of arrivals like Poisson, normal and Pareto. We showed that, however, we can reach the network performance provided by deterministic arrivals by ensuring that the arrival of packets follows a normal process with SD values of less than 1000 microseconds or a Pareto process with a shape parameter of greater than 6.

We also showed how the waiting time and queue length values increase with increasing packet size for a fixed network size in the case of deterministic packet arrivals. Then we showed how the increase in network size increases the backoff time and hence the waiting time and queue length for deterministic arrivals.

Acknowledgments

The authors are grateful to Bhagawan Sri Sathya Sai Baba, the revered chancellor of Sri Sathya Sai University for His constant inspiration.

References

1. *IEEE Standard for Wireless LAN Medium Access Control (MAC) and Physical Layer (PHY) Specifications,* 2007 Edition (Revision of IEEE Std 802.11 – 1999 Edition) (June 2007).
2. G. Bianchi, Performance analysis of the IEEE 802.11 distributed coordination function, IEEE Journal on Selected Areas in Communications, vol. 18, pp. 535 – 547, March 2000.
3. D. Bertsekas and R. Gallager, *Data Networks.* Englewood Cliffs, NJ: Prentice – Hall, 1987.
4. L. Kleinrock, *Queueing Systems,*vol. I : Theory. Wiley Interscience, New York, 1975.

A LOCALIZATION ALGORITHM FOR A GPS-FREE SYSTEM WITH STATIC PARAMETER TUNING*

K. PADIA, G. A. VIKAS, H. S. IYER, V. R. DARSHAN, N. P. GANESH PRASAD, A. SRINIVAS

Department of Computer Science, PES Institute of Technology, 100 feet Ring Road, BSK 3rd Stage Bangalore, Karnataka 560085, India

H. KHAN, A. GUPTA, S.OLARIU

Department of Computer Science, Old Dominion University, Norfolk, Virginia 23508, USA

Localization in wireless network refers to determining the location of a mobile user which may either be stationary or in motion. This paper presents the design and evaluation of an algorithm for localization of mobile nodes in GSM networks. The proposed algorithm does not use GPS and has the advantages of being cost effective and reliable. The received signal strength from the base stations in the proximity of the mobile form the basis for the proposed algorithm. The algorithm concentrates on improving the accuracy of estimated location of the mobile by using a prediction-interpolation technique. The key aspects of the proposed localization technique are that it assumes linear dependency between the accuracy of the estimated mobile location and the received signal strengths from the neighboring base stations, and tunes the location estimate based on this mapping.

Keywords: Received signal strength, Deviation detection, Prediction, Triangulation, Interpolation.

1. Introduction

One of the major challenges in GSM networks is determining the relative position of the mobile nodes with respect to surrounding base stations. This involves tasks which strive to annul the effects of motion of the mobile node. Recent surveys have revealed that 25 percent of cell phone users are not able to provide their location information. The use of GPS in emergency location management is problematic, the reason being the requirement of the GPS system to have three or more satellites visible to the GPS receiver. Moreover GPS does not work indoors and is seen to be inaccurate in poor atmospheric conditions. Also, GPS based devices are expensive and less compact. Hence there is a need to develop efficient GPS-free localization algorithms which provide for high levels of accuracy and subsequently yield reliable results.

The existing localization techniques can be classified into two categories: range based and range free. Range based techniques exploit the range of base station and the distance of mobile node from it. Examples of this category include RSS, TOA, TDOA, AOA based techniques. These techniques call for extra hardware requirements. Range free methods are less accurate and used for applications which can tolerate small permissible errors in location estimation.

In [1], the described technique uses the RSS based measurements as the starting point. At this instant, a prediction method based on the mobile velocity and direction is employed. The author then suggests an interpolation technique using the above two coordinate values to obtain a better estimate of the mobile location coordinates. It is also stated in [1] that either RSS estimate or the predicted position may be responsible for deviation. The algorithm proposed by us in this paper initially concentrates on determining the factor responsible for deviation and then uses this information to fine tune a parameter defined to counter the effect of deviation. We have also presented a method to predict the position of the node at any time instant. All computation is done at the mobile device.

In the next section we briefly present some of the available range based techniques and related localization techniques. In section 3, we explain our algorithm using progressive prediction and interpolation. Section 4 presents case studies and the associated NS-2 simulation results. Conclusion and scope for future work is addressed in section 5.

2. Related Work

A wide variety of approaches to mobile localization have been developed previously. These include

* The results of this paper are a part of the PESIT – ODU collaborative research initiative.

popularly used methods like AOA, TDOA, TOA, TA, U-TOA and their variants. More information can be found in [3], [4], [6], [10] and [11]. The accuracy of these range based techniques depends on the accuracy of the range measurements. Considerable amount of inaccuracy is introduced in these measurements due to two factors, viz. Non-Line of Sight (NLOS) error and measurement error. The measurements in cellular systems, taken by Nokia [12], show that NLOS error dominates the standard measurement noise, and tends to be the main cause of the error in range estimation. They also show that the location estimation error linearly increases with the distance error. Following these measurements, Wylie and Holtzman propose a method for the detection and correction of NLOS errors [14]. They show that it is possible to detect a NLOS environment by using the standard deviation of the measurement noise and the history of the range measurements. They propose a method for LOS reconstruction and they show that the correction is only possible if the standard measurement noise dominates the NLOS error. In [13], Chen presents a Residual Weighting Algorithm for localizing mobile nodes which relies on the basis that correction of the localization estimation errors is possible when the number of range measurements exceed the required minimum.

[15] presents a significantly different approach to mobile localization. The algorithm in [15] describes a connectivity metric method which utilizes the RF communication capabilities of the mobile devices and at the same time addresses the problem of bad environmental conditions. In [16], Srdan proposes an algorithm for mobile localization in Ad hoc networks. The GPS-free algorithm devised in [16] uses the distances computed between mobile nodes to build a relative two dimensional coordinate system. [17] puts forth a two phase TOA based distributed mobile localization algorithm to minimize the number of messages exchanged and the coordinate setup time. The algorithm as proposed in [17], assumes that establishing a network with small subset of mobile nodes can successfully establish the coordination system for the overall network.

The Global System for Mobile Communications (GSM) is the most prevalent phone and data service in use today. GSM provides only RSS measurements and hence GSM based mobiles cannot make direct use of location techniques based on TOA, AOA and TDOA [5]. Hence new techniques have to be devised to localize GSM mobiles and at the same time strive to achieve high accuracy. Consequently, significant research has been made in providing solutions to the localization of GSM mobiles. Some of the developed techniques in this regard and their variants can be found in [2], [5], [7], [8] and [9].

The next section describes the proposed GPS-free static parameter-tuning algorithm for localization in mobile ad-hoc networks which is the main contribution of this paper.

3. Prediction–Interpolation with Static Parameter Tuning

As described in [1], the real path of the mobile user is indicated by a sequence of points R_i. The sequence of prediction based coordinates P_i represent the predicted path. Similarly, the RSS path is represented by the sequence S_i of RSS based estimation coordinates. As proposed in [1], we have:

$$L_n = \lambda * S_n + (1-\lambda) * P_n \qquad (1)$$

Here S_n is the RSS based estimation at time instant T_n. P_n is the prediction based point and finally L_n is the final estimate achieved after interpolation. λ is the parameter defined to counter the deviations in prediction and RSS based coordinate estimations.

The prediction process starts with the premise that the velocity (speed and direction) of the mobile in continuous transition is available. These parameters are measured by a speedometer and an odometer on the mobile. Figure 1 depicts a scenario at time instant Tn. With reference to Figure 1, d is the distance travelled by the moving node and this value is computed using the velocity information. The predicted coordinate P_i is then obtained from L_{i-1} by traversing a distance equal to d in the direction indicated by the odometer. The distance between P_{i-1} and P_i is designated as d_p. The angle made by the line segment $P_{i-1}P_i$ with the direction of motion of the mobile (represented here by a dashed line) is represented by θ_p. Similarly, the angle made by the line segment $S_{i-1}S_i$ with direction of motion of the mobile (represented by another dashed line) is designated as θ_s. The distance between S_{i-1} and S_i is represented as d_s .

It is important to note that we consider only the acute or right angles between the direction of real motion and the direction of predicted (or RSS) path. If the angle between the two of them, θ, is obtuse, we consider the angle to be π – θ.

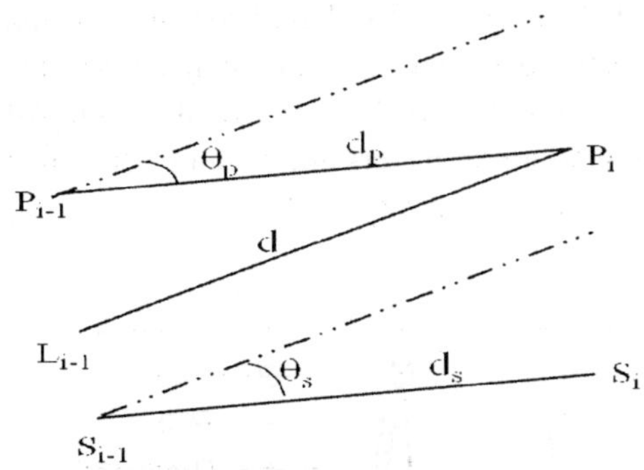

Figure 1. The prediction process

The next step is the determination of the parameter that is responsible for deviation from the real path and forms the basis of this paper. This procedure is primarily based on determining the projections of the real path on both predicted path and RSS coordinate based path.

As shown in figure 2, we first compare $|(d_p\text{-}d)|$ with $|(d_s\text{-}d)|$. This comparison is made to figure out which among the two is closer to 0 and hence determine the distance (either d_p or d_s) that is closer to d. Next θ_p is compared with θ_s. If θ_p is found to have a lower value than θ_s and d_p closer to d than d_s, it is inferred that the majority of the deviation is caused by the RSS estimate and hence the predicted value better approximates the real value than the RSS value. Thus the value of λ is reduced as per [1] in order to give more priority to the predicted value.

The proof for the above deduction is explained using figure 2.

Proof. In figure 2,

$$CD = d.\ cos(\theta_p) \quad (2)$$

$$GH = d.\ cos(\theta_s) \quad (3)$$

If,

$$\theta_p < \theta_s,$$

then,

$$cos(\theta_p) > cos(\theta_s) \quad (4)$$

Thus,

$$d.\ cos(\theta_p) > d.\ cos(\theta_s) \quad (5)$$

i.e.

$$CD > GH \quad (6)$$

This implies that the component of real path is more in triangle BCD than in triangle FGH or equivalently the projection of real path is more in the predicted path than in RSS path, hence the greater preference for the predicted coordinate and subsequent reduction in the value of the parameter λ. □

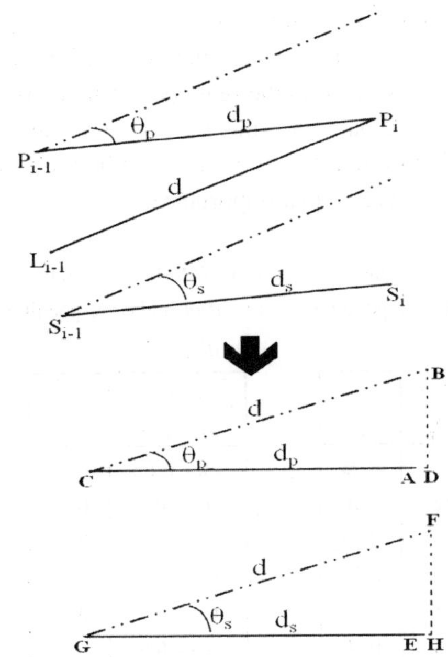

Figure 2. Detecting the parameter that experiences more deviation

Similarly, if θp is greater than θs and $|(dp\text{-}d)|$ has a lower value compared to $|(ds\text{-}d)|$, the reason for deviation from the real path is ascribed to the errors in prediction and hence preference is given to the RSS based estimate over the predicted value. In this case, the value of λ is increased to annul the effect of incorrect prediction. For all other situations apart from the two previously discussed, decision is made based on previous history, i.e., the value of λ which was calculated and employed in the previous iteration is reused in the current iteration.

Once the parameter to be preferred in the current iteration is determined by the method discussed above, the value of λ for the present step is determined. This represents the amount of preference given to the chosen parameter.

The method employed is based on two static look up tables. Table 1 is referred to when the prediction based coordinate is preferred over RSS estimate and Table 2 is referred to if it is the other way round.

The value of λ in Table 1 ranges from 0.0 to 0.5 to ensure that the interpolated point is closer to the predicted point than the RSS point. It can be observed from Table 1, that the algorithm assumes linear dependency of λ on the value of $|d_p-d|/d_p$. The lowest value of λ as shown in Table 1 indicates maximum amount of preference given to the prediction based coordinate which infers that the prediction based coordinate is very close to the real coordinate compared to the RSS coordinate. A value of λ = *0.5* infers that RSS based coordinates and the prediction based coordinates are given equal importance.

Table 1. Value of the ratio $(d_p - d)/d_p$ and corresponding value of λ

Range for $(d_p - d)/d_p$	λ
0 – 0.1	0.05
0.1 – 0.2	0.10
0.2 – 0.3	0.15
0.3 – 0.4	0.20
0.4 – 0.5	0.25
0.5 – 0.6	0.30
0.6 – 0.7	0.35
0.7 – 0.8	0.40
0.8 – 0.9	0.45

Table 2. Value of the ratio $(d_s - d)/d_s$ and corresponding *vaue of* λ

Range for $(d_s - d)/d_s$	λ
0 – 0.1	0.95
0.1 – 0.2	0.90
0.2 – 0.3	0.85
0.3 – 0.5	0.80
0.4 – 0.5	0.75
0.5 – 0.6	0.70
0.6 – 0.7	0.65
0.7 – 0.8	0.60
0.8 – 0.9	0.5

Similarly, if the algorithm determines that the RSS based estimate is to be preferred over predicted coordinate values, the value of λ is obtained by hashing the value of the expression $|d_s-d|/d_s$ into the look up table shown in Table 2. Here the value of λ ranges from 0.5 to 1.0. This is to ensure that the interpolated point is closer to the RSS point as per [1]. A value of λ = 0.95 indicates that the RSS based coordinate is extremely close to the real mobile location coordinate compared to the prediction based coordinate.

The number of intervals for either of the look up tables can be varied by varying the step length and hence there is always a flexibility to obtain the desired level of accuracy. For the purpose of simulation, we have used a step length of 0.1. In the next section we discuss the simulation results for different case scenarios and demonstrate the effectiveness of the proposed algorithm in these scenarios.

4. Implementation and Results

The experiments have been conducted on the network simulator NS2. The graphs for each simulation scenario presented below depict the real path of the mobile user, the path obtained by connecting predicted points, the path obtained by connecting RSS based coordinates and finally the path obtained by the connecting the interpolated coordinates which is the final result. All distances measured are in meters and it can be seen that the resolution of accuracy is very high.

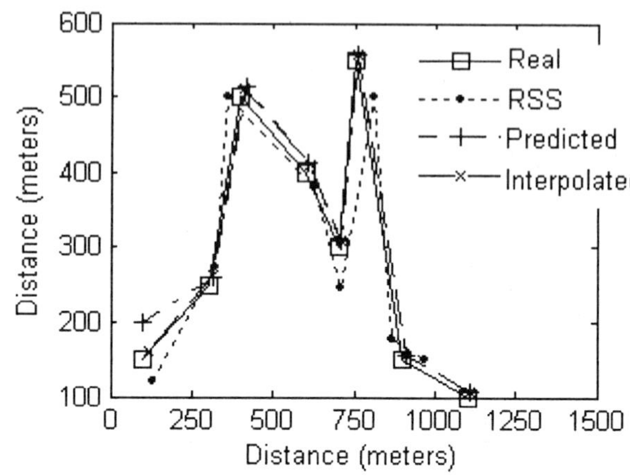

Figure 3. Test Scenario 1

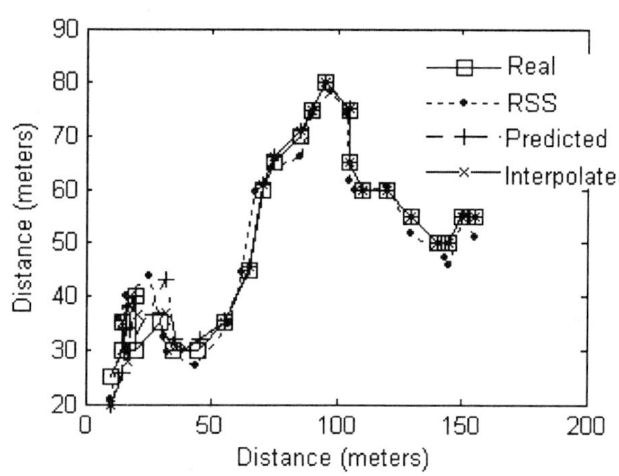

Figure 4. Test Scenario 2

Figure 3 depicts a scenario in which a random path with sharp and prominent deviations has been chosen as the real path of mobile user for simulation. Inaccuracies in prediction and RSS based estimation are clearly depicted in Figure 3. The objective is to bring the interpolated point close to the real point at any time instant Tn. The measurements are taken at regular intervals of 0.8 seconds under the assumption that either the direction of movement of the mobile node or its velocity cannot vary by a large amount in this very short interval of time. From figure 3, it can be observed that the inevitable inaccuracies associated with the prediction and RSS based estimation are addressed suitably by the proposed algorithm and the interpolated path converges towards the real path with a maximum deviation of 10-15 meters towards the end of simulation.

In Figure 4, the path chosen as the real path comprises of sudden deviations, curves, vertical and horizontal movements of the mobile node. Since the proposed static look up table approach controls and assigns the amount of preference to either prediction based coordinates or RSS based coordinates depending on the deviations caused by either of them, the algorithm handles the scenario depicted in figure 8 effectively and convergence is achieved with a maximum deviation of 5-10 meters as is evident from the results in Figure 4.

5. Future Work

The future work lies in predicting the position of mobile node without the use of additional hardware like odometer and compass which may not be provided by a mobile device. The challenge here lies in prediction of mobile location based on only the received signal strength information. The static method makes use of predetermined look up tables and thus reduces the flexibility with which the algorithm can operate. Thus a method for dynamically computing the value of the parameter λ has to be devised. The dynamic choice of λ to adapt to the ambient conditions is likely to result in more accurate interpolated mobile location coordinates. Work is underway in this direction.

References

1. Haseebulla Khan, *Robust and Efficient Localization Techniques for Cellular and Wireless Sensor Networks*, MS Thesis, Old Dominion University, December 2005
2. F. Cesbon and R. Arnott, *Locating GSM Mobiles Using Antenna Arrays*, Electronic Letters, 34(6), 1998, 1539-1540
3. K. W. Cheung, H. C. So, W.-K. Ma, and Y. T. Chau, *Received Signal Strength Based Mobile Positioning via Constrained Weighted Least Squares*, Proc. IEEE International Conference on Acoustics, Speech and Signal Processing, (ICASSP'03), Hong Kong, April 2003
4. P.K. Chrysanthis, *On indoor position location with wireless LANs*, Proc. IEEE ISPIRC-02
5. G. Heine, *GSM networks: Protocols, Terminology and Implementation*, Artech House, MA, 1999
6. M. Pent, M. A. Spirito and E. Turco, *Method for Positioning GSM Mobile Station Units Using Absolute Time Delay Measurements*, Electronic Letters, 33(24), 1997, 1567-1568
7. M. Spirito, *On the Accuracy of Cellular Mobile Station Location Estimation*, IEEE Transactions on Vehicular Technology, 59(3), 2001, 674-685
8. S. Y. Willassen, *A Method of Implementing Mobile Station Location in GSM*, http://willassen.no/msl/node6.html
9. C. L. L. Wong, M. C. lee and R. K. W. Chan, *GSM-based Mobile Positioning Using WAP*, Proc. IEEE Wireless Communications and Networking Conference, (WCNC'2000}, Chicago, IL, September 2000
10. J. K.-Y. Ng, S. K. C. Chan and K. K. H. Kan, *Providing Location Estimation within Metropolitan Area Based on a Mobile Phone Network*, Proc. IEEE International Workshop on database and Expert Systems Applications, (DEXA'02), Aix-en-Provence, France, September 2002
11. M. Spirito, On the Accuracy of Cellular Mobile Station Location Estimation, *IEEE Transactions on Vehicular Technology*, 59(3), 2001, 674-685
12. M.I. Silventoinen and T. Rantalainen, *Mobile Station Emergency Locating in GSM*, Personal Wireless Communications, IEEE International Conference on 1996
13. P.-C. Chen, *A non-line-of-sight error mitigation algorithm in location estimation*, IEEE Wireless Communications and Networking Conference, 1999
14. M.P. Wylie and J. Holtzman, *The non-line of sight problem in mobile location estimation*, 5th IEEE International Conference on Universal Personal Communications, 1996
15. Nirupama Bulusu, John Heidemann, and Deborah Estrin, *GPS-less Low-Cost Outdoor Localization for Very Small Devices*, University of Southern California/Information Sciences Institute
16. Srdan ˇCapkun, Maher Hamdi, Jean-Pierre Hubaux *GPS-free positioning in mobile Ad-Hoc networks,* Proceedings of Hawaii International Conference on System Sciences, 2001, 3481-3490
17. Rajagopal Iyengar and Biplab Sikdar, *Scalable and Distributed GPS free Positioning for Sensor Networks*, Proceedings of IEEE ICC, 2003, 338-342

Session 2

HELLO EXPIRED TIME BASED GREEDY ROUTING SCHEME FOR MOBILE AD HOC NETWORKS

SACHIN SHARMA

Tejas Networks India Limited, Bangalore India, Permanent Address:
Village Niihal (near ITI) Bilaspur, Himachal Pradesh, India, Email: sharon_sachin@yahoo.co.in

In wireless mobile ad hoc networks, nodes change their topology very frequently and unpredictably over time. In such environment, routing protocol needs to update neighbor information very frequently. Many routing protocols suggest that each node should periodically broadcast HELLO packet to their direct neighbors. In these protocols, if node does not receive HELLO packet till HELLO expired time, it deletes the entry of that neighbor from its neighbor table or routing table. This paper presents a metric which mitigates the problems due to higher value of this HELLO expired time. We also incorporate this metric in greedy routing decision of geographical protocols. Performance evaluation of greedy routing and proposed greedy routing is through NS simulation. Simulations show that our proposed greedy routing outperforms existing greedy routing with respect to packet delivery, throughput and overheads.

1. Introduction

Mobile Ad hoc Network (MANET) represents a system of wireless mobile nodes that can freely and dynamically self organize into temporary network topology. This allows mobile nodes to communicate with each other without any preexisting infrastructure. The topology of such networks changes dynamically as mobile nodes join or depart the network. So, to improve the performance of ad hoc networks, routing protocol should adjust its behavior according to network conditions. Thus, designing a routing protocol is a challenging task.

Many routing protocols such as Ad hoc On Demand Distance Vector [1], Optimized Link State Routing [2], Geographical Routing protocols [3,4] have been proposed for wireless ad hoc networks. In these protocols, neighbor information is known through periodically broadcasted HELLO packets. These packets are broadcasted after every HELLO interval. Now if nodes do not receive HELLO packet from their neighbors till HELLO expired time, link with those neighbors are considered as broken.

In this paper, we first investigate pros and cons of keeping large HELLO expired time, and then propose a metric that mitigates the problems due to higher value of HELLO expired time. Finally, we integrate our proposed metric in greedy routing decision of geographical routing protocols. Based on simulation results, we found that performance of greedy routing by adding our proposed metric increases significantly in term of packet delivery, throughput, and overheads.

The rest of the paper is organized as follows: Section 2 gives background to previous research. Section 3 gives analysis of keeping higher value of HELLO expired time. Section 4 describes our methodology. Section 5 describes simulation environment. Section 6 presents analysis of results and finally, we conclude in section 7.

2. Background

This section first describes brief introduction to geographical routing, and then discusses the previous research on HELLO protocol.

2.1. *Geographical Routing*

Greedy routing [3] is the basic mode of operation in most geographical routing protocols, where next hop node is chosen to minimize the distance from destination.

Every node in geographical routing periodically broadcasts HELLO packets within its own radio range. HELLO packet carries node ID (Identification number) and its current position information. Neighbors that receive this HELLO packet store received information in neighbor table. Now if next HELLO packet does not arrive till the HELLO expired time, the neighbor information is removed from table. Greedy routing is based on minimum distance from destination. The header of the packet destined to a particular node contains the destination ID as well as its position. When a node has a data packet to forward, it consults its neighbor table and forwards the packet to the neighbor which is closest to destination. Though this greedy approach works well in many cases, it is not away from pitfalls. In some cases, node reaches a situation of dead-end where it finds that it is the only one among all its neighbors that is closest to the destination.

Well known recovery technique is given in Greedy Perimeter Stateless Routing (GPSR) [3] protocol. In this protocol, when a node finds dead-end situation, the greedy forwarding mode is changed to perimeter forwarding. In perimeter forwarding mode, packet is traversed along the planar graph until it reaches a neighbor that is closer to the destination

2.2. *Research on HELLO protocol*

Significant research [5, 6] has already been proposed on HELLO packet frequency. A low HELLO frequency leads to obsolete tables while a higher one may saturate bandwidth and may cause congestion in network. An adaptive HELLO protocol [8] for AODV has been proposed, in which nodes evaluate two parameters: Time Link Failure (TLF) and Time Without Change (TWC). The nodes first broadcast HELLO packets at low frequency. If at any time node notices that the measured TWC is greater than a threshold, it broadcasts HELLO packets at a higher frequency. On the contrary, if the estimated TLF becomes smaller than a threshold, it broadcasts HELLO at low frequency. Moreover, a turnover based adaptive HELLO protocol (TAP) [7] has been proposed, which enables nodes in mobile networks to dynamically adjust their HELLO packet frequency depending on the current speed of nodes.

Nevertheless, only a few studies have been carried on HELLO expired time. It has been experimentally proved [12] that performance on higher value of HELLO expired time greatly depends on speed of nodes. But no solution till now has been provided which will mitigate bad effects of increasing HELLO expired time.

3. Analysis on HELLO Protocol

This section first explains the reasons of link failure. Link failure means that the node is not able to receive HELLO packet till HELLO expired time. The reasons may be:

1. **Congestion:** Due to congestion, neighbor has not transmitted/received the HELLO packet.
2. **Media Access Control (MAC) layer issues:** Due to interference, fading, shadowing and collisions at MAC level [9], packet loss may happen. As the HELLO packets are not acknowledged, sending node has no clue about its loss and will not retransmit it again. Moreover, if the channel is busy then this may be the reason for not transmitting packet to physical layer.
3. **Mobility:** Due to mobility, neighbor has crossed the radio range.
4. **Energy:** Energy of neighbor is less than threshold. Here threshold is the energy needed to transmit the packet. (In this paper, we do not consider energy)

Secondly this section gives pros of large HELLO expired time than HELLO interval. We assume in this explanation that MAC layer issues exist only for smaller amount of time. We also assume that link failure happened due to MAC layer issues.

If the entry is deleted from neighbor table, entry will again be added only when it receives next HELLO packet. AODV and OLSR maintain routing table for forwarding the data packet. If the entry from routing table is deleted then these protocols search for new path. However, a new path may not exist or may not be a shorter one. If path does not exist then packets are dropped in these protocols. Suppose that longer path exists then packet will increase packet delivery time. Furthermore, path searching also takes some time, this in turn also increases packet delivery time. Thus, HELLO expired time should be greater than HELLO interval. Generally, this parameter is arbitrarily chosen to be three times more than HELLO Interval.

Like AODV and OLSR, same problems exist for geographical protocols as well. In these protocols, routing table is not maintained but neighbor table is maintained. So, if neighbor entry is removed then there is a chance that no suitable neighbor exist or if exist then packet may be forwarded through longer path.

Thirdly, this section gives the cons of keeping large value of HELLO expired time. We assume in this explanation that mobility or energy is the reason of link failure. In this case, nodes believe that they can communicate with the neighbors that have crossed the radio range or have less energy. Thus more packets will be dropped in this case.

Henceforth, it is difficult to recommend any value of HELLO interval or HELLO expired time in wireless ad hoc networks. Nodes in MANET are mobile. Each node can move with different speed and direction. Speed and direction are also not constant. Both changes randomly and unpredictably over time and that is also without any prior notification. Moreover, if the nodes are mobile; congestion, MAC issues are also random. Thus, the issue of recommending HELLO expired time is still open.

Keeping in mind the different problems and constraints described above, we believe that routing protocol should be adaptive to face any value of HELLO expired time. Thus, we propose a metric, which makes routing protocol stronger against HELLO expired time.

4. Our Methodology

This section describes our proposed metric, integrated metric for greedy routing and our algorithmic approach for modified greedy routing.

4.1. *Our Proposed Metric*

Let t_0 is the time when first HELLO packet of neighbor N is received by node A. Now we calculate the expected number of HELLO packets (Say E_{HP}) that should be received by node A in a duration of $[t_0,t]$ (Eq. 1). Say, nodes broadcast HELLO packet after each H_I interval.

$$E_{HP} = \lfloor \frac{(t - t_0)}{H_I} \rfloor + 1 \qquad (1)$$

Assume that within the span of $(t\text{-}t_0)$ time, only N_P number of HELLO packets have been received. Now we calculate the fraction of HELLO packets (P_M) that have not been received by node A in a duration of $[t_0, t]$.

$$P_M = 1 - \frac{N_P}{E_{HP}} \qquad (2)$$

Eq.2 gives our proposed metric, where we believe that value of P_M should be less when we select a node for forwarding the data packet.

4.2. *Metric for Greedy Routing*

Our way of calculating greedy routing metric resembles with Energy Aware Greedy Routing (EAGR) metric [10].

In this greedy routing metric, we believe that, those neighbors are not reliable for packet forwarding, which have more value of P_M.

We use following variables to describe our proposed metric for greedy routing. A is the node which wants to forward the packet to node B. Distance between node A and node B is D and distance between neighbors of A and B are d_1, d_2 ...... d_n.

Greedy routing forwards the packet among its neighbors whose distance from destination (d_i) is less than D. Thus, for (d_i < D), value of (di/D) is less than 1. Now, packet should be forwarded to the neighbor which has less value of both the parameters, P_M and (d_i/D). P_M is always less than 1. Thus, addition of both the values gives equal fairness between number of hops traveled and number of HELLO packets received in time $(t - t_0)$.

Our proposed metric for greedy routing is given in Eq. 3. Here P_{Mi} is the value of PM for i_{th} neighbor.

$$C_i = \frac{d_i}{D} + P_{Mi} \qquad (3)$$

4.3. *Modified Greedy Routing*

Like greedy routing, HELLO packet in modified one consists of neighbor ID and its position. Neighbor table of nodes consists of following information: (1) neighbor ID, (2) position, (3) t_0 time and (4) number of HELLO packets (N_P) received by that time. Each time node receives the HELLO packet; it checks that if it is the new neighbor. If so, then it creates new neighbor entry in which N_P is assigned a value equals to 1, t_0 is made equal to current time, and position and node id are kept in neighbor table. But if the neighbor is old, then it updates the neighbor entry with new position and increases the value of N_P in that entry by one.

Like Greedy routing, header of packet destined to B, contains the B's ID as well as its position. First phase of our simulated greedy routing and modified greedy routing is same, where nodes first check that destination ID is present in its neighbor table or not. If so, then, packet is forwarded directly to destination. Second phase of greedy routing and modified one is different, where destination ID is not present in neighbor table. In this phase, modified greedy calculates C_i for those neighbor whose d_i < D. Now the packet is forwarded to the node, which has least value of C_i.

Nodes in modified greedy routing can also reach to the situation of dead-ends where no neighbor exists whose d_i < D. In the simulation of greedy and modified greedy routing, we recover from this situation by applying Karp and Kung's GPSR solution [3].

5. Simulation Environment

We calculate the performance of greedy routing and modified greedy routing in mobile networks where 60 nodes are randomly distributed in square region of 1500×1500 sq. meter. NS code for greedy routing is taken from [11]. We modified this code for the implementation of our modified greedy routing. The maximum radio range is fixed to 250 meters. Simulations last 100 seconds, where constant bit rate (CBR) traffic flows from 0 seconds to 100 seconds. Total of 10 CBR connections are taken to forward packets from source to destination. HELLO interval in all the simulations is taken as 1 second. Source and destination nodes are taken randomly from 60 nodes. CBR traffic sends data packets of 128-byte length. We assume in our simulation that nodes are able to calculate their own position, may be with the help of global positioning system (GPS).

To obtain the performance, we use random way-point model, where we show two results of measured metrics, one by varying HELLO expired time and other by varying maximum speed of nodes. Maximum speed of node is taken as 20 m/s when we vary HELLO expired time and HELLO expired time is taken as 6 seconds when we vary maximum speed of node. Pause time in all the simulation is taken as 0 seconds.

6. Analysis of Results

This section analyzes the simulation results. We measure packet delivery fraction, latency, average throughput and overheads for calculating the performance of modified greedy and greedy routing.

Table 1. Packet Delivery Fraction-I

Expired time	Modified Greedy	Greedy
3.0	0.637	0.615
4.5	0.578	0.510
6.0	0.546	0.422
7.5	0.498	0.388
9.0	0.437	0.349

Table 1 and Table 2 show that packet delivery fraction of modified greedy is always greater than that of greedy routing. Let, due to congestion or mobility of neighbor, node is not able to receive HELLO packet within HELLO interval. While forwarding the data packet, greedy routing sees only minimum distance from the destination; it does not matter for greedy routing that next forwarding neighbor is highly congested or at the out of radio range. Thus, nodes in greedy routing may transmit the data packet to this highly congested or out of radio range neighbor. At this situation, neighbor may not be able to receive the packet because it is busy with some other task due to congestion. Secondly, if it transmits the packet to the out of radio range node, the packet drops. Both the reasons together give less packet delivery in greedy routing. On the other hand, cost computational parameter Ci of modified greedy routing gives the probable hint for the congestion or mobility of node. Thus probability of forwarding the packet to congested or out of radio range neighbor is less for modified greedy routing. These in turn gives more packet delivery in modified greedy.

Table 2. Packet Delivery Fraction-II

Max. Speed	Modified Greedy	Greedy
30 m/s	0.546	0.422
40 m/s	0.483	0.399
50 m/s	0.427	0.344

Modified greedy can decrease or increase the latency of one packet in wireless ad hoc networks. This is explained in next paragraphs. Table 3 and Table 4 show latency behavior of greedy and modified greedy.

As explained above, that greedy routing may forward the packet to the node, which is highly congested. Thus, one packet can take more time to reach the destination. Furthermore, it also increases the congestion of that neighbor, which in turn causes other packets which are in queue, to take more time to reach the destination. This is the reason for more latency of greedy routing. On the other hand, chance of forwarding the data packet to the congested neighbor is less for modified greedy. Thus, modified greedy can give less latency than existing one.

Since the MAC layer issues exist only for smaller amount time. Thus, if due to these issues, the HELLO packet is not arrived to the node, packet in modified greedy routing may take longer path to reach the destination. On the other hand, greedy routing may perform better in this situation because it does not have clue about these issues. This is the reason of more latency of modified greedy routing at maximum speed of 40 m/s (Table 4).

Table 3. Average Latency of one packet in ms -I

Expired time	Modified Greedy	Greedy
3.0	4482	4826
4.5	5233	5326
6.0	5257	5839
7.5	5827	5921
9.0	5733	5978

Table 4. Average Latency of one packet in ms-II

Max. Speed	Modified Greedy	Greedy
30 m/s	5257	5839
40 m/s	5791	6320
50 m/s	7195	6873

Table 5 and Table 6 show average throughput of modified greedy and greedy routing. Due to more packet delivery in modified greedy routing, bytes received per second are always more for modified greedy routing.

Table 7 and Table 8 give normalized overheads of modified greedy and greedy routing. It is calculated as number of packets transmitted/received or forwarded per unit received data packets by destination.

Table 5. Throughout in bytes received per sec. -I

Expired time	Modified Greedy	Greedy
3.0	6066	5856
4.5	5497	4856
6.0	5199	4013
7.5	4743	3697
9.0	4161	3325

Table 6, Throughout in bytes received per sec. -II

Max. Speed	Modified Greedy	Greedy
30 m/s	5199	4013
40 m/s	4595	3800
50 m/s	4059	3272

It may happen that while moving to destination, a data packet drops at some point. So, data packet overheads from source to that point are wasted. It is explained that data packet delivery of modified greedy routing is always more than greedy routing. Thus, wastage of these overheads is less in modified greedy routing. As we do not change the size and interval of HELLO packet, all other overheads of modified greedy routing is same as greedy routing.

Table 7. Normalized Overheads-I

Expired time	Modified Greedy	Greedy
3.0	39.39	39.54
4.5	40.05	45.45
6.0	41.36	53.54
7.5	44.40	55.07
9.0	50.49	59.63

Table 8. Normalized Overheads-II

Max. Speed	Modified Greedy	Greedy
30 m/s	41.36	53.54
40 m/s	47.24	55.68
50 m/s	56.00	65.06

7. Conclusions and Future Work

In this paper, we proposed a metric which gives a clue about congestion, mobility, and MAC layer issues. We also presented modified greedy routing, where we integrated our proposed metric in well known greedy routing of geographical routing protocols.

Based on simulation results, we assume that our proposed metric would also perform well in other protocols which also use concept of HELLO packets. Thus simulation can be carried to integrate our proposed metric in other protocols as well.

There are some remaining open issues that we did not consider in this paper. One of them is to find the optimum value of HELLO expired time. We indeed focused on to prove that our proposed metric mitigates the bad effect of higher value of HELLO expired time. Since performance of a protocol depends on the chosen HELLO expired time, recommending a value of HELLO expired time is important.

Acknowledgments

Author wishes to thank his parents Sh. Shyam Lal Sharma and Smt. Kesari Devi for their love and blessings.

References

1. C. Perkins, E. Belding-Royer, and S. Das. Ad hoc On-demand Distance Vector Routing, RFC 3561, 2003.
2. T. Clausen and P. Jacquet, Optimized Link State Routing Protocol (OLSR), RFC 3626, 2003.
3. B. Karp and H. T. Kunz, GPSR: Greedy Perimeter Stateless Routing for Wireless Networks, IEEE/ACM Mobicom, pp. 243-254, 2000.
4. M. Mauve, A. Widmer and H. Hartenstein, A Survey on Position-Based Routing in Mobile Ad hoc Networks, IEEE Network, Vol. 5, No. 6, pp. 30-39, 2001.
5. V. C. Giruka and M. Singhal, Hello protocols for ad hoc networks : Overhead and accuracy trade-o_s, WoWMoM, pp. 354{361, 2005.
6. G. Alonso, E. Kranakis, R. Wattenhofer and P. Widmayer. Randomized protocols for node discovery in ad hoc, single broadcast channel networks, IPDPS, pp. 22-26, 2003.
7. F. Ingelrest, N. Mitton, and D. Simplot-Ryl A Turnover based Adaptive HELLO Protocol for Mobile Ad Hoc and Sensor Networks, MASCOTS, pp. 24-26, 2007.
8. C. Gomez, A. Cuevas, and J. Paradells. A Two State Adaptive Mechanism for Link Connectivity Maintenance in AODV, REALMAN, pp. 98-100, 2006.
9. T. Raza_ndralambo, T. Mitton, Analysis of the Impact of Hello Protocol Parameters over a Wireless Network SelfOrganization, 4th ACM Workshop on performance of wireless ad hoc, sensor and ubiquitous, pp. 46-53, 2007.
10. Sachin Sharma, H. M. Gupta, S. Dharmaraja, EAGR: Energy Aware Greedy Routing Scheme for Wireless Ad hoc Networks, SPECTS, pp. 122{129, 2008.
11. www.cn.uniduesseldorf.de/sta /kiess/software/hlsns2-patch.
12. W. A. Mandhari, K. Gyoda, N. Nakajima, Performance Evaluation of Active Route Time-Out parameter in AODV, WSEAS, pp. 47-51, 2008.

A ROLE BASED TRUST MODEL FOR PEER TO PEER SYSTEMS

CHTHRA SELVARAJ
Asst. Professor
Easwari Engineering College
Chennai.
chithraselva@yahoo.co.in

SHEILA ANAND
Dean (Research) Computer Studies
Rajalakshmi Engineering College
Thandalam, Chennai.
sheila.anand@gmail.com

ABSTRACT
In P2P computing, peers dynamically organize themselves to support knowledge sharing and collaboration. The dynamic and decentralized nature of P2P systems causes the issues of maintaining security and trust between peers to become critical. Establishing trust among anonymous peers is a challenging task. This paper discusses a Role Based Trust model for building credential graphs. Loops in the directed graph may lead to cyclic dependency problem causing deadlock in the trust computations. We propose using the DFS algorithm, to convert the graph into a tree to avoid the cyclic dependency problem. The resulting credential tree can be used for trust computation and delegation.

1. Introduction

Peer-to-Peer (P2P) systems enable sharing of various resources and services among peers without the need for central authorities or servers. Peers can join and leave the network dynamically, enabling malicious software to exploit this nature of P2P networks. Security mechanisms which are suitable for centralized systems are not directly applicable for P2P systems, as there is no centralized server and the peers are anonymous.

Decentralized trust schemes are one security measure that can help peers to determine the trustworthiness of other peers. Trust in P2P systems is a peer's belief in another peer's identity, reliability and capability based on its own experiences. Trust Management entails collecting the information necessary to establish a trust relationship and dynamically monitoring and adjusting the existing trust relationship. [1].

In this paper, we describe a Role Based Trust (RT) approach for the construction of trust credentials for P2P applications. Typically, Role Based Access Control (RBAC) is provided as a security mechanism for a single host at the operating system level [2]. The operating system ensures that authenticated users have access to resources based on their assigned roles. Role Based Trust (RT) combines the strengths of role-based access control and trust management systems. [3]. In order to implement efficient trust management in P2P systems, a trust model needs to be incorporated that will allow peers to have dynamic trust score in other peers.

The rest of the paper is structured as follows. Relevant work related to this area is discussed next, followed by our approach of RT. The next section gives the implementation details followed by conclusion and suggestions for future work.

2. Related Work

Various trust models have been proposed based on reputation and recommendation of peers. Kazaa defines a participation level for each peer based on some QOS parameters. An agent based Trust model allow to assess trust by computing binary trust (the agent could be either trustworthy or not) based on the agents' reputation from its former interactions with other agents [4]. In NICE model, each peer at the end of an interaction creates a cookie with feedback about the other peers. The cookie is signed and is exchanged among them for future Trust [5]. Eigen Trust Model is designed for the reputation management of P2P system.

The global reputation of each peer is marked by the local trust values assigned to the peer by other peers, and it is weighted by the global reputation of other peers as mentioned in [5]. A reputation based trust model is used for quantifying and assessing the trustworthiness of peers in P2P ecommerce communities.

Some of the problems that have not yet been satisfactorily solved about trust management in P2P systems include:

- Anonymity – Peers can join the communities with ease without disclosing their identities in most previous P2P systems. Anonymity will assist malicious users to shelter and disguise themselves behind the scenes, or to provide false trust ratings.

- Cyclic Dependency Problem – Peers and its relationships can be viewed as a directed graph's nodes and edges. When there is a loop existing in the directed graph, the trust computation would cause deadlocks between two or more peers on the loop.

- Distributed trust data and communication management in P2P systems – The problem of how to effectively store trust data either as a local score or dynamic calculation.

- Techniques used to aggregate the trust scores of intermediate peers has to be enhanced.

This paper now discusses further about other work related to Role Based Trust model. The Role Based Trust management Framework has been introduced to support credential generation and to form credential graph [6].

RT framework is a family of Role-based Trust management languages for representing policies and credentials for distributed authorization and authentication [7]. This paper introduces a metric that combines a peer's trust value for each its roles in to a single, relative, probabilistic guarantee of trust [8]. The various Trust Management Systems which uses RT Framework are SPKI/SDSI [10], Policy Maker, KeyNote and Delegation Logic.

The process of making access control decisions involves finding a chain of credentials that delegate the authority from the source to requester. A problem in Trust Management is to determine whether the chain exists. This problem is called *Chain Discovery Problem.* It is different from certificate path discovery problem for X.509 certificates because credentials in TM systems have more graph rather than a linear path. The Bottom-up algorithm is used for chain discovery in which all credentials are stored in one location. The credentials are considered in demand-driven manner in Goal directed Algorithm[11].

3. Our Approach

This paper offers a Role Based Trust Model using RT Framework. The process of making access control decisions involves finding a chain of credentials that delegates the authority from the source to the requester. This is called Credential Chain discovery. The construction of the credential graph will help to determine the trustworthiness of the peer. However the construction of the graph may lead to cyclic dependency problem causing deadlock in the trust computations. .Our approach is to convert the credential graph to a credential tree using DFS algorithm. This would avoid having cycles which may in turn avoid the problem of deadlock.

3.1 Credential Chain Construction using RT Framework

The key concept of Role based Trust Management is delegation. A Principal (Entity) may transfer limited authority over one or more resources to other principals. This is done by means of credentials which are pieces of information, passed from one principal to another and used to establish the sending principal's access rights.

Roles are represented by an Entity followed by a role name as

University.Student, A.r, B.r1

Where A is the owner of the role A.r and only A can determine which entities are the members of A.r. In the University.Student example, only University has the authority to determine who are the students or members of the role University.Student.

The credentials can be of any 4 types as shown in Table 1.

Credential	Semantic Expression	Role functionality and chain relationship
Simple Member	A.r ← D	A 'asserts' D is a member
Simple Inclusion	A.r ← B.r1	A asserts that A.r includes all members of B.r1
Linking Inclusion	A.r ← A.r1.r2	A asserts that A.r includes B.r2 for every B that is a member of A.r1
Insertion Inclusion	A.r ← B1.r1 ∩ B2.r2 ∩ ... ∩ Bk.rk	A asserts that A.r includes every principal who is a member of both B1.r1 and B2.r2

Table 1 – Credential Construction Rules

Credential chain construction is explained with an example scenario: IEEE would a discount on the Registration Fee for its conference, provided the person who wishes to register is a student and also an IEEE member. We assume an University which functions from two different campuses say A and B, and School of Information and Technology (SCIT) is an Institution working in the Campus A. Computer Science and Engineering (CSE) is a department of SCIT. Consider a student of the CSE department.

The set of credentials for this scenario are:

IEEE.discount <- IEEE.preferred ∩ IEEE.member
IEEE.preferred<-SCIT.CSE.Student
SCIT.CSE <- CampusA.accredited
CampusA.accredited <- University
University.Student<-Registrar.Student
Registrar.Student <- Alice
IEEE.member <- Alice

These set of credentials can be reduced step by step as follows:

Step 1: If the credential is of the form A.r <- e, it can be added to the chain directly.
For i=1, (i=iteration)
CampusA.accredited <- University Registrar.Student <- Alice, IEEE.member <- Alice

Step 2: If the credentials are not of the form A.r <- e, apply reduction to get the following links.
For i=2,
SCIT.CSE <- University, University.Student <- Alice

Step 3: The credentials are still reduced in the next iteration
For i=3, IEEE.Preferred <- Alice

Step 4: on Further reduction, we arrive at the required link.
For i=4, IEEE.discount <- Alice

Credential Graph can be constructed using the set of credentials based on the closure property defined by RT framework. Each credential graph for C is parameterized by a finite set of role expressions Q $\subseteq$ RoleExpression.. The credential graph $G_{C:Q}$ has node set $N_{C:Q}$ and edge set $E_{C:Q}$, defined as follows: $N_{C:Q=FExps}(C)$ U Intersect ions(C) U Q $E_{C:Q}$ is the least set of edges over $N_{C:Q}$ that satisfies the following three closure properties:

Closure Property 1: If A.r <- e€C, then A.r <- e€$E_{C:Q}$. We call A.r<-e a credential edge.

Closure Property 2: If there is a path A.r1 <-* B in $G_{C:Q}$, then A.r1.r2 <- B.r2 € $E_{C:Q}$. We call A.r1.r2 <- B.r2, a derived link edge, and call the path A.r1 <-* B a support set for the edge.

Closure Property 3 : If D, f_1 ∩ ....∩ f_k € $N_{C:Q}$, and for each j € [1..k] there is a path f_j <-* D in $G_{C:Q}$, then f_1 ∩ ....∩ f_k <-D € $E_{C:Q}$. We call this a derived intersection edge, and say the union of the paths { f_j <-* D | j € [1..k] } is a support set for the edge.

3.2 Conclusions from Closure Properties

- *Every credential has a credential edge*
- *Every support set for the edge has derived link edge*
- *To add A.r1.r2 <- B.r2, the role node A.r1 must have an incoming edge and the entity node B must have an outgoing edge*
- *A node with intersection must have an incoming edge and an outgoing edge*

Using these conclusions, the Credential graph can be obtained for the example scenario as shown in fig. 3.1

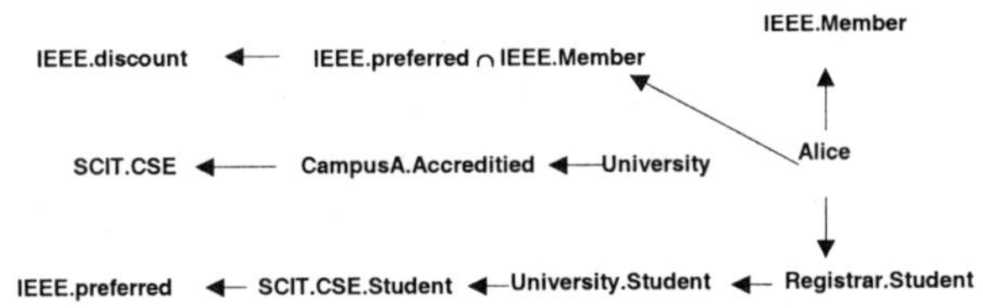

Fig 3.1 Credential Graph

4. Implementation

Linked List has been used for the implementation of the credential graph. The roles have been represented as nodes and the relationship between the roles is represented as edges. The Linked List has been constructed using the following algorithm.

1. A new node is created and visited flag is set to 0.
2. New node is added to the list
3. Adjacency list is created.
4. The graph representing the relation can be arrived using the closure properties.

The credential graph using the steps mentioned earlier in this paper. For Chain discovery, the Backward Search algorithm has been used and the credential graph has been converted to Credential tree, using the Depth First Search (DFS) Algorithm.

.DFS Algorithm

```
dfs(graph G)
{
 list L = empty
 tree T = empty
 choose a starting vertex x
 search(x)
 while(L is not empty)
 {
  remove edge (v, w) from beginning of L
  if w not yet visited
  {
   add (v, w) to T
   search(w) } } }
search(vertex v)
{
 visit v
 for each edge (v, w)
  add edge (v, w) to the beginning of L}
```

The credential graph shown in fig 3.1 is converted to credential tree and is shown in fig. 4.2.

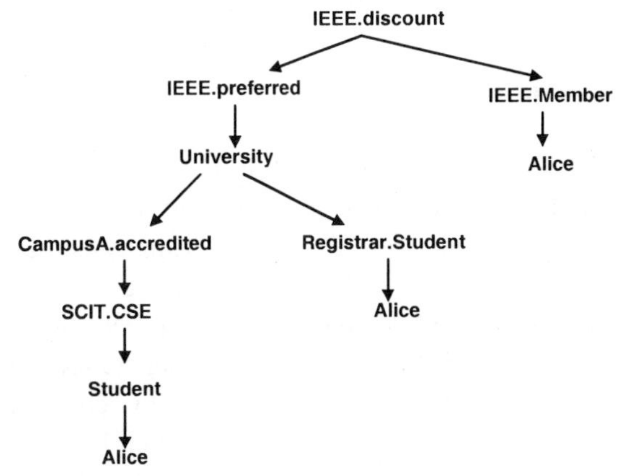

Fig 4.2 Credential Tree

5. System Architecture

We have implemented this process in P2P networks using JXTA platform. The JXTA architecture is given in Fig 5.1.

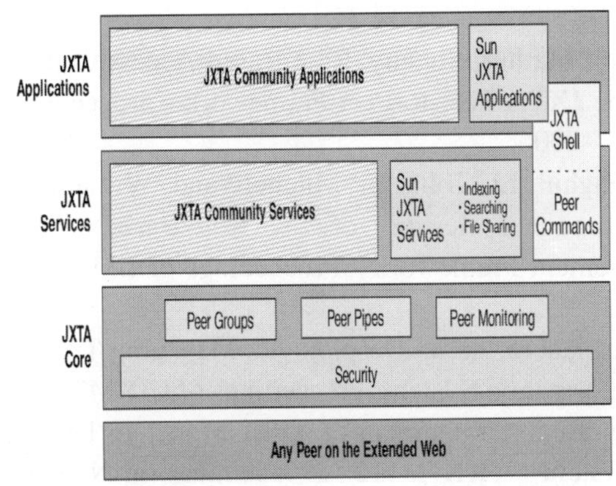

Fig 5.1 JXTA Architecture

Peers can join or leave the Peer group. The trust overlay network is responsible for checking the authentication of the peers. The roles of the users are represented in the form of credentials which is used for constructing trust chain in the Trust overlay. The overall system architecture is shown in the figure 5.2.

5.1 Peer Group Generation

This module takes care of forming a Peer group by providing new Peer ID when a Peer joins the group and deleting the peer ID when that Peer leaves the group.

6. Conclusion

This paper has presented a Role based Trust System for P2P systems, where trust of peers is established using credential trees. Credential chain construction has been explained with an example. The conversion of credential graph to credential tree has been adopted to avoid the problem of cyclic dependency. As future work, we propose to extend RBT by combining credential tree construction with reputation-based trust and trust score calculations, which would enable peers to quantify and assess the trustworthiness of other peers.

References

[1] Huaizhi Li and Mukesh Singhal, Trust Management in Distributed Systems –
Huaizhi Li and Mukesh Singhal – IEEE Journal – Feb 2007.

[2] Amit Mathur, Suneuy, Role Based Access Control and the JXTA Peer-to-Peer Framework - proceedings of Kim –2006.

[3] Ninghui Li, John C. Mitchell and William H. Winsborough, Design of a Role-Based Trust Management Framework - Proceedings of LMW02 – 2004

[4] Karl Abere, Zoran Desplotovic, Managing Trust in P2P Information Systems proceedings of CIKM2001

[5] Hai Ren, Comparison of Trust Model in Peer to peer system - TKK T-110.5290 Seminar on Network Security 2006-12- 11/12

[6] Ninghui Li and John C Mitchell, A Role Based Trust Framework - 2003

[7] Ninghui Li, John C Mitchell and William H. Winsborough, Design of a Role Based Trust-management Framework – Proceedings of LMW02

[8] Mujtaba Khambatti, Partha Dasgupta, Kyung Dong Ryu, A Role based trust model for Peer-to Peer Communities and Dynamic Coalitions - proceedings of Information Assurance Workshop, 2004, Second IEEE International

[9] San Jose, Q- Chain: Building Reputation Basted Trust Chains in Decentralized Peer to-Peer networks – First International Conference on collaborative Computing, 2005

[10] Carl Ellison, SPKI / SDSI , 6 October 2004

[11] Ke Chan, Kai Hwang and Gang Chen, Heuristic Discovery of Role-Based Trust Chains in Peer-to-Peer Networks – IEEECS March 2008

[12] Ninghui Li, William H. Winsborough, John C. Mitchel, Credential Chain Discovery in Trust Management-ACM Conference – Nov2001.

INTERNETWORKING INTERFACE FUNCTION FOR CHARGING AND BILLING IN IP TELEPHONY SERVICES

CHINMAY CHAKRABORTY[1], PARTHA SARATHI CHAKRABORTY[2]

[1]*G. S. Sanyal School of Telecommunications, Indian Institute of Technology Kharagpur, India*
[2]*Department of Computer Science & Engineering, KIIT University, Bhubaneswar, India*

S. S. PATHAK[3], SASWAT CHAKRABARTI[4]

[3]*G. S. Sanyal School of Telecommunications, Indian Institute of Technology Kharagpur, India*
[4]*Department of Electronics and Electrical Communication Engineering, Indian Institute of Technology Kharagpur, India*

The recent development in the field of telecommunication technology and the popularity of the internet have caused the changes in the field of communication, which moves towards to new innovative communication through IP networks like IP telephony. Therefore, IP Telephony requires the support of guaranteed quality of services and charging to provide service for potential customers, which makes some significant changes in the billing network model of telecommunication. The billing model support different level of services in terms of quality and charging requirement made by the users and would be the most efficient in terms of prices to be paid. This paper suggests a methodology to resolve the specific problem of internetworking between IP and PSTN networks for supporting quality voice calls to make true charging. The main objective of the paper is to propose the internetworking interface function (IIF) with the charging and billing methods over the IP telephony and PSTN networks.

1. Introduction

In the recent time, Voice over Internet Protocol (VoIP) becomes popular technology which is used for making telephone calls using a broadband access connection (e.g. ADSL), instead of a regular phone lines. Therefore, it is also called IP Telephony. Through the VoIP support software, a person makes long distance calls for the price of local call to their internet service provider (ISP). This makes it an easy setup and become popular in the new generation cost effective market. Way2Talk of *Sify iWay* is an example of IP telephony for long distance call i.e. international call which is providing at incredible rates. Solutions for providing IP telephony are currently based on IETF's SIP Protocol or ITU's H.323 standard. Both SIP and H.323 were originally developed for establishing multimedia services like VoIP over the internet [1]. But the Session Initiation Protocol (SIP) is considered to be a powerful alternative of the H.323 standard as the signalling systems for the dominant VoIP. SIP [2] is also an application layer signaling protocol for creating, modifying and terminating sessions with one or more participants.

2. Internetworking of Heterogeneous Networks

SIP and PSTN internetworking occurs whenever a call originates in one network and terminates in another network. To set up calls between the PSTN and the internet, gateway nodes have been introduce in the network and to established an end-to-end call between the internet and the PSTN, SIP gateways terminate the SIP signaling on the internet telephony side and usually ISDN signaling on the PSTN side. The gateway also sets up the voice path for each call within the gateway by controlling the gateway resources. The appropriate choice of IP telephony gateways depends on many factors. There are two basic approaches to building these gateways—*complete protocol internetworking* and *protocol encapsulation*. The latter approach is known as SIP Telephony (SIP-T), which is not a separate protocol, but rather the SIP protocol plus a number of extensions. The gateway appears to the SIP network to be a user agent for many different users, and to the PSTN as a terminating telephone switch depending on the design. The primary role of SIP is to initiate sessions but it is widely used for signalling. Signalling inside PSTN is based on SS7. The PIG (PSTN – IP Gateway) architecture is an important element in the signaling conversion between SS7 and IP networks. The inter-networking of signalling protocol between PSTN and IP network through Internetworking Interface Function is shown in figure 1. The IP telephony gives the cost effective and flexibility advantage, but how the process of charging and billing is done for the internet telephony from the traditional PSTN charging and billing methods. This paper illustrates the interworkability between SIP and PSTN networks along with the process of charging. Then the paper explains the proposed different charging schemes over existing scenario for IP Telephony which introduction leads to the main advantage of it.

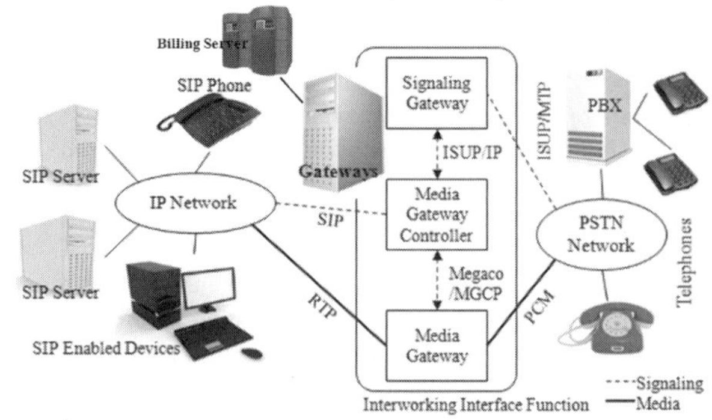

Figure 1. Gateways, IP and PSTN networks.

The Figure 2 illustrates main functions of charging architecture that consists of entities of which input is traffic data over the network and produces invoices for business parties and the end-users. For charging and billing purpose over the IP-PSTN network interworking, the following functions are needed - *Authentication*: It is a process that validates the traffic data and protects the system from untrusted IP networks or devices as independent from the phone manufacture. *Metering:* It is the function of capturing all data related to network resources' consumption (e.g., volume of exchanged data) and is performed by network devices. *Pricing:* The process deals with the determination of the price and traffic model for service usages.

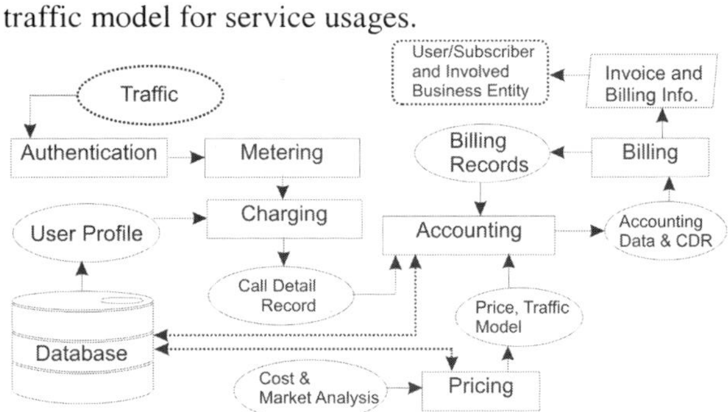

Figure 2. Charging Architecture.

Charging: The charging process applies the agreed traffic on the metered data. *Accounting:* It is a centralized process that deals with charging records or CDR and it maintains the account for billing records of all call signaling events, including call establishment, call termination, abnormal abort that are known to the softswitch. *Billing:* It deals with the preparation of invoice and sends the processing CDR to the accounting node to store in database for future use.

3. Overview of Session Initiation Protocol (SIP)

3.1. *Network Architecture*

IP Telephony services include Internet telephone calls, multimedia distribution, and multimedia conferences. SIP defines two preliminary classes of network entities - clients and servers. Basic entities in SIP are called User Agents (UA). They can be operated in client mode (User Agent Client, UAC), in server mode (User Agent Server, UAS) or in both modes at the same time. For reliable and flexible operation SIP needs the following servers: *Proxy Server* - Forwards SIP requests and responses. *Redirect Server* - Provides up to date routing information as well as returns "contact this address" responses. *Registrar Server* - Handles the location of registered messages. *Location Server* - It is a SIP/SIMPLE application framework. It has also database for proxies, redirect servers and registrars. *Presence Server* - It's to make the most of users presence information in any type of internet or telecom application. *Event Server* - it is used for the network element, acting as Notifier, which receives SUBSCRIBE messages for different SIP Event types, such as Registration and MWI (Message Waiting Indication).

3.2. *Signaling*

SIP transaction is the request/response model depicted in Table 1 based on RFC 2543 by IETF [3]. RFC 2543 defines a set of different message headers. SIP is a text-based protocol and uses the UTF8 char set.

Table 1. SIP Request/Response Model.

SIP Message	Description
INVITE	Invites a user to a call.
ACK	Used to confirm that a transaction is completed successfully.
OPTIONS	Used to query options & capabilities of the remote peer.
BYE	Used to terminate a session between user agents.
CANCEL	Terminates a request for a user.
REGISTER	Used to register the UA with location server.
INFO	Used for mid-session signaling.

After a request message is received and interpreted, the recipient responds with a SIP response message. The response messages contain a numeric status code (three digit numbers) and it's associated textual phrase, for example 100 Trying, 180 Ringing, 200 OK etc.

4. Basic Architecture of SS7 Signaling

The SS7 signalling system [4] is a global standard for telecommunications defined by the ITU-T. It is a protocol for performing call establishment, billing, routing, and exchange of information in PSTN networks. The protocol stack of SS7 protocol (shown in figure 3) is designed to facilitate these functions and to maintain the network.

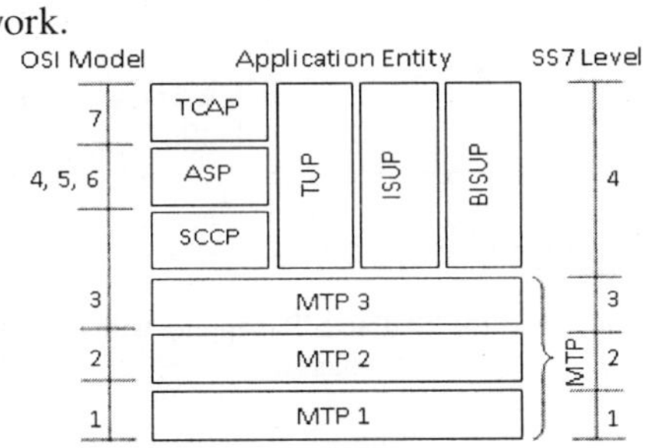

Figure 3. SS7 Protocol Stack.

5. Call Flow Representation with Charging and Metering

5.1. *Call Flow between ISUP to SIP*

This part of the article focuses on the translation of ISUP messages into SIP messages [5]. The ISUP parameters are mapped into SIP headers. The purpose of translation is to allow SIP elements (such as proxy servers) to understand ISUP messages and make routing decisions, for ISUP calls that traverse a SIP network. The mapping between ISUP and SIP is described using PSTN to IP Telephony call flow diagram (in figure 4) with Charging, Authentication and Metering.

Procedure

1. When a PSTN user wishes to begin a session with a SIP user, the PSTN network generates an IAM message towards the signaling gateway.
2. On receipt of the IAM message, the gateway generates an INVITE message, and sends it to an appropriate SIP node.
3. On receipt of a provisional response of 180 or greater, the gateway will generate an ACM message. If the response is not 180, the ACM will carry a called party status value of no indication.
4. After an ACM is sent, all provisional responses will be translated into ISUP CPG messages.
5. When the SIP answers the call, it will send a 200 OK message.
6. On receipt of the 200 OK messages, the gateway will send an ANM message towards the ISUP and ON_CHARGING message to metering entity that results charging entity to accept the message and start charging process.
7. The gateway will send an ACK to the SIP node to acknowledge receipt of the INVITE final response.
8. On receipt of the REL, the gateway sends BYE to SIP node and metering node.
9. Metering entity sends the STOP_CHARGING message to charging entity and SIP sends RLC message to ISUP to acknowledge REL.

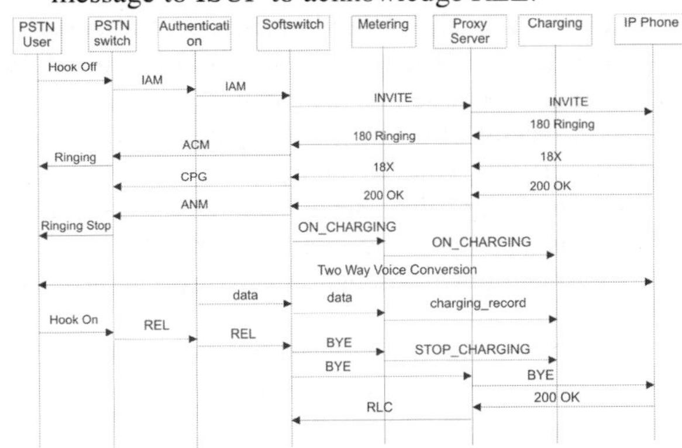

Figure 4. Call Flow from PSTN to IP Network.

5.2. *Call Flow between SIP to ISUP*

Basically, the work is focused on mapping between the two signaling protocols: the SIP and ISUP. The IP to PSTN call flow is described (in the figure 5) with Charging, Authentication and Metering.

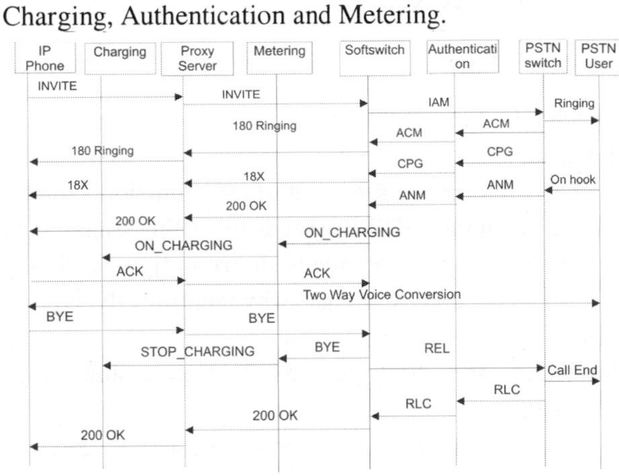

Figure 5. Call Flow from IP to PSTN Network.

Procedure

1. When a SIP user wishes to begin a session with a PSTN user, the SIP entity issues an INVITE request.

2. Upon receipt of an INVITE request, the gateway maps it to an IAM message and sends it to the ISUP network.
3. The remote ISUP entity indicates that the address is sufficient to set up a call by sending back an ACM message.
4. The called party status code in the ACM message is mapped to a SIP provisional response.
5. The remote ISUP may issue a Call Progress (CPG) messages to indicate a change in the progress of the call, for example, that the call is being forwarded.
6. Upon receipt of a CPG message, the gateway will map the event code to a SIP provisional response.
7. Once the PSTN user answers, an Answer (ANM) message will be sent to the gateway.
8. Upon receipt of the ANM, the gateway will send a 200 message to the SIP entity.
9. The gateway also sends an ON_CHARGING message to metering entity which informs the charging entity through the message to start charging.
10. The SIP node, upon receiving an INVITE final response (200), will send an ACK to acknowledge receipt.
11. Upon receipt of the BYE, the gateway sends 200 to SIP and BYE message to metering entity; sends REL message to ISUP.
12. On receipt of the BYE message by metering entity, it sends the STOP_CHARGING message to charging entity.
13. PSTN will send RLC message to the gateway to acknowledge REL.

6. Flow Chart

Flowchart for ISUP to SIP Conversion with Charging

The internetworking interface function should convert incoming ISUP messages to SIP messages. The procedure for the conversion is shown in figure 6. If any ISUP message comes, the gateway identifies the type of the message.

Flowchart for SIP to ISUP Conversion with Charging

If any SIP message comes, first the gateway identifies the type of SIP message. The procedure for the conversion is shown in the figure 7.

In both cases, the messages are monitoring by the charging entity that initiate the ON_CHARGING massage and send the CDR data information to accounting for further processing for bill generation. When it gets the BYE message, it sends the STOP_CHARGING message.

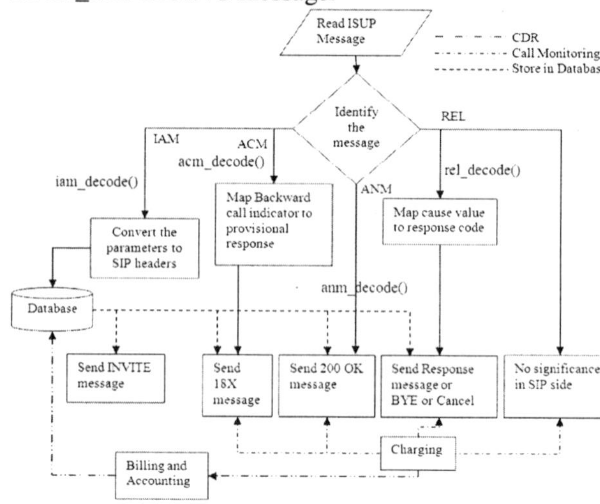

Figure 6. Flowchart for ISUP to SIP mapping with Charging and Accounting.

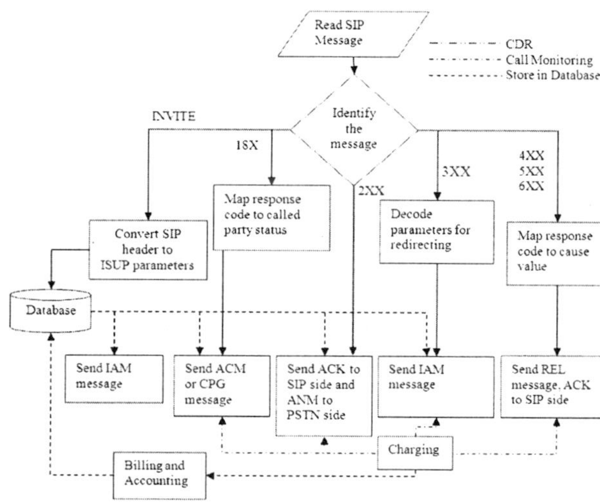

Figure 7. Flowchart for SIP to ISUP mapping with Charging and Accounting.

7. Charging in IP Telephony Services

The two way of charging schemes are done – *offline charging* and *online charging* [6]. *Offline charging* is when the charging is executed at the end of the service usage and the market need right now is to have the service charged in real-time. Another one is *Online charging* uses the rating before the service usage and based on the advice of charge the service usage is allowed for the defined interval.

There are various proposed economic and technical models for charging and billing for IP telephony.

- *Metered Charging:* In this model the consumer is charged with a monthly fee irrespective of the time spent using the network services. Once the consumers have used the time allocated to them, they will be charged for the extra usage time. The duration of the call is proportional to the call's cost.

- *Packet Charging:* It involves capturing and counting the number of packets exchanged in a session, without considering the time the user has spent.
- *Time-based Charging:* In this model the user is charged based on the time he or she is connected to the network even if no data is transferred. Subscribers will have to pay for any amount of air-time each call connection lasts even if no one speaks during the connection time. However, during off-peak hours subscribers will be offered a discounted rate.

8. Accounting and Billing in IP Telephony Services

The call is identified by a globally unique Call-ID. Within a call, each leg can be identified by a unique combination of the To, From, and Call-ID fields [7]. A proxy performing the call accounting function should be able to distinguish different legs and create CDR for each call leg. It should also be able to recognize RE-INVITE messages that only change the media description, not the participants; in this case it should not create a new call leg.

In the PSTN, a call is usually paid by the customer who initiates it. A proxy relaying all signaling from the terminal of a user can create appropriate accounting records by logging the INVITE (RE-INVITE request are ignored), CANCEL, and BYE requests, as well as the replies. The duration of each leg can be derived from the first accepted INVITE request (200 OK) up to the first BYE request [8]. In order to establish a call, user must not be bypassing the network proxy. It is easily done by restrict SIP signaling traffic on the routers connected to the all VoIP devices which are configured to accept calls only if the INVITE comes from the service provider proxy. Then as per the accounting data, the process of billing has done that produce invoice without including the false charging information to the user.

9. Conclusion

Session Initiation Protocol (SIP) has a bright future and it is still very much in the development phase. But the rate at which SIP voice gateways are being developed, is tremendously high. However, potential problems exist, when the softswitch network provides a transit function between PSTN and SIP based VoIP networks. The problem of internetworking has to address the differences between state machines, timers etc. Consequently, there are many issues associated with ISUP-SIP internetworking that need resolution. In this paper, the internetworking interface function between IP and PSTN networks is presented to understand the internetworking issue related to IP telephony, and the authentication, charging and billing aspect for generating invoice without including the false charging information. The decoding of ISUP and SIP message is explained through the call flowchart with charging module. The charging procedure starts when the softswitch or gateway receives the answer message (ANM), and the procedure is stopped, when it receives the BYE message (200 OK). The softswitch approach would be recommended as the best choice for smooth migration to the next generation networks.

Acknowledgement

This work has been supported by Santech-IIT Research Initiative.

References

1. C. Huitema *et. al.*, *An Architecture for Residential Internet Telephony service*, IEEE Internet Computing, pp. 73-82 (2003).
2. J. Rosenberg *et. al.*, SIP: Session Initiation Protocol, RFC 3261 (2002).
3. IETF: *Session Initiation Protocol*, RFC 2543.
4. ITU-T Q.763 *Signaling System No. 7 – ISDN user part formats and codes*, (1999).
5. A. Johnston *et al.*, *Session Initiation Protocol (SIP) Public Switched Tele phone Network (PSTN) Call Flows*, IETF RFC 3666 (2003).
6. Ravikiran A, Intricacies of Charging Telecom Services, Siemens Public Communication Networks Limited India, India.
7. ITU-T Recommendation D.212, ITU-T Study Group 3 (10/96), Series D: General Tariff Principles, General tariff principles – Charging and accounting principles for international telecommunication services provided over the ISDN, Charging and Accounting Principles for the use of Signalling System No. 7, (1996).
8. O. Hersent, J. Petit, D. Gurle, *IP Telephony*, Wiley Publication (2006).

OPTIMIZED ROUTE REQUEST ALGORITHMS FOR ON DEMAND MULTICAST ROUTING PROTOCOL

B.VENKATALAKSHMI†

Velammal Engineering College, Chennai, Tamil Nadu 6000, India

DHIVYA.C

Velammal Engineering College, Chennai, Tamil Nadu 6000, India

GEETHANJALI JAYACHANDRAN

Velammal Engineering College, Chennai, Tamil Nadu 6000, India

Multicast provides a more efficient routing strategy for multimedia applications in mobile environments with large numbers of simultaneous receivers. Many multicast routing protocols of MANET operates in an On-Demand basis. Multicast Routing Protocol relies on periodic, network-wide flooding for route discovery and maintenance. While forwarding the packets the Packet Delivery Ratio (PDR) is a critical metric to be considered. Many methods were proposed to improve PDR which in turn will improve the reliability of transmission in MANET. By handling request (JOIN-QUERY) and reply (JOIN-REPLY) phases in an opportunistic way, the intermediate node's forwarding mode can be changed. This paper proposes algorithms to improve PDR and power consumption of the nodes in an optimal fashion. The results obtained confirmed that a medium network of size 20 to 50 can give best performance by following the proposed algorithms.

1. Introduction

1.1. *Producing Hard Copy Using MS-Word*

A mobile Ad hoc network (MANET) is a fast deployable self configuring wireless network. It is characterized by various parameters like dynamic topology structure, node mobility, unreliable media and limited power supply. With today's third era of computing, applications like [1] on line gaming, classroom communication, battlefield communications, science explorations etc., highly demands Ad-hoc networks. However the protocols developed for wired networks tends to be unsuitable for deployment of MANET. This is why because the wired protocols never take into account the node mobility or increased sensitivity to network load and congestion.

A lot of research in recent years has concentrated on providing routing functionality in unicast [AODV [2], DSR [3]] and multicast [ODMRP [4], MAODV [5]] applications. With limited power and bandwidth as well as, frequently changing topology, these protocols are unable to outperform. To overcome these limitations, various optimization algorithms are proposed towards each of these protocols. The optimization can be introduced in several stages of data transmission [route discovery, route reply, data transmissions, Error handling etc.] In an ad-hoc network, the success of data transmission depends on the characteristics of a group of hosts in a network. Therefore multicast protocols play a major role in MANET. The paper proposes 3-different algorithms in the route discovery phase of ODMRP .The rest of the paper is organized as: The 2nd section quotes various proposals and solution of ODMRP protocol .The new method to optimize ODMRP by using 3-different algorithms are elaborated in section 3. Section 4, analyze the performance of all the proposed algorithms. Finally section 5 concludes, with future possible directions of ODMRP enhancement.

2. Background

On-Demand Multicast Routing Protocol (ODMRP) is a multicast routing protocol designed for Ad-hoc networks

† Work supported by Tifac core of the Velammal Engineering College.

with mobile hosts. ODMRP is a mesh based rather than a tree based multicast scheme. It uses [6] forwarding group concept. It applies On-Demand procedures to dynamically build routes and maintain multicast group membership. Similar to On-Demand unicast routing protocols, a request phase and a reply phase comprise the protocol.

ODMRP's outperformance compared to the tree based multicast protocol AMRIS was explored in [4]. The various properties of ODMRP were also well demonstrated in the network simulator, GloMoSim. The performance behavior of ODMRP with that of MAODV was compared in [7] and suitability of ODMRP for large areas and high mobility nodes was proved. In contrast MAODV suits for denser traffic situations.

Performance metrics of ODMRP like Packet delivery Ratio can be preserved with improved, normalized packet overhead [8], by dynamic refresh rate adaption. The real time performance analysis of ODMRP, carried out in [9] proved the efficiency of ODMRP than the static, Distance Vector Multicast Routing Protocol (DVMRP). Packet Delivery Ratio improvement by using multicast paths technique in ODMRP was proved in [1] using OPNET simulator. A work of improving the resilient property of ODMRP under node failure was suggested in [10] which provide higher PDR with minimal overheads.

3. Proposed Algorithms

ODMRP works with the concept of Forwarding Group Concept. Join-Query (JQ) messages are originated initially. The nodes receiving JQ will react by either setting FG flag and relaying the JQ or by generating Join-Reply (JR). In original ODMRP when a neighbor node receives the JQ, it will check for merely the duplication. The nodes those who are not registering for membership also will overhear this JQ. When registered members are facing any failure problem the route failure may occur. By making use of the neighbors those who have not registered i.e. with NFG flag set status, we can overcome this issue of failure. As an attempt towards this the algorithm 1 is proposed.

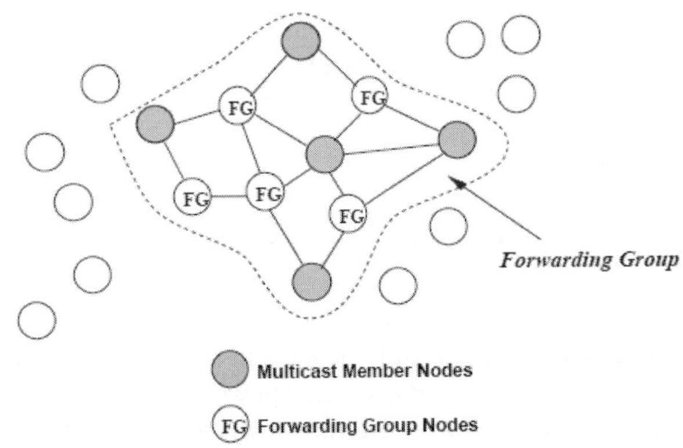

3.1. *Algorithm 1: Static Threshold*

```
Start
    Initialize Counter C; (for counting JQs)
    Initialize Threshold τ; (maximum no. of JQs)
    If not member
            {
              if JQ duplicate
              Increment C;
              If C> τ
              Then set as member;
            }
End;
```

This algorithm works well with improvement in PDR but consequently the power level of the nodes will be increasing. To overcome that algorithm 2 is proposed.

3.2. *Algorithm 2: Dynamic Threshold*

```
Start
    Initialize Counter C; (for counting JQs)
    Initialize Thresholds τ1 and τ2;(maximum no. of
JQs)
    Fix power values;
    If P1
    If not member
            {
              if JQ duplicate
              Increment C;
              If C> τ1
              Then set as member;
            }
If P2
    If not member
            {
              if JQ duplicate
```

```
                Increment C;
                If C> τ2
                Then set as member;
            }
End;
```

This improves the PDR with reasonably good power saving.

Both algorithms 1 and 2 suits for cases with node failures by balancing with increase in overhead (OH). In case if the requirement is to save power by avoiding the nodes unnecessarily registering, algorithm 3 can be used.

3.3. *Algorithm 3: Converting members as non-members*

```
Start
    Initialize Counter C; (for counting JQs)
    Initialize Threshold τ; (maximum value of power)
     If member
            {
                if JQ duplicate
                Increment C;
                If C> τ
                Then set as non member;
            }
    End;
```

4. RESULTS

To evaluate all the proposed algorithms the original ODMRP is simulated and its performance was analyzed for a selected set of inputs. Same inputs were allowed for testing the algorithms.

We evaluated the performance of the existing ODMRP by carrying out simulations in a GlomoSim environment [11]. It is a C-based simulation language developed discrete event simulation model. It employs the parallel discrete-event simulation capability provided by Parsec (PARallel Simulation Environment for Complex Systems).
The nodes position is considered to be random. MAC layer protocol is IEEE 802.11 and the number of packet to be sent is 40 for two multicast member group and 30 for one member group where there will be 1 source sending packet to a multicast member group. Each group consists of 3 destinations. The performances of ODMRP and simulation results are analyzed. The other input for the simulation is given as mentioned in the following table.

TABLE I. INPUTS IN CONFIG FILE

Parameters	Values
Terrain dimension	1000*1000
No of nodes	40
Node input	Random
Mobility	10 – 40 m/sec
Mobility type	Random Way point
Simulation time	200sec

The algorithm is evaluated for the metrics of packet delivery ratio, throughput by changing the mobility of the nodes and number of nodes in the specified terrain with averaging with respect to multiple seed values and the results are shown in figure 1, 2 & 3.

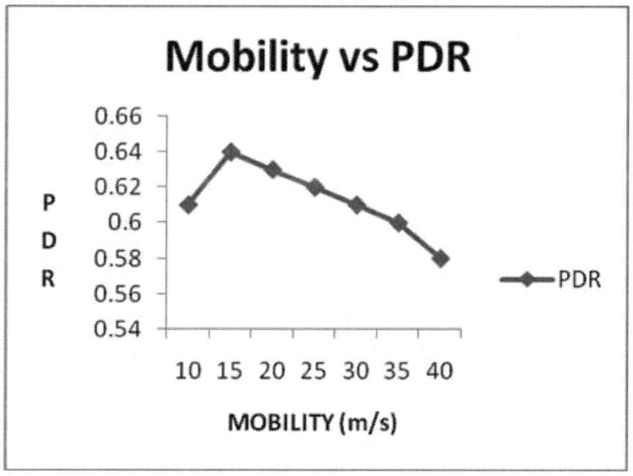

Figure 1. Mobility Vs PDR

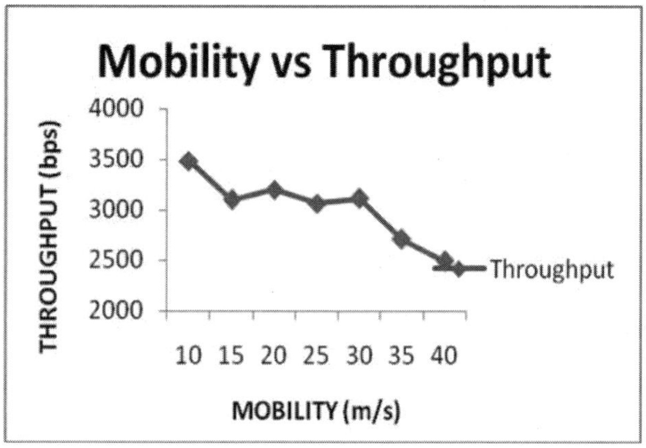

Figure 2. Mobility Vs Throughput

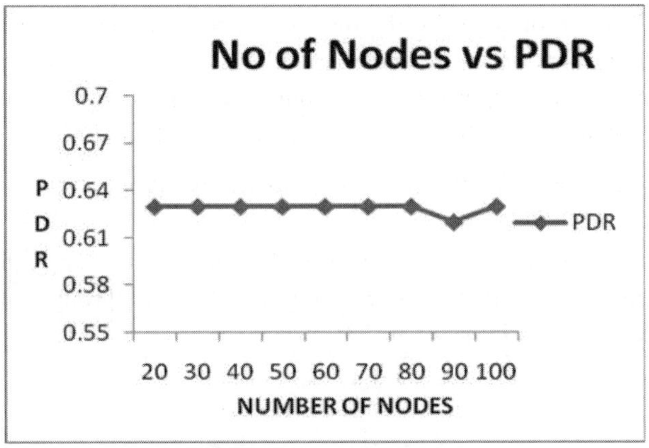

Figure 3. No of Nodes Vs PDR

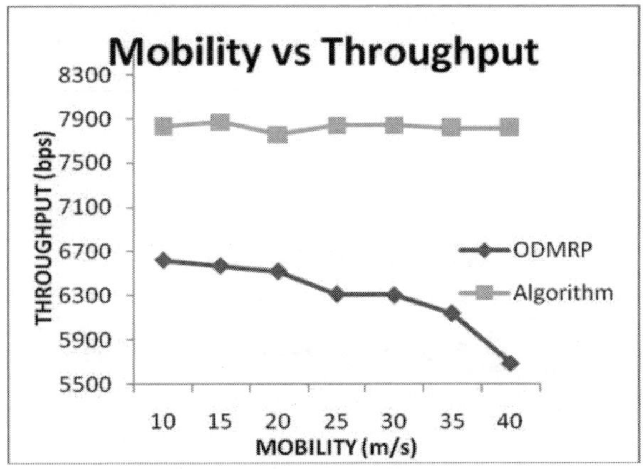

Figure 5. Mobility Vs Throughput

4.1. *Algorithm 1: Static Threshold*

The static threshold value selected was 40. With the same input parameters the simulation was repeated for many seed values and the average output is plotted as in Fig. 4, 5 and 6.

TABLE II. INPUTS IN CONFIG FILE

Parameters	Values
Terrain dimension	500*700
No of nodes	20
Node input	Random
Mobility	10 – 40 m/sec
Mobility type	Random Way point
Simulation time	33sec

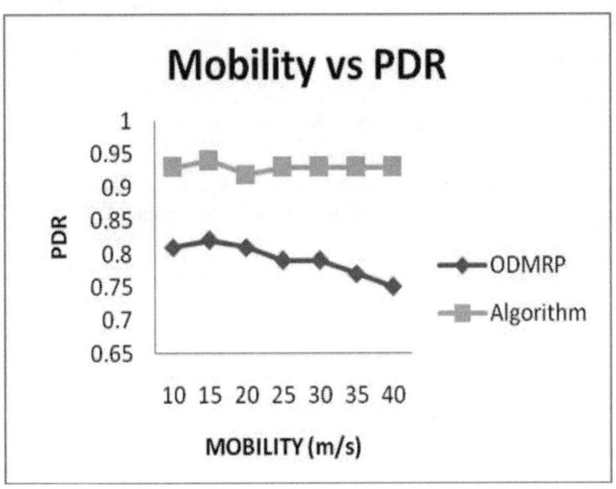

Figure 4. Mobility Vs PDR

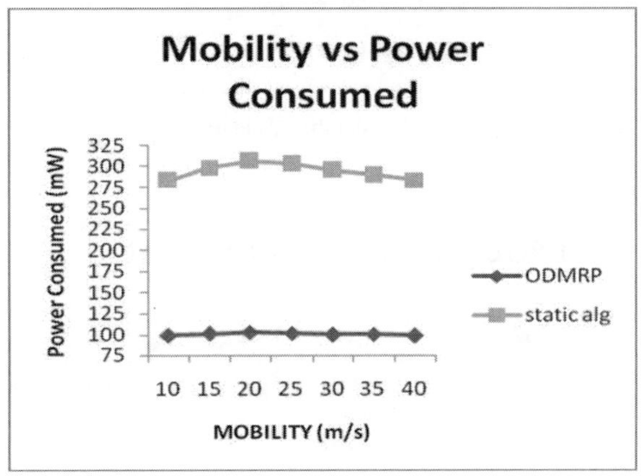

Figure 6. Mobility Vs Power

The results confirmed the improvement in PDR and throughput whereas the power consumed has drastically increased. As a step to avoid this algorithm 2 was simulated.

4.2. *Algorithm 2: Dynamic Threshold*

Here we used a set of power values and corresponding thresholds as given below. With all rest of the configuration same the simulation was performed and the results are as in Fig. 7, 8 and 9.

TABLE III. THRESHOLDS TABLE

Power	JQ Counter
0-50	40
50-100	50
100-150	60
150-200	70

Power	JQ Counter
200-250	80
>250	90

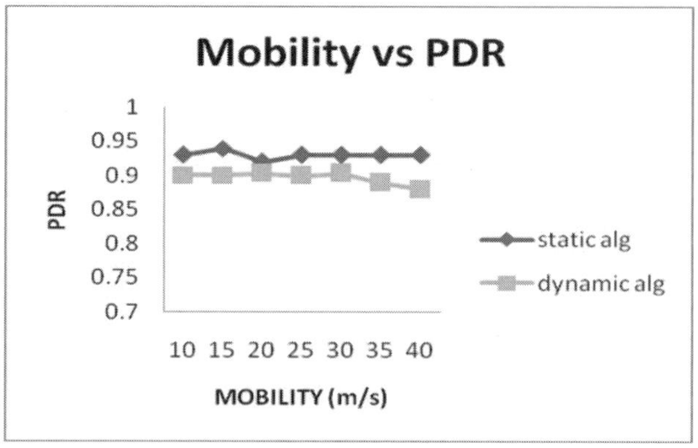

Figure 7. Mobility Vs PDR

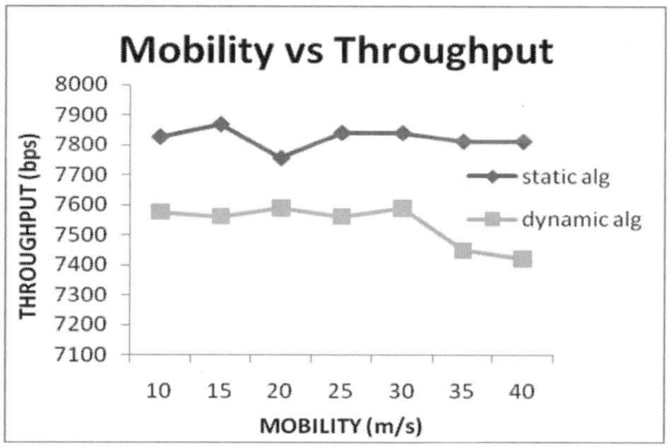

Figure 8. Mobility Vs Throughput

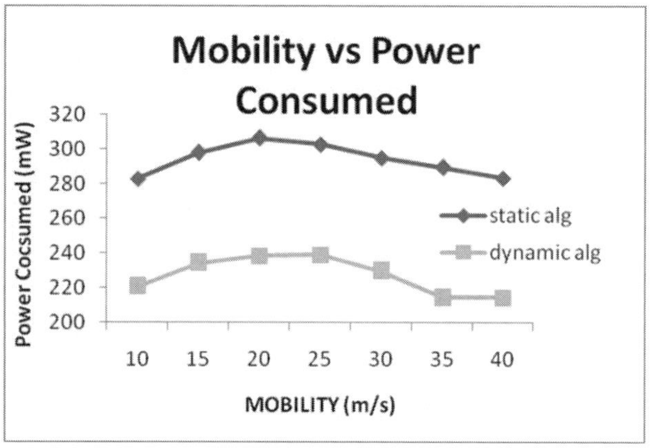

Figure 9. Mobility Vs Power

The results proved the enhancement in power consumption at the nodes. Finally as an effort of saving power the algorithm 3 is simulated and its results are obtained for a JQ count of value 3 as threshold.

4.3. *Algorithm 3: Converting members as non-members*

The figures 10-13 confirm that the algorithm can improve the power by retaining the PDR and throughput as that of original ODMRP.

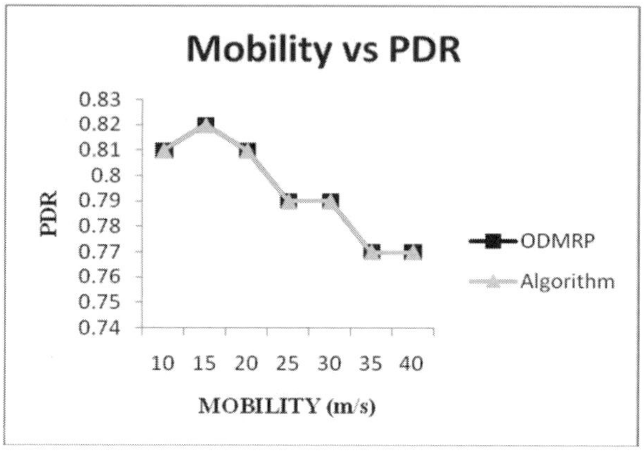

Figure 10. Mobility Vs PDR

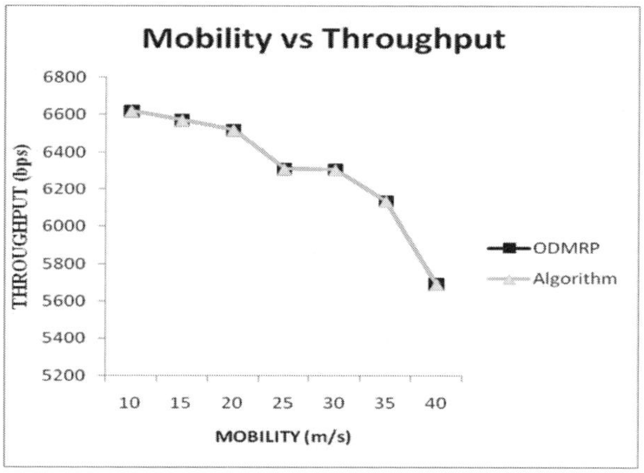

Figure 11. Mobility Vs Power Throughput

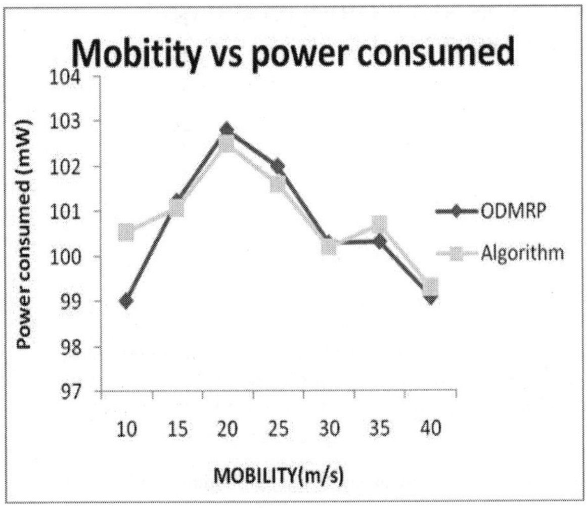

Figure 12. Mobility Vs Power

5. Conclusion

The results obtained by all the three algorithms confirmed that enhancement in ODMRP is achieved. The future work will focus on the optimization efforts in route reply phase of ODMRP

References

1. Shapour Joudi Begdillo, Mehdi Asadi, Improving Packet Delivery Ratio in ODMRP with Route Diversity, IJCNS , Vol7 No.12, December 2007.
2. C. Perkins. Ad Hoc On Demand Distance Vector (AODV) Routing. In Ad Hoc On Demand Distance Vector (AODV) Routing IETF, Internet Draft, draft-ietf-manet-aodv-00.txt, November1997. http://citeseer.ist.psu.edu/article/perkins99ad.html.
3. D. Johnson and D. Maltz. Dynamic source routing in ad hoc wireless networks. In T. Imelinsky and H. Korth, editors, Mobile Computing, pages 153–181. Kluwer Academic Publishers, 1996.
4. S. Ho Bae, S. Lee,W. Su, and M. Gerla. The Design, Implementation, and Performance Evaluation of the On-Demand Multicast Routing Protocol in Multihop Wireless Networks. In IEEE Network Magazine, volume 14, pages 70–77, January 2000.
5. E.Royer and C.Perkins, Multicast Operation of the Ad-Hoc On-Demand Distance Vector Routing protocol, Proceedings of Mobicom,1999
6. Yunjung Yi, Sung-JuLee,William Su, ODMRP for Ad-Hoc Networks,IETF MANET, <draft-ietf-manet-odmrp-04.txt>
7. Alexandros Vasiliou and Anastasios A.Economoides,'Evaluation of Multicasting algorithms in MANETs', proceedings of World Academy of Science,Engineering and Technology, volume 5, April 2005, ISSN 1307-6884
8. Oh, S.Y. Joon-Sang Park Gerla, M. , E-ODMRP: enhanced ODMRP with motion adaptive refresh, 2nd International Symposium on Wireless Communication Systems, 2005.
9. Sang Ho Bae, Sung –Ju Lee, William Su and Mario Gerla, The Design Implementation and Performance evaluation of the On-Demand Multicast Routing Protocol in Multihop Wireless networks, Network IEEE, Jan-Feb 2000
10. Dhammika Pathirana, and Minseok Kwon. RODMRP: Resilient On-Demand Multicast Routing Protocol. 21st International Conference(AINAW'07) IEEE Paper May 2007.
11. http://pcl.cs.ucla.edu/projects/glomosim/

A CLASS OF CAYLEY GRAPH INTERCONNECTION NETWORKS BASED ON ROSENBLOOM - TSFASMAN METRIC

W.B. VASANTHA † and R. RAJKUMAR *

Department of Mathematics , Indian Institute of Technology Madras, Chennai, Tamilnadu 600 036, India

*† E-mail: vasantha@iitm.ac.in, * E-mail: rajkumar.iitm@gmail.com*

www.iitm.ac.in

Rosenbloom and Tsfasman introduced a new metric (RT metric) which is a generalization of the Hamming metric. In this paper we propose a Cayley interconnection network based on the RT metric. We also introduce a new family of Cayley graphs on symmetric groups with respect to the RT metric. We also describe various algebraic and topological properties of these networks and propose optimal routing algorithm.

Keywords: Interconnection networks; Cayley graphs; Rosenbloom-Tsfasman metric; Symmetric groups; Optimal routing.

1. Introduction

Interconnection networks play a key role in the design and implementation of communication networks. Design of interconnection networks are often modeled by finite graphs. The interconnection networks based on the binary n-cubes have been extensively studied because of having many desirable properties. The generalized form of these n cubes are basically product of complete graphs of various sizes.[3] Generally, a class of graphs called Cayley graphs that are having many advantages properties (like symmetry). Various Cayley graphs based on symmetric groups, like hyprcubes,[3] star graphs,[1,2] pancake graphs[2,14] and orthogonal graphs[18] ect., are also surveyed.[13]

Rosenbloom and Tsfasman introduced a series of metrics on the class of $m \times n$ matrices over a finite field.[17] These metrics are defined by using column weight of matrices. Equivalently S. T. Dougherty and M.M. Skriganov defined these metrics using row weight of matrices.[5] Both of these metrics are known as the RT metric or m-*metric*. The study of theory of codes based on RT metric is also done by many researchers.[6,7,19,20] The structure of metric spaces with respect to some well known metrics can also obtain by the study of its distance graphs.[8,9,11,12,16] The well known Hamming graphs, in particularly binary n-cubes are also distance graphs with respect to the Hamming metric.[4]

In this paper we propose a class of Cayley graphs which are based on the RT metric. These graphs can be viewed as distance graphs of metric spaces with RT metric.[21] We also introduce a new class of Cayley graphs based on the symmetric groups. These graphs are basically graph unions and joins of multipartite graphs in a special way. The proposed family of graphs of graphs are having many desirable properties like symmetry, low diameter, higher vertex connectivity, ect.,. We also describe various algebraic and topological properties of these graphs. A part of the paper is available online.[21]

The rest of the paper is arranged as follows. Section 2 gives the preliminary notions of graph theory and introduce the notion of distance graphs. The definition of RT metric also given. Section 3 deals with the study of Cayley graphs of the group Z_q^n based on RT metric and describes various algebraic and topological properties of these graphs. We also propose a optimal routing scheme. Section 4 introduce the study of RT metric on the symmetric groups and describes the Cayley graphs of the symmetric group. Various algebraic and topological properties of these Cayley graphs are also given. In the final section we give the conclusions based on our study.

2. Preliminaries

In this section we just recall the basic concepts[10,12] which are essential to make this paper a self contained one.

Let $G_1(V_1, E_1)$ and $G_2(V_2, E_2)$ be two simple graphs. The *union graph* denoted by $G_1 \cup G_2$ has vertex set $V_1 \cup V_2$ and edge set $E_1 \cup E_2$. The *join graph* denoted by $G_1 + G_2$ consists of $G_1 \cup G_2$ and all lines joining V_1 and V_2.

For any connected simple graph G we write nG for the graph with n components each isomorphic to G.

In this paper we denote by $[G]^m$, the join of the graph G with itself m times. i.e.,

$$[G]^m = G + \cdots + G \quad (m \text{ times}).$$

A complete graph with n vertices is denoted by K_n and a complete r-partite graph $K_{m,\ldots,m}$ is denoted by $K_r(m)$.

The *connectivity*, denoted by $\kappa(G)$ of G is the minimum number of removal of vertices required to make the graph disconnected. The *independence number* of G denoted by $\alpha(G)$ is the maximal cardinality of a set $I \subseteq V(G)$ such that no two vertices of I are adjacent. The *matching number* of G denoted by $\alpha^{'}(G)$ is the maximal cardinality of a set $S \subseteq E(G)$ such that no two edges in S are adjacent. The *dominating number* of G, denoted by $\gamma(G)$ is the minimum cardinality of a non-empty subset S of $V(G)$ such that any vertex of G is either in S or adjacent to some vertex in S. The *diameter* of G, denoted by $d(G)$ is the maximum length among all the shortest path between any two vertices of G.

Let H be a group and $S \subset H$ such that S is closed under inversion and the identity element of H, $1_H \notin S$. The *Cayley graph* $\mathcal{C}(H, S)$ is the graph with vertex set H and where for any $g, h \in H$, g and h are adjacent if and only if $g^{-1}h \in S$.

The distance graph[8,9,11] of a metric space is defined as follows. Suppose S is a subset of a metric space X with metric d. Denote by dist(S) the set of all distances realized by pairs of distinct points in S, i.e.,

$$dist(S) = \{d(x, y) : x, y \in S \text{ and } x \neq y\}.$$

For each subset D of dist(S) the *distance graph* $G(S, D)$ with *distance set* D is the graph with vertex set S and edge set $E(S, D) = \{xy : x, y \in S \text{ and } d(x, y) \in D\}$.

Thus for a metric space X, $\bigcup\limits_{k \in dist(X)} G(X, \{k\})$ is a complete graph on X.

Let $Z_q = \{0, 1, \ldots, q-1\}$. We proceed on to recall the definition of RT metric[5] on Z_q^n .

Let $x = (x_1, \ldots, x_n) \in Z_q^n$. Then

$$\omega(x) = \begin{cases} max\ \{i \mid x_i \neq 0\}\ , & x \neq 0 \\ 0 & , x = 0 \end{cases}$$

is called the *RT weight* of x.

The *RT distance* between x and y in Z_q^n is defined by

$$\rho(x, y) = \omega(x - y).$$

ρ is a metric on Z_q^n.

Thus for any two distinct vectors $x, y \in Z_q^n$ we have

$$\rho(x, y) = d \Leftrightarrow x_d \neq y_d \text{ and } x_i = y_i,\ \ \forall\ d < i \leq n.$$

For example if we take (10211) and (00111) in Z_3^5 then $\rho((10211), (00111)) = 3$.

3. Cayley graphs of Z_q^n based on RT metric

Here note that dist$(Z_q^n) = \{1, \ldots, n\}$.

Theorem 3.1. *For the metric space (Z_q^n, ρ), where ρ denotes the RT metric, suppose $D = \{d_1, \ldots, d_k\} \subseteq$ dist(Z_q^n) with $1 \leq d_1 < \cdots < d_k \leq n$ then the distance graph $G(Z_q^n, D)$ of (Z_q^n, ρ) is isomorphic to*

$$q^{n-d_k}\left[q^{d_k-d_{k-1}-1}\left[\cdots\left[q^{d_2-d_1-1}K_q(q^{d_1-1})\right]^q\cdots\right]^q\right]^q. \quad (1)$$

Proof. Note that

$$G(Z_q^n, D) = \bigcup_{i=1}^{k} G(Z_q^n, \{d_i\}). \quad (2)$$

So first we give the structure of the graphs $G(Z_q^n, \{d\})$ for $d \in \{1, \ldots, n\}$.

Let $x = (x_1, \ldots, x_d, \ldots, x_n) \in Z_q^n$ be a fixed vector.

A vector $y = (y_1, \ldots, y_d, \ldots, y_n) \in Z_q^n$ is adjacent with x in $G(Z_q^n, \{d\})$ if and only if $\rho(x, y) = d$. But $\rho(x, y) = d \Leftrightarrow x_d \neq y_d$ and $x_i = y_i, d < i \leq n$.

By fixing the coordinate y_d in y such that $x_d \neq y_d$, the remaining coordinates $y_1, \ldots, y_{d-1}$ can be chosen in q^{d-1} different ways. Thus we get a set of q^{d-1} vectors such that all of its dth coordinates are same and equal to y_d and they are at a distance d from x. We also note that this set of q^{d-1} vectors are not adjacent with each other since the distance between any two of them is strictly less than d.

Now the dth coordinate in y can vary in $(q-1)$ different ways. By including the vector x , we get totally q sets of q^{d-1} vectors such that the vectors are not adjacent with each other with in each q sets, but all q^{d-1} vectors in each one of these q sets are adjacent to the remaining sets of vectors. Thus they form a complete q-partite graph $K_q(q^{d-1})$. Now the vector x can vary in q^{n-d} ways. Thus correspondingly we get q^{n-d} copies of $K_q(q^{d-1})$.i.e.,

$$G(Z_q^n, \{d\}) \cong q^{n-d}K_q(q^{d-1}).$$

So for each elements of distance set D we have

$$G(Z_q^n, \{d_i\}) \cong q^{n-d_i}K_q(q^{d_i-1}). \quad (3)$$

Now we construct the graph $G(Z_q^n, \{d_1, d_2\})$.

From the definition of the distance graph of a metric space two vertices in $G(Z_q^n, \{d_1, d_2\})$ are adjacent if and only if the RT distance between them is either d_1 or d_2.

So $G(Z_q^n, \{d_1, d_2\})$ is the edge disjoint union of $G(Z_q^n, \{d_1\})$ and $G(Z_q^n, \{d_2\})$. Thus to get the graph $G(Z_q^n, \{d_1, d_2\})$ it is enough to add edges to

$G(Z_q^n, \{d_2\})$ in such a way that if (u, v) is an edge added to $G(Z_q^n, \{d_2\})$ then (u, v) is an edge in $G(Z_q^n, \{d_1\})$.

Now the graph $G(Z_q^n, \{d_2\})$ can be written as ,

$$G(Z_q^n, \{d_2\}) = G_1 \cup \cdots \cup G_{q^{n-d_2}},$$

with each

$$G_i \cong K_q(q^{d_2-1}), i = 1, \ldots, q^{n-d_2}.$$

For each $i = 1, \ldots, q^{n-d_2}$ let V_i be the vertex set of G_i. Thus the space Z_q^n has been partitioned into q^{n-d_2} disjoint sets V_i , $i = 1, \ldots, q^{n-d_2}$ with $| V_i |= q^{d_2}$.

Since each $G_i \cong K_q(q^{d_2-1})$, its corresponding vertex set V_i is also partitioned in to disjoint sets V_{ji} such that,

$$V_i = V_{1i} \cup \cdots \cup V_{qi}\ , \quad | V_{ji} |= q^{d_2-1},\ j = 1, \ldots, q$$

with the condition that each edge in G_i joins a vertex in V_{li} and a vertex in V_{ji}, $l, j = 1, \ldots, q$ with $l \neq j$, for all $i = 1, \ldots, q^{n-d_2}$.

In $G(Z_q^n, \{d_2\})$ two vertices x and y are adjacent if and only if $\rho(x, y) = d_2$.

In the construction of $G(Z_q^n, \{d_2\})$ we note that the partitioned sets of Z_q^n have the following properties: For any $x = (x_1, \ldots, x_n)$ and $y = (y_1, \ldots, y_n) \in Z_q^n$,

(1) If $x \in V_i$ and $y \in V_j$ for some $i, j = 1, \ldots, q^{n-d_2}$ with $i \neq j$ then $(x_{d_2+1}, \ldots, x_n) \neq (y_{d_2+1}, \ldots, y_n)$; i.e., $\rho(x, y) > d_2$.

(2) If $x, y \in V_i$ for some $i = 1, \ldots, q^{n-d_2}$ then $x_r = y_r$ $\forall\, r = d_2 + 1, \ldots, n$; i.e., $\rho(x, y) \leq d_2$.

(3) If $x, y \in V_{ji}$ for some $i = 1, \ldots, q^{n-d_2}$ and $j = 1, \ldots, q$ then $x_r = y_r$ $\forall\, r = d_2, \ldots, n$; i.e., $\rho(x, y) < d_2$.

(4) If $x \in V_{li}$ and $y \in V_{ji}$ for some $i = 1, \ldots, q^{n-d}$ and $l, j = 1, \ldots, q$ with $l \neq j$ then $x_{d_2} \neq y_{d_2}$ and $x_r = y_r$ $\forall\, r = d_2 + 1, \ldots, n$; i.e., $\rho(x, y) = d_2$.

For a fixed $i \in \{1, \ldots, q^{n-d_2}\}$ consider the component G_i of $G(Z_q^n, \{d_2\})$.

Let $x = (x_1, \ldots, x_n) \in V_i$ then $x \in V_{ji}$ for some $j \in \{1, \ldots, q\}$ (say). Consider $y = (y_1, \ldots, y_n) \in Z_q^n$ with $\rho(x, y) = d_1$. We show that any such y must be in V_{ji}. Suppose

(i) if $y \in V_k$ for some $k \neq i$, $k = 1, \ldots, q^{n-d}$ then by using property (1) and $d_1 < d_2$, we have $\rho(x, y) > d_2 > d_1$, which is a contradiction. So $y \in V_i$.

(ii) if $y \in V_{li}$ for some $l \neq j$, $l = 1, \ldots, q$ then by using property (4) we have $\rho(x, y) = d_2$, which is a contradiction. So $y \in V_{ji}$.

Hence all the vectors which are at a distance d_1 from x must be in V_{ji} .

Since x is an arbitrary point in V_{ji} and the component of $G(Z_q^n, \{d_1\})$ which has x as a vertex is isomorphic to $K_q(q^{d_1-1})$, it follows that all the edges in the component containing x must be added in V_{ji}.

Since each component $K_q(q^{d_1-1})$ of $G(Z_q^n, \{d_1\})$ has q^{d_1} vertices and $|V_{ji}| = q^{d_2-1}$, we can attach $q^{d_2-d_1-1}$ number of components $K_q(q^{d_1-1})$ in V_{ji}.

In this way attach components $K_q(q^{d_1-1})$ of $G(Z_q^n, \{d_1\})$ in all partitioned vertex sets of G_i.

Thus after adding edges from $G(Z_q^n, \{d_1\})$ to the component G_i of $G(Z_q^n, \{d_1, d_2\})$ which we are considering is isomorphic to

$$\left[q^{d_2-d_1-1} K_q(q^{d_1-1})\right]^q$$

One can in this way attach $q^{d_2-d_1}$ components $K_q(q^{d_1-1})$ of $G(Z_q^n, \{d_1\})$ in each component of $G(Z_q^n, \{d_2\})$.

But the number of components of $G(Z_q^n, \{d_2\})$ is q^{n-d_2}, thus totally we are attaching $q^{d_2-d_1} q^{n-d_2} = q^{n-d_1}$ i.e, all the components of $G(Z_q^n, \{d_1\})$ in $G(Z_q^n, \{d_2\})$ and hence

$$G\left(Z_q^n, \{d_1, d_2\}\right) \cong q^{n-d_2} \left[q^{d_2-d_1-1} K_q(q^{d_1-1})\right]^q.$$

Now by using the similar type of argument we can construct $G(Z_q^n, \{d_1, d_2, d_3\})$.

Note that

$$G(Z_q^n, \{d_1, d_2, d_3\}) = G(Z_q^n, \{d_1, d_2\}) \cup G(Z_q^n, \{d_3\}).$$

Any component of $G(Z_q^n, \{d_1, d_2\})$ is isomorphic to $\left[q^{d_2-d_1-1} K_q(q^{d_1-1})\right]^q$. By attaching these components in $G(Z_q^n, \{d_3\})$ as in the method described in the previous case one can show that any component of $G(Z_q^n, \{d_1, d_2, d_3\})$ is isomorphic to

$$\left[q^{d_3-d_2-1} \left[q^{d_2-d_1-1} K_q(q^{d_1-1})\right]^q\right]^q.$$

Since $G(Z_q^n, \{d_3\})$ has q^{n-d_3} components, we have $G(Z_q^n, \{d_1, d_2, d_3\})$ is isomorphic to $q^{n-d_3} \left[q^{d_3-d_2-1} \left[q^{d_2-d_1-1} K_q(q^{d_1-1})\right]^q\right]^q$.

Proceeding in this way, at the kth stage, we can arrive at the graph $G(Z_q^n, D)$ as described in the statement of this theorem. □

Suppose $D = \{d_1, \ldots, d_k\} \subseteq \text{dist}(Z_q^n)$ with $1 \leq d_1 < \cdots < d_k \leq n$, then let S_D denote the subset of the group $(Z_q^n, +)$, where addition is done modulo q, such that

$$S_D = \{s \in Z_q^n : \omega(s) \in D\}.$$

It is easy to check that S_D is closed under inversion and doesn't contain the identity element (the all zero sequence). This gives raise to the Cayley graph $\mathcal{C}(Z_q^n, S_D)$.

The next Theorem shows that the graph $G(Z_q^n, D)$ is in fact a Cayley graph.

Theorem 3.2. $G(Z_q^n, D) = \mathcal{C}(Z_q^n, S_D)$.

Proof. The result follows from the fact that
$\forall\, x, y \in Z_q^n\ ,\ \rho(x,y) = \omega(x-y)$. □

Remark 3.1. A Cayley graph representing an interconnection network must be connected. Note that from (1), $\mathcal{C}(Z_q^n, S_D)$ is connected $\Leftrightarrow q^{n-d_k} = 1 \Leftrightarrow d_k = n$; i.e., $n \in D$. In this case S_D becomes a generating set of the group $(Z_q^n, +)$. So in our forgoing discussions we always include the condition that the distance set D of $\mathcal{C}(Z_q^n, S_D)$ contains n.

Fig.1 gives the Cayley graph $\mathcal{C}(Z_2^3, S_{\{1,3\}})$ and its corresponding vertex labeling of this graph. Here we denote a vertex $v = (x_1, x_2, x_3) \in Z_2^3$ as $x_1x_2x_3$.

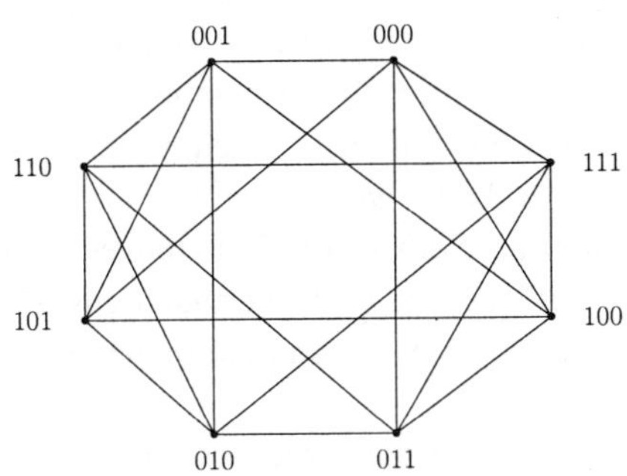

Fig. 1. $\mathcal{C}(Z_2^3, S_{\{1,3\}})$

Lemma 3.1. *Let G be the graph*

$$\left[m_k\left[m_{k-1}\left[\cdots\left[m_1K_p(s)\right]^{r_1}\cdots\right]^{r_{k-2}}\right]^{r_{k-1}}\right]^{r_k}, \qquad (4)$$

where $m_i, r_i, p, s \in \mathbb{N}$ and $p, r_i > 1$, $i \le i \le k$, then

(1) $\alpha(G) = m_k m_{k-1}\cdots m_1 s$.

(2) $\alpha'(G) = m_k \cdots m_2 m_1 r_k \cdots r_2 r_1 [\frac{p}{2}]s$,
where $[x]$ denotes the integral part of x.

(3) $\gamma(G) = m_k m_{k-1}\cdots m_1 s$.

(4) $\kappa(G) = (r_t r_{t+1}\cdots r_k - 1)m_t \cdots m_1 r_t r_{t-1}\cdots r_1 ps$,
where $t = max\{i : m_i > 1, 1 \le i \le k\}$.

Proof of Lemma. (a) The maximum number of vertices in $K_p(s)$ such that no two vertices are adjacent is s. So the maximum nuber of vertices in $[m_1K_p(s)]^{r_1}$ such that no two of them are adjacent is $m_1 s$. Proceeding like this, at the kth stage we can show that the maximum number of vertices in (4) such that no two of them are adjacent is $m_k m_{k-1}\cdots m_1 s$.

(b) The maximum number of edges in $K_p(s)$ such that no two of them are adjacent is $[\frac{p}{2}]s$. So the maximum number of vertices in $m_1K_p(s)$ such that no two of them are adjacent is $m_1[\frac{p}{2}]s$. Thus the maximum number of vertices in $[m_1K_p(s)]^{r_1}$ such that no two of them are adjacent is $r_1 m_1[\frac{p}{2}]s$. Proceeding in this way, at the k the stage we can obtain the edge independence number of (4).

(c) Note that $\gamma(K_p(s)) = s$ and so $\gamma([m_1K_p(s)]^{r_1}) = m_1 s$. Thus in this way we can show that $\gamma(G) = m_k m_{k-1}\cdots m_1 s$.

(d) Let $t = \max\{i : m_i > 1, 1 \le i \le k\}$. Then the graph G can be written as,

$$\left[m_t\left[m_{t-1}\left[\cdots\left[m_1K_p(s)\right]^{r_1}\cdots\right]^{r_{t-2}}\right]^{r_{t-1}}\right]^{r_t r_{t+1}\cdots r_k}.$$

Since $m_t > 1$, from the graph structure it is easy to see that the minimum number of points required to make the graph disconnected is
$(r_t r_{t+1}\cdots r_k - 1)m_t m_{t-1}\cdots m_1 r_t r_{t-1}\cdots r_1 ps$. □

Theorem 3.3. *Suppose $D = \{d_1, \ldots, d_k\} \subseteq \{1, \ldots, n\}$ with $1 \le d_1 < \cdots < d_k = n$ then the graph $\mathcal{C}(Z_q^n, S_D)$ has the following properties.*

(1) $\mathcal{C}(Z_q^n, S_D)$ *has q^n vertices and* $\frac{1}{2}(q-1)q^{n-1}\sum_{i=1}^{k} q^{d_i}$ *edges.*

(2) $\mathcal{C}(Z_q^n, S_D)$ *is symmetric and regular of degree*
$$(q-1)\sum_{i=1}^{k} q^{d_i - 1}.$$

(3) $\alpha(\mathcal{C}(Z_q^n, S_D)) = q^{d_k - k}$.

(4) $\alpha'(\mathcal{C}(Z_q^n, S_D)) = q^{d_k - 1}[\frac{q}{2}]$,
where $[x]$ denotes the integral part of x.

(5) $\gamma(\mathcal{C}(Z_q^n, S_D)) = q^{d_k - k}$.

(6) $\kappa(\mathcal{C}(Z_q^n, S_D)) = (q^{k-t+1} - 1)q^{d_t + 1}$,
where $t = max\{i : d_{i+1} - d_i > 1, 1 \le i \le k\}$.

(7)
$$d(\mathcal{C}(Z_q^n, S_D)) = \begin{cases} 2, & D \neq \{1, \ldots, n\} \\ 1, & D = \{1, \ldots, n\} \end{cases}$$

(8) $\mathcal{C}(Z_q^n, S_D)$ *has a Hamiltonian cycle.*

Proof. (a) $|Z_q^n| = q^n$ and the number of edges in $K_q(q^{d-1})$ is $\frac{1}{2}(q-1)q^{2(d-1)}$. So from (2) the result follows.

(b) Let $x \in Z_q^n$.Then

$$|\{y \in Z_q^n : \rho(x,y) = d\}| = (q-1)q^{d-1}.$$

Hence the degree of a vertex in $G(Z_q^n, D)$ is

$$|\{y \in Z_q^n : \rho(x,y) \in D\}| = (q-1)\sum_{i=1}^{n} q^{d_i - 1}.$$

Also every Cayley graph is symmetric [12,theorem 2.2.15], the proof follows.

(c),(d),(e) and (f) follows from lemma (3.1).

(g) If $D = \{1,\dots,n\}$ then $\mathcal{C}(Z_q^n, S_D) \cong K_{q^n}$ and $d(K_{q^n}) = 1$.

If $D \neq \{1,\dots,n\}$ then form (2), we note that $\mathcal{C}(Z_q^n, S_D)$ contains $K_q(q^{n-1})$ as a induced subgraph. But $d(K_q(q^{n-1})) = 2$, so the result follows.

(h) Note that from (2), $\mathcal{C}(Z_q^n, S_D)$ contains $K_q(q^{n-1})$ as a induced subgraph. But $K_q(q^{n-1})$ is Hamiltonian. So the result follows. □

3.1. *A simple routing algorithm for $\mathcal{C}(Z_q^n, S_D)$*

Let $V(\mathcal{C}(Z_q^n, S_D)) = \{x_i\}_{i=1}^{q^n}$ The following algorithm SHORTEST-ROUTE describes a optimal path between any two distinct nodes x and y in $\mathcal{C}(Z_q^n, S_D)$.

Step 1: if $\rho(x,y) \in D$ **then** xy is a path
else go to step 2
Step 2: for i= 1 to q^n **do**
if $\rho(x,x_i) \in D$ **then** xx_iy is a path.

Theorem 3.4. *The algorithm SHORTEST-ROUTE actually describes a optimal path between given any two arbitrary nodes in $\mathcal{C}(Z_q^n, S_D)$ for $n, q > 1$.*

Proof. Let x and y be given two nodes in $\mathcal{C}(Z_q^n, S_D)$, $n, q > 1$. we have to find a path from x to y. If $\rho(x,y) \in D$ then by the definition of Cayley graph, x and y are adjacent. So xy is the optimal path. Otherwise find a node x_i in $\mathcal{C}(Z_q^n, S_D)$ such that $\rho(x, x_i) \in D$. Such a node x_i always exist, since $d(\mathcal{C}(Z_q^n, S_D)) = 2$ and $n, q > 1$. Then xx_iy describes an optimal path. □

4. Cayley graphs of S_n based on RT metric

In this section we prove for the first time that RT distance is also a metric on the space of symmetric group S_n on the set $W = \{1,\dots,n\}$. Let e denote the identity permutation in S_n.

We define the RT distance on S_n as follows:
Take $\alpha \in S_n$. Let

$$W(\alpha) = \{i \in W : \alpha(i) \neq i\ ,\ i \leq i \leq n\}$$

and

$$\omega(\alpha) = \begin{cases} max\ \{i \mid \alpha(i) \neq i\ ,\ i \leq i \leq n\}\ , & \alpha \neq e \\ 0 & , \alpha = e \end{cases}$$

$\omega(\alpha)$ is called the RT weight of α.

Now we define the RT distance between α and β in S_n by

$$\rho(\alpha, \beta) = \omega(\alpha^{-1}\beta).$$

where α^{-1} is the inverse of α in S_n.

Example 4.1. Let $\alpha = (12)(45)$ and $\beta = (23)$ in S_6. Then $\omega(\alpha) = 5$ and $\omega(\beta) = 3$; $\rho(\alpha, \beta) = 5$.

Theorem 4.1. *ρ is a metric on S_n .*

Proof. We prove that ρ satisfies all the axioms of a metric.

(i) Clearly $\rho(\alpha,\beta) = \rho(\beta,\alpha)$, for all $\alpha, \beta \in S_n$.

(ii) Since the identity permutation is the only one that keeps every element of W fixed, we have $\rho(\alpha,\beta) \geq 0$ and $\rho(\alpha,\beta) = 0$ only when $\alpha = \beta$.

(iii) Next an element of W is moved by $\alpha\beta$ must be moved by at least one of the permutations α, β. Hence $W(\alpha\beta) \subset W(\alpha) \cup W(\beta)$ and consequently, $\omega(\alpha\beta) \leq \omega(\alpha) + \omega(\beta)$.

Now let λ, μ, ν be any three elements of S_n. We have $\rho(\lambda,\nu) = \omega(\lambda^{-1}\nu) = \omega(\lambda^{-1}\mu\mu^{-1}\nu) \leq \omega(\lambda^{-1}\mu) + \omega(\mu^{-1}\nu) = \rho(\lambda,\mu) + \rho(\mu,\nu)$.

So the function ρ satisfies the triangle inequality. In this way we see that ρ is a metric on S_n. □

Remark 4.1. Since two permutations cannot differ exactly in the first position, we have dist(S_n) = $\{2, 3, 4, \dots, n\}$.

The next theorem gives the structure of $G(S_n, D)$.

Theorem 4.2. *For the metric space (S_n, ρ), $n \geq 2$, where ρ denotes the RT metric, suppose $D = \{d_1,\dots,d_k\} \subseteq dist(S_n)$ with $2 \leq d_1 < \cdots < d_k \leq n$ then distance graph $G(S_n, D)$ of (S_n, ρ) is isomorphic to*

$$\frac{n!}{d_k!}\left[\frac{(d_k-1)!}{d_{k-1}!}\left[\cdots\left[\frac{(d_2-1)!}{d_1!}K_{d_1}((d_1-1)!)\right]^{d_2}\cdots\right]^{d_{k-1}}\right]^{d_k}$$

Proof. Clearly $G(S_n, D) = \bigcup_{i=1}^{k} G(S_n, \{d_i\})$.

First we give the structure of the graphs $G(S_n, \{d\})$ for $d \in \{1, \ldots, n\}$.

Fix a permutation $\alpha \in S_n$. A permutation $\beta \in S_n$ is adjacent with α $G(S_n, \{d\})$ in if and only if $\rho(\alpha, \beta) = d$. But $\rho(\alpha, \beta) = d \Leftrightarrow \alpha(d) \neq \beta(d)$ and $\alpha(i) = \beta(i),\ d < i \leq n$.

Since β is a permutation, each $\beta(i) \in \{1, \ldots, n\}$ is distinct. The last $n - d$ coordinates of β are such that $\alpha(i) = \beta(i), d < i \leq n$. So by fixing $\beta(d)$ such that $\alpha(d) \neq \beta(d)$, the remaining $\beta(1), \ldots, \beta(d-1)$ can be chosen in $(d-1)!$ different ways.

Thus we get a set of $(d-1)!$ different permutations β such that all of its dth coordinates are same and they are at a distance d form α. Also this set of $(d-1)!$ permutations are not adjacent with each other since the distance between any two of them is strictly less than d.

Now the dth coordinate in β can vary in $(d-1)$ different ways. By including the permutation α , we get totally d sets of $(d-1)!$ permutations such that the permutations are not adjacent with each other with in each d sets, but all $(d-1)!$ permutations in each one of these d sets are adjacent to the remaining sets of permutations. Thus they form a complete d-partite graph $K_d((d-1)!)$. Now the permutation α can vary in $n!/d!$ ways. Thus correspondingly we get $\frac{n!}{d!}$ copies of $K_d((d-1)!)$. i.e.,

$$G(S_n, \{d\}) \cong \frac{n!}{d!} K_d((d-1)!).$$

So for each elements of distance set D we have $G(S_n, \{d_i\}) \cong \frac{n!}{d!} K_{d_i}((d_i - 1)!)$

To get $G(S_n, D)$ we follow the same procedure as used in theorem (3.1). □

Suppose $D = \{d_1, \ldots, d_k\} \subseteq \text{dist}(S_n)$ with $2 \leq d_1 < \cdots < d_k \leq n$, then let $S_D^{'}$ be a subset of the group S_n,where the binary operation is the usual composition of mappings, such that

$$S_D^{'} = \{\alpha \in S_n : \omega(\alpha) \in D\}.$$

Note that $S_D^{'}$ is closed under inversion and doesn't contain the identity permutation. This defines the Cayley graph $\mathcal{C}(S_n, S_D^{'})$.

The next Theorem shows that the graph $G(S_n, D)$ is in fact a Cayley graph.

Theorem 4.3. $G(S_n, D) = \mathcal{C}(S_n, S_D^{'})$.

Proof. The result follows from the fact that

$$\forall \alpha, \beta \in S_n\ ,\ \rho(\alpha, \beta) = \omega(\alpha^{-1}\beta).$$ □

Remark 4.2. A cayley graph representing an interconnection network must be connected. Note that from (2), $\mathcal{C}(S_n, S_D^{'})$ is connected if and only if $n \in D$. In this case $S_D^{'}$ becomes a generating set of the group $(S_n, \circ)$. So in our forgoing discussions we include the condition that the distance set D of $\mathcal{C}(S_n, S_D^{'})$ contains n.

Fig.2 gives Cayley graph $\mathcal{C}(S_3, S_{\{3\}})$ and its corresponding vertex labeling of this graph.

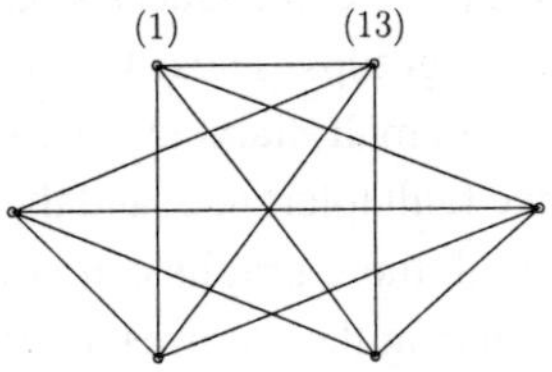

Fig. 2. $\mathcal{C}(S_3, S_{\{3\}})$

Theorem 4.4. *Suppose* $D = \{d_1, \ldots, d_k\} \subseteq \{2, \ldots, n\}$ *with* $2 \leq d_1 < \cdots < d_k = n$ *then* $\mathcal{C}(S_n, S_D^{'})$ *has the following properties*

(1) $\mathcal{C}(S_n, S_D^{'})$ *has* $n!$ *vertices and* $\frac{n!}{2}\sum_{i=1}^{k}(d_i - 1)(d_i - 1)!$ *edges.*

(2) $\mathcal{C}(S_n, S_D^{'})$ *is symmetric and regular of degree* $\sum_{i=1}^{k}(d_i - 1)(d_i - 1)!$.

(3) $\alpha(\mathcal{C}(S_n, S_D^{'})) = \frac{(d_k - 1)!}{d_1 \cdots d_{k-1}}$.

(4) $\alpha^{'}(\mathcal{C}(S_n, S_D^{'})) = \frac{d_k!}{d_1}\left[\frac{d_1}{2}\right]$.
where $[x]$ *denotes the integral part of* x.

(5) $\gamma(\mathcal{C}(S_n, S_D^{'})) = \frac{(d_k - 1)!}{d_1 \cdots d_{k-1}}$.

(6) $\kappa(\mathcal{C}(S_n, S_D^{'})) = (d_t \cdots d_k - 1)d_t!$,
where $t = max\{i : d_{i+1} - d_i > 1, 1 \leq i \leq k\}$.

(7)

$$d(\mathcal{C}(S_n, S_D^{'})) = \begin{cases} 2 & , D \neq \{2, \ldots, n\} \\ 1 & , D = \{2, \ldots, n\} \end{cases}$$

(8) $\mathcal{C}(S_n, S_D^{'})$ *has a Hamiltonian cycle.*

Proof. Proof of (c),(d), (e) and (f) follows from lemma (3.1). Proof of (a),(b),(g) and (h) are similar to theorem (3.3). □

Remark 4.3. Optimal route algorithm for $\mathcal{C}(S_n, S_D^{'})$ is similar to the SHORTEST-ROUTE algorithm described for $\mathcal{C}(Z_q^n, S_D)$ except the number of vertices.

5. Conclusions

In this paper we proposed a new family of Cayley graphs which are based on the RT metric. In particularly we defined these Cayley graphs on the groups Z_q^n and on the symmetric groups. Thus we introduces a family of Cayley graphs on Symmetric groups. These Cayley interconnection networks having small diameter, higher vertex connectivity (and hence fault tolerance) and they have Hamiltonian cycles. Though these graphs can not be iteratively generated but by varying the parameters of the graph we can get various Cayley graph structures. Further study of the propose graphs is needed to make it really useful in network design. In particularly to study the embedding of other well known graphs like hypercubes and meshes etc., and the study of Cayley graphs on the general direct product of groups,[21] is also needed. We are working in this direction for further investigation.

References

1. S.B. Akers and B. Krishnamurthy, The star graph: An attractive alternative to n-cube, *Proc. Int'l Conf. Parallel Processing (ICPP 87),* pp. 393-400,St. (Charles, Ill., Aug. 1987).
2. S.B. Akers and B. Krishnamurthy, A Group-Theoretic Model for Symmetric Interconnection Networks, *IEEE Trans. Computers,* vol. 38, no. 4, pp. 555-566, Apr. 1989.
3. L. Bhuyan and D.P. Agrawal, Generalized hypercube and hyperbus structure for a computer network,*IEEE Trans. Computers,* vol. 33, no. 3, pp. 323-333, Mar. 1984.
4. A.E Brouwer and A.M.Cohen, A.Neumaier, *Distance-Regular Graphs.* (Springer-Verlag, 1989).
5. S.T.Dougherty and M. M. Skriganov, MacWilliams duality and the RosenbloomTsfasman metric, *Mosc.Math.J.,* vol 2, no.1,(2002), 81-97.
6. Steven T. Dougherty and Keisuke Shiromoto, Maximum Distance Codes in $Mat_{n,s}(Z_k)$ with a Non-Hamming Metric and Uniform Distributions, *Designs, Codes and Cryptography,* v.33 n.1, p.45-61, August 2004.
7. Steven T. Dougherty and Maxim M. Skriganov, Maximum Distance Separable Codes in the ρ Metric over Arbitrary Alphabets, *Journal of Algebraic Combinatorics,* v.16 n.1, p.71-81, July 2002.
8. Eggleton RB, Distance graphs and their chromatic numbers. In: Workshop notes of conference of graph theory and combinatorics, Manila (1991).
9. M. Furedi and J.H Kang , Distance graphs on Z^n with l_1 norm, *Theor.Comput.Sci,* 319, 357-366, 2007.
10. F. Harary, *Graph Theory,* (Addison-Wesley, Reading 1969).
11. Jer-Joeng Chen and G.J.Chang , Distance graphs on R^n with 1 norm, *J.Comb.Optim,* 14, 267-274, 2007.
12. Jumming Xu, *Topological structure and analysis of interconnection networks,* (Kluwer Academic Publishers, 2001).
13. S. Lakshmivarahan,J.S. Jwo, and S.K. Dhall,Symmetry in interconnection networks based on Cayley graphs of permutation groups: A survey, *Parallel Computing,* vol. 19, pp. 361-407, 1993.
14. K. Qiu, S.G. Akl, and H. Meijer, On Some Properties and Algorithms for the Star and Pancake Interconnection Networks, *J. Parallel and Distributed Computing,* vol. 22, pp. 16-25, 1994.
15. A.M Raigorodski, The chromatic number of a metric space with the metric l_q, *UMN,*59:5(539), 161-162, 2004,.
16. A.M Raigorodski, Borsuk's problem and the chromatic number of some metric spaces, *UMN,* 56,106-149, 2001.
17. Michael Yu. Rosenbloom and Michael A. Tsfasman, Codes for the m-metric, *Problems of Information Transmission,* 33, 55-63, 1997.
18. I.D. Scherson, Orthogonal graphs for the construction of interconnection networks, *IEEE Trans. Parallel and Distributed Systems,* vol. 2, no. 1, pp. 3-19, 1991.
19. M. M. Skriganov, On linear codes with large weights simultaneously for the Rosenbloom–Tsfasman and Hamming metrics, *Journal of Complexity* , Volume 23, Issue 4-6, 926-936, 2007.
20. Pascal O. Vontobel and Ashwin Ganesan, On universally decodable matrices for space-time coding, *Designs, Codes and Cryptography* Vol.41, Issue 3, 325 - 342, 2006.
21. W.B.Vasantha and R.Rajkumar, Distance Graphs of Metric Spaces with Rosenbloom-Tsfasman metric, in http://arxiv.org/abs/0902.4364v2

RESEARCH ON THE FRAMEWORK OF NETWORKING SIMULATION TRAINING SYSTEM

LIANG LUO
School of Computer Science and Engineering, Beijing University of Aeronautics and Astronautics
Beijing, 100191, China

YUAN GAO
The Second Artillery Equipment Academy
Beijing, 100089, China

In the modern simulation training, networking simulation must be situated on its' appropriate important position. To solve the problem of networking process simulation in the simulation training systems, related works were firstly introduced and the deficiency analysis of the framework of traditional simulation training systems was also provided. Then the framework of separated mode and embed mode based on networking simulation were analyzed in detail. On the basis of this, a distributed embed networking simulation training system framework and the realization strategy of the networking simulation proxy node were brought out. The research provides new idea and available solution for taking the battlefield communication network environment effect into account in simulation training system.

1. Introduction

In the prepare period for the military warfare, it is a important approach to heighten the decision capability, command capability and operation capability of the crew in different levels through the way of execute assistant decision-making and training using the method of computer simulation. Now, the simulation training system based on traditional model theories and approaches can not meet the development requirements to new military revolution character by the symbol of integrated union battle and network centric warfare. So it is urgent to thoroughly research on modeling theories and approaches and to construct the new generation simulation training systems to meet the requirements of military training revolution accompanied by the new military revolution.

Directed by the development trend of networking, basement and simulation training, so many academies and departments have carried out research on the development of simulation training systems and the exertion of simulation training methods. Under this circumstance, a set of engineering standards and technical criterions were established. Also a set of simulation training systems adapted to different training requirements in vary level were developed. But in these systems, few took the battlefield communication network effect on training into account. Especially when the training system was allocated in the local area network or special network, one training federate can transmit and receive telegraph and command messages directly, which resemble the chatting face to face. But in the realistic battlefield environment, especially under the wireless communication circumstance, this mode resembles chatting will never come true.

In the union simulation system, such as JWARS and JMASS, the battlefield communication environment effect on training has been considered to different extend. JWARS introduced the communication delay for all the messages, which is decided by the network type of BSE accessed and the background network traffic load at the same time of message transmitted [1]. JMASS has constructed special communication server to accomplish the actions of links adding, links delete and nodes in the simulated battlefield communication network according to the SNR of communication nodes and LOS degradation analysis [2]. The General Dynamics that responsible for many simulation training systems has brought out the idea of Network-in-the-loop, which refers to the concept of Man-in-the-loop and Hardware-in-the-loop [3]. But in the literatures, the architecture of communication simulation in simulation training systems has not been definitely brought out. So the paper research on the system substratum framework of the simulation training system architecture and organized as follows. Section 2 analyzed the substratum framework of traditional simulation training systems.

Section 3 compared two modes of framework based on networking simulation. Section 4 brought out a novel framework of distributed embed networking simulation training system. Finally in Section 5, we concluded our work.

2. Analysis of the Substratum Framework in Traditional Simulation Training Systems

Now the distributed simulation technology has evolved from DIS architecture and ALSP architecture to HLA (High Level Architecture). And HLA is now and will be the mainstream standard for the development of simulation systems. At present, most of the simulation systems and simulation training systems are developed based on HLA architecture in that HLA separates the three main parts of the simulation systems, namely simulation function realization, simulation running management and substratum communication. So it is benefit for the re-usability of the models [4].

The framework of most simulation training systems based on HLA is shown in Figure 1. The trainee federate communicates with other federates via RTI. The typical flow of transmitting and receiving traffic or messages inner federates can be concluded as the Inside the Federates in Figure 1 shows.

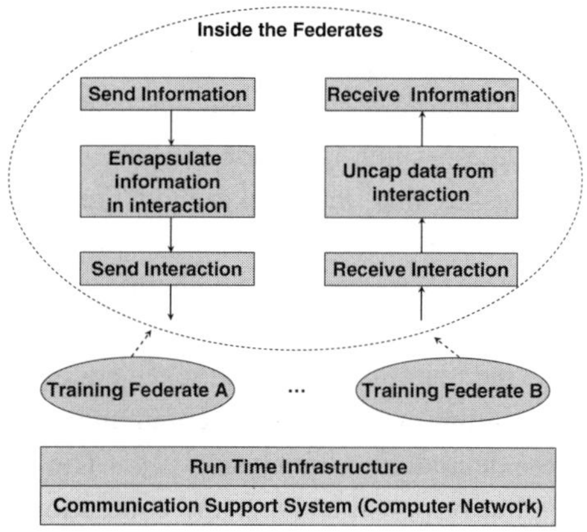

Figure 1. Traditional simulation training systems substratum framework.

As Figure 1 shows, the typical flow of transmitting and receiving messages between Federate A and other federates can be described as follows:

1. In federates initialization process, each one registers its own message Publish/Subscribe relationship.
2. When Federate A needs transmit message to Federate B, A encapsulates messages to be transmitted into a interaction class in HLA. And then A call for the Send Interaction service of RTI to send the interaction to RTI.
3. If Federate B subscribed the anterior interaction class in the initialization, RTI will inform Federate B via the callback Receive Interaction as soon as it finds the interaction class instance.
4. Federate B picks up the interaction parameters from the interaction class instance, and then we can consider that B received the messages from Federate A.

In the instance that training is actualizing via Local Area Network or special network, RTI will never confiscate the interaction from Federate A to Federate B. So the messages communication between federate A and B is equal to talking face to face. The circumstance of package loss, bit error or delay for the message delivering in the battlefield communication environment will never take place. But it is really in existence for the actual warfare and training, which should also be paid more attention to in constructing the simulation training systems.

3. Two Kinds of Simulation Training System Framework Based on Networking Simulation

When the battlefield communication environment effect on training is considered in the simulation training system, two kinds of frameworks as Figure 2 shows can be adopted. The networking simulation part in Figure 2 accomplishes the task to simulation the battlefield communication network running circumstance and to add lose, error and delay on the messages delivered among federates that mentioned above.

In the separated mode in Figure 2, the function of simulating battlefield communication network running is accomplished by Networking Simulation Federate, which communicates with other federates via RTI, too. In the training system, the information interaction among different trainee federates that logically carry through the battlefield communication network. The information include the message transmitting between trainee federates and the director federate that act as superior. It also include the information between trainee federates and the intercessor federate that act as junior and fellow. All the information mentioned above must be sent to Networking Simulation federate firstly, which will be injected into the simulated virtual battlefield communication network in Networking Simulation federate. The transfer process of the messages is simulated in Networking Simulation federate, and then whether the message can be delivered to the receiver and the amount of delay and bit error can be judged. Then the processed message is sent to receiver and transmitter by Networking Simulation federate. The disadvantage of this mode is that Networking Simulation federate takes on almost all the information transmit in the simulation training process, which will be readily to result in bottleneck of the information transmit in the simulation training system.

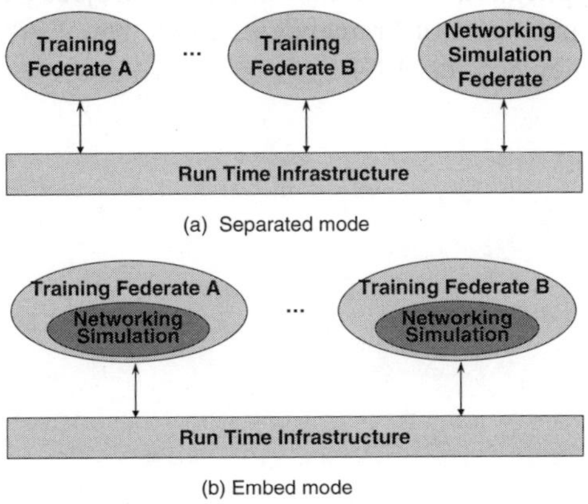

Figure 2. The simulation training system frameworks based on networking simulation.

The embed mode insets the Networking Simulation part into each trainee federates' model. The information transmission of the battlefield communication network is simulated by the interaction among trainee federates. The merit of this mode is that the complex communication network topology modeling task can be omitted. But mostly it is inconsistent between the topology of battlefield communication network and the information terminals that refer themselves on the network to transmit information. For example, for the sake of safety, the communication nodes are not set up in the same place with command post nodes. As regarded to the simulation training system, the trainee federates are really not the communication nodes in the battlefield communication network. For this sake, it is difficult to access communication departments in the simulation training system framework to execute command training, brain men exercise training and signal soldier's equipment operation skill training. It is also not suitable to simulate the network adjustment, communication counterwork and communication equipments destruction that special aimed at communication systems.

So we can see that whether the separated mode or the embed mode is not the ideal solution for the simulation training system framework based on networking simulation.

4. A Distributed Embed Networking Simulation Training System Framework

To heighten the importance of networking simulation in the simulation training systems or war-gaming systems and refer to the idea of Network-in-the-loop, we names the simulation training based on networking simulation as networking simulation training. The basic idea of it is constructing the substratum architecture that includes networking simulation part as a platform and setting up consummated networking simulation training platform. Then the trainee federates in different levels can be inserted into the platform to carry out training, such as synthesized command trainee federate, communication command trainee federate, electrical counterwork trainee federate and others federates. So the information interaction among federates can relatively incarnate the information transfer affect in the real battlefield communication network. Summing up the idea as networking simulation training for that we think it is trend in the field of simulation training, so it is named networking.

Based on the idea of networking simulation training and considering the deficiency of the former two kinds of simulation training system framework, we designed a distributed embed networking simulation system framework as Figure 3 shows.

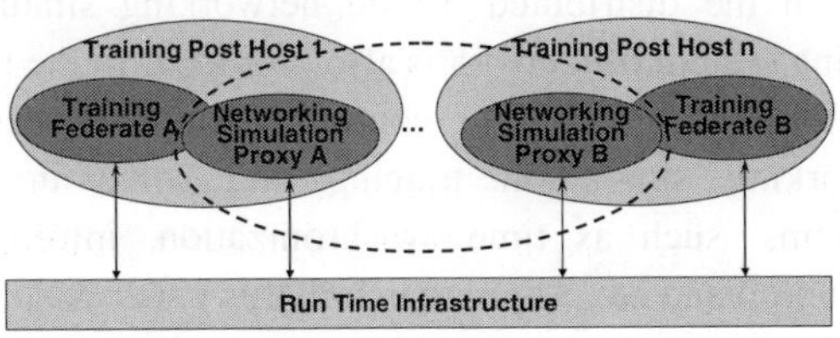

Figure 3. Distributed embed networking simulation training system framework.

The framework in Figure 3 sufficiently utilizes the distributed simulation technique. Each training post is located with a networking simulation proxy, which interacts with others via RTI. The whole networking simulation task is accomplished by all the networking simulation proxy nodes in the dash line in Figure 3. Each proxy node simulates a part of the whole battlefield communication network and the partition can base on different district or different network. The essential of this approach is to connect the proxies via HLA to buildup the networking simulation federate in the separated mode in Figure 2 to take on the task of battlefield communication network simulation. But the differentia between this approach and the embed mode in Figure 2 is that there will never be information transfer bottleneck in the training system of distributed embed framework.

Based on the distributed embed networking simulation training system framework and share the networking simulation burthen to each platform, it is useful for improving the simulation speed to meet the real time requirement of Man-in-the-loop. The realization of networking simulation proxy in the framework can utilize the maturate network simulation tools, e.g. OPNET. The HLA interface of OPNET can be used to be the interface with RTI and the powerful process modeling tool can not only complete the performance simulation of communication network but also simulate the networking process states change by its modeling based on Finite State Machine.

5. Conclusion

The networking simulation system framework was researched in the paper. An idea of networking simulation training and a distributed embed networking simulation training system framework were brought out. The realization strategy of networking simulation proxy node in the distributed embed networking simulation training system framework is also provided. In the future research, we will further consummate the concept of networking simulation training and solve the key problems, such as time synchronization, information interaction and etc. The research in this paper is not only useful to simulation training but to war-gaming.

References

1. Daniel T. Maxwell, Ph.D. An overview of the Joint Warfare System (JWARS). MITRE Corporation. 1820 Dolley Madison Drive McLean, Virginia 22102. Submitted to: Phalanx. July 2000.
2. Bob McCauley, Jerry Hill, Peggy Gravitz. JMASS98-Engagement Level Simulation Framework++. Proceeding of the 2000 Spring SIW Conference, 00S-SIW-148, 2000.
3. Eric Biegeleisen, Mike Eason, Craig Michelson. Network in the loop using HLA, distributed OPNET simulations, and 3D visualizations. Proceedings of the 2002 Spring SIW Conferences, 02S-SIW-176, 2002.
4. Fayad, M.E. D.Schmidt, R.Johnson. Building Application Frameworks: Object-Oriented Foundations of Framework Design. NewYork: John Wiley & Sons, 1999.

COMBINED APPROACH OF SERVICE AND ROUTE DISCOVERY IN MOBILE AD HOC NETWORKS

KIRIT MODI
Ganpat University, Kherva, Gujarat – 382711, India

KULDIP SINGH
Indian Institute of Technology, Roorkee – 247667, India

Service discovery is an integral part of constructing self-configuring Mobile Ad Hoc Networks (MANETs). By combining service and route discovery, both the identity of the node providing the service and the route to the service are discovered at once. This approach differs from related work on service discovery in ad hoc networks, which perform service discovery only at the application layer without discovering a route to the service. The idea of adding service discovery to reactive routing protocols for MANET was earlier proposed in an Internet-Draft using AODV as the routing protocol. In this paper, we propose modifications and extensions to the Internet-Draft. This paper presents the performance evaluation of Reactive routing protocols (AODV and DSR) for service discovery.

1. Introduction

Mobile ad hoc network is a multihop wireless network consisting of a set of mobile nodes not requiring any preexisting network infrastructure. In contrast to traditional wired networks, it has limited resource and energy. Service discovery is defined as the problem of automatically locating different services within a network. Currently, some well-known service discovery protocols for wired networks are Service Location Protocol (SLP) [1], Jini [2], Salutation [3]. SLP is not fully distributed due to the use of directory agents which aggregate service information. Jini uses Java and provides a Jini lookup service which clients use to discover services. Jini is bulky and would not be suitable for nodes in ad hoc network which have limited memory and computation power. Salutation makes use of an entity called Salutation Manager (SLM) in each node. The SLMs communicate using Remote Procedure Calls (RPCs). This would not work in an ad hoc network.

2. Service Discovery protocols for MANETs

GSD [4] is a Group-based distributed Service Discovery protocol for mobile ad hoc networks. It is based on the concept of peer-to-peer caching of service advertisements and group-based intelligent forwarding of service requests to reduce the broadcast storm problem. It does not require a service to register to a lookup server. This protocol uses DAML+OIL [5] to define ontology to describe services in a MANET. DAML supports XML and semantic definition and semantic matching. The services present on the nodes are classified into several groups based on the class-subclass hierarchy present in DAML.

Nom [6] is a fully distributed resource discovery protocol proposed by Doval and O'Mahony. It is designed to provide name resolution i.e. mapping between a string and a node id within an ad hoc network. Nom operates above the network layer and below the application layer. This protocol operation is similar to the on-demand route discovery process of sending a route request and reply. However, the Nom algorithm only returns the identity of the node providing the resource. A route to the node has to then be obtained using the underlying routing protocol.

Java Enhanced Service Architecture (JESA) is a Java based implementation. It has a service discovery protocol known as JESA Service Discovery Protocol (JSDP) which is presented in [7] by Preuß. JSDP consists of two protocols, Provider Location Protocol (PLP) and Proxy/Attribute Request Protocol (PARP). PLP is used to find the location of a service provider based on a service type. The id of a service provider or broker which can provide more information about the service is returned. This id is then used by PARP to obtain attributes of a service or to obtain a service access method. This information is returned in serialized Java objects.

3. Integrated Approach for Service and Route Discovery

In Internet-Draft [8], Koodli and Perkins proposed a method for integrating service discovery with route discovery. This method allows a node to discover the address of a service provider and to discover a route to this provider at the same time.

3.1. *Service Specification*

A service is specified using either the TCP/UDP port at which the service can be accessed or the service type and predicate as defined in the Service Location Protocol RFC [1].

3.2. *Service Binding*

Service discovery involves finding a mapping from the service specification to the IP address of a node providing the service. This mapping is also known as a service binding. Each service binding has an associated lifetime after which the binding is no longer considered valid.

3.3. *Service Table*

This is the table used for storing the service bindings. Each entry in the service table has the service port, service string (service type), address of the node providing the service, the expiry time and the number of hops to the service. The entries in the service discovery table expire after a maximum of 10 seconds. However, when a node itself provides a service, the lifetime of the entry for this service in its service table is set to 600 seconds.

3.4. *Combined Service and Route Discovery*

If a node needs to access a service (initiator) has a valid binding and a valid route to the service, it doesn't need to initiate any discovery process. Otherwise, the node broadcasts a route request with a service request extension. Such a request is called a service request (SREQ). The discovery process is complete when the node receives a route reply with a service reply extension. Such a reply is called a service reply (SREP).

3.5. *Message Formats*

1. Service Request Port Extension

The format of the service request port extension is given in Figure .1. The purpose of each field is as follows: Type: To Be Determined (1 byte), Length: Length of the extension (1 byte), Port Number: TCP/UDP port number used by the service (2 bytes).

The format of the service request url extension is given in Figure .2. The purpose of each field is as follows: Type: To Be Determined (1 byte).Length: Length of the extension (1 byte), ServiceTypeLen: Length of the service type field (1 byte), Reserved: For future use (1 byte).Service Type:

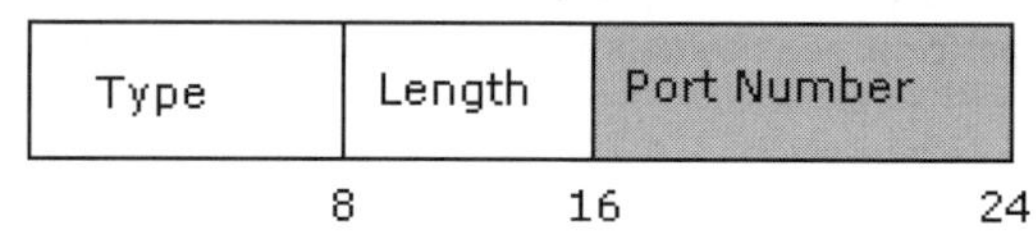

Figure 1: Service Request Port Extension

2. Service Request URL Extension

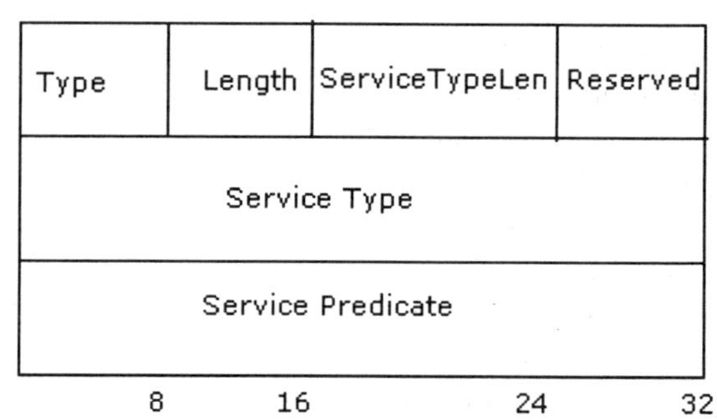

Figure 2: Service Request URL Extension

3. Service Reply Extension

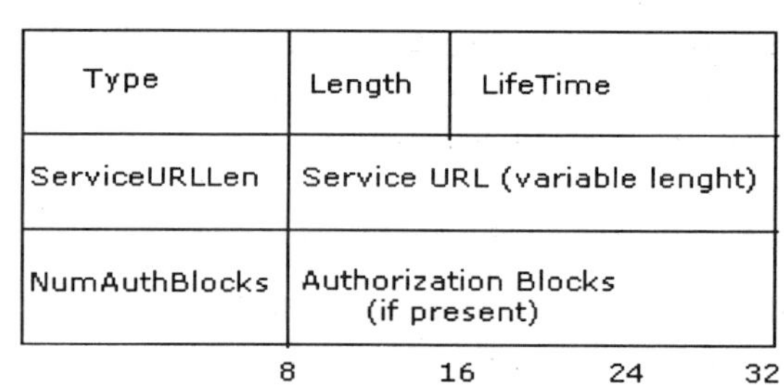

Figure 3: Service Reply Extension

Service type as defined in RFC [1] (variable length), Service Predicate: Service predicate as defined in RFC [1] (4 bytes).

The format of the service reply extension is given in Figure .3. The purpose of each field is as follows: Type : To Be Determined (1 byte), Length : Length of the extension (1 byte), Lifetime : Lifetime of the service binding (2 bytes), ServiceURLLen : Length of the service URL field (1 byte), Service URL : Service URL as defined in RFC [1] (variable length), NumAuthBlocks : Number of authorization blocks as defined in RFC [1] (1 byte), Authorization Blocks : Authorization blocks as defined in RFC [1] (3 bytes)

4. Integration of Service Discovery with AODV

4.1. *Modifications to Internet-Draft Specification*

We propose the following additions and modifications to the Internet-Draft:

1. A service binding lifetime field of 2 bytes is added to the service request URL extension. This is done so that a node which adds a binding to a request but doesn't have a route to the service, can add the binding lifetime to the request. The modified format of the service request URL extension is given in Figure .4.
2. No mention was made in the draft about retransmission of SREQs. The approach we follow for retransmitting SREQs is similar to that followed for retransmitting RREQs.

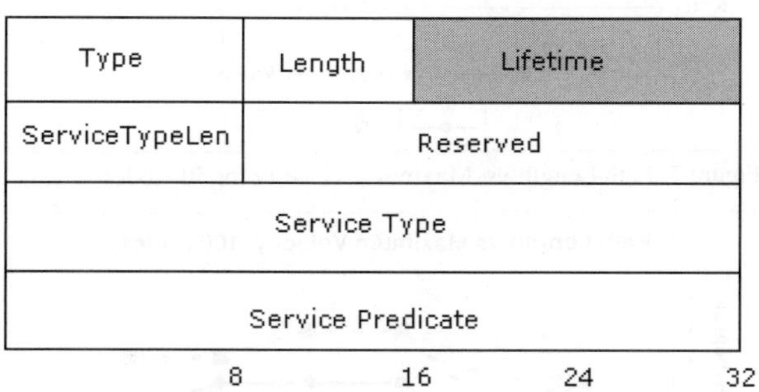

Figure 4: Modified Service Request URL Extension

3. If a network wide SREQ with known service destination has timed out, subsequent network wide retransmissions of the SREQ must be sent with unknown destination. This ensures that other providers of the same service can also send a SREP. This way, if the known service provider is not responding or no longer provides the service, alternate providers can be found.
4. When a SREQ is received at a node which is the request destination or which provides the requested service, the node must send a SREP for its service. Only if the request destination is not this node and this node does not provide the service, will a different service destination be considered.
5. When a SREQ is received at the request destination but the node no longer provides the service, it still sends a SREP with binding lifetime set to 0.
6. When a SREQ with a service binding is received at a node, if the node does not have any binding for this service then add the binding from the request to this node. Otherwise, if this node has a binding but it has expired and there is no pending request for this service, then replace this binding with the binding from the request.
7. When a SREP with service binding lifetime set to 0 by the service provider is received by a node which has a valid binding for this service and provider, this binding should be removed.
8. When a SREP is received by a node which has a better binding for the service and a shorter route to the service destination, the binding and route in the SREP should be replaced with the node's binding and route. Note that the Internet-Draft does mention that a node should replace the binding in a SREP with a better binding, if it has one. However, no mention is made of also checking for a route to the service destination.

5. Integration of Service Discovery with DSR

The same packet formats and OTcl [11] interface are used as in the modified integration of service discovery with AODV [13]. All the modifications to the Internet-Draft proposed in the earlier sections have been implemented in the integration of service discovery with DSR [14] in ns-2. Hence, the integration of service discovery with DSR is similar to the modified integration of service discovery with AODV.

5.1. *Service Table*

Each entry in the service table includes the service port, string, destination address, service expiry time and number of hops. To facilitate retransmission of SREQs, each entry also has the time of the last arp, time of the last service request, the number of outstanding service requests and the type of the last service request. These fields serve the same purpose as the corresponding fields in the request table.

5.2. *Service Timer*

A service timer is added to the DSR agent. This timer expires every 0.1 seconds. When the timer expires, all entries in the service table which have expired and for which there are no pending service requests are deleted. The check for pending service requests is also done in the service timer.

6. Simulation

We have performed simulation using ns-2 [9], [10] simulator (version 2.28) developed by the Virtual InterNetwork Testbed (VINT) project at the University of California at Berkley for our simulations.

6.1. *Simulation Setup*

We have tested the service and route discovery process for different conditions of mobility and number of nodes. We run our tests for the 50 nodes and 100 nodes in an area of 500 meters by 500 meters. Each simulation runs for 180 seconds. During this time, 30 service requests are made for either a service port or string. The values of latency and path length calculated are the average values over all the requests. Note that there are five different servers in the network — a web server at port 80, a mail server at port 60, a print server at port 25, a name server at port 53 and a tftp server at port 69. All these servers are started one second after the start of the simulation and remain up until the end of the simulation. In other words, for these tests, no service termination is done.

The average pause time between node movements is set to 30 seconds. The simulation is run for different values of maximum velocity of the nodes. The values of maximum velocity considered are 2, 4, 6, 8, and 10 meters/second. The Average latency and path length are plotted for the different values of maximum velocity and the results using AODV and DSR for 50 and 100 nodes are shown in Figures 5, 6, 7 and 8 respectively. The latency is the average of the time delays for each individual successful discovery while the path length represents the number of hopes in the route to the service provider.

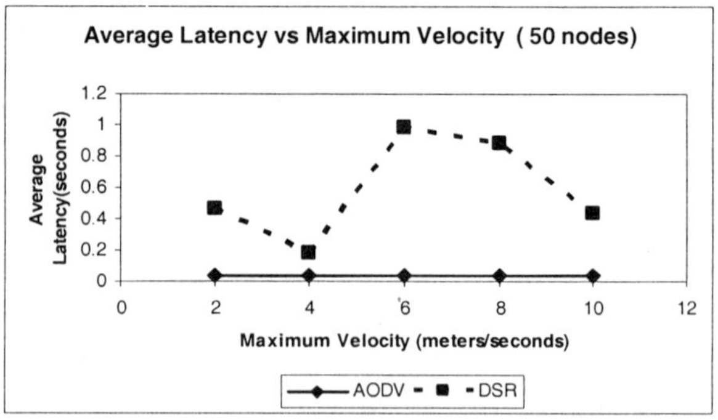

Figure 5: Average Latency vs Maximum Velocity for 50 Nodes

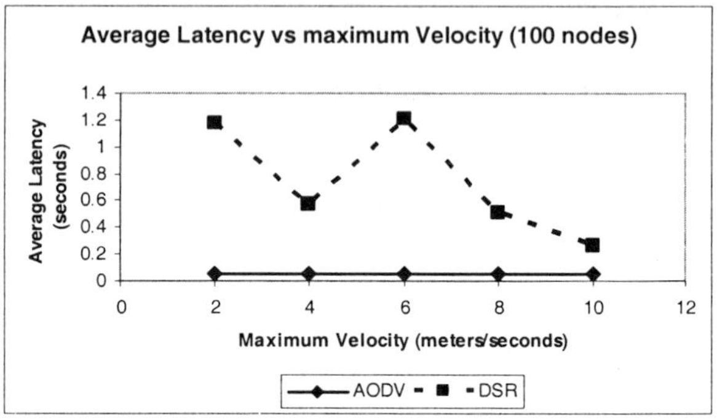

Figure 6: Average Latency vs. Maximum Velocity for 100 Nodes

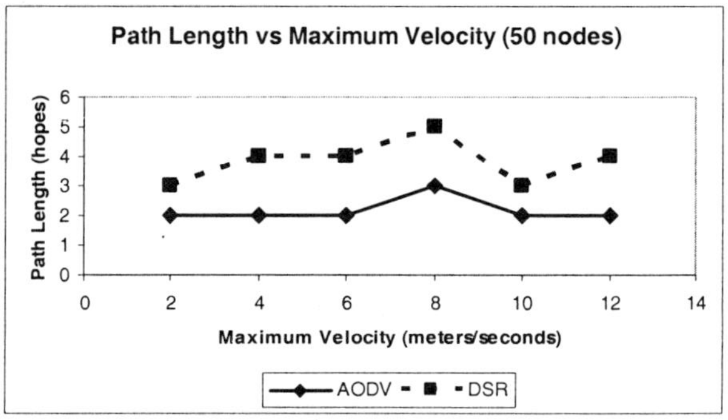

Figure 7: Path Length vs. Maximum Velocity for 50 Nodes

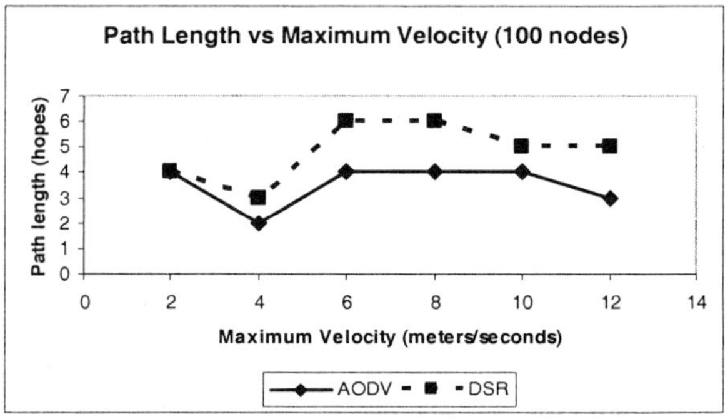

Figure 8: Path Length vs. Maximum Velocity for 100 Nodes

From the graphs, we can conclude that the average latency and path length when using AODV is always smaller than that when we use DSR as the routing protocol. We also note that there is no monotonic increase or decrease in average latency and path length with variation in the maximum velocity. Overall, we can conclude that integration of service discovery with AODV yields better results.

7. Conclusions and Future work

We find that the values of Average latency and path length obtained for both AODV and DSR are reasonable, thus confirming that the integrated approach is a viable method of service and route discovery. The results also indicate a better Average latency and path length when using AODV. We conclude that the integrated approach of service discovery with AODV performs better than the integration with DSR. For future work, we proposed the following:

On-demand routing protocols like DSR and AODV use broadcast of request messages. In a wireless network, broadcast involves a lot of overhead which causes scalability problems for large networks. This is known as the broadcast storm problem. Future work could involve reducing the broadcast overhead in service discovery using DSR and AODV.

References

1. E. Guttman, C. Perkins, J. Veizades, and M. Day. Service location protocol, version 2, RFC 2608, June 1999.
2. Sun Microsystems. Jini architecture specification, version 1.2, December 2001.
3. Salutation Consortium. Salutation architecture specification, version 2.1, 1999.
4. Dipanjan Chakraborty, Anupam Joshi, Yelena Yesha, and Tim Finin. GSD: A novel group-based service discovery protocol for manets. In 4th IEEE Conference on Mobile and Wireless Communications Networks (MWCN 2002), 2002, pages 140–144.
5. DARPA Agent Markup Language and Ontology Inference Layer. http://www.daml.org/2001/03/daml+oil.daml.
6. Diego Doval and Donal O'Mahony. Nom: Resource location and discovery for ad hoc mobile networks. In Proceedings of The First Annual Mediterranean Ad Hoc Networking Workshop, Med-hoc-Net 2002, Sardegna, Italy, September 2002.
7. Stephan Preuß. JESA service discovery protocol. In Proceedings of Networking 2002, Pisa, Italy, 2002, pages 1196–1201.
8. Rajeev Koodli and Charles E. Perkins. Service discovery in on-demand ad hoc networks, Internet Engineering Task Force (IETF) Internet-Draft, draft-koodli-manet-servicediscovery-00.txt, work in progress, October 2002.
9. Marc Greis. Tutorial for the network simulator ns. http://www.isi.edu/nsnam/ns /tutorial.
10. The ns manual (formerly ns notes and documentation), the VINT project. Available from http://www.isi.edu/nsnam/ns/ns-documentation.html
11. Otcl tutorial, version 0.96, September 1995. ftp://ftp.tns.lcs.mit.edu/pub/otcl/doc/tutorial.html.
12. Vincent D. Park and M. Scott Corson. A highly adaptive distributed routing algorithm for mobile wireless networks. In Proceedings of IEEE INFOCOM 1997, Kobe, Japan, pages 1405–1413.
13. Charles E. Perkins and Elizabeth M. Royer. Ad-hoc on-demand distance vector routing. In Proceedings of Second IEEE Workshop on Mobile Computing Systems and Applications (WMCSA 1999), New Orleans, LA, 1999, pages 90–100.
14. David B. Johnson and David A. Maltz. Dynamic source routing in ad hoc wireless networks. In Mobile Computing, Kluwer Academic Publishers, 1996, volume 353, chapter 5, pages 153–181, 1996.
15. Charles E. Perkins. Service location protocol for mobile users. In The Ninth IEEE International Symposium on Personal, Indoor and Mobile Radio Communications, 1998, volume 1, pages 141–146.

ADVANCED LINK STATE PROTOCOL *

K. PRABHAKARAN†

IIIrd year Computer Science, MNM Jain Engineering College, Thoraipakkam
Chennai, Tamil Nadu 600088, INDIA

Internet environment faces a lot of vulnerability at the present situation. The pervasive and ubiquitous nature of the internet coupled with growing concerns about cyber terrorism demand immediate solutions for securing the internet infrastructure. In these Routing table poisoning is more pronounced. So far the solutions for these attacks are the Intrusion detection. . Using an attack analyzer in the fast moving internet environment is not scalable solution. More over it causes failure of the network or heavy loss to the network which is later detected by the attack analyzer based on some criteria and then the network is notified about the attack. So I suggest an alternate for this solution, i.e., a Protocol driven solution for the routing table poisoning attack. In this the router security is enables by the cryptographic techniques, sharing and managing of a public key among the routers. Then the routing table updates are done with certain rules that are enforced by the protocol.

1. Introduction

1.1. *Problem Definition*

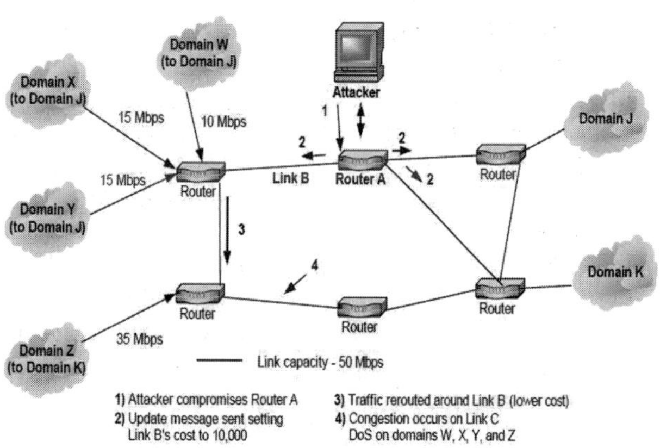

Figure 1.

This is a sample attack in which the 'Router A' is attacked by an attacker. With the identity of the Router A the attacker sends the bogus information to all the participating routers. Thus the weight of the 'Link B' is arbitrarily changed to a higher value which results in the breakdown of the 'Domain Z' this is due that when the Link B has high vale then the packets form the domains X,W and Y are routed through the router where the domain Z has connected. Hence the congestion occurs on the Router mentioned and finally the services to domain Z are shut down. Thus the attacker attacks the Domain Z.

1.2. *The Impact of Poisoning*

- Suboptimal Routing.
- Access to Data.
- Routing table poisoning can lead to Artificial Congestion
- Partition.
- Overwhelmed Host

Routing table poisoning is used as a weapon for *Denial of Service* (DOS) (9) attacks

2. Routing Table Poisoning Attacks

Routing tables are generated by exchange of routing information or updates between routers. Core network routers generally maintain their routing tables dynamically using a routing protocol, whereby the routers exchange routing information with each other.
The Attacker may attack as well as from outside and from inside. Hence the data security should be more to protect our data

2.1. *Modification/Fabrication*

In this the attacker reaches the goal by changing the link capacity. Hence, Routing Information can be intercepted by an adversary; Information can be stopped from propagating. Thereby he reaches the Goal of acquiring the data. Represented in Figure 2.(a).

---

* This work is supported by my college (MNM Jain Engineering college).
† Work partially supported by grant Management of MNM Jain Engineering College.

2.2. *Insertion*

This is arbitrarily changing the link capacity of the network, thus the protocols decide that path as the trusted and it gets affected. Represented in Figure2.(b).

2.3. *Deletion*

In the form of replication of old message. Represented in Figure 2. (c).

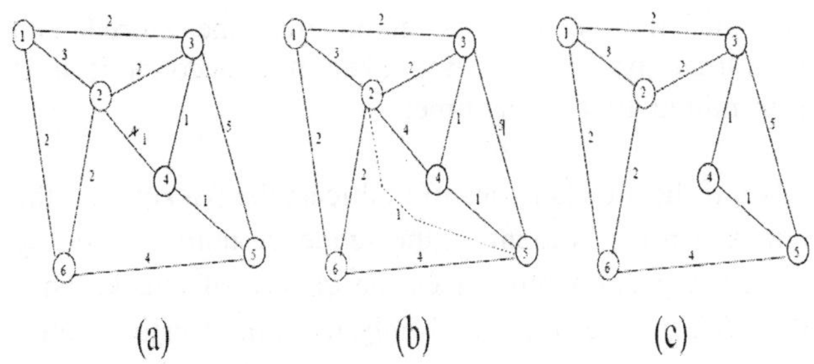

Figure 2.

2.4. *Routing Protocols*

Open Shortest Path First (OSPF) (2) is used for distributing routing information between routers belonging to an AS. OSPF is a link-state protocol based on the Dijkstra algorithm. The OSPF definition states that only trusted routers can participate in the Autonomous System's routing

3. Link State Routing Protocol

While considering the routing protocol security, one naive assumption about routing protocols is that all participating trusted routers are always trustable. That is, if a *link state advertisement* (LSA) (2) is sent from to and this LSA contains valid authentication, then will trust this LSA and update its routing table accordingly. This naive assumption goes in vain when the intruder gets hold of the network router.

3.1. *Faulty Source*

It is compromised and it could send out false LSAs about itself to its neighbors. That is, lying about its status such that the remaining router in the network believes the information passed by the router is unusable when it is up or available when the link does not even exist.

3.2. *Faulty Intermediate Router*

In link-state routing protocols like OSPF, LSAs are flooded through the entire network such that eventually every router will have identical topology information about the whole network. In other words, an LSA might visit many intermediate routers before reaching one particular destination. An evil intermediate router can potentially cause much greater damage than the source router

4. Solution

4.1. *Proposed Protocol*

We propose the protocol named **"Secure link state protocol"**

The options that are added for the secure routing are

- Cryptographic checksums to protect against outsiders generating fraudulent routing messages.
- Per-message sequence numbers and timestamps to protect against outsiders re-ordering or delaying genuine routing information.
- Strong origin authentication, using shared-key or public key cryptography
- Comparing the information in the LSA packets with the LSA packets of other routers.
- Providing Double Authentication scheme to ensure the integrity of the data

4.2. *Cryptographic Technique*

Digital signature is used to authenticate the source. An unauthorized route request would fail verification and be roped by each of the requesting node's immediate neighbors, preventing the request from ooding through the network

4.3. *Shared key architecture for routing protocols*

The proposal for providing security services to routing protocols was to use a shared key-based authentication scheme. In this one (Public / Private) key is used to encrypt the message and the other is used to decrypt the cipher text. The public key algorithms like RSA (5), *Advanced Encryption Standard* (AES) (1), *Hash Message Authentication Code* (HMAC) (4) can be used for the shared key cryptography

4.4. *Shared Key Management for Routing Protocols*

One of the critical issues for the previously described security schemes is the number of shared keys involved. In order to calculate the authentication data appended to the routing messages, the routers maintain one or more keys per interface. A critical issue may be the number of routers (interfaces) that share the same secret. There are mainly two approaches for this problem A single globally-shared key is used to authenticate all routing messages exchanged in an as Pair wise keys are configured for all possible pairs of routers

4.5. *Digital Signature Authentication for OSPF*

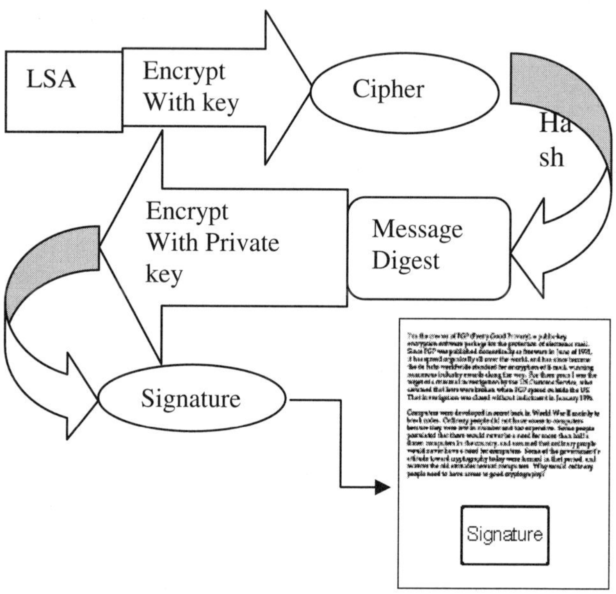

Figure 3.

4.6. *Proposals for the authentication scheme for OSPF*

- Digital signatures are added to all OSPF LSA data. A LSA contains the state of a router adjacent links
- A method is defined to distribute certified router information and keys.
- A neighbor-to-neighbor authentication algorithm (e.g., keyed MD5) (4])is used to protect local protocol exchanges. The LSAs that are flooded inside the link State Update packets are individually protected by a digital signature.

Each LSA is signed by the originator of that information and the signature stays with the data in its travel via OSPF flooding. This provides end-to-end integrity and authentication for LSA data. The digital signature attached to a LSA by the source router guarantees that the data comes from the advertising router

5. Sequencing of Router Dates

In this the LSA packets that are passing through the network are given individual number. These numbers are unique for a router and gets incremented every time an LSA packet has been broadcasted.

By this the security is given that the stored and forwarded packets are not taken into account if it is transmitted after a long time.

Also, if the attacker tries to multicast the packet with the attacked router's identity, the sequence number used by the LSA packets minimizes the chance of attack. Thus the LSA can be originated only from the trusted router. The hacker has no chance to induce his packets to the network

5.1. *Authentication and Key Management*

When a new member comes to the network, then the router is authenticated by the members of the group and a group key is produced at the time when the fresher enters the network.

There are four basic protocols that form the TGDH (3) protocol suite: join, leave, merge, and partition. All protocols share a common framework with the following notable features:

Each group member contributes an equal share to the group key. The key is computed as a function of all current group members' shares.

- Each share is secret (private to each group member) and is never revealed.
- As the group grows, new members' shares are factored into the group key and, upon each new member's joining; one of the old members changes its share.

As the group shrinks, departing members' shares are removed from the new group key, and at least one remaining member changes its key share. Based on the members entering or leaving, a new shared key is generated

5.2. *Comparing With Neighbors Information with Double Authentication*

Thus, we propose a novel *secure group communication keying scheme* (SGCKS) (3), which is based on hash function. Using SGCKS, a group of routers can construct any sub-group communication within the group without collusion problem. Based on SGCKS, we propose *double authentication* (DA) scheme (5). DA is an authentication scheme that authenticates search *link state advertisement* (LSA) twice, with two different sub-group keys. One sub-group key is used by a router and its communication adjacency and another sub-group key is used by the sub-group containing every other group member except its communication adjacency. Thus, an authentication chain can be built along the propagation path of a LSA. We have found that DA scheme to be able to prevent insider attacks when there is only one subverted router, *and* multiple non-colluding subverted routers, and help to detect multiple colluding subverted routers, but they cannot partition the network.

Whenever a new LSA packet has been multicast, the router updates will be transmitted to all the participants in the network using the *Double Authentication* (DA) (8).

The link capacity between the two routers is same when considered on both the directions of travel. In this, the router update received from the router at one end of the link is checked with the router update received on the other end of the link. Thus the attacked router is easily marked by the bogus or the contrasting values about the link. This can be also done as when the huge change in the link capacity has been encountered then the participants who receive those updates might request for the update at the other end. After the confirmation that the two values are same the update can be made. This is not done for the lighter change in the link capacity since request for updates by all the participants might lead to heavy traffic at the router which wants to serve. Hence we can notify the link attack and thus we could stop the intruder to mislead us to wrong information. Using this DA we could stop the insider's attack, since the authentication chain is built along the propagation path of a LSA.

5.3. *Proposed Header for the LSA Transmission*

```
                    1 1 1 1 1 1 1 1 1 1 2 2 2 2 2 2 2 2 2 2 3 3
0 1 2 3 4 5 6 7 8 9 0 1 2 3 4 5 6 7 8 9 0 1 2 3 4 5 6 7 8 9 0 1
+-+-+-+-+-+-+-+-+-+-+-+-+-+-+-+-+-+-+-+-+-+-+-+-+-+-+-+-+-+-+-+-+
|            LS Age             |    Options    |    LS Type    |
+-+-+-+-+-+-+-+-+-+-+-+-+-+-+-+-+-+-+-+-+-+-+-+-+-+-+-+-+-+-+-+-+
|                        Link State ID                          |
+-+-+-+-+-+-+-+-+-+-+-+-+-+-+-+-+-+-+-+-+-+-+-+-+-+-+-+-+-+-+-+-+
|                     Advertising Router                        |
+-+-+-+-+-+-+-+-+-+-+-+-+-+-+-+-+-+-+-+-+-+-+-+-+-+-+-+-+-+-+-+-+
|                     LS Sequence Number                        |
+-+-+-+-+-+-+-+-+-+-+-+-+-+-+-+-+-+-+-+-+-+-+-+-+-+-+-+-+-+-+-+-+
|         LS Checksum           |            Length             |
+-+-+-+-+-+-+-+-+-+-+-+-+-+-+-+-+-+-+-+-+-+-+-+-+-+-+-+-+-+-+-+-+
|                          LSA Data                             /
/ ...                                                           /
+-+-+-+-+-+-+-+-+-+-+-+-+-+-+-+-+-+-+-+-+-+-+-+-+-+-+-+-+-+-+-+-+
|                          Signature                            /
. . . . . . . . . . . . . . . . . . . . . . . . . . . . . . . . .
```

Figure 4.

- LS age – Time to live
- Options – control for other information
- LS Type- Standard LSA Type with the first bit set to indicate the presence of security data and a signature. This creates a new signed LSA type for each existing type.
- LS No – Link state sequence number
- LS checksum – Check sum for the packet
- Length - Length of the whole Packet
- LSA data-LSA message data content
- Signature-Digital Signature added

6. Algorithm

Advanced Link State Protocol

6.1. *Transmitting*

The information of the connected routers;
Encrypt it with randomly generated key;
Cipher text;
Encrypt the key with private key;
Form the digital envelope
Transmit it as the multicast message

6.2. *Receiving*

Collect the LSA packets;
Decrypt the cipher using the private key to get the information of signature and message digest;
If there is large change in the link capacity than threshold;
Then request for link capacity of the participant at other end of link;
If match occur
Then Update the routing table;
Else notify the link attack;
Else
Update the routing table

6.3. *New Member Added*

Using authentication check whether it is a valid member or not; if valid member then proceed; else intimate it as intruder; create a new public key with all members participating

6.4. *Transmit the generated key to all the members encrypted with the old shared key*

Transmit the generated key to all the members encrypted with the old shared key

6.5. *Member Exit*

Create a new public key with all members remaining; Transmit the generated key to all remaining members

7. Algorithms that are best suited for this protocol

7.1. *For the digital signatures the algorithms used are*

Symmetric key algorithm: *Advanced Encryption Standard* (AES)
Asymmetric key algorithm:RSA (1024 bits)

7.2. *Key management*

Tree Group Diffie Hellman (TGDH)

7.3. *Check sum*

MD5 Message Digest - check sum

8. Implementation Issues

One of our design goals is to minimize the modifications. OSPF itself has the extensibility for introducing new types of LSA (2). The DA can be carried out through this extension. . All other functions and structures of OSPF remain the same.

Current generation router handle the add in complexity of cryptographic operations?. Note that using SGCKS will increase the memory requirement of a router .Furthermore, signing/verifying and encrypting/decrypting operations will increase the CPU processing usage time

Acknowledgments

All the faculty members of ***Misrimal Navajee Munoth Jain Engineering College, Thoraipakkam, Chennai-97*** gave enough support to publish this paper.

References

1. AES Algorithm (Rijndael) Information, http://csrc.nist.gov/CryptoToolkit/aes/rijndael/.

2. R. Coltun, .The OSPF Opaque LSA Option., RFC 2370, July 1998.

3. Aniraban Chakrabarthi, *"Security and Privacy in Network World"*, (IEEE 2002) Jan 2003

4. Andrew Nash, William Duance, Celia Joseph and Derek Brink, *"PKI Implementing and Managing E-Security"*, Tata McGraw-Hill, 2002.

5. Uyles Black, *"Internet Security Protocols", Tata McGraw-Hill*, 2001.

6. S. Murphy, B. Wellington, *"OSPF with Digital signatures"*, RFC2154, Jun. 1997

7. S. Kent, R. Atkinson, *"Security Architecture for the Internet Protocol*",RFC 2401, Nov.1998

8. Dijiang Huang, *"secure Link State Routing Protocol: A Framework"*

9. G. Manimaran, *"Internet Infrastructure Security – a Taxonomy"*,IEEE Network, (Security), vol 10, Nov /Dec 2002

Session 3

Improving Basic Cases of Data Mining

Hassan Samavarchi
Yazd University, Yazd, Iran

Mohammad Reza Dehghani
Peyam Noor University, Tehran Branch, Iran

Heydar Ghasemzadeh
Higher Education Institute of Jahad Daneshgahi,Yazd, Iran

Abstract
In a regular fashion, industries and businesses have been highly related to data mining, in such a manner that they are ready to expend a great deal of money for solving their problems, since user can not easily take advantage of data mining in their businesses. The goal of the present study is to investigate the basis of data mining formation in order to understand some semi-automatic parts being created in the past to solve the problems. Therefore, we put stress upon general data mining model from the beginning and expand our procedure through details and shapes of basic storage form, intermediate user functions model, as well as its applicability which make easy the related theory and accompanying procedures. Hence, we take advantage of different choices and expenditure routines in order to lessen and shorten the procedure immediately.

1. Introduction

Data mining is increasingly getting popularity. Due to its principle aids, many organizations are using data mining to gain help in overall phases of costumer relation's management like acquiring new customers, increasing profit by maintaining current customers and gathering appropriate potentially-good customers as well. By acquisition of good customer specifications, a company may predict its future goals with respect to the same specifications. Through documentation of a customer that purchase a specific product, the company may pay its attention to those customers who do not buy the same product. Hence, by documenting those customers who leave the company, the respected organization can keep up customers who are on the verge of leaving there, since keeping current customers is truly less costly than acquisition of new customers. Data mining proposes some values by investigating a wide spread spectrum of companies. Tele-communication companies and credit cards are two main stem of data mining for recognition of frauds that may arise during rendering their related services. Insurance and income generating companies are also having enthusiasm in using this technology to reduce frauds. Pharmaceutical applications are another area of interests therein data mining may play an upper hand. Data mining may be used to recognize the effect of surgery operations, as well as medicinal and therapeutical examinations. Organization activated in financial procedures use data mining to determine market and industry features in order to identify income efficiency. Retailers, moreover, use data mining to decide what product is more profitable in the stores in such a manner they can enhance their workability. Pharmaceutical companies are now investigating the great databases comprised of different chemical compounds and genetic material to discover those materials that may be sought as appropriate alternatives as a basis of medicine creation compounds. Two points are existed to prove that data mining is considered as a successful phenomenon. The first one is about an exact formulation of a problem to be solved. The second one is about using correct data. After choosing in-access data or buying external information, you may have to transfer or classify them through using some methods. Graphical methods may play a prominent role in displaying of communication structure. In the following picture, each circles show a quantity or an event. Communicative lines between these circles show a relation. Bolder lines show a stronger and more frequency communication.

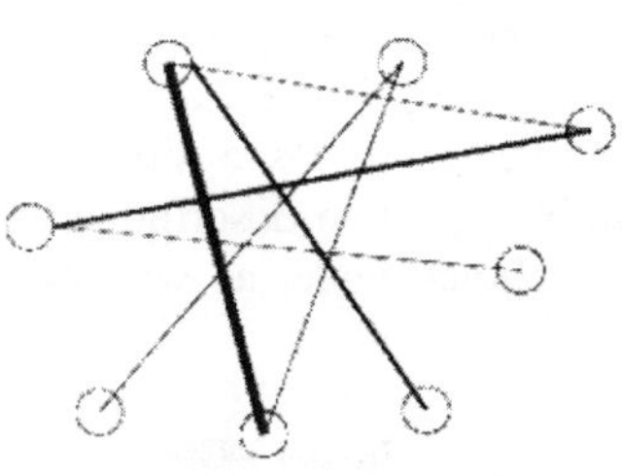

Models and algorithms of data mining

Know let's study some algorithms and models are being used in data mining procedures. The products, mostly, use various types of algorithms set assigned in computer science or statistical topics as well as their specific implementation in order to achieve the goals of customers. For example many sellers embark on selling some versions of CART or CHAID decision trees with some utilities, facilitate works on parallel computers. Some others have their own-based algorithms that can work well, although they may not enjoy from extra utilities and achievements. An important point in this regard is that any model or algorithm could and may not be used alone. For any assigned problem, there would be an effect upon nature of used data that you have chosen. Any model or algorithm may not be called as the best. Therefore, you need a series of tool and technology in order to find the best possible model.

Neural networks

Neural networks are being used in a particular manner, since they are considered a an affective tools for modeling very great and sophisticated issues therein hundreds of proposing variables are set which themselves own a great deal of interactions (bio-neural networks are non-comparably more complex). Neural networks may be used in classification issues or recursive conjectures (therein output parameter is continuous).

A Neural network starts with an interior layer in which each node is assigned to a predictor variable. These input nodes are connected to a number of nodes in the hidden layer. Nodes in the hidden layer may be connected to nodes in another hidden layer or to an output layer. Output layer is comprised of one or more solution variables.

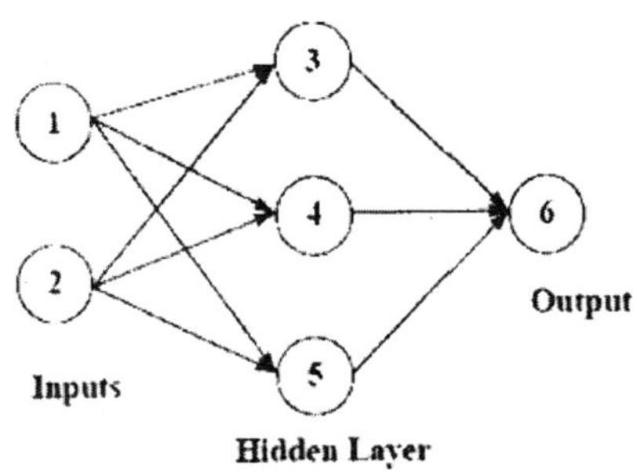

A neural network with a hidden layer

Choice trees

Choice trees is a way to show a set of rules which lead to a class or an amount. For example, you may classify loan request according to the validity risk of good or bad. The next picture shows a simple model from a choice tree with respect to description of all its basic bundles that is choice node, as well as branches and Leafs.

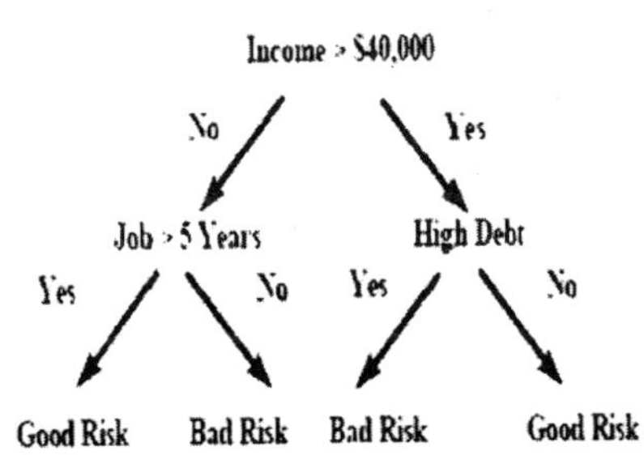

The first bundle of upper node is decision or root, which makes a survey to establish a certain condition. Root group in this example is "Income > $40000". The results of this survey cause tree to be divided into two branches, each indicates possible solutions. In this approach the investigation of mentioned condition may lead to Yes or No answer; therefore, there are two branches. With regard to type of algorithm each node may have two or more branches. For example, CART produces trees that own only two branches in each node. This type of tree is a binary. Generally, different types of decision trees are used in data mining for data exploration and deduction of a tree and its rules that are exploring for prediction purposes. Some amount of different algorithms may be used to make decision trees like CHAID, CART, QUEST, C5.0. The size of a tree may be controlled by ceasing regulations which make growth of a tree restricted.

Deduction of rule

Deduction of rule is a method for accessing a set of regulations in order to categorize the cases. Although decision trees may create some set of regulations, the deduction methods make a set of relevant rules which essentially do not create a tree. Since the rule's deduction agent may not necessarily put branch at each level and may recognize the next step, a better and various patterns might be found sometimes for classification. Unlike trees, producing rules may not cover all of the possible cases.

Genetic Algorithms

Genetic Algorithms are not used to find patterns; rather they are mostly used as a guide about learning procedure of data mining algorithms like neural networks. Genetic Algorithms act as a method for performing a directed search routine for good models at the solution space.

They are called generic algorithms, since they irregularly follow bio-evolution pattern therein member of a generation compete each other upon transferring of their characteristics to next generation so as to find the best model. Transferring data are being set in the pattern of chromosomes comprised of parameters for making a model.

The main steps of data mining to find knowledge are as follows:

1- Defining a problem	2-Building database for data mining
3- Searching of data	4-Preparing data for modeling
5- Building model	6-Assessing model
7- Making model and results	

Data storage: A setting of subject oriented, integrated, time variant, and non volatile of data which is used to support decision making management process.

When required data are chosen and exploring data are set, there usually needs some certain kind of conversion on data. This kind of conversion is related to the working data mining functions and techniques. Conversions are being defined in the range of simple conversion from one type of data to other up to more sophisticated conversions like definition of new traits by performing mathematical and logical functions upon existed traits.

Data exploration
In order to discover requested patterns, converted data are being explored by using different data mining techniques and functions.

Data mining cases
From definition and cases of data mining one may infer one of the 5 following sections:

1-Duties 2-Data
3-Operator 4-Models
5-Data flow process

We show these 5 sections more seriously in the picture. Data mining resembles a tree which comprised of several levels. The first level is as follows:

- Industrial type
- Problems type
- Working subject
- Data mining goal
- Name of the company and organization

Four first elements are pricing for simulations and the other two are used for group cases. In this situation data mining of information are composed of data and data body. In the case of the table's data position, data names, and data types, we may refer to the following items:

1-Key 2-Table's data number
3-Name of table 4-Type of field
5-Number from field

Which comprised of:

1-Name field 2-Type field
3-Value of data 4-Statistical data
5-Ultimately, data comprised of:
5-1 Table number
5-2 Cases of operators
5-3 Next operators

In the case of operator data mining of elements are as follows:

1-Path 2-Name
3-Operators' set 4-Functions
5-Input number 6-Parameters
7-Output number 8-Lines guide

The parameter element is also comprised of:

1-Name 2-Type
3-Type value 4-Different values
5-Minimum value 6-Guide lines maximum value

These are for storing and retrieval of knowledge database on the base of what questions should be asked and how the answers should be; as well as their value which is determined in a central manner. In general model process of data mining, we may not use models for a specific format. We only use PMML language as a representative of other models. This model uses for industrial standard. Data mining case of the model is as follows:

1-Type 2-Parameter
3-Coding paths 4-Coding Name

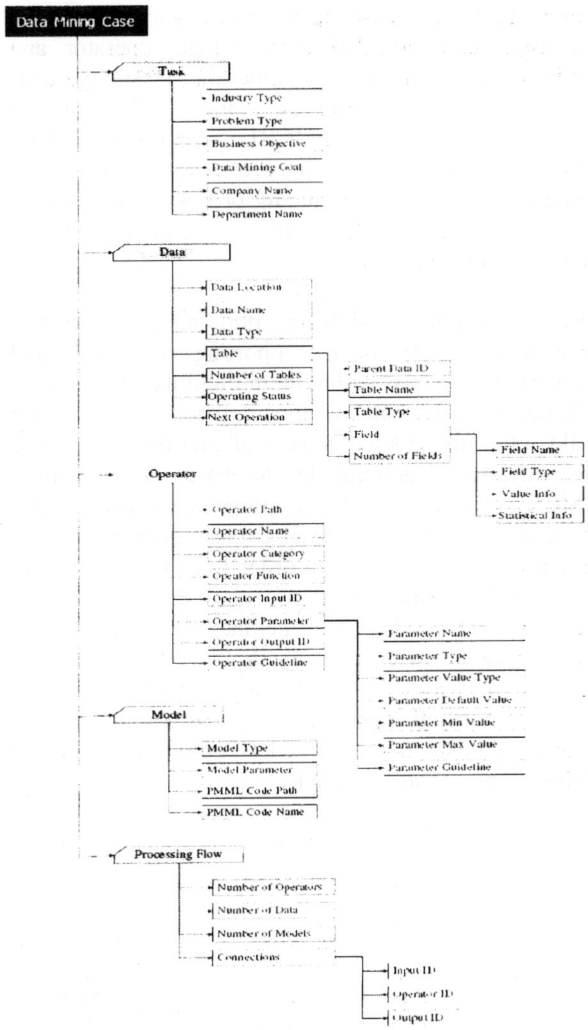

Data Mining Case Model

Finally, data flow process is in the form of data relational connectivity, as well as applying operators and models. Therefore, numbers of data, operators, and models are including some elements; hence, some important part of flow process connectivity is as follows:

1-Input number
2-Operator number
3-Output number

One case of data mining can only include analog flow process. A flow process would be matched with data mining case.
We assume XML as a representative of data mining case, since it may be easily changed and is compatible with DMCRL language, which is a compatible situation about different types of data mining case. PMML causes a set of cases to be easily manipulated.

Case shaping of the base for data mining
In this situation there are four sources for the base storage and five functions which belong to four cases of storage process: data case, operator case, model case, and DMCRL source.

Among them, data case, operator case, and models case are used relatively. For data storage, operator and model of different parts are some kind of storage case that embark on coding procedure. (p7) Data in DMCRL is physically; DMCRL for knowledge base case is a source in this picture, since it is able to recognize again the data mining process, that is to say when it codifies in the DMCRL source in order to make a storage operation.

The five function models are: building case, retrieval case, connectivity data, supporting operators, and transferring models, within them building case may be referred to as a center of model functions. This case builds other models by the help of data mining process and different functions. In the case of simulation, DMCRL is used; after implementing each duty, retrieval case and connectivity data are being used. One may use connecting data in order to connect data case with building case in ODBC or JDBC. Supporting operators are used as intermediatory interfaces with building case, since operators should implement three sections. We may design those operators which are resembled to all operators prepared from different figures. Finally transfer model are being used for PMML representative models.

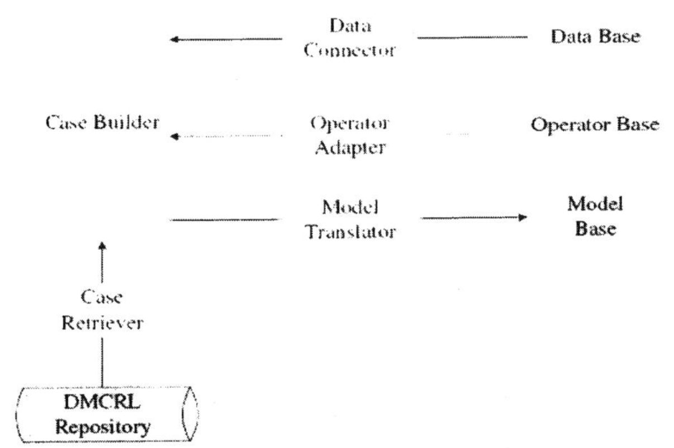

Architecture of knowledge based data mining platform

Conclusion

Data mining is a complete method enjoys from a high time process. Data mining is implemented in the industry, which shows a great dependency with professional data mining activities, in order to help the users to tackle their problems efficiently. Out goal in the present study is to enhance the case of data mining and therefore the application of knowledge based sections from past cases of data mining is simulated in order to solve new incoming problems. This case is being used in "developing" subsection. Basic case of XML is assumed as the base of storage, models' functions, and application of intermediatory interface as languages representatives. To apply this figure we may see the defined picture accordingly. In each step we are understood which operators should be used and displayed to eliminate a lot of problems. A common occupation may easily use the codified knowledge in the form of data mining, which produce a new shape respectively. Those systems employ data mining process as an easy routine; may reduce their procedures according to professional abrupt implementation of data mining and defined working time.

References

1. Cox,e.,(2009), " A Protocycling Methodology For Knowledge-Based Data Mining Project", Pc AI magazine,vol,16(3),pp 21-33-2007.
2. Data Mining Group(2004),Predictive Model Markup Language(PMML) version 2.0, http://www.dmg.org/pmml-v2.0.htm
3. Kotasek p.and Zendulka j.(2002),"Describe the data mining process with DMSL", in: Manolopulos,Y. and N'avrat.p.(Eds),processing of the ADBIS 2002 Communications, Bratislava, Slovak Republic, September 2002,pp.131-140.
4. Krishnaswamy,S., and Zaslavasky, A.,(2006) "Towards data mining service on the internet with a multiple service provider model: An Xml based approach", Journal of Electronic Commerce Research, vol.2(3),pp.103-130
5. VBDM.net consultant(2002), visual basic data mining.net,http://www.visual-basic-data-mining.net/
6. Introduction to data mining and knowledge discovery by Two Crows Corporation 2005
7. Jeffery W.seifert, Analyst in information science and technology policy, "data mining: An overview" December 2004.
8. David J.Hand, Data mining: Statistics and more? December 2007.
9. EmonnKeogh, Stefanol Lonardi, Chotirat Ann ratanamahatana,"Towards Parameter-Free Data Mining" September 2005.

HIGH-PERFORMANCE FPGA IMPLEMENTATION OF COMPACT SINGLE ROUND AES DESIGN

VISHWANATH PATEL

Department of Electronics & Computer Engineering, Indian Institute of Technology Roorkee, Roorkee, Uttarakhand -247667 India

RAMESH C. JOSHI

Department of Electronics & Computer Engineering, Indian Institute of Technology Roorkee, Roorkee, Uttarakhand -247667 India

ASHOK K. SAXENA

Department of Electronics & Computer Engineering, Indian Institute of Technology Roorkee, Roorkee, Uttarakhand -247667 India

This paper presents high-performance and compact architecture for single round Advance Encryption Standard (AES) security algorithm using feedback mode. Two design based on stated architecture has been implemented on virtex-4 Field Programming Gate Array (FPGA) device. These two designs differ in method used for sub-bytes function implementation, in first design Look-Up Tables (LUTs) and in second design fully combinational gates using Composite Field Arithmetic (CFA) has been employed for sub-byte function implementation. Fair performance comparison of these two designs with each other and with other well known previous claims has also been presented. Finally, LUTs based and CFA based designs are achieved with encryption rate and number of Configurable logic blocks (CLBs) slices 1.0497 Gbps/2571 and 880.81 Mbps/1668 respectively. These results are among the fastest hardware implementations with better area utilization.

1. Introduction

The AES algorithm is a private-key encryption algorithm. In January 1997, the National Institute of Standards and Technology (NIST) invited proposals for new algorithms for the Advanced Encryption Standard (AES) to replace the old Data Encryption Standard (DES). After two rounds of evaluation on the 15 candidate algorithms, NIST selected the Rijndael as the AES algorithm [1] in October 2000.

The AES algorithm has broad applications, including smart cards, cellular phones, automated teller machines (ATMs), and digital video recorders. The need for secure electronic data exchange will become increasingly more important. Most of the low-end applications instead of high encryption speeds require low area design, like current wireless networks and mobile communication. This paper attempts to fulfill the requirement of performance and area requirements of such applications. As a result, a low-cost AES implementation for FPGA devices was developed and evaluated.

The structure of this paper is as follows. In Section II, we briefly describe the AES algorithm .The detailed proposed architecture along with round unit, key scheduling and control unit are presented in Section III. Composite Field Arithmetic based Sub-byte function explained in Section IV. Section V outlines the details Implementation results. After making performance comparisons with prior efforts in Section VI, finally we conclude the topic in Section VII.

2. AES Algorithm

The AES is a substitution permutation network allowing the encryption/ decryption of data by blocks of 128-bits and supporting key lengths of 128, 192 and 256 bits. In the following, we focus on the 128-bit key version. Its internal state, usually represented as a 4×4 matrix of bytes, is updated by iterating through the round structure (10, 12 or 14 times according to the key size). The round is described as four different byte-oriented transformations. As shown the full AES encryption algorithm in Figure 1.

First, SubBytes introduces the non-linearity by taking, for each byte, the modular inverse in $GF(2^8)$ and then applying an affine transformation. Instead of computing distinctly these two steps, the full transformation is achieved by passing each byte through

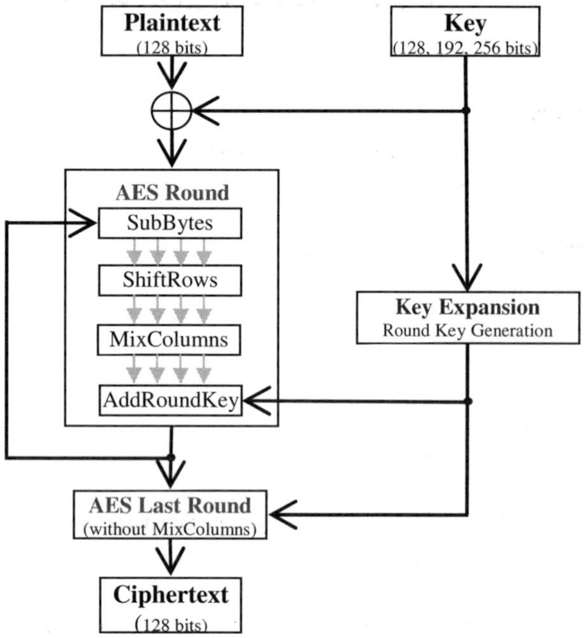

Figure 1. AES Encryption algorithm.

a S-box. Then ShiftRows modifies the state. It simply consists of a circular left shift of the state's rows by 0, 1, 2 and 3 bytes respectively. Third, MixColumns applies a linear transformation to the state's columns. Each of them is regarded as a polynomial and is multiplied by a fixed polynomial $C(x) = 3.x^3 + x^2 + x + 2 \cdot (\text{mod} \quad x^4 + 1)$. Finally, the AddRoundKey transform mixes the key with the state. As each subkey has the same size as the state, the combination is performed by a simple bitwise XOR between subkey bytes and their corresponding state bytes. A first key addition is performed before entering the first round, and the last round omits the MixColumns transformation.

Prior to the en/de-cryption process, the subkeys have to be generated. The key schedule takes the main key *K*0 and expands it as shown in Figure 5 in section III, for the case of a 128-bit key. In encryption mode, this can easily be performed "on-the-fly", *i.e.* in parallel to the rounds execution in order to get the subkey at the exact time it is needed. In decryption mode, the round keys generally have to be derived prior to the decipher.

Let us finally mention that the decryption process slightly differs from the encryption one. In order to decipher data blocks, the inverse transformations have to be applied to the state. These operations are respectively called *Inv-Transform*, except for the AddRounKey as it is its own inverse, and are applied in the same order as described above. This may result in a different performance of the AES in encryption and decryption. Regarding the key schedule, the operations remain the same as for encryption but the subkeys have to be introduced in reverse order. For more details, we refer to [1].

3. Single Round AES Architecture

The working of proposed architecture is straight forward, as we can see in Figure 2. There are three main units i.e. Round unit, Key Scheduler unit and control unit. We will discuss one by one later part of this section.

The multiplexer named as MUX direct particular input by using 2bit selective line data_reg_mux_sel to the input of Data Register at proper clock cycle and that particular 128 bits data store in 128 bits register, for being used by Round unit as a input. Since round 0 is just a XORing between 128 bits data and 128 bits original user-key, performed externally using 128 bits 2 input XOR as shown in Figure 2.

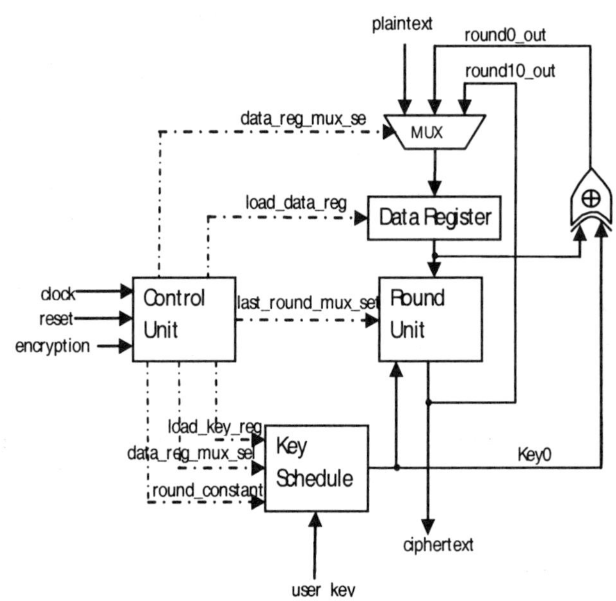

Figure 2. Compact single round AES FPGA architecture.

3.1. *Round Unit*

As we have discuss earlier that round 1 to round 9 are the combination of four functions i.e. sub SubBytes, ShiftRows, MixColumns and AddRounKey and round 10 combination of three function except Mixcolumns. Figure 3 show round unit that also take care of round 10 using MUX that controlled by Last_round_mux_set 1bit selection line.

The concept of parallel processing has been used in this architecture for calculating the sub bytes. Instead of calculating the sub bytes sequentially, which consumes a lot of time, the 16 sub bytes are generated simultaneously using 16 S Boxes [2] and that can be realized by16 look-up tables with 8bit-input/output or by CFA. ShiftRows is a bit shuffling function, requiring no hardware. For MixColumns and AddRoundKey realization general procedure adopted as describe in [1].

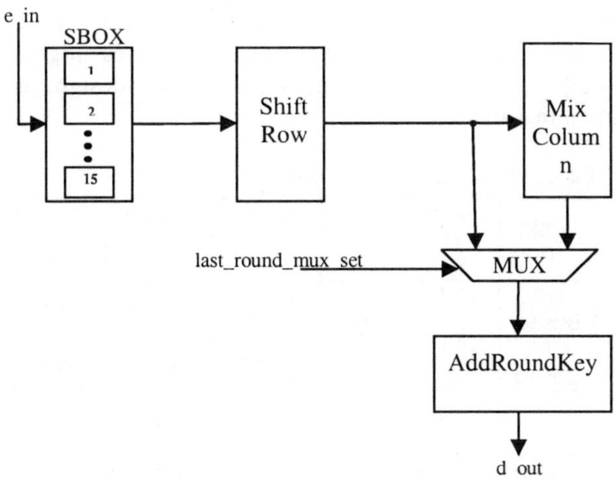

Figure 3. Round unit.

3.2. *Key Scheduler Unit*

Figure 4 is a Key Scheduler (Expansion) Unit [3] used to generate round keys on the fly in the encryption process. The hardware required to generate one set of

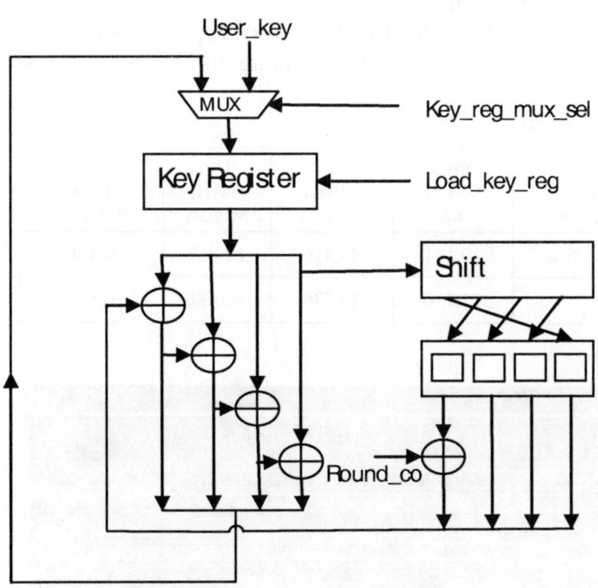

Figure 4. Key Scheduler Unit.

round key is implemented and re-used it for calculating the rest of the round keys. This results in reduction in space used for storing the sub keys values and also improves the speed of operation since round key is generated simultaneously while the sub bytes, shift rows and mix columns take place.

3.3. *Control Unit*

Control unit is brain of the system, which used to control and maintains proper synchronization between different components of design. As shown in Figure 5, Control unit realized using Finite State Machine (FSM) having thirteen states, one for initiation, one for load input and remaining eleven for eleven round of AES. Each state defined by their specific value of state variable (control signal).

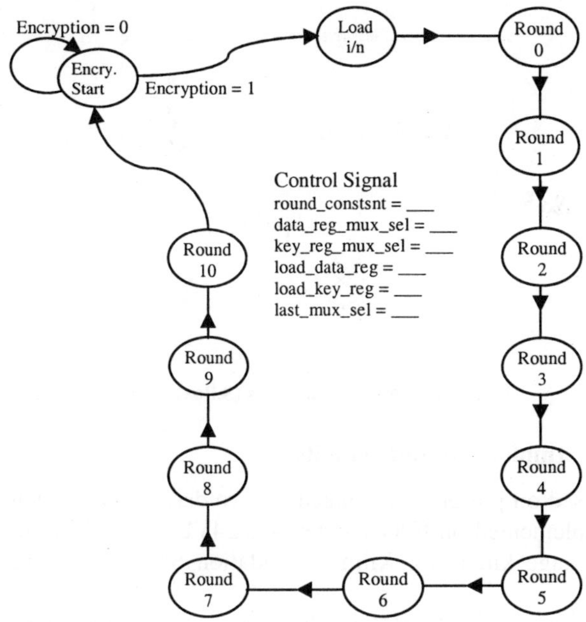

Figure 5. State diagram.

4. Composite Field Arithmetic based SubBytes function

The composite field approach reduces not only the hardware complexity but also exhibits the advantages of inner round pipelining [8], but here we are not interested in pipelining. The Galois field $F1: GF(2^8)$ is mapped into composite field $F2: GF((2^4)^2)$ or sometimes $GF(((2^2)^2)^2)$ [4].

In this paper, we construct the isomorphic composite field by using the fields defined in (1) [5]. The field conversion matrix δ is given in (2).

$$\begin{cases} GF(2) \Rightarrow GF(2^4): p(x) = x^4 + x + 1 \\ GF(2^4) \Rightarrow GF((2^4)^2): q(x) = y^4 + y + \beta, \\ \quad where \quad \beta = \{0b1000\}_2 \ or \quad x^3 \end{cases} \quad (1)$$

$$\delta = \begin{bmatrix} 1 & 0 & 0 & 0 & 0 & 1 & 0 & 1 \\ 0 & 0 & 1 & 0 & 0 & 0 & 0 & 0 \\ 0 & 0 & 1 & 1 & 1 & 1 & 1 & 1 \\ 0 & 0 & 0 & 1 & 1 & 0 & 0 & 0 \\ 0 & 0 & 0 & 0 & 1 & 1 & 1 & 0 \\ 0 & 1 & 0 & 0 & 1 & 0 & 1 & 1 \\ 0 & 0 & 1 & 1 & 0 & 1 & 0 & 1 \\ 0 & 0 & 0 & 0 & 0 & 1 & 0 & 1 \end{bmatrix} \quad (2)$$

Figure 6 describes the optimized design of SubBytes transformation over composite field based on the work in [4].

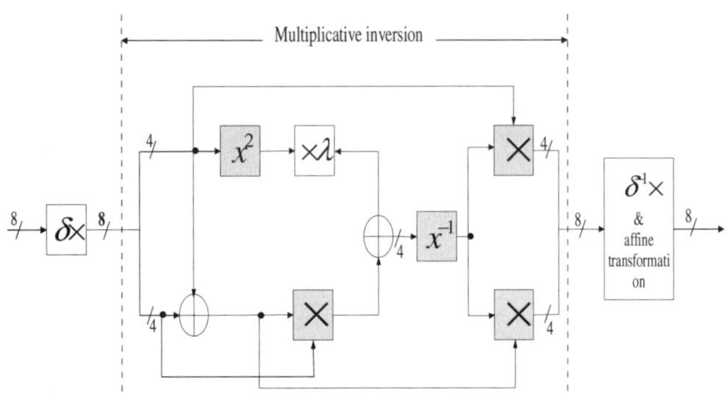

Figure 6. CFA based SubBytes (S Box) design.

5. Implementation Results

Based on presented architecture, two designs have been implemented on FPGA virtex-4 XC4VLX100-12ff1148 package kit, using Xilinx Foundation Series f 9.2i as synthesis and Modelsim 6.3f as simulation tool. The design was coded using VHDL language.

On comparison, we find that LUT based design is 19.18% faster than CFA based design and on the other hand CFA based design proved more cost effective, since it required 35.55% smaller area than LUT based design. But as whole CFA based design is More efficient than LUT based because it gives higher throughput to slices ratio than LUT based design, as shown in Table 1.

Table 2. The logic and routing delay.

Desig n	Perio d ns	Logi c ns	Percen t %	Routin g ns	Percen t %
LUT Based	10.16 1	7.96 6	78.4%	2.194	21.6%
CFA Based	12.11 0	3.82 6	31.6%	8.283	68.4%

6. Performance Comparison with other Designs

There are very few number of designs proposed for small AES design in literature. After intensive search we encountered few single round AES designs, as shown in Table 3 with their performance. Wide trade-off is possible in area and speed of design, so throughput to slices ratio has been taken as comparison parameter for various designs.

As we can see Table 3, throughput to slices ratio design [6] is 0.747, highest among all design but it takes

Table 1. Synthesis and Place & Route results of AES designs on xc4vlx100-12ff1148.

Design	LUT (Syn.) #	Slices (Syn.) #	Period (Syn.) ns	Slices (PAR) #	Blocks RAMs (PAR) #	Usage (PAR) %	Period (PAR) ns	Freq. (PAR) Mhz	Thr. (PAR) Mbits/s	Thr./sli. (PAR) Mbit/s/slice
LUT Based	4296	2222	5.294	2571	20	05%	10.161	98.416	1049.7	0.408
CFA Based	3230	1668	7.285	1657	00	03%	12.110	82.576	880.81	0.532

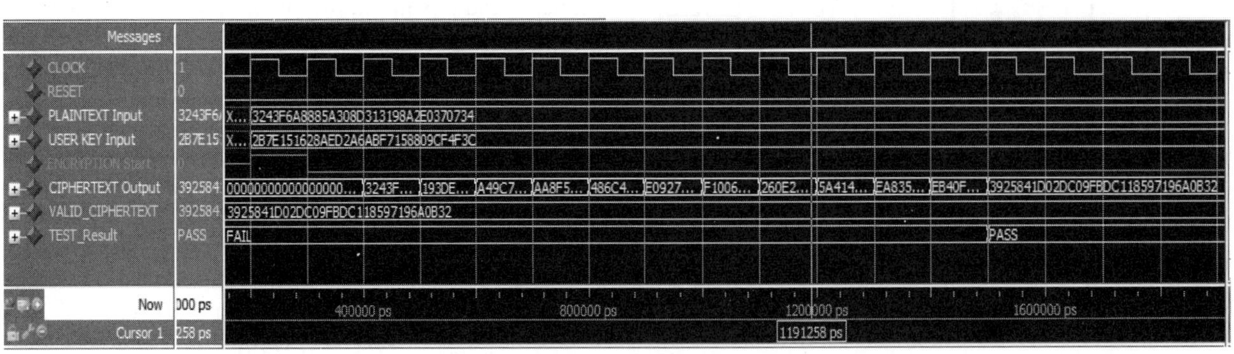

Figure 7. Simulation window

four clock cycles to complete one round and also required three block RAMs and above all very small throughput of 166 Mbps. On the other hand, our composite field arithmetic based design is pure memory less design having 0.532 throughputs to slices ratio, which is second highest among all and first in all design of one clock cycles per round, in addition of that it shows a high throughput up to 880.81 Mbps.

7. Conclusion

In this paper, high-performance architecture for small single round AES security algorithm is presented and then implemented on FPGA virtex-4 kit. The CFA is employed for SubBytes function implementation instead of LUTs, as a result further area reduction is achieved on the cost of small speed reduction. The proposed architecture of the AES algorithm reduces the covered area and achieves a good data throughput. Thus, the combination of security, and cost effective implementation, makes it a very good choice low-end application.

Table 3. Performance comparison of small AES designs.

Design		Area		Throughput [Mbps]	Thr./Slices [Mbits/s/slices]	clock cycles per round
		CLB Slices	Block RAMs			
Pawe_l Chodowiec and Kris Gaj [6]		222	03	166	0.7470	4
P. Chodowiec et al. [7]		~1230	18	577	0.4690	1
A. Dandalis et al. [8]		5673	00	353	0.0620	1
A.J. Elbirt et al. [9]		3528	00	294.2	0.0834	1
K. Gaj et al. [10]		2902	00	331.5	0.1142	1
Proposed Designs	LUT Based	2571	20	1049.7	0.4080	1
	CFA Based	1657	00	880.81	0.5320	1

References

1. National Institute of Standards and Technology, Federal Information Processing Standards Publications – FIPS 197 Announcing the "ADVANCED ENCRYPTION STANDARD (AES)", November, 2001.
2. Henry Kuo and Ingrid Verbauwhede,"Architectural Optimization for a 1.82Gbits/sec VLSI Implementation of the AES Rijindael Algorithm", in 3rd international workshop cryptographic Hardware and embedded systems (CHES 2001), LNCS2162, Paris, May 2001,pp 51-64.
3. Kimmo U. Järvinen, Matti T. Tommiska, and Jorma O. Skyttä. A fully pipelined memoryless 17.8 Gbps AES-128 encryptor. In Proceedings of the 11th ACM International Symposium on Field-Programmable Gate Arrays, FPGA 2003, pages 207–215. ACM Press, 2003.
4. X. Zhang, K.K. Parhi, High-speed VLSI architectures for the AES algorithm, IEEE Transactions on Very Large Scale Integration (VLSI) Systems 12 (9) (2004) 957–967.
5. Kimmo U. Järvinen, Matti T. Tommiska, and Jorma O. Skyttä. A fully pipelined memoryless 17.8 Gbps AES-128 encryptor. In Proceedings of the 11th ACM International Symposium on FPGA 2003, pages 207–215.
6. P. Chodowiec and K. Gaj. Very Compact FPGA Implementation of the AES Algorithm. In *Cryptographic Hardware and Embedded Systems, CHES 2003*, pages 319–333. Springer, Sept. 2003.
7. Chodowiec P., Gaj K., Bellows P., Schott B.: Experimental Testing of the Gigabit IPSec Compliant Implementations of Rijndael and Triple DES Using SLAAC-1 VFPGA Accelerator Board, Information Security Conference (ISC 2001), Malaga, Spain, 2001.
8. Dandalis A., Prasanna V.K., Rolim J.D.: *A Comparative Study of Performance of AES Final Candidates Using FPGAs*, Cryptographic Hardware and Embedded Systems Workshop (CHES 2000), Worcester, Massachusetts, 2000.
9. Elbirt A.J., Yip W., Chetwynd B., Paar C.: *An FPGA-based performance evaluation of the AES block cipher candidate algorithm finalists*, IEEE Transactions on Very Large Scale Integration (VLSI) Systems, Volume: 9 Issue: 4, August 2001.
10. Gaj K. and Chodowiec P.: *Comparison of the hardware performance of the AES candidates using reconfigurable hardware*, Third Advanced Encryption Standard (AES3) Candidate Conference, New York, 2000.

SECURE PROTOCOL FOR DELIVERY OF SMS BANKING SERVICES

Shubat S. Ahmeda
Department of Computer Engineering, El-fath University,
Tripoli-Libya

Ashraf M. Ali Edwila
Department of Electrical and Computer Engineering, 7th of April University
Sabratha-Libya.

Abstract- Short Message Service (SMS) is increasingly being adopted and utilized in banking industry. However SMS does not guarantee confidentiality and integrity of message content, it was specifically intended for sending non-sensitive information in a GSM network. In the mobile communication systems, security offered by the network operator only applies on the wireless link; data delivered through the mobile core network may not be secured enough. Therefore end-to-end security mechanisms are required. The existing end-to-end security mechanisms are provided at application level and typically based on public key cryptosystem. The main concern in a public-key setting is the authenticity of the public key; this issue can be resolved by identity-based (ID-based) cryptography where the public key of a user can be derived from public information that uniquely identifies the user. This paper presents an encryption mechanism based on the ID-based scheme using Elliptic curves to provide end-to-end security for delivery of SMS-banking services. This mechanism has been implemented over the standard SMS network architecture and the Performance analysis showed that the encryption speed on the mobile device is faster than the duration of the transmission.

Keywords: Identity-based Cryptography; Public Key; End-to-end Security; ECC; SMS banking services.

1. Introduction

The most popular type of data transmission is Short Message Service (SMS). This service allows the user to send plaintext messages to the destination mobile phones. The advantages of using SMS are that it is relatively inexpensive and it is reliable for sending non-sensitive messages. The problems with using SMS in banking services are that the SMS message is not entirely secured. There are many flaws in the GSM architecture which lead to security shortfalls for SMS banking. Other limitations of SMS services, is that the size of the message is limited to 160 characters in total length. A Security Mechanism offered by GSM network operator only applies on the wireless link; data delivered through the mobile core network may not be secured. The network does not provide important security facilities such as authentication, end-to-end security, non-repudiation and anonymity [1]. This vulnerability enables an attacker with the right equipment to eavesdrop on the information being sent, therefore a better SMS communication protocol is needed to transmit text data between clients and server. Therefore end-to-end security mechanisms are required. The existing end-to-end security mechanisms are provided at application level and typically based on public key cryptosystem.

In public-key cryptosystem each user has a key pair (PK, SK), where PK is the public key and SK is the private key. The main concern in a public-key setting is the authenticity of the public key. If an attacker convinces a sender that a receiver's public key is some key of the attacker's choice instead of the correct public key, he can eavesdrop and decrypt messages intended for the receiver. This is the well known man-in-the-middle attack [2]. This authentication problem is typically resolved by the use of verifiable information called certificate, which is issued by a trusted third party consisting of the user name and his public key. Shamir [3] introduced the concept of identity-based (ID-based) cryptography where the public key of a user can be derived from public information that uniquely identifies the user. A major advantage of ID-based cryptosystem is that no certificate is needed to bind user names with their public keys.

ID-based cryptosystem transparently provides security enhancement to the mobile applications without requiring the users to memorize extra public keys. Hence sending an ID-based encrypted short message is exactly the same as sending a normal short. This feature is especially desirable for transaction-type mobile applications such as bank or stock transactions [4]. This paper presents an encryption mechanism based on the ID-based scheme using Elliptic curves

Cryptography (ECC) to provide end-to-end security for delivery of SMS-banking services.

2. ID–Based Elliptic Curve Cryptography

Elliptic curve cryptography was introduced by Victor Miller and Neal Koblitz as an alternative to established public-key systems such as DSA and RSA. The main reason for attractiveness of ECC is the fact that there is no sub-exponential algorithm known to solve the discrete logarithm problem on properly chosen elliptic curve [5]. This means that significantly smaller parameters can be used in ECC than in other competitive systems such as RSA and DSA. This helps in having smaller key sizes, hence faster computations. Elliptic curves do not introduce new cryptographic algorithms, but they implement existing public-key algorithms using elliptic curves. The implementation of elliptic curve cryptography requires several choices like the type of finite field, algorithm for implementing the elliptic group operation and elliptic curve protocols which influence the performance of ECC [6].

In 1984, Shamir [3] introduced the concept of identity-based (ID-based) cryptography. The first complete and efficient ID-based encryption scheme was proposed by Boneh and Franklin[7], which uses a bilinear map called Weil pairing over elliptic curves. The bilinear map transforms a pair of elements in group G1 and sends it to an element in group G2 in a way that satisfies some properties. The most important property is the bi-linearity that it should be linear in each entry of the pair. Assume that P and Q are two elements (e.g., points on elliptic curves) of an additive group G1. Let e(P, Q) be the element of a multiplicative group G2, which is the pairing applied to P and Q. Then the pairing must have the following property: $e(rP, Q) = e(P, Q)r = e(P, rQ)$.

Where r is an integer and rP denotes the element generated by r times of additions on P [7]. Weil and Tate pairing on elliptic curves is selected as the bilinear map [8]. That is, the elliptic curve group (the set of point collection on elliptic curves) is used as G1 and the multiplicative group of a finite field is used as G2. The ID-based scheme consists of four algorithms: Setup, Extraction, Encryption, and Decryption. In order to ensure security of SMS banking services, ID-based ECC cryptography algorithm are used, the generated key pair (160-bit) Pk , Sk are used to encrypt and decrypt the message.

3. Secure SMS Protocol Based On ID-Based Cryptography

There are two main challenges that were encountered during the design of secure SMS protocol. The first is the limited CPU strength and physical memory size of the mobile station. The second Challenge is the SMS message structure and its length.

To ensure confidentiality and integrity of SMS messages, cryptographic algorithms are required. Cryptography can be computationally expensive to perform especially when public key cryptographic functions are used. In order to be compliant with all the requirement of SMS, the encryption algorithm should possess three attributes, namely [9]: The encrypted message should be in the form of cipher text in order to meet the SMS message body standards. The encryption algorithm cannot alter the size of the message; the encryption algorithm should be simple and computationally inexpensively used. ID-based cryptosystem provides greater efficiency in terms of computational overheads, key sizes and bandwidth. Hence sending an ID-based encrypted short message is exactly the same as sending a normal short message. Every mobile user involved in the ID-based cryptosystem is given a subscriber identity module (SIM) card at the subscription time, The ID and its corresponding private key PK are loaded in the SIM card by the end-to-end security service provider. The mobile station contains two security modules: ID-based encryption module, and ID-based decryption module. Both modules can be pre-loaded into the SIM card.

The secure SMS protocol has been integrated with banking server. The SMS message is protected for the entire duration of its transit through the network. The underlying carrier network illustrated in Figure 1 depicts the path of encrypted SMS messages being sent between a mobile station and the banking server over a GSM network. The MS captures all the required security information from the user. This information is used to generate the secure SMS message to be sent to the banking server. The server verifies the authenticity of the person who is in possession of the MS. Once the banking server has verified the user, it will send an acknowledgement SMS message back to the MS. Few types of transactions has been simulated in this research.

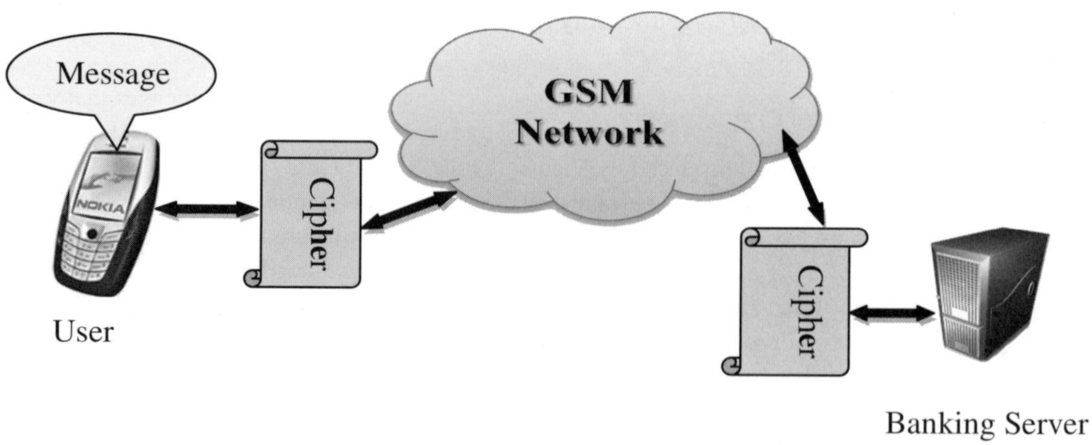

Figure 1. Encrypted SMS experimental environment

4. Results

To deliver short messages, notebook or PC is plugged in a NOKIA Card Phone or Light Wave (GSM-GPRS) and the short message is sent via AL-MADAR GSM network from the sender to the Banking server. SMS message has been encrypted using the ID-based cryptography scheme and sent over AL-MADAR GSM network at different time 11:00 AM, 12:00 PM, 2:00 PM, 7:00 PM. The times required to encrypted and decrypted the message have been measured. And the time taken by the GSM network to deliver the message to the banking server has been measured as well. The experiment has been repeated ten times the encryption time; decryption time and end to end transmission delay have been measured. The average value has been calculated and represented in the figure 2. The result showed that the encryption and decryption speeds on the mobile device are faster than the duration of the transmission. The Elliptic curve cryptosystems have the potential to provide security equivalent to that of existing public key schemes, but with shorter key lengths. Having short key lengths is a factor that can be crucial in the securing of SMS for banking services.

CONCLUSION

Public key cryptographic systems are often employed to transmit short message. In this paper, an applicable end-to-end security mechanism for SMS-banking server based on the ID-based scheme are presented and implemented. The ID-based scheme provides a great simplification of key distribution. That is, all public keys can be derived from the identities of the users. Therefore obtaining someone's public key, for encryption or verification, becomes a simple and transparent procedure. ECC provides greater efficiency in terms of computational overheads, key sizes and

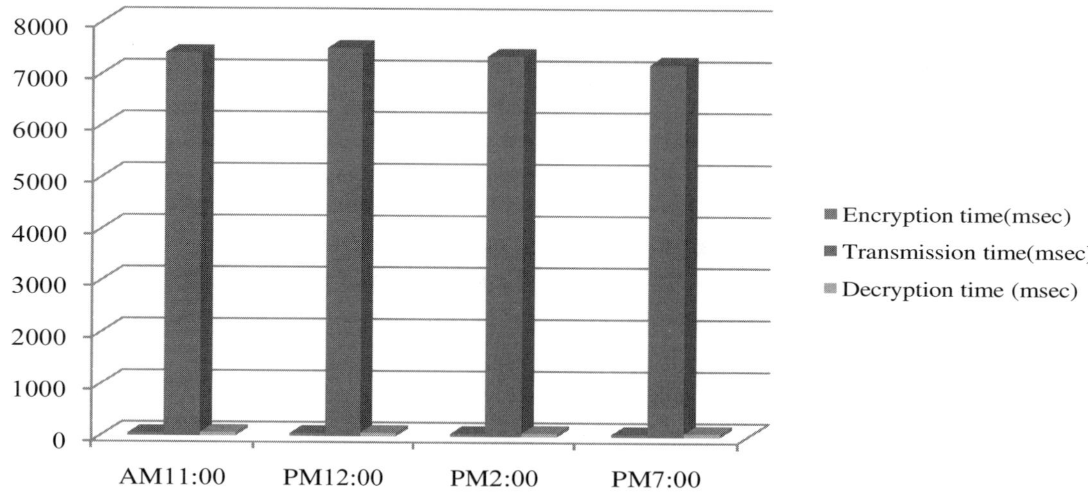

Figure 2. Encryption time, transmission time and decryption time of transaction messages

bandwidths. In implementations, these savings mean higher speeds, lower power consumption, and code size reductions.

REFERENCES

[1] Ratshinanga, H., Lo, J., Bishop, J. "A Security Mechanism for Secure SMS". (Online) http://polelo.cs.up.ac.za/papers/SecureSMS.pdf. 2004

[2] W. Stallings. "Cryptography and Network Security. Prentice Hall, fourth Edition". 2006.

[3] A. Shamir, "Identity-based Cryptosystems and Signature Schemes", Advances in Cryptology–CRYPTO 84, PP. 47-53.

[4] H.-N. Hung, Y.-B. Lin, M.-K. Lu, and N.-F. Peng, "A Statistic Approach for Deriving the Short Message Transmission Delay Distributions", IEEE Trans. on Wireless Communications, vol. 3, No. 6, 2004.

[5] V. Vijayalakshmi and. T.G. Palanivelu. " Secure Localization Using Elliptic Curve Wireless Sensor Networks", IJCSNS International Journal of Computer Science and Network Security, VOL.8 No.6, June 2008.

[6] Vikram V Kumar, S. Doraiswamy, Z. Jainullabudeen, "Elliptic Curve Cryptography Design and Analysis of Algorithms", December 2007.

[7] D. Boneh and M. Franklin, "Identity-based Encryption from the Weil Pairing", Advances in Cryptology-CRYPTO'01, PP. 213–239.

[8] Ben Lynn. "On The Implementation Of Pairing-Based Cryptosystems", Published Doctor's Dissertation, Stanford University. June 2007.

[9] N.J Croft and M.S Olivier. "Using an approximated One-Time Pad to Secure Short Messaging Service (SMS)". In Proceedings of the Southern African Telecommunication Networks and Applications Conference (SATNAC) 2005. PP. 71-76.

THE APPLICATION OF AUTOMATIC MONITORING SYSTEM FOR ELECTROSTATIC PRECIPITATOR

KAIXING WU
School of Information Science and Electrical Engineering
Hebei University of Engineering, Handan, Hebei, China

YUQING ZHENG
School of Information Science and Electrical Engineering
Hebei University of Engineering, Handan, Hebei, China

YONGQIANG MA
School of Information Science and Electrical Engineering
Hebei University of Engineering, Handan, Hebei, China

Electrostatic precipitator is an advantageous choice for air cleansing and pollution control. Volumes of industrial dust, fly ash, fumes and mist particulates are easily collected and the air cleaned through their use. The paper introduces the application of automatic monitoring system for electrostatic precipitator in a steel plant. In order to improve the automation level of electrostatic precipitator, to reduce administrative personnel's labor intensity and arrive the energy conservation goal, the automatic monitoring system for electrostatic precipitator is provided which is based on ifix configuration software. The implement of the system will monitor how electrostatic precipitator works. Considering reducing the energy, it adopts turbidity close-loop control strategy and the method of online detecting removal efficiency. Its function includes detection, display, control, protection, alarming and management. It can storage the running parameters and the information about what the operators do to the database. The system has provided fast, accurate, the comprehensive information basis for the operator about the monitoring and the maintenance. It has realized the electrostatic precipitators long-distance monitoring and the automated management goal.

1. Introduction

One of the major air pollution problems is due to the particulate emissions from many large industrial units, such as the power-generation stations utilizing solid fuels, the cement and mining installations and the petroleum and chemical industries. The concentration of solid air pollutants in the vicinity of the industrial areas constitutes a constant offence to all inhabitants and the environment. Therefore, electrostatic precipitators are frequently used to clean dust and fly-ash from many industrial processes, removing solid particles from the exhaust gas and other smoke. They are useful for providing cleaner air in many industrial applications that result in exhaust gas or smoke. Nevertheless as a result of many sorts of reasons, ESP also has many problems which cause workers unable to find the faults promptly and analyze the position and reason correctly, causing the dust removal efficiency to drop, mist and dust emissions exceeding the allowed figure. Along with the environmental protection standard stricter, the industry control level gradually enhanced and the application in the steel mill and other process industries [1], EPS will inevitably develop the energy conservation, high effecting and intellectualization. In view of above questions the automatic monitoring system was conducted. It is designed based on the electrostatic precipitators in some steel plant, which is shown in Figure 1.

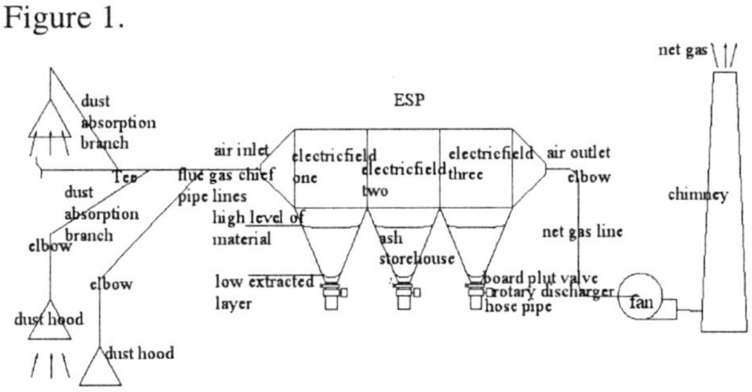

Fig.1. ESP flow chart

What the automatic monitoring system controls is ESP's dust removal process. An electrostatic precipitator [2] is a device that removes particles from a gas stream, typically in the form of smoke, after combustion occurs. An electrical charge is imparted to the particles, causing them to adhere to metal plates inside the precipitator. Finally, tapping the plates causes the particles to fall into a bin for disposal. Within an electrostatic precipitator are collection plates or tubes charged with negative voltage, which dry harvest particulates and dust from polluted air, smoke and gases.

The performance of an electrostatic precipitator is significantly affected by its complex running parameters. Once they are set inappropriately, the failure rate will be increasing. The automatic monitoring system is capable of actively controlling, monitoring and recording the voltage, current, spark rate as well as optimizing the performance of an electrostatic precipitator. It can analyze the information data of the trend and grasp operation problems of the electrostatic precipitator in real-time by monitoring all data related with operation of the electrostatic precipitator in real-time.

2. Theory

2.1. *The design of operating station*

The operating station was developed secondarily by iFix configuration[3] software. IFix is a HMI / SCADA Component based on WINDOWS in Intellution automation software family. It can shorten the automation project design cycle, shorten the system upgrade and maintenance time, realize seamless integration with the third party application, and enhance the productivity of automation project.

IFix's SCADA provides monitor-management, alarm and control function. It attains the process data from OPC server through disposing I/O driver as OPC client. The data will be stored in iFix's real-time and history database and dynamically displayed in manipulate show interface. The production parameter can be input manually if needed to be modified or added by users. Data flow chart is shown Figure2.

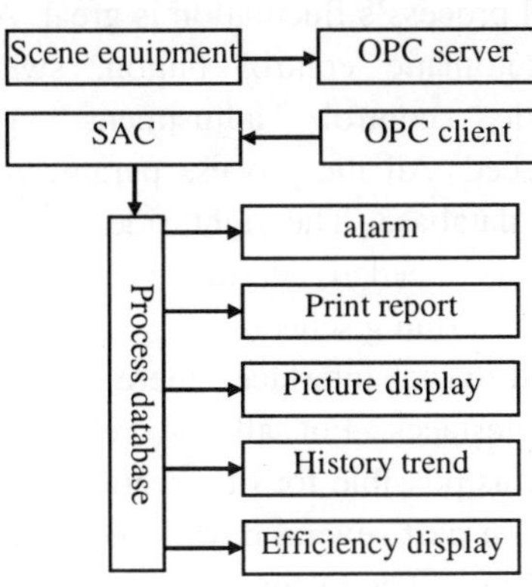

Fig.2. Data flow chart

2.2. *Data Communication*

The process data produced by PLC are read by PC operating station's software of Siemens, then provided to iFix which is installed OPC client programs in OPC (OLE for process Control) data server form. The process data is collected into real-time database through SAC by iFix.

2.3. *Closed loop control*

An ESP first must guarantee the dust removal efficiency to meet the requirements, in this foundation, requests the electrical energy consumption to be as low as possible. In the past, the electrostatic precipitators' running parameters were set manually. One disadvantage was precision poor, more tedious. Another aspect, the changes of smoke concentration which were caused by units load changed, can not be set the parameters correctly. The flue gas concentration increased and electrical energy consumption wasted. The automatic monitoring system will be solving the problem effectively. It meets the least energy consumption and guarantees the collection efficiency standard. In the closed-loop control situation, the flue gas turbidity is basically invariable, but the energy consumption may drop, and also may set the definition turbidity scope. It adopts antihypertensive vibration to improve the vibration effect when the flue gas viscosity is big and the collected ash can not be beating easily in running process. It can set the antihypertensive scope automatically according to the signal provided by the turbidmeter and get back the running parameters quickly.

Turbidity close-loop feedback control principle is based on the continuous monitoring of dust emission export value, adjusting feedback of electric power distribution, or adjusting each stage of intermittent power output voltage and current than that of discharging standard. On the base of emission standard; optimize configuration and save the largest power. Principle as figure3 shows.

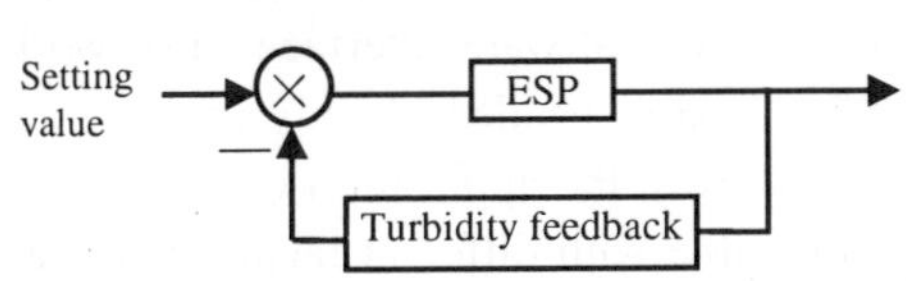

Fig.3. Turbidity close-loop control principle

Turbidity meter installed in emissions export will convert the turbidity into standard current signal and feedback to the comparator. In order to prevent emissions exceeding the standard when condition changes, the value of comparator is set slightly lower than state emissions standard. The difference value of setting and feedback is calculated by comparator and produces a demand signal transmitted through the network to the power supply device controller, realizes instruction and configuration. PC can set the comparator value directly on the dust removal efficiency

2.4. *Online detecting removal efficiency*

The basic model makes the following assumptions: Electrical precipitator actual removal efficiency can be calculated by import turbidity and export net gas turbidity. It can reflect the effect of ESP and provide reference for the closed-loop control. The expression of the efficiency of dust is in the benchmark of dust concentration and shown as Eq (1)

$$\eta = \frac{C_{in} - C_{out}}{C_{in}} \times 100\% \qquad (1)$$

C_{in} is import turbidity, mg/Nm3 ; C_{out} is export net gas turbidity, mg/Nm3;

3. Results

3.1. *The realization of data acquisition*

Data acquisition is used to get data from scene lower computer and processes them into useful form [4]. IFix may write the data into the lower computer, which establishes a both-way junction what the control software needs. The scene data can be got and utilized by iFix in OPC which is a client/server module provided with public interface and supports the communication between iFix and standard object, mode and attribute. IFix obtains data without other special hardware, however, communicates directly with I/O equipment through I/O driver software interface. IFix works with the scene hardware installed already in most cases. In the same network in the application of scene, I/O driver is even compatible with different factory hardware, it is especially important.

In this system, the work process of high-voltage power supply devices and the low-pressure control system is the key in dust removal. The high-voltage power supply devices consist of silicon rectifier, the reactor and the control cubicle. They make sure that ESP works smoothly when average voltage is lower slightly than the spark discharge voltage through adjusting the highest voltage according to the character of flue gas and dust, which makes the collection efficiency best and saves energy. The low-pressure control system consists of rapping control, discharging ash control, incubator constant temperature control and safety chain control. An additional software-power control rapper is also introduced for decreasing secondary blowing dust, so that the dust removal efficiency of ESP can be enhanced and the energy saved[5].

3.2. *The design of operating interface*

1. Technological process interface, the whole dust removal flowchart and details subsystem flowcharts are designed according to ESP's working process. They are visual display for real-time data in graphic and animation. The history trend curve of real-time data will be shown when clicked.
2. Adjusting operating interface, in order to control operating process easily, six adjusting interfaces are designed. Real-time diagrams for monitoring points are located in the left of every picture. Real-time data are displayed below diagrams, such as the value of flue gas turbidity and temperature, the enactment for voltage and piezoelectricity, the rapping period control and the net gas turbidity. In the middle of the picture, there are values of control model PID parameters, such as measured value, set value SV, proportion P, integral I, differential D, modified coefficient K and control mode. Manual work should be operated through clicking the manual control button, when the dust removal process's fluctuation is great. After stable, click automatic control button, switch to the automatic control adjustment way again undisturbed. All the process parameters are input experts database. The right side is the important parameters needed alarm. The below part is dynamic alarming schedule.
3. Historical trend interface, there are 6 historical trend interfaces. Put all the related parameters together as possible for observation. The historical trend from past several days to now can be shown in the picture(The history data can be kept 2—200

days based on setting). All parameters show us in different colors. Clicking a parameter below the picture may cause the Y axis only to appear this parameter scale interval for convenient observation. When the mouse moves over some point in the curve, the corresponding time and data will be displayed simultaneously below the picture.

4. Real-time information interface, the value of 29 parameters are shown dynamically in the picture whose colors are related to the number range. Red color represents the alarm status, green normal. Alarming lamp is set before the parameter in the database which is needed alarm. Alarm status occurs when the alarming lamp turns red. Clicking corresponding data area may open its historical trend interface, which is convenient for observing the parameter changing trend.

3.3. *Data report function*

IFix holds two report output functions; one is that exchanging data with Microsoft's EXCEL procedure by the dynamic data exchange (DDE) form through setting proper DDE data address. The other is exchanging data with database which supports ODBC interface through other ODBC interface. The managers who need long-distance produce process data may scan and print the data from the database.

3.4. *Key technology*

1. Saving-energy optimal control, energy-saving operation is an increasingly important in ESP running. Control system calculates every electric field energy-saving space dynamically combined with the concentration of dust, carries on the systematic optimization to dispose and to coordinate through the energy conservation optimization control strategy, which greatest degree displays the installment energy conservation potential. The efficiency-improving and energy-saving and the dynamically optimization design idea of the lower computer can realize single electric field saving-energy optimal control. Macroscopical and microcosmical saving-energy optimal control make sure ESP running total power consumption lowest without reducing the efficiency of dust removal.
2. Fault Diagnosis[6], the system may give an alarm timely when ESP equipment goes wrong, simultaneously, help user analyze the fault reason according to the correlate content in repository, instruct operator and maintenance workers prompt diagnosis position and solution, and deposit the fault time, type, reason and solution in fault database for later use in consultations and analyses.
3. Redundancy technique, enable the system smoothly work, this system has used the redundant technology. PLC controller and I/O station connect through PROFIBUS—DPField-bus, double nets redundancy, when one bus goes wrong in communication, controller and interface unit will automatically switch to the other one undisturbed and makes communication normal; hardware redundant in PLC controllers, when a fault occurs in master controller, the hot backup secondary will prompt switch undisturbed, I / O module control for scene facility and signal receiving may run smoothly; Two set of monitor-operating station are prepared, respectively independent, may be used at the same time, which compose hot redundancy backup and improve the whole system security for long continuous operation.

4. Conclusions

Applications of electrostatic precipitator's automatic monitoring system make electrostatic precipitators achieve high and reliable performance. The system was developed with the iFIX configuration software which has friendly interface and convenient operation. It can be capable of actively controlling, monitoring and recording the voltage, current, spark rate as well as optimizing the performance of electrostatic precipitator. So its realization not only enhance dust removal efficiency and the level of management, but also facilitates engineering personnel's daily maintenance , more importantly, it can save half energy and meet the national dust discharge standard, promote the purpose of the environmental protection.

References

1. KOCIK M, DEKOWSKI J, MIZERACAYK J. Particle precipitation efficiency in an electrostatic precipitator *Journal of Electrostatics*,2005,63.
2. Gary Tepper, Royal Kessick. A study of ionization and collection efficences in electrospray-based electrostatic precipitators. *Aerosol Science* 39(2008)609-617.

3. J.D. Bapat. Application of ESP for gas cleaning in cement industry—with reference to India. *Journal of Hazardous Materials B81 (2001) 285–308*
4. Agamemnon A.Varonos, John S.Anagnostopoulos,George C.Bergeles. Prediction of the cleaning efficiency of an electrostatic precipitator. *Journal of Electrostatics 55 (2002) 111 -133*
5. GaoJunkai, HuangChao, Tian Li. Advancements in technologies for improving dust removal effectiveness of electrostatic precipitator. *ENVIRONMENTAL POLLUTION & CONTROL* 2007,10
6. Yiqiong Li, Ting Xu, Jin Wang, Zefeng Lu,ESP automatic monitored control system. *Proeeedings of 12th Conferenee of ESP* 2007,10.

KEY ESTABLISHMENT AND MANAGEMENT SCHEME FOR MOBILE SENSOR NODES IN A LIMITED GEGORAPHIC REGION

NIRAV SHAH

Department of Computer Engineering, Charotar Institute of Technology, Changa, Gujarat 388421, India

E-mail: niravleo@yahoo.com

www.ecchanga.ac.in

Key establishment and management is the heart of secure communication. Most key pre-distribution schemes for mobile sensor networks assume that there is no fixed infrastructure available to mobile sensor nodes. Applications of sensor networks are increasing in civil area where fixed infrastructure facility is available to sensor nodes. Proposed scheme of key establishment and management can be used in situation where fixed infrastructure is available to mobile sensor nodes. Proposed scheme exhibits noteworthy properties like node authentication, resilience and connectivity.

1. Introduction

A wireless sensor network is composed of a large number of tiny sensor nodes with limited capability in terms of power, communication range and computing.[1] Sensor networks can be categorized in static wireless sensor networks and mobile sensor networks. Mobile sensor networks are also called MANETs. MANETs are mainly used for military purposes but now MANET has applications in civil areas. Sensor nodes can be deployed by air plane or by a vehicle and thus which node will reside with which one can not be known a prior. The node gets energy from battery and no external source for energy is available. Nodes are mobile and therefore we should take care of establishing secure communication between nodes quickly and efficiently keeping low computation and communication overhead. Nodes are not monitored constantly and in turn it can be captured or destroyed, [2] so the security is essential problem for sensor networks.

Communication between sensor nodes should accumulate or relay secret or captured information. Sensor nodes can establish secure connection in different ways. Existing public key infrastructure can be used for establishing pairwise communication, but due to resource constraints and high memory, computation cost and computation power requirement of this scheme, it is not suitable for sensor networks.[3] key predistribution schemes, where keys are stored off-line in sensor nodes before deployment of nodes, nodes establish secure connection using secret key with its neighboring node using common keys or information between them. Several key predistribution schemes have been proposed in literature. These schemes are measured on different parameters.

Key pre-distribution schemes can be measured on parameters like

- Scalability - Whether addition of new nodes in a network is possible or not
- Network connectivity - How many nodes in a network can successfully establish secure connection between them which leads to connectivity of whole network
- Node authentication - Node authentication can be done for non-repudiation
- Node revocation - Detecting misbehaving node and removing it from the network
- Network size – Number of nodes accommodated by the scheme
- Memory required - Minimum memory required for scheme
- Resilience - How well it can protect the communication between non-captured nodes when nodes are captured by adversary

All schemes[4–7] makes trade-off to achieve good scalability or resilience or connectivity. These schemes can be categorized in probabilistic, keys are randomly selected, or in deterministic, keys are deterministically selected, category.

In a network, nodes can establish secure connection through shared key discovery.[4] Network connectivity can be increased by path-key establishment and forwarding of key.[8] "Random key pre distribution for sensor networks" [6] uses multipath key reinforcement to increase the resilience of network. The entire process of establishing secure connection between nodes incurs more computation and communication overhead.

In this paper, a new key establishment and management scheme for mobile sensor network in a limited geographic region is proposed. Proposed scheme provides perfect connectivity and resilience compared to existing schemes. Node authentication, node addition, prevention against node replication and large network size are features of proposed scheme.

The rest of the paper is organized as follows. In Section II, provides necessary background and related work in the area of key establishment and management schemes. Section III describes the proposed key establishment and management for mobile sensor nodes in a limited geographic region. Section IV presents the analysis of proposed scheme with existing schemes. Section V summarizes the work and points out some future work.

2. Related Work

A lot of work has been done in MANETs regarding key management. Key management technique can be categorized in probabilistic or deterministic key management. This section provides the brief review and analysis of these schemes.

"A key management scheme for distributed sensor networks" proposed by Eschenauer and Gligor[4] was based on the pairwise key distribution. In this scheme keys are selected randomly from large key pool and stored in sensor nodes. This whole process is done before deployment, after that node can establish secure connection if they share any common key. If no common key is available, then path-key establishment can be done to establish connection. It has been shown that if two nodes share at least one common key then whole network can be connected with high probability.

"q-composite key scheme" variant of Eschenauer and Gligor scheme[4] is proposed by Chan *et al.*[6] In this scheme secret connection can be established between two nodes only when they have q-common keys. Idea of sharing q-common keys led to improvement in resilience of network. In the same paper random pairwise key scheme is also given; which achieves perfect resilience at the cost of network size. Scheme proposed by Eschenauer and Gligor[4] and "q-composite" key scheme reuses the same keys and this leads to the compromise of the link between non-captured nodes when any node is captured by the adversary.

Polynomial based key predistribution schemes are proposed by Blundo *et al.*[7] and by Liu and Ning.[9] In these schemes bivariate polynomial operations are used to compute a common key in a group of certain number of nodes. In these schemes, network remains safe until no more than threshold numbers of nodes are compromised.

Das and Roy[5] proposed the key pre-distribution scheme for highly mobile sensor nodes. In this scheme keys are deterministically selected and stored in a sensor node before deploying. This scheme achieves high connectivity and low computation and communication overhead. Scheme has poor resilience, when only few selected nodes are compromised then majority of keys are revealed to the adversary.

Another matrix based scheme was proposed by Cheng and Agrawal.[10] In this scheme, keys are selected by a position of a node in a matrix. This design allows any node in network to share at least two keys with any node. This scheme has good property of connectivity and resilience.

All proposed schemes in[4,6,7,9] do not provide or state that how efficiently one node can find out the key ring of the other node. In these schemes, either computation overhead or communication overhead or both are more. Besides, these schemes including[5] can not provide enough resilience against node capture attack.

In this paper, a new key establishment and management scheme for mobile sensor nodes in a limited geographic region is proposed, which will improve the limitations of current key pre-distribution schemes like connectivity and resilience.

3. Key Establishment and Management Scheme for Mobile Sensor Nodes in a Limited Geographic Region

In proposed scheme, "A New Key-Predistribution Scheme for Highly Mobile Sensor Networks (Matrix Layout (ML) Scheme)" [5] is used with modifications for initial key establishment between nodes. In the ML scheme key is distributed based on matrix layout, a feature that provides high connectivity and low computation and communication overhead. Due to these features this scheme is used with modification for initial key setup between nodes. ML Scheme is briefly described in next section.

3.1. *ML scheme*

ML scheme performs key predistribution by the use of specific matrix layout. Keys are selected according to matrix layout specified in scheme. Matrix layout allows computing key ring of other node with less overhead. Communication overhead is decreased by providing only position of a node in matrix layout and from position one node can find out the key ring of the other node and common key, if any. In this scheme each sensor node contains the t keys and their key ids, position in matrix layout, and node id. Maximum number of keys and nodes supported by scheme are $2((t + 2)/2)^2$. Matrix layout will be formed of size $d \times d$, where $d = t+2$ and keys will be selected according to position of node in matrix layout. After key predistribution, shared key discovery will be done to find the common key, if any, between nodes.

For this scheme the matrix layout given in Das and Roy's scheme[5] is used which is modified for key establishment and management scheme. In next section, detailed scheme with different phases of key establishment and management is presented.

3.2. *Assumptions*

Few assumptions are made for the proposed scheme.

- No node in the network is malicious
- It is assumed that all nodes are deployed randomly and thus no deployment knowledge is available
- Base stations (Infrastructure) are placed in such a way that it can cover the whole network
- Base station has high processing power, large communication range and enough memory to store the network wide keys

There are different phases in proposed scheme to establish secret

1. Key pre-distribution
2. Shared key discovery
3. Sharing of secret key for communication
4. Key re-establishment

Details of each phase are provided in next section.

3.3. *Key pre-distribution*

Key predistribution is an off-line process in which keys are selectively selected and stored in sensor nodes. Proposed scheme has two entities, one, Sensor node and second, Base station for which keys will be selected and stored.

Mobile sensor node - Each node contains

1. One unique private key - This key will be used by node to make a secret hashed key.
2. Ad-hoc private keys and key ids - This will be used only during shared key discovery. Ad-hoc keys will be distributed according to matrix layout.
3. Ad-hoc private keys and key ids - This will be used only during shared key discovery. Ad-hoc keys will be distributed according to matrix layout.
4. Node id - This will act as public key during exchange of messages between nodes or between node and base station.
5. Pre-compiled hash of base stations and base stations id - This hash will be used by sensor node to communicate with base stations. Hash in the form of h(private key of base station || node id).
6. One way hash function - This is used to generate secure hash.

Base Stations - Each base station contains

1. Pre-compiled hash of each node and corresponding node id - This will be used for communicating with node. Hash will be h(private key of node || base station id).
2. Pre-compiled hash of base stations and base station id - This will be used for communicating with other base stations.

Stored hashed keys provide secure communication between base stations and nodes.

3.4. *Shared key discovery*

This phase will be invoked when nodes are first time deployed in a network. After deployment of nodes, each node will send probe request asking neighbor nodes position. In reply to that, each neighbor responds with their matrix layout position. According to matrix layout position source node can find the key ring of the other nodes and if any common key is found, then both nodes can establish a secure connection. If no common key is found then secure connection can be established through common base station. How this will be done is explained in section 3.6.

Proposed scheme can also work without the use of matrix layout scheme, in that case formation of network will take considerable time and to reduce that matrix layout scheme is used for forming initial secure connection between nodes.

3.5. *Sharing of secret key for communication*

Once secure connection is established between nodes then nodes can set pairwise key for a session with other node. The pairwise key will be, stored in sensor nodes memory with node id, used for current session communication only. Use of pairwise key communication prevents the decryption of past communication, because for every session, new key will be generated and used for communication. For example, node u and v are two nodes and they established secure connection. Node u will make pairwise key and send it to v. This pairwise key will be used by u and v to send any messages. Now u and v can communicate using the available pairwise key. Encrypted message send with its own node id.

All stored ad-hoc keys and their respective key ids in a sensor node will be removed from memory. Hence if a node is captured in future it does not reveal any secret information other than its own private key, session keys and secret hashed keys. Motivation behind the process of removing ad-hoc keys is that most of the nodes hold a few common keys which are used by other nodes for communication and capturing only few nodes leads to compromise of communication between non-captured nodes. The use of the matrix layout allows us to carry out shared key discovery process with less computation and less communication overhead during shared key discovery.

3.6. *Key re-establishment*

The nature of mobile sensor node requires key reestablishment. This phase is invoked in two conditions. First, when node moves from one place to another place, second, when it finds that new nodes exist in its neighborhood. This can be identified by periodic broadcast of probe request. Probe request of source node will ask the neighbor nodes to give their node ids and getting ids from neighbor nodes it will check the ids stored in its memory. If major change
is found then key re-establishment phase will be executed and it's explained through key re-establishment algorithm. When node v is no longer available as a neighbor then u deletes the pairwise key with v and its node id from its memory. v also removes the pairwise key with u and its node id from its memory.

Following notations are used for describing the scheme,

u, v - Sensor nodes, ID_u - Id of nod u, PR_{ku} - Private key of node u, h - One way hash function, $Session_{k\_uv}$ - Randomly generated pairwise key by node u for node v, H - Stored hash value, H_u -Computed hash value with own PR_{kv} and ID_u, EM - Encrypted message using pairwise key, DM - Decrypted message using pairwise key, m - Plain message, M - Final message sent to other node, Src_u - Source node id, and Dst_v - Destination node id.

Algorithm: Key re-establishment

for each node u in the network **do**
  for each physical neighbor v of u with which u does not share a key **do**
    u broadcasts a probe message asking for ID of v
    v sends the ID_v to u
    if v is a new neighbour of u
    then
      u generates a pairwise key $Session_{k\_uv}$ encrypts $Session_{k\_uv}$ and ID_u with H of base station b
      Send the encrypted message and Src_u and Dst_v to base station b through intermediate nodes
      Base station b decrypts the message by H_u and sends received message to Dst_v by encrypting with H of v
      v decrypts the message by creating own H_b
      v send message securely to u using $Session_{k\ uv}$

3.7. *Communication scenarios*

This section describes three scenarios for communications. First, node communicates with base station. Second is base station communicates with node and third, node to node communication.

1. Node to base station communication: This communication can happen during initial key establishment or during key re-establishment. In initial phase when no common keys are found, node can find the common base station by listening periodic broadcast done by base station with its id. Node sends the randomly generated pairwise key by encrypting with particular base stations secret hashed key, H, which is pre-loaded in all nodes. Intermediate nodes just forward the message to base station. Received message is decrypted at base station by generating secret hashed key for a source node, H_u, this can be found by source node id, Src_u, with message. Proposed scheme do not allow intermediate node to decrypt the message.
2. Base station to node communication: Base station to node communication done to send the pairwise key received from node Srcu to node Dst_v. Base station b will encrypt the message by H of Dst_v and send the encrypted message to Dst_v. At v it generates hash H_b and decrypts the message with it. Now both u and v has pairwise key for secure communication for current session (as long as both are neighbor).
3. Node to node communication: Before communicating with node, it setup a pairwise key through base station. Pairwise key is used for secure communication between nodes. Let u and v be two nodes which already setup a pairwise key. u wants to send any message m to v then u will encrypt the message and own node id using $Session_{k\ uv}$ and sends it to v with its own node id, $EM = Session_{k\ uv}(m||ID_u)$, $M = (EM, ID_u)$.

On the receiver side v will get node id, u, and encrypted message, M. By getting ID_u, v decrypts the message using $Session_{k\_uv}$, $DM = Session_{k\_uv}(EM)$. If it gets the same node id ID_u then accept the message otherwise discard the message.

4. Performance Analysis of Proposed Scheme

4.1. *Connectivity*

However, the initial secure connection among nodes follows ML scheme, proposed scheme achieves the complete connectivity. This is due to the fact that the nodes which do not share ad-hoc keys can establish secure connection through base stations.

4.2. *Scalability*

Characteristic of sensor node that it runs on limited battery power, nodes may be dead due to drain batteries. Application demand can lead to network growth. Network can grow by adding more new nodes to the existing network. The proposed scheme allows addition of new nodes and achieves complete connectivity among new nodes and existing nodes. The procedure of key predistribution, shared key discovery and sharing of secret key will be done for the newly deployed node and can setup the secret key as done earlier. Pre-compiled hash of new nodes will be added to the base stations with new node ids. The new node can not directly communicate with the existing nodes. For secure connection among existing nodes and the new node can be done through following procedure.

Let u be new node and v be the existing node and u wants to establish a secure connection with v. u will send message asking for the node id of v and in turn v will respond with its node id. Now u generates the pairwise key and transmits it through the base station. Once pairwise keys are transmitted, the base station is not required to communicate among these nodes. If a node moves from one location to other or finds that the existing neighbors are no longer present then it removes pairwise keys from its memory for those nodes. It is important to observe that the matrix layout scheme [5] does not support node addition and the network is hardly scalable.

4.3. *Resilience*

Resilience term is used in.[4] When any node is captured by the adversary then the fraction of the network compromised between non-captured nodes can be defined by resilience. This is one of the parameter used for comparing different key predistribution schemes. The proposed scheme achieves perfect resilience. Node captured by the adversary, it reveals the private key, pairwise keys and hashed keys in that node. This does not affect the communication among non-captured nodes in the network.

4.4. *Node authentication*

Proposed scheme provides node authentication to support non-repudiation. Before establishing secure connection, probe request is generated by source node. Probe request asks for node id from neighbor nodes. Source node first gets the neighbor node id and then pairwise key will be provided by source node through the base station which takes care of verifying neighbor node id. As the base station has pre-compiled hashed key of all nodes with their ids so it encrypts the message using the stored hashed key and sends it to the neighbor node. This encrypted message can only be decrypted by neighbor node because it is having the private key and base station id and hence node authentication is employed inherently.

4.5. *Restricting node replication*

If any node is captured by adversary then the same node can be cloned and used for capturing secret information from network. Proposed scheme restricts node replication, as node establish secure connection only with neighbor node by confirming node id through matrix layout position during initial shared key discovery or it will be done through base station. Thus it discards the messages from the unknown node id and prevents node replication. It is worth to note that each node has unique private key and per session pairwise key thus by replicating the captured node adversary can not get any more information about other nodes from network.

4.6. *Performance evaluation*

Proposed scheme is measured on different parameters. For comparison number of keys stored in sensor node is kept at 200. Table 1 shows the comparison of proposed scheme with existing schemes. "Efficient Pairwise Key establishment and Management in Static Wireless Sensor Networks (EPKEM)" provides perfect resilience and connectivity, proposed scheme also provides perfect connectivity and resilience and at the same time it provides double network size than the EPKEM. Proposed scheme can also be used for static sensor network but EPKEM can not be used for mobile sensor networks.

Table 1. Comparison with different schemes when number of keys stored in sensor node = 200

Scheme	Network Size	Resilience*	Connectivity
Matrix layout scheme	20402	0.409	0.987
EPKEM	10000	perfect	1.0
Random pairwise key scheme	400	perfect	0.5
Proposed scheme	20402	perfect	1.0

*When 50 nodes are captured

ML scheme provides good connectivity, close to one, but at the cost of security. In ML scheme selectively capturing only a few nodes leads to compromise of the whole network. Proposed scheme achieves perfect connectivity and capturing a node does not reveal any information to the adversary.

Proposed scheme provides larger network size and complete connectivity than random pairwise key scheme, which also provides perfect resilience.

5. Conclusion

Applications of mobile sensor networks in civil area are growing. Most of the schemes in literature are designed by assuming that no fixed infrastructure support is available to sensor nodes. In this paper the key establishment and management scheme for mobile sensor nodes in a limited geographic region is presented where infrastructure is available. Proposed scheme achieves complete connectivity and perfect resilience. However, key establishing time between nodes during key re-establishment phase is high and in this area further improvement can be made.

References

1. I. F. Akyildiz, W. Su, Y. Sankarasubramaniam and E. Cayirci, *Computer Networks* **38**, 393 (2002).
2. A. Perrig, J. Stankovic and D. Wagner, *Communications of the ACM* **47**, 53(June 2004).
3. D. Carman, P. Kruus and B. Matt, *Constraints and Approaches for Distributed Sensor Network Security*, Technical Report #00-010, NAI Labs (September2000).
4. L. Eschenauer and V. D. Gligor, A key-management scheme for distributed sensor networks, in *ACM Conference on Computer and Communications Security*, (ACM, 2002).
5. A. Das and B. K. Roy, A new key-predistribution scheme for highly mobile sensor networks, in *ICDCN*, LNCS Vol. 4904 (Springer, 2008).
6. H. Chan, A. Perrig and D. Song, Random key predistribution schemes for sensor networks, in *Proceedings of the 2003 Symposium on Security and Privacy*, (IEEE Computer Society, May 11–14 2003).
7. C. Blundo, A. D. Santis, A. Herzberg, S. Kutten,U. Vaccaro and M. Yung, *Inf. Comput* **146**, 1 (1998).
8. A. K. Das, A. Das, S. Mohapatra and S. Vavilapalli, Key forwarding: A location-adaptive key establishment scheme for wireless sensor networks, in *IWDC*, LNCS Vol. 3741 (Springer, 2005).
9. D. Liu and P. Ning, Location-based pairwise key establishments for static sensor networks, in *SASN*, (ACM, 2003).
10. Y. Cheng and D. P. Agrawal, Distributed pairwise key establishment in wireless sensor networks, in *PSC*, (CSREA Press, 2006).

EPR DATA HIDING IN MEDICAL IMAGES WITH INTEGRITY CHECKING*

SUNITA DHAVALE †
STUDENT, DEPARTMENT OF COMPUTER ENGINEERING, VIT, 666, UPPER INDIRA, BIBWEWADI, PUNE, 411048, INDIA

SURESH MALI
DEAN, DEPARTMENT OF COMPUTER ENGINEERING, VIT, 666, UPPER INDIRA, BIBWEWADI, PUNE, 411048, INDIA

RAJESH JALNEKAR
DEAN, DEPARTMENT OF COMPUTER ENGINEERING, VIT, 666, UPPER INDIRA, BIBWEWADI, PUNE, 411048, INDIA

While transferring electronic patient report (EPR) data along with corresponding medical images over network, confidentiality must be assured. This can be achieved by embedding EPR data in corresponding medical image itself. But checking the integrity of this embedded data must be needed so to assure that retrieved EPR data is original and not manipulated by different types of attacks. This paper proposes checking the integrity of EPR while hiding the data bits in Discrete Cosine Transform (DCT) domain.

High imperceptibility is achieved by adaptively selecting the efficient DCT blocks. Even a slight modification of stego image in embedded region as well as in ROI (Region of Interest) can be detected at receiver so to confirm that attack has been done. The embedding scheme also takes care of ROI which is diagnostically important part of the medical images and generates security key automatically.

1. Introduction

Telemedicine application requires transferring EPR data and corresponding medical images over network for further diagnostic purpose. There is a demand for the protection of both medical images and EPR data[1].
Hiding this EPR in medical image[3] can be done in robust manner so that it prevents the EPR data removing unless the quality of the image is greatly reduced. This robust data hiding can be done by embedding EPR data directly in transform domain coefficients like DCT coefficients. Before embedding, high imperceptibility is achieved by adaptively selecting the area of an image in which to hide data using energy thresholding method[2]. Blind data hiding is achieved by hiding data in fixed DCT locations in all selected image blocks.
Further one must also guarantee that the region in which we have embedded sensitive and confidential EPR data is not tampered by any malicious manipulations[4]. Thus there is a need for integrity checking that must assure both EPR data and image has not been modified by unauthorized person and authentication that must assure that both EPR data and image belongs indeed to the correct patient and is issued from the correct source.
So secure hash can be calculated over this sensitive region and these hash bits can be embedded in diagnostically less important region[4] like border (black surrounding) or very low frequency region outside ROI of medical image using fragile spatial domain techniques like simple LSB substitution method. So even simple cutting or cropping the image at border region can loose these embedded hash bits and attack can be confirmed.
Hash functions are one-way functions as it is easy to determine the hash from the message but mathematically infeasible to determine the message from the hash. It is a cryptographic checksum or message integrity code (MIC) that each party must compute to verify the message. This MIC is invisibly embedded in the image itself so the image can authenticate itself without accessing any side information and makes the MIC less sensitive to attacks. A key can be used to create the hash for the selected region. So both sender and recipient will use the same key to carry out the hash function.

* This work is encouraged by VIT, Pune as part of our ME Post graduation Program.

In this paper, we propose a method by which we can hide EPR data and check the integrity of that embedded region as well as ROI for secure EPR data retrieval at receiver side. The rest of paper organized as follows. In section 2, proposed method is explained. Then in section 3, experiment and results are given followed by conclusions drawn in section 4.

2. Proposed System

2.1. *Transmitter Side Processing*

1. First the image is divided into 8x8 image blocks. Exclude ROI i.e. exclude all blocks falling inside ROI.
2. Apply DCT2 for remaining blocks and calculate energy of each blocks using following equation,

$$Ek = \sum\sum(Cij)^2$$

Where Ek=energy of kth block and Cij = DCT2 coefficients at (i, j) th position and values for i, j ranges from 1 to 7 each.

3. While calculating DC coefficient i.e. C (0, 0) is neither taken for the calculation of energy nor is it used for embedding [8].
4. Classify the remaining blocks by define two different energy thresholds w1 and w2 in such a way that,

w1>>>w2

As blocks having more energy can embed information bits with minimal distortion, we select all blocks having energy greater than w1 as very high frequency DCT blocks and treated as (VBs) Valid Blocks where actual EPR data is to be embedded while blocks having energy lesser than w2 are selected as very low frequency DCT blocks (LFBs) where a small size hash bits can be embedded safely without causing more distortion to medical image.

5. Embed encrypted EPR data bits into DCT coefficients of VBs after quantization that is defined by JPEG quality factor. Dequantize and apply inverse DCT.
6. Take secure hash of Embedded VB's as well as ROI blocks and encrypt and embed these hash bits into LSB's of randomly selected pixels of LFBs.
7. Reconstruct final medical stego image.
8. Secret key can be generated as a part of transmitter side processing whose bit fields can decide values of w1, w2 and JPEG Quality factor, randomization scheme used for LSB substitution, encryption keys or technique used for EPR and Hash bits.

2.2. *Receiver Side Processing*

At receiver side, medical stego image along with secret key must made available.

At receiver side, one has to carry all steps from 1-5 as it is to get all VB's and again recalculate secure hash of those embedded VB's as well as ROI blocks.

Extract the encrypted hash bits from LSB's of randomly selected pixels of LFBs and decrypt it.

Compare both hash bits if equal, then image is authenticated and we can retrieve embedded EPR data safely and decrypt it.

3. Experimental Results

We used grayscale 512 x 512 L-Spine (Lumbar Spine) medical images as shown in following figure 1 for our experiments. Experimentation is performed to check tamper detection capability of the system under various attacks (intentional and unintentional).

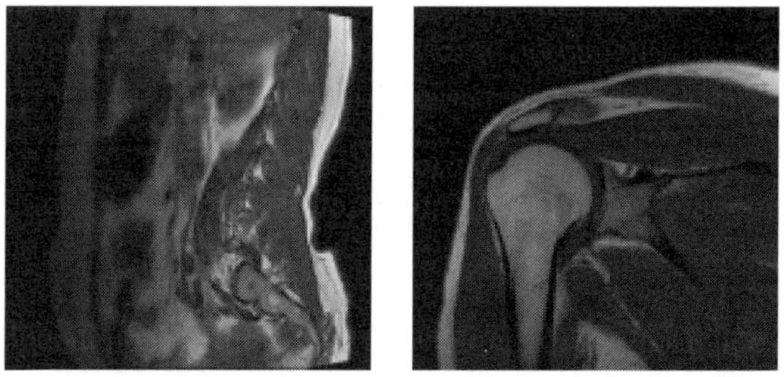

(a) L-Spine image (b) Shoulder image

Figure 1. Original Medical Test Images

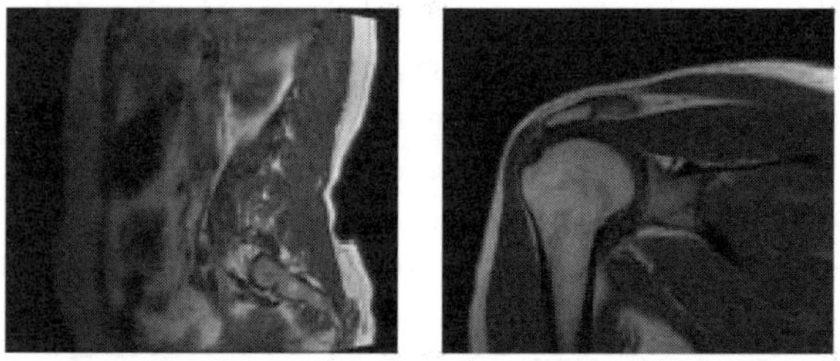

(a) Stego L-Spine image (b) Stego Shoulder image

Figure 2. Correponding Stego Medical Images

Figure 2 shows corresponding stego images, when 4 bits of EPR are embedded per 8 x 8 DCT block. The locations chosen for each VB block are (2,2), (3,0),

(0,3) and (0,2). The 320 bit encrypted hash code is embedded in LSBs of 8 pixels per LFB block.
The quality factor QF=50 chosen.
For a given choice of W1 and W2 values in Table 1, Figure 3 shows corresponding VB Blocks or region of images where EPR data is embedded while Figure 4 shows corresponding LFB Blocks or region of images where Hash data is embedded. So w2 is selected in such a way that all LFBs fall generally in border black region.

Table 1. Result Table

Medical Image	EPR data (in bits)	W1	W2	PSNR of stego	PSNR after attack
L-Spine	2534	3705	10	44.65	40.43
Shoulder	2098	1977	10	47.14	46.61

The PSNR observed for the stego images is above 40db and there is no perceptible difference between original and stego images.

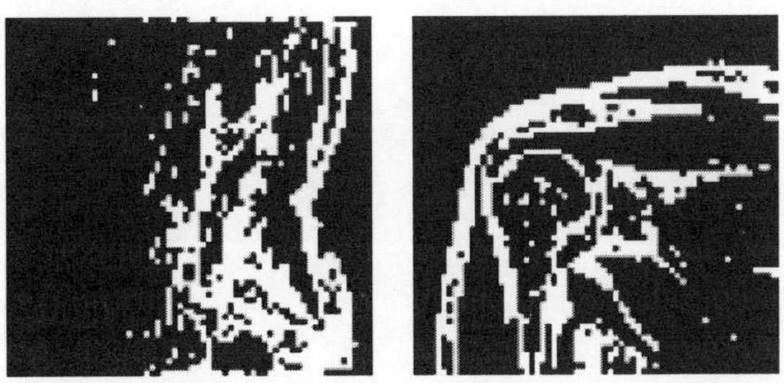

(a) VB Region for L-Spine (b) VB Region for Shoulder

Figure 3. Valid Block Region

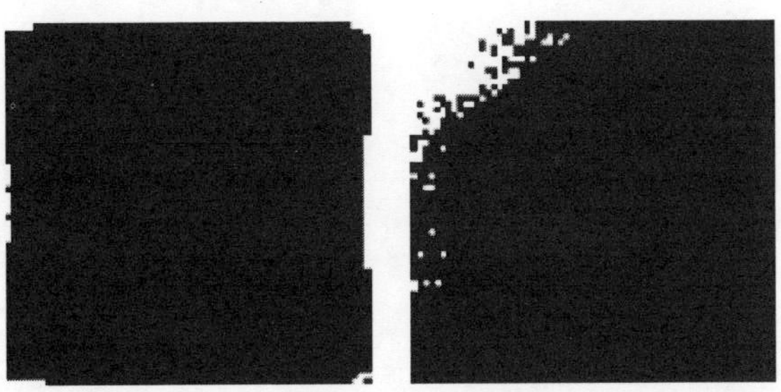

(a) LFB Region for L-Spine (b) LFB Region for Shoulder

Figure 4. LFB Region

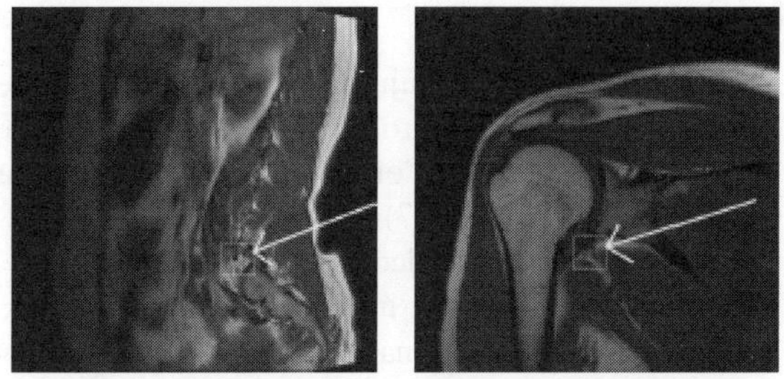

(a) Attacked L-Spine image (b) Attacked Shoulder image

Figure 5. Attacked Stego Medical Images

Figure 5 shows attacked images in which first small pixel stains are made in rectangular area (within VB region where EPR is embedded) as shown, which could not be visible by normal eye and in second image resize attack done. All these attacks are detected at receiver side successfully.
The experimental results shows that any distortion such as compression, noising, resizing, filtering, and little pixels stained on embedded region or ROI of the medical image would be detected at receiver.

4. Conclusions

In this paper, we proposed a method for the secure transmission of medical images by using both DCT and LSB substitution. First we embedded EPR data into the medical images and then we embedded hash bits to guarantee the integrity of the medical images transmitted.
To get high imperceptibility, adaptive energy thresholding method is used and also ROI protected while embedding EPR data. Based on the experimental results, the proposed method can guarantee that even slight modification to embedded region and ROI part can be detected unambiguously at receiver side.
In future we shall focus on the issue of how to locate the area of the image within embedded region and ROI that has been maliciously tampered.

Acknowledgments

We would like to thank Dr. S. Tungenvar, Radiologist, Bajaj Hospital, India for making us available required medical images for testing.

References

1. Gonzalo Alvarez1, Shujun Li and Luis Hernandez: Analysis of security problems in a medical image encryption system. Computers in Biology and Medicine, vol. 37 (2007) 424-427
2. Jasni Zain and Malcolm Clarke: Security in Telemedicine: Issues in Watermarking Medical Images. 3rd International Conference : Science of Electronic, Technologies of Information and Telecommunications (2005)
3. B. Planitz, A. Maeder: Medical Image Watermarking: A Study on Image Degradation. Proc. Australian Pattern Recognition Society Workshop on Digital Image Computing, WDIC 2005, Brisbane, Australia (2005)
4. K. A. Navas, S. Archana Thampy, and M. Sasikumar. : EPR Hiding in medical images for telemedicine. International Journal of Biomedical Sciences Volume 3.1 (2008) 44- 47
5. Kaushal Solanki, Noah Jacobsen, Upamanyu Madhow, B.S.Manjunath and Sivkumar Chandrashekhar.: Robust Image-Adaptive Data hiding using Erasure and Error Correction. IEEE Transactions on image processing, Volume 13, (2004) 1627-1639.
6. Suresh N. Mali and Rajesh M. Jalnekar. : Imperceptible and Robust Data Hiding using Steganography Against Image Manipulation International Journal of Emerging Technologies and Applications in Engineering, Technology and Sciences, (IJ-ETA-ETS) (2008) 84-91.

AN OPTIMIZED METHOD FOR SCHEDULING PROCESS OF SCANNING FOR HANDOVER IN MOBILE WIMAX

MOHAMMAD KAWSER, NAFIZ IMTIAZ BIN HAMID, M.A.NASER, ADNAN MAHMUD

Department of Electrical and Electronic Engineering (EEE), Islamic University of Technology (IUT), BoardBazar Gazipur-1704, Bangladesh

IEEE 802.16e standard for 4G Cellular Technology-Mobile WiMAX is proposed to support mobility. As a result, handover has become one of the most important QoS factors. Because of lack of clarification in the conventional algorithm for handover process, there exists wastage of channel resource along with undesired delay. Again, it causes significant degradation in the overall system performance. Existing standard for handover includes scanning as one of the most vital processes. But scanning requests without proper response and delayed initiation of scanning only deteriorates the scenario. In this paper, a modification of the scheduling process of scanning is proposed to reduce redundant scanning requests and overall handover operation delay.

1. Introduction

Mobile WiMAX is one of the most promising technologies for broadband wireless communication based on the IEEE 802.16e-2005 [1] standard. IEEE 802.16e provides enhancements to 802.16-2004 [2] to support subscriber stations moving at vehicular speeds. Key advantages of 802.16e include- tolerance to Multipath and Self-Interference, Scalable Channel Bandwidth, Orthogonal Uplink Multiple Access, Support for Spectrally-Efficient TDD, Frequency Selective Scheduling, Fractional Frequency Reuse, Fine Quality of Service (QoS), Advanced Antenna Technology [1] [2]. The Physical layer of Mobile WiMAX is based on OFDMA technology. The new technologies employed for Mobile WiMAX result in lower equipment complexity and simpler mobility management due to the all IP core network and provide many other advantages over CDMA based 3G systems [6].

As in the current standard, there is the support for mobility; handover has become a very vital issue. Handover of IEEE 802.16e broadband wireless network had been studied in several literatures. Up to now various fast handover schemes had been proposed. An enhanced fast handover algorithm was proposed to reduce the waste of the wireless channel resources and handover delay in [3] [4]. Target BS estimation using mean CINR and arrival time differences had been proposed for reducing unnecessary neighbor BS scanning and association process in [3]. Single neighbor BS scanning, fast ranging and pre-registration had been proposed in [4].

Again, a scheme for the reduction of data transmission delay and packet loss probability for real-time downlink service had been proposed in [5]. A delay timer to reduce the initiation of unnecessary handover had been proposed in [7]. In that proposal the timer deals with unnecessary handover caused by inaccurate signal level assessment.

In our paper, an optimized scheduling method of scanning is proposed to reduce wireless resource waste and delay in the initiation of scanning process. The remainder of this paper is organized as follows. Section 2 provides an overview of the handover process of the IEEE 802.16e. Section 3 shows the shortcomings in the scheduling process of scanning. Section 4 depicts our proposed scheme. Analysis of the performance of our proposal and conclusion of this paper are given respectively in section 5 and 6.

2. Handover in IEEE 802.16e

In IEEE 802.16e standard, three kinds of handover types can be supported- Hard Handover (HHO), Macro Diversity Handover (MDHO) and Fast Base Station Switching (FBSS). HHO is the simplest one among them; whether other two types having more complicacy are regarded as optional. Again, handover can be both MS and BS initiated. In this paper, when handover is mentioned, it refers to MS initiated HHO.

MS initiated hard handover as seen by MS starts from neighbor BS advertisement message and goes on through request and response related messages for scanning and HO; provided that the corresponding criteria are met. Figure 1 shows the step by step procedure for this. The final indication of handover process is performed via transmission of MOB_HO-IND message. Scanning interval and normal operations appear alternately by frame basis. This is shown in figure 2. for scanning without association case. Figure 3. shows the same process for scanning with non coordinated association. To our view, reduction of unnecessary scanning and HO delay mostly deals with the request, response and other MAC management messages regarding handover.

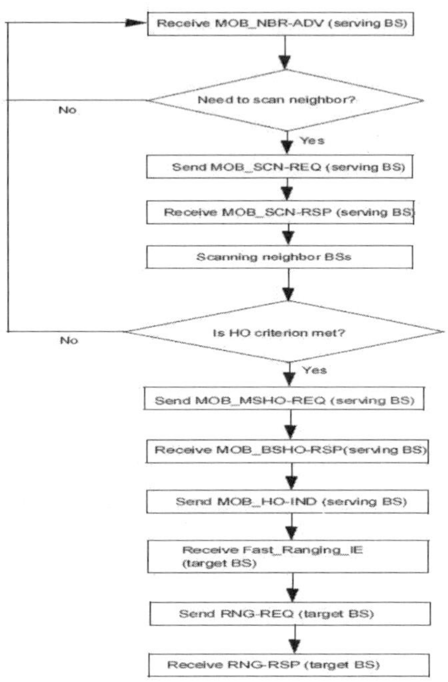

Figure 1. MS initiated hard handover as seen by MS.

So, for the level of significance of those messages in our proposal along with the clarification purpose we here state a brief explanation of some of them as follows:

2.1. *Neighbor Advertisement (MOB_NBR-ADV) Message*

BS supporting mobile functionality is capable of transmitting a MOB_NBR-ADV management message at a periodic interval to identify the network and defines the characteristics of neighbor BSs to potential MS seeking initial network entry or handover. Serving BS keeps mapping-tables of neighbor BS MAC addresses and neighbor BS indexes transmitted through MOB_NBR-ADV message, for each Configuration Change Count for the compression of neighbor BSIDs in MOB_SCN-REP and MOB_MSHO-REQ message.

Parameters included in the MOB_NBR-ADV are mainly Operator ID, Configuration Change Count, N_NEIGHBORS. For each advertised neighbor, important parameters are: Length, Neighbor BSID, Preamble Index/Sub channel Index, PHY Profile ID, FA Index, BS EIRP. Scheduling Service Support, HO Process Optimization.

2.2. *Scanning Interval Allocation Request (MOB_SCN-REQ) Message*

A MOB_SCN-REQ message may be transmitted by an MS to request a scanning interval for the purpose of seeking available BSs and determining their suitability as targets for HO. An MS may request the scanning allocation to perform scanning or non-contention Association ranging.

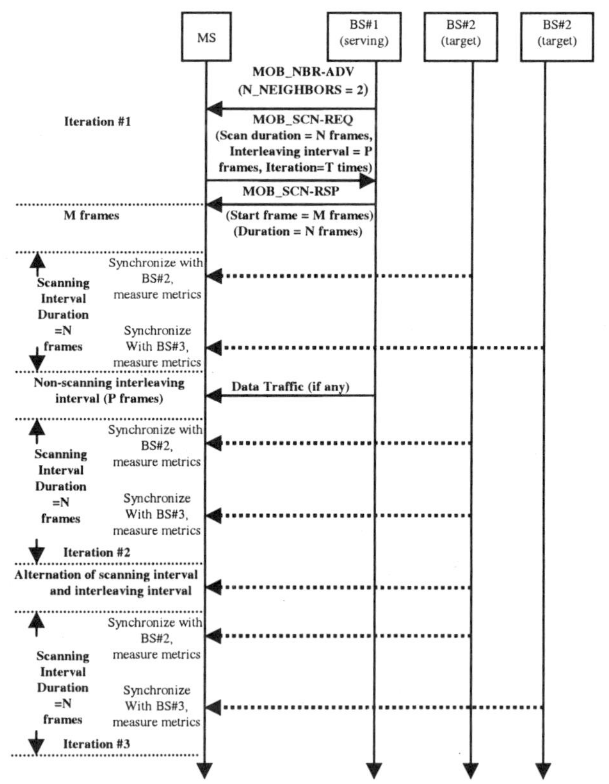

Figure 2. Neighbor BS advertisement and scanning without association by MS request.

Vital parameters of this message are: Scan duration & iteration, Interleaving Interval, N_Recommended_BS_Index, Configuration Change

Count for MOB_NBR-ADV, Neighbor_BS_Index, Scanning type- whether Scanning without or with association; N_Recommended_BS_Full, Recommended BS ID.

2.3. *Scanning Interval Allocation Response (MOB_SCN-RSP) Message*

A MOB_SCN-RSP message is transmitted by the BS either unsolicited or in response to an MOB_SCN-REQ message sent by an MS. A BS may transmit MOB_SCN-RSP to start MS scan reporting with or without scanning allocation. If the Report mode is event-triggered, the MS responds once according to the trigger action specified in the MOB_NBR-ADV or the serving BS DCD. A subsequent MOB_SCN-RSP message may be sent to reset the trigger procedure.

Parameters included in MOB_SCN-RSP message are: Scan duration, Report mode, period and metric containing BS CINR, RSSI; Start Frame, Interleaving interval, Scan iteration, Rendezvous time, CDMA code, Transmission opportunity offset.

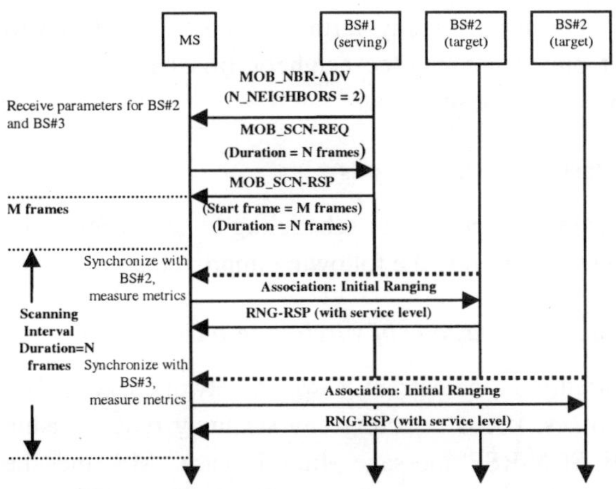

Figure 3. Neighbor BS advertisement and scanning with non-coordinated association by MS request.

3. Shortcoming in Scheduling Process for Scanning in IEEE 802.16e

The IEEE 802.16e standard has the provision of T44 timer for retransmitting scanning request [1]. It has been found as one of the main causes that deteriorates the scheduling process.

According to this standard, when the Trigger action in the DCD message is encoded as 0x3 the trigger condition is met and MS sends the MOB_SCN-REQ message to the BS to begin the neighbor BS scanning process. MS sends the scanning request message repeatedly until serving BS suggests any neighbor BS for scanning. Through the network analysis, it has been observed that MS keeps trying with MOB_SCN-REQ message repeatedly, but the serving BS keeps sending MOB_SCN-RSP suggesting no neighbor BSs for scanning which is not desired at all.

Such repeated exchange of MOB_SCN-REQ and MOB_SCN-RSP messages is obviously a waste of wireless resource. Again, throughput also gets reduced as scanning and data traffic can't take place simultaneously [1]. So, it makes certain degradation in system performance.

The current standard also does not explicitly suggest the beginning of scanning when the signal quality is getting too poor but still serving BS denies the request for scanning.

4. Proposed Scheme

The previous discussion shows that a major waste of resource may be caused by redundancy in attempts to begin scanning and association process of neighbor BSs when the serving BS rejects scanning requests. This can also cause delay in essential scanning and thus, in actual HO. Currently, neighbor BS estimation via CINR measurement prior to scanning request already exists in the proposition [3] [4]. An optional implementation of a Trigger Value and Trigger Averaging Duration in DCD from serving BS is also already in use which suggests MS to request for scanning when the CINR of the serving BS stays below this trigger value for Trigger Averaging Duration. We propose few additional steps in order to avoid redundant attempts to begin scanning as well as expedite beginning of necessary scanning under certain conditions. Thus, the main purpose of the proposal is to reduce wireless channel resource waste and latency in HO decision.

Figure 4 gives a brief overview of our proposed scheme for scanning with MS initiated Hard HO. We propose introduction of a second Trigger Value (Lower Trigger Value) and associated Trigger Averaging Duration in DCD and name the existing Trigger Value as Higher Trigger Value. Regardless of the CINR of the serving BS, MS measures CINR of all BSs in MOB_NBR-ADV message which satisfies QoS requirements. When MS finds that the CINR of the serving BS is in between the Higher Trigger Value and the Lower Trigger Value for Trigger Averaging

Duration associated with Higher Trigger Value, MS selects up to three top neighbor BSs on the basis of their CINR values and sends MOB_SCN-REQ message for scanning of the selected neighbor BSs.

If the serving BS sends MOB_SCN-RSP message suggesting certain neighbor BSs for scanning with or without association, MS will scan Neighbor BSs as per suggestion. Optionally, MS may also scan few neighbor BSs which were not suggested by serving BS. In this case, MS will select neighbor BSs only from what were requested in MOB_SCN-REQ and scan them without association.

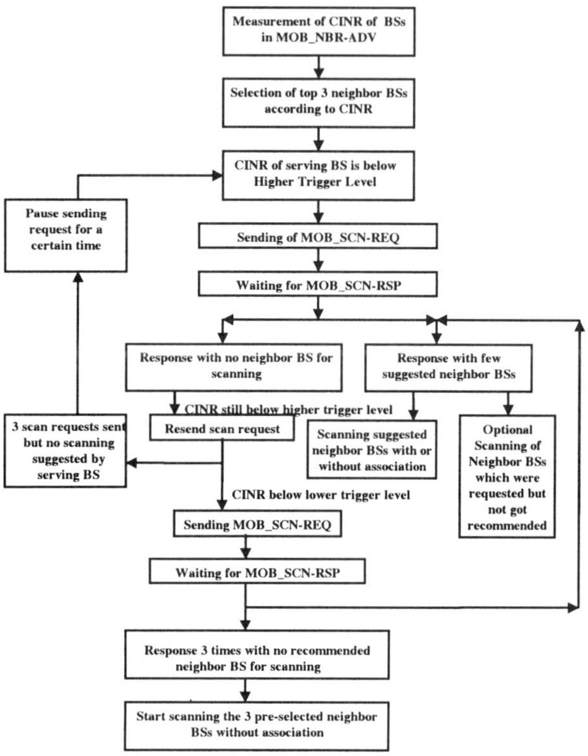

Figure 4. Proposed method for scheduling process of scanning.

However, if the serving BS sends MOB_SCN-RSP suggesting no neighbor BSs for scanning, MS will send MOB_SCN-REQ again. If the serving BS does not again suggest any neighbor BSs for scanning over MOB_SCN-RSP, MS will send MOB_SCN-REQ for the third time. Now, if the serving BS rejects any scanning for the third time, MS will pause sending MOB_SCN-REQ for certain period in order to reduce wireless channel resource waste even if the CINR of serving BS is still found to be below Higher Trigger Value. After waiting for certain period, MS may resume sending MOB_SCN-REQ if the CINR of serving BS is still below Higher Trigger Value.

As long as the CINR of serving BS is found to be in between Higher Trigger Value and Lower Trigger Value, MS will repeat sending MOB_SCN-REQ three times and then pausing if the serving BS keeps rejecting any scanning. The manufacturer of the MS may gradually increase the period for pause with time.

Now, if CINR of the serving BS falls below Lower Trigger Level and stays as such for its associated Trigger Averaging Duration, MS will immediately send MOB_SCN-REQ and check MOB_SCN-RSP from the serving BS. If the serving BS suggests certain neighbor BSs for scanning with or without association in MOB_SCN-RSP, MS will select neighbors BSs and scan them like before. However, if the serving BS suggests no neighbor BSs for scanning over MOB_SCN-RSP, MS will send scanning requests two more times like before. If the serving BS rejects any scanning in these three consecutive attempts, MS will spontaneously trigger 'scanning without association' without waiting for any further events. Here, MS will select only the top three neighbor BSs based on their CINR values for scanning.

5. Performance Analysis

Our proposed scheme for scheduling of scanning can be expected to provide the following improvement.

5.1. *Stopping wastage of wireless resources*

Reportedly, in the current WiMAX network serving BS, sometimes, keeps rejecting any scanning request using MOB_SCN-RSP message. In this case, MS and the serving BS keep exchange MOB_SCN-REQ and MOB_SCN-RSP messages repeatedly with no benefit. Such unnecessary exchange of messages takes place numerous times. This is an evident wastage of wireless resources. In our proposal, MS pauses sending MOB_SCN-REQ message when it finds that the serving BS will most likely reject the scanning request. MS may also gradually increase the pause period in subsequent attempts with additional saving of wireless resources.

5.2. *Justified wait time as scanning requests rejected repeatedly*

According to our proposal, when the serving BS keeps rejecting scanning requests, MS does not keep sending them indefinitely. Rather, after certain attempts, MS initiates either a pause or scanning depending on the situation. Our proposal includes a justified number of attempts for MS to wait here. In both the cases, when CINR of serving BS is in between Higher Trigger Value and Lower Trigger Value and when it is lower than Lower Trigger Value; MS sends MOB_SCN-REQ message exactly three times if serving BS keeps suggesting no neighbor BSs for scanning. These three attempts allow the provision that serving BS may like to check on the continuity of the changed CINR level of serving BS before suggesting neighbor BSs for scanning. On the other hand, consecutive three MOB_SCN-RSP messages suggesting no neighbor BSs can be enough to indicate that serving BS is disinclined to suggest any neighbor BSs for scanning.

5.3. *Scanning confirmed before losing service*

When the CINR of the serving BS becomes too poor, MS may soon go out of service and so an attempt for handover is very much expected then. However, if the serving BS does not realize this dire need of MS, it might still suggest no neighbor BSs for scanning. Our proposal introduces Lower Trigger Level which allows MS to begin scanning in this situation. MS, after getting denied three times by the serving BS, will spontaneously begin scanning. This can actually expedite the decision for handover and help avoid radio link failure as well.

5.4. *Scanning scheduled only when necessary*

MS performs scanning only under certain conditions which are deemed to substantiate its necessity. Scanning can take place when either CINR of the serving BS is in between Higher Trigger Value and Lower Trigger Value and serving BS suggests neighbor BSs for scanning. Also, it can take place when CINR of serving BS goes below Lower Trigger Value. However, scanning will not take place if these conditions are not met. An appropriate setting of values for Higher Trigger Value and Lower Trigger Value can ensure that scanning is justified only under these conditions. This can save unnecessary time allocation and MS power consumption

5.5. *Scanning scheduled only for potential BSs*

MS scans neighbor BSs which the serving BS suggests using MOB_SCN-RSP message. MS may optionally scan neighbor BSs which have been requested using MOB_SCN-REQ message as potential candidates for handover. Also, when CINR of the serving BS falls below Lower Trigger Level but it suggests no neighbor BS for consecutive three times, MS selects only the top three neighbor BSs based on their CINR values for scanning. Thus, it has always been ensured that MS scans only the potential neighbor BSs.

6. Conclusion

Handover is obviously a vital factor in IEEE 802.16e mobile WiMAX network. In this paper an optimized HHO scheme is proposed with a modified scan scheduling. Method proposed here consisted of two trigger levels in DCD in terms of CINR value to reduce unnecessary scanning and quicken the initiation of justified scanning. Starting with MAC layer handover process in mobile WiMAX along with the related major MAC management messages; this paper gives the vivid idea of a probable problematic scenario of the scheduling process of scanning. It also provides the proposed solution scheme with performance analysis verifying the efficacy. In fine, the proposed scheme if properly implemented should enhance the overall performance radically solving the obstacles mentioned.

References

1. IEEE STD 802.16e-2005. "IEEE Standard for Local Metropolitan Area Networks- Part 16: Air Interface for Fixed and Mobile Broadband Wireless Access Systems", 28 February 2006.
2. IEEE STD 802.16-2004, "Air Interface for Fixed Broadband Wireless Access Systems", October 2004.
3. Lee D.H., Kyamekya K., Umondi J.P., "Fast Handover Algorithm for IEEE 802.16e Broadband Wireless Access System", ISWPC 2006.
4. Wang L., Liu F., Ji Y., "Performance Analysis of Fast Handover Schemes in IEEE 802.16e Broadband Wireless Networks", Asia Pacific Advanced Network, Network Research Workshop, August 2007, China.
5. Choi S., "Fast Handover Scheme for Real-time Downlink Services in IEEE 802.16e BWA Systems", Proc. of IEEE 61st Vehicular Technology Conference, 2005
6. WiMAX Forum White Paper- www.wimaxforum.org
7. Becvar Z., Zelenka J., "Implementation of Handover Delay Timer into WiMAX", 6th Conference on Telecommunication. Peniche, Portugal, 2007.

IMPROVING TCP PERFORMANCE WITH SELECTIVE NEGATIVE ACKNOWLEDGEMENT IN HYBRID OPTICAL PACKET NETWORK*

YONGMAO REN * +, HAINA TANG *, JUN LI *, HUALIN QIAN *

* *Computer Network Information Center, Chinese Academy of Sciences*

+ *Graduate University of Chinese Academy of Sciences*

Beijing, 100190, China

The Hybrid Optical Packet Network (HOPnet) is a kind of high-speed network with the development of optical network. The traditional TCP transport protocol performs poorly in this kind of environment. This paper investigates the characters of HOPnet and the issues of TCP performance over HOPnet. A negative acknowledgement scheme, namely selective negative acknowledgement (SNACK), is applied to TCP over HOPnet and a series of NS-2 simulations are performed to compare its performance with the standard TCP. The simulation results confirm that the SNACK scheme outperforms the conventional TCP scheme in HOPnet.

1. Introduction

As the massive data generated in large scale science grid applications such as high energy physics and astronomical observation needs to be transported between many research centers distributed all over the world for analysis and handling, high speed network and high performance transport protocol are needed. However, it's difficult for the traditional IP packet network to satisfy this requirement because of its bandwidth limit. As the fast development of optical network that has obvious advantage of high bandwidth and high QoS guarantee, combined with traditional IP packet network, hybrid optical packet network (HOPnet) emerged.

The GLORIAD (Global Ring Network for Advanced Applications Development) [1] network is a typical hybrid optical packet network. In the practical applications and network measurements based on GLORIAD, the authors discovered that using TCP protocol for transmission, there is bottleneck at the bandwidth utility (less than 70% of available bandwidth). Through theoretic analysis and practical measurement, the authors find the conventional TCP scheme has drawbacks over HOPnet because of its error and congestion detection method and congestion control mechanism.

The TCP performance issues exist in many kinds of network environment, such as satellite network, ATM network, high speed network, wireless network and sensor network. So, it's a very hot research topic, and many TCP variants have been proposed for using TCP in these networks. And, much work has been done for improving TCP performance over high speed network [2], but little particularly for HOPnet.

This study aims to enhance the TCP performance over HOPnet. By investigating the problems of TCP over HOPnet, the authors propose using SNACK option to improve TCP performance and have evaluated its performance by NS-2 [3] simulation. The simulation results confirm that the SNACK scheme outperforms the conventional TCP scheme over HOPnet.

2. HOPnet Background

As the requirement of applications especially the large scale E-science applications such as high energy physics for the network infrastructure has become higher and higher, it's becoming more and more difficult for the traditional IP packet switched network to satisfy this requirement [4]. It is generally believed that the next generation Internet must have high speed and high performance. Compared to IP packet switched network, the optical circuited switched network have obvious advantages such as high speed and high QoS guarantee. So, a hybrid of packet and circuit switched network, which combines them into a coherent and scalable architecture for next generation networks, has emerged and is becoming more and more popular.

There are many HOPnets all over the world. For example, the HOPI (Hybrid Optical and Packet Infrastructure) project [5] supported by Internet2 in America is a large testbed for examining a hybrid of packet and circuit switched infrastructure to satisfy extreme requirement of large scale science applications. The CHEETAH [6] and UltraScience [7] Net are

* This work was supported in part by the National Ministry of Science and Technology of China for International Cooperation and Communications Project under Grant No. 2006DFA11990 and the Knowledge Innovation Program of Chinese Academy of Sciences under Grant No.0814061101.

another two large hybrid networks in America. The GEANT2 [8] pan-European research and education network will be a hybrid optical and packet switched network. And the GLORIAD formerly mentioned is a typical hybrid network around the north earth. Additionally, KREONet2 [9] is an advanced hybrid network in Korea.

The architecture of HOPnet combines the optical circuit switched infrastructure and the IP packet switched infrastructure. The optical layer consists of optical switches nodes or SONET/SDH ADMs nodes and raw lambdas paths or SONET/SDH channels, which can provide end-to-end "lightpaths" with dedicated bandwidth. And the packet layer consists of Ethernet switches or IP routers nodes, VLAN paths or MPLS L2 VPN tunnels which might also have dedicated bandwidth, and common route paths. Usually, the traffics are firstly converged by router before entering into the high speed lightpath.

Compared to the traditional IP network, the hybrid network has particular characters. First, it has high bandwidth, usually 1Gbps (OC-24), or 2.5Gbps (OC-48), 10Gbps (OC-192), and even 40Gbps (OC-768). Second, it has high delay. Because the e-science grid applications usually need cooperation distributed all over the world, the hybrid network infrastructure covers many countries with extreme long distance link. For example, in GLORIAD, the round trip delay (RTT) from Beijing to Netherland is about 340ms while RTT in common LAN is less than 1ms. In addition, it still has packet loss, which may come from the IP access network, some security devices and some management devices like rate control devices.

3. Performance Issues of TCP over HOPnet

The TCP protocol is suitable for low speed and low delay network environment such as Ethernet LAN. But its performance is not good in many kinds of network environment, such as satellite network, ATM network, high speed network, wireless network and sensor network. When using TCP over HOPnet, there are some problems as follows:

Firstly, TCP can't differentiate congestion and error. It relies on RTO timeout and duplicate ACKs to detect packet loss resulted by error or congestion. If the packet loss is resulted by error, TCP will think it as congestion, and reduce its congestion window drastically, which is unnecessary and result in a long time to recover since the delay is large in long distance optical network. Moreover, the RTO value relies on RTT estimation. However, for HOPnet, the RTT value varies largely.

Secondly, the conventional TCP AIMD (*Additive Increase Multiplicative Decrease*) congestion control scheme is too slow in HOPnet. Once TCP enters into the *slow-start* and *congestion avoidance* process, it needs a long time to recover to large congestion window. Moreover, the BDP (*Bandwidth Delay Product*) of HOPnet is extremely large, but the TCP window size is limited and less than the BDP value.

In conclusion, as the traditional TCP's error control and congestion control mechanism is not suitable for HOPnet, the TCP transmission performance is not good. The authors have studied these problems deeply by theoretical and experimental analysis in another paper [10]. Up to now, most enhanced TCP variants for high speed network focus on congestion control, while this paper focuses on error control. For this point, a SNACK scheme is proposed.

4. SNACK Scheme

Some options have already been proposed to solve the TCP performance issues over satellite network or wireless network, such as NAK (*Negative Acknowledgement*) option [11] and SACK (*Selective Acknowledgement*) option [12]. Before describing SNACK, a brief introduction on NAK and SACK is given.

4.1. *NAK*

The NAK option was originally proposed for satellite network. NAK is a negative acknowledgement, which means it tells the TCP sender which packet has not been received. With NAK, TCP sender will know which sent packet has been lost exactly without needing to wait for duplicate ACKs. And, then, it can only retransmit the lost packet immediately. NAK can differentiate loss from congestion by using negative acknowledgement to indicate loss and RTO timeout to indicate congestion. This advantage is especially useful for using TCP over error-prone link like satellite link and wireless link.

The drawback of NAK is that it can only indicate a single hole in the sequence space buffered by the receiver, while, in the HOPnet, there are fewer opportunities to send ACKs since the delay is very high. So, it's not efficient that one ACK only indicates one hole.

4.2. *SACK*

SACK option was motivated through work in high speed network. SACK is a kind of positive acknowledgement, which allows the receiver to specify exactly which data has been received. After receiving the SACK, the TCP sender will know which data have been lost from the gap of sequence space. Like NAK, with SACK, TCP sender will know exactly which segments to retransmit without waiting for a long time. SACK can specify three blocks at a time [13], which is better than NAK, but it's still not bit-efficient for large window size in HOPnet. Another problem is that SACK relies on Fast Retransmit algorithm to detect loss and trigger retransmission, which needs four duplicated ACKs. However, in hybrid network, because the RTT delay is very large, before receiving so many duplicated ACKs, if the RTO timer expires, Fast Retransmit will be triggered and the SACK information will be cleared.

4.3. *SNACK*

By integrating the respective capabilities of NAK and SACK, a novel transport layer acknowledgement scheme named SNACK (*Selective Negative Acknowledgement*) is proposed [13][14]. Like NAK, SNACK is a negative acknowledgement, but it can specify a large number of holes in a bit-efficient way. The SNACK option format is as Fig. 1 shows.

0		16 31
Kind	Length	Hole 1 Offset
Hole 1 Length		Bit Vector
Bit Vector (Variable Length)...		

Fig. 1 SNACK Option Format

The *Hole 1 Offset* field specifies the starting location of the first hole that is being indicated by this SNACK option and the *Hole 1 Length* field specifies the size of the first hole. Both the offset and length values are expressed as the number of MSS (Maximum Segment Size) units. The *Bit Vector* then specifies following blocks after the first hole. Each "0" in the *bit-vector* indicates there are missing data in the corresponding MSS-sized block of the receiver's queue (namely "hole"). The *Bit Vector* field can signal more additional holes and its length is variable and determined from the option length.

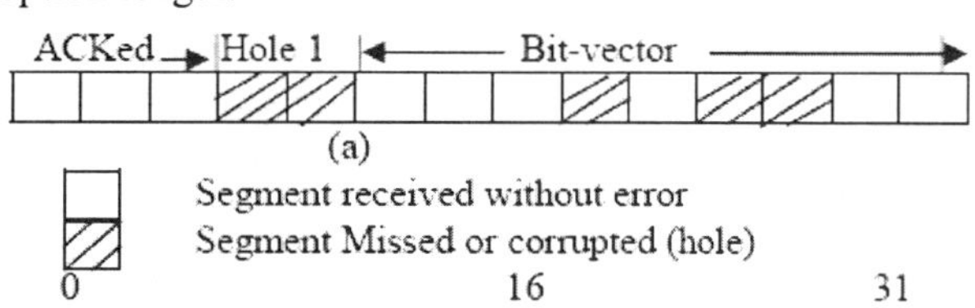

0		16 31
Kind	Length = 8	Hole 1 Offset = 0
Hole 1 size = 2		11101001 1111 0111

(b)

Fig. 2 SNACK example: (a) Receiver buffer, (b) SNACK option

Fig.2 gives an example. Fig. 2(a) illustrates a hypothetical sequence queue at the receiver's buffer. Fig.2 (b) illustrates the corresponding SNACK option. There are two bad blocks in the first hole, and then the bit-vector indicates the successive blocks including four bad blocks.

Compared to NAK and SACK, SNACK is more bit efficient. Moreover, because SNACK option triggers a retransmission, there is no dependence on the Fast Retransmit to detect loss, which avoids the drawback of SACK, and it's especially suitable for high speed and high delay HOPnet.

5. Performance Evaluation

To evaluate the performance of using SNACK over HOPnet, a series of simulations are made to compare the performance between SNACK and standard TCP. The simulations are performed on the well-known network simulation platform NS2 in Linux. Fig. 3 illustrates the simulation topology, which is a typical link of HOPnet. In this topology, the backbone link is a high speed long distance link between two optical devices (typically MSTP devices used in GLORIAD). At each access end, the terminal (may be observing equipment or server in real e-science application) connects to the switch which connects to the optical device through Gigabit Ethernet link. The bottleneck bandwidth is 1Gbps, and the round trip delay is set as 300ms. The packet loss module adopts NS2's Uniform ErrorModel and the default bit error rate for the whole link loss is 1e-7, which simulates all the packet losses resulted by all kinds of reasons in the whole end-to-end link. (Namely, the bit error rate is used to simulate the packet loss rate.) The packet size is 1000B and each simulation time is 1000s.

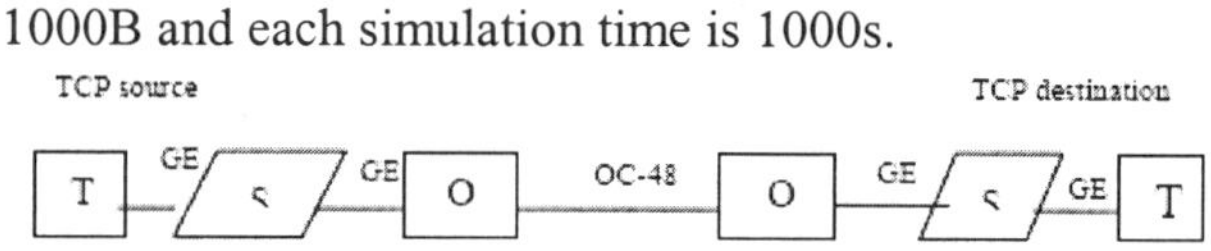

Fig. 3 Simulation topology

Fig. 4 illustrates the throughput changes verse time. The heavy line with diamond point means the throughput of SNACK TCP, and the other is standard TCP. From this figure, it can be found that the traffic of SNACK TCP is obviously higher and much smoother than the standard TCP. The total throughput of SNACK TCP is about 121% than standard TCP.

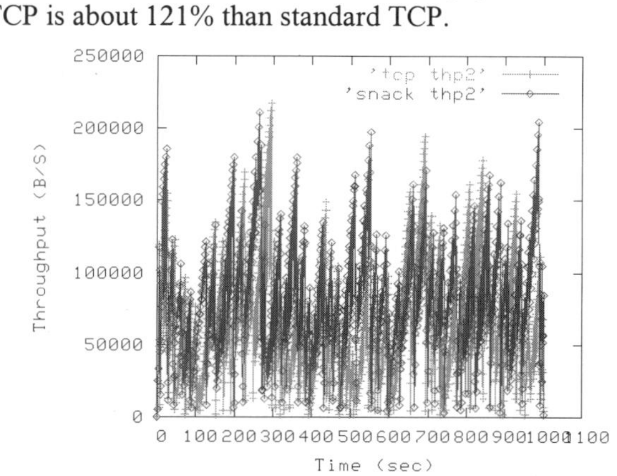

Fig. 4 Throughput changes

The change of traffic throughput is mainly resulted from the change of congestion window size. To study more deeply, the authors further investigated the change of congestion window size. Fig. 5 illustrates the changes of congestion window size.

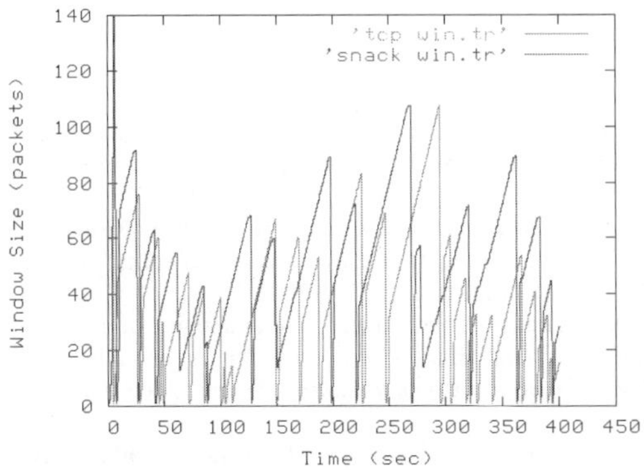

Fig. 5 Window size changes

From Fig. 5, it can be found that the congestion window size change of standard TCP (the thin line) is much more frequent than SNACK (the heavy line). Because when there is error happened in the link, using standard TCP (Tahoe TCP), the sender will get duplicated ACKs or RTO timeout, and it will change the congestion window size to initial value (1 segment) and start the *Slow Start* and *Congestion Avoidance* process, which is not necessary for loss resulted from non-congestion. Using SNACK, the sender can know exactly which data needed to be retransmitted. It doesn't depend on Fast Transmit algorithm to detect loss. There are no more duplicated ACKs. So, the congestion window size doesn't need to change correspondingly. It only resets when the RTO timeout has happened. So, SNACK avoids unnecessary frequent changing of the congestion control and keeps smooth traffic.

Using SNACK, TCP sender can differentiate loss from congestion, which is useful when packet loss occurs in the link resulted by non-congestion reasons. Fig. 6 illustrates the throughputs under different bit-error rate conditions. The simulation result indicates that

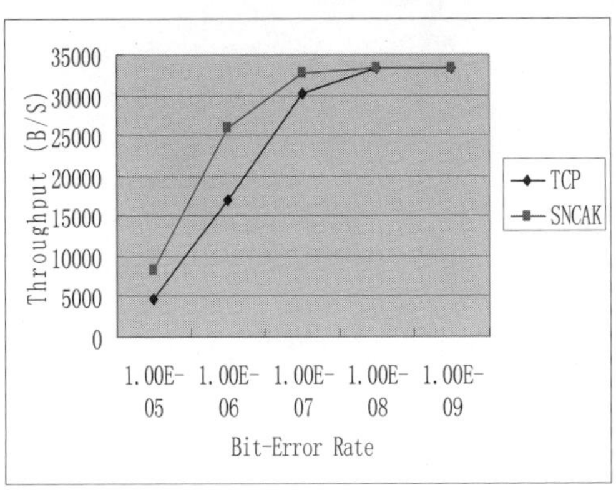

Fig. 6 Effect of error on throughput

SNACK has higher throughput than standard TCP, especially when the packet loss rate is high.

In conclusion, the simulation result verifies that SNACK TCP can reduce unnecessary *Slow Start* and *Congestion Avoidance* process and has higher and smoother throughput than the standard TCP.

6. Related Work

There are some TCP variants for high speed network and some work on SNACK in satellite and wireless networks.

6.1. *TCP Variants for High Speed Network*

A number of TCP variants have been proposed for high speed network. The enhancing methods can be roughly divided into two categories:

(1) Modifying AIMD congestion control algorithm. A number of improved algorithms have been proposed, such as High Speed TCP (HSTCP) [15] and Binary Increase Congestion TCP (BICTCP) [16]. HSTCP adopts more aggressive way to increase and slowly way to decrease congestion window size. And BICTCP uses a particular congestion window size increasing function.

(2) Modifying congestion detection and notification scheme. For instance, FAST TCP [17] uses increasing RTT as a measure of congestion instead of packet loss and defines the congestion window size to be a function of the measured RTT. eXplicit Control Protocol (XCP) [18] adds a congestion header into packet. The sender writes current congestion window size and RTT into the header for router to compute available bandwidth, and router writes computed throughput feedback information into the header for sender to adjust congestion window size. And Variable-structure congestion Control Protocol (VCP) [19] uses ECN [20] field of IP header to notify congestion status (link utilization).

Simulation results indicate that many of these TCP variants improve TCP performance over high speed network at some aspects, but they usually bring forward new problems [21] at the same time. And, these protocols mainly focus on congestion control with none or little consideration on error control. Moreover, they are mainly proposed for high speed network rather than for HOPnet.

6.2. *SNACK over Satellite and Wireless Network*

As mentioned above, SNACK also uses the way of modifying congestion detection and notification scheme to improve TCP performance.

SNACK is firstly proposed for satellite network. The stand TCP transfer performance is poor in satellite network, because the RTT delay is large and error rate is also high. SNACK is efficient in this kind of environment. Some research and simulation results indicate that SNACK can improve TCP performance over satellite obviously [13] [22] [23]. Some researchers also apply SNACK into wireless network [24] [25] [26].

This paper differs from other TCP variants for that it focuses on error control instead of congestion control. And as far as the authors know, it's the first time to adopt SNACK scheme in hybrid optical packet network.

7. Conclusion

This study has proposed adopting the selective negative acknowledgement (SNACK) scheme to improve the performance of TCP over HOPnet. By integrating the respective capabilities of NAK and SACK, SNACK uses selective negative acknowledgement mechanism, which is efficient for TCP sender to retransmit data and avoid unnecessary congestion response. The simulation results verify that using SNACK can increase throughput significantly in HOPnet.

References

1. GLORIAD (Global Ring Network for Advanced Applications Development), [Online]. Available: http://www.gloriad.org/
2. Huang Xiao-Meng, Lin Chuang, Ren Feng-Yuan. "Recent Development of High Speed Transport Protocols," *Chinese Journal of Computers*,2006,29(11):1901–1908 (in Chinese with English abstract)
3. Network Simulator, NS-2, [Online]. Available: http://www.isi.edu/nsnam/ns/
4. REN YM, TANG HN, LI J, QIAN HL. "Optical network control and management for grid applications," *Journal of Software*, 2008, 19(6):1481-1490 (in Chinese with English abstract).
5. HOPI, Hybrid Optical Packet Infrastructure, [Online]. Available: http://networks.internet2.edu/hopi/
6. Zheng X, Veeraraghavan M, Rao NSV, Wu Q, Zhu M, "CHEETAH: Circuit-switched High-speed End-to-End Transport ArcHitecture testbed.," *IEEE Communication Magazine*, 2005, 43(8): s11–s17.
7. Rao NSV, Wing WR, Carter SM, Wu Q., "Ultrascience net: network testbed for large-scale science applications," *IEEE Communications Magazine*, 2005, 43(11):s12-s17.
8. GEANT2, [Online]. Available: http://www.geant2.net/
9. Dongkyun Kim, "The Hybrid Network Initiative in Korea : KREONet2," presented at the 7th Annual LambdaGrid Workshop in Prague, Czech Republic, 2007
10. REN Yong-Mao, QIN Gang, TANG Hai-Na, LI, Jun, QIAN Hua-Lin, "Transport Protocol Performance Analysis over Fast Long Distance Optical Network," *Chinese Journal of Computers,*2008, 31(10):1679-1686 (in Chinese with English abstract)
11. R. Fox, "TCP Big Window and Nak Options," RFC 1106, June 1989
12. M. Mathis, J. Mahdavi, S. Floyd, and A. Romanow, "TCP Selective Acknowledgement Options," RFC2018, October 1996
13. Robert C. Durst, Gregory J. Miller, and Eric J. Travis, "TCP Extension for Space Communications," in *Proc. ACM MOBICOM'96*, Nov. 1996, pp.15-26.
14. SCPS Transport Protocol (SCPS-TP), [Online] Available: http://www.scps.org/scps/
15. Floyd S, "High Speed TCP for Large Congestion Windows," IETF RFC 3649, December 2003
16. Xu L, Harfoush K, Rhee I, "Binary Increase Congestion Control for Fast Long-Distance Networks," in *Proc IEEE INFOCOM*, Hong Kong, 2004
17. Jin C, Wei D X, Low S H, "FAST TCP: motivation, architecture, algorithms, performance," in *Proc. IEEE INFOCOM*, Hong Kong, 2004
18. Dina Katabi, Mark Handley, Chalrie Rohrs, "Congestion Control for High Bandwidth-Delay Product Networks," in *Proc. ACM SIGCOMM*, Pittsburgh, USA, 2002
19. Yong Xia. Lakshminarayanan Subramanian, Ion Stoica. Shivkumar Kalyanaraman, "One more bit is enough," *ACM SIGCOMM Computer Communication Review*, 2005, vol.35, no. 4, pp. 37-48
20. Ramakrishnan K. K., Floyd S., "Proposal to add explicit congestion notification (ECN) to IP," RFC 2481, 1999
21. REN Yong-Mao, TANG Hai-Na, LI, Jun, QIAN Hua-Lin, "Performance Comparison of TCP Variants for High-speed Network Based on NS2," *Computer Engineering*, 2009, 35(2):6-9. (in Chinese with English abstract)
22. Wang Ru-Hai, "A novel acknowledgement scheme for space Internet," in *Proc. 2004 IEEE Vehicular Technology Conference* (VTC-2004/Fall), Los Angeles, 2004, pp. 4061-4065
23. ZHANG Run-Tong, FAN Ning, ZHANG Wei-Jun, "An Experimental Study of the Performance of SNACKTCP in the LEO Satellite Networks," Chinese Journal of Computers, vol. 30, No. 2, pp. 298-304
24. R. S Cheng and H. T. Lin, "TCP selective negative acknowledgment over IEEE 802.11 wireless networks," in *Proc. ICNS2006*, (Silicon Valley, USA), July 2006
25. Rung-Shiang Cheng, Hui-Tang Lin, "Improving TCP Performance with Bandwidth Estimation and Selective Negative Acknowledgment in Wireless Networks," *Journal of Communications and Networks* , vol. 9, no. 3, pp. 236-246, September 2007
26. Fanglei, Sun, Victor O. K. Li, Soung C. Liew, "Design of SNACK Mechanism for Wireless TCP with New Snoop", in *Proc. IEEE WCNC 2004*, Atlant, pp. 1051-1056

Session 4

Behavioral analysis of reactive MANET routing protocol for streaming multimedia applications

A Valarmathi
Department of Computer Applications
Anna University Tiruchirappalli
Tiruchirappalli -620 024, India
valar1030@yahoo.com

RM Chandrasekaran
Department of Computer Science and Engineering
Anna University Tiruchirappalli
Tiruchirappalli-620 024, India
rmc@sify.com

Abstract- ***The dynamic topological change in mobile ad hoc networks hinders the possibility of predicting the behavior under different communication and data transfer requirements. In this paper, a detailed analysis and interpretation was made by simulating the network with DSR protocol, specifically for streaming multimedia applications, under different scenarios set by varying the pause time, workload and data rate. The effect of these variables is evaluated in terms of average throughput, average end-to-end delay and average jitter. It is evident from the analysis that the performance of the DSR protocol is superior under medium mobility compared to high and low mobility scenarios. The influence of workload and data rate on the performance metrics under low, medium and high mobility scenarios were also discussed.***

key words: MANET; DSR; throughput; end-to-end delay, jitter, mobility, multimedia.

I. INTRODUCTION

A mobile ad hoc network (MANET) is one among the computer networks that consists of mobile nodes which establishes connectivity via multi hop communication [1]. The mobile nodes in MANET are free to move, enter and exit in a random manner, resulting in unpredictable change in network topology. This change in network topology must be adapted by the routing protocols, which also need to be reliable and efficient [2]. There are two main categories of routing protocols commonly used in MANET environment, namely, proactive and reactive.

Proactive (or) table-driven routing algorithms employ distance vector based or link state based routing strategies. In these protocols, each node in the network maintains an up to date routing table that reflects topological map, indicating a route to every other node in the network. This is best suited for network topologies when routing to a large number of destinations. However, the main drawback of these algorithms is that the need for frequent table updation consumes significant amount of memory, bandwidth and battery power [3]. Example of such protocols is Optimized Link State Routing (OLSR) [4] and Destination Sequenced Distance Vector routing (DSDV) [5]. In reactive routing protocols, a node searches and maintains a route to another node only when it requires transmitting data to that particular node. This on-demand reactive approach minimizes bandwidth utilization compared to proactive routing protocols. Ad-hoc On-Demand Distance Vector (AODV) [6], Dynamic Source Routing (DSR) [7], Temporally Ordered Routing Algorithm (TORA) [8] and Associatively-Based Routing (ABR) [9] are examples of such protocols. Among these, DSR is a simple and efficient routing protocol which is widely used in MANET. It operates based on two mechanisms such as route discovery and route maintenance. These two functions allow nodes to discover and maintain routes to arbitrary destinations in the network. The DSR protocol initiates a process of route discovery when a mobile node intends to transmit data to a destination node. At this instance, the source node transmits a route request (RREQ) message. Nodes within the transmission range which receive the RREQ will issue a route reply (RREP) message, provided an existing route should present in their caches. If there is no existing route exists, the nodes that received the RREQ attach itself to the end of the message and forward the RREQ message to other possible nodes till the destination is reached. Once the RREQ reaches the desired destination, a RREP message is broadcasted back to the originator of the RREQ. This RREP message ensures a usable and valid path from source to destination. Once the source node discovered the optimum path, the complete path detail is placed in the header of each packet to be transmitted. This will be further processed by each intermediate node until the packet reaches its destination.

In recent years, the use of wireless networks for streaming multimedia applications is significantly increased due to the advancement in video compression and transmission technologies. This would increase the traffic load and influence throughput, delay and packet loss in a wireless ad hoc network. Considering this fact, in the present investigation, a random MANET environment with DSR protocol is created and simulated using NS-2 by varying pause time, data rate and workload. The performance of the network was evaluated in terms of average throughput, average end to end delay and average jitter.

II. SIMULATION MODEL

A. *Simulation Tool and Setup*

NS-2 simulator was used to analyze the network performance under different scenarios. It is a discrete event simulator for networking research in which packet level analysis is employed [10]. It supports and closely resembles OSI model which was developed using C++ and Tcl. It also provides substantial support for simulation of routing protocols over MANET. The Network Animator Tool (NAM), a part of NS-2, was used to visualize, troubleshoot and verify the outcomes of simulation scenarios. The scenarios were established using tcl programming. The CBR multimedia traffic flows and movement patterns were randomly created using cbrgen.tcl and setdest.exe which are available as NS-2 utilities. The cbrgen.tcl includes number of mobile nodes, seed, maximum number of CBR connections and data rate. The pause time, maximum speed, simulation time and topology are defined in setdest.exe. These utilities create text files for repeatable use and testing. It also contains random CBR multimedia streams and connections, which are referenced within the tcl files. Random Waypoint model was used in the simulation [11]. In this model, a mobile node chooses a random destination and moves at a maximum velocity of 10 m/s. Once it reaches the destination, the node is idle for the duration corresponds to the set pause time. At the end of the pause time, it chooses another random destination and the process is repeated till the simulation ends.

B. *Simulation Scenarios*

The parameters set for simulation is listed in Table-I. This simulation incorporates IEEE 802.11b with two-ray ground radio model.

TABLE I. SIMULATION PARAMETERS

Parameter	Value
Toplogy Size	670m x 670m
Number of nodes	15
Simulation time	300s
Traffic type	CBR
Packet Size	512 bytes
Routing protocol	DSR

The pause time, data rate and workload are varied at three levels as shown in Table-II.

TABLE II. SIMULATION VARIABLES

Simulation Variables	Levels		
	Low	*Medium*	*High*
Pause Time (s)	10	100	150
Workload (CBR)	4	8	12
Data rate (PPS)	10	100	200

The scenarios were set by varying pause time, workload and data rate. In figures, the scenarios are named 1 to 27 with a combination pattern of pause time-workload-data rate. The 27 scenarios are: 150-4-10, 150-4-100, 150-4-200, 150-8-10, 150-8-100, 150-8-200, 150-12-10, 150-12-100, 150-12-200, 100-4-10, 100-4-100, 100-4-200, 100-8-10, 100-8-100, 100-8-200, 100-12-10, 100-12-100, 100-12-200, 10-4-10, 10-4-100, 10-4-200, 10-8-10, 10-8-100, 10-8-200, 10-12-10, 10-12-100, 10-12-200.

C. *Performance metrics*

To evaluate the performance of the network under different mobility, workload and data rate, the following performance metrics were used.

C.1 Average Throughput

The average throughput is calculated using the ratio of total number of processed data packets to the total simulation time.

C.2 Average End-to-End Delay

The average end-to-end delay is a measure of average time taken to transmit each packet of data from the source to the destination. A congested network is indicated by higher end-to-end delays.

C.3 Average Jitter

Jitter is a measure of variation in delay across multiple packets associated with a given traffic flow. This metric is important for streaming multimedia applications where small and limited amount of jitter is tolerable.

These performance metrics were derived with the help of awk scripts, using the data extracted from the trace files generated during a particular simulation. The output of the awk scripts are text based data which are used to provide statistical and graphical results.

III. PERFORMANCE ANALYSIS

A. *Average Throughput*

The average throughput measured for different scenarios is shown in Figure 1. The average throughputs were lower and almost same for 10 PPS data rate irrespective of the mobility and workload. Under low mobility, the average maximum throughput was 409 Kbps for 4 CBR flow and 100 PPS data rate. An increase in data rate to 200 PPS leads to slight reduction in average throughput of 386 Kbps. Since DSR uses already cached routes when the mobility is low, the reduced throughput could primarily be attributed to the increase in data rate. Under medium mobility of 100s pause time, average maximum throughputs vary between 798 to 820 Kbps at 200 PPS, irrespective of the workload. When mobility increases, the possibility of alternate routes to destination also increases. This may result in better alternative multi hop paths than at low mobility. In high mobility scenarios, the measured average throughput reflects a completely different phenomenon.

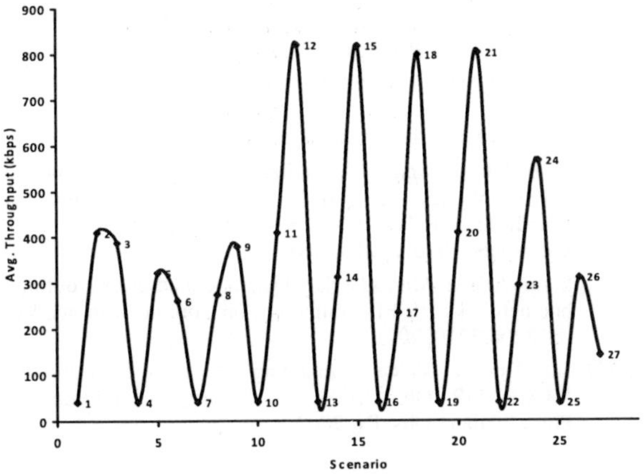

Figure 1. Average throughput at different scenarios.

At workloads of 4 and 8 CBR, an increase in data rate leads to an increase in average throughput. However, at a workload of 12 CBR, highest average throughput was recorded at 100 PPS and the average throughput reduced drastically at 200 PPS. The number of route reconstruction process could be large in high mobility scenarios due to the frequent possibility of route breakage [12]. In this situation, when a source sends a RREQ, many intermediate nodes flood RREP back to the source to restore broken route. This may substantially increase routing overhead and cause poor throughput levels in a combination of high workload and high data rate.

B. Average end-to-end delay

The average end-to-end delay measurements for each scenario are shown in Figure 2.

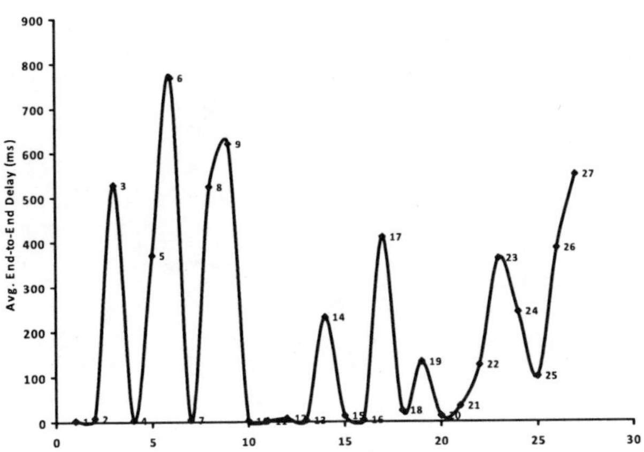

Figure 2. Average end-to-end delay at different scenarios.

When mobility is low, maximum delays were observed at higher data rate of 200 PPS, irrespective of workloads. Under medium mobility scenario, the network behaves exceptionally better with minimum delays at lower workload of 4 CBR with all set data rates of 10, 100 and 200 PPS. As the workload increases, the delay also increases independent to data rate. In high mobility scenarios, the influence of workload on average end-to-end delay is significant compared to data rate. However, in combinations of 10-12-10, 10-12-100 and 10-12-200, the delay increases linearly with respect to both workload and data rate.

C. Average Jitter

Excessive jitter normally caused by unavailable data which may lead to discontinuity in streaming of multimedia applications [13]. The computed average jitter values for different scenarios are shown in Figure 3. In low and medium mobility scenarios, the average jitter behaves similar to average end-to-end delay pattern. During high mobility, maximum jitter levels are experienced at work loads of 4, 8 and 12 CBR flows with data rate at a constant value of 10 PPS. This clearly indicates the dominance of workload on average jitter compared to the influence of data rate.

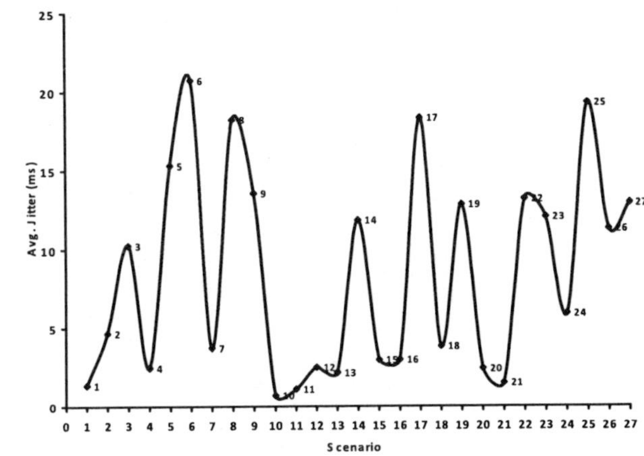

Figure 3. Average jitter at different scenarios.

IV. CONCLUSION

The performance of the MANET was simulated using NS-2 under different scenarios and evaluated using performance metrics such as average throughput, average end-to-end delay and average jitter. Based on the analysis, the following conclusion was made.

When mobility was low, data rate primarily influencing average throughput and average end-to-end delay than workload. The DSR protocol performs better under medium mobility even at higher data rates irrespective of the workload. As mobility increases, both workload and data rate have significant influence on average throughput. However, the workload has substantial effect on average end-to-end delay and average jitter compared to data rate.

REFERENCES

[1] C. Perkins, Ad Hoc Networking, Addison Wesley, 2001.

[2] E. M. Royer and C. -K. Toh, "A Review of current routing protocols for ad hoc mobile networks", IEEE Personal Communications, Vol. 6, pp.46-55, April 1999.

[3] J. Macker, M. Corson and V. Park, "Mobile and wireless internet services: Putting the pieces together", IEEE Communications Magazine, Vol. 36, pp. 146-155, 2001.

[4] T. Clausen and P. Jacquet, "Optimized link state routing protocol", IETF RFC 3626, network Working Group, October 2003.

[5] C. E. Parkens and P. Bhagwat, "Highly dynamic Desination-Sequenced Distance-Vector Routing (DSDV) for mobile computers", ACM SIGCOMM'94 Conference on Communications Architecures, Protocols and Applications, pp. 234-244, 1994.

[6] C. Perkins, E. Belding-Royer and S. Das, "Ad hoc on-demand Distance Vector Routing", RFC 3561, July 2003.

[7] D. B. Johnson, D. A. Maltz and J. Broch, " DSR- The dynamic source routing protocol for multi hop wireless ad hoc networks", In Ad hoc Network, Chapter 5, C. E. Perkins, Eds. Addison-Wesley, 2001.

[8] V. D. Park and M. S. Corson, "A highly adaptive distributed routing algorithm for mobile wireless netwok", Proceeding of the IEEE INFOCOM, pp. 1405-1413, 1997

[9] C. K. Toh, "A novel distributed routing protocol to support ad-hoc mobile computing", Proceeding of IEEE 15th Annual International Phoenix Conference on Computers and Communication, pp. 480-486, 1996.

[10] The Network Simulator - NS-2. http:/www.isi.edu/nsnam/ns/index. html.

[11] D. B. Johnson and D. A. Maltz, "Dynamic Source Routing and Ad oc Wireless Networks", In Mobile Computing, Tomasz Imielinski and Hank Koth, Eds. Chapter 5, Kluwer Academic Publishers, 1996, pp. 153-181.

[12] Sung- Ju Lee, Mario Gerla, "Dynamic load-aware routing in ad hoc networks", IEEE Conference on Communications, Vol. 10, pp. 3206-3210, 2001.

[13] Jim Durkin, Voice - Enabling the Data Network: H.323, MGCP, SIP, QoS, SLAs and Security, 1st Edition, CISCO Press, Indianapolis, IN, 2002.

IMPROVING HANDOVER LATENCY BY USING CROSS-LAYER DIRECT COMMUNICATION MODEL IN IEEE 802.16E BROADBAND WIRELESS ACCESS NETWORKS

SEYYED REZGAR POORAHMADI

Information Technology Department, Sharif University of Technology

Kish Island, Iran

HAMID BEIGY

Computer Engineering Department, Sharif University of Technology

Tehran, Iran

Broadband wireless access networks, such as the IEEE 802.16e standard for wireless metropolitan area networks (WMANs), aim to provide high bandwidth, low-cost and scalable solutions that extend multimedia services from backbone networks to mobile users. Handover is one of the most critical components in mobility management and its related latency plays an operative role in performance of mobile WiMAX environment. By cooperation of MAC and IP Layers, the overall handover latency in IEEE 802.16e networks would be reduced. In this paper, we propose a fast and seamless handover scheme in mobile WiMAX networks that uses the cross-layering design model to create a new interface between layers and improve the quality of services regarding to the real-time multimedia applications demand.

1. Introduction

WiMAX (Worldwide Interoperability for Microwave Access) is the IEEE 802.16 standards-based wireless technology that provides MAN (Metropolitan Area Network) broadband connectivity. WiMAX network would be used to transmit signals as far as 30 miles [2]. The fixed WiMAX standard, IEEE 802.16-2004 [2] (also known as 802.16d) is approved by the IEEE in June 2004 which provides fixed, point to multi-point broadband wireless access services in the range of 10 to 66 GHz bands and its product profile utilizes the OFDM (Orthogonal Frequency Division Multiplexing) 256-FTT system profile. In December 2005, IEEE approved the mobile WiMAX standard, IEEE 802.16-2005 [2] (also called as 802.16e) which adds mobility features to WiMAX in the 2 to 11 GHz licensed bands. IEEE 802.16e allows for fixed wireless and mobile Non-Line-of-Sight (NLOS) applications primarily by enhancing OFDMA.

Mobile WiMAX solution includes many advantages, such as robust security feature, good Quality of Service (QoS), and mesh and smart antenna technology that will allow better utilization of the spectrum resources. But, behind the all of these factors, mobility feature plays the most significant role in the current and the future WiMAX networks in effectively delivering services to the mobile users on the move. In IEEE 802.16e, the mobility management architecture and protocol should be able to seamlessly redirect packets to the mobile's new point of attachment with minimum latency.

For implementing a mobile WiMAX network, a handover process must be defined to maintain uninterrupted user communication session during his/her movement from one location to another and Handover mechanism handles Mobile Station (MS) switching from one Base Station (BS) to another. Handover latency is partially due to the link layer (L2) scanning/ranging as well as the network Layer (L3) re-entry procedure which may result in a delay of hundreds of milliseconds, for exceeding the requirements of typical real-time services (e.g. 150 ms for VOIP). The state-of-the-art is understanding how to apply L3 handover protocol over the existing IEEE 802.16e L2 handover scheme.

In the next two future sections, we are going to address the mechanism of L2 and L3 handover in IEEE 802.16e networks and their effect on the overall network latency. In section 4, we will describe the latency problem in IEEE 802.16e handover process. Then section 5 uses a cross-layering architecture model to integrate the link layer and IP layer that decreases the overall handover latency maintaining the desired quality of services demanded by VOIP or other real-time multimedia applications in IEEE 802.16e network. Finally, the conclusion is provided in section 6.

2. Link Layer Handover in Mobile WiMAX

To realize connectivity in broadband wireless networks such as WiMAX, effective mobility management is critical. Mobility management consists of location management and handover management. A general WiMAX handover process typically involves the following basic entities: Mobile Station (MS), Serving Base Station (SBS), Target Base Station (TBS), Serving Access Router (SAR), Target Access Router (TAR), and Home Agent (HA). The BS is the air link attachment point for the MS. The AR is defined as the node that is the IP layer attachment point for the MS and serves as the first point for IP forwarding. The MS registration and authentication would be done by HA every time it moves from SAR to TAR.

Layer-2 handover (L2HO) is often referred to as "micro-mobility" [1]. It only changes the air interface attachment point but keeps the IP attachment point unchanged. During this process, a comparison of neighboring BSs would be executed based on specific metrics, such as signal strength or other QoS parameters. So, the MS chooses the TBS by making immediate decision for a future handover based on gathered information.

Figure 1 illustrates the basic IEEE 802.16e link layer handover procedure. The SBS sends neighbor advertisement messages (MOB_NBR-ADV) periodically. By listening to messages during these periods, the MS understands the current network identification, gathers information about neighboring BSs, and attempts to be synchronized by configuration of some physical metrics such as decoding the neighboring BS's radio frequency channels. In necessary cases, the MS runs a scanning operation to detection and acquire the candidate neighboring BSs by exchanging scanning request message (MOB_SCN-REQ) and scanning response message (MOB_SCN-RSP) with SBS. Note that at this point, the service via the TBS is not yet available and packets would be released to MS through the SBS.

After selection of candidate BS(s) by the mobile station, it sends a MOB_MSHO-REQ message to SBS and commence the handover process. This message is a notification sign from MS to inform the SBS that there is a demand for changing the air interface attachment point. The SBS then exchanges HO-pre-notification and HO-pre-notification-response messages with the candidate base station(s). This is a mechanism to make a dialog between SBS and candidate base station(s) and candidate responses if it has suitable condition satisfying the QoS constraint of the mobile station . So, the SBS replies to the MS with an MOB_BSHO-RSP message that carries the list of recommended base stations.

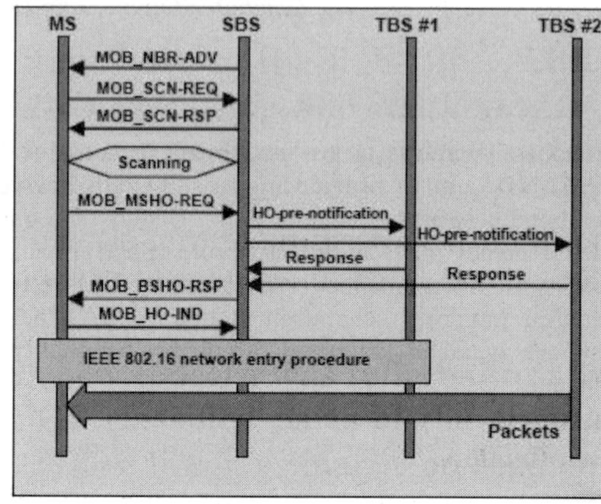

Figure 1. The IEEE 802.16e link layer handover procedure.

After the handover initiation, the handover execution happens. At this point, the MS chooses the desired TBS and starts the handover procedure by sending a MOB_HO-IND message to the SBS. At this critical point, the MS disconnects its relationship with the SBS and naturally later on, network access provider can not release any data packet to the MS through the SBS. Next, the MS connects to the TBS and ranges with it. It means that the MS procures all frequency channel specification of the TBS and synchronize its own parameters to it. After ranging, the MS negotiates its basic capabilities and performs authentication and key exchanges with the TBS, finally registering with the TBS. At this point, the TBS becomes the current base station (new SBS) and begins to serve the MS with an active communication channel.

According to the L2 handover procedure in IEEE 802.16e, after sending the MOB_HO-IND message to the SBS, the MS waits as long as the network access provider completes the IEEE 802.16 network entry procedure and reorganized the data packet release to the MS by the new serving base station (candidate target base station). During this period, there is no air interface attachment point for the MS, therefore, the handover process sustains an undesirable delay and packet loss that can be harmful for real-time IP-based multimedia applications (such as VOIP) on the IEEE 802.16e network.

3. IEEE 802.16e IP layer handover

If the MS moves to a different subnet, the MS must re-configure a new IP address and re-establish its IP connection based on the new IP address. Mobile IP enables the MS to maintain its connectivity to the Internet when moving from one access router to another, a process referred to as layer-3 handover. During L3 handover, there is a period during which the MS is unable to send or receive packets. This handover latency resulting from standard Mobile IPv6 procedures, namely movement detection, new Care of Address configuration, and Binding Update, is often unacceptable to real-time traffic such as Voice over IP. Thus, to retrieve the active session after the link layer handover procedure described previously, the terminal must conduct a network layer mobility mechanism. FMIPv6 [6] (Fast handover for Mobile IPv6) is designed to address issues related to IP layer movement detection.

FMIPv6 procedure is demonstrated in figure 2. When FMIPv6 is used over the IEEE 802.16e network, the MS first performs a link layer handover. The result of the handover procedure is that the MS selects a target base station through the all of candidates. After the selection, the MS exchanges the router solicitation for proxy (*RtSolPr*) and proxy router advertisement (*PrRtAdv*) messages with the SAR to obtain the new subnet prefix of the TBS. After receiving a *PrRtAdv* message, the MS configures its prospective new IP address, called a care-of-address (*CoA*), based on the subnet prefix of the TBS. When the MS receives the indication of an impending handover (e.g. decreasing the signal strength), it sends a fast binding update (*FBU*) message to the SAR to notify the router that there is a binding between the current CoA at the current subnet and the new CoA at the target subnet.

After the FBU message is sent, two parallel processes are activated. First, the router sends the handover initiation (*HI*) message to the TAR. On receiving an HI message, the TAR executes the confirmation procedure (i.e., uniqueness test) for the new CoA and responds with the handover acknowledge (*HAck*) message to the SAR. At this time, the tunnel between the current CoA of MS and its new CoA at the TAR is established. The TAR intercepts the tunneled packets and stores them in a buffer until it receives a fast neighbor advertisement (*FNA*) message from the terminal (The *FNA* message is the first message delivered from the MS when it completes re-association with the TBS). The reception of an *FNA* message allows the TAR to release the buffered packets to the MS. As soon as the MS attaches to the new link, it transmits the FNA message to inform the TAR of its presence.

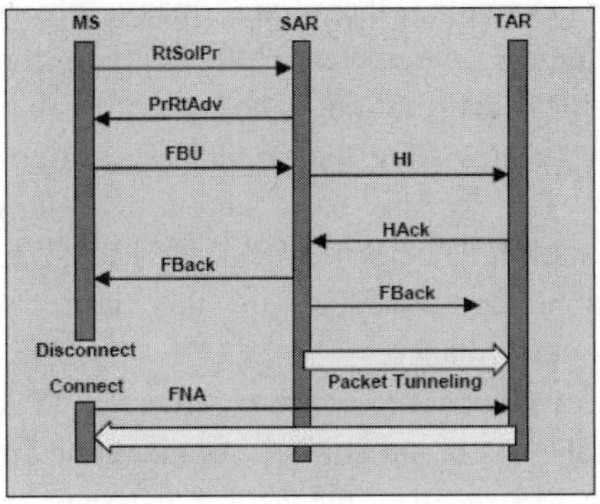

Figure 2. The FMIPv6 procedure.

The second process activated by the *FBU* message (after the *FBU* message is sent) is that the MS waits as long as possible for a fast-binding acknowledgement (*FBAck*) message to arrive from the SAR. If the MS receives the *FBAck* message in the current subnet before the link layer handover takes place, then the predictive FMIPv6 procedure has enabled the MS to move to the target subnet and begin to quickly receive packets from the TAR. This is possible because the packets already were tunneled by the SAR to the TAR via the new CoA. If the MS does not receive an *FBAck* from the SAR before the MS is forced to move to the TAR, (e.g., by low signal strength), then the predictive FMIPv6 procedure was not executed and FMIPv6 must continue in reactive mode, that is, the MS must wait for packet rerouting to be executed before it can receive any packets from the TAR.

4. Problem Statement

Based on handover schemes detailed in previous sections, the performance of IEEE 802.16e network may be vulnerable by incidence of delay problem during both link and IP layer handover procedures. The overall handover latency in mobile WiMAX networks is illustrated in figure 3. As mentioned previously, the link layer handover latency depends on the time interval between sending MOB_HO-IND message by the serving base station and completing the network entry procedure by the target base station. This is an unwanted interrupt during the handover process that is caused by some factors which they are out of control.

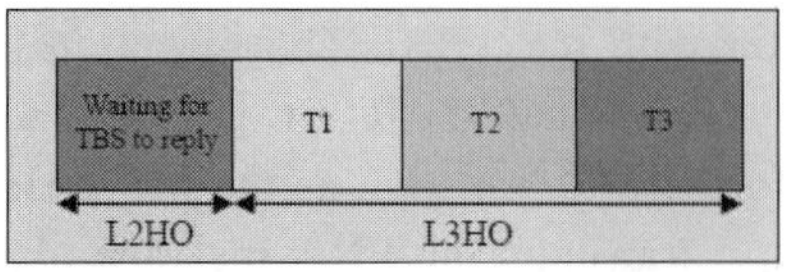

Figure 3. The overall handover latency in IEEE 802.16e.

For example, there are many physical and environmental parameters like signal strength or geographical distribution of base stations that may be effective in how long the target base station takes to response the serving base station by allowing the mobile station to be served. So, we had to accept the undesirable consequences of this issue over the network performance.

All of that makes concern, occurs in IP layer and fortunately it is in our control. As mentioned in section 3, if the MS receives the *FBAck* message before the occurrence of link layer handover, then the predictive FMIPv6 procedure has enabled the MS to move to the target subnet. Our focus is on predictive mode where the latency problem appears in three time segments:

- T1: the elapsed time after receiving the last packet (*FBAck*) through the SAR until sending an MOB_HO-IND message to the SBS.
- T2: the elapsed time after completing the network re-entry procedure until sending an FNA message to the TAR.
- T3: the elapsed time after sending an *FNA* message to the TAR until receiving the first packet from the TAR.

In fact, the absence of interaction between the network layer and the link layer for proper performance causes these latencies in IEEE 802.16e handover process. It should be minimized to reach the better performance in mobile WiMAX networks. For this reason, a straightforward solution must be presented to allow runtime information sharing between layers respecting to the reference architecture.

In the following section, we are going to manipulate the architecture of FMIPv6 procedure by addressing the cross-layer design, where the MAC layer knowledge of the wireless medium is shared with IP layer, in order to provide efficient methods of allocating network resources and applications over the Internet.

5. Proposed Cross-Layering Solution

In the framework of a reference layered architecture (e.g. OSI), the designer has two choices at the time of protocol design. Protocols can be designed by respecting the rules of the reference architecture. In a layered architecture, this would mean designing protocols such that a higher-layer protocol only makes use of the services at the lower layers and is not concerned about the details of how the service is being provided. Following the architecture also implies that protocols would not need any interfaces present in the reference architecture.

Alternatively, protocols can be designed by violating the reference architecture [3], for example, by allowing direct communication between protocols at nonadjacent layers or sharing variables between layers. Such violation of a layered architecture is cross-layer design with respect to the reference architecture.

There are many cross-layer design proposals in the wireless communication literature. One of them is the Direct Communication Model [4] (DCM) that is illustrated in figure 4 schematically. It means making the variables at one layer visible to the other layers at runtime. By contrast, under a strictly layered architecture, every layer manages its own variables, and its variables are of no concern to other layers. Practically speaking, DCM creates new interfaces between the layers. The new interfaces are used for information sharing between the layers at runtime. The architecture violation here is obviously the creation of a new interface not available in the layered architecture.

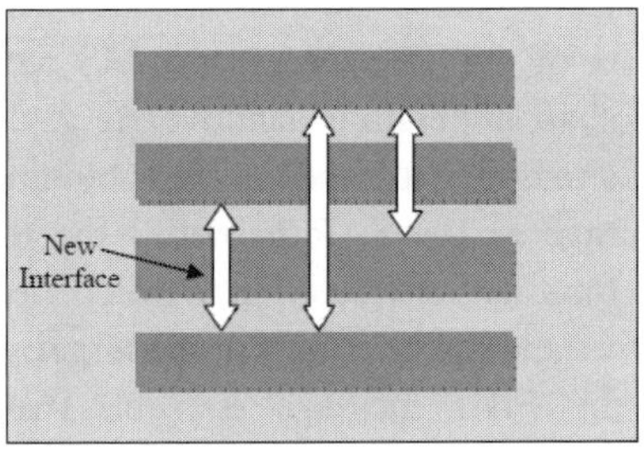

Figure 4. The Direct Communication Model (DCM).

Now, we want to create a new interface for decreasing the scale of delay in IEEE 802.16e handover process. Based on the DCM, there is a demand for a shared variable between link layer and IP layer to make some indication during the handover procedure. So, we suggest a *Boolean Variable* as a flag to directly communicate between layers. The initial value of this variable is set to zero. Two layers have the ability of checking the variable's value continuously. They are also authorized to manipulate the content of the flag under the predefined conditions.

Consider the handover process in IEEE 802.16e where the MS is waiting for *FBAck* message. At this moment, the flag is equal to zero and upon the receiving the *FBAck* message by MS from the SAR, IP layer changes the flag's value to 1. As the link layer checks the flag continuously, it would be informed to trigger the L2HO procedure by sending the MOB_HO-IND message to the SBS. So, the latency time segment T1 would be decreased by applying a direct communication model. In this case, a pseudo code like the following sample must be run at IP layer procedure:

```
boolean flag = 0;
while (1)
 {
        check the MS;
        if (MS received FBAck )
              {   set the flag to 1;
                  exit;            }
 }
```

Also at the link layer side, some of instructions would be executed in parallel as it mentioned below:

```
boolean flag = 0;
while (1)
 {
        check the flag's value;
        if (flag is equal to 1)
              {   send the MOB_HO-
IND;
                  set the flag to 0;
                   exit;
```

Applying the DCM to another delay time segment (T2) has the same effect on declining the overall latency in IEEE 802.16e handover process. In this case, we suppose the same flag as an interface to control the network entry procedure in link layer. By completing the procedure, the value of the flag would be changed:

```
boolean flag = 0;
while (1)
 {
        check the network entry
procedure;
        if (completed )
              {   set the flag to 1;
                  exit;            }
```

This causes the IP layer to perform some actions upon the conversion of the flag status:

```
boolean flag = 0;
while (1)
 {
        check the flag's value;
        if (flag is equal to 1)
              {   send the FNA message to TAR;
                  set the flag to 0;
                  exit;                }
 }
```

Therefore, the *FNA* message would be sent to target access router to grant the release of buffered data packets to the mobile station. It means that the re-association of MS with the TAR is completed.

6. Conclusions

In this paper, we presented two handover protocols for the IP layer and the link layer used in mobile WiMAX networks. These procedures were developed to make a fast and seamless handover process, but it is strongly dependent on cooperation between IP layer and link layer to overcome the latency problem. We presented a cross-layering design to apply the Direct Communication Model (DCM) for supporting the indication between the layers. In this model, a common variable used to guarantee the information sharing between the IP layer and the link layer to decrease the overall handover latency in IEEE 802.16e networks.

References

1. R.Q. Hu, D. Paranchych, M.H. Fong, and G. Wu, "On the Evolution of Handoff Management and Network Architecture in WiMAX", *IEEE Proceeding*, 2007, pp. 144-149.
2. IEEE 802.16 Working Group, "IEEE Standard for Local and metropolitan area networks Part 16: Air Interface for Fixed and Mobile Broadband Wireless Access Systems Amendment 2," IEEE Std. 802.16e-2005, Feb. 2006.
3. S. Shakkottai, T.S. Rappaport, and P.C. Karlsson, "Cross-Layer Design for Wireless Networks", *IEEE Communications Magazine*, Oct. 2003, pp. 74-80.
4. V. Srivastava, and M. Motani, "Cross-Layer Design: A Survey and the Road Ahead", *IEEE Communications Magazine*, Dec. 2005, pp. 112-119.
5. IETF RFC 5270 "Mobile IPv6 Fast Handovers over IEEE 802.16e Networks", June 2008.
6. IETF RFC 4068 "Fast Handovers for Mobile IPv6", July 2005.

SWARM FORMATION IN A MULTI-SWARM NETWORK CENTRIC WARFARE

POOIA LALBAKHSH, NASRIN SOHRABI

Computer Engineering Department, Islamic Azad University – Borujerd Branch
Borujerd, Lorestan, Iran

MEHDI N. FESHARAKI

Computer Engineering Department, Islamic Azad University – Science & Research Campus
Tehran, Iran

The paper comprehensively explains the vital role of swarm intelligence in network centric warfare. It describes the various types of existing NCW swarms and proposes some new forms of this strategy to improve the efficiency of such critical environments. To accomplish this goal, the paper presents the NCW swarm taxonomy including different types of this strategy such as human swarm, swarm robots, sensor swarm, service swarms and swarm coordinating strategies together with their formation process in NCW related areas. We also take a look at the existing tools and infrastructures to implement these technologies in such heterogeneous environments.

1. Introduction

The dawning of the information age had considerable impacts on different areas, particularly on Information related systems. Domination of network enabled systems and power distribution to the edges of the system, have greatly changed the features of traditional systems. On the other hand, increasing the complexity and heterogeneity of computing systems in this era introduced new scalability, dependability and management challenges that should be handled [1].

Nature abilities to manage its huge complexity persuaded scientists to model and simulate these abilities into their complex artificial and non-artificial distributed systems. Swarm intelligence is one of the most important lessons learned from this sophisticated teacher. Having a swarm based system; different complicated missions can be accomplished using distributed simple organs with low level and even binary interactions [2]. Moreover the system granularity in swarm-based system, prepares good levels of flexibility, adoptability and robustness particularly against unpredicted situations [3].

According to the features mentioned above, it is evident that swarm strategy would be a good solution for unpredicted and dynamically changing environments such as warfare domains. However matching the swarm factors with battlefield environments contains critical challenges that should be comprehensively considered.

This paper studies the different types of swarm behavior that can be applied on different layers of NCW and also the required infrastructures for their implementation.

2. Swarming in NCW

The consequences of the information age and the requirements of the modern battlefield environments such as coalition and asymmetric missions and the need for reducing the mission accomplishment time led to the introduction of a new integrated concept of network centric warfare. It should be noted that NCW is not about using sophisticated and intelligent systems, or warfare robots. It is not also about networking warfare equipments only. NCW looks for the efficiently use of situational information to generate a shared awareness and finally to create an acceptable level of sense making towards the mission goals. It can be viewed as heterogeneous multi-agent system acting dynamically towards its mission.

After the appearance of network enabled systems and transforming the value from technology to information, new information management challenges were introduced. These challenges were more important in battlefield environments because of their special and vital responsibilities. Moreover, the great importance of military applications and the growing complexity of heterogeneous distributed systems in such environments, and the need for special military requirements such as coalition missions, introduced special complexity, security and maintainability challenges that should be handled [4]. These interwoven environments were too complex to be justified only by using some stove-piped technology-based strategies such as traditional C4ISR systems [5].

Network Centric Warfare or NCW was proposed to handle the modern battle space complexity by an information age matching strategy. Simulating a cognitive structure, NCW tries to solve the complexity and scalability problems autonomously. Swarm intelligence and its related aspects play important roles in solving mentioned problems in the NCW. This strategy makes use of simple elements to carry out complicated missions through their integration. Nature has demonstrated swarm effectiveness and efficiency [6].

2.1. *Swarming in control*

One of the most important goals of NCW is known as power to the edge [1]. Making use of this advantage, NCW tries to eliminate the previous hierarchical top-down command process. In this strategy instead of a series of direct commands to reactive soldiers the commander tries to imply its main intensions to the lower units so they can use their creativity to accomplish the high level goal through their cognitive nature. This strategy makes use of multiple swarm groups, cooperating with each other according to the mission. Taking advantage of specialized individuals, decreasing the amount of resources involved, and self-synchronization within and between the groups are the main characteristics of the swarm strategy in the modern warfare. In such a distributed swarm-based environment the high level commanders are not considered with the very detail battlefield processes and only deals with the overall theater like a chess player. Appropriate situational awareness strategies such as sophisticated COPs will heighten the efficiency of the commander decisions.

2.2. *Swarming in sensors and effectors*

Situational awareness is a key factor for sense making among different NCW entities. Sensors and trackers are the basic elements of situational awareness by which other higher level services such as common operational and/or tactical pictures are generated. It is evident that, more information gathering entities result in more comprehensive situational awareness if good data fusion strategies are applied. Sensor fusion is a challenging topic of NCW in which the gathered data should be appropriately processed and integrated to generate a comprehensive, correct, and understandable information about adversary or sometimes our own warfare resources. JDL is one of the popular models of data fusion as a threat-oriented model [7]. Since the focus is on swarm behavior, we discuss two categories namely: swarming between sensors identifying a track and sensor to shooter swarms.

The former refers to a group of identical/different sensors trying to identify a track according to predefined processes and online inner/outer negotiations. Figure 1 tries to display such a situation in which a radar swarm and a camera swarm try to identify a track. In this structure, both swarm groups are responsible for matching their inferred information with each other to deliver accurate identification outputs. Each of the groups may take advantage of other resources or swarm groups for their specific processes.

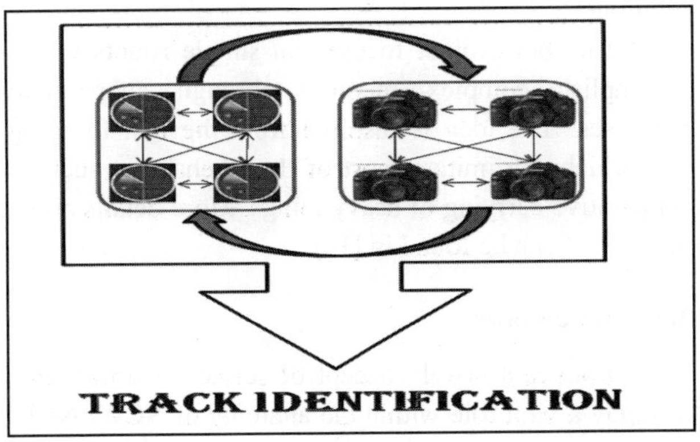

Figure 1. A radar swarm and camera swarm cooperating towards track identification.

Body sensors can also be considered as a modern sensor network. Using NCW textiles, the clothes of each soldier collects a huge amount of information about the battlefield environmental occurrences and even the soldier biological and/or emotional conditions [8].

On the other hand, sensor to shooter systems involve a closed control loop from a sensor (or a sensor swarm) to an effector (or effector swarm) against an invader. In these autonomous systems, an invader is identified and tracked by a sensor swarm and a shooter or a group of shooters are considered to behave against the invader. The shooter selection may be accomplished through a predefined plan or using a dynamically online algorithm.

2.3. *Swam robots*

Swarm robot is an important concept which will change the feature of the future warfare. There is an increasing growth in such applications in military domains such as unmanned vehicles [9] and swarm-bot project [10]. It can be said that such semi-cognitive (or cognitive) artificial soldiers will be replaced by the human ones, which would decrease the cultural consequences and increase the manageability and maintainability of wars.

Unmanned vehicles as an important project in this category, focuses on the communications between swarm nodes (vehicles). According to the mobility of such systems, a kind of wireless network should be applied to connect mobile vehicles. Each vehicle may involve independent swarm sensor or even a sensor to shooter structure by its own. It is also possible for different UVs to work with each other complementally using different signal frequencies for different swarm subgroups.

Swarmbot project focuses on simple robots which accomplish complex missions through cooperative processes. The idea is inspired from the real foraging ants which can imitate most of their behaviors such as cooperative carrying of heavy things. More details about the project can be found in [10].

2.4. *Service swarm*

We introduce a novel concept of service swarm which can play a vital role within the anatomy of NCW. NCW is based on service oriented architecture, in which various services are delivered through a common underlying networked infrastructure [11]. All of the services work as independent serving entities, making use of a common language and some predefined standards. In the real engineering world, SOA concepts are implemented as web services using XML and available standards such as WSDL, SOAP, and FDDI. The main advantage of SOA which matches the NCW tenets is reusability. Moreover, the dispersed independent services increase the system granularity, flexibility, and finally adaptability which are the vital requirements of NCW. Each task in the battlefield environments may involve more than one service. Combination of the dispersed services is a challenging aspect of SOA which can be accomplished as a swarming process. Some of the existing challenges in service composition are:

1. In the case of replicated services, which services should be chosen?
2. Since battlefield environments involve high levels of uncertainty, the composition process should be accomplished dynamically. Such dynamic algorithms can be implemented through goal-based strategy [12] or a predefined ontology [13].

Although the philosophy of service orientation can be applied in different aspects of a system, we only consider the software services in our discussions. Common operational picture, an important layer of situational awareness can be considered as a service swarm. In this layer, different services are joined together to provide a comprehensive and understandable picture of the battlefield. COP can even be considered as visualized NCW, while an ideal COP should be dynamically generated according to its user, the organizational level of the user, the mental and psychological characteristics of the user, and other similar factors. Service swarms may take advantage of the other swarms such as service swarms to enrich the prepared picture. Many different service swarm applications are proposed on dynamic/static composition algorithms. As an example, authors in [14] proposed a service oriented steganography process, which is a service swarm approach. In the proposed system, the service composition process is accomplished semantically through a predetermined plan according to the current system conditions.

3. Multi-swarm NCW

Although all the mentioned swarm structures are involved in NCW concept, they are working independently but in a cooperative environment. The output of each swarm cluster can be a semantic statement to be processed by the other clusters. For example, the output of a sensor swarm will be the concept of a threat together with the appropriate data for a cluster of effectors. Figure 2 shows a multi-swarm NCW in which all swarm groups are working together. All the results of each swarm group (and sometimes each node) is connected to a network infrastructure as a service. Each task is accomplished through the composition of these services. As shown in the figure, COP service is generated through a sensor swarm and other information collecting entities and also other distributed databases which may be updated by other services. All of the outer negotiations (interactions between the groups) are accomplished through SOA standards.

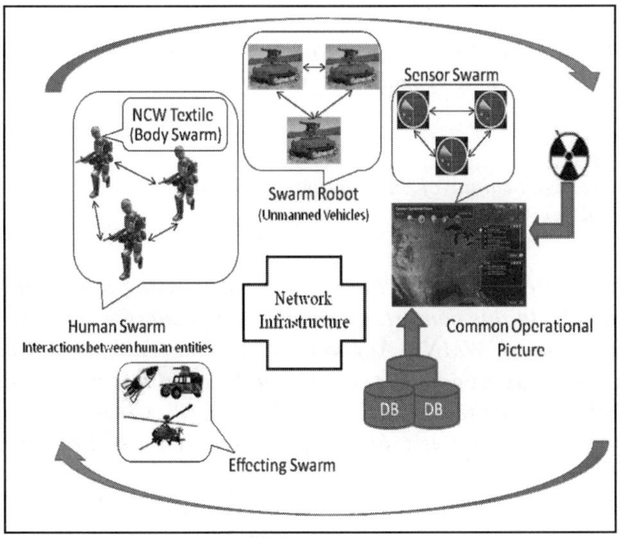

Figure 2. A multi-swarm NCW. Each entity is connected to the network infrastructure using SOA standards to handle the inconsistencies.

4. Conclusion

Although swarming in NCW covers a very extensive topic, we tried to express the most important formations and aspects of swarm behavior from human to software processes. We classified swarming in control, sensor, robot, and service swarms and studied the characteristics of each category. We finally illustrated the NCW anatomy as a multi-swarm structure on a network infrastructure in a service oriented architecture. Since SOA prepares an open, highly available structure, other services can be added to the system as outsourced products. On the other hand, internal products of the system can also be exported as enterprise services according to specific security policies.

References

1. D. Alberts, R. Hayes, Power to the edge: Command and control in information age, CCRP Publications, 2003.
2. G. Theraulaz, J. L. Deneubourg, Swarm intelligence in social insects and the emergence of cultural swarm patterns, Proc. NATO ASI, Series D: Behavioral and social sciences, Vol. 78, 1994, pp. 107-123.V.
3. P. Lalbakhsh, M. N. Fesharaki, Basic concepts and anatomy of swarm intelligence and its roles in today and future network centric environments, Proc. Int. Multi-conference of Engineering and Computer Scientists, Hong Kong, March 2008, pp. 78-83.
4. K. Herman, G. Muhl, K. Geihs, Self Management: A solution to complexity or just another problem, IEEE Distributed Systems Online, Vol. 6, No. 1, 2003, pp. 5-18.
5. P. Lalbakhsh, M. N. Fesharaki, Highly reliable interconnection network for C4ISR framework, M. S. c Thesis, School of Computing, Islamic Azad University, Science & Research Campus, Tehran, IRAN, Summer 2006.
6. H. Z. Chavez, Artificial intelligence benefits from biological lessons, IEEE Distributed Systems Online, Vol. 5, No. 5, 2001.
7. E. Franklin, Jr. White, Data Fusion Lexicon, Joint Directories of Laboratories, Technical Panel for C3, Data Fusion Sub-panel, Naval Ocean Systems Center, San Diego, 1987.
8. T. Tassinari, P. Leitch, extileD. Alberts, Interactive textiles for soldier systems, Proc. Int. Conf. Soldier Systems, 2004.
9. K. Mathia, G. Lafferriere, A. Williams, Cooperative Control of Unmanned Vehicle Formations, Proc. Int. Conf. Euro UAV, Paris, june, 2006.
10. R. Groβ, M. Bonani, F. Mondada, M. Dorigo, Autonomous Self-Assembly in Swarm-Bots, IEEE Transaction on Robotics, Vol. 22, No. 6, 2006, pp. 1115-1130.
11. M. P. Papazoglou, W. J. Heuvel, Service Oriented Architecture: Approaches, Technologies and Research Issues, The International Journal on Very Large Data Bases. Vol. 16, Issue 3, 2007, pp. 389-415.
12. P. Lalbakhsh, M. N. Fesharaki, Towards Autonomic Computing using Goal-Based Translation Strategy in Heterogeneous Distributed Environments, Proc. Int. Conf. Automatic Control, Modelling and Simulation, Turkey, 2007, pp. 65-71.
13. P. Lalbakhsh, A. Goodarzi, M. N. Fesharaki, Towards Virtual Audio/Video Environments using Semantic Service Composition on a Service Oriented Infrastructure, Proc. Int. Conf. Advanced Computer Control, Singapore, 2008, pp. 485-492.
14. P. Lalbakhsh, S. Ravanbakhsh, M. N. Fesharaki, N. Sohrabi, Service Oriented Steganography steganography-A novel approach towards autonomic secured distributed heterogeneous environments, Proc. Int. Con. Computer Design and Applications, Singapore, 2009, [In press].

CHANNEL ASSIGNMENT IN WMNS: ISSUES AND SOLUTIONS*

ATHOTA KAVITHA

Department of Computer Science and Engineering, Jawaharlal Nehru Technological University Hyderabad, Hyderabad, Andhra Pradesh, India. athotakavitha@gmail.com

ATUL NEGI†

Department of Computer Science and Engineering, Prestige Institute of Engineering and Science, Indore, India-452 010. atul.negi@ieee.org

Wireless Mesh Networks (WMNs) are recently gaining much attention due to the scope for increasing aggregate network throughput by utilization of non-overlapping channels. In this context, Channel Assignment (CA) is a key issue in offering optimal performance multi-radio multi-channel WMNs. A good CA scheme can maximize number of simultaneous transmissions, which in turn maximizes aggregate network throughput. In this paper we address key issues in designing CA Algorithms for multi-channel multi-hop networks. We classify various state-of-the-art Channel Assignment Schemes and present a comparative analysis. Some future research directions for CA are also suggested.

1. Introduction

Wireless networks have serious capacity limitation when compared with their wired counterparts. IEEE802.11b/g offers 11 Mbps peak transmission rate in ideal conditions. Conventional IEEE 802.11 supports usage of one channel assigned to one network interface. IEEE802.11b/g offers 3 non-overlapping and IEEE 802.11a offers 12 non-overlapping channels. Using multiple channels for data transmission improves network throughput [1]. Research is in progress to offer optimal network throughput by efficiently utilizing multiple channels in multi-hop networks.

Wireless Mesh Networks (WMNs) are characterized as multi-channel multi-hop networks. Research in WMNs is gaining momentum in recent past due to their low cost solution for broadband internet access. Some application areas of WMNs include community networks, campus networks, enterprise networks and municipal networks.

The typical architecture of WMN is as shown in Fig-1. As shown in architecture it consists of three types of nodes: Internet Gateways(IGW), Mesh Routers(MR) and Mesh Clients. IGW is connected wired to internet. MR can operate on orthogonal channels to facilitate (Multi-Radio) Multi-Channel communication. MR collaboratively forwards the network traffic of Mesh Clients towards IGW. Mesh Clients connect to the nearest MR in a single-hop fashion to connect to IGW and get internet services.

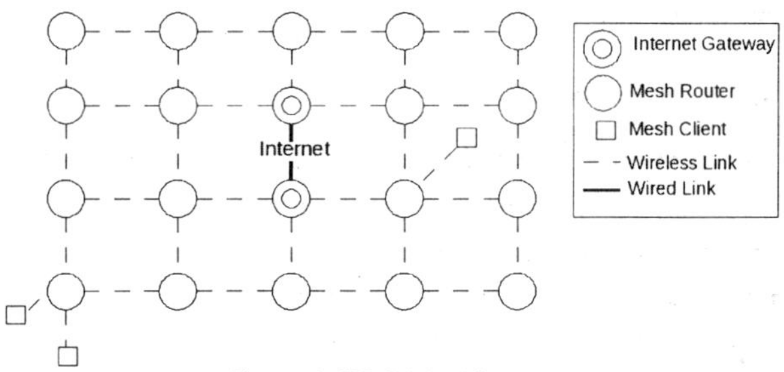

Figure 1. WMN Architecture

The rest of this paper is organized as follows. Section II gives an overview of the challenges in designing channel assignment algorithm. Section III provides classification and survey of proposed channel assignment algorithms. Section IV presents a comparative study follows by conclusion section.

2. Challenges in designing CA algorithm

Channel here refers to range of frequencies assigned to network interface on MR for the purpose of communication with the neighboring MRs. Channel Assignment problem is all about mapping available channels to the network interfaces at MRs in order to achieve optimal network performance. There are some

* This work is supported by AICTE-RPS project F.No.:8023/BOR/RPS-90/2006-07

† Atul Negi is on leave from Dept. of CIS, University of Hyderabad, Hyderabad, A.P., India

common design issues considered in designing Channel Assignment Algorithms. They are interference, connectivity, stability, throughput, delay, fault tolerance, fairness.

Interference is one of the key factors in wireless networks that affect network performance. Interference can be modeled as a protocol model or a physical model. The protocol model considers that each node has transmission range and interference range. In physical model of interference, the transmission is successful if signal to interference and noise ratio (SINR) of transmitter's signal at the receiver is larger than a threshold. Physical model is capable of detecting interference from all transmitters

Connectivity is an important issue in WMNs as Channel Assignment decisions can change network topology. Connectivity is modeled as disk model or graph model. In the disk model the nodes connectivity is defined based on their geometric distances. In general two types of graphs used by most of the CA approaches, reachability graph and conflict graph. The reachability graph, $G<V,E>$ is defined as undirected graph where V is the set of nodes in the network and E represents the communication link between the nodes in the node set. A communication link $(v1,v2)$ in E if and only if the distance or received power between the two nodes $v1$ and $v2$ is less than some threshold.

Stability of the network plays an important role in Channel Assignment. Inefficient Channel Assignment method may cause network unstable due to 'Ripple Effect' and 'Channel Oscillation'. Ripple Effect is caused by the constraint that two radios in the communication range must share a channel. For example, Node *A* is using interface I_A operating on channel C_1 for communicating with Node *B* and Node *C* is operating on Channel C_2. If Node *A* switches interface I_A from channel C_1 to C_2 for communicating with Node *C*. Then Node *B* has to switch from C_1 to C_2 in order to keep transmission with Node *A* in progress. Channel Oscillation may result due to dynamic metric used by CA algorithms. For example, If Node *A*, Node *B* identifies a traffic-free channel they simultaneously switch to that channel. When they find increased traffic in that channel they switch back to the previously used channel simultaneously. Channel Oscillation problem due to CA decisions make network unstable.

Throughput, Delay are two desirable characteristics of Channel Assignment as they can give good indicators of network performance. For WMNs obtaining optimal throughput is possible by reducing interference and Delay can be reduced by choosing links that are assigned to lightly loaded channels.

Fault Tolerance is an important issue that can be handled by CA in performing self healing when some nodes fail due to some internal or external problems. Failure of one or few mesh nodes should not bring operation of network down.

Fairness is another necessary issue in WMNs. CA decisions should be taken such a way that not only highly loaded links get all network share but also lightly loaded links get their proportionate share in the network.

CA solutions found in literature, typically address more than one of these issues as they are related to each other. For example, reducing the transmission range will increase energy efficiency, improve throughput, reduces interference but also reduces connectivity. CA algorithms should be carefully designed to enhance aggregate network performance and service requirements of the mesh nodes are satisfied.

3. Classification of Multi Channel CA Algorithms

There are other ways of classifications for WMNs are possible. Here our purpose is to classify channel assignment schemes taking into various aspects into consideration. Multi Channel CA algorithms for WMNs can be broadly classified based on number of radios/interfaces employed by CA approach into Single Radio Multi Channel(SRMC) and Multi Radio Multi Channel(MRMC) approaches as shown in fig-2.

In SRMC case, each node is equipped with one interface which can be configured to operate in non-overlapping channels. Single Radio works in half duplex mode i.e., it cannot receive and transmit simultaneously. So, SRMC approaches may still experience capacity limitation.

In MRMC case, each node is equipped with multiple radios. MultiRadio nodes are effectively full duplex. So, they can simultaneously transmit on one interface and receive on another interface operating on orthogonal channels which in turn increases network throughput.

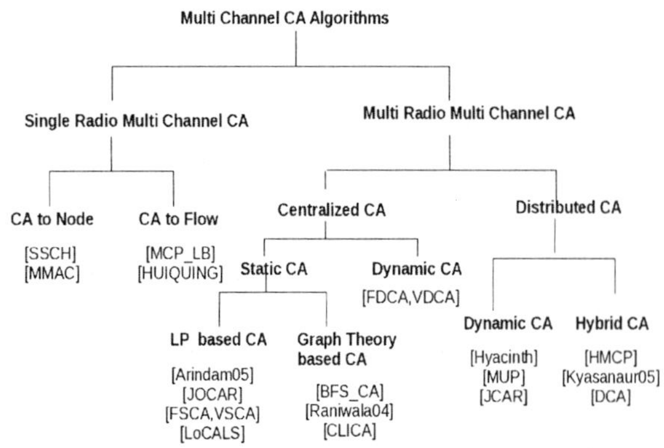

Figure 2. Multi-channel CA Algorithms Classification

3.1. Survey of Single Radio Multi Channel Approaches

SRMC CA algorithms can be further classified based on two approaches [2]. First approach is CA to nodes, nodes do not change channel to participate in flow. For example, in sample network shown in Fig-3 assume Nodes *A,B,C,D* and *E* are operating channels 1,2,3,4 and 5 respectively. If Node *A* to communicate with Node *C* it should switch its interface to the channel 2 for communicating with intermediate node *B*. Then Node *B* switches its interface to channel 3 for forwarding traffic to node *C*. In CA to node approach every node on the path should have knowledge about next hop node and channel it is listening on. This approach decouples route discovery and channel assignment. One drawback of this approach is it may cause deafness problem, two nodes cannot communicate because they are listening on different channels. For ex, in fig-3 If Node *B* is forwarding traffic from Node *A* to Node *C* on channel 3, It can not listen to the communication from Node *D* on channel 2. Second approach is to assign channels to flows instead of nodes. When the route is established, all nodes are assigned with a common channel. Nodes on the path do not need to know which channel the next hop node is listening. In this case, channel assignment need to be coupled with route discovery.

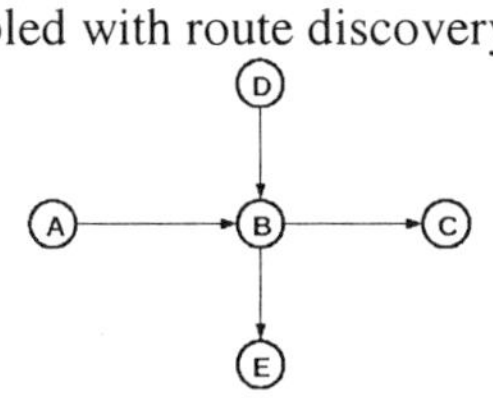

Figure 3. Sample network topology

In this subsection we present review of present SRMC CA approaches. In [3], [4], [5], [6] authors present SRMC CA approaches. In fig-2 and rest of the document we refer to these CA approaches given in [3], [4], [5], [6] are referred by [SSCH], [MMAC], [MCP_LB] and [HUIQING] respectively. [SSCH], [MMAC] follow the CA to node approach and [MCP_LB], [HUIQUING] follow CA to flow approach. [SSCH] allows nodes to switch between all channels in some predetermined order. In this scheme interface switches between available channels in different slots, based on a random pattern. Nodes which wish to communicate need to wait for a slot when their interfaces are in the same channel. [SSCH] allows traffic load balanced across all available channels reducing overall interference. As [SSCH] implementation requires per packet channel switching it cannot be supported by present IEEE 802.11 commodity hardware.

CA approach in [MMAC] utilizes one interface and all nodes need to maintain traffic information about all channels. All the nodes in the network share a common channel. The communicating nodes negotiate for their communication channel on common channel. The bottleneck in [MMAC] is usage of the common channel by all nodes in the network.[MMAC] also requires clock synchronization among nodes.

In [MCP_LB] nodes connected to IGWs should follow the channel as that of IGW. Assumes each node should know at least one path to IGWs because it facilitates nodes to switch channels to associate with an IGW with minimum load. Traffic load at each node is estimated considering traffic at IGW for that node and as well as hop length between IGW and that node

As [MCP_LB], [HUIQUING] also requires that each mesh node has to associate with spanning tree formed with IGW. [HUIQUING] proposes a new load metric to measure load considering interference at different geographic tiers. All nodes on route to IGW use same channel. For Load balancing the mesh node choose IGW such that load of tree after joining it will be less than that of current spanning tree.

3.2. Survey of Multi Radio Multi Channel Approaches

In MRMC networks availability of multiple radios and multiple channels at each node raises two important issues. First, which radio need to be used to communicate with a particular neighbor and Second, which radio need to be assigned which particular channel.CA problem in MRMC network is proven to be NP-Hard in [7].

As shown in fig-2 MRMC Channel Assignment approaches can be further classified into Centralized and Distributed approaches based on where network information maintained and CA algorithms are executed.

Another dimension of classifying MRMC CA approaches is based on how long a channel is associated with an interface into Static, Dynamic and Hybrid CA. In Static CA, the CA algorithm is executed in longer intervals compared to packet transmission duration i.e., an interface associates with a channel relatively longer time. Dynamic CA algorithms try to obtain optimal performance by allowing channel switching on per-packet basis. In Hybrid CA case, few interfaces of a node are assigned some channels statically and remaining interfaces are assigned channels dynamically. Static CA approaches are well-suitable to the WMNs where traffic demands are constant over a period of time. For WMNs with variable traffic demands, Dynamic CA approaches are suitable. Hybrid CA has flexibility of both static CA and dynamic CA. Hybrid CA approaches follow default channel approach or receiver-based channel approach. In common channel approach, all the mesh nodes have to dedicate one interface to listen on common channel and the remaining interfaces are allowed to configure to other channels. In Default-channel approach each node configures an interface to listen on specific channel for receiving information from neighbor nodes.

3.3. *Survey of Centralized Multi Radio Multi Channel Approaches*

Most of the proposed CA approaches for problem formulation and solving CA problem are classified into two classes based Linear Programming (LP) and Graph Theoretic approaches. LP a based approach require network topology, network load as inputs and obtains optimal CA satisfying given constraints. Graph theoretic approaches view the problem as node coloring or edge coloring problem on reachability graph satisfying given constraints. Graph Theoretic approaches given network topology, number of colors (i.e., channels) the goal is to assign the colors to edges while satisfying constraints.

The Centralized CA approaches can be classified under static CA and dynamic CA approaches. The CA approaches proposed in [7], [8], [9], [10], [11], [12] and two of the algorithms proposed in [13] are classified into static CA approach. In this paper these static CA approaches are referred as [Raniwala04], [Arindam05], [JOCAR], [BFS_CA], [CLICA], [LoCALS] and [FSCA,VSCA] respectively. As given in fig-2 CA algorithms [Arindam05], [JOCAR], [LoCALS] and [FSCA,VSCA] follow LP-based approach. CA algorithms [Raniwala04], [CLICA], [BFS_CA] are based on graph theory. The two distributed CA approaches proposed in [13] are referred in this paper as [FDCA, VDCA].

In [Arindam05] authors formulated CA problem as linear programming problem taking input as number of interfaces on node, network topology with constraint that no interface can be assigned more than one channel and objective function to maximize the number of links that can be active simultaneously. Authors tried to derive global optimal solution for achieving network throughput.

In [JoCAR] authors first mathematically formulated the joint CA, routing and link scheduling problem as linear programming problem. The CA problem takes into account the interference constraints, the number of channels in the network and number of radios available at each mesh router. [JoCAR] proposes a solution that optimizes overall network throughput ensuring fairness.

In [13] authors consider two types of application traffic demands. One type of applications objective is to minimize the time to transport all the data. The other type of applications the objective is to satisfy bandwidth requirement as much as possible. Two CA solutions are given for each application class: static and dynamic. Dynamic solutions are discussed in the next part of this subsection. Static CA algorithms [FSCA,VSCA] proposed for hardware which do not have fast switching capabilities.

Authors of [LoCALS] formulated Load aware Channel Assignment and Link Scheduling problem as Mixed Integer Linear Programming (MILP) problem. The algorithms perform two steps before reformulate problem to solve in polynomial time, Channel Assignment step followed by link scheduling step. In

Channel Assignment step, Weights are assigned to edges based on load. Starts with edges with highest load and assigns a channel to interface of incident nodes. If all the interfaces of node are assigned a channel (i.e., saturated) then remaining edges emanating from these nodes are assigned the same channel. This is step is repeated until edges left channels unassigned. Second step, performs link scheduling so that no two edges assigned the same channel and belonging to interference range are not scheduled at the same time. Edges are sorted in the order of their interference degree in conflict graph. Slots are allocated starting from the edges with highest degree.

In [BFS_CA] approach authors addressed interference in WMN from external wireless networks for the first time. Proposed algorithm is a spanning tree based CA rooted at IGW node or any other node called as Channel Assignment Server (CAS) that can receive channel information from all other nodes in the WMN. Channels with least interference in the neighborhood are assigned to nodes in the breadth first order. A common channel is selected by the CAS based on the channel information received from all the mesh nodes.

Authors of [Raniwala04] proposed Centralized, load-aware, joint channel assignment and routing algorithm. The steps of the Load-Aware Channel Assignment algorithm are as shown in fig-4. Initially the load on each link is estimated based on the traffic rates, then repeatedly channel assignment followed by routing steps are performed to meet given traffic load on all the links

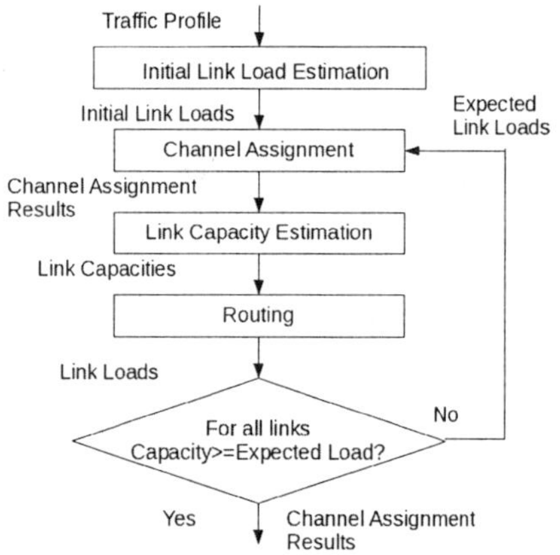

Figure 4. Load aware channel assignment

[CLICA] proposes Channel Assignment independent of traffic pattern. Non-overlapping channels are distributed among different links such that interference is reduced and connectivity is preserved.

[FDCA,VDCA] offers dynamic CA for best-effort(ftp) and real-time (video broadcasting) applications.

3.4. *Survey of Distributed Multi Radio Multi Channel Approaches*

In this subsection details about Distributed Multi Radio Multi Channel Approaches are presented. Distributed Approaches can be further classified as Dynamic approaches and Hybrid approaches. Dynamic approaches are proposed in [14], [15] and [16] are referred by the names [Hyacinth],[MUP] and [JCAR] respectively. In this paper hybrid approaches are proposed in [17], [18] and [19] are referred to as [DCA], [Kyasanaur05] and [HMCP] respectively.

[Hyacinth] is distributed, spanning tree-based, load-balancing routing algorithm that can adapt to traffic load changes as well as network failures. The CA algorithm proposed is load-aware and assigns least used channels to highly loaded links. Load-balancing is achieved by distributing routes towards distance nodes from IGW nodes which are relatively less loaded .

[MUP] is a layer2.5 solution that combines multiple interfaces into single logical interface as seen by higher layers. Each MR selects the interface with lowest round trip time for forwarding packets to specific neighbor.

In [JCAR] a distributed joint channel assignment and routing algorithm is proposed and a new metric called Channel Cost Metric (CCM) is proposed. [JCAR] performs channel selection based on the traffic information measured and exchanged among the two-hop neighbors. CCM is an indicator of interference level of a channel and is computed as sum of expected transmission time (ETTs) weighted by channel utilization overall interfering channels. [JCAR] algorithm selects a JCAR pattern that results in smallest CCM at each node locally. JCAR algorithm guarantees both feasibility and connectivity

Authors of [DCA] proposed hybrid CA by assigning one interface of each node statically to common control channel. Other interfaces are allowed to switch among other channels in order to communicate with neighboring nodes.

[Kyasanaur05] proposes a hybrid, distributed CA where a set of fixed interfaces are assigned to specific channels for longer duration of time. The remaining set of interfaces switch between channels based on communication requirements. The fixed interfaces of a node are assigned the least-used channels in the neighborhood and the information is communicated to the node's neighbors.

[HMCP] classifies interfaces into fixed interfaces, which are tuned to channel for longer duration and switchable interfaces can switch among remaining non-fixed channels. [HMCP] assigns fixed channels of successive nodes along the chain to different channels. When an intermediate node is receiving data using one interface, it can simultaneously forward data to the next node using second interface which increases end to end throughput.

4. Comparative analysis of MultiChannel CA algorithms

In this section summary of CA approaches for MultiChannel WMNs with reference to important factors is presented in Table-1. The Parameters used in comparison MRMC CA algorithms are in the order of CA/Routing/Link Scheduling proposed, Default Channel is offered for the purpose of control message transfer and connectivity preservation, Ripple Effect is handled (N/A entry in table represents not applicable), Channel Oscillation problem addressed, Fault Tolerance addressed, Fairness Offered to give low priority flows their proportionate share of bandwidth, and CA decisions are based on Traffic Load information.

5. Conclusion

WMNs are playing crucial role in offering low-cost connectivity in campus-wide, community, enterprise networks. IEEE 802.11 is promising solution for deploying WMNs. Utilizing non-overlapping channels to increase aggregate throughput satisfying connectivity, fairness is challenging. In this paper we presented importance of Channel Assignment problem and issues in designing solution to Channel Assignment Problem. We provided the classification of state-of-the-art Channel Assignment Algorithms. A review of Multichannel CA algorithms is presented. As observed in comparison of Channel Assignment approaches still there is scope for improvement. Dynamic CA approaches are more appropriate to adapt to the Changes in the network load, network topology. Flow fairness and Quality of Service are two important issues that need to be addressed to support real-time applications like VoIP, Video Surveillance. It is advisable to couple service differentiation with CA in order to support QoS for real-time traffic in WMN. One important issue raised in multi radio multi channel networks is broadcasting due to fact that nodes listen on different channels. Broadcast messages need to be copied on to all channels in order to reach all the nodes in network. Enhancements can be proposed for broadcast protocol to reduce overhead. Common channel reduces overhead to some extent at

Table 1. Comparative analysis of multichannel CA Algorithms

CA Scheme /Parameters	*CA/Routing/Link Scheduling Proposed*	*Default Channel Supported*	*Ripple Effect Addressed*	*Channel Oscillation Addressed*	*Fault Tolerance Offered*	*Fairness Offered*	*Traffic Load Considered*
[Arindam05][8]	CA+LS	No	N/A	N/A	No	No	Yes
[JOCAR][9]	CA+RA+LS	No	N/A	N/A	No	Yes	Yes
[FSCA,VSCA, FDCA,VDCA][13]	CA+LS	No	N/A	N/A	No	Yes	Yes
[LoCALS][9]	CA+LS	No	N/A	N/A	No	No	Yes
[BFS_CA][10]	CA	Yes	N/A	N/A	No	No	Yes
[Raniwala04][7]	CA+RA	Yes	Yes	No	Yes	Yes	Yes
[CLICA][11]	CA	No	N/A	N/A	No	No	No
[Hyacinth][14]	CA+RA	No	Yes	No	Yes	Yes	Yes
[MUP][15]	CA	No	N/A	N/A	Yes	No	Yes
[JCAR][16]	CA+RA	No	Yes	No	No	No	Yes
[HMCP][19]	CA	Yes	N/A	N/A	No	No	Yes
[Kyasanaur05][18]	CA+RA	Yes	No	Yes	No	No	No
[DCA][17]	CA	Yes	N/A	Yes	No	No	Yes

the cost of dedicating one interface on common channel. Channel Assignment schemes offering load balancing still need to be explored.

References

1. Ian F.Akylidz, Xudong Wang and W.Wang, "Wireless mesh networks: A Survey",*Computer Networks Journal, Elsevier*, 2005.
2. N.H.Jungmin So and Nitin H Vaidya " A routing protocol for utilizing multiple channels in multihop wireless networks with a single transceiver", Computer Science Department, UIUC, Technical Report, Oct 2004.
3. V.Bahl, R.Chandra and J.Dunagan,"SSCH: Slotted Seeded Channel Hopping for capacity improvement in IEEE 802.11 adhoc wireless networks",in *Proceedings of ACM Mobicom*, 2004.
4. J.So and N.H.Vaidya, "Multi-channel MAC for adhoc networks: Handling multi-channel hidden terminals using a single transceiver", in *MobiHoc*,2004.
5. J.So and N.H.Vaidya, "Load-balancing routing in multichannel hybrid wireless networks with single network interface", in *IEEE Transactions on Vehicular Technology*, 2007.
6. H.Wang and K.C.Yow, "QoS routing in multi-channel multihop wireless mesh networks with infrastructure support", in *Intersense*, 2006.
7. A.Raniwala, K.Gopalan, and T.Cker Chiueh,"A centralized channel assignment and routing algorithms for multi channel WMNs", in *ACM SIGMOBILE Mobile Computing and Communications Review*, 2004.
8. A.K.Das, H.M.K.Alazemi, R.Vijayakumar, and S.Roy,"Optimization models for fixed channel assignment in wireless mesh networks with multiple radios", in *proceedings of Second Annual IEEE Wireless Communications Society Conference on Sensor and Adhoc Communications and Networks*, 2005.
9. M.Alicherry, R.Bhatia and L.E.Li,"Joint channel assignment and routing for throughput optimization in multiradio wireless mesh networks",in *ACM MobiCom*, 2005.
10. K.N.Ramachandran,E.M.Belding,K.C.Almeroth, and M.Buddhikot,"Interference aware channel assignment in multi-radio wireless networks", in *IEEE Infocom*, 2006
11. M.K. and S.R.Das,"A topology control approach for utilizing multiple channels in multi-radio wireless mesh networks", in *Proceedings of Second Annual Conference on Broadband Networks*, 2005.
12. A.Kanagasabapathy, A.Franklin and C.S.R.Murthy, "A load aware channel assignment and link scheduling algorithm for multi-channel multi-radio wireless mesh networks", in *Proceedings of High Performance Computing,* 2008.
13. H.Yu, P.Mohapatra, and X.Liu,"Channel assignment and link scheduling in multi-radio multi-channel wireless mesh networks", in *Springer*, 2008.
14. A.Raniwala and T.Cker Chiueh, "Architecture and algorithm for an IEEE 802.11 based multi-channel wireless mesh networks ", in *Infocom*, 2005.
15. A.Adya, P.Bahl, J.Padhye, A.Wolman, and L.Zhou, "A multiradio unification protocol for IEEE 802.11 wireless networks", in *Proceedings of the First International Conference on Broadband Networks*, 2004.
16. H. Wu, F.Yang, K.Tan, J.Chen, Q.Zhang and Z.Zhang," Distributed channel assignment and routing in multi-router multi-channel multi-hop wireless networks", in *IEEE Journal on Selected Areas in Communications*, 2006.
17. S-L Wu, C-Y Lin and Y-C Tseng, " A new multi-channel mac protocol with on-demand channel assignment for multi-hop mobile adhoc networks", in *International Symposium on Parallel Architectures, Algorithms and Networks (I-SPAN)*, 2000.
18. P.Kyasanaur and N.H.Vaidya, "Routing and interface assignment in multi-channel multi-interface wireless networks", in *WCNC*, 2005.
19. P.Kyasanaur, J.So, C.Chereddi and N.H.Vaidya, "Multichannel mesh networks: Challenges and Protocols", in *IEEE Wireless Communications*, 2006.

IDENTIFYING COVERT MESSAGES INSIDE AN STEGNOGRAPHIC IMAGE USING NEURAL NETWORK

IMRAN KHAN

Technocrat's Institute of Technology (IT Department), Rajiv Gandhi Technical University
Bhopal, Madhya Pradesh, Pincode-462023, INDIA

BHUPENDRA VERMA

Technocrat's Institute of Technology (IT Department), Rajiv Gandhi Technical University
Bhopal, Madhya Pradesh, Pincode-462023, INDIA

ABSTRACT:

Steganographic techniques are being applied across a broad set of different digital technologies. The steganographic method will be used for internet/network security, watermarking and so on. So, the steganography is the process of hiding one medium of communication (Text, Sound, and Image) within another. It can work on JPEG 2000 compressed images & Stir Mark images.

The 'Steganalysis' is the field of detecting the covert messages. Almost all steganalysis consist of hand-crafted tests or human visual inspection to detect whether a file contains a message hidden by a specific steganography algorithm.

The new method of steganalysis based on neural network to get the statistics features of images to identify the underlying hidden data. We first extract the features of image embedded information, then input them into neural network to get the output. Experiment result indicates this method is valid in 'Steganalysis'

The neural network in still images is used to overcome the hurdles by hiding the data indirectly into graphical image using neural network algorithm to get cipher bits, The generated cipher bits are then placed in the least significant bit position of the carrier image. The XOR propagation network model is used which acts as a multilayer perceptron.

Keywords: cipher bits, StirMark filtering, cover image, regression model

Introduction

Steganographic techniques have been used for centuries and being applied across a broad set of different digital technologies. It has been observed that terrorists have been utilizing steganographic techniques within digital images to communicate to the internet[3].

A. Implementing steganography

Secrets can be hidden inside all sorts of cover information: text, images, audio, video and more. However, there are tools available to store secrets inside almost any type of cover source. A possible way of storing a secret inside a text is using a publicly available cover source, a book or a newspaper, and using a code which consists for example of a combination of a page number, a line number and a character number[3].

Hiding information inside images is a popular technique nowadays. An image with a secret message inside can easily be spread over the world wide web or in the newsgroups. The use of steganography in newsgroups has been researched by German steganographic expert, who created a 'scanning cluster' which detects the presence of hidden messages inside images that were posted on the net.

To hide a message inside an image without changing its visible properties, the cover source can be altered in "noisy" areas with many color variations, so less attention will be drawn to the modifications. The most common methods to make these alterations involve the usage of the least-significant bit or LSB, masking, filtering and transformations on the cover image.

The LSB method [4] uses bits of each pixel in the image. When using a 24 bit color image, a bit of each of the red, green and blue color components can be used, so a total of 3 bits can be stored in each pixel.

Masking and filtering techniques usually restricted to 24 bits or grayscale images. These methods are effectively similar to 'paper watermarks', creating markings in an image. This can be achieved for example by modifying the luminance of parts of the image. While masking does change the visible properties of an image, it can be done in such a way that the human eye will not notice the anomalies.

A more complex way of hiding a secret inside an image comes with the use and modifications of Discrete Cosine Transformations (DCT). DCT are used by the JPEG compression algorithm to transform successive 8 x 8 pixel blocks of the image, into 64 DCT coefficients each.

A simple pseudo-code algorithm to hide a message inside a JPEG image could look like this

```
Input:   message, cover image.
Output:  steganographic image containing message.
while    data left to embed do
           get next DCT coefficient from cover image
           if DCT ≠ 0 and DCT ≠ 1 then
               get next LSB from message
               replace DCT LSB with message bit
           end if
           insert DCT into steganographic image
end while
```

'Steganalysis' is the field of detecting these covert messages. Almost all steganalysis consist of hand-crafted tests or human visual inspection to detect whether a file contains a message hidden by a specific steganography algorithm. The process of detecting steganographic messages is known as 'Steganalysis' and a popular Steganalysis technique is called an 'attack'. the 'Steganalysis' is simply : 'Discovering and rendering useless such covert messages is a new art form known as 'steganalysis'. Steganalysis usually consist of brute force attacks using some tools. Brute force attacks usually consist of simply running tools against images.

III. Neural Network Approach

'Steganalysis' has recently attracted researchers' interests with the development of information hiding (data hiding) techniques. We consider a new method based neural network to get statistics features of images to identify the underlying hidden data. We first extract features of image embedded information, then input them into neural network to get output. And experiment results indicate this method is valid in steganalysis. This method was used for internet/network security,Watermarking and so on.

The positive application of information hiding technology is that it can maintain the owner's legal rights. But there must exist the negative aspect for everything. The Terrorist may be communicated with each other by data hiding technology. US today printed an article "Terror groups hide behind web encryption". In this case, the data hiding in digital media on Internet has proven to be a boon for terrorists. So how to determine whether digital media has hidden information become a emergency problem for social security and stability. This new research area is called as 'Seganalysis'.

A. Information detection based on neural network

The information detection [1] is based on result that host image must be difference with hidden information host image. Maybe because human eye's mask features, we can't find any difference between host images and hidden information host images. But in essentially, data hiding process have to alter host image for embedding data. In other words, data hiding algorithms reveals statistical evidence or traces which can be used to detect the existence of hidden information in still images. Because now popular data hiding methods can be divided into two major classes: spatial domain and transform domain. Spatial domain is simple and easy to implement, but their robustness is weaker than other methods. Transform domain includes discrete Fourier transform, discrete cosine transform, discrete wavelet transform . And in spatial domain, mainly data hiding method is least significant bit (for short writing LSB) including all kinds of improved LSB methods. In transform domain, methods can be divided into several classes, quantization based, LSB based. Because we hope our method is feasible to all kinds of hiding methods no regardless embedding information in spatial or transform domain. So we try our best to consider all kinds' methods' features. But due to methods is too much, so we only consider transforms used in common data hiding methods. we only consider following transforms, DFT, DCT and DWT. Firstly we analysis object digital image according these three different kinds transforms in this method. The object image is algorithm to be able to detect methods as many as possible. These selected features should be significantly impacted by the data hiding processing. But it is difficult to find those features, so we select neural network to process this problem, neural network as the super capability to approximation any nonlinear functions. For these features which have more effected by data hiding process, neural network will assign larger weight coefficients and for these features which have less effected by data hiding process, neural network will assign less weight coefficients.

B. Image features extracting

First we analysis image's discrete cosine transform domain's statistics features. We divide each image into 8×8 sub-block and then take DCT of each sub-block. Based on analysis of Image Quality Measures (IQMs)[2] that depends on image features i.e. the good IQM should be accurate, consistent and monotonic in predicting quality.

We consider following IQMs[2]. We denote multispectral components of an image at the pixel position i, j, and in band 'k' as $C_k(i,j)$ where k = 1….3 for color images. The C(i,j) , $\hat{C}(i,j)$ indicate the multispectral pixel vectors at position C(i,j). Use M_i, i=1…10 to describe ten IQM features used in the detector.

a.Minkowsky Measures

The L_γ norm of the dissimilarity of two images can be calculated by taking the Minkowsky average of the pixel differences spatially and then chromatically (that is over the bands)

$$M_\gamma = \frac{1}{K}\sum_{k=1}^{K}\left\{\frac{1}{N^2}\sum_{i,j=1}^{N}\left|C_k(i,j)-\hat{C}_k(i,j)\right|^\gamma\right\}^{1/\gamma}$$

………..(1)

γ = 1 corresponds to mean absolute error (M_1) , and γ=2 to mean square error(M_2) , respectively.

c. Correlation Measures

A measure to compare vectors with strictly nonnegative components, as in the case of images, is the Czekanowski distance.

$$M_3 = \frac{1}{N^2}\sum_{i,j=0}^{N-1}\left(1-\frac{2\sum_{k=1}^{K}\min\left(C_k(i,j),\hat{C}_k(i,j)\right)}{\sum_{k=1}^{K}\left(C_k(i,j)+\hat{C}_k(i,j)\right)}\right).$$

……(2)

A correlation-based measure is the statistics of the angles between the pixel vectors of the two images. So, the angular correlation between two vectors $\mathbf{C}, \hat{\mathbf{C}}$, is defined as follows :

$$M_4 = 1-\frac{1}{N^2}\sum_{i,j=1}^{N}\frac{2}{\pi}\cos^{-1}\frac{\left\langle \mathbf{C}(i,j),\hat{\mathbf{C}}(i,j)\right\rangle}{\left\|\mathbf{C}(i,j)\right\|\left\|\hat{\mathbf{C}}(i,j)\right\|}.$$

.(3)

c. Spectral Measures

The Discretė Fourier Transforms (DFT) of the k th band of the original and embedded image be denoted by $\Gamma_k(u,v)$ and $\Gamma_k(u,v)$ respectively.

The spectra are defined as:

$$\Gamma_k(u,v) = \sum_{m,n=0}^{N-1} C_k(m,n)\exp\left[-2\pi i m\frac{u}{N}\right]\exp\left[-2\pi i n\frac{v}{N}\right], \quad k = 1\cdots K. \quad (10)$$

……(4)

***d.** HVS Based Measure*

The incorporation of human visual system (HVS) model into objective measures has led to a better correlation with We assume that the human visual system can be modeled as a band-pass filter with a transfer function in polar coordinates.

$$H(\rho) = \begin{cases} 0.05e^{\rho^{0.554}} & \rho < 7 \\ e^{-9[|\log_{10}\rho-\log_{10}9|]^{2.3}} & \rho \geq 7 \end{cases}$$

……….(5)

C. Performance Analysis & Experiment Results

From the measured statistics of training sets of images with and without hidden information, the destination is to determine whether an image has been hidden information or not. Because data hiding process is a nonlinear process, if we only use linear classifier to classify images, it is not a good simulation. And neural network has an excellent capability to simulate any nonlinear relation, so we make use of neural network to classify images. so that it uses following regression model, each decision label *'y'* in a sample of *'n'* observations as a linear function of the image quality measure scores *x's* plus a random error 'ε'

$$\begin{aligned} y_1 &= \beta_1 x_{11} + \beta_2 x_{12} + \ldots + \beta_q x_{1q} + \varepsilon_1 \\ y_2 &= \beta_1 x_{21} + \beta_2 x_{22} + \ldots + \beta_q x_{2q} + \varepsilon_2 \\ &\vdots \\ y_n &= \beta_1 x_{n1} + \beta_2 x_{n2} + \ldots + \beta_q x_{nq} + \varepsilon_n \end{aligned}$$

………(6)

In this expression, x_{ij} denotes the IQM score, where the first index indicates the i th image, i=1….N . and the second one the quality measure, j=1…..q , q being the total number of quality measures considered. The β_s denote the regression coefficients.

$$\hat{y} = \hat{\beta}_1 x_1 + \hat{\beta}_2 x_2 + \cdots + \hat{\beta}_q x_q$$

..(7)

for $\hat{y} \geq 0$ the image contains watermark, and for $\hat{y} < 0$ it does not.we found that neural network is more feasible to process nonlinear problem, so we take use of BP neural network to train and simulate images. This BP neural network uses three levels: input level, hidden level and output level. In neural network, the important issue is the slow of convergence The following figure shows the three levels of the back propagation neural network.

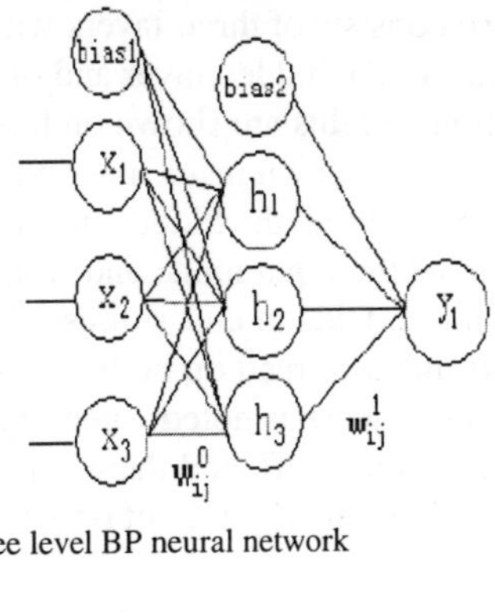

Fig. 1. Three level BP neural network

IV. Neural Network Based Camouflaging In Still Images

A. Neural design Architecture

Initially, training the patterns that are formed from the original data and the selected bits from the graphical image produces cipher text. The cipher text is embedded in the LSB of the image and then transmitted to the receiver. The secrecy lies in the design of the neural algorithm that trains the pattern. The neural algorithm has to be exchanged between the sender and receiver through a secure channel. A neural algorithm accepts "n" input pattern that has to be trained, equals to 2^K+1, for an input pattern having k+1 bits. Here 1 bit is selected from the secret message and k bits from carrier image. Input layer is designed with k+1 neurons. The no. of neurons in the hidden layer depends on the problem domain. An "m" bit secret message can be hidden in m pixels of the image and k+1 bit is encrypted at a time.

XOR-Propagation algorithm is implemented in training the bit patterns. On the decryption section, the input patterns bits are formed by the merging of cipher and selected bits from the image. The retrieval process returns back the original graphical image.

Figure 1/Design Architecture

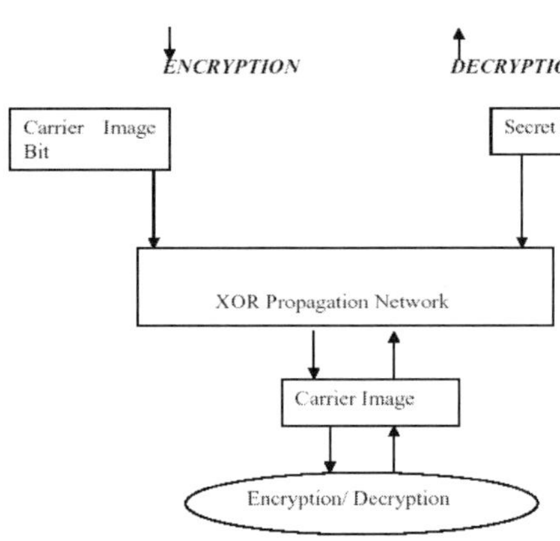

Fig 2. Design Architecture

B.XOR Propagation Network

The network consists of three-layers with two input units, one unit in the hidden layer and one output unit. The connection weights are shown on links and the threshold of each unit is shown inside the unit. As far as the hidden unit is concerned, the hidden unit is no different from both of the input units, and simply provides another input. Hidden unit's threshold of 1.5 means that it is off unless turned on both the inputs on. The behavior of the network is noted when inputs are off (00), the hidden unit is also off, and there is no net input to the output unit. When the right input only is on (01), the hidden unit does not receive enough net input to turn it on, so it remains off. The output unit sees a net input of +1, which exceeds its threshold, and so it turns it on. The same happens when the left unit only (10) is on. When both inputs are on (11) the hidden unit receives a net input of +2, which exceeds its threshold value, and so it turns on. The output unit now sees a net input of +1 from each of the input units, making +2, and –2 from the hidden unit, making 0 in all. This is less than threshold and so the unit is off.

The hidden unit detects and acts as a feature detector, detecting when both the inputs are on. It can be viewed as recording the basic inputs and mapping of input patterns to output ones.

The neural based steganography is explained by choosing text as a secret message and the graphical image as the carrier medium. The LSB of the 256 Bitmap Picture (bmp) is used as the graphical image. The secret message and the graphical image bits are combined to form the cipher bits, which are referred as trained input patterns. A single bit secret text is combined with single bit graphical image to form possible input patterns. The neural algorithm is designed with respond to binary. The output bits generated called cipher bits embedded in the LSB of the image. Thus secret message is indirectly hidden in the cover.

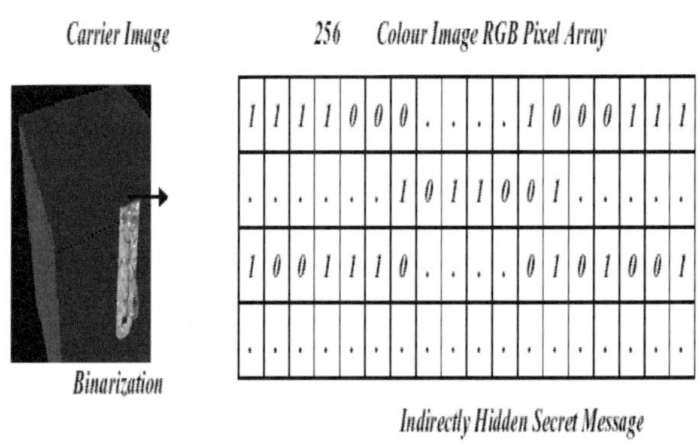

Fig 3. LSB Encoding Symbolic Representation

C. Illustration with an example

A message "Attack Postponed" is converted to binary bits equivalent through the process of binarization.In this example, MSB (Most Significant Bit) of the RGB components are selected bits of the graphical image. The secret data bits and selected graphical image bits acts as input. The neural network for the above example is designed with 2 input neurons, 1 hidden neurons and an output neuron. The training pattern is nothing but the XOR. The weight values are set to train the input pattern with definite thresholds. The trained neural network fires the output neurons (cipher bits) after satisfying the thresholds in the network. The output from the output layer is placed in LSB[4] (Least Significant Bit) of the image placing as 7 bits in a pixel array sequentially in rows.

D. Algorithm

The neural based steganography algorithmic system design as follows.

INPUT: Message Bits, Selected cover image bits

OUTPUT: Stego image.

Step 1: Design Principles of Training Pattern

Form the input pattern by selecting one bit of secret text and k image bit. Choose the number of bits required in the target output pattern.

Step 2: Deign of Neural Network

Design the neural network with the above training pattern by deciding the number of input neurons, middle layer neurons and output neurons.

Step 3: Train the Pattern

While data bits of secret message present do The input is fed into the trained network and the output generated is stored in the LSB of image.

end while

V. Future Enhancement

Steganography is renewed nowadays merging with different fields like neural network, Fuzzy system, increasing a feasible security and privacy. Using steganographic technique, software can easily transmit private user information without user's knowledge. Steganography is of immense importance and it is indispensable in the fields of digital watermarking, Digital fingerprinting, Internet security, Network security, Authentication, Copyright issues etc.

Since detection can never give a guarantee of finding all hidden information, it can be used together with methods of defeating steganography, to minimize the chances of hidden communication taking place.

In the near future, the most important use of steganographic technique will probably be lying in the field of digital watermarking. Content Providers are eager to protect their copyrighted works against illegal distribution and digital watermarks provide a way of tracking the owners of these materials. Although it will not prevent the distribution itself, it will enable the content provider to start legal actions against the violators of the copyrights, as they can now be tacked down.

Steganography might also become limited under laws, since governments already claimed that criminals use these techniques to communicate. More restrictions on the use of privacy -protecting technologies are not very unlikely, especially in this period of time with great anxiety of terrorist and other attacks.The Steganalysis approaches may be appearing in future in the fields of Artificial Neural Network, Genetic Algorithms, Simulated annealing, other standard signal processing techniques

VI. Conclusion

Detection technique development in this area of data hiding will continue. We find image's statistic features are important clues to determine whether hiding information or not from the detection process. So this suggests us to develop more robustness method with statistic features altered as little as possible.

The neural approach to embed information satisfying a secure steganography. Neural approach adds the complexity for the hackers accessing and also presents high potentiality in Defence operations. Neural Steganography is a powerful tool that enables people to communicate without possible eavesdroppers even knowing there is a form of communication.

Steganography, especially combined with cryptography, is a powerful tool which enables peoples to communicate without possible eavesdroppers even knowing there is a form of communication in the first place. The methods used in the science of steganography have advanced a lot over the past centuries, especially with the rise of the computer era. Although the techniques are still not used very often, the possibilities are endless. Many different techniques exist and continue to be developed, while the ways of detecting hidden messages also advance quickly.

Equally important are the ethical concerns of using steganography and steganalysis. Using steganographic techniques, software can easily transmit private user information without the user's permission or knowledge. Watermarks- already an issue in the hosty disputed domain of digital rights management – could be comprised by advanced steganalysis tools. Similar abuses of steganography and steganalysis can easily enumerated.

References

[1] Liu Shaohui, Yao Hongxun, Gao Wen "Neural Network based Steganalysis in Still Images" Proceedings of IEEE ICME 2003.

[2] I.Aveibas, N.Memon, B.Sankur. "Steganalysis based on image quality metrics". Multimedia Signal Processing, 2001 IEEE Fourth Workshop on, 2001

[3] Neil F.Johnson and Sushhil Jajodia. "Steganalysis: The Investigation of Hidden Information". Proceedings of the IEEE Information Technology Conference, Syracuse, New York, USA.1998

[4] R.Chandramouli and N. Memon, "Analysis of LSB based image steganography techniques," in Proc. ICIP, Oct. 2001.

SPEECH ENHANCEMENT USING INDEPENDENT COMPONENT ANALYSIS BASED ON ENTROPY MAXIMIZATION

SANGEETA NAKHATE

Deptatment of Electronics and Communication Engineering,

Maulana Azad Naional Institute of technology, Bhopal-462007 (India).

R. P. SINGH

Deptatment of Electronics and Communication Engineering,

Maulana Azad Naional Institute of technology, Bhopal-462007 (India).

AJAY SOMKUWAR

Deptatment of Electronics and Communication Engineering,

Maulana Azad Naional Institute of technology, Bhopal-462007 (India).

Abstract — Speech enhancement from the mixture of blind sources has been a challenge for many researchers for almost three decades. Blind source separation (BSS) is an emerging technique, which enables the extraction of target speech from observed mixed speech signals. In order to enhance the quality and intelligibility of speech it can be assumed that the original speech signal and the noise signal are mutually independent. BSS algorithms are based on restoring the statistical independence of the source signals. This paper is concerned with blind source separation of mixtures of acoustic signals, especially speech in which the source signals are instantaneously mixed in unknown nonlinear processes. A statistical and computational technique, called independent component analysis (ICA), used for BSS. Speech enhancement is done by according to the Entropy Maximization theory for minimizing the mutual information. By using real speech signals, the entropy of the power spectrum of the extracted unmixed signal is maximized, corresponding change in weights for the feedback loop is find out. The cross power spectral density and cross correlation coefficient of observed unmixed signal and test signal is check to conform the received signal is the original signal. The model is verified and compared with the existing algorithms on the basis of signal to noise ratio. Simulation results demonstrate that the proposed new algorithm has good Performance in speech enhancement.

Index Terms—: speech enhancement, Blind Source Separation (BSS), Independent Component Analysis (ICA), Entropy, power spectral density and Cross correlation coefficient.

1. Introduction

Extraction of Speech signal is becoming more and more important as in numerous applications such as mobile phones, conference equipments and surveillance. The quality of speech signal deteriorates radically in the presence of background noise, especially when the speech signal is subjected to subsequent processing, for example in telecommunications, speech enhancement, data communication, speech coders and automatic speech recognition systems. Consequently, modern communications systems, such as cellular phones, employ some speech enhancement procedure at the preprocessing stage, prior to further processing. To provide a good quality of communication, many speech enhancement algorithms and techniques have been proposed. Traditionally filters are used for the extraction of required signals, Kaman filtering was proposed by Paliwal and Basu [1] for speech enhancement another approach is division of noisy speech into narrow bands which was used to individually estimate speech and noise energies. Based on this concept, a novel method [5] is proposed to continuously estimate the SNR across the frequency bands; the noise spectrum is estimated during segments of no speech activity and used for SNR computations. Wiener filtering of the noisy speech based on spectral estimation of the noise (in non-speech frames) and an AR (auto regressive) modeling of the speech is another method where speech model is continuously improved by using the filtered speech obtained in the preceding iteration. The performance of the post filter is improved by combining the coherent nonlinear filter with the Wiener filter [7]. The well-known coherence function is usually used to measure the similarity between two signals. However the filtering technique does not provide the complete signal extraction because it also filtered out some desired signal lies within the filter band.

The blind source separation (BSS) technique has emerged as an efficient tool to perform speech signal extraction. Strictly, BSS as the name implies, is a technique for estimating original sources from observed mixed signals without information about the array geometry and source localization. BSS has been a major area of interest in audio research, received extensive interest signal processing due to its potential applications in numerous fields - pattern reorganization, feature extraction, noise cancellation, compression, biomedical signal processing, sonar and radar. Extraction of unknown hidden factors/components from multivariate data using only the assumption that the unknown factors are mutually independent is termed as Independent Component Analysis (ICA).It is a statistical technique for revealing hidden factors that underlies sets of random variables. Since the introduction of ICA concepts in the early 1980s in the context of neural networks and array signal processing, many new successful algorithms have been proposed that are now well-established methods. ICA defines a generative model for observed multivariate data. Recently the high-order statistics and information-theoretic criteria are used for speech enhancement which exploited to measure the non-Gaussian state or independence.

Many real-world signals, including speech signals are Super-Gaussian signal. In the proposed algorithm maximizing the entropy means minimizing the mutual information is taken as the one of the best contrast function for speech enhancement using ICA.

In the proposed model, network structure used for speech enhancement using ICA is feedback (FB) structures. As with this structure less distortion is obtained if compared with feed forward (FF)-BSS structures on the basis of transmission time difference [13]. the entropy of the power spectrum of the mixed signal is maximized, corresponding change in weights for the feedback loop is find out. The cross power spectral density and cross correlation coefficient of observed unmixed signal and test signal is check to conform the received signal is the original signal. The model is verified on the basis of signal to noise ratio for the unknown signals.

2. Proposed ICA based algorithm for speech enhancement

Proposed Algorithm attempts to separate unknown signal $s(t) = [s_1(t), s_2(t), \ldots\ldots s_n(t)]$

Where $s_1(t)$ to $s_n(t)$ are n statistically independent signals are recorded with the help of n separated microphones. Let's take $x_1(t), x_2(t) \ldots\ldots x_n(t)$ are mixtures of signals observed at different m icrophone signals at n different microphones, can be written as

$$x(t) = A\,s(t) \tag{1}$$

Where $s(t)$ is the vector of sources at instant t, A is the mixing matrix and $x(t)$ is the observed signal.

$$u(t) = Wx(t) \tag{2}$$

Where W is unknown matrix have to find out As shown in fig. 1, the number of microphones and the number of sources are the same as n. The measured mixed signals at the nth microphone at τ^{th} sampling time may be represented as

$$x_n(\tau) = s_n(\tau) + \sum_{m \neq n}^{N} \sum_{d=0}^{D-1} A_{nm}[d]\, s_m[\tau - d] \tag{3}$$

Where n =1,2,…..N.

$$u_n(\tau) = x_n(\tau) + \sum_{m \neq n}^{N} \sum_{d=0}^{D-1} W_{nm}[d]\, u_n[\tau - d] \tag{4}$$

$s_n(\tau)$ denotes the nth source signal at τ^{th} sampling time and $A_{nm}[d]$ is the convolutive mixing coefficient from m^{th} source to n^{th} microphone with d^{th} time delays. D is the number of longer time delay and $W_{nm}(d)$ is unmixing coefficient from m^{th} source to n^{th} microphone with d^{th} time delays. The proposed algorithm estimates the unmixing coefficients for enhancement of original signals $s_1(t)$ to $s_n(t)$. This work based on ICA in which the adaptation is made towards the extraction of statistically independent sources by maximizing entropy at the output end. The cross correlation coefficient of observed unmixed signal and source signal is check to conform the received signal is the original signal.

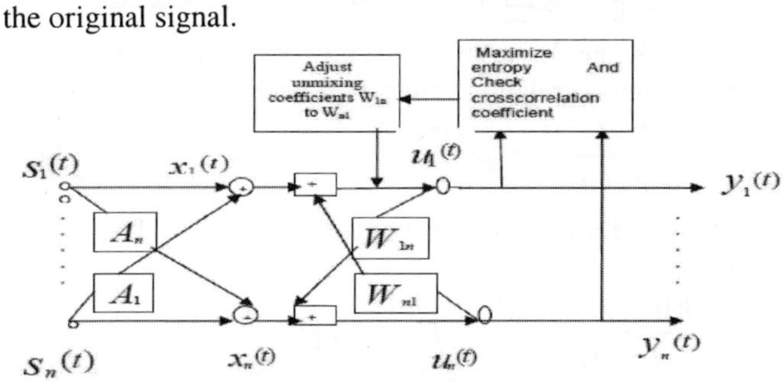

Fig. 1. Network architecture for speech enhancement

2.1. *Maximum entropy spectral estimation*

The power spectrum of a stationary signal is defined as the fourier transform of autocorrelation sequence.

$$p_{xx}(f) = \sum_{n=-\infty}^{\infty} r_{xx}(m)\, e^{-j2\pi fm} \tag{5}$$

Equation (5) requires the autocorrelation $r_{xx}(m)$ for lag m in the range of ± ∞, but in practice an estimate of the autocorrelation $r_{xx}(m)$ is available only for the value of m in a finite ranges of say ± p. In general there are an infinite number of different correltion sequences that have the same values in the range $|m| \leq |M|$ as the measured values. The particuar estimate used in the nonparametric methods assumes the correation values are zero for the lags beyond ±p, for which no estimates are available. This arbitary assumption result in spectral leakage and loss of frequency resolution. The maximum entropy estimate is based on the principle that the estimate of the autocorrelation sequence must correspond to most random signal whose correlation values in the range of $|M| \le p$ coincide with measured values.

The maximum entropy principle is appealing because it assumes no more structure in the correlation sequence than that indicated by measured data.

The randomness or entropy of a signal is defined as

$$H[p_{xx}(f)] = \int_{-1/2}^{1/2} \ln p_{xx}(f)\, df \tag{6}$$

To obtain the maximum entropy correlation estimate, differentiate (6) with respect to the unknown values of correlation coefficients and set the derivatives to zero.

$$\frac{\partial H[Pxx(f)]}{\partial r_{xx}(m)} = \int_{-1/2}^{1/2} \frac{\partial \ln Pxx(f)}{\partial r_{xx}(m)} df = 0 \tag{7}$$

for $|m| > M$

For stochastic signals, the quantity of interest is the power spectral density, defined as the Fourier transform of the autocorrelation function as given in (5).

$$p_{xx}(f) = \sum_{-\infty}^{\infty} r_{xx}(m) e^{-j2\pi fm} \tag{8}$$

From (8) the derivative of the power spectrum with respect to the autocorrelation values is given by

$$\frac{\partial[Pxx(f)]}{\partial r_{xx}(m)} = e^{-j2\pi fm} \tag{9}$$

from (9) for the derivative of the logarithm of the power we have

$$\frac{\partial[\ln Pxx(f)]}{\partial r_{xx}(m)} = p_{xx}^{-1}(f) e^{-j2\pi fm} \tag{10}$$

From(10) substituting derivative of the logarithm of the power in (7)

$$\int_{-1/2}^{1/2} p_{xx}^{-1}(f) e^{-j2\Pi fm} df = 0 \tag{11}$$

for $|m| > \mathrm{M}$

Assuming that $p_{xx}^{-1}(f)$ is integrable, it may be associated with an autocorrelation sequence $C(m)$

$$p_{xx}^{-1}(f) = \sum_{m=-\infty}^{\infty} C(m) e^{-j2\Pi fm} \tag{12}$$

Where $C(m)$ is autocorrelation sequence

$$C(m) = \int_{-1/2}^{1/2} p_{xx}^{-1}(f) e^{j2\Pi fm} df \tag{13}$$

From equation (11) and (12) we have $C(m) = 0$ for $|m| > \mathrm{M}$

Hence from the equation (12) the inverse of the maximum entropy power spectrum can be obtained from the fourier transform of a finitelength autocorrelation sequence as

$$p_{xx}^{-1}(f) = \sum_{m=-M}^{M} C(m) e^{-j2\Pi fm} \tag{14}$$

Maximum entropy power spectrum is given by

$$p_{xx}^{\wedge ME}(f) = \frac{1}{\sum_{m=-M}^{M} C(m) e^{-j2\Pi fm}} \tag{15}$$

Since the denominator polynomial in equation (15) is symmetric, it follows that for every zero of this polynomial situated at radius r, there is a zero at radius 1/r, Hence this symmetric polynomial can be factorised and expressed as

$$\sum_{m=-M}^{M} C(m) z^{-m} = \frac{1}{\sigma^2 u(x) u(x^{-1})} \tag{16}$$

Where $\frac{1}{\sigma^2}$ is a gain term

$u(x)$ and $u(x^{-1})$ is a polynomial of order p (can be any natural value n) defined as

$$u_q(x) = 1 + W_{11} x^{-1} + W_{12} x^{-2} + \cdots + W_{1p} x^{-p} \tag{17}$$

$$u_q(x^{-1}) = 1 + W_{11} x^{1} + W_{12} x^{2} + \cdots + W_{1p} x^{p} \tag{18}$$

Assume $W_{11} = W_{12} = \text{------} = W_{1p} = 1$ without any time delay component to avoide signal whitening

From equation (13) and (14) the maximum entropy power spectrum can be expressed as

$$p_{x_q x_q}^{\wedge ME}(\mathrm{f}) = \frac{\sigma^2}{u_q(x) u_q(x^{-1})} \tag{19}$$

Equation (19) shows that the maximum entropy power spectrum estimate is the power spectrum of an autoregressive model which is obtained by maximising the entropy of the power spectrum with respect to unknown autocorrelation values.

p is order of the polynomial can be any natural number and q is the number of rows of the ummixing matrix where maximum value of q is equal to p.

Thus from euation (19) equation for maximum entropy power spectrum estimation can be written as

$$p^{\wedge ME}_{x_q x_q}(f) = \frac{\sigma^2}{[1+\sum_{p=1}^{n} W_{qp}\, x^{-p}][1+\sum_{p=1}^{n} W_{qp}\, x^{p}]} \quad (20)$$

Let's take the order of the polynomial $p = 3$ and $q = 1$ equation (18) can be written as

$$p^{\wedge ME}_{u_1 u_1}(f) = \frac{\sigma^2}{u_1(x)+x_1 u_1(x)+W_{12}x_2^2 u_1(x)+W_{13}x_3^3 u_1(x)}$$

Thus the equation for maximum entropy power spectrum in generalized form can be written as

$$p^{\wedge ME}_{xx}(f) = \frac{\sigma^2}{u_q(x)[1+\sum_{p=1}^{n} W_{qp}\, x_p^{p}]} \quad (21)$$

Let's Put value of $u_q(x)$ and $u_q(x^{-1})$ for q=1 and p=3 in (19)

$$p^{\wedge ME}_{x_1 x_1}(f) = \frac{\sigma^2}{[1+x_1^{-1}+W_{12}x_2^{-2}+W_{13}x_3^{-3}][1+x_1^{1}+W_{12}x_2^{2}+W_{13}x_3^{3}]} \quad (22)$$

Differentiating equation (22) with respect to W_{12} and W_{13} for getting change in weight ΔW_{12} and ΔW_{13} respectively.

$$\Delta W_{12}\ \alpha\ \frac{\partial P^{\wedge ME}_{x_1 x_1}(f)}{\partial W_{12}}$$

$$\Delta W_{12} = \eta \frac{2W_{12}}{[u_1(x_1^{-1})\, u_1(x_1^{1})]^2} \quad (23)$$

Where η is the praportionality constant, in the generalized form equation (23) can be written as

$$\Delta W_{qp} = \eta \frac{2W_{qp}}{[u_q(x_q^{-q})\, u_q(x_q^{q})]^2} \quad (24)$$

$$W_{qp}^{(new)} = W_{qp}^{(old)} + \Delta W_{qp}$$

2.2. *Check for power spectral density*

Power spectral density of signal $x_n(\tau)$ is given as

$$\gamma x_n x_n(\tau) = \int_{-1/2}^{1/2} p^{-1}_{x_n x_n}(f)\, e^{2\pi fm}$$

At maximum power spectral density $u_n(\tau)$ is find out using equation (4)

Then reconstructed signal $y_n(t) = \frac{1}{1+e^{-u_n(\tau)}}$ is most approximately equal to the original signal $s_n(t)$.

3. Experimental results and comparison

Actual voices as source signals $s_1(t)$ and $s_2(t)$ male and female voices respectively are taken. The unknown nonlinear mixture structure is specified as

$$A1=\begin{bmatrix}0.7 & 0.5\\ 0.5 & 0.7\end{bmatrix} \qquad A2=\begin{bmatrix}0.7 & 0.5\\ 0.5 & 0.7\end{bmatrix}$$

In the iterative procedure following parameters have been setup as

The number of samples taken: 15000

The order of polynomial: p = 2

The weight of criterion: σ = 0.5

Initial value of weights: $W_{max} = 3$

Final value of weight: $W_{min} = 0.1$

the results of the nonlinear blind source separation using proposed algorithm from the mixtures of male and female voices is shown in fig. (2) and (3).

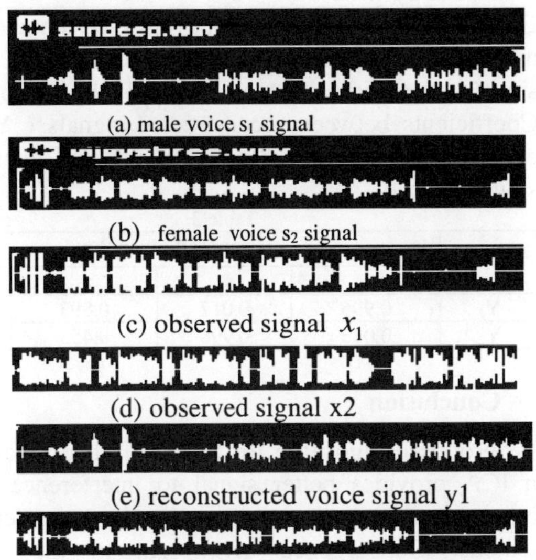

(a) male voice s_1 signal

(b) female voice s_2 signal

(c) observed signal x_1

(d) observed signal x2

(e) reconstructed voice signal y1

(f) reconstructed voice signal y2

Fig. 2

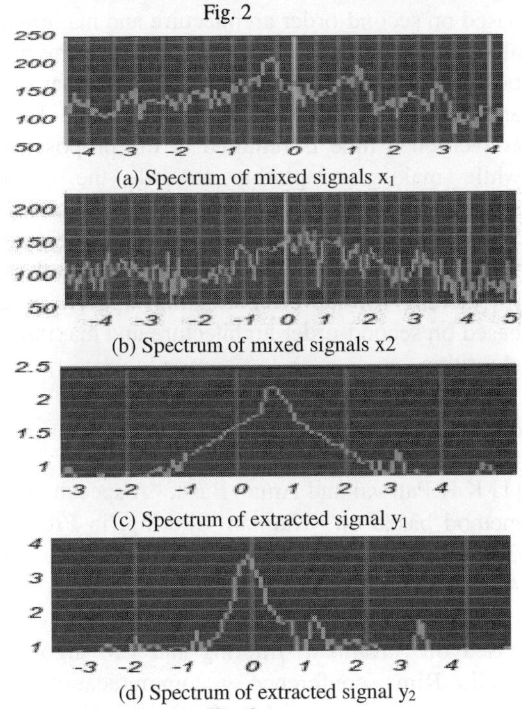

(a) Spectrum of mixed signals x_1

(b) Spectrum of mixed signals x2

(c) Spectrum of extracted signal y_1

(d) Spectrum of extracted signal y_2

Fig. 3

Table 1 gives the comparison between adaptive

parameters used in the iteration procedure of Mutual Information Based Separation Algorithm and proposed algorithm.

Table 1.

Methods for BSS	Adaptive Parameters			
	P	σ	W_{max}	W_{min}
Speech enhancement based on second-order architecture and maximum entropy algorithm	2	0.5	16	-0.6
Proposed algorithm	2	0.5	6	0.1

Cross correlation coefficient of observed unmixed signal and source (test) signal is check to conform the received signal is the original signal. Table II shows Correlation Coefficients between reconstructed signals (Y_1, Y_2) and original source signals (s_1, s_2) and intermediate signals (x_1,x_2).

Table 2.

	Proposed algorithm			
	s_1	s_2	x_1	x_2
Y_1	0.996	0.017	0.893	0.476
Y_2	0.013	0.998	0.453	0.899

4. Conclusion

The proposed algorithm for Speech Enhancement based on ICA provides better signal to interference ratio as compare to the existing computationally quite demanding methods. Convergence of weight in the proposed algorithm is from 6 to 0.1 and for Speech enhancement based on second-order architecture and maximum entropy algorithm is from 16 to 0.6. Although the order of the polynomial taken same that is 2 less number of iteration are required with proposed algorithm. Less weight convergence time is required in the proposed algorithm while making adaptation towards the extraction of statistically independent sources by maximizing entropy. When the proposed algorithm is convergent, the output SNR is 41.983 db much better as compared to 35.59db [6] obtain with already existing Speech enhancement based on second-order architecture and maximum entropy algorithm.

Referances

[1] K.K.Paliwal and Anjan Basu, "A speech enhancement method based on Kalman filtering,"in Proc. *IEEE* Int. Cod. Acoust., Speech, Signal Processing, pp177-180, Apr. 1987,.

[2] Weixiu Du and P. Driessen " Speech enhancement based on Kalman filtering and EM algorithm",IEEE pacific Rim conference on communications, computers and signal processing, May 9-10, 1991 Pp 142 to 145.

[3] Yariv Ephraim, "Statistical-Model-Based Speech Enhancement Systems", Proceedings of the IEEE, vol. 80, No. 10, pp 1526-1555, October 1992 .

[4] A.J.Bell and T.J.sejnowsh. "An information maximization approach to blind separation and blind deconvolution." Neural Computation, vol7(6) ppl129-1159,1995

[5] Patrik Sorqvast, Peter Handel and Bjorn Ottersten, "Kalman filtering for low distortion speech enhancement in mobile communication", Proceedings of the IEEE 1997 ,pp 1219-1222, 1997.

[6] Yu Xiao; Hu Guangrui "Speech enhancement based on second-order architecture and maximum entropy algorithm"; Proceeding of ICSP '98 Fourth International Conference on signal processing", Page(s):572-75vol.1,12-16Oct.1998.

[7] Djamila Muhmoudi and Andrzej Drygujlo ," Combined wiener and coherent filtering in wavelet domain for microphone array speech enhancements." IEEE Proceedings 1998,pp 385- 388.

[8] Lieven De Lathauwer, Bart De Moor and Joos Vandewalle "An introduction to Independent component analysis" journal of chemometrics; pp 123–149, 2000.

[9] Chang-Min Kim, Hyung-Min Park, Taesu Kim, Yoon-Kyung Choi, and Soo-Young Lee,"FPGA Implementation of ICA Algorithm for Blind Signal Separation and Adaptive Noise Canceling, IEEE Transaction on Neural Networks, VOL. 14, NO. 5, *pp-1038-1046 september 2003.*

[10] K.Nakayama, A.Hirano and Y.Dejima, "Analysis of signal separation and distortion in feedforward blind source separation for convolutive mixture"Proc. MWSCAS2004, Hiroshima, Japan, pp. 111-207-111-210, July 2004.

[11] Marcel Gabrea Robust adaptive Kalman filtering-based speech enhancement algorithm" IEEE international Conference on Acoustics, Speech, and Signal Processing, Proceedings. (ICASSP '04). Volume 1, Page(s):I - 301-4 vol.1, 17-21 May 2004.

[12] Jordi Sole-Casalsa and Marcos Faundez-Zanuyb "Application of the mutual information minimization to speaker recognition/identification improvement" Neurocomputing Dec 2005.

[13] Akihide Horita, *Student Member, IEEE*, Kenji Nakayama, Akihiro Hirano Members, IEEE, and Yasuhiro Dejima "A Distortion Free Learning Algorithm for Feedforward BSS and Its Comparative Study with Feedback BSS" International Joint Conference on Neural Networks Sheraton Vancouver Wall Centre Hotel, Vancouver, BC, Canada pp 3911-3918, July 16-21,2006.

MULTI OPERATOR DELIMITER BASED DATA ENCRYPTION STANDARD (MODDES)

PROSANTA GOPE

M.Tech in Computer Science and Engineering,National Institute of Technology Durgapur, West Bengal, Zip-713209, India

D. GHOSH

Professor of Computer Science and Engineering,National Institute of Technology Durgapur, West Bengal, Zip-713209, India

A. R. KRISHNA CHELLURI

M.Tech in Computer Science and Engineering,National Institute of Technology Durgapur, West Bengal, Zip-713209, India

PINAKI CHATTOPADHYAY

M.Tech in Computer Science and Engineering,National Institute of Technology Durgapur, West Bengal, Zip-713209, India

Designing a secret key algorithm needs high-level security against all kinds of unauthorized attacks like active and passive attacks. Here we have introduced a new block cipher algorithm named Multi Operator and Delimiter based Data Encryption Standard (**MODDES**). It is an unique independent approach, which uses the concept of stack of operators and randomized delimiters selection along with some suitable mathematical logic and lookup table concept as well. Thus a new protocol has been designed to encrypt a given text, which allows a high-level security and higher throughput. The algorithm is implemented and is successfully tested on text file as well as corresponding digital text file for image, audio signals as well.

Keywords- Data encryption and decryption methodology, MODDES, Randomized operators and delimiters, Codesequence, Lookup table

1. Introduction

An assault on system security derived from an intelligent threat is an intelligent act , which is a deliberate attempt to evade security services and penetrate into the security policy of a system. In this paper we have introduced a new approach which will put real challenge in the world of network security[6]. It is basically a secret key algorithm where we have introduced a 32-bit key and also used multiple binary operators and some delimiters, which are chosen randomly from predefined stacks along with a code sequence. As it is a secret key algorithm, the complexity is also less. In spite of a secret key algorithm [7], it does not entirely depend on the key. As such, if the key value is known, then also it is impossible to decipher it without the knowledge of decryption algorithm as well as code sequence generated from that particular processing. It is worthwhile to note here that for the same text and the same key, cipher code is different for each and every processing. The MODDES algorithm protects the cipher code from the attacks like brute force because of, by using all possible combination of keys and substitution of each and every ciphered character using substitution process (mono alphabetic substitution or poly alphabetic substitution)[6] one cannot decipher

2. Encryption Procedure using MODDES

In this algorithm we have taken two predefined stacks and a lookup table. The first stack consists of different combinations of operators and the other stack consists of combinations of delimiters, which are chosen randomly at the code sequence. The lookup table consists of the code words of the corresponding operators present in first stack . The steps of the algorithm are given below.

i) Read a character from the text file corresponding to a text, audio or image to be encrypted. Now get the ASCII value of that character.

ii) Take the binary equivalent of that ASCII value.

iii) Now read the binary string.

iv) Next step consists of performing mathematical operation using operators from the operator stack over the bits, using the secret key.

v) To maintain secrecy of operators used as above, encode the operators using lookup table.

vi) Generate a random number.

vii) Depending on the nature of the key a suitable mathematical operation is performed with the random number.

viii) Add the corresponding character of the generated random number to the code sequence.

ix) Choose a random delimiter from the predefined stack and add it at the end of the code sequence.

Continue step (i) to step (ix) for the next characters of the file until eof is reached.

3. Decryption Procedure using MODDES

i) Read the first character from the cipher text and get the corresponding ASCII value of it.

ii) Check the key and examine the character before the delimiter in the code sequence.

iii) Perform similar mathematical operations with this character depending on the nature of the key.

iv) Decode the code sequence and perform inverse operation for each and every character of the code sequence.

v) Repeat the steps (i) to (iv) till the end.

vi) If the file happens to be an audio or image file, then after deciphering to plain text form, it is now converted back to its respective audio or image file using various softwares like MATLAB 7.6.

4. Languages suitable for MODDES

The algorithm MODDES may be implemented in all the languages supporting Unicode system facility like Java, C#.Net,etc.. However, this may as well as be implemented using C,C++ with restrictions.

5. System Model suitable for MODDES

It appears that star topology[7] is the most suitable network architecture for implementation of the algorithm. Firstly, both sender and receiver clients have to agree upon a common key value to be stored in the server having central database. Now the text, image and audio files (all in textual form) will be sent by the sender after encryption using MODDES with the corresponding code sequence for that particular encryption cycle. It is worthwhile to note that the same text with same key value will have different cipher text at different processing, practically making it impossible for the hacker to break it, even if the key value is known to him. The code sequence generated along with the cipher text is also sent to the server.

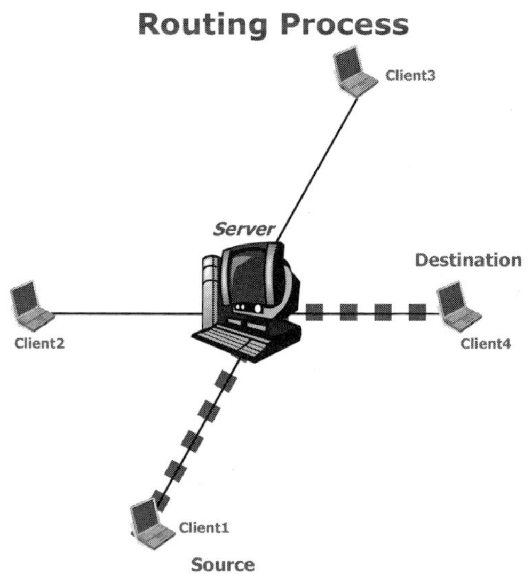

Fig 1.

Now the receiver client on request may get the cipher text only from the server on production of key value. However, if he wants to decrypt the cipher text, he is required to use a key value, the same code sequence available in the server and the decryption algorithm.

The server has to be distributed in nature as well as multithreaded. So, each and every request will be handled by a certain thread. So, only the thing kept in mind at the time of designing the server program is, it must be thread safe.

If the server doesn't support multi-threading facility, then for better performance, server maintains storage for the code sequence along with an indicator. If the corresponding client (who asks for that particular file) can decipher that cipher text successfully, by using the code sequence which is already delivered to the server from the sender end it sends a green signal to the server (i.e. true).

Unless and until the server gets the green signal it will not clear the code sequence storage and the indicator value will remain false. In the mean time it will not receive any further request from that particular client for that same file.

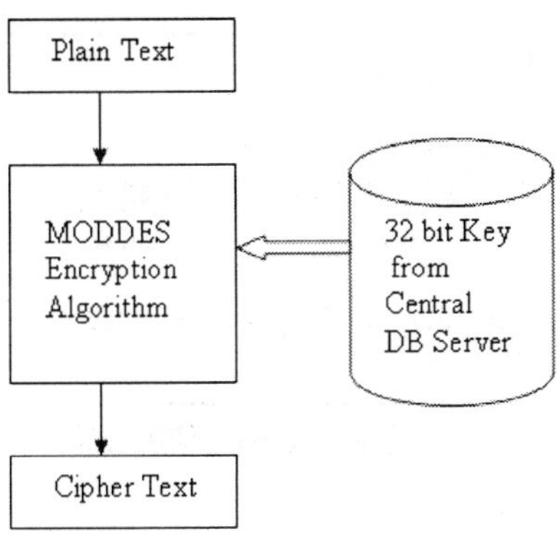

Fig 2. Basic block diagram of MODDES at the Sender System

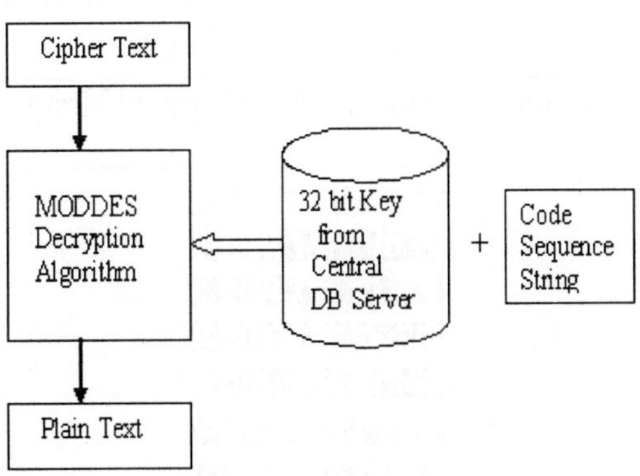

Fig 3. Basic block diagram of MODDES Receiver System

6. Conclusion and Future work

This paper introduces a new secret key algorithm named **MODDES** which was successfully tested for text, image and audio/speech files. As compared to DES, **MODDES** is simple and efficient which does not fully emphasize on the key. In the mean time it was seen that if the file size is in between 25000 bytes then it can even beat the DES [6], 3DES, AES(Rijindael)[4] in terms of total execution time. A proposed direction for the future work could analyze the performance/security trade off MODDES as compared to other algorithms including DES, 3DES, AES (Rijindael).

7. Result

MODDES applying on Text

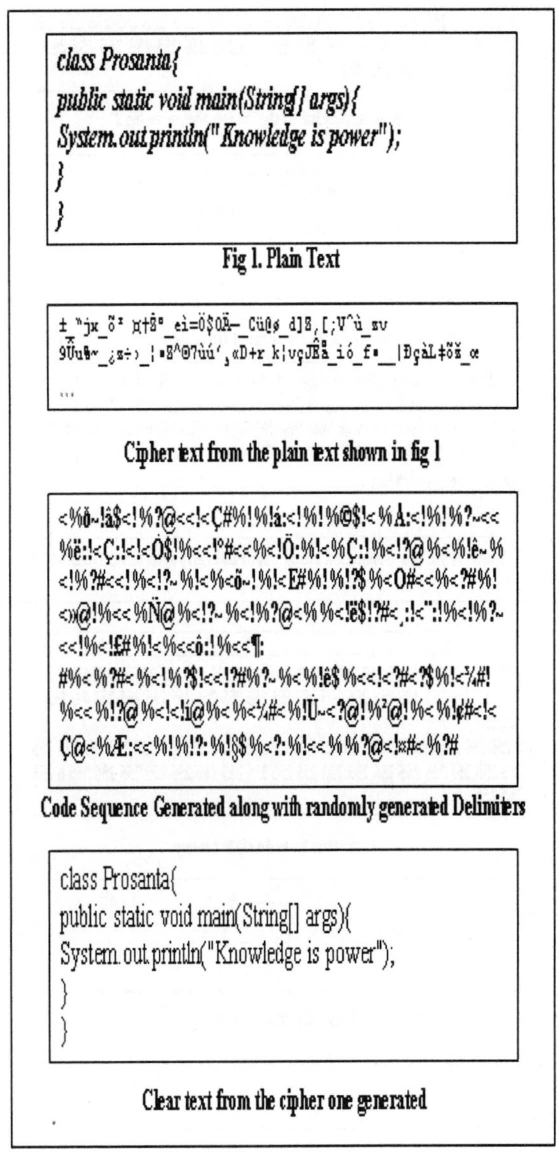

Fig 4.

MODDES applying on Image

Fig 2. Image File

```
0 255 255 255 255 255 255 255 255 255 255 255 255 255 255 255 255 255 255
255 255 255 255 255 255 255 255 255 255 255 255 255 255 255 255 255
255 255 0 0 255 255 255
0 255 255 255 255 255 255 255 255 255 255 255 255 255 255 255 255 255 255
255 255 255 255 255 255 255 255 255 255 255 255 255 255 255 255 255
255 255 255 0 255 255 255
```

Digital text value of the image shown in fig 2

```
â3þ$°Y⊕⊕Ȅš_±□(Wü]•)×¢ïçoœtÔhΓ _uvH_°v|m°_²01ò÷‡ÐáV___,,²
oδk_¸uÚÛ‰y³²ó|¯£þâ/m7'w™Žõ_³Û¶:ØΈ–
†Ðq□_yN7×bÐ[ULÀ«ÓÅ¤3òßØtÒµ£í_+□–zb£ËÑ¶Çw
‰□¯¦ÊáÞoàt‰□Î ª?þÀùT‡šöRB«бãô`_,¸¿âG¢D<Š¼I@²Ő_|aíš–Ñwÿ_ó_²œª<,9
Φäȇwµ_4__Ø^,;Ô:÷ f□ófŸ=ó
```

Cipher text from the plain text generated from the image shown in fig 2

```
<%!Ñ#%!%¥@<İ@%<<%!?@<%%<!%µ#!<%!£#%!%?:<?~%<!%<
?$<%%è#!<%!Á:%!<%!?$<%?:%<!<Ç#<%!<?$!<!<?:%!<%?~<!<!?:
<<!<<?~%%<%!¬~<%<<%ð~!â$<!%?@<<!<Ç#%!%!á:<!%!%©$
©$!<%Å:<!%!%?~<<%ë:!<Ç:!<!<Ȯ$!%<<!°#<<%<!Ö:%!<%Ç:!%<!?
@%<%!ê~%<!%?#
```

Code Sequence Generated along with randomly generated Delimiters

```
0 255 255 255 255 255 255 255 255 255 255 255 255 255 255 255 255 255 255 255 255
255 255 255 255 255 255 255 255 255 255 255 255 255 255 255 255 255 255 0 0 255
255 255
0 255 255 255 255 255 255 255 255 255 255 255 255 255 255 255 255 255 255 255 255
255 255 255 255 255 255 255 255 255 255 255 255 255 255 255 255 255 255 0 255
255 255
```

Text value from the cipher image

Image file from text value

Note: In above the text value from the image or image to text value conversion takes place with the help of MATLAB 7.6 software.

Fig 5.

MODDES applying on Audio/Speech

```
-8.093262e-002 -8.093262e-002
-7.696533e-002 -7.696533e-002
-6.951904e-002 -6.951904e-002
-5.535889e-002 -5.535889e-002
-3.369141e-002 -3.369141e-002
-8.361816e-003 -8.361816e-003
1.568604e-002 1.568604e-002
3.240967e-002 3.240967e-002
```

Digital text value of the audio that says "WELCOME"

```
o_änp»Ė¬%HŘ<_#e†ÄS_□
_2"^¿
D¡wû_l¬""4Lo_"ÐþNaI¡ýß__Öþèi5_'±<}–
ÖS ¯øöí¥FáÖt|□NQ"__÷h□Ii¾¡Iä‡dv4šßû`bÏÜš_ECþ…E‹
      ×¢â[z_fâF·ú•Ä'Ö_9 š      _Ì¢Pqßf_ÎtHé□œN
      _ØⒸXPØ¿}Ï™□°¯±_´o|`İ–
ÄÜŸ^□ÏLš>8DjjÄAGœy_|Ðë^,YHßœþ⊖_Q_Ȯâ}ž801aGF‰`E!¥£œ
ëoDUQÞ|iF_i¥‰_Ⓔns,Ä
```

Cipher text of speech "WELCOME"

```
§<æ$!<%ä~!%¶$<!~%!%!Ä$%Æ#!<<%Ö$!<<i$<%!<Þ@%<!%!?@<<%
?$!%!%ö$<<:<%%<?@%!%<?:<!<%?:!<!@<!Å:%!«:%<!<?@!²:<
<!¶#%<°~%%<%®$!<<<I$!<<?#!%<!§~<!<©:%!<Ø:%<!<ã~!%<!%¤$!<
%%®:<!<%Ö$<!%<?#<%Ȯ~%!Ø#%×$!<?$%<!<?~<!<µ$
```

Code Sequence Generated along with randomly generated Delimiters

```
-8.093262e-002 -8.093262e-002
-7.696533e-002 -7.696533e-002
-6.951904e-002 -6.951904e-002
-5.535889e-002 -5.535889e-002
-3.369141e-002 -3.369141e-002
-8.361816e-003 -8.361816e-003
1.568604e-002 1.568604e-002
3.240967e-002 3.240967e-002
```

Text value of speech "WELCOME" from the Cipher one

Note: In the above fig. text to audio or audio to text value conversion takes place with the help of MATLAB 7.6 software.

Fig 6.

References

1. National Bureau of Standards – Data Encryption Standard, FIPS Publication 46, 1977.
2. NIST, "Advanced Encryption Standard Call", NIST, 1997. http://www.nist.gov/aes/.
3. Twenty Second National Radio Science Conference (NRSC 2005), RDEA Algorithm.
4. Daemen, Jijmen, V.: "AES Proposal: Rijndael", Banksys/Katholieke., R Universiteit Leuven, Belgium, AES submission, June 1998.
5. http://www.rsasecurity.com/company/news/releases/pr.asp?doc_id=462
6. W.Stallings "Cryptography and network security principles and practice," Fourth edition, Prentice hall, 2007.
7. Computer Networks b y Andrew S.Tanenbaum, Fourth edition, Prentice hall, 2004.

A COMPARATIVE STUDY OF PERFORMANCE BASED CRYPTO ANALYSIS FEATURES FOR STANDARD DATA ENCRYPTION ALGORITHMS WITH (MODDES)

A R KRISHNA CHELLURI

M.Tech in Computer Science and Engineering,National Institute of Technology Durgapur, West Bengal, Zip-713209, India

D. GHOSH

Professor of Computer Science and Engineering,National Institute of Technology Durgapur, West Bengal, Zip-713209, India

PINAKI CHATTOPADHYAY

M.Tech in Computer Science and Engineering,National Institute of Technology Durgapur, West Bengal, Zip-713209, India

PROSANTA GOPE

M.Tech in Computer Science and Engineering,National Institute of Technology Durgapur, West Bengal, Zip-713209, India

While designing an encryption algorithm, apart from security, one of the most important parameter that are required to be considered is it's performance and cost analysis. Here we have tried to highlight the performance of some well known data encryption algorithms like DES, 3DES, AES (Rijndael) and compare them with the MODDES. Based on the experiment, it can be said that the MODDES algorithm is one of the best performing partially symmetric key algorithm among the algorithms chosen for implementation, particularly for the text message with limited size.
Keywords- DES, 3DES,AES, MODDES, Cryptanalysis

1. Introduction

All symmetric key algorithms[6] like DES, 3DES, AES[4], Blowfish etc.. are efficient in terms of time, which however invariably use the concept of symmetric key. According to the definition of symmetric key, same key is used for both encryption and decryption. Here, a plain text (message) is encrypted to a cipher text using a key through some unique processes, and reversing the process and applying the same key on the cipher text for decryption regain the same text. Thus while deciphering a cipher text, knowing the key value (Brute Force method etc..) , enables a hacker to decipher the cipher text by reducing the security of the text to a great extent.
Here, in MODDES[8], we introduce the concept of partial symmetric key. At the time of decipher, knowing the key value only does not allow a hacker to decipher. The following information invariably have to be known for deciphering a cipher text using MODDES technique.

i) Key value.
ii) Code sequence string generated from a particular process.

Code sequence string invariably consists of multiple operators and delimiters in an encoded form with random arrangement changing every time with a process. Thus for deciphering the cipher text apart from key value, code sequence string for ith processing is a must. This really increases the security of the text multifold and makes it impossible to decipher.
Further MODDES method can also be used for encryption and decryption of images and voices, apart from text messages.

2. Implemented Algorithms

In Here we have chosen the following symmetric key algorithms like:-

- DES
- Triple DES
- AES (Rijndael)
- MODDES (Partially symmetric key)

2.1. *Data Encryption Standard*

In January 1977, the US Government adopted a product cipher developed by IBM as its official standard for unclassified information. This cipher, DES was widely adopted by the industry, specially banking sector for use in security products. Here a plain text is encrypted in blocks of 64 bits, yielding 64 bits of cipher. The algorithm which is parameterized by a 56 bit key, has 19 distinct stages. Although the DES standard is public, the deign criteria used are classified. There has been considerable controversy over the design particularly when IBM reduced the key from 128 bits to 56 bits.

It has been proved that if the number of iterations are increased in DES the complexity of the algorithm increased exponentially. It was particularly based on a cipher developed and patented by IBM called the Lucifer. In 1977, two Stanford cryptography researchers have proved that DES key can be broken as well.

2.2. *Triple Data Encryption Standard*

In 1979, IBM realized that DES key length is too short and even single key is not enough. So, as a replacement of DES, they proposed a new data encryption standard, where the algorithm can take two or three 56 bit keys. Thus, the effective key length is upto 168 bits.

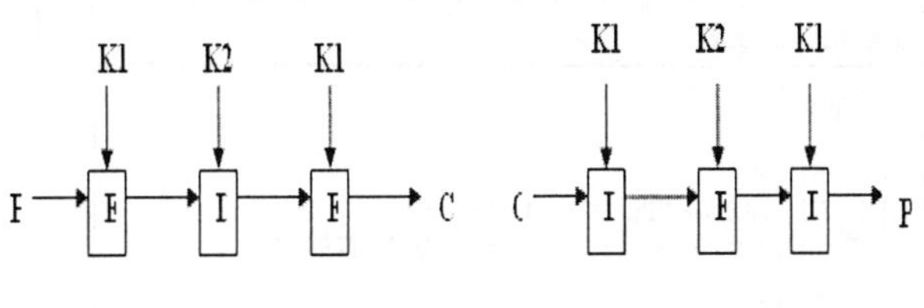

(a) Triple encryption using DES (b) Decryption

Figure 1

In the first stage, the plain text is encrypted using DES in the usual way with K1. In the second stage DES is run in the decryption mode using K2 as the key. Finally another DES encryption is done with K1.

It has been proved that in ECB (Electronic Code Book) mode, although the Triple DES algorithm is much more secure than DES, it takes execution time greater than DES both for encryption and decryption.

2.3. *Advanced Data Encryption Standard*

In January 1977, the researchers from all over the world were invited to submit proposals for new standards to be called AES (Advanced Data Encryption Standard) along with some bake off rules. The symmetric block cipher algorithm must support the key length of 128, 192 and 256 bits and it can be implemented both by hardware and software.

After exhaustive analysis and evolutions it has been proved that Rijndael AES is one of the finest one and it supports the key length and block size from 128 bits to 256 bits in steps of 32 bits. Although this technique is more secure than DES and Triple DES, it takes greater execution time than both DES and Triple DES.

2.4. *MODDES*

It is basically a new partial symmetric key algorithm which is unique in nature, where we have introduced a 32 bit key and also used multiple binary operators and some delimiters chosen randomly from predefined stacks along with a code sequence. Here with the same partial symmetric key and for the same plain text, the code sequences and the cipher texts generated from different processes are different as shown in fig 2. So, in this case the system for keeping track of each and every cipher along with code sequences are required to be

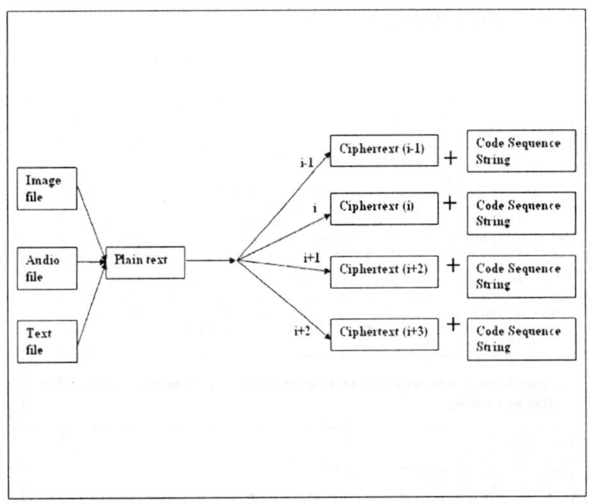

Figure 2

multithreaded in nature. In other standard algorithms, in most of the cases, iteration of key values are required and depending upon this key value only, decryption can be made. However using same technique deciphering is an uphill task in case of MODDES. For the plain text in fig.3 below, using the same key we have generated a separate set of cipher text with its corresponding code sequence string as shown in fig3(a) to 3(f). 3(f).

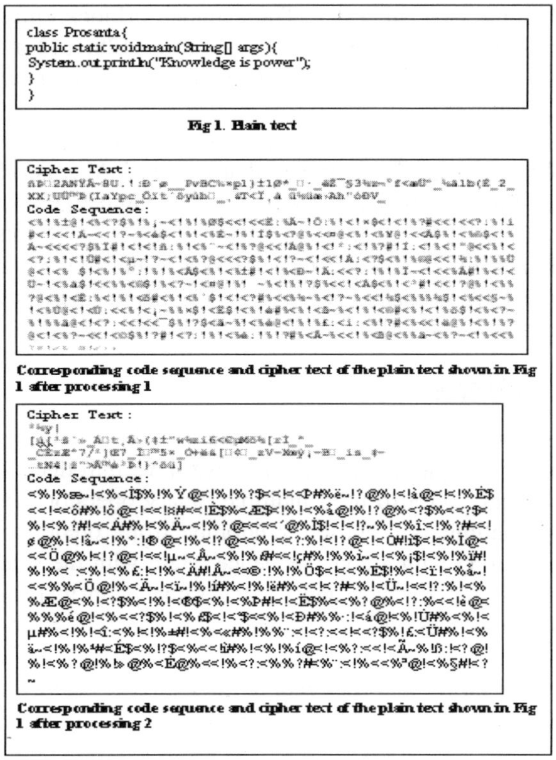

Figure 3 (a) and Figure 3 (b)

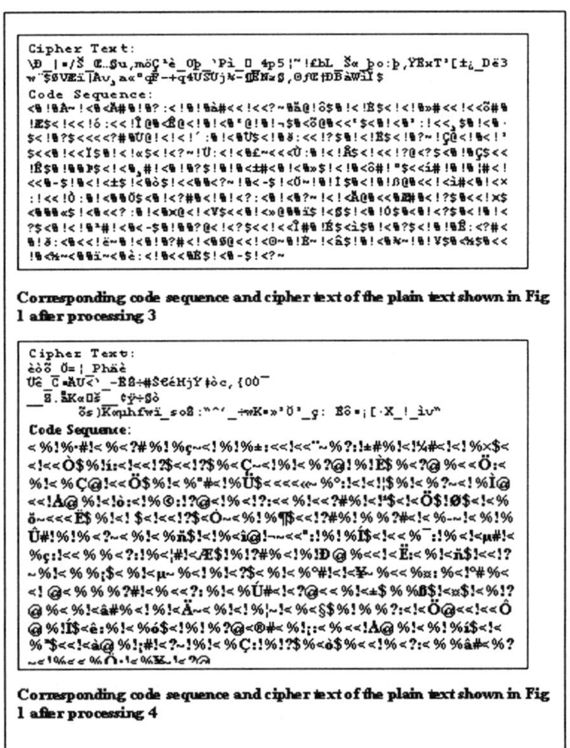

Figure 3 (c) and Figure 3 (d)

Figure 3 (a) to Figure 3 (f) indicates six versions of different cipher texts for six processing p1 top6 for the same text and same key value. In the process, six different sets of code sequence sets of code sequence strings are generated.

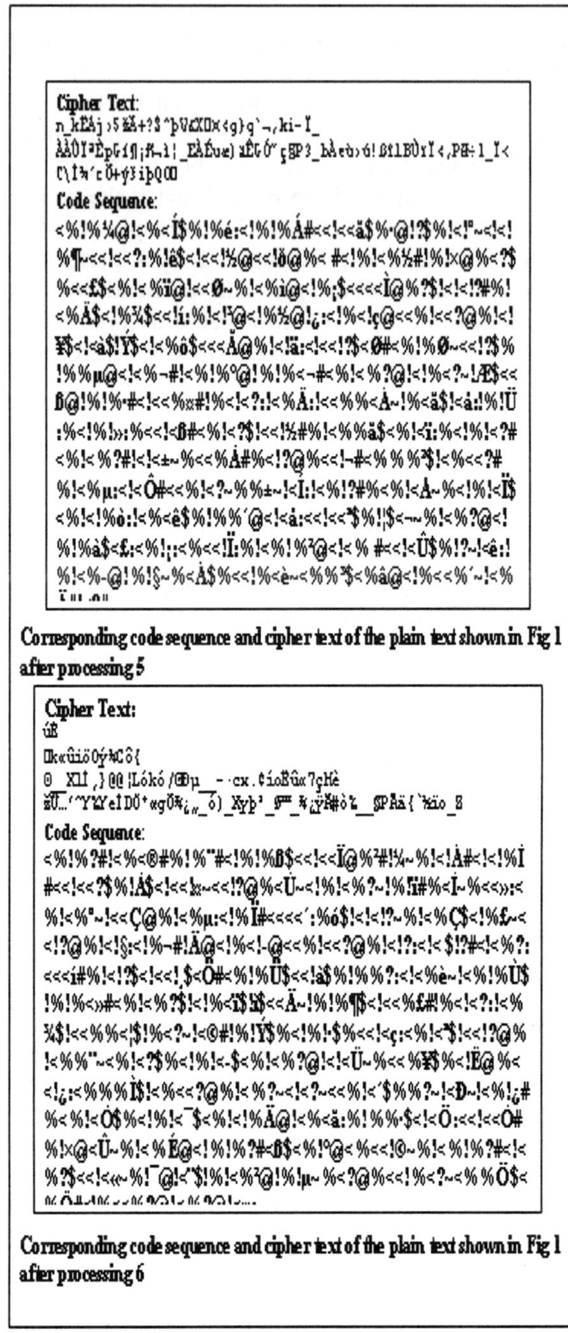

Figure 3 (e) and Figure 3 (f)

3. BENCHMARKING AND PERFORMANCE ANALYSIS OF MODDES WITH DES, 3DES AND AES.

a) Comparative execution time of encryption in the secret key algorithms

Input Size (bytes)	DES(In 2.4GHZ)	3DES(In 2.4GHZ)	AES(In 2.4GHZ)	MODDES(In 1.8 GHZ)
20,527	2	7	4	12
36,002	4	13	6	39
45,911	5	17	8	66
59,862	7	23	11	119
69,646	9	26	13	167

Figure 4 (a)

b) Comparative execution time of decryption in the secret key algorithms

Input Size (bytes)	DES(In 2.4GHZ)	3DES(In 2.4GHZ)	AES(In 2.4GHZ)	MODDES(In 1.8 GHZ)
20,527	17	58	62	2
36,002	30	99	94	3
45,911	41	130	125	3
59,862	52	181	174	3
69,646	69	201	200	3

Figure 4 (b)

c) Comparative execution time for encryption as well as decryption in the secret key algorithms

Input Size (bytes)	DES(In 2.4GHZ)	3DES(In 2.4GHZ)	AES(In 2.4GHZ)	MODDES(In 1.8 GHZ)
20,527	19	65	66	14
36,002	34	112	100	42
45,911	46	147	133	69
59,862	59	204	185	122
69,646	78	227	213	170

Figure 4 (c)

However although the benchmarking of all the standard algorithms for encryption and decryption has been carried out in 2.4 GHZ machines, for the same text size performance of MODDES has been studied using 1.8 GHZ machines. As such, it is expected that the time taken will be further reduced if 2.4 GHZ machines are also used for MODDES. From the above results we can conclude that performance of MODDES in terms of execution time is better than other well known secret key algorithms like DES, Triple DES and AES etc.. for the text file size less than 25,000 bytes.

Further, as discussed, since the usage of secret key here is only partially symmetric, this increases the security of the data as compared to other standard algorithms.

This algorithm is best suited for languages (Java, C#) which supports Unicode system facility with larger RAM size.

4. CRYPTANALYSIS

Modern high quality encryption methods have few known flaws and are subjected to extensive attack by cryptography experts through cryptanalysis. This is a science (or art) of reading encrypted traffic without prior knowledge of key. Hence while considering as to what encryption to use, it is important to choose a well known method that has been rigorously examined by the wider community. Many high security algorithms have turned out to be ultimately insecure. The cryptanalysis will be used against a condition, if some one tries to break encrypted traffic. The methods used vary, both due to the nature of the attacks and the encryption algorithm they are trying to break. Some well known attacks like Brute Force[7] is probably the most rigorous technical attack in use today , simply because most modern algorithms and their implementations have few known holes that attacker can exploit. An 8 bit key has 2^8 combinations (256), thus a typical pocket calculator has enough power to try out all these combinations against the cipher text in less than a second, by comparison a 40 bit key has 2^{40} combinations (1,099,511,627,776) but this is still computable fairly easily.

In case of MODDES,

- Attack like brute force fails totally because by using all possible combinations of 32 bit key and even getting the key value does not help to decipher.
- Here the usage of key is only partially symmetric.
- The same key and the same text generates different cipher texts associated with corresponding code sequence strings, which is obviously different for each processing.
- Following MODDES therefore deciphering a cipher text C_i is possible only with

Key value (fixed)

Code sequence string S_i associated with that particular version of cipher text C_i for the ith processing

- Further, even if a hacker breaks the key and proceeds to break the cipher text by generating his own code sequence string (since multi operators and delimiters are finite), it is impossible to generate such code sequence string as illustrated below in fig(5) with a word say CALCUTTA.

- Apart from above, as an additional security from possible hacking, MODDES also use
    a) Encoding of operators.
    b) Use of different lookup tables.
    c) Linking the generation of cipher text and corresponding associated code sequence string with generation of random prime numbers both for encryption and decryption, which obviously are different for each processing.
- Almost all the standard methods allow standard English alphabets only where as MODDES allow 65,535 (2^{16}) characters as text for ciphering. Further image and audio files in textual forms can also be encrypted as demonstrated.
- Already as demonstrated if the file size is less than 25000 bytes, it is the most efficient method in forms of security as well as least time for encryption and decryption taken together.

To demonstrate the efficiency of MODDES, let we consider an example as follows. For a given text say, CALCUTTA we have for decryption:-

Alphabet	Corresponding Binary (Last octet)	Number of ones
C	01000011	3
A	01000001	2
L	01001100	3
C	01000011	3
U	01010101	4
T	01010100	3
T	01010100	3
A	01000001	2

Figure 5

For decryption, considering the key value is known and three operators are being chosen randomly so the possible number of attempts to generate the code sequence string, number of combination to be tried will be:-

$3^3 * 3^2 * 3^3 * 3^3 * 3^4 * 3^3 * 3^3 * 3^2 = (3)^{23}$ [on the basis of number of ones available in several bit positions].

$(3)^{23}$ possible combination of operators towards generation of code sequence strings.

Thus even if the key value is hacked by the hacker, generation of code sequence for the word 'CALCUTTA' will take 14.52 hrs in 1.8 MHZ machine.

Further encoding of multi operator and delimiters and linking the generation of code sequence with random prime number generations make it impossible to decipher.

5. Conclusion and Future work

In this paper we have tried to benchmark performance analysis of popular secret key algorithms ie. DES,3DES,AES with MODDES algorithm. It has been proved that performance and security provided by MODDES algorithm is better than other secret key algorithms for small messages.

A proposed direction for the future work could be to analyze the following factors.

i) Key values steganography along with cipher text

ii) Key factors for implementations like features with operating system, networking, etc..

The hardware implementation of MODDES in EVM and other machines.

6. References

1. National Bureau of Standards – Data Encryption Standard, FIPS Publication 46, 1977.
2. NIST, “Advanced Encryption Standard Call”, NIST, 1997. http://www.nist.gov/aes/.
3. Twenty Second National Radio Science Conference (NRSC 2005), RDEA Algorithm.
4. Daemen, Jijmen, V.: “AES Proposal: Rijndael”, Banksys/Katholieke., R Universiteit Leuven, Belgium, AES submission, June 1998.
5. http://www.rsasecurity.com/company/news/releases/pr.asp?doc_id=462
6. W.Stallings “Cryptography and network security principles and practice,” Fourth edition, Prentice hall, 2007.
7. Computer Networks b y Andrew S.Tanenbaum, Fourth edition, Prentice hall, 2004.
8. Multi Operator Delimiter based Data Encryption algorithm

Session 5

A RADIX-2^2 PIPELINE FFT FOR ULTRA WIDE BAND TECHNOLOGY

K. HARIKRISHNA

Dept. of Electronics & Computer Engineering,
Narayana Engineering College, Nellore, AP., India.

T. RAMA RAO

Dept. of Telecommunication Engineering,
SRM University, Kattankulattur, Chennai, TN., India.

VLADIMIR A. LABAY

Dept. of Electrical & Computer Engineering,
Gonzaga University, Spokane, WA., USA.

This paper presents a high level implementation of a high performance FFT for Ultra Wide Band (UWB) applications. The design has been coded in VHDL and targeted into Xilinx Virtex-E XCV400E FPGAs. The hardware requirement comparison shows that our implementation outperforms other implementations of FFT on the same series of FPGAs. Radix-2^2 algorithm has the same multiplicative complexity as the Radix-4 algorithm, but retains the butterfly structure of Radix-2 algorithm. The design is parameterizable in terms of input word length, output word length, twiddle factor word length, and processing word length. Also, it is scalable in terms of number of stages.

1. Introduction

The Fast Fourier Transform (FFT) is one of the most commonly used operations in digital signal processing and, currently, the demands increase towards larger and multidimensional transforms. Some applications require more processing on each data sample, which increases the total quantization noise. This can be avoided by gradually increasing the word length inside the pipeline, but affects memory requirements as well as the critical path in arithmetic components [1]. For large size FFTs, dynamic scaling is, therefore, a suitable trade-off between arithmetic complexity and memory requirements.

The FFT algorithm eliminates the redundant calculation which is needed in computing Discrete Fourier Transform (DFT) and is thus very suitable for efficient hardware implementation [2]. In addition to computing efficient DFT, the FFT also finds applications in linear filtering, digital spectral analysis and correlation analysis, Ultra Wide Band (UWB) applications, etc. A hardware oriented radix-2^2 algorithm [3] is developed by integrating a twiddle factor decomposition technique in divide and conquer approach to form a spatially regular Signal Flow Graph (SFG). Mapping the algorithm to the cascading delay feedback structure leads to the proposed architecture.

In the search for high performance FFT, this paper presents a pipelined architecture called R2^2SDF and its implementation on Field Programmable Gate Arrays (FPGAs) using Very High Speed Integrated Circuit (VHSIC) Hardware Description Language (VHDL). The next section describes architecture & design methodology, followed by its implementation in VHDL code and utilization in UWB technology. Finally we conclude with a comparison of hardware requirement of R2^2SDF and several other popular pipeline architectures.

2. Architecture & Design Methodology

2.1. *Radix-2^2 Decimation in Frequency FFT Algorithm*

A useful state-of-the-art review of hardware architectures for FFTs was given by He et al. [4]. In [4], different approaches were put into functional blocks with unified terminology. From the definition of DFT of size N [5]:

$$X(k) = \sum_{n=0}^{N-1} x(n) W_N^{nk}, \quad 0 \le k < N \qquad (1)$$

where W_N denotes the primitive *Nth* root of unity, with its exponent evaluated modulo N, He [4] applied a 3-dimensional linear index map,

$$n = \left< \frac{N}{2}n_1 + \frac{N}{4}n_2 + n_3 \right>_N$$
$$k = \left< k_1 + 2k_2 + 4k_3 \right>_N \qquad (2)$$

and Common factor algorithm (CFA) to derive a set of 4 DFTs of length N/4 as,

$$X(k_1 + 2k_2 + 4k_3) = \sum_{n3=0}^{\frac{N}{4}-1} \left[H(k_1, k_2, k_3) W_N^{n_3(k_1+2k_2)} \right] W_{\frac{N}{4}}^{n_3 k_3} \qquad (3)$$

where $H(k_1,k_2,k_3)$ is expressed in eqn (4).

$$H(k_1, k_2, n_3) = \left[x(n_3) + (-1)^{k_1} x\left(n_3 + \frac{N}{2}\right) \right] + (-j)^{(k_1+2k_2)} \left[x\left(n_3 + \frac{N}{4}\right) + (-1)^{k_1} x\left(n_3 + \frac{3N}{4}\right) \right] \qquad (4)$$

Eqn (4) represents the first two stages of butterflies with only trivial multiplications in the SFG, as BFI and BFII. Full multipliers are required after the two butterflies in order to compute the product of the decomposed twiddle factor $W_N^{n_3(k_1,2k_2)}$ in eqn (3). Note the order of the twiddle factors is different from that of radix-4 algorithm.

Applying this CFA procedure recursively to the remaining DFTs of length N/4 in eqn (3), the complete radix-2^2 Decimation-in-frequency (DIF FFT) algorithm is obtained. The corresponding FFT flow graph for N=16 is shown in Fig. 1 where small diamonds represent trivial multiplication by $W_N^{N/4} = -j$, which involves only real-imaginary swapping and sign inversion [4].

2.2. *Radix-2^2 SDF Architecture*

Mapping radix-2^2 DIF FFT algorithm derived to the radix-2 SDF architecture, a new architecture of R2^2SDF approach is obtained [3]. Fig 2 outlines an

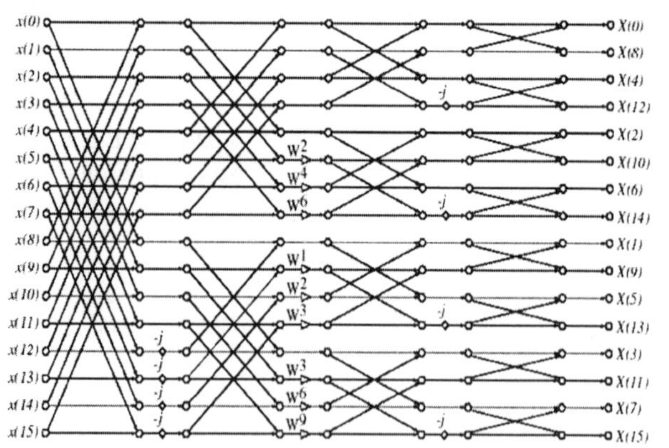

Fig 1. Radix-2^2 DIF FFT flow graph for N=16

implementation of the R2^2SDF architecture for N=1024, note the similarity of the data-path to R2SDF and the reduced number of multipliers. The implementation uses two types of butterflies; one identical to that in R2SDF, the other contains also the logic to implement the trivial twiddle factor multiplication, as shown in Fig 3 (i), (ii) respectively [3].

Due to the spatial regularity of Radix-2^2 algorithm, the synchronization control of the processor is very simple. A ($\log_2$N)-bit binary counter serves two purposes: synchronization controller and address counter for twiddle factor reading in each stage. With the help of the butterfly structures shown in Fig 3, the scheduled operation of the R2^2SDF processor in Fig 2 is as follows.

On first N/2 cycles, the 2-to-1 multiplexers in the first butterfly module switch to position "0", and the butterfly is idle. The input data from left is directed to the shift registers until they are filled. On next N/2 cycles, the multiplexers turn to position "1", the butterfly computes a 2-point DFT with incoming data and the data stored in the shift registers.

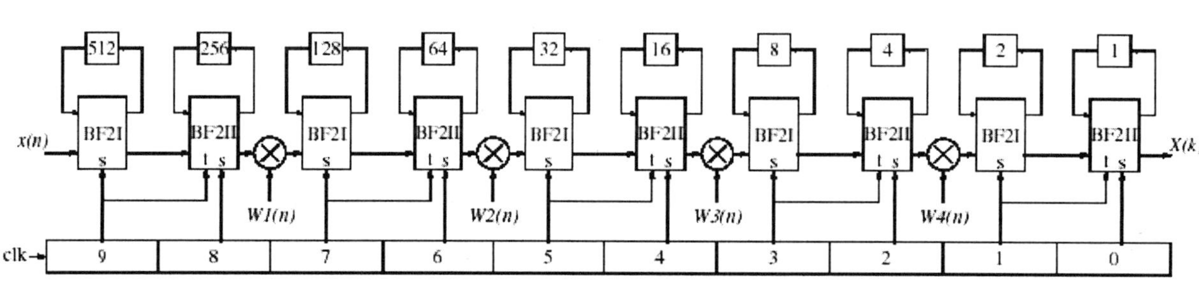

Fig 2. R2^2SDF pipeline FFT architecture for N=1024

$$Z1(n) = x(n) + x\left(n + \frac{N}{2}\right)$$

$$Z1\left(n + \frac{N}{2}\right) = x(n) - x\left(n + \frac{N}{2}\right), 0 \leq n < \frac{N}{2} \quad (5)$$

The butterfly outputs Z1(n) and Z1(n + N/2) are computed according to the equations given in eqn (5). Z1(n) is sent to apply the twiddle factors, and Z1(n + N/2) is sent back to the shift registers to be "multiplied" in still next N/2 cycles when the first half of the next frame of time sequence is loaded in. The operation of the second butterfly is similar to that of the first one, except the "distance" of butterfly input sequence are just N/4 and the trivial twiddle factor multiplication has been implemented by real-imaginary swapping with a commutator and controlled add/subtract operations, as in Fig 3(i) (ii), which requires two bit control signal from the synchronizing counter. The data then goes through a full complex multiplier, working at 75% utility, accomplishes the result of first level of radix-4 DFT word by word. Further processing repeats this pattern with the distance of the input data decreases by half at each consecutive butterfly stages. After N-1 clock cycles, the result of the complete DFT transform streams out to the right, in bit-reversed order. The next frame of transform can be computed without pausing due to the pipelined processing of each stage.

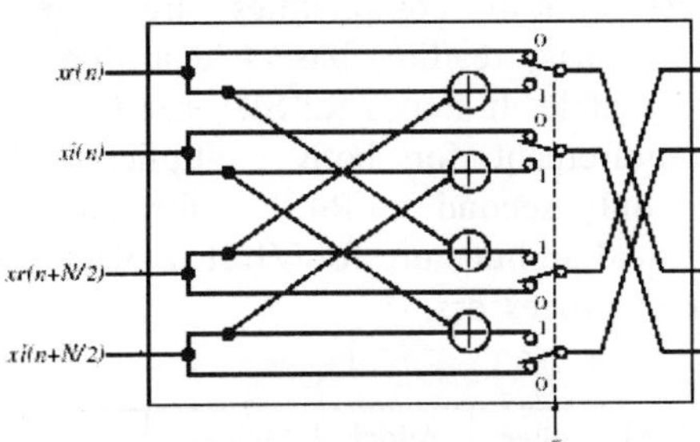

(i) BF2I

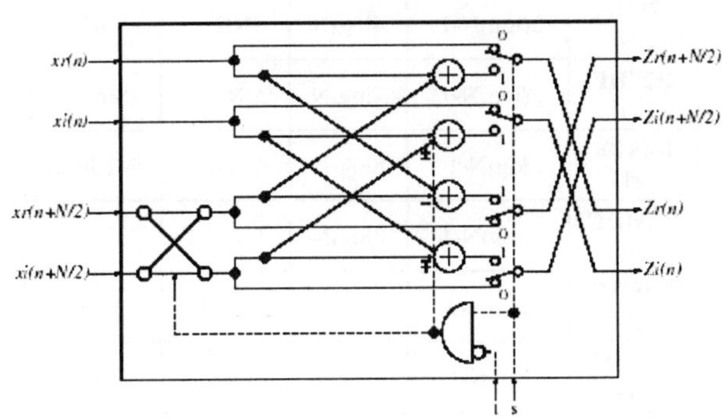

(ii) BF2II

Fig 3. Butterfly structure for R2^{2}SDF FFT

3. Implementation in VHDL

The R2^{2}SDF presented above has been fully coded in Very High Speed Integrated Circuit (VHSIC) Hardware Description Language (VHDL). Once the design is coded in VHDL, the Modelsim XEIII 6.2c compiler [6] and the Xilinx Foundation ISA Environment 9.1i [7] generate a net-list for FPGA configuration. The net-list can then be downloaded into the FPGA using the same Xilinx tools and Texas Instruments prototyping board.

From the architecture of R2^{2}SDF in Fig 2, the butterfly blocks BF2I and BF2II are described as building blocks in VHDL code. Booth multiplication algorithm for signed binary numbers is used for complex multipliers. Thus, the overall latency of the real implementation varies as the processing word length changes [3]. Look-up-table (LUT) based Random Access Memories (RAMs) and Flip-Flops are used to implement feedback memory of the very last stages where are the RAM blocks in the FPGA are used for the rest of the stages. Similarly, LUT-based Read Only Memories (ROMs) are used to implement twiddle ROMs of the very last stages whereas Block RAMs are used for the rest of stages [4]. The FFT is heavily pipelined to achieve as highest clock frequency as possible. Twiddle factors are generated by an external program and embedded to the VHDL code.

The implementation results after implementing in Xilinx Virtex-E XCV400E FPGA [8] are listed in Table 1(a), 1(b). Table 1(a) shows the implementation results where as table 1(b) shows the timing summary.

The resulting figures show that our implementation outperforms the other implementations of that kind. Its speed nearly matches that of the Xilinx core but its throughput is more than 3 times higher due to its pipeline nature.

Logic Utilization	Used	Available	Utilization
No. of Slices	592	4800	12%
No. of Slice Flip flops	527	9600	5%
No. of 4 input LUTs	1030	9600	10%
No. of bonded IOBs	34	404	8%
No. of GCLKs	1	4	25%

Table 1(a). Implementation Result

Minimum period	21.634ns (Max. Frequency: 46.224MHz)
Minimum input arrival time before clock	21.202ns
Maximum output required time after clock	23.743ns
Maximum combinational path delay	23.311ns

Table 1(b). Timing Summary

4. Application in UWB

UWB technology based on Orthogonal Frequency Division Multiplexing (OFDM) has received great attention from both the academia and the industry. It can provide high data rate up to 480Mb/s according to the proposal of IEEE 802.15.3a standardization group[9]. The technology utilizes the unlicensed radio spectrum form 3.168 GHz to 10.56GHz. The carriers are efficiently generated using a 128-point FFT processor. However, the FFT processor must finish the transform in 312.5 ns. It will be a great challenge to meet the strict specification of the UWB systems with traditional approach because of the high requirement of power and performance [10].

In an UWB system, the processes of modulation and demodulation are carried out by means of an Inverse Fast Fourier Transform (IFFT) and a FFT respectively [11]. The specifications of the modern communication standards demand high speed IFFT/FFT processing, and specific hardware is often used. Many different IFFT/FFT cores have been proposed [12-16]. They rely on parallel or pipeline processing to speed up the computation. However, this parallel or pipeline processing can increment significantly the silicon area of the IFFT/FFT core [11].

In this paper, we presented a pipeline architecture that implements the radix-2^2 FFT efficiently. By utilizing the more regular radix-2^2 FFT algorithm, only two sets of complex multipliers are used. Additionally, the number of real multipliers is reduced to $\log_4(N-1)$. Due to efficient pipelining, a maximum frequency of 46.224MHz (Table 1(b)) is achieved which greatly increases the efficiency of the modulator and demodulator in the UWB system. Bahl [17] has implemented a pipeline FFT with an SDF architecture similar to ours but using radix-2^3 algorithm on Virtex-E FPGAs with the performance of 32 MHz. Dick [18] has implemented an FFT based on Systolic array architectures by mapping 1D input data set into a 2D array and use a pseudo 2D transform to compute the 1D DFT, operated at 15.3 MHz. Also the hardware utilization in our architecture is also less when compared to other implementation as shown in Table 1(a). The number of slices and flip flops utilized are less and maximum 12% of the available hardware is used when implemented on Virtex-E FPGAs (Table 1(a)).

Hence, the lesser utilization of hardware and good timing and power criteria make this structure an ideal one of UWB applications. The carriers are efficiently generated using a FFT processor. In the OFDM system, FFT is used as the modulator and demodulator. This proposed R2^2SDF FFT algorithm will serve the purpose of modulator and demodulator with greater efficiency.

The VHDL code developed in the present work is scalable. That means, the code can be utilized for any input point size 8-point, 128-point, 1024-point, etc. The code uses input data, output data and twiddle factors of 8-bit size which can also be increased for greater precision.

5. Conclusions

In this paper, a hardware-oriented radix-2^2 algorithm is derived. Based on this algorithm, new, efficient pipeline FFT architecture, the R2^2SDF architecture, is put forward. The hardware requirement of proposed architecture as compared with various approaches is shown in Table 2, where not only the number of complex multipliers, adders and memory size but also the control complexities are listed for comparison. For easy reading, base-4 logarithm is used whenever applicable. It shows R2^2SDF has reached the minimum requirement for both multiplier and the storage, and only second to R4SDC for adder. This makes it an ideal architecture for VLSI implementation of pipeline FFT processors.

	Multiplier #	Adder #	Memory size	Control
R2MDC [19]	$2(\log_4N-1)$	$4\log_4N$	3N/2 -2	Simple
R2SDF [20]	$2(\log_4N-1)$	$4\log_4N$	N-1	Simple
R4SDF [21]	$\log_4N-1$	$8\log_4N$	N-1	Medium
R4MDC [19]	$3(\log_4N-1)$	$8\log_4N$	5N/2 -4	Simple
R4SDC [22]	$\log_4N-1$	$3\log_4N$	2N-2	Complex
R2^2SDF [4]	$\log_4N-1$	$4\log_4N$	N-1	Simple

Table 2. Hardware requirement comparison

Further, the proposed architecture consumes the minimum required amount of multipliers, storage and finds extensive application in the UWB Applications.

Acknowledgments

The authors wish to acknowledge the support of the SRM University, Chennai to carry out this research work.

References

1. Thomas Lenart and Viktor Öwall. Architectures for dynamic data scaling in 2/4/8k pipeline FFT cores. IEEE transactions on Very Large Scale Integration (VLSI) systems, vol. 14, no. 11, Pages: 1286-1290, November 2006.
2. Mian Sijjad Minallah, Gulistan Raja. Real Time FFT Processor Implementation. IEEE—ICET 2006 2nd International Conference on Emerging Technologies. Peshawar, Pakistan 13-14, Pages: 192-195, November 2006.
3. S Sukhsawas, K Benkrid. A High-level Implementation of a High Performance Pipeline FFT on Virtex-E FPGAs. Proceedings of the IEEE Comp. Society Annual Symp. on VLSI Emerging Trends in Systems Design (ISVLSI'04). 0-7695-2097-9/2004.
4. S. He and M. Torkelson. A new approach to pipeline FFT processor, 10th Int. Parallel Processing Symp. (IPPS'96), p. 766–770, 1996.
5. Digital Signal Processing: Principles, Algorithms and Applications (3rd Edition) by John G. Proakis and Dimitris K Manolakis - Prentice-Hall, Inc., - Oct 5, 1995.
6. Modelsim manual. Mentor Graphics Corporation. http://support.xilinx.com.
7. Xilinx, Inc. http://www.xilinx.com/.
8. Xilinx, Inc. High-Performance 1024-Point Complex FFT/IFFT V2.0. http://www.xilinx.com/ipcenter/.
9. Batra, J. Balakrishnan, A. Dabak, R. Gharpurey, J. Lin, P. Fontaine et al., "Multi-band OFDM physical layer proposal for IEEE 802.15 task group 3a", IEEE P802.15-03, Mar. 2004.
10. Shushan Qiao, Yong Hei, Bin Wu, Yumei Zhou. An Area and Power Efficient FFT Processor for UWB Systems. 1-4244-1312-5/07, IEEE, Pages: 582-585, 2007.
11. Ainhoa Cortés, Igone Vélez, Juan F. Sevillano, and Andoni Irizar, *Member*, IEEE. An Approach to Simplify the Design of IFFT/FFT Cores for OFDM Systems. IEEE Transactions on Consumer Electronics, Vol. 52, No. 1, FEBRUARY 2006. Pg 26-32.
12. C. C. Wang, J. M. Huang, and H. C. Cheng, "A 2K/8K mode small area FFT processor for OFDM demodulation of DVB-T receivers", IEEE Transactions on Consumer Electronics, pp. 28-32, 2005.
13. T. H. Tsai and C. C. Peng, "Design and implementation of a FFT/IFFT soft IP generator for OFDM systems", ICCE: International Conference on Consumer Electronics, pp. 88-97, 2005.
14. Tsung-Han Tsai and Chen-Chi Peng, "A FFT/IFFT Soft IP generator for OFDM communication system", IEEE International Conference on Multimedia and Expo (ICME), pp. 241–244, June 2004.
15. H. Jiang, Hanwen Luo, Jifen Tian, and Wentao Song, "Design of an efficient FFT Processor for OFDM Systems", IEEE Transactions on Consumer Electronics, vol.5, no. 4, pp. 1099-1103, November 2005.
16. F. Argüello, J. D. Bruguera, and E. L. Zapata, "A parallel architecture for the Self-Sorting FFT algorithm", Journal of Parallel and Distributed Computing, pp. 88-97, 1995.
17. S. K. Bahl. A hardware efficient architecture for fast Fourier transform. In Proc. GSPx and International Signal Processing Conference (ISPC'03), Dallas, Texas, Apr. 2003.
18. C. H. Dick. FPGA based systolic array architectures for computing the discrete Fourier transform. In IEEE International Symposium on Circuits and Systems (ISCAS'96), volume 2, pages 465–468, May 1996.
19. L.R. Rabiner and B. Gold. *Theory and Application of Digital Signal Processing*. Prentice-Hall, Inc., 1975.
20. E.H. Wold and A.M. Despain. Pipeline and parallel-pipeline FFT processors for VLSI implementation. *IEEE Trans. Comput.*, C-33(5):414–426, May 1984.
21. A.M. Despain. Fourier transform computer using CORDIC iterations. *IEEE Trans. Comput.*, C-23(10):993–1001, Oct.1974.
22. G. Bi and E. V. Jones. A pipelined FFT processor for word sequential data. *IEEE Trans. Acoust., Speech, Signal Processing*, 37(12):1982–1985, Dec. 1989.

A Key Recovery Attack on Chang-Chang Password Key Exchange Protocol

R.Padmavathy
Dept of Computer Science and Engineering,
National Institute of Technology,
Warangal, Andhra Pradesh, India.

Chakravarthy Bhagvati
Dept of Computer and Information Sciences
University of Hyderabad, Hyderabad
Andhra Pradesh, India.

Abstract

The key exchange protocols using passwords achieved great attention due to its simplicity and efficiency. On the other hand, the protocol should resist all types of password guessing attacks, since the password is of low entropy. Recently Chang and Chang proposed a novel three party simple key exchange protocol. They claimed the protocol is secure, efficient and secure. Unless their claims Yoon and Yoo presented an Undetectable online password guessing attack on the above protocol. In the present paper we demonstrated an another attack called as a key recovery attack on Chang and Chang protocol using the Undetectable online password guessing attack proposed by Yoon and Yon. Further we discussed the efficient methods of computing the ephemeral keys, when the password of one party is exposed.

keywords Chang-Chang password key exchange protocol, Pohlig-Hellman method, Undetectable online password guessing attack.

1 Introduction

The key exchange protocol is one of the most elegant ways of establishing secure communication between pair of users by using a session key. The session key, which is exchanged between two users assures the secure communication for later sessions. The first practical key exchange protocol is proposed by Diffie-Hellman[1]. Since the introduction of key exchange protocol by Diffie-Hellman, various versions and improvements in key exchange protocol have been developed. In the line of key exchange protocol development, password based key exchange mechanism achieved attention due to its simplicity and wide range of applicability, as it requires the users to remember the easily remembrable password. Even though the protocol is simple and efficient, according to Ding and Horster[2], it should not be vulnerable to any type of off line, undetectable or detectable on line password guessing attacks, since the passwords are of low-entropy.

In general the password guessing attacks can be divided into three classes and they are listed below:

- Detectable on-line password guessing attacks : An attacker attempts to use a guessed password in an on-line transaction. He/She verifies the correctness of his/her guess using the response from server. A failed guess can be detected and logged by the server.

- Undetectable on-line password guessing attacks : Similar to an attacker tries to verify a password guess in an on-line transaction. However, a failed guess can not be detected and logged by server, as server is not able to distinguish an honest request from a malicious one.

- Off-line password guessing attacks : An attacker guesses a password and verifies his/her guess off-line. No participation of server is required, so the server does not notice the attack.

Since the first proposal of Bellovin and Merrit (PAKE)[3], many efficient key exchange protocols based on password have been developed. Recently these two party key exchange protocols are extended to three party, in which, the two parties initially communicates the passwords with the trusted server securely. Later the server authenticates the clients when they want to agree upon a session key. The 3-party protocol is introduced by Steiner et al[4]. Subsequently Ding and Hoster published on line and off line guessing attacks on Stener's protocol [2]. Later lin et al. proposed two versions of improved three party protocol[5], one with server's public key and another without. Recently Chang and Chang [6] proposed a novel three party encrypted key exchange protocol without server public key and claimed the protocol is secure, efficient and practical. Unlike their claims Yoon and Yoo [7] pointed out an Undetectable password guessing attack on their protocol, in which one party is able to know the other party's password and furthermore they presented an improved version of it to avoid the above attack. In the similar line Lu and Cao [8] extended the Adbella and Pointcheval protocol (SPAKE)[9] and proposed a simple three party key exchange protocol (S-3PARTY). More recently Phan et al. [10] pointed out the Unknown key share attack and Undetectable password guessing attack on S-3PAKE and Guo et al. [11] proposed man in the middle attack and Undetectable on line dictionary attack. They also presented an improved version of S-3PAKE protocol to resist the above attack.

In this paper we presented a key recovery attack on Chang and Chang protocol using the Undetectable password guessing attack proposed by Yoon and Yon. It causes one malicious party to recover the session key exchanged between two parties with one party's password is known, which is guessed in some other session with the same party. If a malicious party able to guess the password of another, then the same party will act as a third party during the session between two parties and will recover the session key exchanged between them.

The paper is organized as follows: section 2 briefly reviews the Chang and Chang protocol and the undetectable password guessing attack. Section 3 describes the key recovery attack on Chang and Chang. Section 4 reports the method of retrieving the ephemeral key, which aids in recovering the session key and the concluding remarks are made in section 5.

2 Review of Chang and Chang novel three party key exchange protocol and Undetectable password guessing attack

This section briefly explains the Chang and Chang novel three party key exchange protocol and the Undetectable password guessing attack.

Chang and chang three party encrypted key exchange protocol
The notations used in this protocol are listed below:

- A, B : two communication parties.
- S: the trusted server
- ID_A, ID_B, ID_S: the identities of A,B and S, respectively.
- PW_A, PW_B: the passwords securely shared by A with S and B
- $E_{PW}(.)$:a symmetric encryption scheme with a password PW.
- r_A, r_B: the random numbers chosen by A and B, respectively.
- p a large prime.
- g a generator of order $p-1$.
- R_A, R_B, R_S: the random exponents chosen by A,B and S, respectively.
- $N_A, N_B : N_A = g^{R_A} \, mod \, p$ and $N_B = g^{R_B} \, mod \, p$.
- $F_S(.)$: the one-way trapdoor hash function (TDF) where only S knows the trapdoor.
- $f_K(.)$: the pseudo-random hash function (PRF) indexed by a key K
- K_{AS}, K_{AS}: a one time strong keys shared by A with S and B with S, respectively.

The procedure followed in Chang-Chang is given below:

Step 1:

$A \rightarrow B : \{ID_A, ID_B, ID_S, E_{PWA}(N_A), F_S(r_A), f_{K_{AS}}(N_A)\}$
User A chooses a random integer number r_A and a random exponent $R_A \in_R Z_p^*$, and then computes $N_A = g^{R_A}$ and $K_{AS} = N_A^{R_A}$. Then, A encrypts N_A by using his/her password PW_A like $E_{PW_A}, (N_A)$ and computes two hash values $F_S(r_A)$ and $f_{K_{AS}}(N_A)$. Finally, A sends $\{ID_A, ID_B, ID_S, E_{PWA}(N_A), F_S(r_A), f_{K_{AS}}(N_A)\ \}$ to B.

Step 2:

$B \to S$: $\{ID_A, ID_B, ID_S, E_{PWA}(N_A), F_S(r_A), f_{K_{AS}}(N_A)$ $E_{PWB}(N_B), F_S(r_B), f_{K_{BS}}(N_B)\}$. User B chooses a random integer r_B and a random exponent $R_B \in_R Z_p^*$, and then computes $N_B = g^{R_B}$ and $K_{AB} = N_B^{R_B}$. Then, B encrypts N_B by using his/her password PW_B like $E_{PW_B}, (N_B)$ and computes two hash values $F_S(r_B)$ and $f_{K_{AB}}(N_B)$. Finally, B sends $\{ID_A, ID_B, ID_S, E_{PWA}(N_A), F_S(r_A), f_{K_{AS}}(N_A)$ $E_{PWB}(N_B), F_S(r_B), f_{K_{BS}}(N_B)\}$ to S.

Step 3:

$S \to B$:$\{ N_B^{R_S}, f_{K_{AS}}(ID_A, ID_B, K_{AS}, N_B^{R_S}), N_A^{R_S},$ $f_{BS}(ID_A, ID_B, K_{BS}, N_A^{R_S})\}$ Server S decrypts $E_{PWA}(N_A)$ and $E_{PWB}(N_B)$ by using PW_A and PW_B to get N_A and N_B,respectively. Then, S gets r_A and r_B from $F_S(r_A)$ and $F_S(r_B)$ by using a trap door, respectively. To authenticate A and B, S computes $K_{AS} = N_A^{r_A}$ and $K_{BS} = N_B^{r_B}$ and then verifies $f_{K_{AS}}(N_A)$ and $f_{K_{BS}}(N_B)$, respectively. If successful, S chooses a random exponent $R_S \in_R Z_p^*$ and then computes ,$N_A^{R_S}$ and ,$N_B^{R_S}$, respectively. Finally, S computes two hash values $f_{K_{AS}}(ID_A, ID_B, K_{AS}, N_B^{R_S})$ $f_{K_{BS}}(ID_A, ID_B, K_{BS},, N_A^{R_S})$, and sends $\{ N_B^{R_S}, f_{K_{AS}}(ID_A, ID_B, K_{AS}, N_B^{R_S}), N_A^{R_S},$ $f_{BS}(ID_A, ID_B, K_{BS}, N_A^{R_S})\}$ to B.

Step 4:

$B \to A$: $\{ N_B^{R_S}, f_{K_{AS}}(ID_A, ID_B, K_{AS}, N_B^{R_S}),$ $f_K(ID_B, K)\}$ By using $K_{BS} = N_B^{r_B}$, B authenticates S by checking $f_{BS}(ID_A, ID_B, K_{BS}, N_A^{R_S})$. If successful, B computes the session key $K = (N_A^{R_S})_B^R = g_S^R R_A R_B$ and hash value $f_K(ID_B, K)$, and then sends $\{ N_B^{R_S}, f_{K_{AS}}(ID_A, ID_B, K_{AS}, N_B^{R_S}), f_K(ID_B, K)\}$ to A.

Step 5:

$A \to B$:$\{f_K(ID_A, K)\}$ By using $K_{AS} = N_A^{r_A}$, A authenticates S by checking $f_{K_{AS}}(ID_A, ID_B, K_{AS}, N_B^{R_S})$. If successful A computes the session key $K = (N_B^{R_S})^{R_A} = g^{R_S R_A R_B}$, and authenticates B by checking $f_K(ID_B, K)$. If authenticates is passed, A computes and sends $f_K(ID_A, K)$

Step 6:

B authenticates A by checking $f_K(ID_A, K)$. If successful, B confirms A's knowledge of the session key $K = g^{R_S R_A R_B}$.

2.1 Undetectable password guessing attacks on Chang-Chang protocol

This section demonstrates the undetectable password guessing attack on Chang-Chang protocol. Assuming B as malicious party the procedure of the above attack is given below:
Step 1

$A \to B$: $\{ID_A, ID_B, ID_S, E_{PWA}(N_A), F_S(r_A),$ $f_{K_{AS}}(N_A)\}$

Step 2.

B records message $\{ID_A, ID_B, ID_S, E_{PWA}(N_A), F_S(r_A),$ $f_{K_{AS}}(N_A)\}$ from A

Step 3.

B guesses a password PWA' from password dictionary and gets N'_A

Step 4.

B chooses a random integer r_B and then computes $K_{BS} = N_A'^{r_B}$. Then, B encrypts N'_A by using his/her password PW_B like $E_{PW_B}, (N'_A)$ and computes two hash values $F_S(r_B)$ and $f_{K_{BS}}(N'_A)$.

Step 5.

$B \to S$: $\{ID_A, ID_B, ID_S, E_{PWA}(N_A), F_S(r_A),$ $f_{K_{AS}}(N_A)E_{PWB}(N'_A), F_S(r_B), f_{K_{BS}}(N'_A)\}$ B transmits $\{ID_A, ID_B, ID_S, E_{PWA}(N_A), F_S(r_A),$ $f_{K_{AS}}(N_A)E_{PWB}(N_B), F_S(r_B), f_{K_{BS}}(N_B)\}$

Step 6.

$S \to B$:$\{ N_A'^{R_S}, f_{K_{AS}}(ID_A, ID_B, K_{AS}, N_A'^{R_S}), N_A^{R_S},$ $f_{BS}(ID_A, ID_B, K_{BS}, N_A^{R_S})\}$ After receiving the message S can authenticate A and B by verifying $f_{K_{AS}}(N_A)$ and $f_{K_{BS}}(N'_A)$, respectively. S will compute $f_{K_{AS}}(ID_A, ID_B, K_{AS}, N_A'^{R_S})$ and $f_{BS}(ID_A, ID_B, K_{BS}, N_A^{R_S})$ to B.

Step 7.

After receiving the message B simply compares $N_A'^{R_S} = N_A^{R_S}$. If $N_A'^{R_S} = N_A^{R_S}$, it follows that $PWA' = PWA$.

3 A key recovery attack on Chang and Chang protocol

In this section we presented a key recovery attack on Chang and Chang protocol. A malicious party B guesses the password of A using Undetectable password guessing attack as proposed by Yoon and Yoo. B uses the password of A for obtaining the session key between A and C, when A and C wants to communicate. The following procedure presents the attack in detail.

Step 1:

$A \rightarrow C : \{ID_A, ID_B, ID_S, E_{PWA}(N_A), F_S(r_A), f_{K_{AS}}(N_A)\}$ User A chooses a random integer number r_A and a random exponent $R_A \in_R Z_p^*$, and then computes $N_A = g^{R_A}$ and $K_{AS} = N_A^{R_A}$. Then, A encrypts N_A by using his/her password PW_A like $E_{PW_A}, (N_A)$ and computes two hash values $F_S(r_A)$ and $f_{K_{AS}}(N_A)$. Finally, A sends $\{ID_A, ID_B, ID_S, E_{PWA}(N_A), F_S(r_A), f_{K_{AS}}(N_A)\ \}$ to C.

Step 2:

B gets $\{ID_A, ID_B, ID_S, E_{PWA}(N_A), F_S(r_A), f_{K_{AS}}(N_A)\}$ and from $E_{PWA}(N_A)$ decrypts N_A, since password is known and solves the ephemeral key R_A from N_A using the popular Pohlig-Hellman method or index calculus method as discussed in the following section. This is achieved, since the order of the generator used in the protocol is p-1. When the factorization of p-1 is known and small, the exponent can be solved in reduced time, even in polynomial time when the factors of p-1 is in the form of $2^n p1^m$, where p_1 is small and n, m are very large.

Step 4:

$C \rightarrow S$: $\{ID_A, ID_C, ID_S, E_{PWA}(N_A), F_S(r_A), f_{K_{AS}}(N_A)$ $E_{PWC}(N_C), F_S(r_C), f_{K_{CS}}(N_C)\}$. User C chooses a random integer r_C and a random exponent $R_C \in_R Z_p^*$, and then computes $N_C = g^{R_C}$ and $K_{CS} = N_C^{R_C}$. Then, C encrypts N_C by using his/her password PWC like $E_{PWC}, (N_C)$ and computes two hash values $F_S(r_C)$ and $f_{K_{CS}}(N_C)$. Finally, C sends $\{ID_A, ID_C, ID_S, E_{PWA}(N_A), F_S(r_A), f_{K_{AS}}(N_A)$ $E_{PWC}(N_C), F_S(r_C), f_{K_{CS}}(N_C)\}$ to S.

Step 5:

$S \rightarrow C$:{ $N_C^{R_S}, f_{K_{AS}}(ID_A, ID_C, K_{AS}, N_C^{R_S}), N_A^{R_S}$, $f_{CS}(ID_A, ID_C, K_{CS}, N_A^{R_S})\}$ Server S decrypts $E_{PWA}(N_A)$ and $E_{PWC}(N_C)$ by using PW_A and PW_C to get N_A and N_C,respectively. Then, S gets r_A and r_C from $F_S(r_A)$ and $F_S(r_C)$ by using a trap door, respectively. To authenticate A and B, S computes $K_{AS} = N_A^{r_A}$ and $K_{CS} = N_C^{r_C}$ and then verifies $f_{K_{AS}}(N_A)$ and $f_{K_{CS}}(N_C)$, respectively. If successful, S chooses a random exponent $R_S \in_R Z_p^*$ and then computes ,$N_A^{R_S}$ and ,$N_C^{R_S}$, respectively. Finally, S computes two hash values $f_{K_{AS}}(ID_A, ID_C, K_{AS}, N_C^{R_S})$ $f_{K_{CS}}(ID_A, ID_C, K_{CS},, N_A^{R_S})$, and sends { $N_C^{R_S}, f_{K_{AS}}(ID_A, ID_C, K_{AS}, N_C^{R_S}), N_A^{R_S}$, $f_{CS}(ID_A, ID_C, K_{CS}, N_A^{R_S})\}$ to B.

Step 6:

B gets { $N_C^{R_S}, f_{K_{AS}}(ID_A, ID_C, K_{AS}, N_C^{R_S}), N_A^{R_S}$, $f_{CS}(ID_A, ID_C, K_{CS}, N_A^{R_S}$ } and from $N_C^{R_S}$ he computes the session key $(N_C^{R_S})^{R_A}$ is nothing but a session key between A and C $g^{R_A R_S R_C}$

Step 7:

$C \rightarrow A$: { $N_C^{R_S}, f_{K_{AS}}(ID_A, ID_C, K_{AS}, N_C^{R_S})$, $f_K(ID_C, K)\}$ By using $K_{CS} = N_C^{r_C}$, C authenticates S by checking $f_{CS}(ID_A, ID_C, K_{CS}, N_A^{R_S})$. If successful, C computes the session key $K = (N_A^{R_S})^{R_C} = g^{R_S R_A R_C}$ and hash value $f_K(ID_C, K)$, and then sends { $N_C^{R_S}, f_{K_{AS}}(ID_A, ID_C, K_{AS}, N_C^{R_S}), f_K(ID_C, K)\}$ to A.

Step 8:

$A \rightarrow C$:$\{f_K(ID_A, K)\}$ By using $K_{AS} = N_A^{r_A}$, A authenticates S by checking $f_{K_{AS}}(ID_A, ID_C, K_{AS}, N_C^{R_S})$. If successful A computes the session key $K = (N_C^{R_S})^{R_A} = g^{R_S R_A R_B}$, and authenticatesC by checking $f_K(ID_C, K)$. If authenticates is passed, A computes and sends $f_K(ID_A, K)$

Step 9:

C authenticates A by checking $f_K(ID_A, K)$. If successful, C confirms A's knowledge of the session key $K = g^{R_S R_A R_C}$.

4 Solving Discrete Logarithm problem (DLP) for ephemeral keys

From the discussion of key recovery attack on Chang-Chang protocol, it is observed that the computation of R_A from N_A is the key issue. This leads to recover the session key by the mailcious party B. In this section we presents the method of computing the key R_A form N_A using the popular methods to solve Discrete Logarithm Problem (DLP). For a given prime field Z_p^*, a generator $g \in Z_p^*$ of order $p-1$ and an element $y \in Z_p^*$, the problem of finding x, in the range of $0 \leq x \leq p-2$, such that $g^x = y \ (mod\ p)$, is known as the DLP.The security assumption of cryptosystem based on Discrete logarithm problem (DLP) is, one way function : an attacker cannot recover x from g and g^x. Computation of discrete logarithms over a finite field Z_p^* is a difficult problem. No algorithms are known that solve the problem in time polynomially bounded by the size of the field. When factorization of $p-1$, which is the order of a generator is known and small then a popular algorithm Pohlig-Hellman can be used to solve the problem in reduced time. The algorithm solves the DLP in polynomial time for some instances of prime field. This is applicable on Chang-Chang protocol to compute R_A, due to the fact that the prime chosen in the protocol is a random prime and the generator g is of order $p-1$, the DLP of N_A can be solved in reduced time with the assumption of the factors of $p-1$ are known and small. The following section presents the Pohlig-Hellman method.

4.1 Pohlig-Hellman Algorithm

This is an algorithm introduced by Pohlig-Hellman on 1978. If the order of the group is known along with the complete factorization and the factors are relatively small then this attack is possible.
Let $p-1 = p_1^{e_1}.p_2^{e_2}......p_k^{e_k}$ and g be the generator of order $p-1$. Then

$$g^x = y \quad mod \quad p \Rightarrow \text{ can be reduced into}$$

$$\alpha^x = \beta \text{ mod p where} \alpha \text{ is } g^{(\frac{p-1}{p_1^{e_1}})}, g^{(\frac{p-1}{p_2^{e_2}})}, ...g^{(\frac{p-1}{p_k^{e_k}})}$$

and

$$\beta \text{ is } y^{(\frac{p-1}{p_1^{e_1}})}, y^{(\frac{p-1}{p_2^{e_2}})} ......y^{(\frac{p-1}{p_k^{e_k}})}$$

The logarithm in the small subgroups are solved by using one of the popular square root algorithms. Later the Chinese Remainder Method is used to combine the results x_i mod $p_i^{e_i}$ to retrieve x mod p.

4.2 Experimental results

The purpose of the present experiments is to produce the data on which the reliable statement regarding the expected running time to recover the session key can be obtained. The problem is described as follows: First a data file is produced, which contains a list of tuples. A tuple is of the form (m, p, q) with the following properties. m lies between 13 and 200 digits, p is a prime, q is the list of factors of $p-1$. Having built up the data file the Chang-Chang password key exchange protocol is implemented and the session key is recovered.The Table-2 shows the selected list of problems solved and the running time to recover the session key is reported. The trap door hash function mentioned in the above protocol is implemented by using the RSA-trap door hash function [12].
for example a problem of given $p =$ 12354138214723269403533485216332053524660110994963094785247378545048606590980187022168408637245590534058400097769951339145176552219627304115752702394091713106183405557203514035791158676147460937 51 is solved in fraction seconds.

5 Conclusion

In the present paper we demonstrated the key recovery attack on Chang and Chang protocol. The attack is developed by using undetectable online password guessing attack. The attack can be avoided by selecting the generators of large prime order and the computations are to be restricted to prime order subgroup of $p-1$.

References

[1] W. Diffie and M. Hellman, *New Directions in cryptography,* IEEE Transactions on Information theory, 22(6):644-54:1976.

[2] Y. Ding and P. Hoster, *Undetectable Online password guessing attacks,* ACM operatinf system review, 29(4):77-86:1995.

[3] SM. Bellovin and M. Merrit, *Encrypted key exchange: password-based protocols secure against dictionary attacks. In: Proceedings of IEEE sysmposium on research in security and privacy,* IEEE Computer society press :72-84:1992.

[4] M. Steiner and G. Tsudik, M. Waidner *Refinement and extention of encrypted key exchange,*

ACM Operating Systems Review, 29(3):22-30:1995.

[5] CL. Lin, HM. Sun, M. Steiner, T. Hwang *Three-party excrypted key exchange without server public keys* IEEE Communication letters, 5(12):497-9:2001.

[6] CC. Chang and YF. Chang, *A novel three party encrypted key exchange protocol,* Computer Standards and Interfaces, 26(5):471-6:2004.

[7] EJ. Yoon and KY. Yoo, *Improving the novel three-party encrypted key exchange protocol,* Computer Standards and Interfaces, 30:309-314:2008.

[8] R. Lu and Z. Cao, *Simple three-party key exchange protocol,* Computers and Security, 26:94-97:2007.

[9] M. Abdella and D. Pointcheval, *Simple password-based encrypted key excahnge protocols,* CT-RSA 2005, Speinger-Verlag, :191-208:2005.

[10] RCW. Phan, WC. Yau and BM. Goi *Cryptanalysis of simple three-party key exchange protocol (S-3PAKE),* Information sciences, 178(2008):2849-2856:2008.

[11] H. Guo, Z. Li, Y. Mu and X. Zhang *Cryptanalysis of simple three-party key exchange protocol* , Computers and Security, 27(2008):16-21:2008.

[12] Fuw-Yi Yang *Improvement on a Trap door Hash Function,* International Journal on Network Security, Vol 9, No 1, pp 17-21, (2009).

Table 1: Running time to recover the session key

Problem	Running time to recover the session key
432412210443444766536290824808696782 2904858	9ms
405006915689289033885033149435917765 16203	14ms
105488132477042462663174850544801321 14947	8ms
227504758229815122511473898344776598 27887	8ms
310233761222475167061100770470149906 74390	9ms
164838881183106336031117884004666831 843	5ms
295656961335792691161464509394119870 39	5ms

VBR VIDEO TRAFFIC PREDICTION AND ANALYSIS FOR EFFICIENT RESOURCE UTILIZATION

T. RAGHUVEERA

Department of Computer Science and Engineering, Anna University Chennai, Chennai-600025, India

A. DHANALAKSHMI

Department of Computer Science and Engineering, Anna University Chennai, Chennai-600025, India

K. S. EASWARAKUMAR

Department of Computer Science and Engineering, Anna University Chennai, Chennai-600025, India

The allocation of bandwidth and other network resources for VBR Video traffic is a challenging task due to bursty nature of traffic as well as rigid Quality of Service requirements of applications. In this paper, we propose prediction based approach for efficient bandwidth allocation for multimedia applications. In this we demonstrate frame level and GOP level prediction of traffic using MLP networks (Multi Layer Perceptron). D-Bind Model [12] is used for the computation of resource requirements which can be used for resource reservation. Video Traffic Prediction plays an important role to achieve desired QoS, overall network utilization and in determining dynamic resource requirements. We have extensively studied traffic prediction at frame and GOP levels. We show that neural network traffic predictor can successfully predict real-world VBR video traffic, thereby enabling predictive dynamic bandwidth control and allocation. Neural Network Traffic Prediction with D-Bind Model works well with various dynamic bandwidth allocation schemes.

1. Introduction

Almost all of the current day networked multimedia applications rely on MPEG encoded Variable bit rate (VBR) data for providing end-to-end of Quality of Service. VBR based multimedia applications, such as IPTV and online news, are amongst the list of future applications with significant growth potential. Allocation of network resources for such a kind of traffic is a challenging task because of the inherent burstiness of the traffic, and strict Quality of Service requirements. Further more, researchers have found that VBR video traffic typically exhibits burstiness over multiple time scales [1]. Burstiness over shorter time scales is due to I, B and P frame structures and burstiness on a longer time scale is due to scene changes.

Results in [2] has shown that the effective bandwidth of a multiple time-scale stream is determined by the maximum effective bandwidth of its all component subchains' effective bandwidths, which implies that a static traffic descriptor (such as static effective bandwidth) would be wasteful in bandwidth allocation for multiple timescale VBR video traffic. Therefore, dynamic bandwidth allocation on-the-fly based on online network traffic prediction, are called predictive dynamic bandwidth allocation, is considered to be very promising [3], [4] for live VBR video and other real-time VBR video applications such as interactive services where no video stream is known in advance. Three basic frame types are used in MPEG video encoding. They are I, P and B frames. An I frame is an intracoded frame without any reference to other frames. As for P frame, it is obtained by compressing the differential information between original frame and predicted frame where the predicted frame is estimated from previous I or P frame. A 'B' frame is compressed similarly to a P frame, but the predicted frame can be estimated bidirectional from both the previous and future I or P frames. The encoded sequence is of the form IBPBPB or IBBPBBPBBPBB depending on the encoder parameters setting. This sequence repeats throughout the encoded video. A group of frames starting with an I and ends before an I is called Group of Pictures (GOP). MPEG encoded video traffic features complex cyclic ACF patterns due to the GOP structure [5]. For this reason, researchers usually choose to model the video traffic at GOP level [6, 7]. A network traffic predictor is built to predict the future network traffic patterns according to the observed past traffic patterns, and thus bandwidth can be dynamically reallocated based on the predicted traffic. Network traffic predictor thus plays a key role in Network Resource Allocation and Management. We used sample video traces [11] for our experiments.

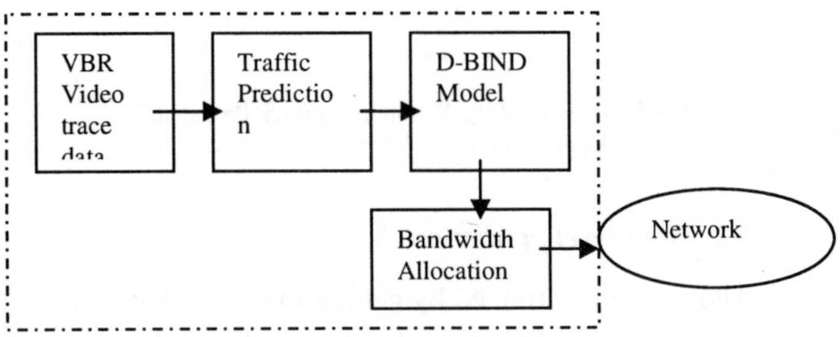

Fig 1. Architectural overview

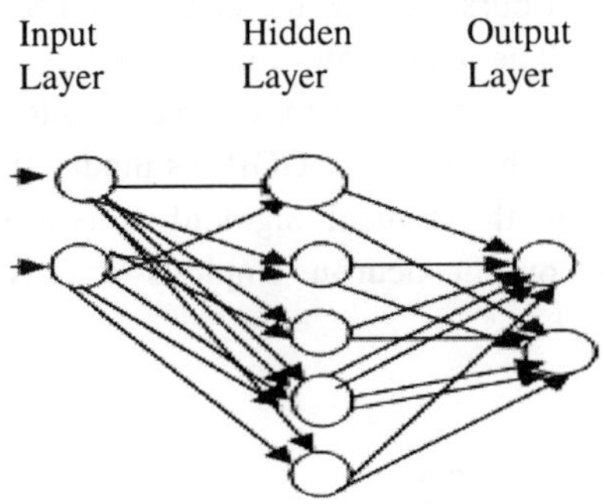

Fig 2. 2-5-2 Feed Forward Network Structure for traffic Prediction

2. Analysis of MPEG VBR video traffic

The characteristic of MPEG VBR video traffic is analyzed. Several video sequences are used for this study, but only representative results based on the sequences from the two films, ''**Star Wars IV"** and ''**Jurassic Park I**'' are presented. The video sequences **Star Wars IV"** and ''**Jurassic Park I**'' are encoded at 25 frames/sec. A typical GOP pattern for video streaming, IBBPBBPBBPBB, is selected. The I, P and B frame-size sequences from ''Jurassic Park I" for the first 4800 frames are shown in fig 3: The frame index value in the Figure is described as follows: frame index value equal to 1 refers to the first frame and frame index value equal to 2 refers to the second frame, and similarly for others. The y-axis refers to the frame-size values. As can be observed, the mean video bit-rate fluctuates noticeably from one mean level to another. Multimedia traffic is inherently bursty. Burstiness is defined as the peak to mean ratio of frames sizes .For a given trace $\{X_i\}$ where I varies from 1 to n.

$$\text{Burstiness} = \frac{\text{Max}\,\{x_i\}}{\text{Mean}\,\{x_i\}} \qquad (1)$$

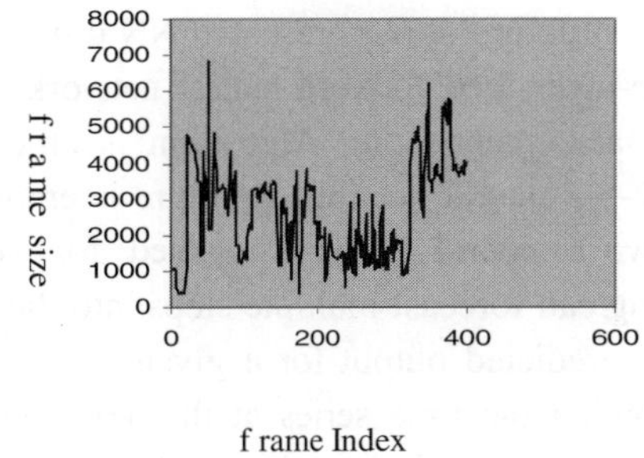

Fig 3. "Jurassic Park" the empirical trace
I frame size sequence

Burstinesss increases as the value of mean (in the formula) decreases. One of the most significant issues in providing Quality-of-Service (QoS) guarantees for the real-time multimedia communications in a network is to estimate the burstiness accurately.

3. Modeling at the frame and GOP levels

3.1. *Frame level prediction*

Every 12 frames contain one Peak Rate. Peak Rate is due to I frames. Frame Level Prediction focuses on Predicting the next few I frames by getting the previous I frames. The Neural Network Predictor is trained for prediction of future I frames.

3.2. *GOP level prediction*

Every 12 frames form a GOP. Peak rate is predicted by using mean and burstiness as input using the equation (1) for burstiness.

4. Traditional Learning Neural Network Traffic Predictor

4.1. *Traditional Learning*

The Back propagation (BP) algorithm (Rumelhart, Hinton, & Williams, 1986; Rumelhart, Durbin,Golden, & Chauvin, 1992) [13] is perhaps the most widely used supervised training algorithm for multi-layered feed forward neural networks.. We follow Freeman and Skapura's book (1992) to describe the procedure of training feed forward neural networks using the back propagation algorithm.

4.2. *Neural Network Traffic Predictor*

The basic structure of our presented NN traffic predictor is a three-layer feed forward neural network, shown in Fig. 1. Back Propagation Algorithm is employed for training.2-5-2 neural network structure is employed. As we know, a neural network trained for single-step forecasting can forecast multiple steps into the future by using the predicted output for a given step as an input for computing the time series at the next step, and all other inputs are shifted back one time unit. This is referred to as iterated multi-step ahead predictor. With iterated multi-step prediction, an NN traffic predictor can predict as many steps ahead as needed, as iterated multi-step prediction thus, the long-term traffic prediction. Obviously, long-term prediction is much more difficult than one-step prediction, and as the prediction is conducted *iterated* forward, the prediction accuracy will continuously degrade.

5. Experiments

5.1. *Frame Level prediction*

The network is trained by getting two I frames from the 2 GOPS and next two I frames are predicted using Back Propagation Algorithm. Jurassic Park and Star Wars IV video trace been used First few I frames have been trained and next few I frame have been predicted. Prediction of next 270 I frames, by training first 100 I frames is shown in fig 4 and fig 5.

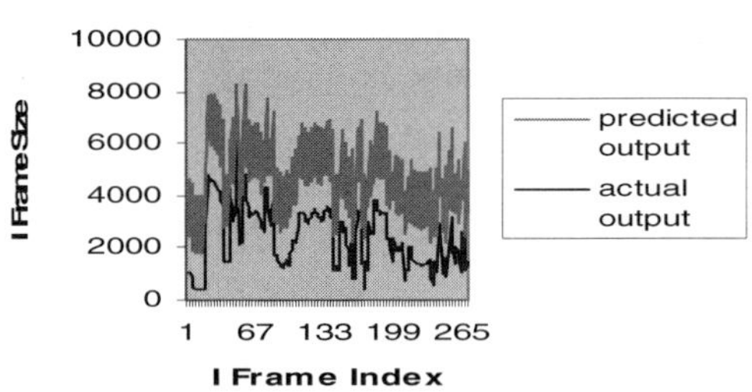

Fig 4. Frame level Prediction using Back Propagation Algorithm for Jurassic Park video trace

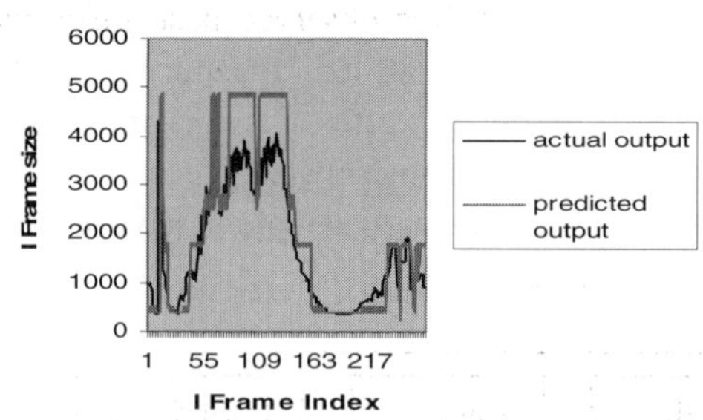

Fig 5. Frame level Prediction using Back Propagation Algorithm for Star Wars IV video trace

5.2. *GOP level prediction*

The network is trained by getting mean and burstiness of few frames. NN Predictor using Back Propagation Algorithm successfully predicts peak rate for next 4 GOPs. Mean and burstiness of the first 4 GOPs is given as input and mean and burstiness of the next 4 GOPS is predicted as output. The peak rate can be computed from the mean and burstiness. The input layer employs mean and burstiness of the first four GOPs as inputs, the hidden layer employs the typical sigmoid activation function, while the output neuron employs a linear activation function.

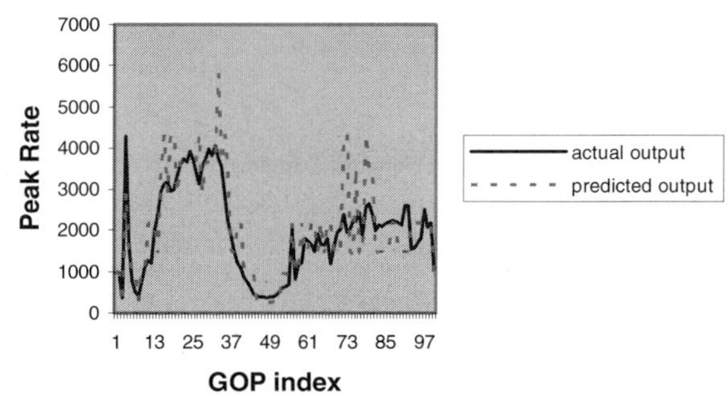

Fig 6. GOP level prediction using Back Propagation Algorithm for Star Wars IV video trace

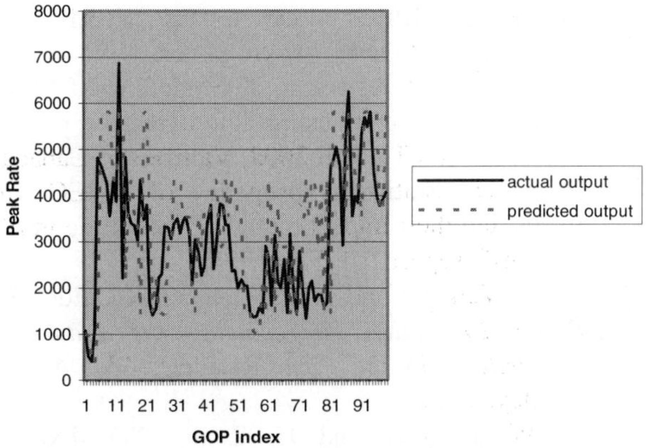

Fig 7. GOP level Prediction using Back Propagation Algorithm for Jurassic Park video trace

6. Performance Analysis

The performance of prediction based on Traditional Learning highly depends on Neural Network Structure. 2-5-2 structure is employed for prediction shown in fig 2. Table II and III shows the results of iterated multi-step ahead frame prediction using Traditional Learning for Star Wars IV and Jurassic Park. To quantitatively assess forecasting performance, the normalized mean squared error (NMSE) is also used [11]. The NMSE is defined as

$$\text{NMSE}=\frac{1}{\sigma^2}\frac{1}{n}\sum_{i=1}^{n}[X_i-\overline{X}]^2$$

TABLE II
Frame level based Prediction Errors for Various Video Traces (NN Traffic Predictor)

Video Trace	NMSE using traditional learning
Star Wars IV	0.45770024
Jurassic Park	2.051351

TABLE III
GOP based Prediction Errors for Various Video Traces (NN Traffic Predictor)

Video Trace	NMSE using traditional learning
Star Wars IV	0.395770024
Jurassic Park	0.947908111

The NMSE is widely used for evaluating *multi-step* prediction performance. It means that the prediction performance is better if NMSE <1 which has been given in table III. Frame Level Prediction Error result is shown in table II.In Frame level Prediction X_i is the observed I frame size value of the time series, $\overline{X}$ is the predicted I frame size of the time series and σ^2 is the variance of the time series over the prediction duration. In GOP level Prediction Xi is the observed value of the time series $\overline{X}$ is the predicted peak value of the next four GOPS and σ^2 is the variance of the time series over the prediction duration.

7. Computation of Traffic Descriptor

A traffic model, also called traffic descriptor, describes the characteristics of certain traffic with the use of countable traffic parameters. Several traffic models have been proposed in recent years. One popular traffic model is the deterministic bounding interval-length dependent (D-BIND) traffic model [9]. It has been widely recognized and utilized in NRAM systems for multimedia applications. After prediction of next few frames using Neural Network Traffic Predictor, D-BIND model can be used for computation of bounding rates which can be used for future resource reservation.

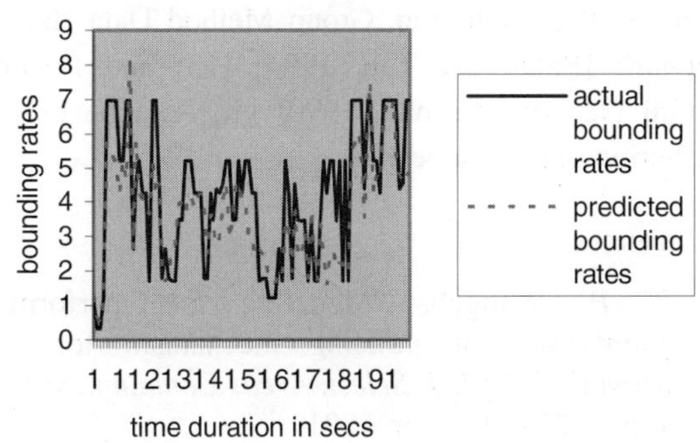

Fig 8. Computation of bounding rates using D-Bind Model for Jurassic Park video trace

The bounding rates computed after prediction of next few frames which can be used for reservation .The bounding rates of the actual frames will be compared with that of the reserved as shown in fig 8. If the reserved resource is not sufficient then the frame segment will be blocked.

8. Predictive Dynamic Bandwidth allocation

The multi-step ahead frame prediction works successfully on various dynamic bandwidth allocation algorithms. In [10] RED VBR a renegotiated deterministic variable bit rate service (RED-VBR) is proposed. Optimized allocation of resources can thus be achieved by predicting GOP level traffic because the prediction error is negligibly low. This predictive method works well with R-VBR Renegotiated variable bit rate service [12].

9. Conclusion

The statistical characteristics of MPEG VBR-encoded video sequence have been studied. We propose a new approach of NN traffic predictor, i.e., statistical characteristics based NN traffic predictor, and demonstrate that NN traffic predictor can consistently achieve significantly better long-term prediction performance.

10. Future work

Our future work includes extensive simulations for evaluating various dynamic bandwidth allocation algorithms within the framework based on the long-term online traffic prediction. Group Method Data Handling Network [Pham and Liu, 1994] [13] and Recurrent Neural Network [Elman, 1990] [13] can be used for prediction in this framework.

References

1. E. P. Rathgeb, "Modeling and performance comparison of policing mechanism for ATM network," *IEEE J. Select. Areas Commun.*, vol. 9, pp. 325–334, Apr. 1991.
2. D. Tse, R. Gallager, and J. Tsitsiklis, "Statistical multiplexing of multiple time-scale Markov streams," IEEE J. Select. Areas Commun., vol. 13, pp. 1028–1038, Aug. 1995.
3. A. A. Lazar and G. Pacifici, "Control of resources in broadband networks with quality of service guarantees," *IEEE Commun.*, pp. 66–73, Oct. 1991.
4. S. Chong, S. Li, and J. Ghosh, "Predictive dynamic bandwidth allocation for efficient transport of real-time VBR video over ATM," *IEEE J.Select. Areas Commun.*, vol. 13, pp. 12–23, Jan. 1995.
5. Ansari, N., Liu, H., Shi, Y., and Zhao, H "On modelling MPEG video traffic", IEEE Trans. Broadcast., 2002, 48, (4)
6. Galaup, A and Aghvami, A"Modelling of MPEG4 traffic at GOP level using autoregressive process". Presented at VTC Fall 2002, Vancouver, Canada.
7. Rose, O "Statistical propeties of MPEG video traffic and their impact on traffic modelling in ATM systems", report 101, Feb 1995.
8. A. S. Weigend and N. A. Gershenfeld, Eds., *Time Series Prediction: Forecasting the Future and Understanding the Past.* Reading MA:, Addison-Wesley, 1994.
9. E. W. Knighly and H. Zhang, "D-BIND: An accurate traffic model for providing QoS guarantees to VBR traffic," IEEE/ACM transactions on Networking, vol. 5, pp. 219-231, 1997.
10. H. Zhang and E. W. Knightly, "RED-VBR: A new approach to support delay sensitive VBR video in packet-switched networks," in Proceedings of Workshop on Network and Operating System Support for Digital Audio and Video (NOSSDAV'95), pp. 275-286, April 1995.
11. Public library of frame-size video traces:http://www-tkn.ee.tu-berlin.de/research/trace/trace.html.
12. Yao Liang and Mei Han "Dynamic Bandwidth Allocation Based on Online Traffic Prediction for Real-Time MPEG-4 Video Streams", Hindawi Publishing Corporation, EURASIP Journal on Advances in Signal Processing, Article ID 87136, 10 pages, Volume 2007 (2007).
13. James A. Freeman,David M. Skapura:Neural NetworksAlgorithms, Applications, and Programming Techniques : Addison-Wesley Publishing Company
14. Y. Liang, "Real-Time VBR video traffic prediction for Dynamic Bandwidth allocation", IEEE Transactions on Systems, vol. 34, pp. 32-47, 2004.

ADVANCED AUTHENTICATION & PASSWORD RESET MANAGER

P. A. BAMNODKAR[↓]
Pune Vidyarthi Griha's College of Engineering & Technology, Pune, India

H. K. SAWANT[↓]
BVCOE,Pune

G. V. GARJE[↓]
Pune Vidyarthi Griha's College of Engineering & Technology

PANKAJ KULKARNI[↓]
Synechron, Pune

Abstract: It happens many times! A user tries to log into a corporate network but fails to remember his or her Windows password when prompted and is locked out of everything. Lock outs have cost associated with it because the user can't work and has to call the company's helpdesk to reset the password. As much as 30 percent of all helpdesk calls are password-reset requests, on average every request takes 20 minutes to resolve and costs more than $23 on helpdesk operations alone, says market research firm- Gartner.' *Advanced Authentication and Password Reset Manager*' eliminates those minutes and dollars too. It provides self-service to users to reset their passwords on their own in few minutes even before login to the system. *Advanced Authentication and Password Reset Manager* should automate the process of resetting passwords. This will reduce the help desk calls and hence will increase the productivity and reduce the cost. THE ULTIMATE GOAL - Lower cost and higher productivity

1. Technical Objectives:

Automating process of resetting password involves –
->Minimum footprint and no dependency upon any third-party software already being installed.
->Modifying Windows authentication mechanism to launch Client Application for resetting password.
->Develop Client Application which will communicate with Authentication Web Service.
->Develop Authentication Web Service which will communicate with Database server (SQL Server 2005) and Directory Server (Active Directory) for secondary Authentication and Reset Password.
->Develop a Configuration Manager Web Application which will allow user to configure Challenges/Responses.

2. *Basic Concepts:*

The figure specified below shows the different client workstation (where *Advanced Authentication and Password Reset Manager's* Client Application is installed) communicating to the Authentication Web Service over HTTP for Challenge-Response authentication and password reset. End user will use his/her current desktop without actually logging into the system to use the reset password functionality. Authentication Web Service communicates with the

↓ Prof. P.A. Bamnodkar is lecturer in Pune Vidyarthi Griha's College of Engineering & Technology (phone: 9823031243; (e-mail:pab_comp@pvgcoet.ac.in).

↓ Prof. H.K. Sawant is Prof. in BVCOE,Pune(phone:9822007653);(email:hemant1960@gmail.com)

↓ Prof. G.V. Garje, is Assistant Professor & Head, Department of Computer Engineering & IT in Pune Vidyarthi Griha's College of Engineering & Technology. He is also a Chairman Board of Studies Computer Engg.,University of Pune(phone: 9850809413; (e-mail:gvg_comp@pvgcoet.ac.in).

↓ Mr. Pankaj Kulkarni is with Synechron, Pune (phone: 9823013243; (email: pankajcoolkarni@gmail.com).

Database server for Challenge Response Authentication and if authentication succeeds, Reset Password screen will be presented to the user and s/he can reset domain password.

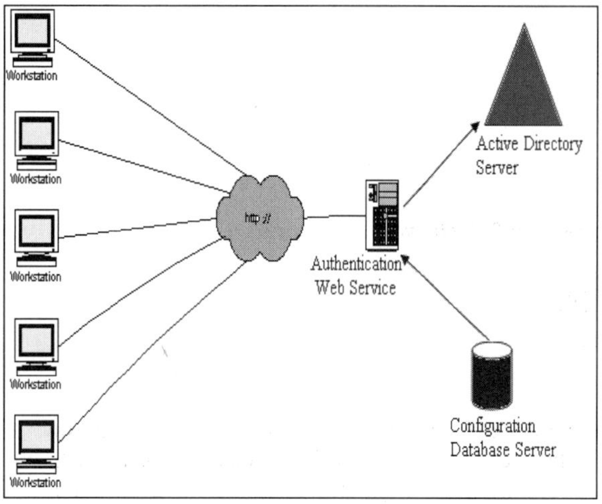

2.1. *Advantages:*

- This product eliminates help-desk calls and costs associated with password reset. Up to 30 percent of all helpdesk calls are password-reset requests, on average taking 20 minutes to resolve and costing more than $23 per call says market research firm, Gartner Group.
- This product provides unparalleled usability, enabling users to enroll, reset passwords, and unlock accounts on their own in seconds.
- It increases network security by allowing the end user to reset his/her own password instead of a helpdesk person resetting the password.
- This product essentially gives 24x7 support desk for password reset requests.
- Because helpdesk calls are costly and current password reset processes unproductive, an increasing number of organizations have evaluated self-help tools. However, many tools are inconvenient to use because they cannot be accessed from the computer on which the user is currently locked out.
- This product seamlessly and securely includes the enrollment and password-reset process into the Windows logon, providing users with a simple enrollment, reset, and unlock process where and when they need it. This easy to use process dramatically increases user adoption of the password reset tool, resulting in less time spent on resetting passwords and unlocking accounts.
- The product facilitates user to reset the password quickly and in-turn reduces the user downtime dramatically.
- Password Manager provides several mechanisms to ensure that users enroll and use self-service when they need to change passwords, reset forgotten passwords or unlock their account. Without these mechanisms, users will continue making expensive support calls and prevent your organization from realizing a **high Return On Investment**.
- Improves user and IT satisfaction since the product will be simple to use and easy to deploy.

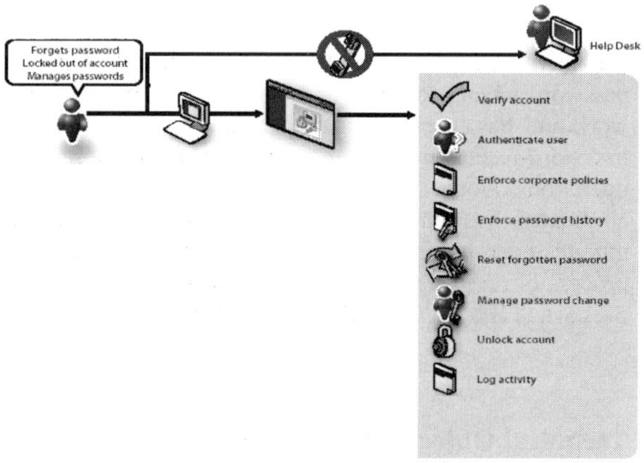

2.2. *Disadvantages Application and Limitations:*

1. *Advanced Authentication and Password Reset Manager* supports Windows 2003 and later operating systems only.
2. *Advanced Authentication and Password Reset Manager* can be configured for Active Directory only

3. Problem definition:

As organizations adopt increasingly tougher security standards, today's users are required to remember more passwords for more systems. These passwords are more complex and have a shorter lifetime than ever before. The increased likelihood of errors in recalling passwords generates an increase in calls to the Helpdesk for password resets. Overall, this decreases the productivity of the user. These are two factors affecting the bottom-line of the business.

Consider an organization having thousands of employees having individual workstations. As per a study, in such a big environment, on an average, as much as 30 percent of the help desk requests are for resetting passwords. Lock outs have cost associated with it because the user can't work and has to call the company's helpdesk to reset the password.

Password management is the most common IT support issue bringing the most help desk workload in many organizations. Password complexity and expiration policy requirements lead to frequently forgotten passwords and account lockouts, increasing the overall administrative burden.

Advanced Authentication and Password Reset Manager is a simple and cost effective solution that gives end-users the ability to securely manage their passwords and resolve account lockout incidents in a self-service fashion without calling help desk personnel.

With Advanced Authentication and Password Reset Manager, you can increase your overall IT department efficiency through enabling the user self-service password management, plus reduce the delegation and rights assignment issues with Help Desk Portal which gives you a convenient and secure interface for managing user accounts. Even further reduce the IT department load with account lockout monitoring, which lets users examine and identify account lockouts in real time and without contacting support teams.

4. Technical Specification

GINA DLL(Graphical Identification & Authentication)

This component, developed in C++, will get invoked by windows operating system. This in turn will invoke windows default authentication mechanism. In addition this component will add ''reset password'' button on windows log in screen.To quote from Microsoft documentation, "[GINA} Graphical Identification and Authentication component that serves as the gateway for interactive logons. GINA is the pluggable part of WinLogon that third parties may replace in order to customize the functionality or the UI of the logon experience in Windows®. By replacing GINA, one can choose the authentication mechanism Windows will use for interactive users. This is often useful for smartcard or biometric logons or hooking some other authentication mechanism. To deploy the GINA, the installer program will copy the DLL onto the target machine in the System32 directory, and update that machine's registry by adding a named value under WinLogon's key: HKLM\SOFTWARE\\CurrentVersion\WinLogon

Credential Provider

In Windows Vista and Windows 2008, GINAs are replaced with a new modular Credential Provider model that is easier to program to. Credential Security Service Provider (CredSSP) is a new security service provider that is available through the Security Support Provider Interface (SSPI) in Windows. The Credential Provider, COM-based architecture, requires each provider to enumerate its UI elements. For example, in a given scenario, a provider might indicate to LogonUI that it requires two edit boxes, two captions, a checkbox, and a bitmap. In turn, LogonUI renders those controls on behalf of the credential provider. Hence Credential providers are the Plug-Ins to LogonUI. LogonUI can interact simultaneously with multiple credential providers.

Client Application: This desktop application developed in C#.NET will facilitate user to answer configured questions and will also allow user to reset his/her password. For Windows 2003 EE and SE GINA DLL will be responsible to invoke this application while for Windows Vista and Windows 2008 Credential Provider will be responsible for invoking this application.

Authentication Web service: This .NET web service will be responsible for authenticating user using challenge response mechanism and if user succeed in answering configured questions correctly then this will enable user to reset the password.

Configuration Manager: This is a ASP.NET (C#) web application where user can configure challenge response. The challenges and responses will be stored in the database SQL Server 2005. These challenges will be displayed to the user for authentication purpose.

4.1. *Hardware and Technical requirement*

General Access Minimum Requirements

RAM and Processor: Minimum: 256 MB RAM and 550 MHz Processor.

Internet Explorer 6.0/7.0

Platforms : Windows XP (SP2+), Windows Server 2003, Windows Vista and Windows 2008

Server Requirements

RAM and Processor: Minimum: 512 MB RAM and 733 MHz processor

Platforms : Windows Server 2003

Microsoft Internet Information Server 5.0/6.0

Microsoft .NET 2.0

Microsoft Active DirectoryB, Microsoft SQL 2005

References

[1]Journal:" **The usability of pass phrases for authentication: An empirical field study**" byMark Keith, Benjamin Shao and Paul John Steinbart ,Department of Information Systems, W. P. Carey School of Business, Arizona State University, Box 4606 Tempe, AZ 85287-4606, USA

[2]IEEE Paper: "**Password Management** "by Matt Bishop Dept. of mathematics and computer science Dartmount college, Hanover.NH03755

[3]"**Create a Password Reset Disk**"Publisher : Microsoft Tips White Papers

[4]"**NetWrix Password Manager**"Publisher: NetWrix Corporation

[5]"**Reducing helpdesk costs using self-service password reset tools**" by Bejoy V G, Wipro

[6]"**Password Management for Windows and Beyond**" by Stephanie Collins, Product Manager, Quest Software

[7]"CryptoBytes Identity Theft: An Introduction "by J. Black

[8]"Quantifying the Security of Preference-based Authentication" by Markus Jakobsson ,Palo Alto Research Center Palo Alto, CA 94304 mjakobss@parc.com, Liu Yang, Susanne Wetzel Stevens Institute of Technology Hoboken, NJ 07030 {lyang,swetzel}@cs.stevens.edu

[9]"Personal knowledge questions for fallback authentication: Security questions in the era of Face book" by Ariel Rabkin, UC Berkeley asrabkin@cs.berkeley.edu

INTRUSION DETECTION IN WIRELESS MESH NETWORK USING INCOMPLETE NON-COOPERATIVE GAME THEORY

VINAY SHARMA

M.Tech (computer science and eng.), VIT University,
Vellore, Tamil Nadu-632014, India

P. VENKATA KRISHNA

Asso. Professor, VIT University
Vellore, Tamil Nadu-632014, India

V. SARITHA

Asst. Professor, VIT University
Vellore, Tamil Nadu-632014, India

Wireless MESH network is a new pattern that allows the enhancement of existing wireless Network with multi hop connection. The medium for transmission of wireless network is air, which is unprotected medium therefore the challenging problem facing by wireless network is network security, some of network security problems such as eavesdropping of the wireless signal, jamming of the wireless channels, network intrusions. Here we are focusing on network intrusions detection. Intrusion is used to describe attacks from the outside hence intrusion detection is detection of outside attacks. We are using game theory, a study of how to mathematically determine the best strategy for given conditions in order to optimize the outcome for detecting intrusion in wireless mesh network. We represent the interaction between intruder and intrusion detection system (IDS) as the 2x2signaling game which comes under non-cooperative game with incomplete information where one player is informed player i.e. intruder and other is uninformed player i.e. IDS, who is unaware of intruder source.

1. Introduction

1.1. *Mesh Network*

Mesh networking is a way to route data between nodes. It allows reconfiguration and connections without interruption around broken or blocked paths. Wireless Mesh Networks (WMN) [2] is the networks in which each node can communicate directly with one or more peer nodes. Each node plays the role of host as well as of router. It can forward packets on behalf of other nodes that may not be within direct wireless transmission range of their destinations. Mesh networks differ from other networks in that the mesh network parts can connect to each other via multiple hops, and they are not mobile generally. Mesh networks properties make it as one type of ad hoc network. Mesh networks are self-organized, self-healing, the network can still operate even when a node breaks down or a connection goes bad. Because of it, a very reliable network is formed. WMNs having two types of nodes: mesh routers and mesh clients. A wireless mesh router not only has the capability as of gateway but it has additional routing functions to support mesh networking. Mesh clients have a higher variety of devices such as laptop/desktop, pocket PC, PDA etc. Architecture of wireless mesh network is of following type:-

1.Infrastructure wireless mesh networks: Mesh routers form an infrastructure for clients such as laptop/desktop PC, PDA etc.

2.Client wireless mesh networks: Client nodes constitute the actual network to perform routing and configuration functionalities

3. Hybrid wireless mesh networks: Here mesh functions are performed by mesh clients with other mesh clients as well as they access the network through mesh routers.

Communication medium of wireless mesh network is air so the security issue of the network has major concern. Here the focus is on a key area of security that is intrusion detection. Intrusion in networks has many forms including denial of service attacks, viruses introduced into the networks, etc. Here the particular intrusion problem is considered. In this problem, the intruder attempts to send a malicious packet to a destination node in the network

1.2 Game theory

Game theory [6] has been successfully applied to many disciplines including economics, political sciences, and computer sciences. Game theory is a strong candidate to provide mathematical framework for analysis, modeling, decision, and control processes for information security and intrusion detection. The concept of game theory is to maximize the profit and minimize the loose. It involves in finding the best actions for individual decision makers in these conditions and knowing stable outcomes. The object of study in game theory is the game, defined to be any situation in which:

• There are at least two players. A player may be an individual, a company, or a wireless node.
• Each player has a number of possible strategies, courses of action he or she may choose
• The strategies chosen by each player decide the outcome of the game.
• The each possible outcome of the game is a collection of numerical payoffs, one to each player. These payoffs are the value of the outcome to the different players.

Games are generally categorized as non-cooperative and cooperative games.

Non-cooperative game theory is concerned with the analysis of strategic choices and specifically models the process of players' making choices out of their own interests.

A cooperative game is a game in which the players can make binding commitments, as is not the case in the non-cooperative game. Analysis in cooperative game theory is centered on coalition formation and distribution of wealth gained through cooperation.

With the application of game theory, we can address problems where players with different, and in many cases, unique behavior. A specific branch of game theory that has been often used is non-cooperative game theory. Non-cooperative game theory studies situations in which a number of players are involved in an interactive process whose outcome is determined by the node's individual decisions and affects each agent in a possibly different way. In this paper, we model the interaction between an attacker and an intrusion detection system as a basic signaling game which comes under the non-cooperative game theory with incomplete information.

Signaling games [7] refer a class of two-player games of incomplete information in which one player has information and the other has not. The informed player's strategy set consists of signals based on information and the uninformed player's strategy set consists of actions based on signals. More generally, a signaling game includes any strategic setting in which players can use the actions of their opponents to make believe about hidden information.

The rest of the paper is organized as follows. Section ii overviews the related work. In Section iii, we present the problem statement and then model of the game. Section iv presents the conclusion and future work.

2. Related Work

Hadi Otrok et al. [1], developed a network packet sampling policy to reduce the success chances of an intruder by finding the value of the game using a min–max strategy. Non-cooperative game theory with complete information about the players is used to express the problems, where the players are the cooperative intruders or a smart intruder (depends on which way we are solving) and the intrusion detection system. In this game model the IDS has an best sampling strategy in order to detect the malicious packets. The strategy for each intruder is the chances of opting each possible path to send its malicious packet to the non-attacker node. The best strategy for the IDS is to choose the sampling rates to each link to maximize the chances/probability of detection while not exceeding the total budget. Here author has taken many assumptions, one of them is the intruder source is known to the IDS i.e. they assume the complete information about intruder source.

Liqiang Zhao et al. [5], use incompletely cooperative game theory to improve the performance of MAC protocols in WMNs. In this game, first, each node guesses the current game state (e.g., the number of participating nodes). Second, the node adjusts its equilibrium strategy by tuning its local disputed parameters to the guessed game state. The game is repeated several times to get the best performance. To use the game successfully in WMNs, the authors present a CSMA/CA protocol by integrating a proposed virtual CSMA/CA and the standard CSMA/CA protocol. When a node has no packet to send, it proceeds with effort for the channel in virtual CSMA/CA mode. In this way the node can guess the game state and obtain the best strategy. When a node has packets to send, it efforts for the channel in standard CSMA/CA mode with the optimal strategy obtained in virtual CSMA/CA mode. Here Liqiang Zaho used cooperative game theory approach where players have complete freedom of pre-play communication to make joint binding agreement.

There exit several schemes to secure wireless ad hoc Networks and wireless sensor networks which share similarities with WMNs to some extent. Bo Sun et al. [4], used incompletely cooperative game theory to improve the system performance of WSNs. Clear cooperation among nodes is clearly impractical in WSNs as it causes additional energy and bandwidth utilization. Here a new concept of incompletely cooperative game theory to improve the performance without any external cooperation among nodes is presented. In this game, firstly, each player estimates the game state; secondly, the player adjusts its equilibrium strategy to the estimated game state by tuning its local contention parameters. Results show that when using the game in WSNs, the key problem is how to design a proper equilibrium strategy based on the game. The incompletely cooperative game can be classified as an arbitrary game, which starts when a new packet arrives at the node and ends when the packet is transmitted successfully or discarded.

Signaling games refer [7] a class of two-player games of incomplete information in which one player is informed and the other is not. The informed player's strategy set consists of signal based on information and the uninformed player's strategy set consists of actions based on signals. More generally, a signaling game includes any strategic setting in which players can use the actions of their opponents to make believe about hidden information.

Zhiqi Tao et al. [3], differentiate between wireless and standard intrusion detection. Commercial network intrusion detection systems are normally used to protect the boundary of an organization's network, or to secure a network within the organization. By deploying a network intrusion detection system at a network location can not only detect many of the known malicious packets, it can do so with accuracy. But the loophole of such a network intrusion detection system is that they does not generally detect network intrusions originating from internal hosts of the network, whether these attacks are from insiders or from outside attackers

3. System Model

In the model of the signaling game, a node is the sender and the host based IDS is the receiver to which the message is directed. A sender can be of two types, a variable that summarizes private information (in an incomplete information game). The sender node could be a regular node or he could be a malicious node. In other words, the type space of a given sender is given by Θ = [Attacker; Regular]. The IDS earlier beliefs that the probability that any other node in the system is either an attacker or a regular node can be described by a single number $q \in [0;1]$. The malicious node's decision is a choice between malicious behavior and normal behavior. Let the probability of a particular malicious node shows openly malicious activity be s, and the probability of the same node shows normal behavior be $1-s$. The IDS detects this decision with a probability t and misses it with a probability $1-t$ depending on his beliefs.

Consider the attacker-IDS game shown in Fig 3.1.1. The IDS has a gain of –d1 for detecting an attack whereas there is a cost involved whenever the IDS misses an attack d2 or when it raises a false alarm f. On the other hand, the intruder has a gain of –c2 on a successful undetected intrusion and a cost of c1 on being detected and blocked. We consider false alarms have a zero cost value to the attacker.

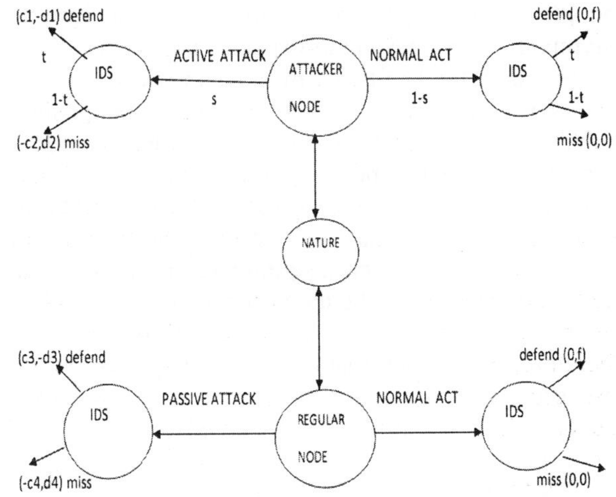

Fig. 3.1 Signaling game

A payoff function for a player is a mapping from the cross-product of players' strategy spaces to that player's set of payoffs (normally the set of real numbers)

Table 3.1 Payoff of signaling game

	Attacker, attack	Attacker, normal	Regular, attack	Regular, normal
Defend	c1 , -d1	0 , f	c3 , -d3	0 , f
Miss	-c2 , d2	0 , 0	-c4 , d4	0 , 0

As type θ's payoff to strategy σ1(·|θ) when Player 2 plays σ2(·|a1) is

$$u1(\sigma 1.\sigma 2.\theta) = \sum_{a1}\sum_{a2}\sigma 1(a1|\theta)\sigma 2(a2|a1)u1(a1.a2.\theta) \quad (1)$$

Therefore for the attacker in all cases the expected payoff is:

$$s[tc1-(1-t)c2] \quad (2)$$

As Player 2's payoff to strategy σ2(·|a1) when Player 1 plays σ1(·|θ) is

$$\sum_{\theta} p(\theta)(\sum_{a1}\sum_{a2}\sigma 1(a1|\theta)\sigma 2(a2|a1)u2(a1.a2.\theta)) \quad (3)$$

Therefore for IDS in all cases the expected payoff is:

$$sd2+tf-st(d1+f+d2). \quad (4)$$

Where: spaces of mixed actions are A1 and A2 with elements a1and a2 respectively; ui(α1, α2, θ) is player i's payoff; $\sigma1(\cdot|\theta)$ is probability distribution over actions a1 for each type θ; $\sigma2(\cdot|\alpha1)$ is probability distribution over actions a2 for each action a1

The Nash Equilibrium for such a signaling game is described by the following condition

For the attacker/ regular node: Given the strategy of the IDS, each type θ of a node evaluates the utility from sending a message a1 as $\sum_{a2} \sigma2(a2|a1)u1(a1,a2,\theta)$ and $p(\theta)$ puts weight on a1 only if its amongst the maximizing messages in this expected utility.

For the IDS: The IDS will move in two steps. First for every message a1 that is sent with positive probability by some type θ, the IDS uses Bayes' rule to compute the posterior probability analysis that a1 comes from each type θ. According to the Nash equilibrium condition, for all a1 that are sent by some type θ with positive probability, every response a2 in support of the IDS's response should be the best response to a1 given the beliefs that are computed using Bayes' rule. Therefore, we can say that the IDS strategy will be the best response to the sending nodes behavior strategy if and only if it maximizes its expected utility over all possible pure strategies.

EXAMPLE:

The first move is taken by Nature, with equal probabilities, Nature assigns Player 1 type t € {t1,t2). Player 1 knows her type, and chooses the option whether to play L or R. Player 2 does not know what player's 1 type is, but he observes whether she plays L or R and after her decision he chooses U or D

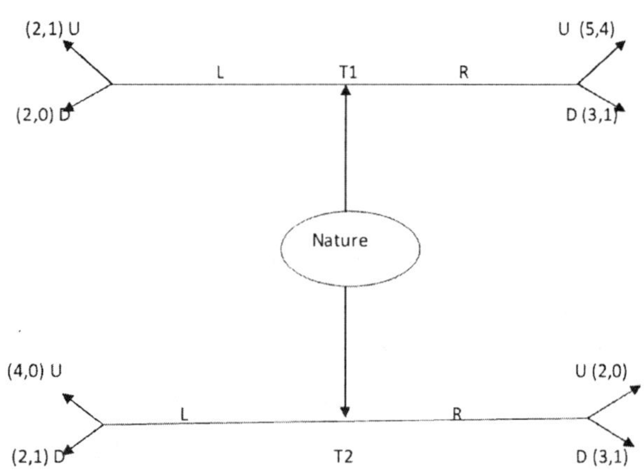

Fig. 3.2 Game

Table 3.2 payoff of the game

	T1,Left(L)	T1,Right(R)	T2,Left(L)	T2,Right(R)
Up(U)	2 , 1	5 , 4	4 , 0	2 , 0
Down(D)	2 , 0	3 , 1	2, 1	3, 1

The extensive form of the game and its payoffs are presented.

If Player 1 is of type t1 and plays R, and Player 2 plays U, the payoffs are 5 to Player 1 and 4 to Player 2. Note that if Player 1 is of type t2 and plays R, and Player 2 plays U, the payoff to Player 1 is 2. Note also that for Player 1 of type t1, R strictly dominates L: playing L, she will always get 2; playing R, she will get at least 3. This means that in any PBE, type t1 will always play R.

Player 1 Strategy

We consider the case of semi-separating PBE.

One type of Player 1 plays a pure strategy while second type plays a mixed strategy. As a result, Player 2 is not able to update perfectly his prior beliefs about Player l's type.

In a 2 x 2 game if there is a semi-separating equilibrium in the game, it must take the form that Player 1 of type tl plays R exclusively, and Player 1 of type t2 mixes L and R. The only uncertainty regards the mixing probabilities for type t2. In other words,

σ 1(t)=R if t=t1

σ 1(t)= pL + (1-p)R if t=t2 where p€[0,1]

Beliefs for Player 2

Let $\mu(t_i/A)$ be the probability Player 2 assigns to type i after observing action A. Now Bayes' rule is applied in both information sets for Player 2.

Bayes' rule:

μ(t1/R)=P(R/t1)*P(t1) / [P(R/t1)*P(t1) + P(R/t2)*P(t2)]

We know from the structure of the game that

P(t1) = P(t2) = 0.5. By construction

we know that

P(R/t1) = 1 and P(R/t2) = (1-p)

After solving, we get

μ(t1/R) = 1/(2-p) (and therefore, μ(t2/R) = (1-p)/(2-p)).

In the same way, we solve for μ(tl/L) = 0.

Best Response for Player 2

Against R

Player 2's expected utility from playing U and D at the right-hand information set, respectively, is

EU2(U,R)= μ(t1/R)*U2(U,R,t1)+μ(t2/R)*U2(U,R,t2) = 4/(2-p) and (1)

EU2(D,R)= μ(t2/R)*U2(D,R,t2)+μ(t1/R)*U2(D,R,t2) = 1. (2)

After comparing (1) and (2), the maximum will be the best response for player 2 against R.

Against L

EU2(U,L)=μ(t1/L)*U2(U,L,t1)+μ(t2/L)*U2(U,L,t2) = 0 and

EU2(D,L)=μ(t1/L)*U2(D,L,t1)+μ(t2/L)*U2(D,L,t2) =1. Here best response for player 2 against L is D.

4.Conclusion

A mesh network (WMN) is a topology that relies heavily on the ad hoc paradigm of "multi hop". In a wireless mesh network we see a series of nodes that communicate with each other constantly. The challenging problem facing by wireless network is network security. Specifically here we are discussing network intrusion problem, whose intention is to insert malicious packets in the network to create various network problems. A non-cooperative with incomplete information game theoretic approach to detect the intrusion, unwanted involvement in wireless network is used. A basic 2x2signaling game which comes under non-cooperative game theory with incomplete information is used to model the interaction between the players, IDS and intruder. We assume that a malicious node attacks only one node at a time. The IDS does one of two things, it either warns on detection of an intrusion or does nothing.

References

1. Hadi Otrok , Mona Mehrandish, Chadi Assi, Mourad Debbabi, Prabir Bhattacharya "Game theoretic models for detecting network intrusions" Computer Security Laboratory, Concordia Institute for Information Systems Engineering, Concordia University, Montreal, Que., Canada H3G 1M8 Received 28 February 2007; received in revised form 22 December 2007; accepted 23 December 2007
2. Ian F. Akyildiz , Xudong Wang , Weilin Wang "Wireless mesh networks: a survey" Broadband and Wireless Networking (BWN) Lab, School of Electrical and Computer Engineering, Georgia Institute of Technology, Atlanta, GA 30332, USA Kiyon, Inc., 4225 Executive Square, Suite 290, La Jolla, CA 92037, USA Received 1June 2004; received in revised form 1November 2004; accepted 20 December 2004
3. Zhiqi Tao Department of Information Systems University of Melbourne Melbourne, Australia , A. B. (Tobias) Ruighaver Department of Information Systems University of Melbourne Melbourne, Australia "Wireless Intrusion Detection: Not as easy as traditional network intrusion detection" zhiqit@pgrad.unimelb.edu.au,anthonie@unimelb.edu.au
4. Bo Sun and Lawernce osborne, "Intrusion Detection techniques in mobile ad hoc and wireless sensor networks" lamar university yang xiao, the university of alabama sghaier guizani, university of quebec at trois-rivieres, IEEE Wireless Communications • October 2007
5. Liqiang Zhao and Jie Zhang, University of Bedfordshire Hailin Zhang, Xidian University "Using Incompletely Cooperative Game Theory in Wireless Mesh Networks" IEEE Network • January/February 2008
6. Renita Machado , Sirin Tekinay "A survey of game-theoretic approaches in wireless sensor networks" Department of Electrical and Computer Engineering, New Jersey Institute of Technology, Newark, NJ 07029, USA. Received 13 December 2007 Received in revised form 7 June 2008 Accepted 16 July 2008
7. "Signaling Games" Joel Sobel, Department of Economics, University of California, San Diego, email: jsobel@ucsd.edu May 31, 2007

TEST CASE MINING

LILLY RAAMESH
Research Scholar, Anna University Chennai,
Chennai 600 025, Tamil Nadu, India.

G.V. UMA
Asst. Prof./C.S.E, Anna University Chennai
Chennai 600 025, Tamil Nadu, India.

Today, the design of test case with enhanced reliability is a real challenge as it needs expert designers with perfect knowledge about the whole system and also the traditional test case generation approach faces a challenge in test results analysis, because of the difference between the generated test cases and the expected results. So, it will be better if we could establish a method for automatic test case generation based on both program structures and the functional requirements in specifications. Mining approach can be used to have a perfect knowledge about the whole system. This paper presents a novel approach of mining test cases.

1. Introduction

Testing is a process finding defects. Even when software is developed using a rigorous discipline, it will contain a significant number of bugs. So, testing is needed to guarantee the software quality and reliability before release.

Testing of system behavior can be categorized into (i) White box testing or Structural testing or Glass box testing:

In this approach the actual implementation is used to generate the tests. While test generation using the white-box approach is not common, evaluation of test effectiveness often requires use of structural information.

(ii) Black box testing or Functional testing:

When test generation is done by only considering the input/output description of the software, nothing about the implementation of the software is assumed to be known. This is the most common form of testing.

2. Test Cases

A test Case is a set of conditions or variables under which a tester will determine if a requirement or use case upon an application or partially or fully satisfied. It may take many test cases to determine that a requirement is fully satisfied. To develop bug free quality software a test plan and test cases are very important.

3. Related Work

There are approaches like Pareto Efficient Multi-Objective Test Case selection[1], An empirical study of test case filtering techniques based on exercising information flows[2], Search algorithms for regression test case prioritization[3], Improving fault detection capability by selectively retaining test cases during test suite reduction[4], Neural Networks Based Test Case Selection[5], A choice Relation framework for supporting Category-partition Test Case generation[7], Test Case Prioritization, A Test generation strategy for Pair-wise testing[9], Prioritizing Test Cases for regression testing[14], Generating software test data by Evolution[10] etc. for test case generation, test case selection & test case prioritization etc.

But none of these uses mining approach. In this paper we propose a mining approach to have better knowledge about the test cases and about the full system.

4. Mining

Data mining is the principle of sorting through large amounts of data and picking out relevant information. It is usually used by business intelligence organizations, and financial analysts, but it is increasingly used in the sciences to extract information from the enormous data sets generated by modern experimental and observational methods. Data mining identifies trends within data that go beyond simple analysis. Through the use of sophisticated algorithms, uses have the ability to identify key attributes of business processes and target opportunities.

Data mining is often used to apply to the two separate processes of knowledge discovery and prediction. Knowledge discovery provides explicit information that has a readable form and can be understood by a user. Forecasting, or predictive modeling provides predictions of future events and may be transparent and readable in some approaches and opaque in others such as neural networks. Moreover, some data mining systems such as neural networks are inherently geared towards prediction and pattern recognition, rather that knowledge recovery.

5. Test Case Mining

5.1. Test Case

A set of test data and test programs and their expected results. A test case validates one or more system requirements and generates a pass or fail. The test case generation results in a collection of test cases known as a test suite. The generation may be done manually or automatically.

The main challenge in testing is to select & execute test cases.

5.2. Mining

The Science of extracting useful information from large data sets or databases.

5.3. Test Case Mining

The collection of large amounts of test cases makes it possible to apply data mining techniques to discover knowledge and patterns in the test cases.

The proposed knowledge discovery process has the following steps as described in figure 1.

- Preprocessing
- Transformation and feature extraction
- Test case mining
- Interpretation and evaluation

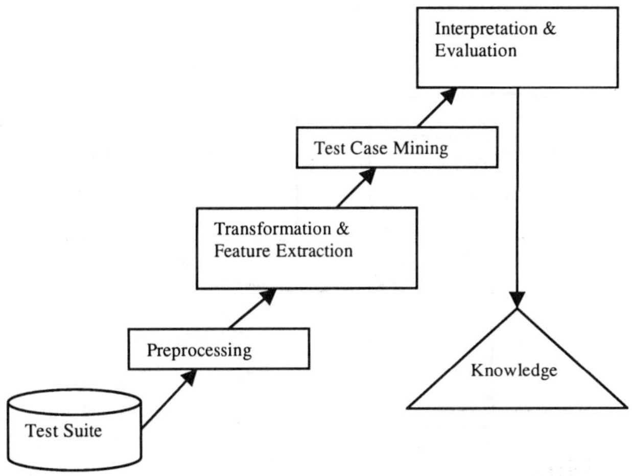

Figure 1. Mining module

Preprocessing is removing noise and inconsistent data from the test suite.

Transformation and feature extraction is where data are transformed or consolidated into forms appropriate for mining by performing summary or aggregation operations.

Test case mining is an essential process where intelligent methods are applied in order to extract data patterns.

Interpretation and evaluation is used to identify truly interesting patterns representing knowledge based on some interestingness measures.

6. Basic Structure of Test Case Mining System

The basic structure of test case mining system (TCM) has a mining module as described in figure 2.

The test suite is given as an input to the mining module. The derived knowledge from the mining module is again applied to the test suite so that a better test suite is provided for testing. The test suite is mined to provide a better set of test cases which best suits to the need of the system.

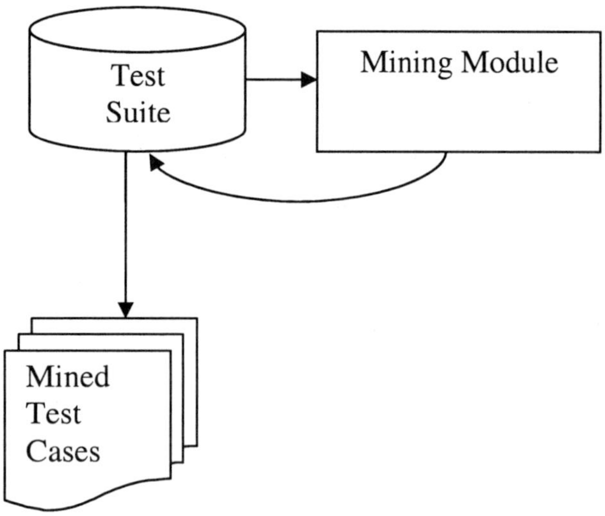

Figure 2. TCM System

7. Conclusion

In this paper we present a mining approach to have better knowledge about the test cases and about the full system. So that better test cases can be generated, selected and are used for testing. Because the main challenge in testing is to select & execute test cases. The proposed TCM has better way of mining the test suite and provides a better set of test cases to test the system performance.

References

1. Shin Yoo and Mark Harman., *Proc. ISSTA '07,* (2007).
2. Wes Masri, Andy Podgurski., *IEEE transactions on software Engineering*, **vol.33, No.7**, (July 2007).
3. Zheng Li, Mark Harman, robert M. Hierons, *IEEE transactions on software Engineering,* vol.33, No.4, (April 2007).
4. Dennis Jeffrey and Neelam Gupta, . *IEEE transactions on software Engineering*, **vol.33, No.2**, (February 2007).
5. Mao ye, boqinFeng, yao Lin 7Li Zhu, *Proc of IEEEtransactions*,(2006)
6. Xu, Z.; Gao, K.; Khoshgoftaar, T.M, *IRI - 2005 IEEE International Conference,(*Aug. 2005)
7. T.Y. Chen, Pak-lok poon, t.h. Tse, *IEEE transactions on software Engineering,* **vol.29, No.7**, (July 2003).
8. Sebastian Elbaum, Alexey G.Malishevsky, Gregg Rothermel, *IEEE transactions on software Engineering*, **vol.28, No.2**, (ebruary 2002)
9. Kuo –Chung Tainand Yu Lei, *IEEE transactions on software Engineering*, **vol.28, No.1**, (January 2002).
10. Christoph C. Michael, gary McGraw, Michael A. Schatz, *IEEE transactions on software Engineering*, **vol.27, No.12**, (December 2001).
11. Gregg rothermal, Ronald H. Untch, Chengyun Chu, Mary Jean Harrold, *IEEE transactions on software Engineering*, **vol.27, No.10**, (October 2001).
12. Scott w. Ambler, *IEEE software*, (2007).
13. Wei-Tek Tsai and Lian Yu, Feng Zhu, Ray Paul, *IEEE software,(2005).*
14. *S. G. Elbaum, A. G.* Malishevsky, and G. Rothermel, I*n International Symposium on Software Testing and Analysis*, **ACM Press**, (2000).

EFFICIENT INTRUSION DETECTION SYSTEM MODELS

URMILA ADSULE[†]
V. K. PACHGHARE

College Of Engineering, Pune, Shivaji Nagar, Pune, Maharashtra, 411009, India.

PARAG KULKARNI

Chief Scientist and Research Head, Capsilon Research Labs, Capsilon India, Pune, India.

This paper investigates the suitability of various techniques to model efficient intrusion detection systems. We briefly describe some of the latest developments made to increase the efficiency and accuracy of intrusion detection using support vector machines(SVMs), artificial neural networks (ANNs) and linear genetic programming (LGP). One approach focuses on reducing training time of SVMs using clustering tree analysis called CT-SVM. Another approach called DT-SVM combines Decision tree and SVM to maximize the detection accuracy. Third uses LGP with feature selection and ranking algorithm. Fourth uses ANN with Back propagation Algorithm. Here we will compare the performances of all the above approaches.

1. Introduction

Whenever an intrusion occurs, the security and value of a computer system is compromised. Network based attacks make it difficult for legitimate users to access various network services by purposely occupying or sabotaging network resources and services. This can be done by sending large amount of traffic exploiting well-known faults in networking services, and by overloading network hosts. Intrusion detection attempts to detect computer attacks by examining various data records observed in processes on the network and it is split into two groups: first is misuse detection, which is an attempt to intrusions that match known attack scenarios. Another is anomaly detection which is scalable solution for detecting network based anomalies.

Anomaly detection is capable of catching new attacks. However new legitimate behavior can also be falsely identified as an attack, resulting a false positive. The current challenge is to reduce false positive as well as false negative rate, consequently to improve the accuracy of intrusion detection systems (IDSs) in an efficient way.

Many machine learning algorithms are being used to develop IDS competing for accuracy and speed. Here we will analyze different algorithms which use different pattern matching/ classification techniques on the basis of their accuracy.

We compare four recent methods: 1. CT-SVM (Clustering tree and SVM) focuses on enhancing training time of SVM, when dealing with large datasets, using hierarchical clustering analysis. It uses dynamically growing self organized tree (DGSOT) [2]. 2. DT-SVM (Decision Tree and SVM) is a hierarchical hybrid intelligent system. It combines individual base classifiers and other hybrid machine learning paradigms to maximize detection accuracy and minimized computational complexity [5]. 3. LGP (Linear genetic programming): Mukkamala uses LGP to improve efficiency and effectiveness. He gave emphasis on feature selection and ranking. Thus only key features give notable performance in terms of detection accuracy [7]. 4. ANN-SOM-BPN (Artificial Neural Networks-Self Organized Map with Back Propagation): Among many neural network algorithms, SOM has the ability to construct topological result. It operates on data regardless of amount and linearity of dataset [3].

2. Related Work

Data mining approach to intrusion detection was first implemented in ‘Mnining Audit Data for Automated Models for Intrusion Detection’, MADAMID in 1999 [10]. ‘A State Transition Analysis Tool for intrusion

† Work partially supported by Pune Vidyarthi Gruha’s College of Engineering and Technology, Pune.

detection', STAT' and 'Intrusion Detection In Our Time', IDIOT are misuse detection systems that use signatures of known attacks. In recent years, there have been several learning-based efforts in intrusion detection. 'Anomaly-based Data Mining For Intrusions', ADMIT is user-profile dependant IDS with host-based data collection and processing. In this effort 'Next Generation Intrusion Detection Expert System', NIDES and 'Event Monitoring Enabling Responses to Anomalous Live Disturbances,' EMERALD creates user profile based on statistical method.

Neural networks are used to extract program behavior profiles instead of user behavior profiles. SOM and SVM have been used as anomaly detectors. SOM is used to cluster and graphically display network data to determine which clusters contain attacks. 'One-class SVM' based on one set of examples performs well. Some more algorithms are developed for feature selection and ranking to improve performance of SVM-IDSs. One technique experimented by Latifur Khan in CT-SVM improves training time of SVMs [2].

LGP is also used for modeling IDS and identifying the key features that help in deciding whether a connection is intrusive or normal activity.

3. IDS Based on Machine Learning

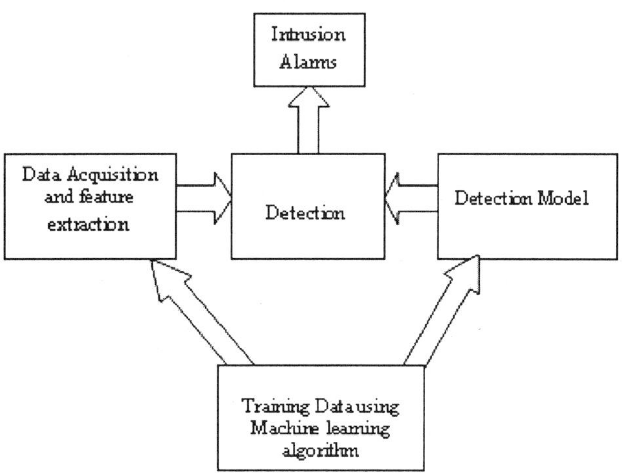

Figure 1. Overall Structure of IDS

To explain the three perspectives of technical challenges, a general framework for IDSs based on machine learning is presented in Fig.1. In our proposed system, we use this framework. To explain the three perspectives of technical challenges, a general framework for IDSs based on machine learning is presented in here. The framework is composed of three main parts. The first one is for data acquisition and feature extraction. Data acquisition is realized by a data sensing module that observes network flow data or process execution trajectories from host computers. After pre-processing of the raw data, a feature extraction module is used to convert the raw data into feature vectors that can be processed by machine learning algorithms and an extraction model based on unsupervised learning can be employed to extract more useful features or reduce the dimensionality of the feature vectors. This process for automated feature extraction is a component of the machine learning part in the framework. In the machine learning part, audit data for training are stored in databases and they can be dynamically updated either by human analysts or by machine learning algorithms. To automatically construct detection models from the audit data, various machine learning methods can be applied, which include unsupervised learning, supervised learning and reinforcement learning. In the following sections, we will apply some recently developed machine learning algorithms to the challenging problems in IDSs and evaluate their performance. The third part in the framework depicted in Fig.1 is for real-time detection, which is to make use of the detection models as well as the extracted feature vectors to determine whether an observed pattern or a sequence of patterns is normal or abnormal.

4. Dataset

The approaches which are discussed here focus on network based anomaly detection. The algorithm is applied to a set of benchmark data namely 1998 DARPA that originated from MIT Lincoln Lab. The KDD Cup 1999 Intrusion detection contest data was prepared by the 1998 DARPA Intrusion Detection Evaluation program [8]. Lincoln lab acquired nine weeks of raw TCP dump data. The raw data was processed into connection records, which consist of about 5 million connection records. The data set contains 24 attack types. These attacks fall into four main categories:

1. Denial of service (DOS):An attacker makes resources too busy or too full to handle legitimate requests, or denies legitimate users access to a machine.
2. Remote to user (R2L): An attacker who does not have an account on a remote machine sends packets to that machine over a network and exploits some

vulnerability to gain local access as a user of that machine.
3. User to root (U2R): An attacker starts out with access to a normal user account on the system and is able to exploit system vulnerabilities to gain root access to the system.
4. Probing: An attacker scans a network of computers to gather information or find known vulnerabilities.

5. Clustering Tree And SVM

This approach for enhancing the training process of SVM is based on the combination of clustering and SVM to find relevant support vectors. In this system, Latifur Khan builds a hierarchical clustering tree for each class in the data set (for simplicity and without loss of generality, we assume binary classification) using the DGSOT algorithm. The DGSOT algorithm, top-down clustering, builds the hierarchical tree iteratively in several epochs. After each epoch, new nodes are added to the tree based on a learning process. To avoid the computation overhead of building the tree, it does not build the entire hierarchical trees. Instead, after each epoch it trains SVM on the nodes of both trees. It uses the support vectors of the classifier as prior knowledge for the succeeding epoch in order to control the tree growth. Specifically, support vectors are allowed to grow, while non-support vectors are stopped. This has the impact of adding nodes in the boundary areas between the two classes, while eliminating distant nodes from the boundaries [2].

6. Decision Tree And SVM

A hybrid intelligent system uses the approach of integrating different learning or decision-making models. Each learning model works in a different manner and exploits different set of features. Integrating different learning models gives better performance than the individual learning or decision-making models by reducing their individual limitations and exploiting their different mechanisms. In a hierarchical hybrid intelligent system each layer provides some new information to the higher level. The overall functioning of the system depends on the correct functionality of all the layers.

The data set is first passed through the DT and node information is generated. Node information is determined according to the rules generated by the DT. Terminal nodes are numbered left to right starting with 1. All the data set records are assigned to one of the terminal nodes, which represent the particular class or subset. The terminal nodes show either red or blue color representing either normal or attack. This node information (as an additional attribute) along with the original set of attributes is passed through the SVM to obtain the final output. The key idea here is the node information provided by the DT will improve the performance of the SVM [5].

7. Linear Genetic Programming

LGP manipulates and evolves program at the machine code level. The settings of various LGP parameters are of utmost importance for successful performance of the system. The population space has been subdivided into multiple subpopulation or demes. Migration of individuals among the subpopulations causes evolution of the entire population. It helps to maintain diversity in the population, as migration is restricted among the demes. Moreover, the tendency towards a bad local minimum in one deme can be countered by other demes with better search directions. The various LGP search parameters are the mutation frequency, crossover frequency and the reproduction frequency: The crossover operator acts by exchanging sequences of instructions between two tournament winners. A constant crossover rate of 90% has been used for all the simulations. After a trial and error approach, the above parameters are used to develop IDS. Five LGP models are employed to perform five class classifications (normal, probe, denial of service, user to root and remote to local). The elimination of useless features (the so-called audit trail reduction) enhances the accuracy of detection while speeding up the computation, thus improving the overall performance of an IDS [7].

8. Artificial Neural Network –Self Organized Map With Back-Propagation

A neural network based IDS ttypically consist of a single neural network based on either misuse detection or anomaly detection. Neural network with good pattern classification abilities typically used for misuse detection, such as 1. Multilayer Perceptron 2. Radial Basis function networks, etc. Neural network with good classification abilities typically used for anomaly detection, such as 1. Self organizing maps (SOM) 2. Competitive Learning Neural Network, etc.

SOM is based on competitive learning. The Winner takes all neuron and Forms a topographic map of input patterns i.e. spatial locations of neurons in the lattice are indicative of statistical features contained in the input patterns. Here Back Propagation algorithm is used for classification. It is a case of supervised learning and typically used for multilayer perceptrons. There are two stages, forward pass and backward pass. In forward pass input signal propagates forward to produce the output. In backward pass, synaptic weights are updated in accordance with the error signal, which is then propagated backwards [3].

9. Performance Evaluation

The accuracy rate of CT-SVM is the best and it is better as compared to pure SVM. It is possible that pure SVM *training* accuracy for testing set may be good but generalization accuracy may not be as good as the accuracy of CT-SVM. DGSOT provides a set of supporting vectors and using SVM hyperplane is generated that would be more accurate for the testing set as compared to the hyperplane generated by pure SVM from entire training data set. Furthermore, False Negative rate is lowest for CT-SVM and False Positive rate is as low as pure SVM.

A hybrid DT–SVM model has two steps for constructing the classifier. The datasets were first passed through the DT and the node information was generated. Training and test data along with the node information is given to the SVM. SVM gives the final output of the hybrid DT–SVM. Hybrid DT–SVM works better than the individual DT and SVM for normal class. For Probe, U2R and R2L classes it performed better than an individual SVM approach.

Since LGP implements feature reduction algorithm along with learning algorithm, it outperforms pure SVM in terms of detection accuracies with the expense of time. The above mentioned four approaches to intrusion detection are best at their places as they emphasize on different aspects to improve the efficiency of detection. However their detection accuracies can be compared as given in Table 1

Table 1. Detection Accuracies For All Approaches

<table>
<tr><th>Methods</th><th>CT-SVM</th><th>DT-SVM</th><th>LGP</th><th>ANN-SOM-BPN</th></tr>
<tr><td>Dataset</td><td>DARPA 1998</td><td>KDD -99</td><td>DARPA 1998</td><td>KDD -99</td></tr>
<tr><td>Attack types</td><td colspan="4"></td></tr>
<tr><td>Normal</td><td>95</td><td>99.70</td><td>99.64</td><td rowspan="5">98.91 % for union of all attacks</td></tr>
<tr><td>Probe</td><td>97</td><td>98.57</td><td>99.86</td></tr>
<tr><td>DOS</td><td>23</td><td>99.92</td><td>99.90</td></tr>
<tr><td>U2R</td><td>43</td><td>48</td><td>64</td></tr>
<tr><td>R2L</td><td>91</td><td>37.80</td><td>99.47</td></tr>
</table>

10. Conclusion

We can summarize that the methods described in this paper are the best methods in their corresponding technological approaches. However it is observed that SVM outperforms in important respects of scalability and training time. LGP outperforms in terms of detection accuracies with expense of time. We proposed a system which will improve the detection accuracy of CT-SVM as this is the only approach emphasizes on reducing training time. It also will be possible to use the algorithms used in above mentioned approaches to further improve efficiency.

References

5. John S. Buaa and Maben Rabi , 'Intrusion Detection with Support Vector Machines and Generative Models' Institute for Systems Reeearch and Department of Electrical and Computer Engineering, University of Maryland, College Park MD 20742, USA (2002).
6. Latifur Khan , Mamoun Awad , Bhavani Thuraisingham , "A new intrusion detection system using support vector machines and hierarchical clustering" The VLDB Journal DOI 10.1007/s00778-006-0002 (2007).
7. P. Ganesh Kumar, "Network Intrusion Detection using Hybrid Neural Network", et al., IEEE – ICSCN, India, pp. 563 – 569 (2007).
8. Pavel, Ptrick, Dussel, Christin Schafer, Konrad Rieck 'Learnng: Usupervised, Unsupervised' in Image analysis and processing, Proc. Of 13th ICIAP Conferences50-57 (2005).
9. Sandhya Peddabachigari, Ajith Abraham, Crina Grosan, Johnson Thomas, "Modeling Intrusion Detection system using hybrid intelligent system" ScienceDirect, Journal of Network and computer Applications 30 114-132 (2007).

10. Srinivas Mukkamala, Andrew H. Sung1,2 and Ajith Abraham 'Identifying Key Variables for Intrusion Detection Using Soft Computing Paradigms' Internationa Journal of Digital Evidence, Volume 1, Issue 4, Winter (2003).
11. Srinivas Mukkamala, Andrew H. Sung, Ajith Abraham, "Modeling Intrusion Detection system using Linear Genetic Approach", In: Robert O., Chunsheng Y., Moonis A., editors. Lecture Notes in Computer Science, vol. 3029. Germany: Springer; a. p. 633–42 (2004).
12. The Third International Knowledge Discovery and Data Mining Tools, http://kdd.ics.uci.edu/databases/kddcup99.kddcup99.html (May 2002).
13. Wenke Lee and Salvatore J. Stolfo. A framework for constructing features and models for intrusion detection systems. ACM Trans. Inf. Syst. Secur., 3(4):227–261 (2000).
14. Wenke Lee, "A Data Mining Framework for Constructing Features and Models for Intrusion Detection Systems", Thesis submitted in Columbia University (1999).
15. Xin Xu, "Adaptive Intrusion Detection Based on Machine Learning: Feature Extraction, Classifier Construction and Sequential Pattern Prediction", International Journal of Web Services Practices, Vol.2, No.1-2, pp. 49-58 (2006).

A SURVEY ON RECONFIGURABLE ARCHITECTURES FOR FUTURE WIRELESS NETWORKS

T. SURESH

Research Scholar, Department of ECE, R.M.K Engineering College
Kavaraipettai, TamilNadu, 601 206, India

JOSEPH HENRY

Professor, Department of EEE, R.M.K Engineering College
Kavaraipettai, TamilNadu, 601 206, India

P. RANGARAJAN

Professor, Department of I.T, R.M.D Engineering College
Kavaraipettai, TamilNadu, 601 206, India

Future wireless communication requires the design of a single wireless user terminal able to autonomously operate in different heterogeneous access networks. A large number of reconfigurable hardware architectures have been proposed both in academia and commercially for the efficient realization of wireless multimedia communication systems. A reconfigurable architecture has evolved from fine-grained to coarse-grained architecture due to some major advantages such as efficient area, high performance and low power. There are several shortcomings for the existing reconfigurable architectures. This paper gives a brief survey of coarse-grained reconfigurable architectures used for multimedia and wireless communications. It is also found that applying agent-based model into a suitable reconfigurable architecture, the overall system flexibility and efficiency will be significantly improved.

1. Introduction

Future mobile communications are envisioned to offer higher data rates, higher mobility support and seamless communication. To achieve seamless communication future wireless communication systems will have to incorporate and integrate different wireless access technologies. The integration should offer seamless interoperability of different types of wireless networks with the wireline backbone. So it requires the design of a single wireless user terminal able to autonomously operate in different heterogeneous access networks. The design of this multistandard/multimode cognitive user terminal faces several problems. There must be reductions in cost, size, power consumption and circuit complexity that will lead to a reconfigurable user terminal, which must be cheap and efficient. For this purpose, advanced reconfigurable architectures, which can dynamically adapt to the changes in access technologies, are currently hot research topics[1].

1.1. *Coarse-grained Reconfigurable Architecture*

During recent years, a number of research efforts are focused on the design of new reconfigurable systems for particular area of application. The work in the area of developing new reconfigurable architectures covers the research on fine-grained and coarse-grained reconfigurable architectures[2]. Coarse-grained reconfigurable architectures offer a high degree of parallelism, sufficient to achieve high throughput. In general, coarse-grained architectures are made upon a set of hard macros (8-bit, 16-bit or even a 32-bit ALU), usually called P*rocessing Element* (PE). The PEs are able to carry few operations such as addition, subtraction or even multiplication. The interconnection is realized either through switching matrices or dedicated busses. The configuration is done by defining the operation mode of the PEs and programming the interconnection between the Processing Elements.

2. Reconfigurable Architectures

The evolving of current and future broadband access techniques into the wireless domain introduces new and flexible network architectures with difficult and interesting challenges. The system designers are faced with a challenging set of problems that stem from access mechanisms, energy conservation, error rate, transmission speed characteristics of the wireless links and mobility aspects. This paper analyzes the major challenges in realizing flexible microelectronic system solutions for future mobile communication applications. Based thereupon, the various architecture designs of flexible system-on-chip solutions in the digital baseband processing for future mobile radio devices are discussed. The motivation of this paper is to find a new parallel and dynamically reconfigurable hardware/software architecture adaptable to various wireless network standards.

2.1. *Montium Architecture*

At the University of Twente, in the *Chameleon* project[1], the steps have been made to define an energy efficient heterogeneous reconfigurable System-on-Chip architecture. Chameleon Systems created one of the first practical commercial implementation of coarse-grained reconfigurable technology for data intensive Internet, DSP and other high performance telecommunication applications[8]. This architecture contains a coarse-grained reconfigurable part called MONTIUM Processor Tiles. The MONTIUM tile is designed to execute highly regular computational intensive DSP kernels using its Multiply and Accumulate operations (MAC). This architecture yields a combination of performance, flexibility and energy-efficiency.

Figure 1. depicts a single MONTIUM Processor Tile. The hardware organization within a tile is very regular and resembles a very long instruction word (VLIW) architecture. The five identical Arithmetic and Logic units (ALU1_ _ _ALU5) in a tile can exploit spatial concurrency to enhance performance. This parallelism demands a very high memory bandwidth, which is obtained by having 10 local Memories (M01_ _ _M10) in parallel. The ALU input registers provide an even more local level of storage. Locality of reference is one of the guiding principles applied to obtain energy efficiency in the MONTIUM. A vertical segment that contains one ALU together with its associated input register files, a part of the interconnect and two local memories is called a Processing Part (PP). The five Processing Parts together are called the Processing Part Array (PPA). A relatively simple sequencer controls the entire PPA.

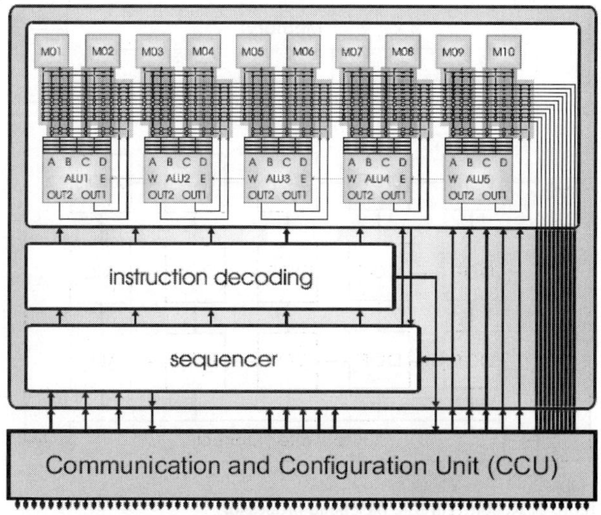

Figure 1. MONTIUM Processor Tile

The Communication and Configuration Unit (CCU) implements the interface with the world outside the tile. The interconnect provides flexible routing within a tile. The configuration of the interconnect can change every clock cycle.

A HiperLAN/2 receiver was implemented in this architecture, which is adaptable depending on the used modulation scheme, as well as a flexible Bluetooth receiver on the same architecture. But the set of multi-standard algorithms is rather incomplete. So more adaptive algorithms are to be developed for the various wireless standards.

2.2. *Reconfigurable Baseband Processor*

This architecture focuses on increasing the granularity of the configurable units without compromising flexibility. Figure 2. shows Reconfigurable baseband processor. This architecture contains five different configurable units (Dominant configurable unit (DOF), CORDIC, ML, ALU and Interconnect unit. The DOF consists of four multipliers, five adders, two accumulators, two shifters, and eight two's complement operations. The CORDIC configurable unit can be configured to perform either polar to rectangular transformation or rectangular to polar transformation. The core building block is the CORDIC stage which is composed of adders and shifters. Any miscellaneous operation is supported by two general-purpose 16-bit ALUs running at the highest speed. The two ALUs

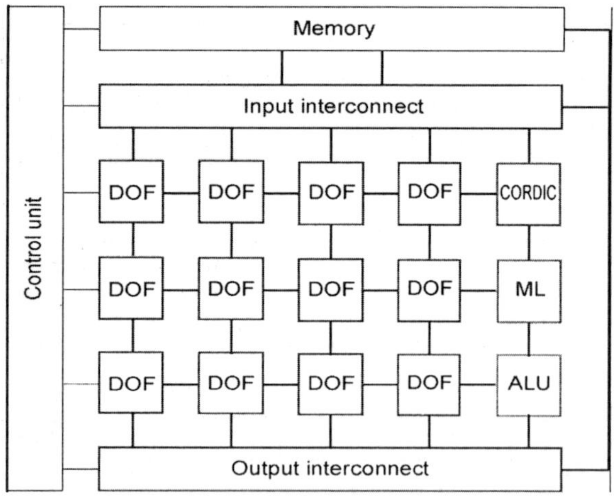

Figure 2. Reconfigurable baseband processor

are serving the real and the complex components of the datapath respectively. Using Multiple Instruction stream, Multiple Data steams (MIMD) approach together with shared memory, the flexibility can be provided.

The processor has two memory banks: data memory and coefficient memory. The data memory has simultaneous read write ports, while the coefficient memory has a read/write port. Using time-multiplexed cross-bar interconnect the number of wires are reduced. It provides a more compact interconnection, but it requires extra circuitry for the multiplexing and demultiplexing of signals and it incurs latency. This architecture was tested in IEEE 802.11 standard and power consumption was estimated for each module, since power efficiency is more critical in wireless communications applications.

2.3. *FleXilicon Architecture*

The architecture proposed in reference[3] addresses three critical design issues with the loop-level-parallelism, wide memory bandwidth, reconfigurable controller, and the support of flexible word length and mapping critical loops into processing elements. Processing element of an instruction-oriented architecture performs sequence of operations, which are defined by instructions, micro-code and/or control signals. Instructions are stored in a configuration memory and fetched by a controller to control the associated processing element. FleXilicon has an array of Processing Elements Slices (PES) and each PES consists of local memories, crossbar switch network, and 16 processing elements and multipliers and a Reconfigurable Controller (RC). This architecture is also a coarse-grained architecture which intends to address various problems faced by the existing architectures like PADDI, Chameleon, AVISPA and RAW.

2.4. Reconfigurable Modem Architecture

In this paper a Reconfigurable Modem (RM) Architecture targeting 3G multi-standard wireless communication systems was proposed. This architecture targeted two 3G wireless standards WCDMA and CDMA 2000 and the design objectives are scalability, low power dissipation and low circuit complexity. This architecture includes cell searcher, rake receiver and viterbi decoder. Cell searcher requires Registers, Adders, Comparators and Multipliers. Rake receiver contains Registers, Counters, Logic gates, Adders, Subtractors, Accumulators, Multipliers, Shifters and Comparators. Viterbi decoder requires Registers, Adders and Comparators. Based on the above four different types, PEs which consists of many functional units are constructed. Each PE is dedicated for one of four basic operations, Bit manipulation, One-Bit Correlation, MAC or ACS (ADD Compare and Select). Then PEs are grouped into four different types of PE modules. PEs inside the PE module communicate with each other reconfigurable bi-directional data paths.

It was proved that this architecture achieves flexibility, scalability and low circuit complexity. It can support multiple standards and easily adapt to rapid change of specification. This architecture has a critical path delay of 13nsec and that for the ASIC implementation is 7.5 nsec. The longer critical path delay is due to long data path inside PEs.

3. Multiagent Based Reconfigurable Architecture

Multagent systems are systems that contain several entities that are called agents[13]. Agents are intelligent autonomous stand-alone processes, continuously sense the environment and over time perform actions, which are designed to alter that environment. These agent-based systems have been successfully applied to a number of problem domains, with one of the most active areas of research being in the area of mobile communication. In the past, multiagent systems have only existed in software. But now with the advent of large-scale commercially available reprogramable logic, it is now possible to extend this agent technology to both software and selected hardware of the system. By applying this agent-based model into a reconfigurable system-on-chip platform, the overall system flexibility and efficiency will be significantly improved.

4. Performance Comparison

Table 1. shows simulation results for a Viterbi decoder. The performance of FleXilicon architecture was compared with ARM920T processor. FleXilicon reduces the number of cycles significantly for Viterbi decoder.

Table 1. Performance comparison for Viterbi Decoder

	Frequency	Cycles	Execute Time (μs)
FleXilicon	200MHz	12	0.07
ARM 920T	200MHz	22706	27.47

Table 2. summarizes the synthesis results of Reconfigurable Modem (RM). The estimated area for the RM is 6.9M equivalent NAND2 gates while that for ASIC is 5.5M NAND2 gates. By optimizing the bit width, the circuit complexity of RM will be lowered significantly. The complete HiperLAN/2 receiver processing would require about 11μs while mapping the HiperLAN/2 receiver algorithms on the MONTIUM Architecture. Reference[2] shows that the Reconfigurable baseband processor implementation is two orders of magnitude more power efficient than Digital Signal Processors (DSP).

Table 2. Performance comparison of an ASIC and RM

	Circuit complexity (NAND2 gates)	Critical path delay
ASIC	5.5M	7.53
RM	6.9M	13.02

In Reference [14] the agent-based platform was implemented for face detection and tracking algorithm and the experiment results showed that the average detection time for software-only is 33.05msec, while the average time for hardware/software co-design approach is 8.375msec. It is obviously that the co-design approach can improve the system performance significantly.

5. Conclusion

In this paper some Reconfigurable Architectures adaptable to multistandard wireless communication systems are analyzed and their performances are compared. In this paper we also addressed the application of the multiagent technology to reconfigurable hardware/software systems. Experiment results of applying agent-based architecture to real-time face detection and tracking task in reference[14], showed that this architecture provides a very flexible platform and much more efficient compared to other approaches. So our future research will focus on multiagent hardware/software reconfigurable architecture adaptable for wireless networks.

References

[1] G.K. Rauwerda, G.J.M. Smit, L.F.W. van Hoesel, P.M.Heysters, "Mapping Wireless Communication Algorithms to a Reconfigurable Architecture", Proceedings, International Conference on Engineering of Reconfigurable Systems and Algorithms (ERSA'03), pages: 242-251, 2003

[2] Ada S.Y. POON, "An Energy Efficient Reconfigurable baseband processor for Wireless Communications", IEEE Transactions on Very Large Scale Integration (VLSI) Systems, Vol. 15, No.3, pages: 319-327 Mar. 2007

[3] Jong-Suk Lee and Dong Sam Ha, "FleXilicon: a Reconfigurable Architecture for Multimedia and Wireless Communications", Proceedings, International Symposium on Circuits and Systems, 2006

[4] Jina Kim and Dong Sam Ha, "A New Reconfigurable Modem Architecture for 3G Multi-Standard Wireless Communication Systems" Proceedings, IEEE International Symposium on Circuits and Systems 2005, Pages: 1051-1054

[5] Hooman Parizi, Afshin Niktash, Amir Kamalizad, Nader Bagherzadeh, "A Reconfigurable Architecture for Wireless Communication Systems", Proceedings, Third International Conference on Information Technology: New Generations, 2006, Pages: 250-255

[6] Alsolaim.A, Becker.J, Glesner.M, Starzyle.J, "Architecture and Application of a dynamically reconfigurable hardware array for future mobile communication systems", Proceedings,

IEEE Symposium on Field-Programmable Custom Computing Machines, 2000, Pages: 205-214

[7] Carl Ebeling, Chris Fisher, Guanbin Xing, Manyuan Shen, Hui Liu, "Implementing an OFDM Receiver on the RaPiD Reconfigurable Architecture", IEEE Transactions on Computers, Vol.53, Issue 11, Pages: 1436-1448, Nov.2004

[8] Reiner Hartenstein, "Coarse Grain Reconfigurable Architectures", Proceedings, Conference on Asia South Pacific Design Automation, Pages: 564-570, Jan.2001

[9] Frank Hannig, Hritam Dutta, and Jurgen Teich, "Regular Mapping For Coarse-Grained Reconfigurable Architectures", Proceedings, IEEE International Conference on Acoustics, Speech, and Signal Processing, Vol.V, pages: 57-60,May 2004

[10] Jurgen Becker, Manfred Glesner, "A parallel Dynamically Reconfigurable Architecture Designed for Flexible Application-Tailored Hardware /Software Systems in Future Mobile Communication", The Journal of Supercomputing, Vol.19, Issue 1,Pages: 105-127,May 2001

[11] Scott Hauck, Thomas W.Fry, Matthew M.Hosler, and Jeffrey P.Kao, "The Chimaera Reconfigurable Functional Unit", IEEE Transactions on Very Large Scale Integration (VLSI) Systems, Vol.12, No.2, Feb. 2004

[12] Andrew A.Gray, Clement Lee, Payman Arabshahi, Jeffrey Srinivasan, "Object-Oriented Reconfigurable Processing for Wireless Networks", Proceedings, IEEE Intenational Conference on Communications, Vol.1, Pages: 497-501,2002

[13] Hamid Reza Naji, B.Earl Wells, "On Incorporating Multi Agents in Combined Hardware/Software based Reconfigurable Systems – A General Architecture Framework", Proceedings, Thirty Fourth Southeastern Symposium on System Theory, Pages: 344-348, 2002

[14] Yan Meng, "A Mobile Vision System with Reconfigurable Intelligent Agents", Proceedings, International Joint Conference on Neural Networks, July 2006

Session 6

DELAY ANALYSIS OF TWO WAY RESERVATION SCHEMES IN OPTICAL BURST SWITCHING NETWORK

M. RAJIV GANDHI

Department of ECE, Pallavan College Of Engineering, Thimmasamudram, Kanchipuram-631 502, Tamilnadu, India
mirajiv@gmail.com

E. MOHAN

Department of ECE, Pallavan College Of Engineering, Thimmasamudram, Kanchipuram-631 502, Tamilnadu, India

R. SATHYAN

Kanchi Pallavan Engineering College, Kolivakkam, Kanchipuram-631 501, Tamilnadu, India

ABSTRACT

The concept of optical burst switching (OBS) aims to allow access to optical bandwidth in dense wavelength division multiplexed (DWDM) networks at fractions of the optical line rate to improve bandwidth utilization efficiency. This project gives an alternative network architecture combining OBS with dynamic wavelength allocation under fast circuit switching to provide a scalable optical architecture with a guaranteed QOS in the presence of dynamic and burst traffic loads. It is assumed that there are no buffers or wavelength conversion in core nodes and that fast tunable laser sources are used in the edge routers. Based on an analytical model, upper bounds for these parameters are derived to quantify the advantages of wavelength channel reuse, including the influence of the signaling round-trip time required for light path reservation. The results allow to quantify the operational gain achievable with fast wavelength switching compared to quasistatic wavelength-routed optical networks and can be applied to the design of future optical network architectures.

Key words: Dynamic Wavelength Allocation, Fast Circuit Switching, Optical Burst Switching (OBS), Optical Networks, Optical Packet Switching

1. Introduction

1.1. *Optical Burst Switching*

The concept of burst switching first emerged in the context of voice communications in early 1980s. More recently, optical burst switching, has received considerable attention as an alternative to optical packet switching [2]. In essence, optical burst switching considers the optical layer merely as a buffer-less transparent media for applications.

- Granularity: the transmission unit size of optical burst switching is between the optical circuit switching and optical packet switching
- Separation of Control and Data control information is transmitted on a separate wavelength (or channel)
- One-Way Reservation: Resources are allocated using one-way reservation. That is, a source node does not need to wait for the acknowledgement back from the destination node, before it starts transmitting of the burst.
- Variable Burst Length: The size of burst is variable
- No Optical Buffering: The intermediate node in the optical network does not require optical buffers. Bursts go through the intermediate node without any delay.

1.2. *One Way Reservation OBS*

Many types of OBS paradigms are available for deployment in future all-optical networks. The concept underpinning most types of OBS is as follows. IP packets destined for a common egress router are assembled into data bursts at an ingress router. A control packet precedes each burst by a time offset; the control packet is electronically processed at a sequence of OXCs to reserve a contiguous sequence of wavelength channels, known as a light path or route, for the pending burst. Then, depending on the type of OBS deployed, the pending burst is entirely switched in the optical domain either with or without acknowledgement; one-way reservation, respectively[3]. OBS types using one-way reservation, such as just enough time (JET), just-in-time (JIT)[6] and Horizon, send a burst before it is confirmed that a light path can be reserved, from the ingress router to the egress router. The mean burst blocking probability is considered the most important measure of quality of service (QoS) in OBS types using one-way reservation.

1.3. *Two Way Reservation OBS*

OBS types using two-way reservation, such as wavelength-routed OBS (WR/OBS)[4], delay a burst at the ingress router until an acknowledgement propagates from the egress router to the ingress router, thus confirming a successful light path reservation. These OBS types overcome burst blocking arising from wavelength contention since if the control packet fails to reserve a light path, the burst is electronically buffered at the ingress router and rescheduled for later transmission. However, two-way reservation prolongs the packet delay since the burst must remain idle until an acknowledgement is received. For OBS types using two-way reservation, the most important measures of QoS[7] is queuing delay at ingress routers. WR/OBS is the only OBS type using two-way reservation for which performance evaluation is considered.

2. WR-OBS

In OBS networks, lower priority bursts experience loss as a penalty. However, given that each burst may contain a large number of transmission control protocol (TCP)–internet protocol (IP) packets or acknowledgment, each lost burst would affect a number of higher layer connections. Thus, in OBS networks, care should be taken to also minimize the loss of lower priority bursts to prevent this.

In this paper, we propose and analyze an alternative OBS network architecture that requires an end-to-end reservation to satisfy specific service criteria such as latency and packet loss rate (PLR) for burst input traffic

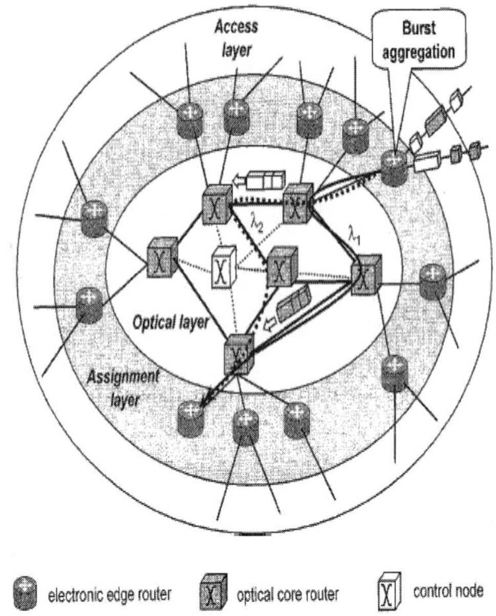

Figure 1. Architecture of the proposed wavelength-routed optical burst-switched (WROBS) network with burst aggregation at the network edge and wavelength routing in the optically transparent core.

This architecture, shown in Fig.1 and termed here wavelength-routed optical burst switching (WR-OBS)[8], assumes a fast circuit-switched end-to-end light path assignment with a guaranteed, deterministic delay, and requires an obligatory end-to-end acknowledgment[5].

The packets are electronically aggregated at the network edge into bursts, according to their destination and class of service (CoS), but with timescale of milliseconds, which is a typical forwarding time of IP routers, making the reservation of resources along the path prior to burst transmission feasible [9]. The aggregation time is strictly determined by the performance parameters such as delay at the edge or the required burst size for the network. At an appropriate point during the aggregation cycle, an end-to-end wavelength channel is requested from a network control node for transmission of the burst between edge routers.

This requires, however, that the bit rate at the input to the buffers at edge routers is sufficiently high to form bursts on a millisecond timescale. Following transmission, the wavelength channel is released and can be reused for subsequent connections. The network core can either be considered as a passive core or as a network of fast-reconfigurable optical routers/cross connects, where the same controller that allocates wavelengths dynamically sets up end-to-end light paths or circuits.It is assumed that wavelength conversion in core nodes is not required, because, as previously shown, it brings little benefit to wavelength-routed networks with wavelength agility at the network edge. A centralized network management was assumed in this work as a worst-case scenario. A distributed control scheme would be preferred; however, such a scheme relies on synchronization and fast distribution of information on the state of the network.

The aim of this work is to analyze the network performance under which dynamic WR-OBS would bring significant operational advantages and, in particular, in the reuse, utilization of wavelength channels that are set up only for the required burst transmission time (termed wavelength holding time) and, thus, increased over a much simpler but less adaptable quasistatic logically fully meshed WRON. The calculated values for WR-OBS[10] represent an upper bound for the achievable network parameters, namely the edge delay, bandwidth utilization, wavelength reuse, and idle time, and give design rules on the speed requirements for dynamic routing and wavelength assignment algorithms to make a core network in which resources are assigned dynamically practical. The results can be applied to optimize the design rules of future optical network architectures and quantify the operation regimes that best make use of the static or dynamic network architectures.

3. Network Architecture And Edge Router Model

In this we are going to discuss about network and edge router architecture assumptions, burst aggregation and timing diagrams, modeling of the Impact of Traffic Statistics on Burst Aggregation

The proposed edge router setup is shown schematically in Fig. 2, where bursts are aggregated from packets that are electronically presorted according to their destination and CoS and stored in separate queues.

After a time-out signal indicates that packets have to be transmitted to meet application specific latency requirements, a wavelength request is sent to a control node, an acknowledgment is received and the buffer content is dynamically assigned to a free wavelength. If a free wavelength channel is not available, packets are not lost and, instead, are stored in edge-router buffers but could incur additional delay. An edge router with dimensions is considered where the number of independent traffic inputs is, represents the number of CoS, and is the number of destinations.

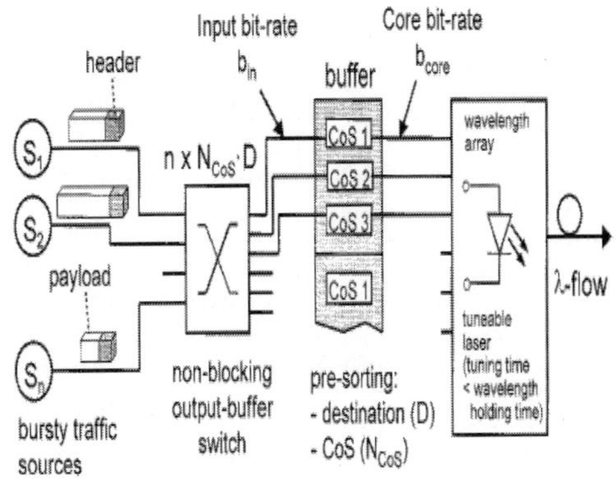

Figure 2. Edge router model with n burst traffic inputs, an output-buffered switch with presorting and a wavelength-tune able laser array for dynamic wavelength allocation. The graph is for N = 3 CoS.

4. Results And Discussion

In this chapter we are going to present the simulation results for the edge router and core network performance. We will present the analysis of DTWR OBS based on the edge router delay. In this we discussed about the delay that accrued in edge router due to two-way reservation

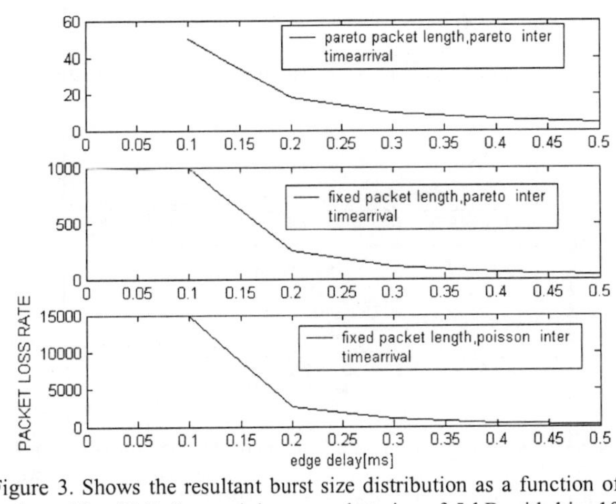

Figure 3. Shows the resultant burst size distribution as a function of and resulting PLR for a minimum packet size of 5 kB with bin=10 Gb/s and an average load of 0.1 (i.e., max. access buffer bandwidth 100 Gb/s) for the following packet and inter arrival time distributions:

Case 1) Pareto (α=1.5) packet length distribution, Pareto (α=1.5) inter arrival time distribution;

Case 2) fixed length packet sizes, Pareto inter arrival time distribution (α=1.5);

Case 3) fixed length packet sizes, Poisson inter arrival time distribution

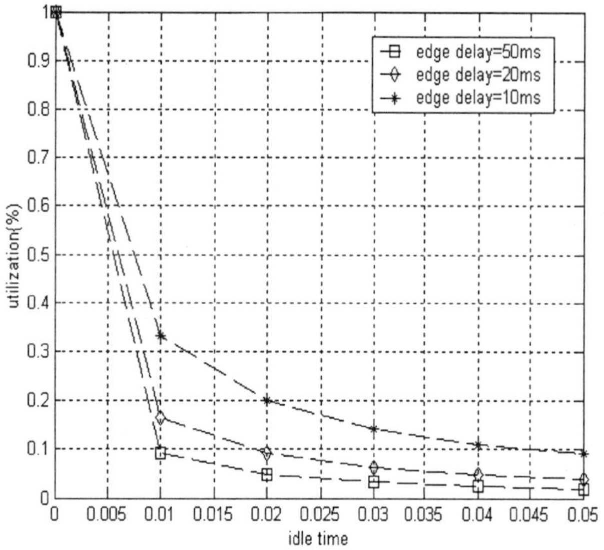

Figure 4. Light path utilization U as a function of the idle time (tidle) for tedge = 10, 20, 50 ms, and bit-rate ratio A = 10

$U= B_{per\lambda} / t_{wht}$

$U= t_{edge} / A.\ t_{idle} / t_{edge}$--------(4.1)

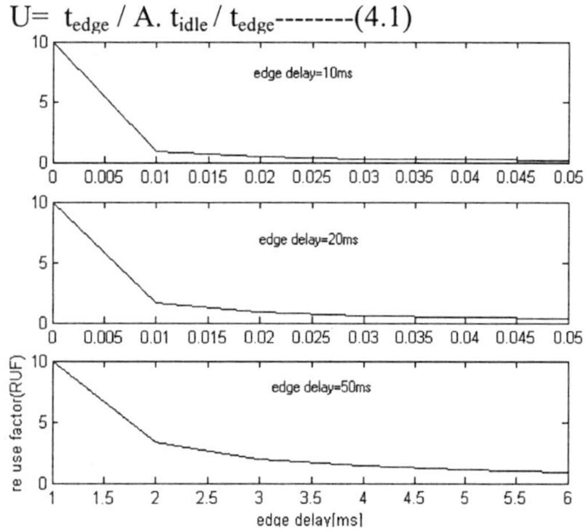

Figure 5. Wavelength RUF as a function of the idle time (t_{idle}) for t = 10, 20, 50 ms, and bit-rate ratio A = 10. Shaded region: network requires more wavelengths than in a static WRON

$RUF= t_{edge} / t_{wht}$

$RUF= A.\ t_{edge} / A.\ t_{idle} / t_{edge} = A.U$-- (4.2)

P=U.RUF------- (4.3)

5. Conclusion

This project describes and analyzes a WR-OBS network that combines the functions of OBS with fast circuit switching by dynamically assigning and releasing wavelength-routed light paths over a buffer less optical core. The potential advantages of this architecture compared to conventional OBS are explicit QoS provisioning and, compared to static WRONs, are in fast adaptation to dynamic traffic changes in optical networks and more efficient utilization of each wavelength channel.

The proposed architecture ensures a deterministic delay for the optical packets through a known, predefined queuing delay at the edge and burst aggregation and the propagation in the core network. Moreover, it guarantees an acknowledgment of the wavelength assignment for QoS-determined provisioning and uses dynamic wavelength routing. Finally in this paper we calculated different parameters in references with edge delay(i.e wave length holding time, band width per wave length).

To investigate the impact of the on the network, both the utilization U and reuse factor RUF are repotted for different values of edge delays (10, 20, 50 ms) and constant in Figs.4.2and 4.3. To ensure that RUF >1requires tidle < (A-1)/A . t_{edge} ⇔ $t_{idle} < t_{edge}$ for A>>1 . A key result is that, for , as in high core bit-rate networks, a high reuse factor can be achieved only for tidle on the timescale of a few milliseconds

6. References

1. 1. C. Qiao and M. Yoo [2000], 'Choices, features and issues in optical burst Switching,' SPIE Opt. Networks Mag., vol. 1, no. 2, pp. 36–44.
2. 2. J. S. Turner [1999], 'Terabit burst switching,' J. High Speed Networks, vol. 8, no. 1, pp. 3–16,
3. 3. K. Dolzer, C. Gauger, J. Späth, and S. Bodamer [, 2001], 'Evaluation of reservationmechanisms for optical burst switching,' AEÜ Int. J. Electron. Commun., vol. 55, no. 1, pp. 1–8.
4. 4. M. Düser, E. Kozlovski, R. I. Killey, and P. Bayvel [2000], 'Design trade-offs in optical burst switched networks with dynamic wavelength allocation,'in Proc. Eur. Conf. Optical

Communication, vol. 2, Munich, Germany, pp. 23–24.

5. 5. C. Qiao, [2000] 'Labeled optical burst switching for IP-over-WDM integration,'IEEE Commun. Mag., vol. 38, pp. 104–114,..
6. 6. J. Y. Wei, J. L. Pastor, R. S. Ramamurthy, and Y. Tsai [1999], 'Just-in-time optical burst switching for multiwavelength networks,' in Proc. IFIP Conf. Broadband '99, Hong Kong, China, , pp. 339–352.
7. 7. M. Yoo, C. Qiao, and S. Dixit [2000], 'QoS performance of optical burst
8. switching in IP-over-WDM networks,' IEEE J. Select. Areas Commun.,vol. 18, pp. 2062–2071,.
9. 8. Y. Xiong, M. Vandenhoute, and H. C. Cankaya [2000], 'Control architecture in optical burst-switched networks,' IEEE J. Select. Areas Commun., vol.18, pp. 1838–1851,.
10. 9. S. Verma, H. Chaskar, and R. Ravikanth [2000], 'Optical burst switching: Aviable solution for terabit IP backbone,' IEEE Network, vol.14, no.6,pp.48-53
11. 10. S. Baroni, P. Bayvel, R. J. Gibbens, and S. K. Korotky[May 1999], 'Analysis and design of resilient multifiber wavelength-routed optical transport networks,'J. Lightwave Technol., vol. 17, pp. 743–758.

REDUCING THE RESOURCE INTENSITY IN ANTNET FOR MOBILE AD-HOC NETWORKS*

D. N. MALLIKARJUNA RAO

Jyothishmathi Institute of Technology and Science,Karimnagar, Andhra Pradesh, India

V. KAMAKSHI PRASAD

Professor in CSE and Additional Controller, Examination Branch, Jawaharl Nehru Technological University, Hyderabad

AntNet[1] is one of the approaches to adaptive learning of routing tables in wide are best-effort datagram networks. The AntNet algorithm, as proposed by Di Caro and Dorigo is resource intensive algorithm. In this algorithm two types of ants are generated viz. Forward ant and Backward ants. While traveling from a source to a destination the forward ants store their paths and of traffic conditions they encounter. After reaching the destination the forward ant transfers its memory to the backward ant and dies. The backward ant retraces the path traversed by the forward ant and updates the routing tables in the path. Since the mobile adhoc networks are dynamic and every effort should be made to reduce the resource intensity. We have made an effort to reduce the resource intensity in the basic AntNet algorithm. We propose three methods. The first method experiments with not generating a backward ant for every forward ant, instead we collect a set of forward ants and generate a subset of backward ants by choosing the best trip times among the received forward ants. In the second method we update the routing tables with the help of forward ants without generating backward ants. In the third method we update the routing table only at the destination node. Since every node is a destination for all other nodes, routing table at every node gets updated. In this method also no backward ants are generated. At the end we compare our results with the basic AntNet algorithm results.

1. Introduction

We first describe the basic AntNet algorithm as proposed by Di Caro and Dorigo and then describe the changes that have been made by us.

Basic AntNet Algorithm as proposed by Di Caro and Dorigo:

A forward ant is launched, at regular intervals, towards a destination 'd' from source 's' to find a feasible path from 's' to 'd'.

1. At each node, each forward ant which is going towards destination d, selects the next node to move on.

2. A cycle is detected when the forward reaches a node which is already present in its memory. If a cycle is detected, the nodes which are forming a cycle are removed from the memory.

3. When the forward ant reaches the destination node, the Ant agenet generates a backward ant, transfers all of its memory to it and the forward ant is killed.

4. The backward ant retraces the same path the forward ant traversed but in the reverse direction.

5. The backward ant updates the routing table at every node in the path.

We want to apply this Antnet algorithm for mobile adhoc networks. Since in mobile adhoc networks the nodes may not have abundant computing power and battery power is also limited, we propose the following changes in the algorithm so that the overhead and the resource intensity are reduced.

Rest of the paper is organized as follows: Section 2 describes the changes that have been proposed. Section 3 gives the simulation results and observations. Section 4 the conclusions and the future work.

* Paper No. F436 in iccnt, 2009

2. Changes Proposed to make the algorithm Less Resource Intensive

In this section we discuss about the propsed changes we make in the basic AntNet algorithm to reduce the resournce intensity.

2.1. *Method 1 – generation of backward ants for chosen forward ants*

Since all the forward ants will not take the best routes, we need not generated a backward ant for every forward ant that reaches the destination. At each node we collect 'm' number of forward ants and generated 'n' number of backward ants where n<m. Since we choose 'n' best backward ants among 'm' forward ants, we are eliminating the forward ants which take longer routes. This will reduce the resource intensity to some extent.

2.2. *Method 2 – updating the routing tables with the use of forward ants*

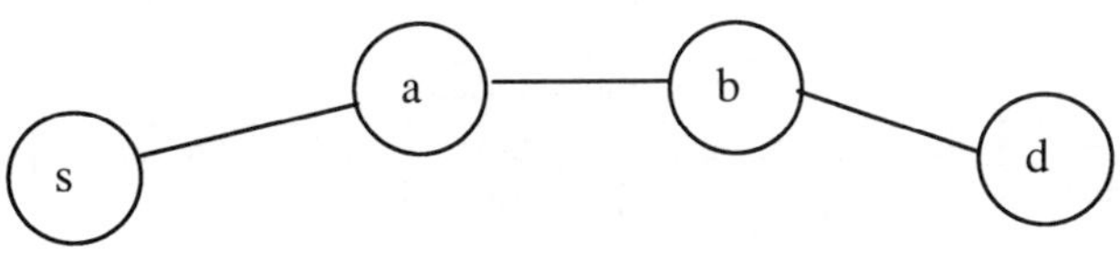

Figure 1. A small segment of a network showing four nodes.

Figure 1 shows a small segment of network containing four nodes namely s,a,b and d for our discussion purpose. With reference to fig.1 suppose a forward ant starts its journey from a source node 's' towards a destination node 'd' and visits a node 'b' in the route. We can update routing table at node 'b' by considering node 's' as destination node and the node visited prior to the node 'b' namely 'a' as next node. Hence the routing table at node 'b' says that if we want to forward a data packet to node 's' one can take 'a' as next node.

2.3. *Method -3 Updating the routing table only at the destination node*

Consider again the same figure above, as per the original algorithm when a backward ant starts at node 'd' towards node 's' it updates all the nodes it visits en route to the destination 's'. Since every node is a destination for all other nodes, and since all the forward ants generated towards a destination probably reach the destination, we can consider updating only the destination node. Wen the forward ant is launched, it starts storing all the nodes it visited and the delay incurred. When it reaches the destination it will update the routing table at the destination by using the memory carried by it.

In this method also total number of ants generated are reduced to half when compared to the original algorithm. Apart from reducing the number of ants it also reduces the computations required to update the routing tables at every intermediate node, since it updates only at the destination node. But it achieves the efficiency of basic Ant algorithm as far as the adapting to the new paths are considered.

3. Implementation

The proposed changes have been implemented in ns-2.33 network simulator[3] based on the [2]AntNet implementation by Lavina Jain. We have used arbitrary topology as provided in the documentation of the above reference for better comparison. We have used the same link capacities viz 155Mbps bandwidth and 155ms propagation delay.

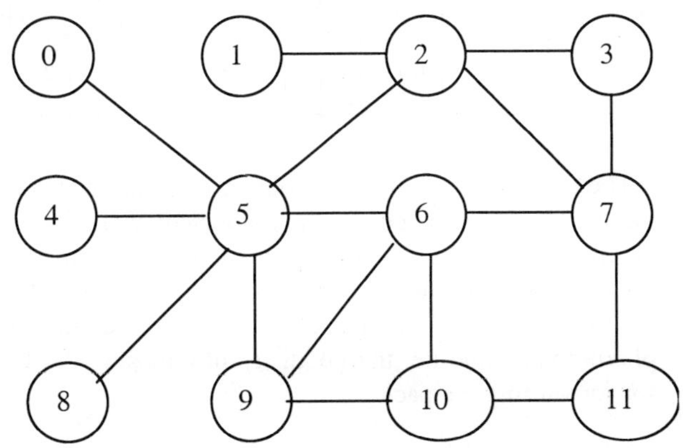

Figure 2. Network used in the simulation

We have simulated the three methods and obtained routing tables in each method. Each routing table is compared with the basic one. The routing tables are converging to more or less same probabilities but the difference is the saving in number of ants being created. Since our methods reduce the total number of ants that are generated, they reduce the load on the network.

We have shown routing table of one node as it is difficult to present all the routing tables for all the methods due to lack of space. We have compared the routing table at node 3 by applying all the three methods with the basic algorithm.

3.1. *Basic method*

Here we present the routing table when basic AntNet algorithm is applied on the topology(figure 2) at node 3.

Table 1. Routing table showing destination, next node and pheromone value for basic method

Routing Table at node 3					
Dest Node	Next Node	Ph Value	Dest Node	Next Node	Ph Value
0	7	0.273717	6	2	0.047743
0	6	0.422875	7	7	0.722928
0	2	0.303408	7	6	0.102545
1	7	0.281825	7	2	0.174526
1	6	0.172239	8	7	0.255596
1	2	0.545936	8	6	0.401245
2	7	0.165806	8	2	0.343159
2	6	0.046219	9	7	0.301843
2	2	0.787975	9	6	0.529727
4	7	0.277198	9	2	0.168430
4	6	0.372067	10	7	0.397410
4	2	0.350735	10	6	0.439464
5	7	0.197638	10	2	0.163126
5	6	0.482314	11	7	0.582402
5	2	0.320048	11	6	0.193428
6	7	0.158613	11	2	0.224170
6	6	0.793644			

The above table shows the routing table at node 3 for the basic method as got by the authors in V. Laxmi[2].,et al. In the table the first coloumn shows the destination node, the second the next node which the packet has to be forwarded to, and the third coloumn specifies the pheromone value i.e. the goodness of choosing the line for forwarding the packet.

3.2. *Reducing the number of backward ants generated*

In this method we capture a set of forward ants at a destination and generate a subset of backward ants. In the table – 2 we have shown the routing table by generating 2 backward ants for every 6 forward ants.

Table 2. Routing table created by generating 2 backward ants for every 6 forward ants in method 1.

Routing Table at node 3					
Dest Node	Next Node	Ph Value	Dest Node	Next Node	Ph Value
0	7	0.350833	6	2	0.150309
0	6	0.348333	7	7	0.780933
0	2	0.300833	7	6	0.104508
1	7	0.396120	7	2	0.114559
1	6	0.259829	8	7	0.285792
1	2	0.344051	8	6	0.378417
2	7	0.198181	8	2	0.335792
2	6	0.097146	9	7	0.255033
2	2	0.704673	9	6	0.495692
4	7	0.300833	9	2	0.249275
4	6	0.350833	10	7	0.550542
4	2	0.348333	10	6	0.277855
5	7	0.170220	10	2	0.171713
5	6	0.377253	11	7	0.697948
5	2	0.452528	11	6	0.172582
6	7	0.259410	11	2	0.129470
6	6	0.590281			

Table 3. Routing table created by generating 3 backward ants for every 10 forward ants in method 1.

Routing Table at node 3					
Dest Node	Next Node	Ph Value	Dest Node	Next Node	Ph Value
0	7	0.333333	6	2	0.054053
0	6	0.333333	7	7	0.732276
0	2	0.333333	7	6	0.181523
1	7	0.249579	7	2	0.086202
1	6	0.199579	8	7	0.333333
1	2	0.550842	8	6	0.333333
2	7	0.213956	8	2	0.333333
2	6	0.094050	9	7	0.213820
2	2	0.691994	9	6	0.565560
4	7	0.333333	9	2	0.220621
4	6	0.333333	10	7	0.447429
4	2	0.333333	10	6	0.444726
5	7	0.349345	10	2	0.107845
5	6	0.368383	11	7	0.627862
5	2	0.282272	11	6	0.209599
6	7	0.193761	11	2	0.162539
6	6	0.752186			

Table 4. Routing table created by generating 4 backward ants for every 20 forward ants in method 1

Routing Table at node 3					
Dest Node	Next Node	Ph Value	Dest Node	Next Node	Ph Value
0	7	0.333333	6	2	0.139373
0	6	0.333333	7	7	0.459265
0	2	0.333333	7	6	0.255208
1	7	0.333333	7	2	0.285527
1	6	0.333333	8	7	0.333333
1	2	0.333333	8	6	0.333333
2	7	0.279621	8	2	0.333333
2	6	0.199579	9	7	0.282779
2	2	0.520800	9	6	0.484442
4	7	0.333333	9	2	0.232779
4	6	0.333333	10	7	0.350833
4	2	0.333333	10	6	0.348333
5	7	0.264009	10	2	0.300833
5	6	0.385437	11	7	0.350833
5	2	0.350555	11	6	0.348333
6	7	0.172544	11	2	0.300833
6	6	0.688082			

We have experimented by creating different number of backward ants. The table – 2 is obtained by generating 2 backward ants for every 6 forward ants received at a node.

Table 3 is obtained by generating 3 backward ants for every 10 forward ants received and the table 4, it is 4 for 20. In this method as the ratio of the backward ants to forward ants is reduced the probability(pheromone) value is tending to 1/n where n is the number of neighbours of that node, when the destination is far away from the source.

3.3. *Forward ants updating the routing tables*

In the table – 5 we have presented the routing table for the method – 2. In this method forward ant not only carries the information along with it but also does the updating of the routing tables en route to the destination. No backward ants are generated.

This method is as good as the basic method s far as the pheromone values are considered and better than the basic algorithm when we consider the number of ants generated. In this method the number of ants generated are only 50% of the basic algorithm.

3.4. *Updating the routing tables at the destination node only*

Table – 6 shows the routing table at node – 3 after applying the method – 3. In this method forward ants only carry the information along with it to the destinations. This information is used to update the routing table only at the destination. Since every node is a destination node for all other nodes, we will get enough information and routing table thus generated reflects the traffic conditions in the network.

Table 5. Routing table updated with the help of only forward ants (method – 2)

Routing Table at node 3					
Dest Node	Next Node	Ph Value	Dest Node	Next Node	Ph Value
0	7	0.134690	6	2	0.007919
0	6	0.607664	7	7	0.984564
0	2	0.257646	7	6	0.000131
1	7	0.195821	7	2	0.015305
1	6	0.002520	8	7	0.165715
1	2	0.801658	8	6	0.501385
2	7	0.164196	8	2	0.332900
2	6	0.000005	9	7	0.103851
2	2	0.835800	9	6	0.868333
4	7	0.117654	9	2	0.027816
4	6	0.585502	10	7	0.635782
4	2	0.296844	10	6	0.328240
5	7	0.107801	10	2	0.035978
5	6	0.674502	11	7	0.896370
5	2	0.217697	11	6	0.056140
6	7	0.088723	11	2	0.047491
6	6	0.903358			

Table 6. Routing table generated with the helpf of the method -3 viz forward ants updating routing table only at the destination.

Routing Table at node 3					
Dest Node	Next Node	Ph Value	Dest Node	Next Node	Ph Value
0	7	0.149939	6	2	0.001527
0	6	0.505691	7	7	0.844541
0	2	0.344370	7	6	0.130694
1	7	0.172313	7	2	0.024766
1	6	0.251855	8	7	0.336550
1	2	0.575832	8	6	0.318846
2	7	0.183622	8	2	0.344604
2	6	0.112873	9	7	0.235847
2	2	0.7.3505	9	6	0723364
4	7	0.253062	9	2	0.040789
4	6	0.441005	10	7	0.482844
4	2	0.305933	10	6	0.479437
5	7	0.241138	10	2	0.037719
5	6	0.418967	11	7	0.806708
5	2	0.339895	11	6	0.126831
6	7	0.145134	11	2	0.066460
6	6	0.853339			

This method is much more efficient than all the other methods due to two reasons. First one is in this also no backward ants are generated therefore the number of ants generated are 50% of the basic AntNet algorithm. The second one is, since we are updating the routing tables only at the destination, we are saving time required to update the tables in the intermediate nodes.

4. Conclusion and Future work

In this paper we have made an attempt to reduce the intensity of original AntNet algorithm by reducing the number of Ants and also making them update only at the destination. The pheromone values we obtained are conforming to the network topology and matching with the original AntNet algorithm.

In this paper we have only generated routing tables. We can also create data packets and measure the delay incurred and the number of packets that have actually reached the destination.

These methods can also be experimented with increased number of nodes and with the real network.

References

1. Gianni Di Caro and Marco Dorigo, AntNet: Distributed stigmergic Control for Communication Networks. Journal of Artificial Intelligence Research (9, 1998).
2. V.Laxmi, Lavina Jain and M.S. Gaur, Ant Colony Optimization based routing on ns-2, International conference on Wireless communication and Sensor Networks(WSCN), India (December 2006).
3. The VINT Project, The ns Manual, http://www.isi.edu/nsnam/ns/ns-documentation.html.

A NOVEL APPROACH FOR ADMISSION CONTROL USING GRACEFUL DEGRADATION IN NETWORKS

ATUL KUMAR SHUKLA

Department of E&ECE, IIT Kharagpur
West Bengal-721302, India

S S PATHAK

Department of E&ECE, IIT Kharagpur
West Bengal-721302, India

Network management and service deployment has thrown new challenges with integration of applications and services in the data networks. Admission Control (AC) is a key mechanism to keep services under controlled load to ensure required Quality of Service (QoS) levels and honor the service level agreements based on priority. The priority can be policy based as in case of government and military networks or based on revenue model or purely based on application sensitivity. The contemporary techniques are based on either rejection of the new flow or pre emption of low priority flow when sufficient capacity is not available. We present a novel approach based on graceful degradation for flow admission called as Inverse Taxation model. The proposed solution also supports the requirement of Military QoS (MQoS).

1. Introduction

There is a requirement of new service management paradigms, protocols and control mechanisms to ensure the constant Quality of Service (QoS) levels and honor the Service Level Agreements (SLA) based on priority while supporting the Internet's service heterogeneity and integration. In multiservice and multiclass networks, Admission Control (AC) is a critical means to ensure high quality communication by safeguarding enough resource availability for customer traffic based on the priority of the request. The priority allotment can be policy based as in case of government and military networks. Revenue model based on platinum service and gold service etc. can be the basis of priorities allotted to the contending flows or the priorities can be application based. AC strategy plays an important role in ensuring the availability of resource for honoring the SLA and allowing the critical government and military flows. AC can be particularly useful for services such as IP telephony and Videoconferencing [1].

Introduction of control mechanisms to honor the QoS specific commitments in the IP networks has not been standardized and easy to resolve. The approach taken by some service providers is over provisioning of communication resources to provide QoS in network backbones to avoid or reduce network control complexity, however, it cannot be a widely used as a permanent solution in view of the likelihood that the number of users and the demands of their applications will continue to outgrow the availability of resources. This necessitates the requirement of new paradigms for service and traffic control mechanisms to guarantee that the QoS and priority commitments can be precisely specified and honored. Keeping the network control plane simple is another key aspect and major objective while deploying such mechanism. It is imperative to reach a good compromise between service guarantees, complexity and resource utilization.

The present strategies of AC in contemporary networks are based on either the rejection of call or flow in case sufficient capacity or resource is not available or when priority based admission to the network is implemented as a solution it leads to the termination of the existing low priority flow or call to accommodate the requesting high priority call or flow. In first case the objective of availability and honoring the priority based agreements is violated and in the later case termination of call or flow takes place. In both the existing strategies the network resources are not optimally used and the service agreements based on priorities either on government policy or on revenue model are not honored. We propose a novel approach based on graceful step down of existing flows leading to termination only as the last measure to support the priority based agreements. The approach is termed as Inverse Taxation approach as it follows the reverse philosophy to existing taxation systems. The proposed solution also works for supporting the military QoS (MQoS). The term M-QoS represents commercial QoS in conjunction with the following three main features. Firstly, if there is contention for network resources in military packet networks, the flows carrying mission critical information should get preference (i.e., higher priority) over less important flows. Secondly, there should be graceful "step down" in the hard QoS of less important military flows in overloaded networks, instead of automatic tear down. Thirdly, higher flow priorities should be given for a restricted time defined by doctrine. Presently, packet based military networks do not support M-QoS [2].

The rest of the paper is organized as follows. The relevant design parameters for AC solution and the present approaches are discussed in section 2. The network resource metrics and capacity estimations used for implementing AC solutions are discussed in Section 3. The proposed Inverse Taxation Solution is presented in section 4. The implementation approach for the proposed solution and its advantages are discussed in section 5.

2. Existing Admission Control Approaches

The design objectives of an AC approach should be able to cover the following aspects, namely: the efficiency of resource utilization for the service levels offered; ability to fulfill the QoS commitments based on the priority; signaling overheads; complexity in network data and control planes; and the latency introduced in making AC decision. The ease of implementation of the desired solution in real networks is a major criterion on the usefulness of the AC approach.

The existing approaches while admitting a requesting high priority flow under resource starved scenario are based either on preemption of low priority flow even when the requesting flow does not require complete capacity which is unfair and leads to violation of principle of availability and fairness or are based on rejection of the new flow or call if the requested resources are unavailable which leads to dishonoring the agreements, under utilization of resources and principle of availability. A comparison of representative AC approaches is discussed by S. R. Lima et al [3].

The AC approach may be centralized or distributed depending on which nodes (e.g., all nodes or specific nodes) are involved and how they participate in the AC process. A node can make an AC decision or only gather information for some other control entity to use. The network model under which AC operates ranges from single-service (best effort) to multiservice architectures, following flow- or class-based paradigms. Their scope in targeting an intradomain, interdomain, and/or end-to-end solution also varies.

3. Network Resource Metrics and Capacity Estimation

In this section we delve upon the basic network resource that is bandwidth and its metrics that will be used in nomenclature of the proposed Inverse Taxation solution. We will define two metrics capacity and available capacity for both individual links and end-to end-path. We also discuss the available methods for capacity estimations to impress upon the practical implementation possibilities of our proposed solution.

Links at the data link layer (layer 2), links at label switching layer such as Multi Protocol Label Switching (MPLS) layer (layer 2.5) and links at the IP layer (layer 3) are different in connotations. A layer 2 link, or segment, can normally transfer data at a constant bit rate, which is the transmission rate of the segment. For instance, this rate is 1000 Mb/s on a gigabit Ethernet segment, and 2.048 Mb/s on an E1 segment. The transmission rate of a segment is limited by both the physical bandwidth of the underlying propagation medium as well as its electronic or optical transmitter/receiver hardware. At the IP layer a hop delivers a lower rate than its nominal transmission rate due to the overhead of layer 2 encapsulation and framing and layer 2.5 labels if MPLS is used. Specifically, suppose the nominal capacity of a segment is C_{L2}. The transmission time for an IP packet of size L_{L3} bytes is

$$T_{L3} = \frac{L_{L3} + H_{L2} + 4n}{C_{L2}}, \tag{1}$$

Where H_{L2} is the total layer 2 overhead (in bytes) needed to encapsulate the IP packet and n is the depth of LABEL Stack in case MPLS is used. So the capacity C_{L3} of that segment at the IP layer is

$$C_{L3} = C_{L2} \frac{1}{1 + \frac{H_{L2} + 4n}{L_{L3}}} \tag{2}$$

We define the capacity C_i of a hop i to be the maximum possible IP layer transfer rate at that hop. From Eq. 2 the maximum transfer rate at the IP layer results from MTU-sized packets. So we define the capacity of a hop as the bit rate, measured at the IP layer, at which the hop can transfer MTU-sized IP packets. Extending the previous definition to a network path, the capacity C of an end-to-end path is the maximum IP layer rate the path can transfer from source to sink. In other words the capacity of a path establishes an upper bound on the IP layer throughput a user can expect to get from that path. The minimum link capacity in the path determines the end-to-end capacity C, that is,

$$C = \min_{i=1,..,H} C_i \quad . \tag{3}$$

Where C_i is the capacity of the ith hop, and H is the number of hops in the path. In case of MPLS implementation the path means Label Switched Path (LSP).

Another important metric is the available capacity of a link or end-to-end path. The available bandwidth of a link relates to the unused or spare capacity of the link during a certain time period. So even though the capacity of a link depends on the underlying transmission technology and propagation medium, the available bandwidth of a link additionally depends on the traffic load at that link, and is typically a time-varying metric. At any specific instant in time, a link is either transmitting a packet at full link capacity or idles, so the instantaneous utilization of a link can only be either 0 or 1. Thus, any meaningful definition of available capacity requires time averaging of the instantaneous utilization over the time interval of interest. The average utilization u_{av}(t –¢ ,t) for a time period (t – ¢,t) is given by

$$u_{av}(t-\phi,t) = \frac{1}{\phi}\int_{t-\phi}^{t} u(x)dx, \tag{4}$$

where $u(x)$ is the instantaneous utilized capacity of the link at time x. We refer to time length ¢ as the averaging timescale. If C_i is the capacity of hop i and u_i *is* the average utilization of that hop in the given time interval, the average available capacity A_i of hop i is given by the unutilized fraction of capacity,

$$A_i = (1-u_i)C_i . \tag{5}$$

Extending the previous definition to an H-hop path, the available bandwidth of the end-to-end path is the minimum available bandwidth of all H hops,

$$A = \min_{i=1,..,H} A_i . \tag{6}$$

Several methodologies for measuring available bandwidth make the assumption that the link utilization remains constant when averaged over time (i.e., they assume a *stationary traffic load* on the network path). While this assumption is reasonable over relatively short time intervals, diurnal load variations will impact measurements made over longer time intervals. The constant average utilization (stationarity) does not preclude traffic variability (burstiness) or long range dependence effects. Since the average available bandwidth can change over time, it is important to measure it quickly. There are four major techniques for capacity estimation: variable packet size (VPS) probing, packet pair/train dispersion (PPTD), self-loading periodic streams (SLoPS), and trains of packet pairs (TOPP). VPS estimates the capacity of individual hops, PPTD estimates end-to-end capacity, and SLoPS and TOPP estimate end-to-end available capacity. There is no currently known technique to measure available capacity of individual hops. An up-to-date taxonomy of network measurement tools is maintained online at [4].

4. Proposed Inverse Taxation Solution

The network resource metrics and the capacity estimation tools mentioned in section 3 are to map the same into the proposed solution being actually applied to the real networks .All the terms defined so far are used in notations of the proposed solution. The network routing algorithm or MPLS signaling schemes have been assumed to find a path/LSP from Ingress node to Egress Node. The proposed AC approach works in a centralized manner at a admission control module at the Ingress node to the network known as Label Edge Router (LER) in MPLS solutions or it is implemented using the concept of Bandwidth Brokers (BB) in normal IP networks. The term path is used as the path from source to destination or the LSP in case of MPLS. The Equal Cost multiple paths between a source destination or Multiple LSP used for load balancing are also included in the proposed solution. We have devised four solutions depending upon the complexity of the problem. The simplest case is of the single existing flow in single path/LSP(SFSL) and then we proceed to solve further complex problems with multiple existing flow in single path/ LSP (MFSL), MFSL with weighted graceful degradation (MFSLWD) and finally multiple existing paths/ LSP multiple flow (MLMF).The notations used are as follows.

The parameter of constrained network resource such as capacity be denoted by C

C_t =total resource existing path/LSP

C_u =used resource existing path/LSP

C_{req} =requested resource on existing path/LSP

C_a=available resource on existing path/LSP

Li= ith LSP

F_{ex}= existing flow

F_{req}= requseting flow

W_{exij}=Weight of existing ith flow in jth path/LSP as per priority of the flow.

T_{exij} = Time of usage of path/LSP by existing ith flow in jth path/LSP

Subscripts used in conjunction are; *sel*=selected, req=requested, *ex*=existing. Our solution is as follows:

4.1. *Single existing flow single path/ LSP (SFSL) solution*

Assumptions:

A flow cannot degrade a flow with $W_{ex}>=W_{req}$

The solution is executed only if $C_{req}> C_a$.The flows which are not elastic and delay/jitter sensitive operate between two thresholds of capacity, the higher one beyond which capacity increase will not lead to increase in any user perceived QoS and the lower threshold below which the intelligibility of the application is lost. The degradation in such flows can be done between these two thresholds. If such a flow breaches the lower threshold during degradation based on lower priority it will be completely terminated. The solution is as follows

#1. if $W_{ex}>= W_{req}$, Admit flow with C_a, C_a=0.
Stop.

#2. else if $C_{req} < C_t$, $C_{uex} = C_t - C_{req}$,
$C_a = C_{req}$, Admit flow with C_{req}, C_a=0.
Stop.

#3. else admit the flow with $\sum C_{uj}$ + C_a for all j i.e $W_j<W_{req}$, C_a=0.
Stop.

4.2. *Multiple existing flow in single path/ LSP (MFSL)*

No of Flows =N i.e. i=1 to N

#1 if min (W_{ex})> =W_{req}, Admit flow with C_a, C_a=0.
Stop.

#2 else If $C_{req}> C_t$ go to SFSL#3
else go to #3

#3(Selection of Flow to be gracefully degraded)

a) for all F_{ex} with $W_{ex}<W_{req}$.
Selected flow F_{sel} =min(W_{ex}) .

b) if for i≠j min(W_{ex})=W_{exi} =W_{exj}

c) if (C_{uexi} >C_{uexj}) select F_{exi}

d) if (C_{uexi} =C_{uexj}) {
if T_{exi} =T_{exj} select any of F_{exi}, F_{exj};
else if T_{exi} > T_{exj} select F_{exi} ,
else select F_{exj} .
}

e) if (C_{uexi} <C_{uexj}) select F_{exj} .

#4 $C_{addl} = C_{req} - C_a$
if $C_{usel} + C_a >= C_{req}$
$C_{usel} = C_{usel} - C_{addl}$, $C_a = C_{req}$, Admit flow with C_{req} , C_a=0.
Stop.
else C_a= C_a+ C_{usel} , C_{usel} =0;
min(W_{ex})=next min(W_{ex})
Go to #3 for selecting next flow to be gracefully degraded.

4.3. *MFSL-Weighted graceful degradation (MFSLWD)*

#1 Solution SFSL and MFSL though simple to implement, may lead to complete demise of the least priority flow. Though solution is simple in implementation it is extremely unfair. With all other assumptions of SFSL and MFSL we propose a weighted graceful degradation technique with additional assumption that if remaining fraction of flow left after degradation is less than a given threshold (T_h) then the flow will be completely terminated to converge the solution.

if min(W_{ex})>= W_{req}, Admit flow with C_a , C_a=0.
Stop.
else If $C_{req}> C_t$ go to SFSL#3
else go to #2

#2(Calculating weighted value for degradation)
Degradation coefficient
if j=1, α_{exj}=1.

else $\alpha_{exj} = (\sum W_{exj} - W_{exj}) / (\sum W_{exj})$ For all j where Wexj<W_{req}
#3(Selection of flow for graceful degradation)
Flow with max $(\alpha_{ex}) = F_{sel}$
if max$(\alpha_{ex}) = \alpha_{exi} = \alpha_{exj}$ for i≠j
go to MFSL #3.c #3.d #3.e and get F_{sel}
#4(Updating the flow parameter)
if $(1-\alpha_{sel}) * C_{usel} < T_h$
$\alpha_{sel} = 1$;
$C_{addl} = C_{req} - C_a$
if $(\alpha_{sel} * C_{usel}) + C_a >= C_{req}$
$C_{usel} = C_{usel} - C_{addl}$, $C_a = C_{req}$,
Admit flow with C_{req}.
Stop.
else $C_a = C_a + (\alpha_{sel} * C_{usel})$
$C_{usel} = (1-\alpha_{sel}) * C_{usel}$
#5 (selecting the next flow for degradation)
max(α_{ex})=nextmax(α_{ex}).
Go To #3.

4.4. *Multiple existing paths/ LSP multiple flow (MLMF)*

#1if $C_{aj} >= C_{req}$, Admit flow in jth LSP with C_{req}
#3 (Selecting the LSP)
For all LSPs find degradation insulated weighted capacity in *n*th path/LSP
$D_{insn} = (W_{in} * C_{uin})$ for all i i,.e $W_{in} >= W_{req}$
Degradation open weighted capacity in jth path/LSP
$D_{openn} = (W_{in} * C_{uin})$ for all i i.e. $W_{in} < W_{req}$
Find max $\{ C_{aj} + (D_{openn} / D_{insn}) \}$
If the max occurs in LSP j $L_j = L_{sel}$
#4Apply MFSL/MFSLWD in L_{sel}

5. Remarks and Discussion

Intuitively the proposed solution will give better network resource utilization, lesser flow rejection and honor the service level agreement based priorities. The simulations for networks based on Poisson distribution are far from reality. We will present our test bed results of implementation of the algorithm on open source MPLS test bed at our institution in next paper. The proposed Inverse Taxation solution can be implemented in a software module located at LER in the MPLS networks. In the existing networks it can be implemented as centralized solution using the concept of bandwidth brokers (BB).

6. Conclusion

We have presented a novel approach for admission control based on graceful step down rather than automatic teardown which will improve utilization of network resources and honoring of service agreements based on priority as well as solution for MQoS. We have presented solutions for all the four possible cases with increasing degree of complexity in the admission control problem.

References

1. J. Babiarz, K. Chan, and F. Baker, "Configuration Guidelines for Diffserv Service Classes," RFC 4594, Aug. 2006, informational; http://www.ietf.org/rfc/rfc4594.txt
2. Marek Kwiatkowski; "A Concept of Defense Core Communication Infrastructure Supporting M-QoS".Report of Communications Division - Electronics and Surveillance Research Laboratory. Department of Defense Science & Technology Organization (DSTO-TR-1220), October-2001.
3. S R Lima, P. Carvalho and V. Freitas, "Admission Control in Multiservice IP Networks: Architectural Issues and Trends", IEEE Communications Magazine, Vol. 45, Issue 4, pp.114 – 121, April 2007.
4. CAIDA, http://www.caida.org/tools/taxonomy
5. L. Massoulie and J. Roberts, "Bandwidth sharing: objectives and algorithms", IEEE/ACM Transactions on Networking, Vol. 10, Issue 3, pp. 320- 328, June 2002.
6. D. Bertsekas and R. Gallager, Data Networks. Englewood Cliffs, NJ: Prentice Hall, 1987.
7. F. Kelly, A. Maulloo, and D. Tan, "Rate control for communication networks: Shadow prices, proportional fairness and stability," J. Oper. Res. Soc., Vol. 49, pp. 237–252, 1998.

COGMAN-A COGNITIVE RADIO BASED SYSTEM FOR INTEGRATING AD-HOC NETWORKS

PARAS JAIN
Thadomal Shahani Engineering College (IT Dept)
Mumbai University, India

NIKHIL NAWATHE
Thadomal Shahani Engineering College (IT Dept)
Mumbai University, India

ABHISHEK MALHOTRA
Thadomal Shahani Engineering College (IT Dept)
Mumbai University, India

Abstract— Today we pack radio waves into the air as tightly as possible. New radio technologies require unique hardware appropriate to its way of transmitting data. To minimize interference, each is restricted to its specific band. As user demands for data services and data rates steadily increase, efficient spectrum usage is becoming a critical issue. However recent measurements hint that 90 % of the available bandwidth is wasted [1]. Hence the need for Software Defined Radio (SDR) or Cognitive Radio (CR) arises. SDR enhances the ability to transmit and receive data using a variety of protocols and modulation schemes (enabled by reconfigurable software rather than hardware) [12]. Furthermore, as the name suggests, such radios can even become "cognitive". As dictated by the software, these radios can adapt their behavior to their wireless surroundings without user intervention.

1. INTRODUCTION

Cognitive radio is a paradigm for wireless communication in which either a network or a wireless node changes its transmission or reception parameters to communicate efficiently avoiding interference with licensed or unlicensed users. Here each radio simply observes its neighbours to check if they are transmitting and accordingly take its own decisions. Thus their primary aim is to use the spectrum in a dynamic manner by allowing the radio terminals to operate in the best available frequency band, maintaining seamless communication requirements during the transition to better spectrum utilization. In other words it figures out which frequencies are quiet and pick one or more over which to transmit and receive data. Hence it is imperative for a Cognitive Radio network to sense spectrum holes. Detecting primary users is the most efficient way to detect spectrum holes [9], for which various sensor sensing techniques such as Transmitter detection, Cooperative detection & Interference based detection [10] can be used. Cognitive radio technology is perfectly suited to opportunistically employ the wireless spectrum in Ad-hoc Networks. The CR technology offers a great deal of improvement over contemporary methods with reference to their frequency agility, dynamic frequency selection, adaptive modulation, transmit power control, location awareness. Through our paper, we make an attempt to analyze these future means of communication and discuss the related engineering and networking issues.

2. LITERATURE SURVEY

FCC [11] defines software radio [SDR] as “radio that includes a transmitter in which operating parameters such as frequency range, modulation type or maximum output power can be altered by software without making any changes to hardware components that affect the radio frequency emissions”. A Cognitive radio is a type of Software Defined radio [SDR] that can make decisions as to the network, modulation, and/or coding parameters based on its surroundings [22]. Their frequency agility, dynamic frequency selection, adaptive modulation, transmit power control, location awareness, and negotiated use meaning ability to incorporate agreements into their behavior- all allow for very flexible spectrum use.

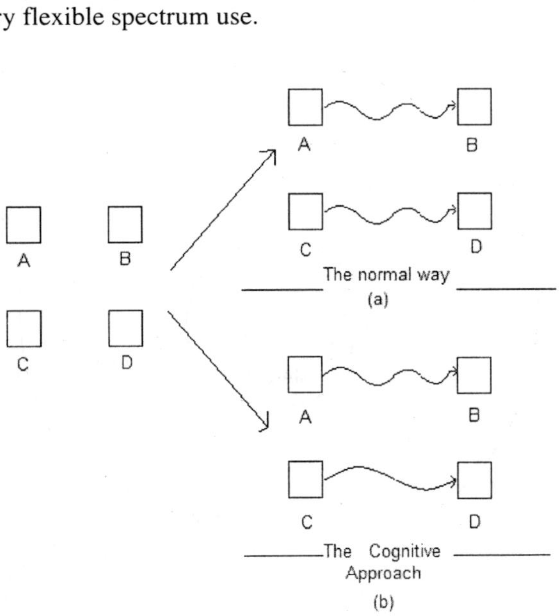

Figure 1. In this scenario, Nodes A and B are communicating using frequency f1. Now if C wishes to communicate with D using the same frequency, it has to wait until there is a break in communication between A and B (a). Using the Cognitive paradigm (b), C and D change to another free frequency and simultaneous communication is possible. In figure 1, the use of Cognitive radio is illustrated. The problem faced by C and D in their communication is overcome by the frequency agility of the Cognitive radio. However, using cognitive radio and some intelligent knowledge sharing the communication can even take place in the same frequency [1].

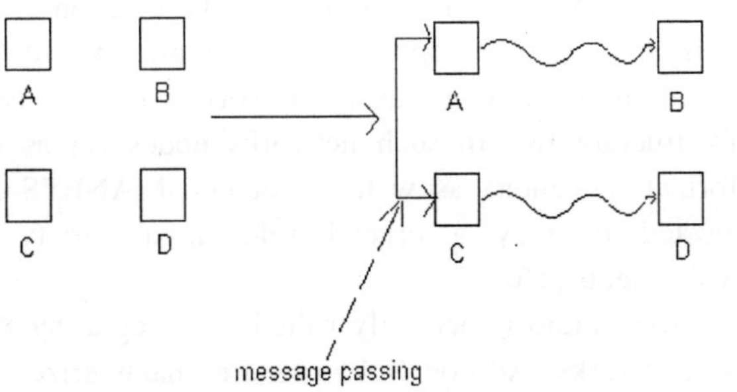

Figure 2. In this scenario, Nodes A and B are communicating using frequency f1. Now if C wishes to communicate with D using the same frequency, it uses intelligent message passing with A to minimize interference.

Cognitive radio can be used to simulate message passing by which a single channel medium can be transformed into a two channel medium. The interference optimization would require two stages. First, it is necessary to measure the received signal power of a primary receiver in the adjacent band since the interference constraints are referenced to it. This power measurement could be obtained from the spectrum sensing, and used to create transmit power mask for the cognitive radio transmitter. Then, the spectrum of the signal generator needs to be shaped to fit the spectrum mask.

There are several spectrum shaping techniques that could be used [5]:

- Introducing guard bands
- Windowing
- Power control per sub-carrier

Introducing guard bands would assign more sub-carriers to zero, thus resulting in significant power loss and inefficient spectrum use. Its only benefit would be preserved user/channel orthogonality. Windowing techniques [6] would pre-filter each sub-carrier to reduce the sidelobes, but would also introduce power loss. The main disadvantages of the windowing approach are the increased complexity due to additional filtering and potential loss of orthogonality. The third option is to assign independent power constraints for each sub-carrier and optimally fit the spectrum mask [20]. This approach would preserve all benefits of OFDM transmission without sacrificing spectrum utilization.

3. COGNET [4]-AN APPROACH TO SDR

While the development of cognitive radio hardware and Software, especially at the physical layer, has received considerable attention, the question of how one organizes a set of cognitive radios into a cognitive network is not well understood. As such, adaptive networks of cognitive radios represent an important but demanding research challenge for both the wireless and networking communities. The extreme flexibility of cognitive radios has significant implications for the design of network algorithms and protocols at both local/access network and global internetworking levels. In particular, support for cross layer algorithms [13] which adapt to changes in physical link quality, radio interference, radio node density, network topology or traffic demand may be expected to require an advanced control and management framework with support for cross-layer information and inter-node collaboration. At the wireless local-area network level, an important technical challenge is that of distributing and managing this inter-node and cross-layer information then using this control information to design stable adaptive networking algorithms that are not overly complex. At the global internetworking level, clusters of cognitive radios represent a new category of access network that needs to be interfaced efficiently with the wired network infrastructure both in terms of control and data. End-to-end architecture issues of importance include naming and addressing consistent with the needs of self-organizing network clusters, as well as the definition of sufficiently aggregated control and management interfaces[14], between cognitive radio networks and the global Internet[3].The COGNET model proposes a way to interface cognitive radios[4][17]. In order to implement the capabilities detailed above, COGNET envisions several inter-module interfaces and protocols, specifically:

• A Global Control Plane (GCP) implemented as a cross layer network management overlay that can interface with the network layer and can provide aggregated representations of the cognitive subnetwork state to the future Internet.

• An API for PHY *layer adaptation* (e.g., agility, change of modulation waveform), and support for collaborative PHY in the form of network coding.

• Spectrum coordination protocols that facilitate dynamic sharing among radio nodes using mechanisms such as etiquette policies or spectrum server [18].

•Autoconfiguration (e.g., bootstrapping and topology discovery) protocols that can be used to establish network connectivity after a cognitive radio device is turned on or enters a new service area.

• Flexible *MAC* framework [15] that permits programmable functionality capable of dynamic selection of channel sharing modes based on observed network conditions and traffic demands.

• Network layer protocols that support service discovery naming, addressing and routing in ad hoc wireless constellations including features that provide economic incentives for collaboration.

4. COGMAN- USE OF COGNITIVE RADIO IN MOBILE AD-HOC SUPPORT

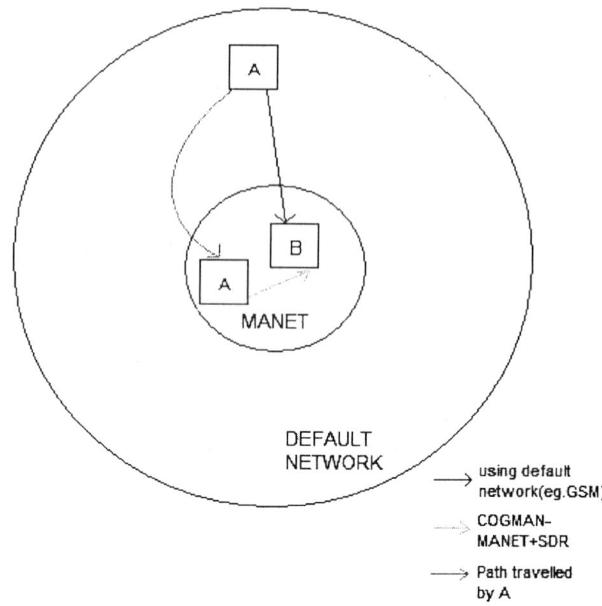

Figure 3. COGMAN in action explains a scenario in which cognitive radio can be used to support a handover between a MANET and a default network.

A mobile, ad-hoc network or MANET is the next generation self-configuring network. We can split the term "Mobile Ad-hoc" to understand the behavior of such network. Firstly, it is a network, i.e., a set of nodes coming together in order to exchange information. This network is "mobile" in the sense that the location of the nodes and network topology is dynamic. As ad-hoc network is a self configuring network it doesn't need infrastructure [8]. In such networks nodes act as the information centers as well as routers. MANETS are expected to play a crucial role in a variety of environments [16].
Cognitive Radio is perfectly suited for integrating Ad-Hoc Networks. Ad hoc Networks are characterized by scare resources and dynamic topologies. COGMAN provides organized solutions compatibility issues between heterogeneous nodes and networks. As SDRs are self-aware, hence strategies for reducing energy consumption of the communication system and increasing the life of nodes can be used more efficiently. Ad hoc networks may or may not have homogenous distribution of routing information and processing on each node. SDRs can help to distribute "responsibility" based on physical capabilities of heterogeneous nodes in

MANETS. The capacity of Ad-Hoc networks is also constrained by mutual interference of concurrent transmission between nodes. COGMAN has multiple reception parameters and can switch between them to communicate efficiently avoiding interference. Let us consider a simple scenario of handovers in Ad-Hoc networks. Let us consider that node A and node B are communicating with the help of the default network. Node A then moves from the default network to a region in which it can communicate with node B by forming a MANET (Mobile Ad-Hoc Network).Let us consider p1 as the set of parameters of the default network. Now node A moves to a region wherein it can communicate with node B via transmission parameters p2. The process of handoff can be explained as follows:

1. If nodes are out of MANET reach, continue normal relay of transmission.

2. If default network + MANET detected, check for free frequencies to transmit through MANET.

3. If no free frequencies found continue with default network.

4. If free frequencies found, use cognitive radio to mutually switch to a frequency by which ad-hoc network can be established.

5. If MANET disabled, use COGNET to switch to regular frequency

6. Repeat steps 1 to 5 every n minutes (where n is a stipulated period)

5. CONCLUSION

COGMAN offers great improvements for integrating Ad-Hoc networks with reference to their frequency agility, dynamic frequency selection, adaptive modulation, transmit power control, location awareness. As shown, cognitive radio can help achieve handovers between basic and MANET network dynamically and in an efficient manner. Main drawback of COGMAN is increase in complexity of the communication system. Design and Analysis of routing protocols remains an important issue in COGMAN deployment.

REFERENCES

1. Natasha Devroye, Patrick Mitran, and Vahid Tarokh.. Limits on Communications in a Cognitive Radio Channel. IEEE Communications Magazine ,June 2006
2. J. Mitola III, "Cognitive Radio: An Integrated Agent Architecture for Software Defined Radio," Ph.D. Thesis, KTH Royal Inst. Technology, Stockholm, Sweden, 2000.
3. D. Raychaudhuri and M. Gerla, New Architectures and Disruptive Technologies for the Future Internet: The Wireless, Mobile and Sensor Network Perspective, Report of NSF WMPG Workshop, August 2005.
4. Dipankar Raychaudhuri, Narayan B. Mandayam WINLAB, Rutgers University: CogNet - An Architectural Foundation for Experimental Cognitive Radio Networks within the Future Internet
5. Danijela Čabrić, Robert W. Brodersen , Berkeley Critical Research Issues in SDR and Cognitive Radio. Wireless Research Center, University of California at Berkeley, USA
6. F. J. Haris,"On the Use of Windows for Harmonic Analysis with the Discrete Fourier Transform", Proc. of the IEEE, vol. 66. January 1978.
7. N Nawathe, A Malhotra."An Appraise of the B.A.T.M.A.N. protocol for MANETS". Prastuti-08.
8. H. B. Kekre, S Thepade, N Nawathe, A Malhotra. "Bolstering B.A.T.M.A.N. with STO", NCAICT Allahabad -08.
9. R Tandra, S Mishra "What is a spectrum Hole and what does it take to recognize one", Dept. of Electrical Engineering and Computer Sciences, U C Berkeley.
10. V Luca' X Wang, L Marco," Multiuser detection for cooperative networks and performance analysis", IEEE transactions on signal processing **ISSN** 1053-587X.
11. "Cognitive Radio Report and Order" ET Docket No. 03-108, 20 FCC Rcd 5486 (2005).
12. S Ashley, "Cognitive radio", Scientific American, February, 2006.
13. G Ding, "Cross-layer algorithms for mobile wireless networks", PHD dissertation, url: http://docs.lib.purdue.edu/ dissertations/ AAI3239771.
14. C. Raman, R. Yates, and N. Mandayam, Scheduling variable rate links via a spectrum server, Proc. of IEEE DySPAN'05, Nov. 2005.
15. V. Bharghavan, A. Demers, S. Shenker and L. Zhang, MACAW: A Media Access Protocol for Wireless LAN, Proc. of ACM SIGCOMM'94, 1994

16. M. Grossglauser and D. Tse, "Mobility increases the capacity of ad-hoc wireless networks" Proc. of IEEE INFOCOM '01, volume 3, pages 1360–1369, 2001
17. D. Raychaudhuri and X. Jing, "A spectrum etiquette protocol for efficient coordination of radio devices in unlicensed bands", Proc. Of IEEE PIMRC'03, Beijing, September 2003
18. S. Che and X. Wan, Network Coding in Wireless Network, Proc. Of 16th Int. Conf. on Computer Communication, China, 2004.
19. B. Zhao, Y. Duan, L. Huang, A. D. Joseph, and J. D. Kubiatowicz, "Brocade: Landmark routing on overlay networks", Proc. of the 1st Int.Workshop on Peer-to-Peer Systems (IPTPS), March 2002
20. D. Raychaudhuri, "Adaptive Wireless Networks Using Cognitive Radios as a Building Block", MobiCom 2004 Keynote Speech, Philadelphia, PA, September, 2004
21. FCC 03-322 NPRM on Cognitive Radio http://hraunfoss.fcc.gov/edocs_public/attachmatch/FCC-03-322A1.pdf.

AN EXPERIMENTAL STUDY ON LOCALIZATION USING MULTIPLE BLUETOOTH DEVICES *

SAURAV KUMAR†, TAVLEEN SINGH

Undergraduate Student Computer Science Department, Delhi College of Engineering
New Delhi, Delhi India

PALLAVI AWASTHI

Undergraduate Student Biotechnology Department, Delhi College of Engineering
New Delhi India

Abstract: In this paper we are presenting a Localization System for a Mobile Server based on Bluetooth Signal Parameters received from Multiple Bluetooth Devices in range. Though Bluetooth technology allows us to keep a low budget and low power system but at the same time it adds a tradeoff of accuracy. Therefore before predicting the distance first we create a lookup table with RSSI and Distance. We calculate the RSSI value by taking a large number of measurements for various distance and picking up the value that occurs most frequently by making the histogram. When we are predicting the distance we are taking reading from the Heading Sensor and Odometer attached to the mobile server and passing it on to an Extended Kaman Filter which model the noise associated with the system.

1. Introduction

Localization is seen as one of the basic necessity in this ubiquitous computing world. Location awareness is very significant and enables new applications and services Global Positioning System (GPS) is one of the world-wide used satellite-based navigation system. However, GPS has very limitations. It fails in the indoor environment as the receiver usually fails due to the loss of line of sight visibility to the satellite.

Localization can be broadly classified as Local and Global. Local positioning refers to the application of technology in restricted area (e.g. inside a building). However, Global positioning refers to the task of determining position and the technology applied in broad area (e.g. in a city) so as to locate itself in outside environment.

Indoor Localization has become one of the hot topics of research these days. Real Time indoor localization technologies are increasingly becoming affordable and portable. These systems aim at locating people and assets based on sensory data obtained from RFID, Wi-Fi, Bluetooth, etc. Indoor localization technologies have applications in different sectors such as military, healthcare, postal/courier, and recently retail and agricultural.

* Work partially supported by DSIR TePP 2007 Research Grant Awarded to Mr. Saurav Kumar.

Development of Wireless Network helped us to meet the requirements of data communication, beyond the Physical link, which have been fuelled by fabrication improvements of digital and radio frequency (RF) circuits, new large-scale circuit integration, and other miniaturization technologies that make portable radio equipment smaller, cheaper and more reliable.

Bluetooth Beacon Placement for Indoor Localization has been discussed in [1].The work only consider the placement of Bluetooth beacon irrespective of signal parameter of Bluetooth. Bluetooth signal just like other radio signal have some loss associated with it when it

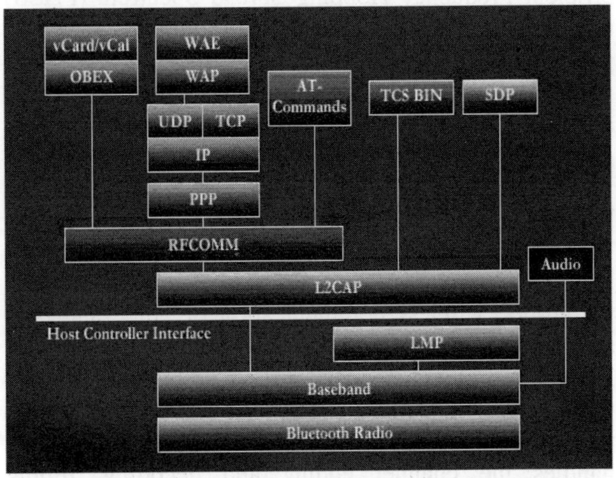

Figure 1. Bluetooth Protocol Stack

propagates in an environment. These wireless signal propagation models have been discussed in [2] and [3]. Another study on Localization has been in [4] which take into consideration of various Bluetooth Signal Parameters like RSSI, TPL and LQ discussed in [5]. Using RSSI value for distance estimation in Wireless sensor networks is one of our main concerns and this has been discussed and experimented using ZigBee in [6] and using Bluetooth we have discussed in this paper.

Section II gives a overview of Bluetooth Technology and propagation model to calculate Looses involved. In Section III we discuss the signal parameters to estimate distance. In next sections we discuss the experimental test bed and Result. Conclusion and future work to improve the accuracy of localization is discussed in Section VI.

2. Overview of Bluetooth & Propagation Model

Bluetooth is a radio frequency specification for short range, point to point and point to multi point voice and data transfer. Operates at the 2.4 GHz range in the globally available license free ISM band. This band is reserved for the general use by Industrial, Scientific, and Medical applications.

This means the Bluetooth has to be robust as there are a great many existing users and interferers of this shared spectrum. The operating band is divided into 79 1 MHz-spaced channels, each signaling data at 1MHz. The modulation scheme used is GFSK (Gaussian Frequency Shift Keying). After each packet, both devices retune their radio to a different frequency, effectively hopping from channel to channel using an efficient Frequency Hopping Spread Spectrum (FHSS) technique. Each Bluetooth slot lasts 625 μsec. The radio power is one of three classes (1mW, 2.5mW and 100mW), which provide an operation that ranges of approximately 10 m, 20m, and 100m; the lowest power gives 10 m range, and the highest power up to 100m.Bluetooth Protocol Stack has been shown in Figure 1.

Bluetooth wireless technology is an open specification for a low-cost, low-power, short-range radio technology for ad-hoc wireless communication of voice and data anywhere in the world. The Physical layer of the Bluetooth protocol stack is represented by the radio and the baseband. The radio acts as the interface between the wireless channel and the digital baseband. The baseband handles the channel coding and decoding, timing control, reliable transmission and management of link for each data packet transfer. The Link Controller (LC) is responsible for link level operations in response to the Link Manager (LM) commands.

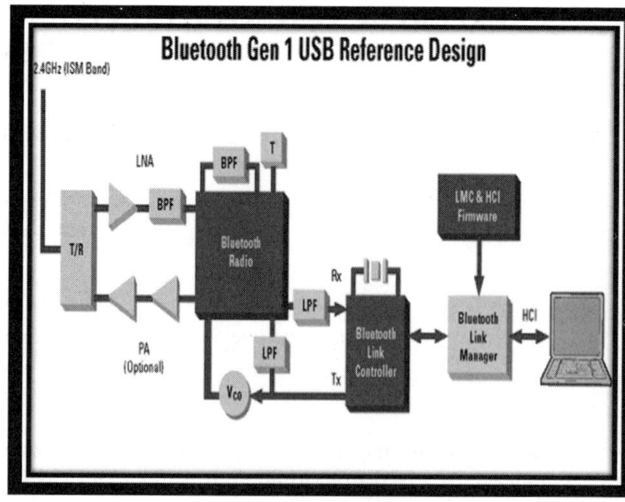

Figure 2. Bluetooth Reference Design

These has been shown in Picture 2.The Bluetooth system provides a point-to-point connection (only two Bluetooth units involved), or a point-to-multipoint connection. Two or more units sharing the same channel form a piconet. One Bluetooth unit acts as the master (which initiates an exchange of data and then controls the channel access) of the piconet, whereas the other unit(s) acts as slave(s). Each Bluetooth device has a 48 bit address known as the Bluetooth Device Address (BD_ADDR). 2 types of links can be established- Asynchronous Connection Less (ACL) & Synchronous Connection Oriented (SCO). ACL is a packet-switched while SCO is a circuit-switched link. The Bluetooth specification also defines Host Controller Interface (HCI) which provides a command interface to the baseband, link manager and access to hardware status. Propagation models are used extensively in network planning, particularly for conducting feasibility studies and initial deployment. Mobile computing applications are becoming increasingly common in outdoor, indoor, pedestrian and vehicular scenarios. These models are mainly used to predict path loss. The deterministic models use the laws governing electromagnetic wave

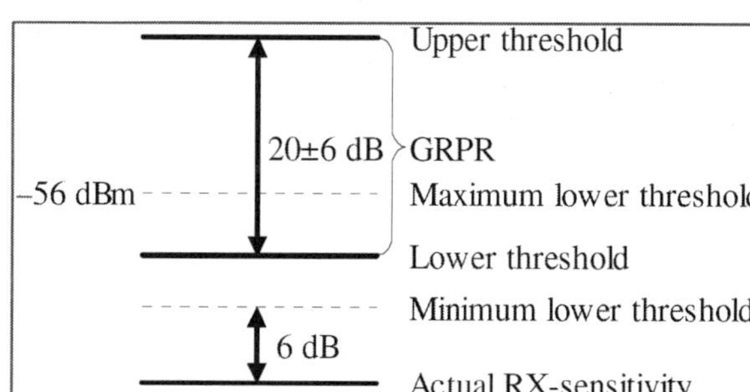

Figure 3. Definition of GRPR

propagation to determine the received signal power at a particular location. Stochastic models, on the other hand, model the environment as a series of random variables. Various Propagation Model that exist for wireless Communication are ***Free space propagation model***(Built on the assumption that the transmitter and receiver are in the line of sight, and there are no obstacles between them. [3]) and L***og Distance model which*** has been derived from analytical, empirical methods . [10]

3. Bluetooth Signal Parameter and Localization

3.1 Bluetooth Signal Parameter

Although there are the 4 signal-related parameters made available by Bluetooth Core Specification but we are using Received Signal Strength Indicator (RSSI), Link Quality (LQ), and Transmit Power Level (TPL) as the Bluetooth signal parameter from which we can predict the status of Bluetooth connection. The Host Controller Interface (HCI) provides access to all the above three connection status parameters. All these status parameters require the establishment of an active Bluetooth connection in order to be measured. [**15**]

3.1.1 Link Quality (LQ)

LQ is an 8-bit unsigned integer that evaluates the perceived link quality at the receiver. It ranges from 0 to 255; the larger the value, the better the link's state. LQ is used mainly for adapting to changes in the link's state, notably to support CQDDR (Channel Quality Driven Data Rate).

3.1.2 Received Signal Strength Indicator (RSSI)

It is a 8-bit unsigned integer value that indicates the value of the received (RX) power level with respect to the Golden Receiver Power Range (GRPR). GRPR is the ideal RX power range. The relationship between GRPR and RSSI is indicated in FIGURE1. A positive or negative RSSI (in dB) means the RX power level is above or below the GRPR, respectively, while a zero implies that it is ideal (i.e., within GRPR). The upper and lower thresholds of GRPR are device specific. Since RSSI is a relative parameter, its absolute accuracy is not mandated in the specifications. The RSSI status parameter of Bluetooth is particularly intended to be used for power control purpose.[6]

3.1.3 Transmit Power Level (TPL)

TPL is an 8-bit signed integer which specifies the Bluetooth module's transmit power level (in dBm). Although there are instances when a transmitter will use its device-specific default power setting, its TPL may vary during a connection due to possible power control.

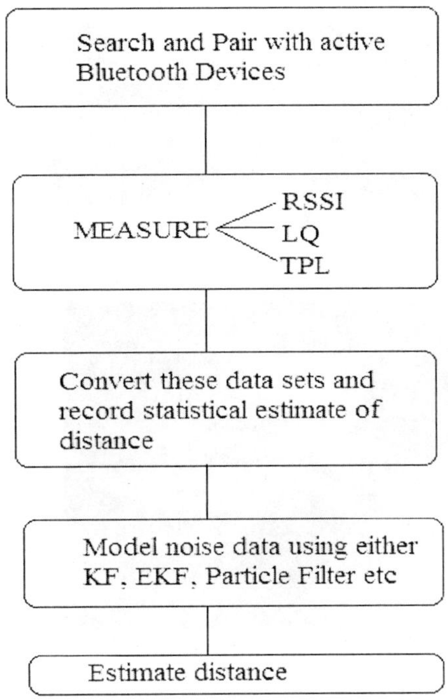

Figure 4. Block Diagram of Estimating Distance

For Class 1 devices, which have a maximum output power of +20 dBm, power control is mandatory when the TPL is between +4 and +20 dBm. In Bluetooth specification, power control is optional for TPL under +4 dBm. Therefore, Class 2 (maximum output power +4 dBm) and Class 3 (maximum output power 0 dBm) devices need not support power control.

3.2 Localization

After receiving the data from RSSI, TPL and LQ, We calculate RSSI* is equal to RSSI if LQ = 255 and TPL = 0 but it becomes equal to zero as soon as either LQ = 0 or TPL < 0. Initially We take the RSSI* data for various point for different range for more than 20 to 30 Minutes thus taking about 1000 Reading at a single Point. We plot a histogram of all the RSSI* value received. The most frequent data RSSI** is taken out from the histogram and a table is prepared in this way with RSSI** and Measured Distance between the main Server and communicating active Bluetooth device.

Next time when we are predicting the distance on the basis of RSSI** observed for any random point we check across the table created above and find out the suitable distance. Since the measurements are corrupted by noise. A larger Number of measurement samples is preferred to decrease the effect of single measurement errors and to evaluate the uncertainty of distance measurement by computing the variance of the sample

5 (a)

(b)

5 (c)

Figure 5. (a) STLC2500 Chip (b) Heading Sensor (c) Experimental Test Bed

set. In predicting the distance we take the help of EKF (Extended Kalman Filter).It help linearize the range measurement in Euclidean space. EKF is formulated to estimate the position of the mobile Bluetooth Server given measurement of odometer, heading change (from heading sensor) and range measurement from measurement from stationary active Bluetooth devices it is communicating with.

Let Mobile Bluetooth Server state (position and orientation) at time k be represented by state vector $Q_k = [X_k^r, Y_k^r, Ø_k^r]$

The dynamics of Moving Bluetooth System can be represented by,

$$q_{k+1} = \begin{bmatrix} x_k^r + \triangle D_k \cos(\phi_k^r) \\ y_k^r + \triangle D_k \sin(\phi_k^r) \\ \phi_k^r + \triangle \phi_k \end{bmatrix} + \nu_k = f(\widehat{q}_k, u_k) + \nu_k,$$

Where V_k is the noise vector,

D_k is the odometric distance travelled,

$\Delta Ø_k$ is the orientation change

For every new control input vector,

$u(k) = [D_{k,}, \Delta Ø_k]$

that is received, the estimates of robot state and error covariance are propagated using EKF.

$X^{\wedge}{}_k^b$ (range measurement received at time k)

$$= [(X_k^r - X_k^b)^2 + (X_k^r - Y_k^b)^2]^{(1/2)} + n_k$$

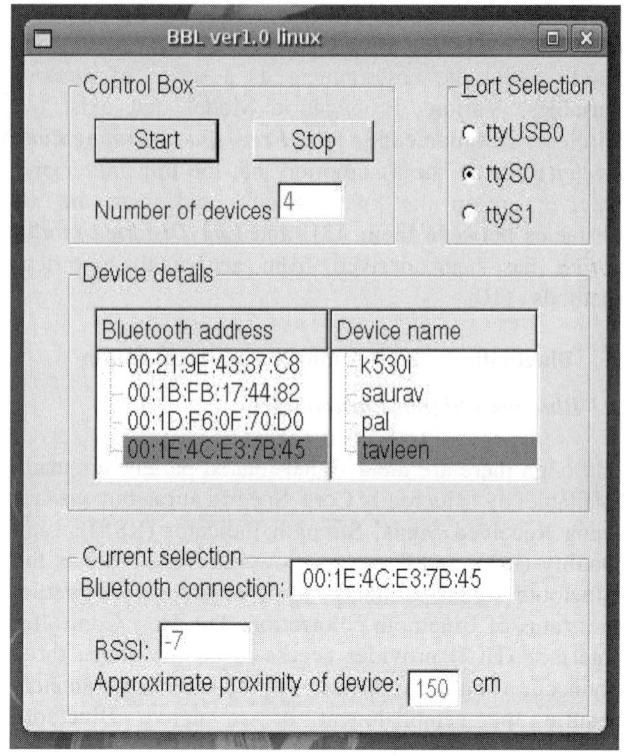

Figure 6. BBL GUI in Linux

Where

$r^{\wedge}{}_k^b$ = range from the one of the active Bluetooth Device

$(X_k^b, {}_k^b)$ = localization of active Bluetooth Device From which the measurement was received

n_k = Gaussian noise with zero mean

4. Experimental Setup

Hardware Setup and Software

For active Bluetooth Devices we took Laptops (SONY VAIO and DELL), Mobile Phones (K530i and E210 from Samsung) and STLC2500 Bluetooth Chipset [7]. We had the main server running on VAIO and all the different Laptop, Mobile Phones and STLC2500 Chips were working as client and were sending the RSSI data when requested. The main server is installed onto a vehicle during the localization which is driven using two Quicksilver Servo Motor. Bumblebee Stereo Vision Camera and Laser Ranger Finder are installed for obstacle avoidance. An Ocean Server Heading sensor is also installed onboard which gives the vehicles heading direction w.r.t to North Pole. Different Hardware and Experimental test bed is shown in Figure 5.

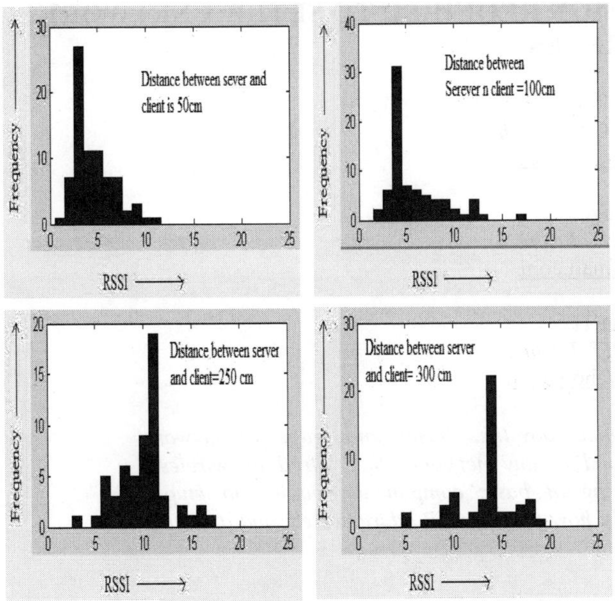

Figure 7.

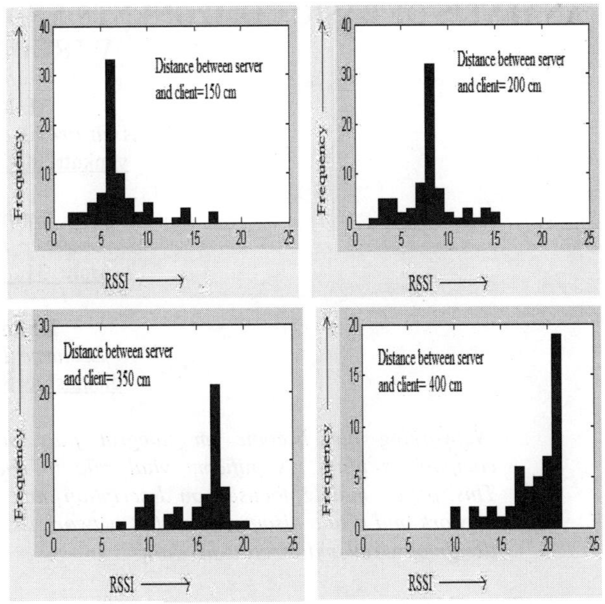

Figure 8.

We created a GUI in QT. Program runs over Ubuntu Linux. The Histograms are calculated using OCTAVE (open source version of MATLAB). It is named as BBL which stands for Bluetooth Based Localization. A snapshot of the software is shown in Figure 6.

5. Results

The above sets of measurements shown in figure 7 & 8, were carried-out using the STLC 2500Chip based Bluetooth module. About 60 Data Sets were taken for RSSI after each 50 cm of difference in distance. A histogram of RSSI was calculated. RSSI* was selected and a table was made.

Measurements were taken in both indoor and outdoor environment in real time condition and not in a Noise-free laboratory. This is because we wanted to place the modules within real working environment, in which they would normally be operating when deployed.

6. Conclusion

We presented a simple Localization system using STLC 2500 Bluetooth chip, Laptop and few mobile phones. Based on the parameters of an established data link, the system computes a plane of Probable Position, which is refined further by taking multiple datasets and Modeling the error using EKF.

The accuracy of Distance measurement obtained from above experiment is not enough to localize a mobile Robot in Indoor Environment. Therefore another feature

Other than Bluetooth has to be added for E.g. Vision and the effect should be studied together so that the localization can be done with a better accuracy

References

[1] Sudarshan S. Chawathe, "Beacon Placement for Indoor Localization using Bluetooth", 11th IEEE,Conference on Intelligent Transportation Systems,Beijing, China, October 12-15, 2008

[2] Paolo Santi: Topology Control in Wireless Ad Hoc and Sensor Networks, ISBN-13: 978-0470094532, September

[3] R. A. Santos, O. Álvarez, A. Edwards, "Experimental Analysis of Wireless Propagation Models with Mobile Computing Applications ", IEEE 2005

[4] Antti Kotanen, Marko Hännikäinen, Helena Leppäkoski, Timo D. Hämäläinen, "Experiments on Local Positioning with Bluetooth", Tampere University of Technology, Institute of Digital and Computer Systems

[5] A. K. M. Mahtab Hossain and Wee-Seng Soh, "A Comprehensive Study of Bluetooth Signal Parameters for Localization", PIMRC' 07

[6] K. Benkic, M. Malajner, P. Planinšic, Ž. Cucej , "Using RSSI value for distance estimation in Wireless sensor networksbased on ZigBee".

[7] STLC2500 Chip Data Sheet http://www.datasheetcatalog.org/datasheet2/1/02u8s89l5yiyiu8pj61eaefy7xky.pdf

ANALYSIS OF BASIC COMPONENTS AND DESIGN REQUIRED TO SETUP A NETWORK WIRED/WIRELESS

M. Kiruthika
Assit Professor, Fr.CRIT, Vashi
venkatr20032002@gmail.com

Smita Dange
Lecturer, Fr.CRIT, Vashi
smm_31@rediffmail.com

Dhanashree H
Lecturer, Fr.CRIT, Vashi
dhanashree812@yahoo.co.in

Networking has become an integral part in day to day life. Basic knowledge of network components plays a significant vital role in understanding any network either wired or wireless. This paper mainly focuses on description and working of basic components required to setup a network and also a discussion on few network issues like how to assign IP addresses etc and a sample design of wired and wireless network.

Keywords
Network, Switch, Router

1. Introduction

Networking has become an upcoming field with evolving of various technologies. Awareness of those technologies and components is becoming very important. Even though basic components are known by everyone, the description and utilization of these components require an emphasis. Also, how to use them while designing a network (wired/wireless) requires some stress. With this in mind, the following sections give some idea about the components and how are they used in designing a network (wired/wireless).

2. Basic Components

2.1 *Hub*

A hub is a simple multiport repeater. There is usually no software to load, and no configuration required (i.e. network administrators don t have to tell the device what to do). Essentially, a hub simply receives incoming packets, possibly amplifies the electrical signal, and broadcasts these packets out to all devices on the network - including the one that originally sent the packet.

2.1.1 *Types of Hubs*

Technically speaking, three different types of hubs exist:

- Passive
- Active
- Intelligent

Passive hubs do not amplify the electrical signal of Incoming packets before broadcasting them out to the network.

Active hubs, on the other hand, do perform this amplification, as does a different type of dedicated network device called a repeater. Some people use the terms concentrator when referring to a passive hub and multiport repeater when referring to an active hub.

Intelligent hubs add extra features to an active hub that are of particular importance to businesses. An intelligent hub typically is stackable (built in such a way that multiple units can be placed one on top of the other to conserve space). It also typically includes remote management capabilities via SNMP and virtual LAN (VLAN) support.

2.2 *Switch*

Switch is layer 2 devices it deals with data link layer of OSI Model. It is a centralized device to connect Computers in a network and traffic handling. Switch receives data packet from source, inspects it and then sends it to the specified destination. It overcomes the drawback of hub. Hub always work on broadcast. Domain that means if any packet comes from the source it doesn't know where to send it so it broadcast it to each and every port of the hub then every port check whether that packet is related to it or not. If yes it receives that packet else it discards it. This creates unnecessary traffic in the network. To avoid that switch receive the packet from the source inspects it and then sends it to specified destination. Switch works on full duplex mode. Transfer of data is bidirectional which is not established in hub.

2.2.1 *How switch communicates*

Switch has its own internal memory where there is a MAC address entry table(Look Up table). It store the MAC address of the computers which are connected to the switch. MAC address is of 48 bits. It has 6 octets separated by dot. When any source sends a Packet (Ethernet frame) it contains the source and Destination MAC address, data and error checking information. Switch reads the receiver MAC address from the header then compares to a list of addresses maintained in the switch's lookup table and then redirects the message to the respective port. Switch uses mainly three methods for handling traffic:

1. **Cut-through**
2. **Store-and-forward**
3. **Fragment-free**

Cut-through : In this switch read, only first 48 bits of the packet i. e. it only reads the MAC address of the destination and it immediately begins sending the packet to the destination. It never checks the error and collision.

Store-and-forward : Switch saves the entire packet to the buffer and check it for CRC errors or other problems before sending. If the packet has an error, it is discarded. Otherwise, the switch looks up the MAC address and sends the packet on to the destination node.

Fragment-free: It is same as cut-through except that it stores the first 64 bytes of thc packet before sending it on. The reason for this is that most errors, and all collisions, occur during the initial 64 bytes of a packet.

2.2.2 *Configuration Options*

1. Unmanaged switch

These switches have no configuration interface or options. You cannot access this switch and it doesn't have a console port so you cannot view and configure this switch.

2. Managed switches

These switches can be accessed, configured and modified. It has a console port via which you can access the whole switch. You can manage switch with a serial console or Command Line Interface accessed via telnet or Secure Shell; an embedded Simple Network Management Protocol (SNMP) agent allowing management from a remote console or management station; a web interface for management from a web browser.

2.3 ***Router***

Router is layer 3(Network Layer) device of OSI Model. It is used to join multiple wired and wireless networks. Router forwards packets from one network to another. Based on internal routing tables, it reads each incoming packet and decide how to forward it. The destination address in the packets determines which line (interface) outgoing packets are directed to. In large company routers are also used to separate networks and for communication between different networks to balance traffic and filter traffic. If any packet come to the Router ,he will inspect that packet based on IP address. instead of the MAC address. Router also has its own memory and operating system. Same as switch, it has internal routing table which keeps the information about networks connected to him as well as other routers in networks. It regularly updates information about change in network.

2.3.1 Types of router

There are two types of router

1. Hardware Routers : Cisco, D-link
2. Software Routers: Operating systems like Windows and Linux and third party software like Mikrotik.

2.3.2 Types Of Routing

There are two types of routing

1. Static
2. Dynamic

2.3.2.1 Static Routing

For communication between different networks administrator should know the source as well as destination networks for manual updates of routing table. It is preferably used for small networks and also where security is required. It is comparatively faster than dynamic routing because administrator configure the path of destination network manually.

2.3.2.2 Dynamic Routing

The individual router share their own network information using a routing protocol. Routing protocols are used between routers to determine paths and maintain routing table. Once the path is determined a router can route the information.

2.3.3 *Routing Protocols*

Routing protocols are classified in two types

1. Distance Vector: RIP, IGRP
2. Link State : OSPF

There is a combination of these two types that is Advanced Distance Vector/ Hybrid : EIGRP In case of Distance Vector router sends periodic large updates to the neighboring routers only. Distance vector algorithms know only about their neighbors. Link-state algorithms (also known as shortest path first algorithms) flood routing information to all nodes in the inter network. Because they converge more quickly, link-state algorithms are somewhat less prone to routing loops than distance vector algorithms. On the other hand, link-state algorithms require more CPU power and memory than distance vector algorithms. Link-state algorithms, therefore, can be more expensive to implement and support. Link-state protocols are generally more scalable than distance vector protocols.

2.3.4 *Example Of How Networks Communicate with each other using Router*

There are three routers A,B,C
A is connected to network 1,2,3
B is connected to network 3,4,5
C is connected to network 5,6,7

As shown figure1

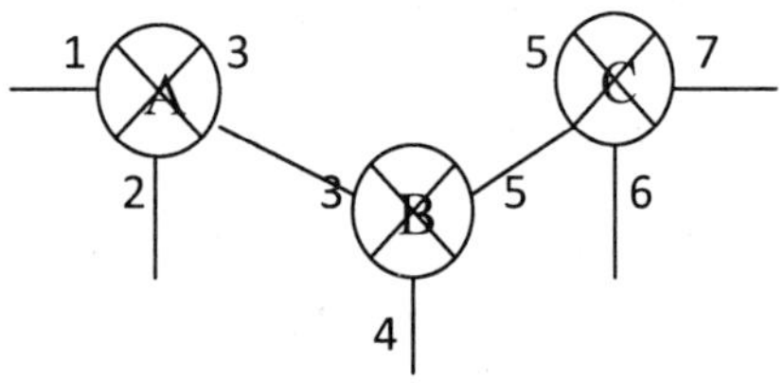

Figure1 : Updating Routing Table

Now in routing table each router is having information about its own connected networks

Router A
1
2
3
Router B
3
4
5
Router C
5
6
7

Now the basic work of the router is to connect to the networks of other router. Routing is the act of moving information across an internetwork from a source to a destination.

That we can achieve by applying different types of routing. After outing each router table is having information about its own connected networks and other networks.

Like
A is updated with
1 2 3 4 5 6 7
B is updated with
3 4 5 1 2 6 7
C is updated with
5 6 7 1 2 3 4
So, all networks can communicate with each other.

2.3.5 *Routing Metrics*

Routing tables contain information used by switching software to select the best route. Routing algorithms have used many different metrics to determine the best route.

1. Path length
2. Reliability
3. Delay
4. Bandwidth
5. Load
6. Communication cost

2.4 ***NIC (Network Interface Card)***

There are two types of network cards .

2.4.1 *Wired NIC*

A network interface card is used to connect a computer to a network. The card provides an interface to the media

2.4.2 *Wireless NIC*

A wireless network interface controller (WNIC) is a network card which connects to a radio-based computer network.

A WNIC is an essential component for wireless desktop computer. This card uses an antenna to communicate through microwaves. A WNIC in a desktop computer usually is connected using the PCI bus. Other connectivity options are USB and PC card.

A WNIC can operate in two modes known as infrastructure mode and ad-hoc modan infrastructure mode network the WNIC needs an access point: all data is transferred using the access point as the central hub. All wireless nodes in an infrastructure mode network connect to an access point. All nodes connecting to the access point must have the same service set identifier (SSID) as the access point, and if the access point is enabled with WEP they must have the same WEP key or other authentication parameters.

In an ad-hoc mode network the WNIC does not require an access point, but rather can directly interface with all other wireless nodes directly. All the nodes in an ad-hoc network must have the same channel and SSID.

3. Assigning Address

3.1 *Subnetting*

Subnetting is a logical division of a local area network, which is created to improve performance and provide security. To enhance performance, subnets limit the number of nodes that compete for available bandwidth. Instead of one network handling all the traffic, the network is divided into groups of clients and servers that interact with each other most of the time. For security, the subnet divisions can be based on servers that have restricted applications. IP address is made up of 32 bits which is divided into four octets which is combination of bits 1 and 0.

As per organization s host requirement it is divided into different classes :Refer Table 1

Table 1. Address ranges and LAN sizes

Address range	Subnet mask	Provides	Addresses per LAN
10.0.0.0 - 10.255.255.255.255	255.0.0.0	1 class A LAN	16,777,216
172.16.0.0 - 172.31.255.255	255.255.0.0	16 class B LANs	65,536
192.168.0.0 - 192.168.255.255	255.255.255.0	256 class C LANs	256

Now depending on the number of hosts connecting to your network you can select one class from above table. Sometimes for security and utilization of IP address we can do subnetting.

Subnetting is the process of allocating bits from the host portion as a network portion. The Figure2 shows an example of how the bitwise "AND" process is being performed on a classful network and how bits are being borrowed to turn a classful network into a subnet.

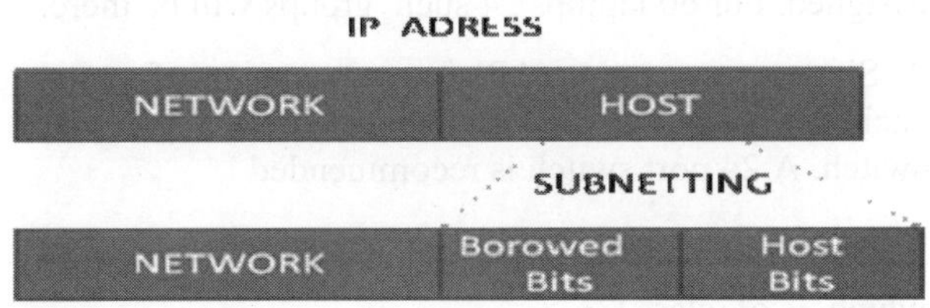

Figure 2 : Subnetting Example

3.2 *IP addresses Allocation*

There are two ways to assign IP addresses in a LAN. You can manually assign a *static* IP address to each computer in the LAN, or you can use a DHCP server that automatically assigns a *dynamic* IP address to each computer as it logs into the network.

3.2.1 *Static IP addressing*

It manually assigns unique IP address to the computer in a network. If you are working under same network then first three octets should be same and the last octet should be a unique number in the network.

3.2.2 *Dynamic IP addressing*

Dynamic IP addressing is accomplished via a server called DHCP (Dynamic Host Configuration Protocol) that automatically assigns a unique IP address to each computer as it connects to the network.

4. Sample Design of Wired Network

Now lets see how above components are used to design a wired network. Example If you want to setup a LAN with 40 PCs then ,

1. Two 24 port switch or three 16 port switch is required.

2. Class C subnet mask can be used for the above network .

3. A class C IP addressing mechanism is used.

4. The switch can be connected to a server if authentication, security and any other issues need to be implemented

Refer Figure 3

5. Sample Design of Wireless Network

Now lets see how above components are used to design a wireless network. Example, if you want to setup a wireless LAN with 60 Laptops then ,

1. We divide them into a group of 15 each so that ,for each group one access point with specific IP address is assigned. For 60 laptops , 4 such groups will be there.

2. Since access point (AP) is an extension of switch, each access point will be connected to a port in a switch. A 24 port switch is recommended .

3. Switch recognizes access points with its IP address which is of class C.

4. Each access point is configured with the MAC address of the laptops within its range. In this case , each AP is configured with MAC address of 15 laptops which would fall under the range of that particular AP. The laptops whose MAC id is not configured under that AP would not fall under the range of that AP .

5. Above is a combination of wired and wireless network since AP is connected to the switch through a cable.. To design a pure wireless network a manageable switch can be used.

6. The switch can be connected to a server if authentication ,security and any other issues need to be implemented

Refer Figure 4

6. Conclusions

In this paper , we have highlighted some of the components required to set up a network (wired/wireless) and how it can be used while designing a network. A sample design layout of both wired and wireless network is given and also which subnet mask and IP addressing mechanism should be chosen.
Thus, it gives an overall idea about the components and basic design required to setup a network.

7. References

1. http://www.answers.com/topic/subnetwork
2. http://compnetworking.about.com/od/hardware network gear/ g/bldef_hub.html
3. http://www.hp.com/rnd/products/switches/ ProCurve_Switch_1800_Series/specs.htm
4. http://www.ybet.be/en-hardware-2-05/hub-switch.htm#hub

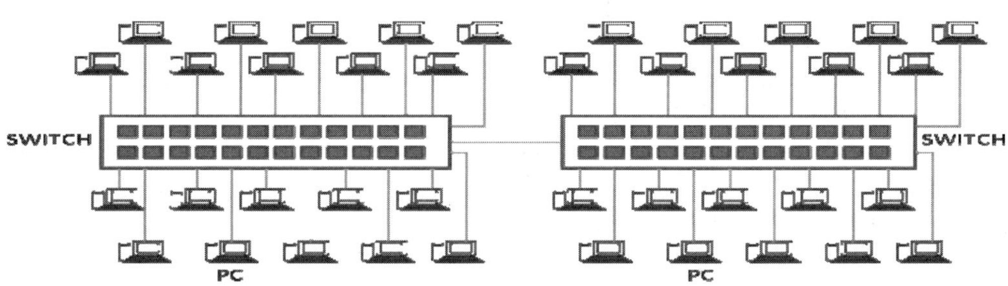

Figure 3 : Sample Design Layout of Wired Network

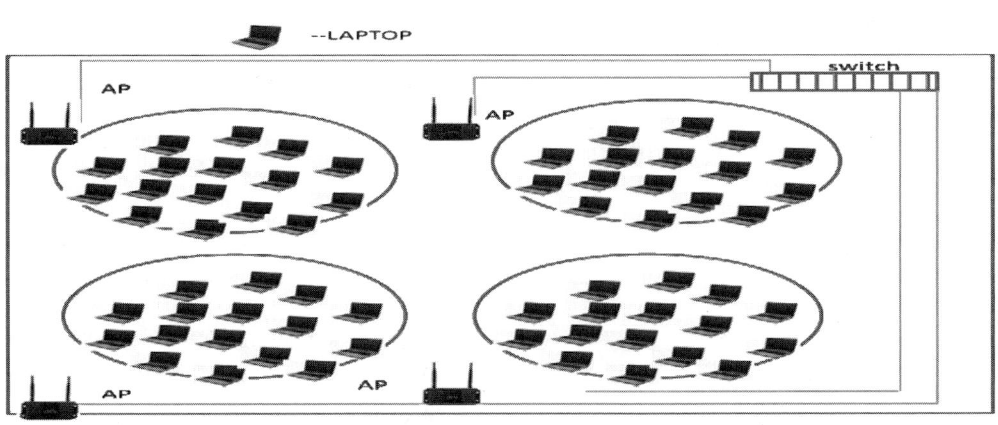

Figure 4 : Sample Design Layout of Wireless Network

DETECTION OF FACES AND FACIAL FEATURES IN COLOR IMAGES

ARCHANA H. SABLE
Department of Computer Engineering
M.G.M's college of Engg, Nanded
(M.S) India -431602
Emailid:helloarchu27@gmail.com

Guided by
K. C. JONDHALE
Department of Computer Engineering
M.G.M's college of Engg, Nanded
(M.S) India-431602
Emailid:kcjondhale@rediffmail.com

Human face detection is concerned with finding the location and size of every human face in a given group image. Face detection plays a very important role in human computer interaction field. It represents the first step in a fully automatic face re-cognition, facial features extraction, and expression recognition. There are many techniques used in face detection, each one has its advantages and disadvantages. The face detection system presented in this paper is a hybrid of known algorithms. First stage of the proposed method is applying skin color detection algorithm to specify all skin locations in the image. Second, face features detection like eyes, mouth and chin In experiments on images of group photos having upright frontal faces with any background our system has achieved high detection rates and low false positives.

1. Introduction

In recent years, face recognition has attracted much attention and its research has rapidly expanded by not only engineers but also neuroscientists, since it has many potential applications in computer vision communication and automatic access control system. Especially, face detection is an important part of face recognition as the first step of automatic face recognition. However, face detection is not straightforward because it has lots of variations of image appearance, such as pose variation (front, non-front), occlusion, image orientation, illuminating condition and facial expression.

Many novel methods have been proposed to resolve each variation listed above. For example, the *template-matching methods* [1], [2] are used for face localization and detection by computing the correlation of an input image to a standard face pattern. The *feature invariant approaches* are used for feature detection [3], [4] of eyes, mouth, ears, nose, etc. The *appearance-based methods* are used for face detection with *eigenface* [5], [6], [7], *neural network* [8], [9], and *information theoretical approach* [10], [11]. Nevertheless, implementing the methods altogether is still a great challenge. Fortunately, the images used in this project have some degree of uniformity thus the detection algorithm can be simpler: first, the all the faces are vertical and have frontal view; second, they are under almost the same illuminate condition. This project presents a face detection technique mainly based on the color segmentation, image segmentation and template matching methods.

2. Face Detection

Our face detection system consists of three steps. The first step is to classify each pixel in the given image as a skin pixel or a non-skin pixel. The second step is to identify different skin regions in the skin detected image by using connectivity analysis. The last step is to decide whether each of the skin regions identified is a face or not. This is done using two parameters. They are the height to width ratio of the skin region and the percentage of skin in the rectangle defined by the height and width.

2.1 Skin Pixel Classification

Different color spaces used in skin detection previously include HSV, normalized RGB, YCrCb, YIQ and CIELAB. According to Zarit et al. _ 10 _, HSV gives the best performance for skin pixel detection. We conducted our own experiments independently and converged to the same fact. Our experiments also showed the superiority of HSV color space over RGB and YCrCb color spaces. Skin color can be modeled using a histogram, a single Gaussian or a mixture of Gaussians. Jones and Rehg _ 4 _ have demonstrated that the histogram model is superior to other models. Also, the histogram is easy to implement and is computationally efficient. In the HSV space, H stands for hue component, which describes the shade of the color, S stands for saturation component, which describes how pure the hue (color) is while V stands for value component, which describes the brightness.

The removal of V component takes care of varying lighting conditions. H varies from 0 to 1 on a circular scale i.e. the colors represented by H=0 and H=1 are the same. S varies from 0 to 1, 1 representing 100 percent purity of the color H and S scales are partitioned into 100 levels and the color histogram is formed using H and S. In order to train for skin color, we downloaded color images containing human faces from the Internet and extracted the skin regions in these images manually. Our training set contained more than 4,50,000 skin pixels to form the color histogram in H and S. For each pixel, H and S values are found and the bin corresponding to these H and S values in the histogram is incremented by 1. After the training is completed, the histogram is normalized. The histogram obtained 2 dimensions in Fig 1 respectively. Though it appears that there are two different regions very much apart with high skin probability, they both belong to the same region, since H is cyclic in nature. Also, we can see that the skin color falls into a very small region in the entire HS space. The height of a bin in the histogram is proportional to the probability that the color represented by the bin is a skin color.

Figure 1. HS histogram for skin pixels in 2D view

So we use a threshold between 0 and 1 to classify any pixel as a skin pixel or a non-skin pixel. If the threshold value is high, all the non-skin pixels will be classified correctly but some of the skin pixels will be classified as non-skin pixels. If the threshold value is low, all the skin pixels will be classified correctly whereas some of the non-skin pixels will be classified as skin pixels. This represents a trade-off between percentage of skin pixels detected as skin and percentage of non-skin pixels falsely detected as skin. There is an optimum threshold value with which one can detect most of the skin pixels and reject most of the non-skin pixels. This threshold is found by experimentation. Given an image, each pixel in the image is classified as skin or non-skin using color information. The histogram is normalized and if the height of the bin corresponding to the H and S values of a pixel exceeds a threshold called skin threshold (obtained empirically), then that pixel is considered a skin pixel. Otherwise the pixel is considered a non-skin pixel. A skin detected image is one in which only the skin pixels are shown. A general image and its skin in Fig 4 (a) and Fig 4 (b), respectively.

2.2 Face feature detection

2.2.1. *Face localization*

In the proposed method, a skin color model is first used to localize the face. Then, spatial segmentation is conducted to regularize face shape. Finally, face features are used to verify the detected face candidatures. The process is as follows: using a skin color model, a map of face candidatures can be achieved. At the same time, watershed transformation is used to get spatial over segmented results. The face candidature map is then superimposed on the top of the spatial segmentation mask to refine the shape of face candidature. That is, if a majority part of spatial segmented region belongs to face candidature, the whole segmented region is considered as part of the face candidature. Next, the connected spatial region is merged together in order to get the regularized face candidate. For every candidate, the shape is evaluated based on the method in [3] because human faces are characterized by elliptical or oval shape. Finally, if eyes and mouth are found in the face candidature, it is considered as a face. Fig.1 shows the face detection results for Akiyo and Carphone sequences. It is shown that the proposed method can detect the face shape precisely.

2.2.2. *Eye detection*

For eye detection, two methods have been proposed. For a large face, a deformable template matching method is used. If the size is small, threshold is conducted on the face after filtering by using a morphological erosion filter. For deformable template matching method, the process is described as follows: Firstly, eye location is detected roughly and a small patch surrounding the eye is extracted; Next, the Hough transform is applied to detect the outer edge of the iris, based on the edge distribution. Unfortunately, not all edge maps of irises are standard circle -like, for example, the upper eyelid can hide part of the iris. In this case, the width of iris mask is chosen to be 3-pixel wide for CIF sequences. Furthermore, edge direction is considered during Hough transform. Many tests show that this is more robust than other published schemes. After detecting the iris position and radius, deformable template matching is used to detect the upper and lower

eyelids. The edge and valley energies are used to adjust the template, which is the same as those in [4].
If the face size is very small, such as a face in a QCIF sequence, one simple method is proposed, which is based on the Morphological Open by Reconstruction Filter (MORF) and thresholding. The process is described as follows: Firstly, MORFs are used for the eye patch. Then, thresholding is used to obtain a binary map. For every column of this patch (from left to right), the first and last columns with zero elements are chosen as the column that the eye corners are located at. The mean value of the row number, in which the elements are zeros, is calculated as the row number of each eye corner. Next, the centre of the eye can be estimated based on the eye corners. The upper and lower eyelid (two points) can be estimated based on the fact that the line joining these two points is perpendicular to the line joining the two eye corners. This method is very simple, but has good performance.

2.2.3. *Mouth detection*

In the proposed method, deformable template matching method, together with lip colour distribution, is used to detect the mouth. At first, the mouth position is detected based on its luminance value and the position of the eyes. After that, the SUSAN corner detector [5] is used to detect the right and left mouth corners. Deformable template matching is used to detect the upper and lower lips based on the edge energy of mouth. In order to reduce the computational complexity of the deformable template matching, we propose that the lip colour distribution is used to reduce the search position of deformable template. The colour distribution inside the mouth is modeled as a Gaussian mixture. There are three prominent colour regions inside the mouth: a dark aperture, pink lips and bright specularity. Experiments show that this information can be used to reduce almost two third of the computational complexity.

2.4. Chin detection

For chin detection, a new method is proposed to increase the reliability of detection. In this method, deformable template matching and an active snake model are combined. Experimental results have shown that deformable template matching cannot detect the chin correctly. It can only be used for chins with parabola -like shapes, for example, the chin of Akiyo. It cannot detect the chin of Carphone correctly. For active snake method, the snake initialisation and the chosen external force affect its performance. In our research, a new chin detection method is proposed in order overcome above disadvantages. The gradient vector flow (GVF) is used as the external force [6]. It can yield a smoother field than the gradient, which was used by the published methods [2].
The process is listed as follows:
1. The detection result of deformable template matching is used as the initialization of active snake model.
2. The external force (GVF) is calculated based on the detected edge and the method in [6].

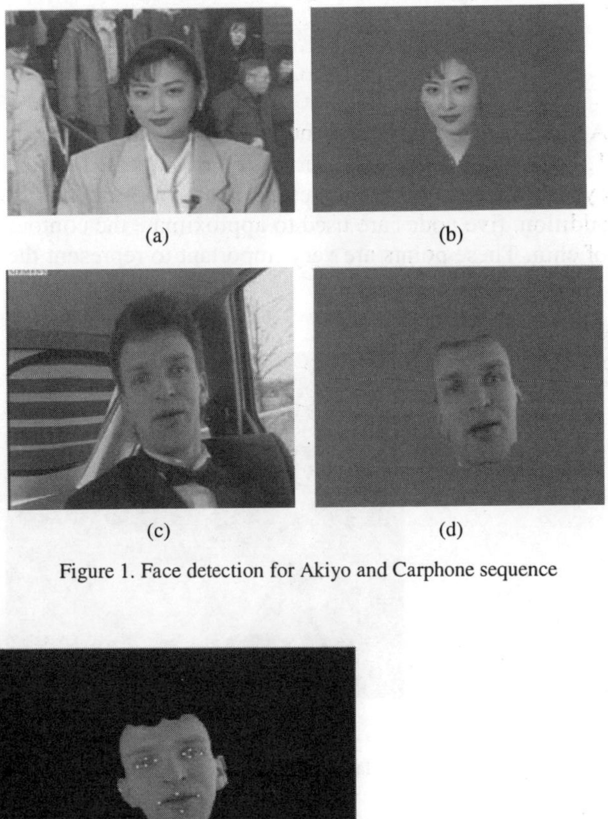

Figure 1. Face detection for Akiyo and Carphone sequence

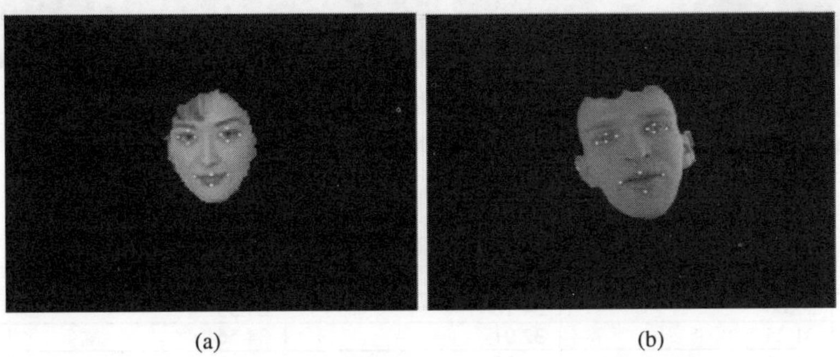

Figure 2. Face feature detection for Akiyo and Carphone sequence

3. Active snake algorithm is used to detect the chin. Fig.2 shows the eyes, mouth and chin detection results of Akiyo and Carphone sequences. It shows that eyes, Mouth and Chin can be detected precisely by using the proposed methods.

3. 2-D Scalable face mode l design

The human face is considered as a special object to be modeled separately in 2-D scalable model-based video coding since the human face undergoes both rigid and non-rigid motion. The nodes should be allocated on the face features in order to reduce the estimation error of movement. In our research, a heuristic scalable face model is constructed, based on the muscle distribution of human faces [7].

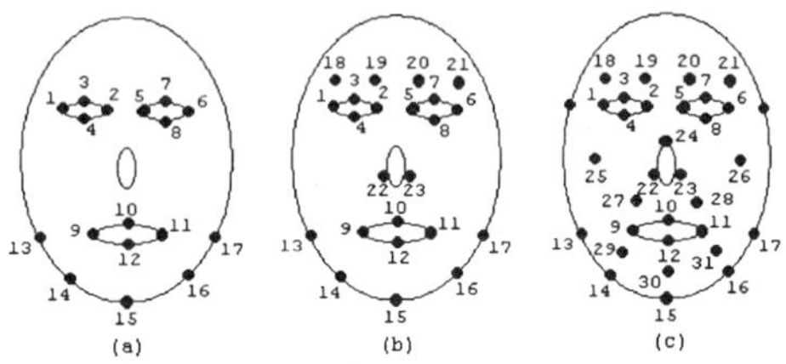

Figure 3. Scalable face model design

A three-level scalable face model is shown in Fig.3.

1. First, eight nodes and four nodes are allocated on the eyes and mouth to represent their movement. In addition, five nodes are used to approximate the contour of chin. These points are very important to represent the movement of the face and are included in the lowest level 1 (from 1 to 17 in Fig.3 (a)).
2. For level 2 shown in Fig.3 (b), six additional points are introduced to represent the movement of eyebrows and nose (from 18 to 23). They are useful for head motion estimation. For node point 22 and 23, if the face size is small, they are merged as one point located at the middle of their positions.
3. For level 3, 8 points are allocated mainly based on the face muscle distribution [7]. The scalable model of level 3 is shown in Fig.3 (c).

This heuristic model is based on the face muscle distribution used to represent the face motion. A more complex model can be designed if more complex face expression needs to be encoded.

4. Experimental results

Some head-shoulder sequences are used to test the performance of the designed scalable face model for representing face motion. For the head-shoulder object, the scalable models of the human face and other parts, such as human body, are designed separately. The scalable face model is designed by using above proposed method. For other parts, the method in [8] is used.

During experiments, four frames (frame 2, 4, 6 and 8) are warped from frame 0 based on the scalable model and motion information. Then, average PSNR values are calculated for four levels. Table 1 listed the PSNR values. Compared with the results in [9] for Akiyo sequence, the proposed method can achieve about 2-5

(a) (b)

Figure 4. Classification of pixels as skin or non-skin (a) Original Image (b) Skin detected Image

Table 1. Average PSNR values (dB) of Carphone and Akiyo sequence for different represent levels

	Average PSNR Value (dB)			
	Level 1	Level 2	Level 3	Level 4
Carphone (CIF)	32.60	34.16	34.58	35.51
Akiyo (QCIF)	31.25	32.91	34.56	35.91
PSNR of Akiyo (QCIF) using method in [9]	28.64	29.27	29.83	30.56

dB improvements. It shows that the designed scalable face models can represent the object motion more precisely than existing published methods.

5. Conclusion

In this paper, face feature detection and a scalable face model design are studied. Some face feature detection methods have been proposed. These methods can achieve precise and reliable eye, mouth and chin detection. Furthermore, a heuristic scalable face model is designed based on face muscular distribution and detected face features. Experimental results show that this scalable model can represent the face motion more precisely than previously published techniques and can be used to achieve scalable model-based video coding.

Reference:

[1]. A.Murat Tekalp, Y.Altunbasak, and G. Bozdagi, 1997,"Two- versus three-dimensional object-based videocompression", **IEEE Trans. CSVT**,7(2),391-397

[2]. Ming-Hsuan Yang, David Kriegman, N. Ahuja, 2002,"Detecting faces in images: a survey", **IEEE Trans. PAMI**,24 (1), 34-58

[3]. K. Sobottka and I. Pitas, 1996, "Face localization and feature extraction based on shape and color information",**Proceedings of Int. Conf. IP (ICIP-96)**, 483-486

[4]. J. Y. Deng and Feipei Lai, 1997, "Region-based template deformation and masking for eye feature extraction and description", **Pattern Recognition,** 30 (3),403-419

[5]. S.M.Smith and J.M.Brady, 1997, "SUSAN-a new approach to low level image processing", **Int. Journal of Computer Vision**, 23(1), 45-78

[6]. Chenyang Xu and Jerry L. Prince, 1997, "Gradient vector flow: a new external force for snakes", **Proceeding of Int. Conf. CVPR'97**, 66-71

[7]. K. Waters, 1987, "A muscle model for animating three-dimensional facial expression", **Computer Graphics,** 21 (4)

[8]. M. Hu, S. Worrall, A. H. Sadka, A. M. Kondoz, 2002, "Model design for scalable 2-Dimensional model-based video coding", **IEE Electronics Letters,** 38 (24), 1513-1515

[9]. P. van Beek, A. M. Tekalp, Ning Zhuang, I. Celasum, Minghui Xia, 1999, "Hierarchical 2-D mesh representation, tracking, and compression for object-based video", **IEEE Trans. on CSVT**, 9 (2), 353-369

FACES DETECTION AND FACIAL FEATURES EXTRACTION IN COLOR GROUP IMAGES

ARCHANA H. SABLE
Department of Computer Engineering
M.G.M's college of Engg, Nanded (M.S) India -431605
Email id: helloarchu27@gmail.com

Guided by
K. C. JONDHALE
Department of Computer Engineering
M.G.M's college of Engg, Nanded (M.S),India-431605
Email id: kcjondhale@rediffmail.com

Human face detection is concerned with finding the location and size of every human face in a given group image. Face detection plays a very important role in human computer interaction field. It represents the first step in a fully automatic face re-cognition, facial features extraction, and expression recognition. There are many techniques used in face detection, each one has its advantages and disadvantages. The face detection system presented in this paper is a hybrid of known algorithms. First stage of the proposed method is applying skin color detection algorithm to specify all skin locations in the image. Second, extract face features like eyes, mouth and nose. At the last, a verification step is applied to ensure that the extracted features are facial features. In experiments on images of group photos having upright frontal faces with any background our system has achieved high detection rates and low false positives.

1. Introduction

In recent years, face recognition has attracted much attention and its research has rapidly expanded by not only engineers but also neuroscientists, since it has many potential applications in computer vision communication and automatic access control system. Especially, face detection is an important part of face recognition as the first step of automatic face recognition. The images used in this project have some degree of uniformity thus the detection algorithm can be simpler: first, the all the faces are vertical and have frontal view; second, they are under almost the same illuminate condition. This project presents a face detection technique mainly based on the color segmentation, image segmentation and template matching methods. Detection rate and the number of false positives are important factors in evaluating face detection systems. Detection rate is the ratio between the number of faces correctly detected by the system and the actual number of faces in the image. Many heuristic and pattern recognition based strategies have been proposed for achieving robust and accurate solution. Among feature-based face detection methods, the ones using skin color as a detection cue, have gained strong popularity. Color allows fast processing and is highly robust to geometric variations of the face pattern. Also, the experience suggests that human skin has a characteristic color, which is easily recognized by humans.

In this paper we discuss pixel-based skin detection methods, which classify each pixel as skin or non-skin individually, independently from its neighbors.

The challenges associated with face detection can be attributed to the following factors:

• Pose. The images of a face vary due to the relative camera-face pose (frontal, 45 degree, profile, upside down), and some facial features such as an eye or the nose may become partially or wholly occluded.

• Presence or absence of structural components. Facial features such as beards, mustaches, and glasses may or may not be present and there is a great deal of variability among these components including shape, color, and size.

• Facial expression. The appearances of faces are directly affected by a person's facial expression.

• Occlusion. Faces may be partially occluded by other objects. In an image with a group of people, some faces may partially occlude other faces.

• Image orientation. Face images directly vary for different rotations about the camera's optical axis.

• Imaging conditions. When the image is formed, factors such as lighting (spectra, source distribution and intensity) and camera characteristics (sensor response, lenses) affect the appearance of a face.

1.1 Face Detection in a Single Image

The techniques for faces detection in a single image were classified into three categories [8].

1. *Knowledge-based methods:* These rule-based methods encode human knowledge of what constitutes a typical face. Usually, the rules capture the relationships between facial features. These methods are designed mainly for face localization.

2. *Feature invariant approaches:* These algorithms aim to find structural features that exist even when the pose, viewpoint, or lighting conditions vary, and then use the these to locate faces. These methods are designed mainly for face localization.

3. *Template matching methods:* Several standard patterns of a face are stored to describe the face as a whole or the facial features separately. The correlations between an input image and the stored patterns are computed for detection. These methods have been used for both face localization and detection.

4. *Appearance-based methods:* In contrast to template matching, the models (or templates) are learned from a set of training images which should capture the representative variability of facial appearance. These learned models are then used for detection.

1.2 Face Detection in Multiple Images

In these techniques faces detection in image sequence depends on detecting the motion of facial features. These techniques use the head and face gesture to detect the face [1], some use the sound and lips motion[3] ,others use hand gesture in an image sequence[4] ,and others use the motion of eyes.

2. Methodology

The methodology that used in this research mainly based on three stages, skin colors detection, facial features extraction, and the last stage is the verification.

2.1 Skin Colors Detection

Human skin color has been used and proven to be an effective feature in many applications from face detection to hand tracking. Although different people have different skin color, several studies have shown that the major difference lies largely between their intensity rather than their chrominance [5]. Several color spaces have been utilized to label pixels as skin including RGB [7], normalized RGB [9], HSV (or HSI) [10], YCrCb [13], YIQ [12], CIE XYZ [14], and CIE LUV [11]. The RGB format is not used; because RGB components are subject to the lighting conditions which causes the face detection may fail when the lighting conditions change. Skin color is one of the most important features in the human face.. The skin detector detects whether certain regions in a color image represent human skin or not. It must define certain decision rules to discriminate between skin and non-skin pixels. To build these rules, a human skin model must be built. Several skin color-modeling methods have been introduced [15], [16-18]. The selection of the color space that will be used in modeling skin color is very important; it is well known that different people have different skin color appearance, but these differences lie mostly in the color intensity not in the color itself. That is why many skin detection methods drop the luminance component of the color space.

Dropping the luminance component achieves two important goals; first the model will be independent of the differences in skin appearance that may arise from the difference in human race, or the difference in the lighting of the image; second the color space dimensions will be reduced so the calculations would be easier. There are lots of color spaces that have been used in early work of skin detection, such as RGB, normalized RGB, YCbCr, HIS and TSL [16]. Although RGB color space is one of the most used color spaces for processing and storing digital images, it is not widely used in skin detection algorithms because the chrominance and luminance components are mixed. Normalized RGB and YCbCr are often used by skin detection techniques. Some work has been done to compare different skin color space performance in skin detection problems [17].

The YCbCr components are used, where In the YcbCr color space, the luminance information is contained in Y component; and, the chrominance information is in Cb and Cr. Many research studies found that the chrominance components of the skin-tone color are independent of the luminance component [18]. Hence, in this implementation, the Cb, Cr components are used to model the distribution of skin colors. The RGB components were converted to the YCbCr components using the following formula [19].

$$\begin{aligned} Y &= 0.299R + 0.587G + 0.114B \\ Cb &= -0.169R - 0.332G + 0.500B \quad (1) \\ Cr &= 0.500R - 0.419G - 0.081B \end{aligned}$$

In the skin color detection process, each pixel was classified as skin or non-skin based on its color components. The detection window for skin color was determined based on the mean and standard deviation of Cb and Cr component, obtained using 164 training faces in 7 input images. The Cb and Cr components of 164 faces are plotted in the color space in Fig.1; their histogram distribution is shown in Fig.

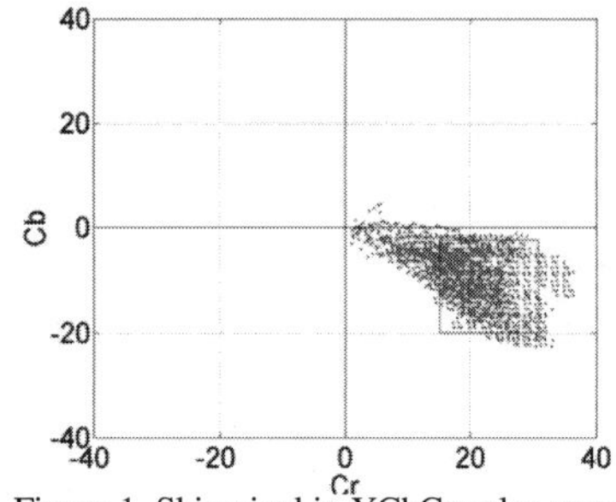

Figure 1. Skin pixel in YCbCr color space.

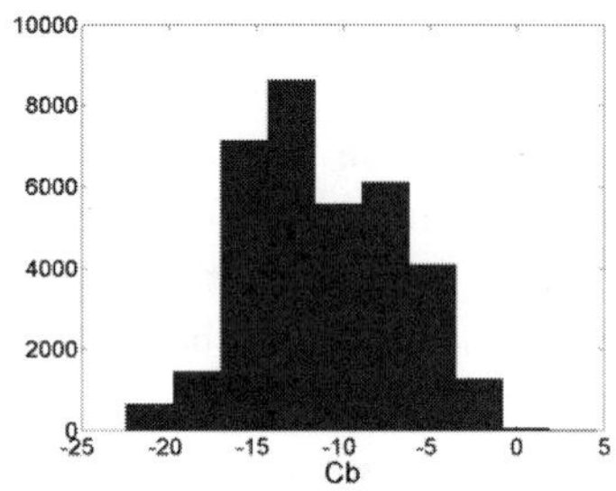

Figure 2 (a). Histogram distribution of Cb.

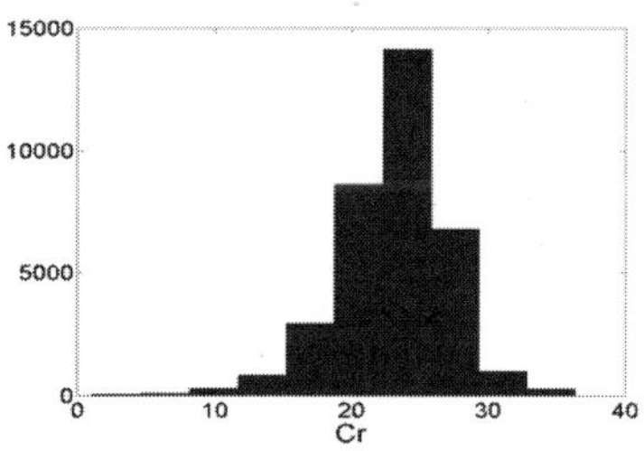

(b). Histogram distribution of Cr.

In our work, we build a skin color model based on explicitly defined skin regions in Cb Cr color space. Cb Cr color space was chosen in our work for many reasons; first, it contains no information about luminance which yields a more general skin color model; also it has only two components which helps to speed up the calculations; also the transformations from RGB color space into Cb Cr color space is done using simple and fast transformations.

To build the model, we collected samples of human skin from different races. For every pixel in the skin samples, the values of Cb and Cr are calculated. After the Cb Cr skin color model is built, it can be used for skin detection. The first step in skin detection is pixel based skin detection, where the skin detector tests every pixel of the input image and computes its Cb and Cr. If Cb and Cr values of the pixels satisfy the inequalities (2), then this pixel is considered skin. The range of values for skin color were according to experimental results of [20].

$$
\begin{aligned}
&137 < Cr < 177 \\
&77 < Cb < 127 \qquad (2) \\
&190 < Cb + 0.6Cr < 215
\end{aligned}
$$

The steps of implemented algorithm are:

Step1: Pixel-Based Skin Detector An image that contains three faces differs in the degree of skin colors and shape of the face is selected to be a good test of the algorithm as shown in Figure 3.

Figure 3. The original image.

Changing the figure 3 to ycbcr color space we see

Figure 4. The original image converted to ycbcr color space.

Applying the color segmentation to the image shown in Figure 3 using Inequalities (2) and the result is shown in Figure 5.

Figure 5. Color segmentation result.

Step2: Image Segmentation

The output of the pixel-based skin detector is a binary image that contains ones in the skin regions and zeros in non-skin regions. The detected skin regions may be discontinuous; this discontinuity may be due to lighting effects that leads to missed skin pixels or due to the presence of non-skin face features like the eyes and brows. In order to make the detected skin regions continuous, the process is to remove white isolated regions, which are smaller in area than a certain threshold that was determined experimentally by applying set of training images. The resulted image is then subjected to erosion stage to leaves the white regions with reasonable regions as illustrated in Fig 6.

Figure 6. The image after elimination of small and narrow regions.

Step 3: Edge detection

Roberts Cross Edge detection algorithm is applied on the grey scale version of the original image. The Roberts Cross Operator performs a simple and quick computation of the 2-D spatial gradient measurement. It thus highlights regions of high spatial gradients that often correspond to edges as shown in Fig 7.

Figure 7. Edges detected by the Roberts cross operator.

The highlighted region is converted into black lines and eroded to connect crossly separated pixel as shown in Fig 8.

Figure 8. Inverted image of edge detected.

The previous images are integrated into a binary image then removing small white regions according to regions determined in training images, we combine two images in Figure 6 and Fig 8 using logic and operation to leave the edges connected to black regions to be as boundaries between faces regions and background. The second result of using and operation is the removing of small details in the segments. The result of this stage is shown in Figure 9. The white regions in Figure 9 are localized and its corresponding regions in Figure 8 are separated into objects or segments. The resulted segments are shown in Figure 10 and each is then processed in the next stage to determine whether it is a face or not.

Figure 9. Integrated binary image.

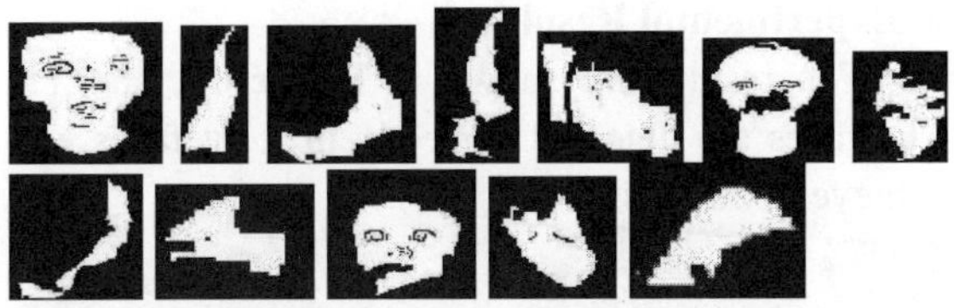

Figure 10. The segments of the image.

Step 4: Optimization

The regions, which have not any details, have been canceled, and keeping the remaining segments which contain details (features) as shown in Fig 11.

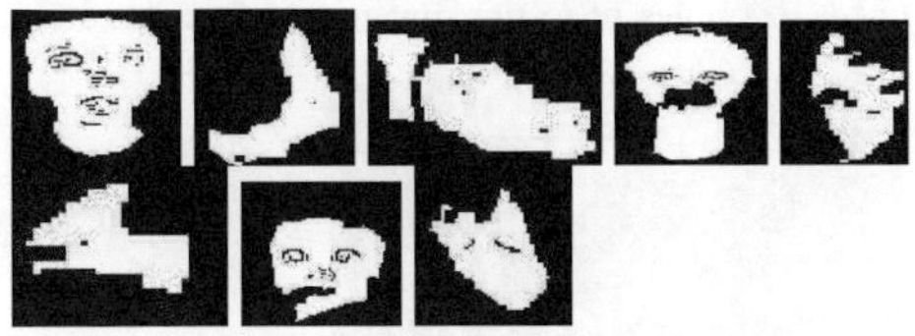

Figure11. The segments after optimization.

2.2 Features Detection

In the proposed method, a skin colour model is first used to localize the face ,in each segment the location of each object and its center (row, column), and half size of each one are computed and located. We search for objects that at the same row These objects may classified as eyes, by calculating the half distance between these two objects and see if there is a another object at this location it may be the nose or the mouth if these features are founded, this will be a face as shown in Fig 12.

Figure 12. The locations of features of faces.

2.3 Verification of eyes, mouth and nose detection

In verification step we try to ensure that features were detected are face features so we make a horizontal and vertical histograms to show the regions, which areblack like eyes, nose, and mouth represent deep curves, as shown in Figure 13.

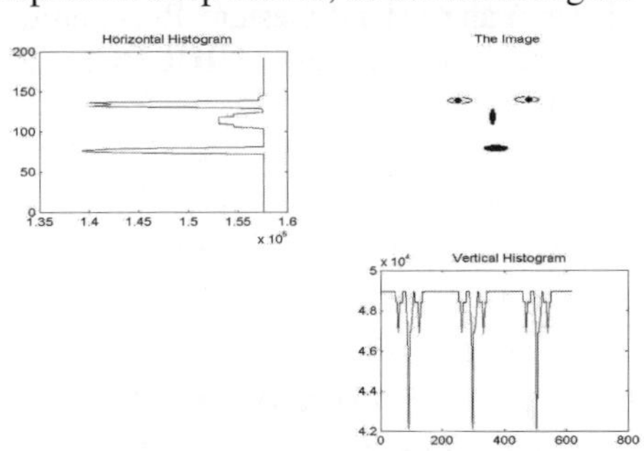

Figure 13. The Horizontal and Vertical Histograms.

Figure 14. The final results.

3. Experimental Results

The results are shown in Figure 14, and 15. The faces are detected correctly in front faces and achieve good results.

a) b)

Figure 15 (a-b). Examples of testing image and face detection results.

Figure 16. The proposed system succeeded in detecting frontal faces, and failed in detecting overlapped faces.

4. Conclusion

In this paper the algorithm used for the detection of faces achieves a high rate of accuracy, because of using many stages for detection, each stage uses different technique, first detect the skin, then detect the features of the face, and at last make a verification step. As shown in the test images in Figure 16, this algorithm succeed in detecting frontal faces, and failed in detecting overlapped faces, this algorithm can not detect it correctly, so the hope for the future, that detect joined faces.

5. References

[1] M. Yang, D. Kriegman, and N. Ahuja, "Detecting Faces in Images: A Survey", **IEEE Transactions on Pattern Analysis and Machine Intelligence** , Vol. 24, no. 1, January 2002.

[3] U. Dieckmann , P. Plankensteiner , T. Wagner 2 "A biometric person identification system using sensor fusion" **Pattern Recognition Letters** 18 (1997) 827–833.

[4] Ming-Hsuan Yang "Hand Gesture Recognition and Face Detection in Images", **UIUCDCS -R-** *2000-2151*, July 2000.

[5]H.P. Graf, T. Chen, E. Petajan, and E. Cosatto, "Locating Faces and Facial Parts," Proc. **First Int'l Workshop Automatic Face and Gesture Recognition**, pp. 41-46, 1995.

[6]M.-H. Yang and N. Ahuja, "Detecting Human Faces in Color Images," **Proc. IEEE Int'l Conf. Image Processing**, vol. 1, pp. 127-130, 1998.

[7]T.S. Jebara and A. Pentland, "Parameterized Structure from Motion for 3D Adaptive Feedback Tracking of Faces," **Proc. IEEE Conf. Computer Vision and Pattern Recognition**, pp. 144-150, 1997.

[8] D. Saxe and R. Foulds, "Toward Robust Skin Identification in Video Images," **Proc. Second Int'l Conf. Automatic Face and Gesture Recognition,** pp. 379-384, 1996.

[9] Crowley and J.M. Bedrune, "Integration and Control of Reactive Visual Processes," **Proc. Third European Conf. Computer Vision**, vol. 2, pp. 47-58, 1994.

[10] Ming-Hsuan Yang, David J. Kriegman, and Narendra Ahuja, "Detecting Faces in Images" **IEEE Tran s. Pattern Analysis And Machine Intelligence** , vol. 24, no. 1, Jan. 2002.

[11] U. Dieckmann , P. Plankensteiner , T. Wagner 2 "A biometric person identification system using sensor fusion" **Pattern Recognition Letters** 18 (1997) 827–833.

[12] Y. Dai and Y. Nakano, "Extraction for Facial Images from Complex Background Using Color Information and SGLD Matrices," **Proc. First Int'l Workshop Automatic Face and Gesture Recognition,** pp. 238-242, 1995.

[13]D. Chai and K.N. Ngan, "Locating Facial Region of a Head-and-Shoulders Color Image," **Proc. Third Int'l Conf. Automatic Face and Gesture Recognition**, pp. 124-129, 1998.

[14]Q. Chen, H. Wu, and M. Yachida, "Face Detection by Fuzzy Matching," **Proc. Fifth IEEE Int'l Conf. Computer Vision**, pp. 591-596, 1995.

[15] L. Mostafa and S. Abdelazeem , "Face Detection Based on Skin Color Using Neural Networks",**GVIP 05 Conference** , 19-21 December 2005, CICC, Cairo, Egypt.

[16] V. Vezhnevets, V. Sazonov, A. Andreeva, "A Survey on Pixel-Based Skin Color Detection Techniques", **In Proceedings Graphicon**-2003, pp. 85- 92, Moscow, Russia, September 2003.

[17] J.C. Terrillon, and S. Akamatsu, Comparative Performance of Different Chrominance Spaces for Color Segmentation and Detection of Human Faces in Complex Scene Images **Proc. Vision Interface**, pp. 180-187, 1999.

[18] J.Yang, W.Lu, andA. Waibel,"Skin Color modeling and Adaptation ", **ACCV**, pp.687-694, 1998.

[19] Inseong Kim, Joon Hyung Shim, and Jinkyu Yang,"face detection", Stanford University.

[20] M.Hu, S.Worrall, A.H.Sadka, A.M.kondoz," A Fast and Efficient Chin Detection Method for 2-D Scalable Face Model Design", **IEEE, VIE, Guildford**- London, UK July 2003.

Session 7

GROUPING OF META KNOWLEDGE BY PROBLEM SOLVING BY CLUSTERING TECHNIQUE

VIJAYALAKSHMI M. N.

Departmen of MCA, R.V. College of Engineering, Mysore Road Bangalore-560059, Karnataka, India

R. VASANTHA

Departmen of ISE, R.V. College of Engineering, Mysore Road Bangalore-560059, Karnataka, India

In an intelligent tutoring system (ITS), the domain expert should present relevant domain knowledge to the tutor so that it will be able to guide the learner during problem solving. However, in several domains, this knowledge is not predetermined and should be captured or learned from expert users as well as from intermediate users. Our hypothesis is that, knowledge discovery (KD) techniques can help to build this domain intelligence in ITS. This paper proposes a framework to capture problem-solving knowledge using a clustering approach of data and knowledge discovery based on a combination of clusters. The framework has been implemented and is used to discover new meta knowledge from the clusters obtained which will serve as a problem space guiding the learners in problem-solving situations. To achieve this two clustering algorithms COBWEB and CHAMELEON are applied. Results show that CHAMELEON yields better clusters than COBWEB.

1. Introduction

In an intelligent tutoring system (ITS), the domain expert should present relevant domain knowledge to the tutor so that it will be able to guide the learner during problem solving. However, in several domains, this knowledge is not fixed and should be captured or learned from expert users as well as from intermediate users. Our hypothesis is that, knowledge discovery (KD) techniques can help to build this domain intelligence in ITS.[4] describe student group interaction data mining that seeks to identify significant sequences of activity. Their objective is to set up communication sequences which indicate problems and successes so that tutors can help students recognize problematic situations in the early stages of the learning sessions. Their aim is not related to learning procedures nor does it seek to find links between significant interaction sequences or patterns. One of the main goals of an intelligent tutoring system is to actively provide relevant feedback to the student in problem-solving situations [9] This paper proposes an approach to support new domain knowledge discovery in field where it is difficult to set up a clear problem space or task models. In such a area, we need to capture new procedures (correct or incorrect), new problem spaces and new problem-solving strategies from users' actions. Cognitive task analysis that aims at producing effective problem space or task model (to support model and knowledge tracing, coaching, errors detection and plan recognition) is a very time consuming process [8]. The approach presented in this paper is based on a clustering technique. We show how the proposed approach is used to discover new knowledge in a given
domain, which then extends domain knowledge and serves as a problem space allowing the intelligent tutor to track learners' actions and give relevant hints when needed. Fig 1 gives the overall architecture of the knowledge discovery and ITS.

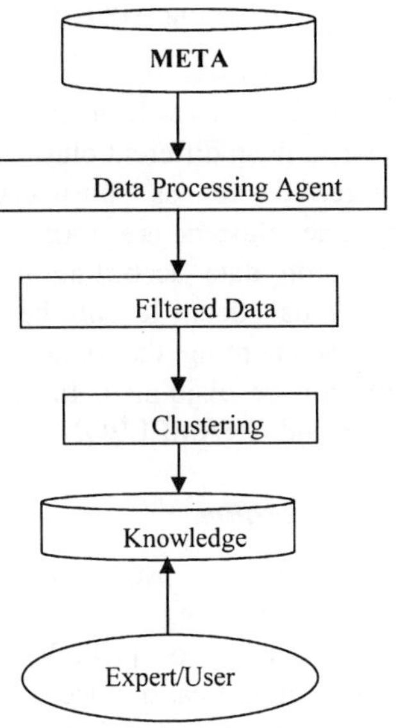

Fig.1 Overall Architecture of Knowledge Discovery

The paper is organized as follows. First, we will present the context of this research work by stating the need of KD to enhance tutoring agent knowledge. Then an overview of clustering algorithms used. Finally results and conclusions

2. Need For KD

Educational data mining is becoming a very important area in the Artificial Intelligence
in Education community [1]. Several techniques are used to extract relevant data, information or knowledge mainly from databases and log files of learning sessions.[11] Very little research investigated ITS automatic procedural knowledge learning [5, 6, 7]. Yet, such a capability could facilitate the development of problem spaces (task model procedural knowledge, etc.) and reduce the need for domain experts. For example, [6] attempted to induce simple production rules using a single example and the analogy mechanism. [7] looks up a set of marked examples, trying to generalize them and generate production rules. Some works focuses on learner or group classification, clustering [2,3]. [3] uses k-means algorithm to show the value of a data-based approach for recognizing learners as an alternative to knowledge-based approaches that tend to be complex and time-consuming even for domain experts. Using k-means is time consuming, and does not give superior groups of knowledge. So this paper an attempt is made to reduce the time by making use of two different clustering algorithms COBWEB and CHAMELEON.

3. Overview of Clustering Algorithms

Clustering is the process of grouping objects into clusters such that the objects from the same cluster are similar and objects from different clusters are dissimilar. So it is referred to as unsupervised learning segmentation. The clusters are formed y finding the similarities between data according to characteristics found in the actual data. It can be thought of as partitioning or segmenting the data into groups that might or might not be disjointed. In this paper we are using COBWEB and CHAMELEON.

3.1. *COBWEB Algorithm*

The COBWEB algorithm constructs a classification tree incrementally by inserting the objects into the classification tree one by one[10]. When inserting an object into the classification tree, the COBWEB algorithm traverses the tree top-down starting from the root node. In classification tree it characterizes each cluster with a probabilistic description. The algorithm operates based on the category utility function (CU) that measures clustering quality. If we partition a set of objects into m clusters then the CU of this particular partition is

$$\mathrm{CU} = \frac{\sum_{k=1}^{m} P(C_k)\left[\sum_i \sum_j P(A_i = V_{ij} / C_K)^2 - \sum_i \sum_j P(A_i = V_{ij})^2\right]}{m}$$

Here Ai stands for ith attribute and Vij is the jth attribute value of Attribute Ai.Ck is the kth cluster and m is the number of clusters. P(Ck) is the fraction of the data set in cluster Ck

3.2. *CHAMELEON Algorithm*

This is a graph partition based algorithm [10]. It finds the clusters in the dataset by using two phase algorithm. During the first phase, it uses a graph partitioning algorithm to cluster the data items into a large number of relatively small sub-clusters. During the second phase, it uses an agglomerative hierarchical clustering algorithm to find the genuine clusters by repeatedly combining together these sub-clusters. It determines the pair of most similar sub-clusters by taking into account both the inter-connectivity as well as the closeness of the clusters. CHAMELEON determines the similarity between each pair of clusters Ci and Cj by looking both at their relative inter-connectivity RI (Ci,Cj) their relative closeness RC(Ci,Cj). This algorithm selects to merge the pair of clusters for which both RI(Ci, Cj) and RC(Ci, Cj) are high i.e., it selects to merge clusters that are well inter-connected as well as close together with respect to the internal inter-connectivity and closeness of the clusters.

4. Results and Conclusions

The two clustering algorithms are applied on the filtered data and the results are analyzed. The table below gives the performance of the COBWEB and CHAMELEON algorithms

Table 1: Performance Evaluation of Clustering Algorithm

Performance Evaluation	Approach	Methodology	Result
COBWEB	Incrementally	Category Utility function	Classification Tree
CHAMELEON	Graph-partition	Relative inter connectivity & relative closeness	Dendogram

From the table it is clear that CHMELEON give better clusters compared to COBWEB, since its uses the graph partition algorithm, which operates on sparse graph in which nodes represent data items, and weighted edges represent similarities among the data items. This sparse graph representation of the dataset allows CHAMELEON to scale to large datasets and to operate successfully on data sets that are available only in similarity space and not in metric space.

5. Conclusions

In this paper clustering technique is been applied using two clustering algorithm COBWEB and CHAMELON and their performance is evaluated. Analysis shows that CHAMELEON yields better clusters when compared to COBWEB which can serve as a problem space allowing the learners to give hint to their problem solving.

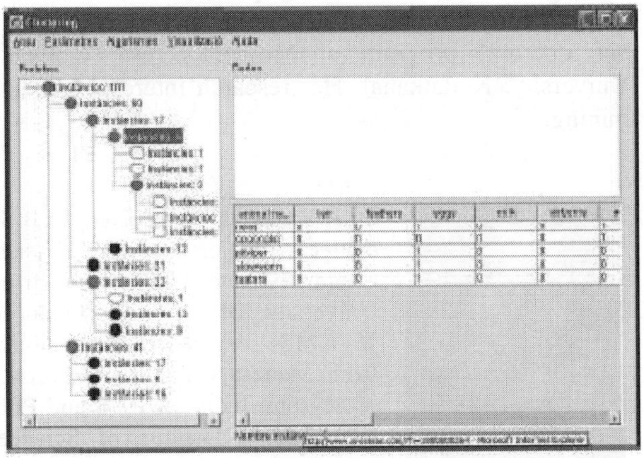

Fig 1. COBWEB results

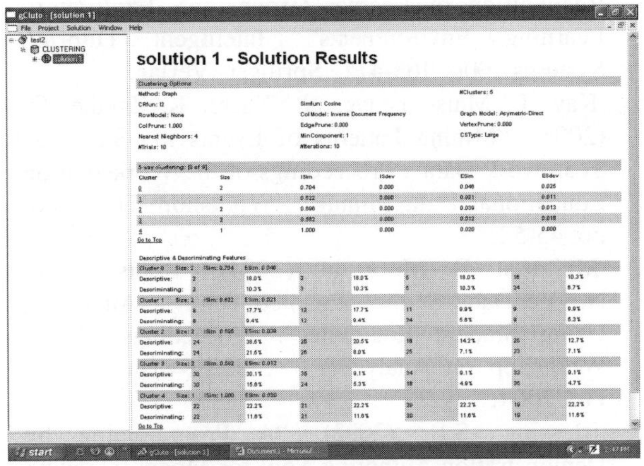

Fig 3. CHAMELEON results

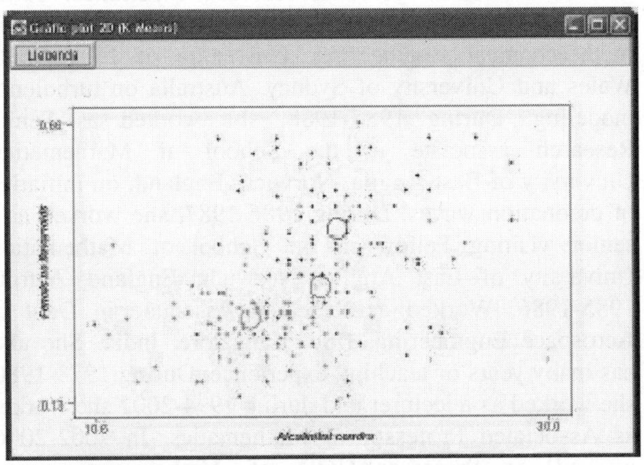

Fig 2. Screen Shot showing the COBWEB Clustering

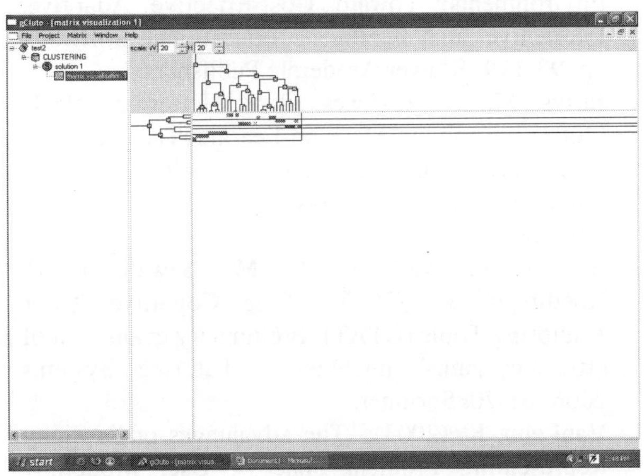

Fig 4. Screen Shot showing the CHAMELEON Clustering

References

1. Heiner, C., Baker, R. and Yacef, K. (2006). Proceedings of the Educational Data Mining Workshop. ITS'2006.
2. Graf, S. and Bekele, R. (2006). "Forming Heterogeneous Groups for Intelligent
3. Collaborative Learning Systems with Ant Colony Optimization". Intelligent Tutoring Systems 2006: 217-226. Springer-Verlag.
4. Amershi, S. and Conati, C. (2006). "Automatic Recognition of Learner Groups in Exploratory Learning Environments". Intelligent Tutoring Systems 2006: 463-472. Springer- Verlag.
5. Kay, J., Maisonneuve, N., Yacef, K, Zaïane, O. (2006). "Mining Patterns of Events in Students' Teamwork Data". Proceedings of the Workshop on Educational Data Mining Workshop. ITS'2006, pp. 45-52.
6. McLaren, B. M. et al. (2004). "Bootstrapping Novice Data: Semi-Automated Tutor Authoring Using Student Log Files". Proceedings of the Workshop on Analyzing Student- Tutor Logs. ITS'2004.
7. Blessing, S.B. (2003). "A Programming by Demonstration Authoring Tool for Model- Tracing Tutors". In, Authoring Tools for Advanced Technology Learning
8. Environments: Toward Cost-Effective Adaptive, Interactive and Intelligent Educational Software, pp. 93-119. Kluwer Academic Publishers
9. Jarivs, M., Nuzzo-Jones, G. & Heffernan. N. T. (2004). "Applying Machine LearningTechniques to Rule Generation in Intelligent Tutoring Systems". Intelligent Tutoring Systems 2006: 541-553. Springer.
10. Aleven, V., McLaren, B. M., Sewall, J., & Koedinger, K. (2006). "The Cognitive Tutor Authoring Tools (CTAT): Preliminary evaluation of efficiency gains". Intelligent Tutoring Systems 2006: 61-70. Springer.
11. VanLehn, K. (2003). "The advantages of Explicity Representing Problem Spaces". User Modeling, Springer Verlag LNAI 2702:3.
12. "Insight into Data Mining theory and Practice " K.P. Soman, Shyam Diwakar, V.Ajay Prentice-Hall India 2006
13. Roger Nkambou,Engelbert Mephu Nguifo,Olivier Couturier,and Philippe Fournier-Viger (2008) "Problem Solving Knowledge Mining from users Actions in an
14. Intelligent Tutoring System"9th International Conference ,Montreal Canada Springer

Vijayalakshmi.M.N was born on June 11, Karnataka, India. She graduated the BSc degree in Electronics at G. S. S. College Belgaum, India in the year 1994. She gained her MCA degree in the year 1998 at Bangalore University and has obtained her Master of Philosophy degree from BharathiDasan University. She is a life member of ISTE. She has written many papers at the national and international conferences and journals. She is pursuing her doctoral program at Mother Teresa Women's University, Kodaikanal. Her research interests are data mining.

Dr.R.Vasantha received B.Sc degree, majored in Physics, Chemistry, and Mathematics from University of Mysore, India in 1976,MSc degree in Mathematics from Manasa Gangotri, University of Mysore, India, in 1978 and PhD from Indian Institute of Science, Bangalore in 1985. Currently she is a professor in the Department of Information Science and Engineering,R.V.College of Engineering, Bangalore. She got more than 20 years of research experience. 1988-1991,she Worked as research Associate in the Department of Mechanical Engineering, University of New South Wales and University of Sydney, Australia on turbulence modeling. During 1987-1988, she worked as Senior Research associate in the School of Mathematics, University of East Anglia, Norwich, England, on initiation of detonation waves. During 1986-1987, she worked as a senior visiting Fellow in the School of Mathematics, University of East Anglia, Norwich, England .During 1985-1986, Worked as Research Associate in Dept of Aerospace Engineering, IISc, Bangalore, India. She also has many years of teaching experience. During 1978-1980, she worked as a lecturer and during 1994-2002 she worked as Associated Professor of Mathematics. In 2002-2006, worked as Professor&HOD of Mathematics in an Engineering College in India. Her research interests are in the field of computational fluid mechanics. She is the author and co-author of several publications appearing in international journals and conference proceedings in the field of applied mathematics and computational fluid mechanics.

Dr.Vasantha is a Gold medal contender for PhD dissertation .She has won scholarship from Bsc till end of PhD

HANDOFF LATENCY AND PACKET DROPPING PROBABILITY IN LAYERED MIPV6: A MATHEMATICAL ANALYSIS

NITUL DUTTA
Computer Science & Engineering Department,
Sikkim Manipal Institute of Technology, Sikkim, India

ITI SAHA MISRA
Electronics & Telecommunication Engineering Department,
Jadavpur University, West Bengal, India

In this work a mathematical analysis for handoff latency and packet dropping probability at different anchor agents in a general n-layered architecture has been made. Through the analysis we want to find an optimal level of hierarchy with respect to handoff latency and packet dropping probability. We assume that each of the anchor agents in the network maintains an M/M/1/K queue. Analysis shows that handoff latency decreases by a ratio of 25-35% with the addition of a new layer up to layer three, around 15% decrease on adding fourth layer and a negligible decrease of 2-3% beyond layer four. Also, packet-dropping probability is directly proportional to the offered load, which in turn is dependent on the number of mobile nodes. As the number of layer increases, the coverage area of the anchor agent as well as the mobile nodes under its coverage increases. A 2-5% of the packets are dropped up to layer four and beyond which it exceeds 5%. A 5% handoff dropping is not considered to be acceptable. So, taking both, handoff latency and packet dropping probability in anchor agent, a three-layered architecture may be considered optimal.

1. Introduction

Quality of services (QoS) in mobile environment is characterized by handoff latency and packet dropping probability during conversation. An agent provides care-of-address (CoA) to visitor mobile node (MN) and informed to its home network through binding registration (BR) process through exchange of Binding Update (BU) and Binding Acknowledgement (BACK) messages. While being in the foreign network, MN may change its current CoA. Then MN needs to update its new CoA to home network. This process is called binding update process and involves BU/BACK exchange. The time taken to complete the binding update process is called handoff latency. During the period of handoff all packets destined to the MN are dropped. Higher the handoff latency, more the number of packets loss during handoff. Again, when users are highly mobile and large number of ongoing sessions is associated, a sufficiently large number of BU/BACK messages as well as data packets are transmitted. In such conditions, either BU or BACK messages or data packets may be dropped at the anchor agent. Dropping of such handoff related message increases handoff latency or may disconnect the on-going communication. Dropping of data packets may lead to unacceptable quality of services to end-users. User is more sensitive to disruption of ongoing communication rather than blocking it during the stage of connection establishment. To provide an acceptable QoS, network architecture must support as minimum handoff latency and packet dropping probability, as possible. There are architectures with one or more hierarchies proposed to minimize handoff latencies. In this paper, we have analyzed the handoff latency and packet dropping probability at anchor agents in a general *n*-layered IPv6 based network. Through mathematical evaluation, we have tried to find out the optimal layers of hierarchy in terms of handoff latency and handoff dropping probability at different anchor agents. We assume,

- Anchor agents are arranged as tree and M/M/1/K queue at each of the anchor agents.
- Packet arrival process at any anchor agent obeys Poison's distribution.

The contribution of this paper may be stated as

- Analysis of handoff latency for a general *n*-layered architecture for optimal hierarchy under various speed of MN.
- Analysis of packet dropping probability at various anchor agents to find the optimal level of hierarchy with acceptable QoS under different packet arrival rate and MN speed.

A survey of related work in hierarchical mobile IP based network is in section 2. Section 3 presents our motivation towards this work. A brief description of proposed multilevel HMIPv6 architecture [1] is found in section 4. Section 5 explains the mathematical background in support of the analysis made in this paper. Performance analysis of our model is done in section 6. Finally, section 7 concludes the paper.

2. Related Work

The first protocol for mobility management in IP based network is Mobile IPv4 [2]. MIPv4 suffers from lack of route optimization as well as shortage of address space. MIPv6 [3, 4] is the enhancement of mobility management in IPv6, and resolves the problem of MIPv4. In MIPv6 the care of address (CoA) assigned to a MN in its visited network is reported to the HA as well as to the Correspondent Node (CN). But, MIPv6 overwhelm both the local and backbone network when MN moves very fast and also suffers long handoff delay and packet loss before the end-to-end path establishment in the new AR [3]. Hierarchical Mobile IPv6 (HMIPv6) [4] divides the entire network into two parts known as backbone and local domain. A Mobility Anchor Point (MAP) at the boundary of the local domain in HMIPv6 minimizes the signaling cost over the backbone network by making MN's mobility transparent to the HA and CNs [4]. But HMIPv6 does not perform well for globally moving MNs.

To provide higher degree of scalability, and handle both slow and fast moving MNs efficiently, there is always a tendency to organize a group of anchor agents in the local domain by placing them in different levels either as a pyramid [5] or as a tree [6]. Although hierarchical arrangement of anchor agents minimize the signaling overhead in one hand but increases the tunneling cost and cost of binding refresh on the other. In section 3, we are briefly discussing few of them and their cons, which are the motivation of the work, presented in this paper.

3. Motivation

Two different proposals made by [3] and [7] use the concept of M/M/1/K queue and handoff dropping probability at anchor agents in layered architecture. The paper [3] has considered the existence of an M/M/1/K queue at the anchor agent. The authors also analyzed the network cost and bandwidth consumption of delivering management messages and data payload in both inside and outside the hierarchical domain. They have proposed a mathematical model of HMIPv6 with the consideration of queuing model in the anchor agent and built an intelligent system called Intelligent Mobility Management Scheme (IMMS), which allows an MN to select a suitable mobility management mechanism from mobile IPv6 and HMIPv6 according to its working parameters. The work of [7] examines the probability of handoff blocking and call dropping in a cellular network based on mathematical modeling. The work of [10] discusses the blocking probability at MAP in HMIPv6. They have compared the performance of Robust Hierarchical-MIPv6 (RH-MIPv6) and HMIPv6 taking the probability of MAP unavailability as one of the factors. They also assume an M/M/C/C queue at the MAP. These works [3, 7, 10] are about single layer architecture and analyzes signaling overhead, tunneling cost, or handoff latency. Despite its significant importance, packet-dropping probability has not been discussed in these papers. These unaddressed issues for mobile IP based network influenced us to write this paper with the intention to investigate and analyze packet-dropping probability at each of the anchor agent in n-layer architecture, along with the handoff latency. This work is based on the mathematical model [1] for general n-layered MIPv6 architecture for wireless IP-based network. Mathematical analysis shows that the packet dropping probability is directly proportional to the offered load in the anchor agent which is dependent on number of mobile nodes which increases as we increase the number of layers. Again, although handoff latency decreases with the increase of layers, we cannot keep on increasing the number of layers as it increases the packet dropping probability at different anchor agents. Keeping in mind these facts, we tried to establish an optimum level of hierarchy through mathematical analysis, which provides optimum values for both handoff latency and packet dropping probability.

4. Proposed Architecture

In the proposed architecture [1] (Figure1), backbone is formed by interconnection of top-level gateways of Internet. A local domain is the region covering all the routers under a single top-level gateway. Mobile Anchor Agents, also called mobile anchor points (MAPs), are organized hierarchically. Lowest layer of MAPs are called level one MAP or L1-MAP; next higher layer is called L2-MAP, and so on. The top layer consists of a single MAP (Global MAP or GMAP) and is located in the border of the local domain. Each L1-MAP covers one or more Access Routers (ARs) that serves one or group of mobile nodes (MN). The region covered by an AR is called a cell. Every MN in receives incoming packets via AR. The coverage of the top-level gateway within which an MN registers permanently is called MN's home domain. When an MN visits a network other than its home domain the visited domain is called foreign domain or foreign network. During the visit to a foreign network the visitor MN has to resister with an AR near to it, that provides a Link Care of Address (LCoA) to the visitor MN and also supplies a group of Care of Addresses (CoA) depending upon the level of hierarchies in the architecture. Every time it changes its AR it has to acquire a new LCoA and needs to perform binding update by exchanging BU/BACK between MN and L1-MAP. If the new AR of the visitor MN is not under the same L1-MAP then BU/BACK exchange takes place with higher-level MAPs. At the moment the visitor MN crosses the L-N MAP (or GMAP), the HA of the visitor MN and all the CNs that the visitor MN communicates with during its stay in the foreign domain, need to be updated.

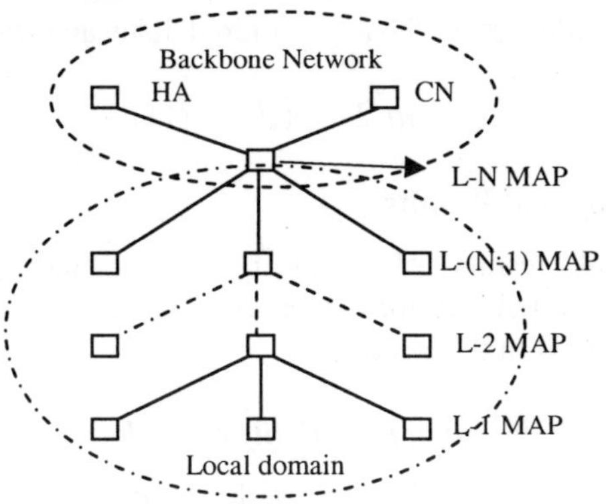

Figure 1. Proposed Network Architecture

5. Mathematical Modeling

Figure 2 shows the packet transmission cost from CN to MN visiting in a foreign network [3]. When a datagram is received by a HA for the MN currently visiting a foreign network, it sends the data packet to the concerned GMAP and also inform the CN about the MN's new location. Then onwards the new datagram for MN is sent directly to GMAP from the CN. Every packet received by the GMAP is tunneled and sent to next lower level MAP, ultimately L1-MAP tunnels it to AR and AR delivers to MN. Any message to CN is sent independently via AR and need no tunneling.

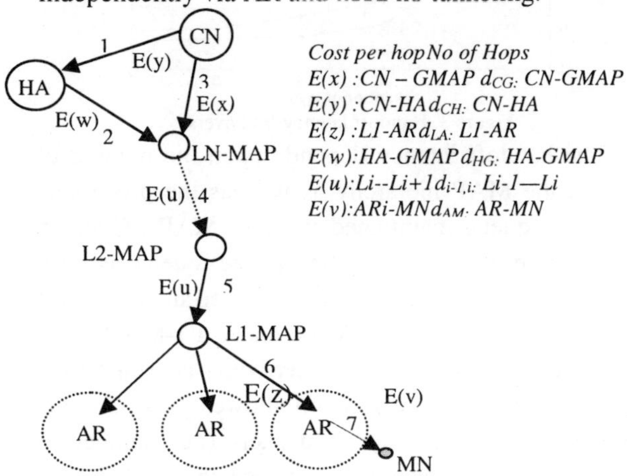

Figure 2. Data Transmission form CN to MN with unit cost

5.1. *Handoff Latency*

Handoff latency is defined as the time taken to complete the location update process, right from the initiation of update process in the old AR to the reception of the first packet in the new AR. The BU/BACK messages to complete the binding update process traverses through various anchor agents. We assume that a queue of type M/M/1/K is maintained at each of the anchor agent in the architecture and the packet arrival rate λ obey Poisson's distribution. Taking these assumptions into consideration, the handoff latency can be characterized by three different time instances. First, the Router Advertisement (RA) processing time t_{p_ra} taken by the visitor MN to construct the LCoA and other CoAs; second, BU/BACK packets' transmission time, t_p between the MN and the respective anchor agent; third, the queuing time, t_q at anchor agent. The visitor MN uses stateless auto configuration [8] to construct LCoA from the RA messages. The t_p is fixed (constant) and depends upon the distance between the MN and the respective anchor agent, which in turn depends upon the levels of anchor agent update required. The third quantity, t_q depends upon the length of the queue at the anchor agent. First let us calculate the queuing delay [3]. Let ρ is the density of the queue, i.e. number of already accepted packets; K is the maximum (and finite) number of packets that could be resided in the queue and t_s is the packet service time, then

$$\rho = \frac{\lambda}{t_s} \tag{1}$$

The probability p_j, for which the queue may have j number of packets, is given by,

$$p_j = \frac{(1-\rho)\rho^j}{1-\rho^{K+1}} = \frac{1}{\sum_{i=0}^{K} \rho^{i-j}} \ldots . j = 0,1, \ldots . K$$

Based on this probability, the length of the queue L at any moment could be calculated as

$$L = \sum_{j=0}^{K} j p_j \tag{2}$$

If L equals to the capacity of the queue then the packet will be dropped, otherwise accepted. The probability of a packet being accepted by the queue η is given by,

$$\eta = 1 - p_K \tag{3}$$

The queuing time t_q, may be now defined according to Little's formula as,

$$t_q = L / \eta \tag{4}$$

Term t_{qi} denotes the queuing time at i^{th} layer anchor agent in the rest of the paper. The cost of propagation of the *BU/BACK* messages from MN to i^{th} layer agent is calculated as

$$t_p = 2.s.t_u.d^i_{MN} \quad (5)$$

where, s is the size of *BU/BACK* packets, t_u is the transmission cost per byte per unit distance, d^i_{MN} is the distance between MN and i^{th} layer anchor agent (figure 2). Hence, the total handoff latency is calculated as,

$$T_l = \sum_{i=1}^{N} 2.s.t_u \{ d^{GMAP}_{MN} + \left\lceil \frac{i}{N} \right\rceil .d^{HA-CN}_{MN} \} + t_{qi} + t_{p\_ra} \quad (6)$$

where,

$$d^{GMAP}_{MN} = E(v).d^{AR}_{MN} + E(z).d^{L1}_{AR} + E(u).d^{Li+1}_{Li}$$

and

$$d^{HA-CN}_{MN} = d^{GMAP}_{MN} + E(w).d^{GMAP}_{HA} + E(x).d^{GMAP}_{CN}$$

When $i=N$, the *BU/BACK* messages are communicated between MN and the HA, otherwise they are not. So, the term $\left\lceil \frac{i}{N} \right\rceil$ contributes to the total handoff only in that condition.

5.2. *Packet dropping probability at anchor agent*

Processing capability, maximum allowed queue length, and available outgoing lines (called channels), restrict anchor agent to allow all the packets to pass through. So, few of the incoming packets destined to various MNs is blocked or dropped at each of the anchor agent. We assume that the average packet arrival rate at an anchor agent per MN is λ and T unit time is required to transmit the complete packet. If there are m number of MNs under the coverage of L1-MAP, then the offered load at L1-MAP is given by,

$$a = m.\lambda.T \quad (7)$$

A packet is queued when all the outgoing routes (channels) are busy and dropped if queue is full. The steady state probability *P(i)* at the M/M/1/K queue of the anchor agent of all the channels are same[9] for all i=0, 1, ····, S, which is given as

$$P(i) = \frac{a^i}{i!} P(0) \quad (8)$$

where, a is the offered load and

$$P(0) = \left[\sum_{i=0}^{s} \frac{a^i}{i!} \right]^{-1} \quad (9)$$

packet dropping probability is calculated as

$$P(S) = \frac{a^S / S!}{\sum_{i=0}^{S} a^i / i!} \quad (10)$$

The packet dropping probability is entirely dependent on the offered load and the queuing capacity at the anchor agent. Also, at each of the anchor agent the offered load is determined by the amount of mobile nodes under its coverage. Alternately, the offered load and hence the packet dropping probability at each of the anchor agent is determined by the number of MNs under it. Equation (10) is the packet dropping probability at L1-MAP. For *n-th* layer anchor agent, value of offered load will be calculated in terms of MNs under L1-MAP and the value of n. That is, offered load at *n-th* layer anchor agent is

$$a_n = m.2^{n-1}.\lambda.T \quad (11)$$

6. Analytical Results

Analytical results of handoff latency and packet dropping probability for a general n-layered architecture are presented in this section.

6.1. *Packet dropping probability at anchor agent*

With a single anchor agent at the border of the local domain the handoff latency is around *300ms* (Figure 3). As layer increases the handoff latency decreases. Latency sharply decreases up to layer four with average deduction of around *80-100ms* and after that it decreases very slowly. Only *10-20ms* deduction in latency is found for layer five and six. The data plotted in the graph is for t_s=*10* and *15 ms* and speed of MN is *10m/s*.

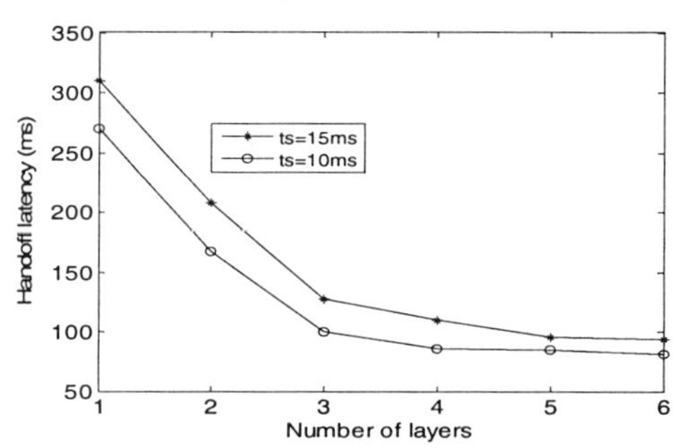

Figure 3. Handoff latency Vs Layers

The handoff latency depends upon the number of layers in the MAP hierarchy as well as the processing time at the queue maintained in these MAPs. Queuing delay or the processing time at the queue is also influenced by the number of lower level anchor agents and hence the number of MNs under L1-MAP. In a queue, the probability of a packet being accepted by a queue is dependent on maximum allowed packets in the queue K and the density of packets (i.e. number of already accepted packets). To reduce the packet loss, density ρ must be kept minimum and the queue capacity K large [3]. If we consider K as constant, increasing the processing ability of the MAP could minimize ρ. The value $t_s=10ms$ and $15ms$ are assumed as processing time of a packet [11, 12] in the observation

6.2. *Packet dropping probability*

In Figure 5, we have plotted the data for average packet arrival rate *15, 25* and *35* per *MN* and the number of MNs under L1-MAP is considered as *50 (i.e. m=50)*. Since anchor agents are organized as tree, there are $2^{n-1}.m$ number of mobile nodes under the coverage of *n-th* layer anchor agent. The graph shows that packet dropping probability remains within *2%* up to layer two, *2-3%* up to layer four and more than *5%* beyond layer four when packet arrival rate is *15*. For average packet arrival rate *25*, packet dropping probability exceeds 5% at layer four and above. For packet arrival rate *35*, 5% of packet dropping probability exceeds at layer three and above. So, from packet dropping probability point of view, three-to-four levels of hierarchy may be considered suitable when packet arrival rate per MN is less than *35* and MNs per L1-MAP is around *50*. But considering both handoff latency and dropping probability three levels of hierarchy in the architecture may be considered optimal.

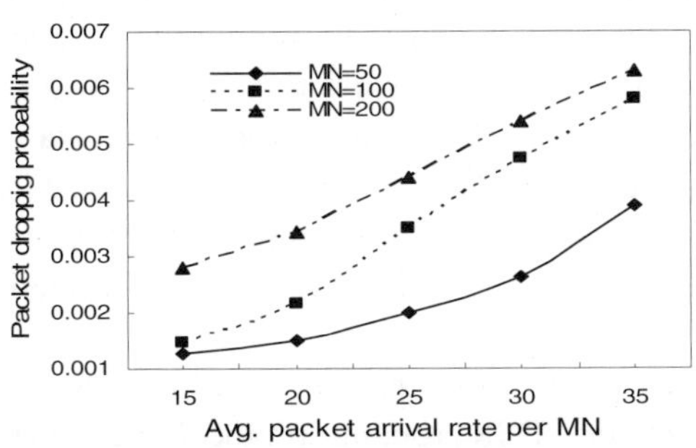

Figure 4. Packet dropping probability Vs packet arrival rate

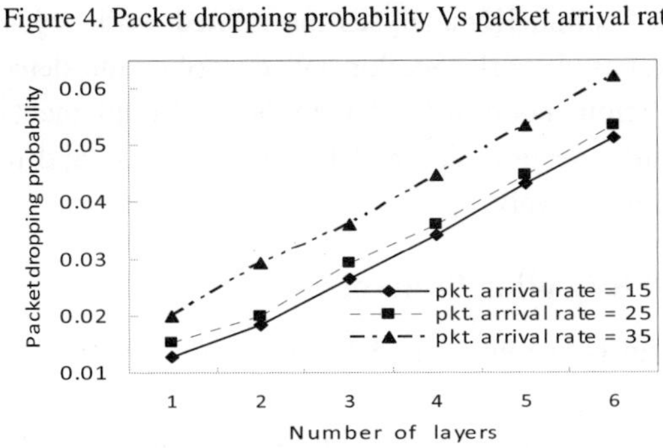

Figure 5. Packet dropping probability Vs layers

7. Conclusion

In this paper handoff latency and packet dropping probability at different anchor agents for *n*-layered MIPv6 based architecture is being analyzed mathematically. We test the model under different traffic arrival pattern and MN density. Analysis shows that handoff latency decreases by a ratio of *25-35%* in addition of a new layer up to three layers, around *15%* decrease on adding fourth layer and a negligible decrease of *2-3%* beyond layer four. A level of three to four in the hierarchy is good in terms of packet dropping probability considering above *5%* packet drop is unacceptable [10]. A three-layered architecture gives optimal handoff delay. So, a three-layered architecture may be adopted for next generation IPv6 based network. Low handoff latency implies a better QoS to the end users. Also, in a situation where users are more sensitive to the disruption in ongoing communication, this model provides better quality of service as only *2-5%* packets are dropped.

Table 1. Parameter used for numerical analysis

<table>
<tr><td>E(z)</td><td>E(u)</td><td>E(v)</td><td>E(w)</td><td>E(x)</td><td>E(y)</td><td>K</td><td>T</td></tr>
<tr><td>1</td><td>1</td><td>1</td><td>1</td><td>1</td><td>1</td><td>20</td><td>10</td></tr>
<tr><td colspan="2">d_{HA}^{GMAP}</td><td colspan="2">d_{CN}^{GMAP}</td><td colspan="2">d_{Li}^{Li+1}</td><td colspan="2">d_{AR}^{L1}</td></tr>
<tr><td colspan="2">6</td><td colspan="2">4</td><td colspan="2">3</td><td colspan="2">2</td></tr>
</table>

References

1. N.Dutta, I.S.Misra, "Mathematical Modeling of Hierarchical Mobile IPv6 Based Network Architecture in Search of Optimal Performance", *IEEE CS 15th International Conference on ADCOM*, 2007 pp. 599-601.
2. C. Perkins, "IP mobility support", *IETF RFC 2002*.
3. PENG Xue-hai, et al "Modeling in Hierarchical Mobile IPv6 and Intelligent Mobility Management Scheme", *Proc. of 14th IEEE 2003 Int. Symposium on Personal, Indoor and Mobile Radio Communication*, pp. 2823-2827.
4. H. Soliman et al. "Hierarchical mobile IPv6 mobility management (HMIPv6)". *Internet draft, 4(1)*, 2003.
5. J. Xie et. al., "A Distributed Dynamic Regional Location Management Scheme for Mobile IP," *IEEE Trans. Mobile Computing*, July 2002, Vol. 1, No. 3, pp.1069-1079.
6. Iti S Misra et.al "An Approach for Optimal Hierarchical Mobility, Management Network Architecture", *IEEE VTC-2006-Spring*, Vol. 1, pp. 481- 485.
7. Y. Fang. "Modeling and Performance Analysis for Wireless Mobile Networks: a New Analytical Approach", *IEEE Trans. on Networking*, October 2005.
8. S. Thomson, T. Narten, T. Jinmei, "IPv6 Stateless Address Autoconfiguration," *IETF RFC 4862*, September 2007.
9. Book: System simulation, Geofrey Gordon, *2nd Edition, PHI*, 2002 pg.147.
10. Sangheon Pack, "Performance Analysis of Robust Hierarchical Mobile IPv6 for Fault Tolerant Mobile Services", *IEICE Trans. Communi*cation. Vol.E87-B, No.5, May 2004.
11. Xavier P´erez-Costa and Hannes Hartenstein, "A Simulation Study on the Performance of Mobile IPv6 in a WLAN-Based Cellular Network," Computer Networks, *a special issue on "The New Internet Architecture"*, September 2002.
12. The ns Manual, formerly ns Notes and Documentation, Chap7: Queue Management and Packet Scheduling.

IDENTIFICATION OF MALICIOUS NODE IN DYNAMIC SOURCE ROUTING PROTOCOL

GANESH GUPTA
School of Computer Science & I.T., Shobhit University
Meerut, U.P.,India

Mobile Ad Hoc Networks (MANET) represents multifaceted distributed systems, allowing no preexisting communication infrastructure and dynamic topology. To facilitate effective communication within such network a routing protocol is used to discover routes between nodes. The goal of the routing protocol is to have an efficient route establishment between a pair of nodes, so that messages can be delivered in a timely manner. The growing interest in mobile ad hoc network techniques has resulted in many on demand routing protocol proposals. But detecting events and attacks in on demand routing protocol is a difficult task. The proposed malicious node detection scheme monitors several parameters on each node in DSR. Suggested scheme analyzes that some intermediate node might act selfishly to drop packets for other nodes in order to save their battery life. Though there have been many works in the recent years on existing routing protocols, the node detection for packet drop scheme amongst the node is not adequately addressed. The paper focuses on the vulnerability and potency of DSR in brief. The results of NS2 simulator demonstrates that proposed scheme can accurately detect malicious node code caused by network layer attack. Further, the results corroborated using comparative analysis of each node.

Keywords- MANET, DSR(Dynamic Source Routing), Ad- hoc.

1. Introduction

There are many new ideas for protocols, services and security has been developed for wireless network. The most popular prevalent research area over some last year is mobile Ad-hoc Networks (MANETs). In Mobile Ad-hoc networks co-operative nodes moves arbitrarily. Routing Protocols have two main categories proactive and reactive (on demand). First, one protocol attempts to maintain up to date routing information to all nodes in regular manner. However, second one (on-demand) attempts to discover the route to a destination only when a node originates a packet sending request for certain destination.

The DSR is also on-demand routing protocol. On-demand DSR protocols generally have lower overhead and faster reaction time than other types of routing protocols that are based on periodic mechanisms [1].

Since the nodes communicate over an air interface, security becomes a very important issue. Compared to a wired link, the wireless link can be intercepted or disrupted by an attacker much more easily, since it is freely accessible and not protected at all. In addition, the constantly changing topology makes it hard to determine which node really left the network, just changed the location, or has been intercepted or blocked [2].

This paper work is primarily concerned with the following two scenarios. First, an intermediate node may behave selfishly to save its own battery power by silently ignoring the source's route request. Second, a more malicious node may participate in the route request, but later may silently drop all the data packets coming to it, which increases the probability of malicious node existence. It presents the parameters by which the malicious nodes are detected considering the above scenarios.

The paper contains six sections. Section II. describes the DSR routing protocols and malicious nodes. Section III. analyses the related work regarding the proposed work. Section IV. describes the detection of malicious node in DSR with detailed implementation & results. Section V. and VI. are conclusion and future work respectively.

2. DSR Routing Protocol

The Dynamic Source Routing protocol (DSR) is a simple and efficient routing protocol designed specifically for use in multi-hop wireless ad hoc networks of mobile nodes. DSR allows the network to be completely self-organizing and self- configuring, without the need for any existing network infrastructure or administration [3].

DSR consists of two on-demand mechanisms: Route Discovery and Route Maintenance. When a source wants to send packets to a destination to which it does not have a route, it initiates a Route Discovery by broadcasting a ROUTE REQUEST. A node receiving a ROUTE REQUEST checks whether it has a route to the destination in its cache. If it has, it sends a ROUTE REPLY to the source including a source route, the concatenation of the source route in the ROUTE REQUEST and the cached route. Otherwise, it adds its address to the source route in the packet and rebroadcasts the ROUTE REQUEST. When the ROUTE REQUEST reaches the destination, the destination sends a ROUTE REPLY containing the source route to the source. When forwarding a ROUTE REPLY, a node stores the route starting from.

3. Malicious node in DSR

A malicious node can promise to forward packets but in fact fails to do so. In DSR routing technique, every node in the network will probe the other nodes periodically to detect if any of them fail to perform the forwarding function. [6]. Watchdog resides in each node and is based on overhearing. Through overhearing, each node can detect the malicious action of its neighbors and report other nodes. However, if the node that is overhearing and reporting itself is malicious, then it can cause serious impact on network performance.

A packet may be dropped under various reasons, which in turn can be grouped into the following categories:

3.1. *Unsteadiness of the medium*

i. A packet may be dropped due to contention in the medium.

ii. A packet may be dropped due to congestion and corruption in the medium.

iii. A packet may be dropped due to broken link.

3.2. *Genuineness of the node*

i. A packet may be dropped due to overflow of the transmission queue.

ii. A packet may be dropped due to lack of energy resources.

3.3. *Selfishness of the node*

i. A packet may be dropped due to the selfishness of a node to save its resources.

3.4. *Maliciousness of the node*

i. A packet may be dropped due to the malignant act of a malicious node.

Though a packet may be dropped in the similar manner by a selfish or a malicious node, they distinctly differ from the others because the packets are dropped intentionally. From the above examination, it is obvious that the intentional packet drop events have to be tackled, which generalized as "Packet Drop Attack" contrast to the accidental packet drop events.

4. Related works

Secure Routing has been interesting research field in MANETs. This section will give a short overview of existing works and entry points for literature. The reason behind researchers try to solving the security problem is many types of attacks identified. A selection among the Wormhole attack is popular. General mechanism, called packet leashes, for detecting and defending against wormhole attacks [7]. Sybil attacks are always possible except under extreme and unrealistic assumptions of resource parity and coordination among entities [11]. Rushing attack is also particularly damaging because it can be performed by a relatively weak attacker [1]. Denial of service attack is also a simple eavesdropping attack.

ARAN (A secure Routing protocol for Ad hoc Networks) is based on certificates and successfully defeats all identified attacks [8]. ARIDANE (A secure on-demand routing protocol for Ad hoc Network) is efficient, using only highly efficient symmetric cryptographic primitives [10]. SEAD (Secure Efficient Distance Vector Routing for Mobile Wireless Ad Hoc Networks)" which is based on the DSDV routing [9]. SEAD has a higher packet delivery ratio than DSDV; it has more overhead and latency.

Zapata has been made first approach for AODV with SOADV [12]. An overview on secure routing in general can be found in the article by Gupte and Singhal [13]. The complete and extensive overview on ad hoc routing challenges and protocols has been presented in [14].

An algorithm to find selfish nodes and deal with them, using a modified Dynamic Source Routing (DSR) protocol called as Efficient Secure Dynamic Source Routing (ESDSR). Packet delivery ratio increases in a network containing selfish/unreliable nodes when compared DSR with ESDSR [15].

Ant-DSR is another recent approach, which implements a distributed topology discovery mechanism through mobile agents to maintain DSR cache [5].

5. To find out the malicious node

Simulating random movement and traffic requires several simulations with changing scenario and traffic files, which is a very time consuming task. Since the objective of the simulations is to find the malicious node in DSR with trust based route selection, using one scenario is considered satisfying.

The results can vary between simulations with different trust based route selection. Given simulation considers six node scenarios connected with TCP agent and Constant Bit Rate (CBR) traffic has been taken. The nodes transfer packets at constant bit rate. To detect malicious node proposed mathematical solutions are implemented as TCL scripts and AWK scripts.

5.1. *Matrices Used for Detecting Malicious Node in DSR*

There are several different metrics that can be applied to measure protocols performance against. Studies of performance evaluations of protocols for mobile ad hoc networks indicate that the following metrics is usually used [4].

i. Packet Delivery Ratio (PDR): Which is the ratio between the number of packets send by the application layer and the number of packets received at the application layer? This is calculated by Eq. (1).

PDR = ∑ CBR Packets received / ∑ CBR Packets sent * 100 .... (1)

ii. Packet Delivery Overhead (PDO): Is the ratio between the number of transmitted packets (Pkttx) at the MAC layer and the number of successfully decoded packets (Pktdcd).

PDO = (No. of Transmitted pkts) / (successfully decoded pkts) . . .. (2)

iii. Dropped Data Packets: This is the number of data packet dropped by particular node in networks.

iv. Dropped Data in bytes: It gives the total information losses by particular nodes in bytes.

v. Packet Delivery Delay (D): It is the average time between the first transmission of a packet and the reception and successful decoding at the destination node.

The proposed work identify malicious node on the basis of above given mathematical parameters.

5.2. *Simulation Methodology*

The simulation starts with movement of six mobile nodes numbering 0 to 5. After some interval of time some node among six (node 3, node 0, node 4) sends packets to rest of node as well as each others. Here it has been assumed that some intermediate nodes are malicious .In such situation packets can be loss as well as more unusual packets can be added without receiving from sender node. That shows the transferring of data packets from sender node to receiver node along with also dropping of data packets. Simulation script written in tcl (Tool Command Language) code simple parameters after compiling it shows this output nam file and one trace file.

In this work of simulation, 6 nodes appears in 800x800 square meter area, which is in two dimensional area (2D) rectangles. The position of each node is represented in 2D grid: the X-axis value is chosen from the range (0,800) and Y-axis value is chosen from the range of (0,800).Table 1 summarizes the simulation parameters of DSR.

Table 1. Simulation Parameters

Parameter	Value
Number of nodes	6
Simulation time	20 minutes
Pause Time	0.1 sec
Environment Size	800x800 m
Traffic Type	Constant Bit Rate
Packet size	512 bytes
Protocol	DSR

6. Implementation and Results

As discussed above the implementation scripts of scenario is in tcl (tool command language). Code for calculating packet delivery ratio named as .tcl in it PDR is calculated for assuming 4 intermediate nodes (node 1, node 3, node 4, and node 0) because here more than one senders and receivers. The packet delivery ratio for node 2 is undefined (0/0), which show this node is ideal node because it neither sends nor receive any packet in network. To calculate all parameters proposed scheme take one parent .tcl codes and all rest codes (in awk) are added on same program.

Now proposed implementation for number of dropped data packets and dropped data along each node. The output comes in .xgr files have given in Table 2.

The last parameter is Packet Delivery Delay (D), which gives the time interval taken by a packet from one node to another node .However the trace results is so long but for calculation point of views only five starting results has been taken and it is enough for analysis. This result also comes in .xgr output file.

Table 2. Information losses

Nodes	packets dropped	Total number of data bytes dropped
On Node no 0	0	0
On Node no 1	1676	1709584
On Node no 3	46	46920
On Node no 4	115	117360
Overall network	1837	1873864

First five Results of Packet Delivery Delay for node 3 to 1:
Time interval for packet frm 3 to 1 is= 0.00067
Time interval for packet frm 3 to 1 is= 0.00067
Time interval for packet frm 3 to 1 is= 0.00070
Time interval for packet frm 3 to 1 is= 0.00067
Time interval for packet frm 3 to 1 is= 0.00067

First five Results of Packet Delivery Delay for node 1 to 3:
Time interval for packet frm 1 to 3 is= 0.20000
Time interval for packet frm 1 to 3 is= 0.20000
Time interval for packet frm 1 to 3 is= 0.20000
Time interval for packet frm 1 to 3 is= 0.20000
Time interval for packet frm 1 to 3 is= 0.20000

The schemes described in the above sections deeply analyze each parameter considering mathematical approaches and the results have been calculated accordingly. The first parameter Packet Delivery ratio for node 4 and 3 are normal (less than 100), however for node 1 and 0 (greater than 100) is abnormal. In case of node 1, it receives information from more than one sender and its dropped data packet is 0, so obviously it increases packet delivery ratio (more than thousands). However, in case of node 1 shown in Fig. 1 it losses huge amount of data packet and still its packet delivery ratio is more (more than 100). Second parameter

Packet Delivery overhead is normal for all nodes its varying between 3 to 4 . Third and fourth parameters i.e., Packet dropped (packets) and Data dropped (in bytes) along each node shows great abnormality for node 1. The fifth parameter, Packet Delivery Delay for each node also shows more time difference in case of node 1 to 3 and 3 to 1, which is due to network congestion or malicious behavior of node 1.

Therefore after considering all these parameters node 1 has detected as malicious node. Hence the proposed scheme can successfully apply to any of Ad hoc network topology.

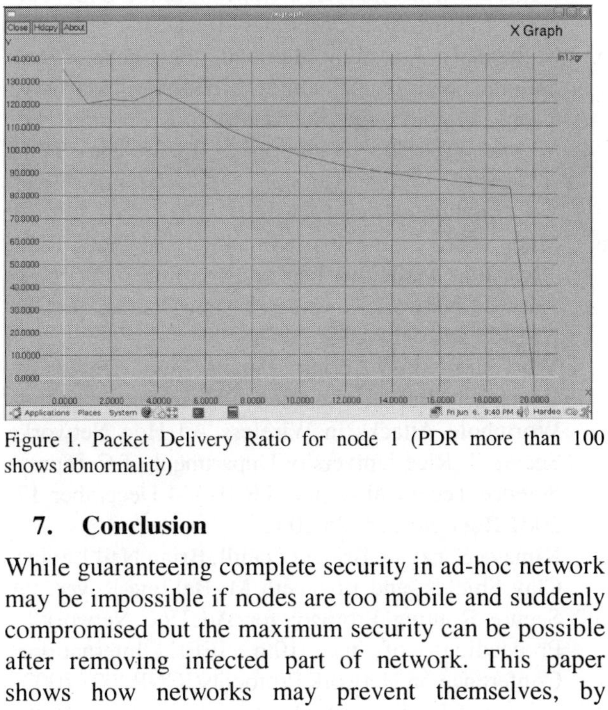

Figure 1. Packet Delivery Ratio for node 1 (PDR more than 100 shows abnormality)

7. Conclusion

While guaranteeing complete security in ad-hoc network may be impossible if nodes are too mobile and suddenly compromised but the maximum security can be possible after removing infected part of network. This paper shows how networks may prevent themselves, by detecting malicious node accurately on the basis of their essential parameters. It also shows all the limitations where the node does not behave as normal, which can be identified immediately using mathematical parameters. The countermeasures are proposed to protect misbehaviors, and then further enhance the security points. Simulation result shows the network performance degradation or abnormality in case of malicious node presence. After incorporating the proposed mechanism in DSR, it can be concluded that presented work is feasible in real world and not expensive to implement.

References

1. Yih-Chun Hu, Adrian Perrig and David b. Johnson, "Rushing Attacks and defense in Wireless Ad Hoc Network Routing Protocols" In Proceeding of ACM Sept 2003.
2. Stephan Eichler and Christian Roman, "Challenges of Secure Routing in MANETs: A Simulative Approach using AODV-SEC", Technical Report LKN-TR-2, Aug 2006.
3. David B. Johnson, David A. Maltz and Josh Broch, "DSR: The Dynamic Source Routing Protocol for Multi-Hop Wireless Ad Hoc Networks", http://www.monarch.cs.cmu.edu
4. Xin Yu and Zvi M. Kedem, "A Distributed Adaptive Cache Update Algorithm for the Dynamic Source Routing Protocol", NYU Computer Science Department Technical Report TR2003-842, July 2003. Last revised: December 20, 2004.
5. Mohamad Aissani, Messoud Fenouche, Hadi Sadour, and Abdelhamid Mellouk, "Ant-DSR: Cache Maintenance Based Routing Protocol For Mobile AD-Hoc Networks", IEEE The Third Advanced International Conference on Telecommunications (AICT'07) 2007.
6. Mike Just, Evangelos Kranakis, and Tao Wan, "Resisting Malicious Packet Dropping in Wireless Ad Hoc Networks", research supported in part by NSERC and MITACS, 2007.
7. Yih-Chun Hu, Adrian Perrig, and David B. Johnson, "Packet Leashes: A Defense against Wormhole Attacks in Wireless Ad Hoc Networks Secure," Rice University Department of Computer Science Technical Report TR01-384 December 17, 2001 Revised: Sep. 25,2002.
8. Kimaya Sanzgiri, Bridget Dahill, Brian Neil Levine, Clay Shields, and Elizabeth M. Belding-Royer, "A Secure Routing Protocol for Ad Hoc Network" , Proceedings of the 10th IEEE International Conference on Network Protocols(ICNP '02),2002.
9. Yih-Chun Hu David B. Johnson and Adrian Perrig, "SEAD: Secure Efficient Distance Vector Routing for Mobile Wireless Ad Hoc Networks " , Proceeding of the Fourth IEEE Workshop on Mobile Computing Systems and Applications (WMCSA'02) 2002.
10. Y.-C. Hu, A. Perrig, and D. B. Johnson, "Ariadne: A secure on-demand routing protocol for ad hoc networks," Proceedings of the eighth annual international conference on Mobile computing and networking (MobiCom 2002), Atlanta, Georgia, USA, September 23–28, pp. 12–23,2002.
11. John R. Douceur, "The Sybil Attack", in Proceeding of the IPTP S02 Workshop, March 2002.
12. Manel Guerrero Zapata, "Secure Ad hoc On-Demand Distance Vector Routing" Mobile Computing and Communications Review, Volume 6, No. 3, Oct. 2001.
13. S. Gupte and M. Singhal, "Secure routing in Mobile wireless Ad Hoc Networks" Ad Hoc Networks ,vol 1,no 1,p. 151 to 174, July 2003
14. Yin-Chun Hu and Adrian Perrig, "A Survey of Secure Wireless Ad Hoc Routing", IEEE Security & Privacy, vol. 4, pp. 28-39, May/June 2004.
15. Michael Weeks and Gulsah Altun, "Efficient, Secure, Dynamic Source Routing for Ad-hoc Networks" , Springer Science+Business Media Journal of Network and Systems Management, Vol. 14, No.4, December 2006.

COMPARATIVE CALL FLOW AND PERFORMANCE ANALYSIS OF H.323 AND SIP PROTOCOLS USING OPNET IT GURU

SHEELA GANESH THORENOOR

Consultant, Talent Transformation, Wipro Technologies
Bangalore, Karnataka, 560100, India, sheela.ganesh@wipro.com

JAYASURYA VENUGOPALAN

Senior Consultant, Talent Transformation, Wipro Technologies
Bangalore, Karnataka, 560100, India, jaya.venu@wipro.com

Abstract— This paper presents a comparative analysis of call set up times, MOS (Mean Opinion Score), packet end to end delay and packet loss for the H.323 and SIP (Session Initiation Protocol) signaling schemes used in Voice Over IP (Voice over Internet Protocol) calls. We compare voice performance parameters like MOS, delay, jitter and call set up times and establish the differences in performance of these two VoIP protocols through an opnet simulation. This detailed simulation study is performed over H.323 and SIP networks where we have shown that the H.323 network performed better in terms of call set up time and packet end to end delay for the signaling messages. However, MOS for the voice packets in both the networks was expectedly the same as the same network topology was used for both the signaling protocols. There has been an influx of a large number of signaling and transport protocols over IP networks, giving rise to unacceptably large delays, most unsuitable for real time applications. SIP and H.323 are used for establishment and release of Voice aver IP calls as well as Video and Media calls. Both these protocols play a very important role in terms of optimizing the call set up time and call reliability and flexibility over IP networks for real time applications like voice and video.

Key words:

VoIP, H.323, SIP, Call Set Up Time, MOS, End to End delay, Packet Loss, OPNET

1. Introduction

Voice traffic will be in the near future a considerable fraction of the total telecom traffic around the world, as the network operators are building high capacity packet switched Internet Protocol (IP) infrastructures. Since IP networks are becoming ubiquitous, voice is just one application over such networks. Voice Over Internet Protocol or VoIP aims at transmitting and receiving voice packets via the internet over the shared media used in IP(Internet Protocol) unlike the dedicated time slots used in the Public Switched Telephone Network.

Packetized communication of voice , video and data can use the H.323 suite of protocols standardized by ITU-T or use Session Initiation Protocol or SIP for setting up or closing down the call as in the case of PSTN (Public Switched Telephone Network) signaling. Since these signaling protocols are application layer protocols in the TCP/IP protocol stack, for their transportation, they depend on either TCP or UDP at the transport layer and IP at the Network layer. However, when the actual voice information packets are to be transmitted across the IP network, they make use of RTP (Real Time Protocol) and RTCP (Real Time Control Protocol) in order to provide the real time or delay sensitivity time stamp., when transmitted over IP networks.

2. VoIP signalling

The first hurdle to overcome when making a VoIP phone call is to establish a connection between the parties involved. In legacy telephony, this is done by switching circuits until a physical wire is established between locations. Generally, for session set up, negotiation, and management, TCP is used for its reliability. For time sensitive media such as voice and video, UDP is utilized as the transport mechanism because of its speed and low overhead. The packet size can be further reduced by using RTP header compression, reducing the combined IP/UDP/RTP header from over 65% to as low as 10% of the entire packet size. Smaller means faster, and in IP Telephony, the name of the game is speed.

2.1 H.323 Signalling

As a session layer protocol, the main function of H.323 is to perform call control and management on an IP network. The H323 specification relies on two additional signaling protocols, H.225 and H.245, for call setup and management. When a session is initiated between two H.323 devices, the H.225 standard uses the Q931 ISDN protocol to perform setup and teardown functions using TCP for a reliable connection. H.245 then opens another TCP connection to establish the capabilities of the devices, negotiate the codecs, and determine which ports will be used for the session. A channel is then opened on which the actual media will travel using UDP for transport because of its speed, and relying on the upper layer Real Time Protocol (RTP) for sequencing and timing information.

An H.323 network is comprised of four logical components, not all of which will be needed on every network and that can reside on a wide variety of devices. A terminal is an endpoint device such as an IP telephone, a computer running an H.323 software application, or a dedicated conferencing device. An H.323 compliant terminal must support H.245 for channel and capabilities negotiation, RAS (Registration, Admission, Status), Q931 for signaling and setup, and support for RTP and RTCP on which to stream the media. Terminals must support audio and T.120 data communications is optional. An MCU provides services to allow three or more terminals to participate in a conference. The MCU consists of a Multipoint Controller (MC) and an optional Multipoint Processor (MP). The MC is responsible for H.245 functions (negotiating common ground) while the optional MP handles the actual mixing of media streams, and manages the streams to avoid bandwidth contention. H.323 supports Centralized, Decentralized, and a Hybrid concept of multipoint conferencing. When terminals participating in a conference reside in both a centralized and decentralized environment (mixed) the MCU acts as a bridge between the two.

MC and MP functions can reside on a dedicated component, terminal, a gateway or a gatekeeper, but when endpoints exist off network like in PSTN, the MC can be utilized on a gateway. Gateways provide a variety of services, not the least of which is protocol conversion between H.323 networks and non-H.323. A gateway performs call setup and teardown, translates audio, video and data formats, and can perform RAS for registration with the gatekeeper. On the H.323 side, the gateway uses H.225 and H.245 for call setup and management. A gateway can be implemented on a gatekeeper, an MCU, or on a voice enabled router or switch. As an optional component that is usually found in larger Enterprise networks, the gatekeeper is the most important component in the H.323 configuration. The gatekeeper manages all the registered terminals, gateways, and MCUs in a single H.323 zone, which can span multiple LAN/WAN segments. Services such as addressing, authorization and authentication of H.323 components, bandwidth management, accounting and billing can all be configured on the gatekeeper. The gateway of the zone can make routing decisions, and can also simplify management of multiple gateways by handling their call control functions in a centralized manner.

Shown in the fig below is the call flow for H.323. the Gateways(GW) as shown are optional. Setup message originates from the End Terminal and is directed to the end system by the Signalling protocol (H.245). Call Proceeding. Progress and Alerting inform about the call progress. When the destination terminal accepts the call a Connect message is sent to the source. The Call is now connected . Once the call is over the call is released with Release Messages. The H.323 messages are encoded in binary format

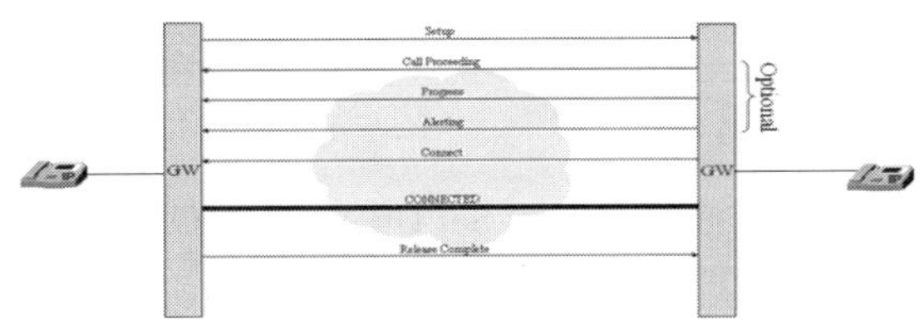

Fig. 1: H.323 Signalling call flow

2.2 *SIP (Session Initiation Protocol) Signalling*

SIP is a text based application layer protocol like HTTP which uses either UDP or TCP as the transport protocol. It is used for creating multimedia sessions and also to locate the end users. It allows modifying of parameters like different CODEC standards associated with the session at any time during the session. It also allows termination of the already created session. SIP User Agent (UA) is a logical entity that can act as both a user agent client and user agent server. User Agent Client (UAC) is a logical entity that creates a new request (initiates a new call), and then uses the client transaction state machinery to send it. The role of UAC lasts only for the duration of that transaction. User Agent Server (UAS) is a logical entity that generates a response to a SIP request (receives the call request). The response accepts, rejects, or redirects the request. This role lasts only for the duration of that transaction. It is an intermediary entity that acts as both a server and a client for the purpose of making requests on behalf of other clients.

A proxy server primarily plays the role of routing and is transparent to end devices. A proxy interprets and, if necessary, rewrites a request message before forwarding it. A proxy server can either maintain state information of transaction (stateful proxy) or simply forward the requests (stateless proxy). A proxy can forward the requests one after the other sequentially. A proxy can fork the requests to multiple servers, in which case, it is known as a forking proxy. This process used by the forking proxy is called Parallel Search. A Registrar is a server that accepts REGISTER requests and places information it receives in those requests into location service for the domain it handles. Typically the registrar may be adapted to provide location services to the SIP network. Location Service is a Data Base containing the SIP URI and its location(s). Location service is used by a SIP redirect or proxy server to obtain information about a callee's possible location(s). DNS query is used to access location service.

SIP supports multiple methods for setting up and closing down the calls like INVITE, ACK, OPTIONS,BYE, CANCEL and REGISTER. The corresponding responses may be 1XX for Provisional response, 2XX for Final response indicating success of request, 3XX for Final response indicating redirection class of treatment, 4XX for Final response indicating failure, 5XX for Final response indicating server failure and 6XX for Final response indicating global failure.

The SIP Call flow is different. Shown below is the SIP Call Flow mechanism.

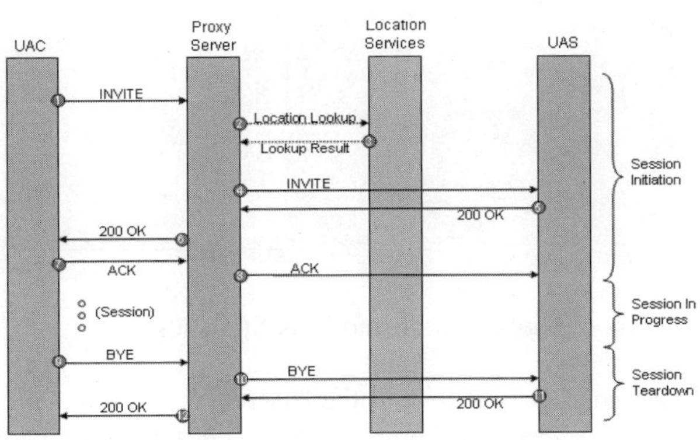

Fig. 2: SIP signalling call flow

The UAC client sends an INVITE message through the proxy server. Location Services could be used to look up the destination.. Destination UAS (server) sends back a 200 OK acknowledging the INVITE. The client then acknowledges this with an ACK. The session is terminated with a BYE. The SIP messages are in text format unlike the binary encoded H.323 messages.

3 *Simulation*

3.1 *Simulation Methodology*

Network is simulated using OPNET® IT Guru. OPNET® is extensive and powerful simulation software with wide variety of possibilities. It enables the possibility to simulate entire heterogeneous networks with various protocols.

The simulated network for H.323 as shown in the fig.3, consist of two different sites located at Baghdad and Shanghai. There are caller and callee clients connected to the routers within the subnets at each of these locations. The Callee terminal is situated in Shanghai and connected to a router which acts as an IP based gateway. The Caller terminal is situated in Baghdad is also connected to a router which acts as an IP based gateway for the VOIP Calls. The voice clients are connected to the router through 100 Base T links, routers in turn are interconnected in the IP network through PPP_DS1 links. Since the background has been set as Asia, the actual distances between the chosen locations and thereby the relevant propagation delays are going to be considered in Opnet IT Guru simulation tool.

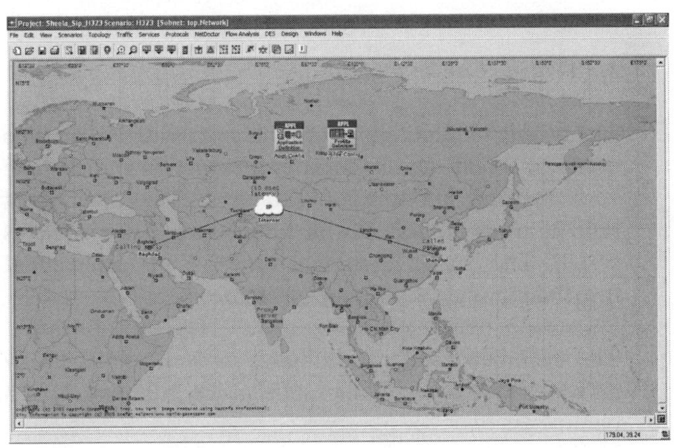

Fig. 3: Virtual Network topology for H.323

A similar kind of virtual network is simulated as show in fig.5, for SIP signalling, with the Redirect server situated in Bangalore, while the caller and callee are at Baghdad and Shanghai as earlier.

3.2 Application Configuration

An application configurator is used in both scenarios to configure the voice application parameter. For SIP, voice Frame per packer is used, signaling parameter is set to SIP, voice encoding scheme is chosen as G.723.1. Type of Service corresponds to DSCP marking of 208 for Interactive Voice Traffic compression and Decompression, the delay is 0.02 secs and the conversation environment is set at Land Phone Quiet room. For H.323 the application configurator is setup with H.323 signalling , other parameters being same, making comparisons easy and meaningful. All standard voice encoding schemes are enabled.

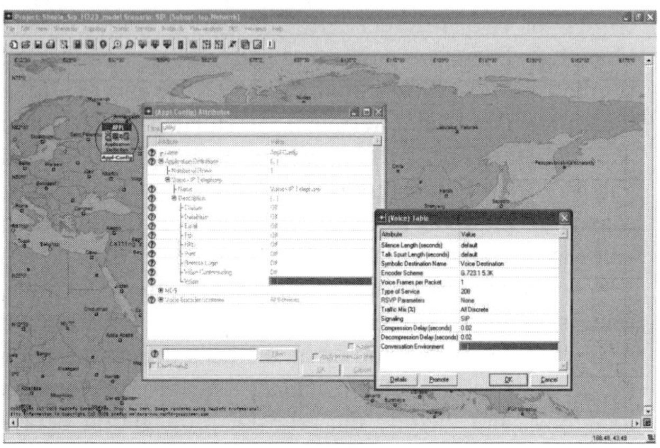

Fig. 5: Application Configuration for Voice

3.3 Profile Configuration

The profile configuration for both is set with a start time offset of 0 and an exponential distribution of call time with average duration of 120 secs. The number of repetitions is unlimited with a repetition pattern that is serial. The inter repetition time is of exponential distribution with an average of 360 secs..

The caller and caller attributes, as well as the proxy server are setup with the appropriate SIP and H.323 parameters .

H.323 options are configured with the Direct Endpoint signalling domain, as the simulated H.323 calls are directly routed from caller to callee. The maximum number of calls is unlimited given the constraints of the simulation time and the call duration and the inter call delay as indicated earlier. The H,323 Device role is as a terminal.

For SIP, the UAC and UAS service is enabled and the call time out is determined by the TCP connection time out.

For SIP a proxy server needs to be set up. Our model has situated the proxy server in Bangalore.. The proxy server is a SUN Ultra 10 333 Mhz system. It uses an Ethernet interface to connect to a router acting as an IP gateway for SIP calls. The proxy service on the proxy server is enabled and the number of maximum simultaneous calls configured as unlimited.

3.4 Network analysis

We have first built the network with H.323 as the signalling protocol and the same model is repeated for analysis as a second scenario using SIP protocol. In order to analyse the network in terms of end to end delay, end to end call set up time, packet loss, throughput, Mean Opinion Score etc, the global, node and link statistics are to be chosen. In the first scenario, under global statistics, H.323 and voice are chosen as the parameters for analysing the results. Under node statistics, IP, IP interface, voice calling party, voice called party, and voice application are the chosen parameters and for link statistic, end to end delay and jitter parameters are chosen. Similarly for the second scenario, instead of H.323 SIP is chosen as the parameter for statistical analysis.

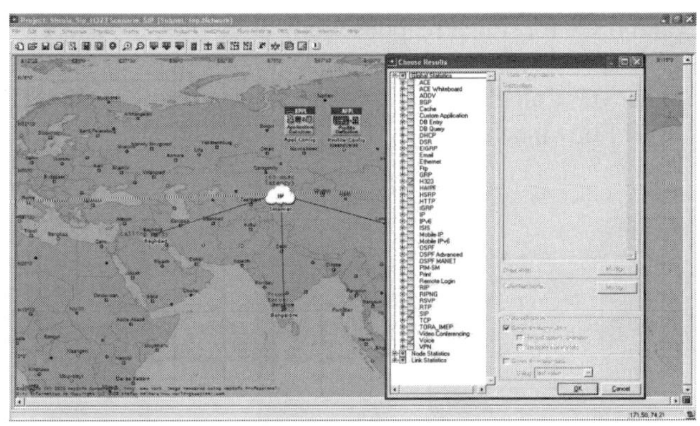

Fig. 6: Global, Node and Link Statistics

The simulation is done as the Discrete Event Simulation, in which case the kernel mode is chosen to be under "optimized" and the simulation duration is for 30 minutes. The results obtained as shown in the following graphs plotted.

A. Call set up time: comparison of H.323 and SIP call set up times.

As can be seen from the results shown the Call set up times for H.323 is on average 400 msec whereas for SIP the average is around 900 msec. One of the major reasons for this is H.323 uses a binary scheme for call signalling and establishment whereas SIP is text based(XML Messages) which take more processing and parsing time at end systems.
The result substantiates the fact that H.323 will afford smaller call set up times vis vis SIP. This has to be traded with the complexity of the H.323 call signalling stack implementation at the end.

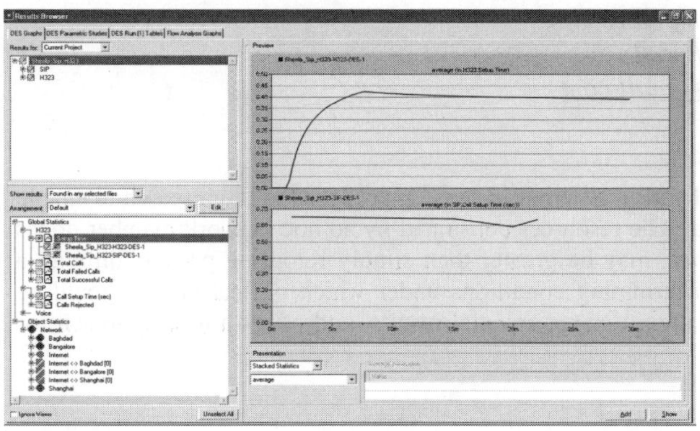

Fig. 7: H.323 and SIP call set up times

B. MOS for SIP and H 323 calls

There is not much of a significant difference in the Mean Opinion Score expectedly as the same network topology is used for both. Voice encoding and decoding is more robust and less errored in H.323 as compared to SIP.

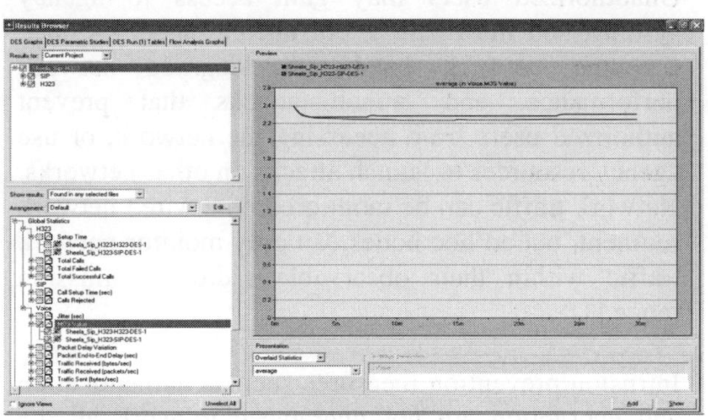

Fig. 8: MOS for H.323 and SIP calls

C. Packet end to end delay

The packet end to end delay is greater in the case of SIP as compared to H.323. for the signalling messages..

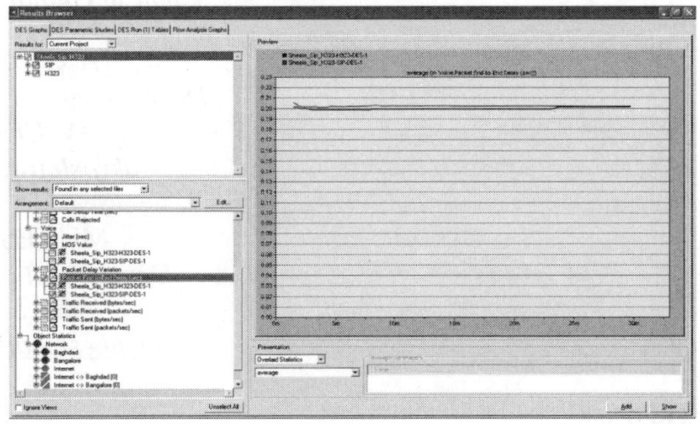

Fig. 9: Packet end to end delay

4 Conclusions

It can be seen that H.323 definitely performs better in terms of:

a) Call set up time
b) End to end Delay
c) MOS Scores
d) Traffic Throughput.

Advantage in SIP implementations is the universal nature of the SIP text based messages.
However we have to be prepared to incur a performance penalty for this. Moreover the number of message exchanges in SIP is much more than in H.323 compounding this problem.

5 References

http://www.iec.org/online/tutorials/int_tele/indes.asp.
http://salaam.cs.buap.mx.VOIP/LIBROS/VoIP%20tutorial.pdf
ITU-T H.323 documentation
RFC 3621 documentation for SIP
OPNET Documentation, OPNET Technologies
Real-time Signaling Transport Protocol for VoIP Zhensheng Shen, Gang Bai, Wendong Wang, Shiduan Cheng, National Laboratory of Switching Technology & Telecommunication Networks
Convert Channels in SIP for VoIP signlaling by Wojciech Mazurczyk, Krzysztof Szczypiorski, Warsaw University of Technology, Faculty of Electronics and Information

Intrusion Detection System for Wireless Ad-hoc network

KAMLESH CHANDRAVANSHI
Department of Computer Technology
V.J.T.I. Mumbai
kamlesh.chandravanshi@gmail.com

AKROSH TIWARI
Department of Computer Technology
V.J.T.I. Mumbai
akrosh.tiwari@gmail.com

MUKESH BATHRE
Department of Computer Engg.
B.I.S.T. Bhopal
mukesh.bathre@gmail.com

Abstract

A number of neighbor-monitoring, trust-building, and cluster-based voting schemes have been proposed in the research to enable the detection and reporting of malicious activity in ad hoc networks. The resources consumed by ad hoc network member nodes to monitor, detect, report, and diagnose malicious activity, however, may be greater than simply rerouting packets through a different available path. In this paper we present a method for determining conditions under which critical nodes should be monitored, describes the details of a critical node test Simulation, presents experimental results, and offers a new approach for conserving the limited resources of an ad hoc network IDS.

KEY WORDS

Mobile ad hoc network, MANET, intrusion detection, IDS, worm model

1. Introduction

Wireless communications offer organizations and users many benefits such as portability and flexibility, increased productivity, and lower installation costs. Wireless local area network (WLAN) devices, for instance, allow users to move their laptops from place to place within their offices without the need for wires and without losing network connectivity. Less wiring means greater flexibility, increased efficiency, and reduced wiring costs. Ad hoc networks, such as those enabled by Bluetooth, allow data synchronization with network systems and application sharing between devices. Handheld devices such as personal digital assistants (PDA) and cell phones allow remote users to synchronize personal databases and provide access to network services such as wireless e-mail, Web browsing, and Internet access.

However, risks are inherent in any wireless technology. Some of these risks are similar to those of wired networks; some are exacerbated by wireless connectivity; some are new. Perhaps the most significant source of risks in wireless networks is that the technology's underlying communications medium, the airwave, is open to intruders, making it the logical equivalent of an Ethernet port in the parking lot.

The loss of confidentiality and integrity and the threat of denial of service (DoS) attacks are risks typically associated with wireless communications. Unauthorized users may gain access to agency systems and information, corrupt the agency's data, consume network bandwidth, degrade network performance, and launch attacks that prevent authorized users from accessing the network, or use agency resources to launch attacks on other networks. Network traffic can be monitored on a wired network segment, but ad hoc nodes can only monitor network traffic within their observable radio transmission range [1].

Intrusion prevention measures such as authentication and encryption are not guaranteed to work all the time, which brings out the need to complement them with efficient intrusion detection and response. If an intrusion is detected quickly enough, the intruder can be ejected before any damage is done or any data is compromised. Effective IDS can not only serve as a prevention to prevent intrusions but also provide information about intrusions to strengthen intrusion prevention measures.

The paper is organized as follows: Section 2 provides some background work on IDS, Section 3 provides the Introduction of Critical Path Detection and Worm Propagation Model, Section 4 Simulation Details, section 5 Simulation Results, Section 6 Conclusion, Section 7 Future Work, Section 8 References.

2. Background

A number of IDS techniques have been proposed in the research literature. Moreover, a number of trust building and cluster-based voting schemes have been proposed to enable the sharing and vetting of messages, and data, generated and gathered by IDS systems. Zhang and Lee describe a distributed and collaborative anomaly detection-based IDS for ad hoc networks [3,4]. Tseng et al. describe an approach that involves the use of finite state machines for specifying correct AODV routing behavior and distributed network monitors for detecting run-time violation of the specifications [5]. Pirzada and McDonald present a method for building confidence measures of route trustworthiness without a central trust authority. The authors also present a concise summary of previous work in the area of establishing trust in ad-hoc networks [6]. Theodorakopoulos and Baras present a method for establishing trust metrics and evaluating trust [7]. Michiardi and Molva assign a value to the "reputation" of a node and use this information to identify misbehaving nodes and cooperate only with nodes with trusted reputations.

3. Critical Path Detection and Worm Propagation Model

In this section first, we describe the definition of a critical path is a path whose failure or malicious behavior disconnects or significantly degrades the performance of the network. Once identified, a critical path can be the focus of more resource intensive monitoring or other diagnostic measures. If a path is not considered critical, this metric can be used to help decide if the application or the risk environment warrant the expenditure of the additional resources required to monitor, diagnose, and alert other path about the problem.
Worm propagation model is mainly described as detailed network and abstract network. The detailed network can be an enterprise network and run by ISPs, the rest of the part is known as abstract network.

3.1 Architecture of IDS

Figure 3.1 shows the architecture of intrusion detection system, we first generate the test traffic using tcl script and find out the critical link in the network and then we block the path, after that worm propagation model is injected in the network through critical link and find out the type of attack, tcp, udp and cbr comparison before intruder and after intruder and we also find the node who spread the malicious activity.

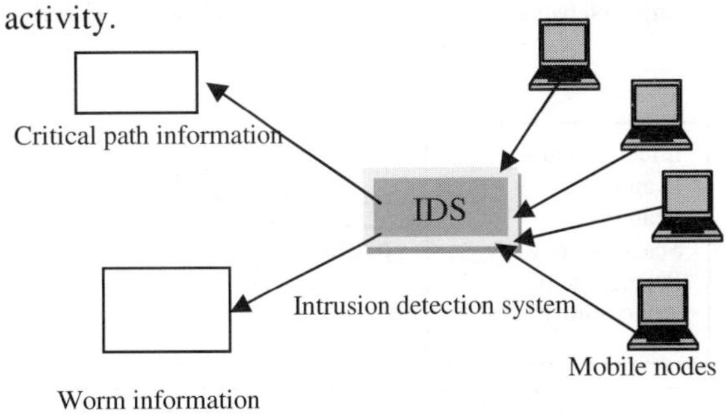

Figure 3.1 Architecture of IDS

3.2 Critical Path Detection

In this simulation module we use the trace file generated by ns-2, which is used as an input for C++ structure file, where we have created two linked lists. One link list stores incoming node numbers and other outgoing node numbers. In this file we used a count variable as global variable. These count variable stores the total number of pair's m-n, where m and n are some positive integer. Whenever first value pair comes then the count variable will increase and in the same manner we read all the incoming and outgoing node number and set the count for this path. After that we check that which incoming and outgoing node count value is greater in all pair's and set the path between these nodes as a critical path. After that we enter a worm propagation model in the network and check the status of the network and then we find out the intruder node.

3.3 Worm Propagation Model

Worm propagation model can be described as detailed network and abstract network. The detailed network could be an enterprise network, the whole network can be considered as detailed network in our simulation. Abstract network is also a part of the detailed network but the only difference is that it can be worm node where the infection occurrence can be assumed, so an abstract network can be called as susceptible infectious removal model. Worm node takes place in the network were we have blocked the path.

The communication between detailed network and abstract network is done through actual packet transmission that is the probing packet generated by compromised node in both parts. A vulnerable node is compromised upon receiving a probing packet. Then it chooses a target node to scan. Probing packet has no effect on invulnerable nodes. Figure 3.2 shows the worm propagation model

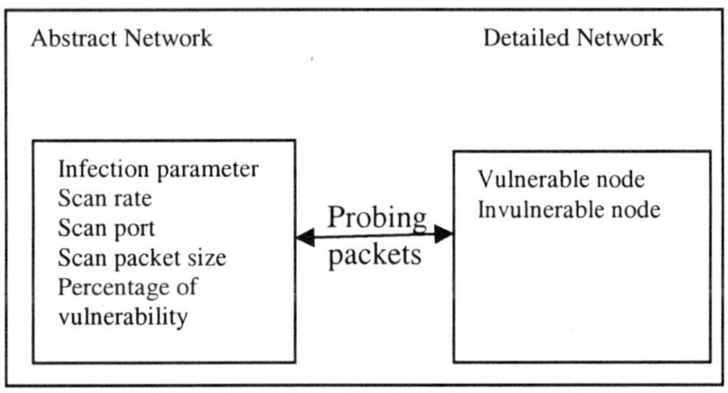

Figure 3.2 Worm Propagation Model

3.4 Intrusion Detection System

An IDS is shown below in figure:-3.3 which have three different modules namely Normal Profile, Worm node and Intrusion information. . Normal profile consists of TCP transmission, UDP transmission and CBR transmission; it also contains the path of packet flow in the network this information is before the worm node enters in the network. After that worm node enter the network in place of critical path, it captures the information of normal profile and infect the vulnerable node in network through message passing (probing packets) between abstract network and detailed network and then worm node set the scan rate, scan port, percentage of vulnerability and infection parameters. If probing port of detailed network and abstract network are same then worm node sends the infected packets to all the vulnerable nodes and infects the network. Intrusion Information takes the information from both normal profile and worm node and detects the intrusion by comparing both the information's. It checks for fields like worm node number, port number, time of intrusion and type of attack.

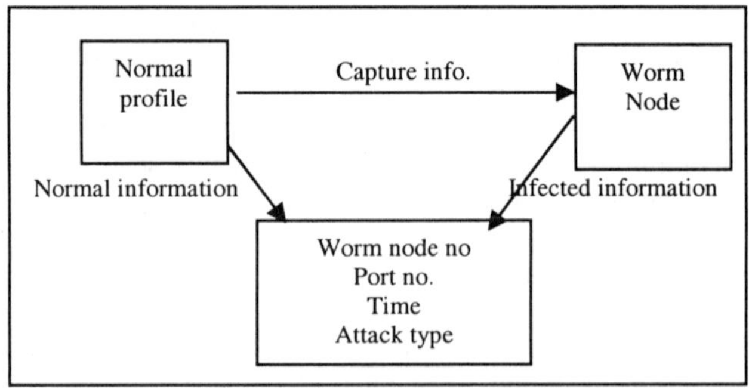

Figure 3.3 Model of Intrusion Detection System

4. Simulation Details

The simulation described in this paper was tested using the ns-2 test-bed that allows users to create arbitrary network topologies [8]. By changing the logical topology of the network, ns-2 users can conduct tests in an ad hoc network without having to physically move the nodes. ns-2 controls the test scenarios through a wired interface, while the ad hoc nodes communicate through a wireless interface.

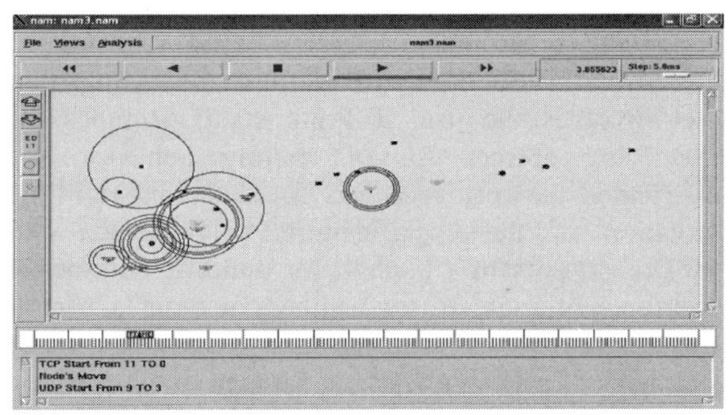

Figure 4.1 A sample topology generated by ns-2

The topology shown in Figure 4.1 is used to show how the IDS collects information and determines if a path and its incident communication links warrant the invocation of the critical path test. In order to illustrate the detection of critical path, we first generate some test traffic in the network. TCP socket servers are initiated at nodes 0, 11 and 19 to generate TCP traffic. Three TCP socket clients are initiated at nodes 0, 12 and 22. These clients send simple socket messages every 2 to 3 seconds to the servers. Node initiates a ping of node 3 and similarly node 5 initiates a ping of node 9 in order to create UDP packet traffic within the network. Finally two Secure Shell (SSH) sessions are initiated between node 0 and node 11, and node 22 and node 19.

The Simulation ends up with generation of a trace file and a nam file. We use the trace file to retrieve **Hs** (id for this source node) and **Hd** (id for next hop towards the destination). AWK utility is used to retrieve those fields from trace file and save them in a different file then the generated out put file can be use for calculating number of packet travel from each path by using C++, after that we find out the path from where the maximum data has travel and set the path as a critical path. Table1 shows the source to destination path and traffic

From_Node	To_Node	No_of_pkt_recorded
6	1	2726
5	3	1640
16	4	322
22	1	1712
0	2	744
From node	**To Node**	**Maximum Traffic**
6	1	2726
Total traffic from all path		7144

Table 1 shows source to destination path Vs traffic

Then after detecting the critical path a worm model replaces the critical path. The test traffic is again generated and then we again monitor the network and record the changes in the network. Changes can be inspected by examining the trace file. If we found any change in the information in any field of the trace file or more losses in TCP, UDP and CBR or infected UDP packet then we can conclude that the path is critical and our assumption of critical path is true otherwise it is not the critical path and we keep on checking the same thing for different paths.

5. Experimental Results

UDP Comparison before Intrusion

Figure 5.1 shows UDP packet transmission which includes packet receive, packet loss and total packet transmission and comparison before intruder node enter in our network. Graph shows that the packet received is much more than the packet loss.

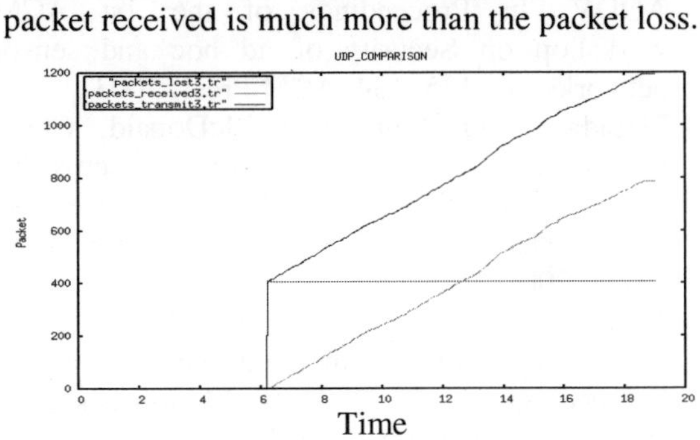

Figure 5.1 UDP packets before intrusion

UDP Comparison After intruder

Figure 5.2 shows UDP packet transmission which includes packet receive, packet loss and total packet transmission and comparison after intruder node enter in our network. Graph shows that the packet received is much less than the packet loss.

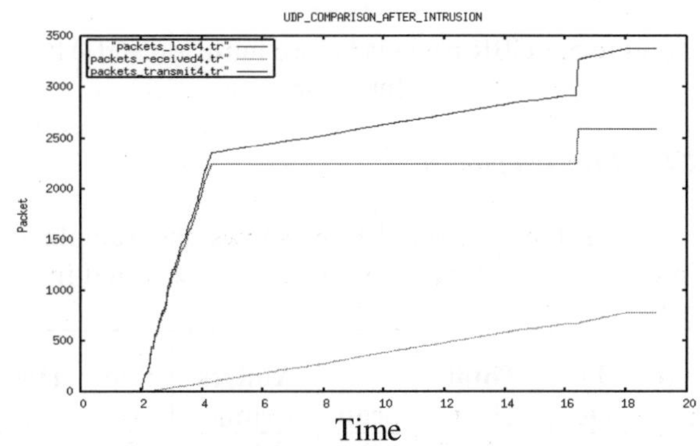

Figure 5.2 UDP packets after intrusion

TCP Comparison

Figure 5.3 shows TCP packet transmission which includes packet receives and total packet transmission and comparison before and after intrusion in network. Graph shows that the packet received is much large before intrusion than after intrusion.

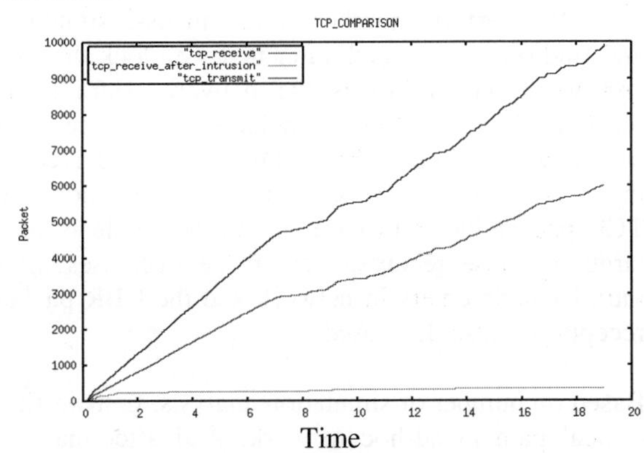

Figure 5.3 TCP packets before intrusion and after Intrusion

CBR Comparison

Figure 5.4 show CBR packet transmission which includes packet receives and total packet transmission and comparison before and after intrusion in network. Graph shows that the packet received is less before intrusion than after intrusion.

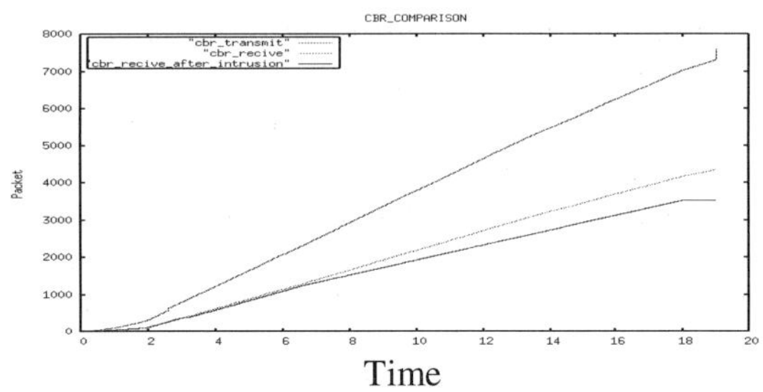

Figure 5.4 CBR packets before intrusion and After Intrusion

UDP Infected packet

Table 2 given below shows the sample of infected packet after the intrusion has occurred in the network

worm node	Ti me	Total Host	scan	Addres s range	Spo rt	Dpor t
A	2	159979	1	39996	0	0
A	3	159977	3	39996	0	0
A	4	159974	6	39996	0	0
A	5	159967	13	39996	0	0
A	6	159956	24	39996	0	0
A	7	159933	47	39996	0	0

Table 2 UDP infected packet

6. Conclusion

We perform number of test in ns-2 simulator and find out critical path after that we block the link and worn model infects the network. Here some result is shown. Table 3 conclude if the number of nodes are minimum than UDP packet received is much large before intrusion than after intrusion and TCP packet block in case of intruder node is also large. Because received percentage decreases after intruder node enters in network and the CBR packet reception is also decreased.

Based on number of simulation analysis, first we find critical path in ad-hoc network. And after that we check the activities of critical node by injecting the worm packets in that critical node and than analyze the UDP, TCP and CBR packets. And we find out the following information that shows when intruder comes in the network

1) In TCP packets : more packets are blocked (more packet loss)
2) In UDP packets: more packets loss and some received packets are also infected.
3) In CBR packets: little bit more loss than without intruder.

UDP				**TCP**		**CBR**	
before intrusion		**after intrusion**		**befor e intrus ion**	**after intrus ion**	**befor e intrus ion**	**after intrus ion**
recei ved %	**lo ss %**	**receiv ed%**	**lo ss %**	**receiv ed%**	**receiv ed%**	**receiv ed%**	**receiv ed%**
66	**34**	**24**	**76**	**62**	**17.2**	**71.4**	**56.2**

Table 3 Packet Comparison before and after intrusion

7. Future work

In this project we detect only single critical path and single intruder node in ad-hoc network. In future we trace all the critical paths and nodes. We injected worm packet in critical node so that it act like an intruder and than analyze TCP, UDP, and CBR packets transmission. So we can also apply the other techniques like packet capturing, false route forwarding, changing source and destination addresses etc.

8. References

1. Karygiannis, E. Antonakakis, and A. Apostolopoulos, Detecting Critical Nodes for MANET Intrusion Detection Systems". Available: {arygiannis@nist.gov }
2. Y. Zhang and W. Lee. Intrusion detection in wireless ad hoc networks. In Proceedings of the 6th annual international conference on Mobile computing and networking, pp. 275–283. ACM Press, 2000.
3. Y. Zhang, W. Lee, and Y. Huang. Intrusion detection techniques for mobile wireless networks. ACM/Kluwer Mobile Networks and Applications (MONET), 2002.
4. C.-Y. Tseng, P. Balasubramanyam, C. Ko, R. Limprasittiporn, J. Rowe, and K. Levitt. A specificationbased intrusion detection system for AODV. In Proceedings of the 1st ACM workshop on Security of ad hoc and sensor networks, pp. 125–134. ACM Press, 2003.
5. Pirzada, Asad Amir, and McDonald, Chris. Establishing trust in pure ad-hoc networks. Proceedings of the 27th conference on Australasian Computer Science - Volume 26, pp 47-54, 2004.
6. Theodorakopoulos, George and Baras, John. Trust evaluation in ad-hoc networks. Proceedings of the 2004 ACM workshop on Wireless security, pp. 1-10, 2004.
7. The Network Simulator – ns

ROUTING OF QUALITY OF SERVICE PACKETS BASED ON AUCTION IN MOBILE AD HOC NETWORKS

PAVAN KUMAR KVVNSD

PG Student, Dept of ECE, SSN College of Engineering, Kalavakkam Chennai-603110, India. Email:pavankondaka@gmail.com

ANANDA KRISHNA B

Associate Professor, Dept. of ECE, Universal College of Engg & Tech Dokiparru, Guntur-522438, India. Email:anand_bk@rediffmail.com

JEGADISH KJ

Senior Lecturer, Dept of ECE, SSN College of Engineering Kalavakkam, Chennai-603110, India. Email:jegadishkj@ssn.edu.in

Mobile ad hoc networks (MANETs) are infrastructure less network consisting of mobile nodes, with constantly changing topologies, which communicate via wireless medium. Routing of packets is done through the co-operation of the relay nodes when source and destination are not in direct transmission range. Because of the selfish nature of the nodes, the nodes would not transmit the packets from source to destination. Pricing is one method to stimulate node co-operation. The requirements of the route differ with the type of application. There are certain applications which require QoS route and which do not require. For the applications which require QoS route, the source node has to pay a higher cost in order to transmit the packets. The parameters used to obtain QoS route are bandwidth, delay and jitter. In this paper, we propose auctions in order to get QoS route for lesser cost.

1. Introduction

A mobile ad hoc network (MANET) is an infrastructure less networks consisting of mobile nodes with constantly changing topologies, which communicate via a wireless medium. The transmission range in MANETs is usually limited, so nodes within a network need to relay data packets over several intermediate nodes to communicate. Hence, MANETs are suitable for applications in which no infrastructure exists such as military battlefield, emergency rescue, vehicular communications and mining operations. Thus, nodes in MANETs act as both hosts and routers. Forwarding of packets for other nodes results in the consumption of the nodes limited resources such as processing power, transmission time and battery power. The researcher's in the wireless network area has taken an effort in studying these problems. Co-operation works and related concepts were first proposed by Buttyan and Hubaux [1], Marti et al [2].

There are different types of applications and the QoS route required by the applications differs. The real time traffic can be divided into two categories: delay sensitive real-time traffic and nondelay sensitive real-time traffic. Based on the type of application, the route can be selected: (i) a route with least cost which does not guarantee the QoS and (ii) a route with QoS which demands higher cost. In this paper we propose to implement auctions, in order to reduce the cost of route with QoS. Until now, auctions have represented an internet based e-commerce applications. We therefore provide a mobile auctions application in order to provide a QoS route for lesser cost.

In this paper, we present the details of the proposed auction model. The rest of the paper is organized as follows. In Section 2 related work is presented, section 3 the methodology is discussed, section 4 gives the simulation results, section 5 gives the conclusion and future work in section 6.

2. Related Work

There are several works related to the auctioning. In [3], [4] and [5], the authors introduced auction like methods where the sender centric Vickrey auction has been adopted to discover the most efficient routes for the cost efficient and truthful routing in MANETs. In

[6] and [7], the least cost route is selected from the available routes based on auction. It is found that none of the existing auction schemes considered about the QoS issues. The QoS routing is of much interest in the area of research recently. The major challenges for designing a routing protocol for ad hoc networks are mobility of nodes, resource constraints, hidden and exposed terminal problems [8]. Routing protocols can be broadly classified in to two different categories. They are proactive or table-driven and reactive or on-demand routing protocols. DSDV, WRP, CGSR, OLSR, etc. comes under proactive and DSR, AODV, etc. comes under reactive protocols. It has been found from [9] that QoS routing can be done as an extension of the existing routing protocols such as DSDV, AODV, TORA and DSR. In this paper, we have taken an effort to minimize the cost of the QoS route by auctioning. Bandwidth, delay and jitter are taken as major constraints to obtain QoS. The available bandwidth can be calculated as [10], if, T_{idle} (sec) → total idle periods in the measurement interval T_S of nodes. Channel capacity→ is the total bandwidth of the channel.

$$B_{avlb} = channelcapacity * (T_{idle} / T_S) \quad (1)$$

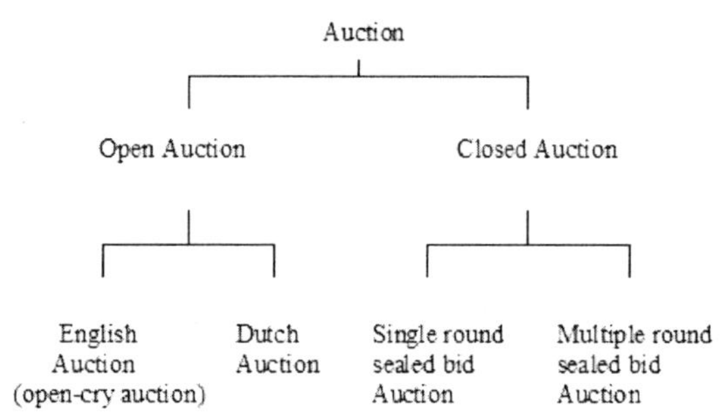

Figure 1. Classification of Auction

The auction process can be created anywhere and as soon as a group of at least three persons agree to participate in the auction. An auction is defined as "a market institution with an explicit set of rules determining resource allocation and prices on the basis of bids from the participants" [11]. The classification of auction is as shown in fig. 1.

In this paper, we propose a fair architecture for deploying auctions over ad hoc networks and operating according to English auction rules. English auctions are the mostly deployed auction type and present simple bidding rules. Auctions generally relay on a central auction server called the auctioneer. In this paper, we consider the source node which initiates auction, as the auctioneer. The auctioneer is responsible for the auction process. The bidders (i.e., the other nodes in the network) must have an equal fair chance for submitting a successful bid. In order to achieve fair auctions, the total time of the auction application is divided into rounds. The number of rounds is defined by the source node (which is the initiator). This number is flooded to the other participating nodes. In the fig. 2, consider node x and node y (bidders) are the farthest nodes in the network. To provide fairness, node x and node y must receive each others bid during the same round.

The necessary round duration, to provide fairness is the Round Trip Time(RTT) also called $T_{fairness}$ which is applied to the longest path in the network i.e., the distance between the two farthest nodes in the network and $T_{fairness}$ is given by

$$T_{fairness} \approx 2 \times \max imalhopnumber \times Timeout \quad (2)$$

Where, Time out→maximal time of retransmission.

3. Methodology

In this paper, we have chosen DSR as the routing protocol. As it is on-demand routing protocol, it discovers the route when it is required. If a source node requires a route to the destination for which it does not have route information, it initiates a route discovery process which goes from one node to another node until it reaches the destination node.

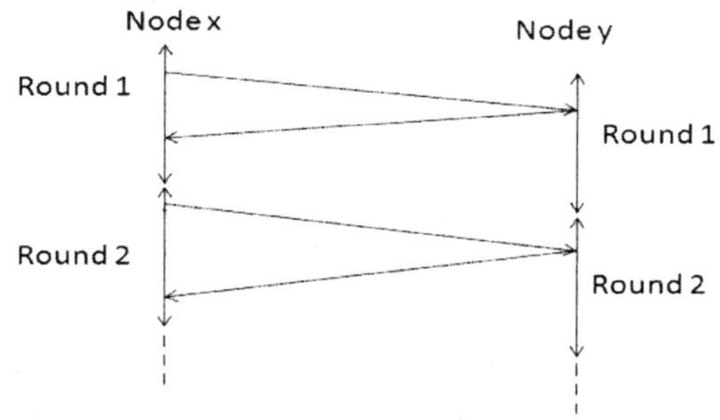

Figure 2. Fair Round Duration

This protocol finds a route on demand by flooding the network with Route Request packets. The destination node, on receiving Route Request packet, responds by sending a Route Reply packet back to the source, which carries the route traversed by the Route Request packet received. The major difference between this and the other on-demand routing protocol is that it is beacon-less and hence does not require periodic hello packet transmissions, which are used by a node to inform its neighbors of its presence. As it is beacon-less, power and bandwidth can be saved. In DSR, Route Request packet contains source address, destination address, sequence number and next hop. In this paper, we have been extended the Route Request packet to one more field called bidding price. Bidding price is the initial price quoted by the sender. Therefore, the new Route Request packet contains source address, destination address, sequence number, next hop and bidding price.

The flowchart of the process is as shown in the fig. 3. When it is needed to transmit number of packets from source to destination, a Route Request packet is flooded in the network.

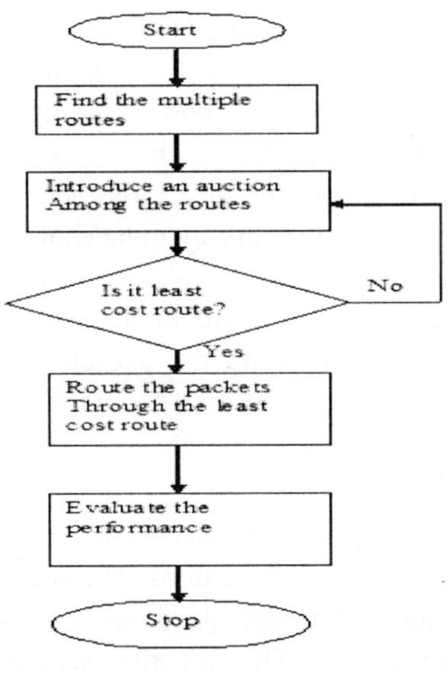

Figure 3. Flow Chart of the Proposed Model

The Route Request packet contains source address, destination address, sequence number, next hop and bidding price. Each intermediate node upon receiving the Route Request packet adds its cost, for forwarding the packets, to the bidding price and finally reaches the destination. The destination node will have multiple routes with different hops and different cost. Therefore, the destination node implements an auction among the routes. The cost with the least cost is selected as the winning route. A route reply is sent to the source with the route information. The cost is distributed by the sender. The packets are routed through the route. This process is done dynamically over time. And finally, the performance is evaluated.

4. Simulation Results

We perform the simulation study using GloMoSim. GloMoSim is a scalable simulation environment for large wireless and wireline communication networks. GloMoSim uses a parallel discrete-event simulation capability provided by Parsec. Parsec is a C-based simulation language, developed by the Parallel Computing Laboratory, for the sequential and parallel execution of discrete-event simulation models. It can also be used as parallel programming language [12].

There are N nodes deployed inside a rectangular region according to two dimensional uniform and random distribution and each node moves according to the random waypoint model. We consider two scenarios for simulation as shown in the table 1. Considering these two scenarios, we have been plotted two plots between number of packets transmitted Vs cost of the route (QoS and NonQoS). Fig. 4 and fig. 5 shows that, as the number of packets transmitted increases cost of the route (QoS and NonQoS) increases. It is found that the cost of the QoS route is higher than the cost of the nonQoS route.

Table 1. Simulation Scenarios

	Scenario1	Scenario2
Simulation Time(sec)	1800	300
Simulation Area(sq.m)	2000*2000	1000*1000
Number of Nodes	30	20
Requested Bandwidth(bits/sec)	700	1000
Traffic	CBR	CBR
Node Placement	Uniform	Random
Packet Size(bytes)	512	256
Routing Protocol	DSR	DSR
MAC Protocol	802.11	802.11
Node Mobility Speed(m/sec)	10	20

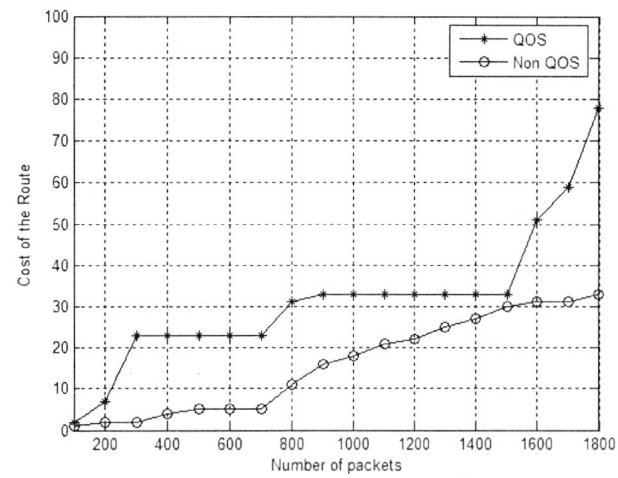

Figure 4. No. of Packets Vs Cost of the Route

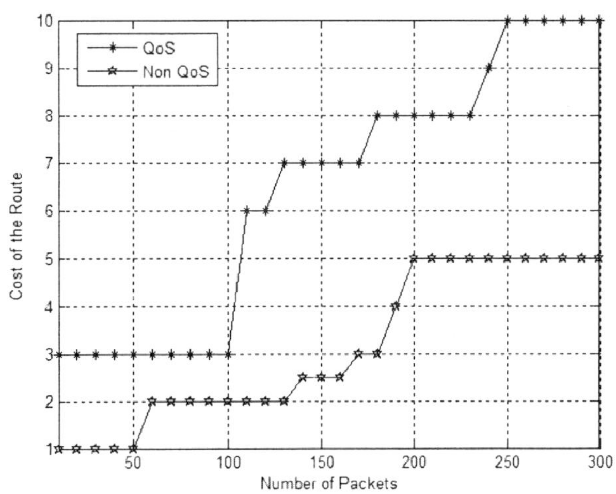

Figure 5. No. of Packets Vs Cost of the Route

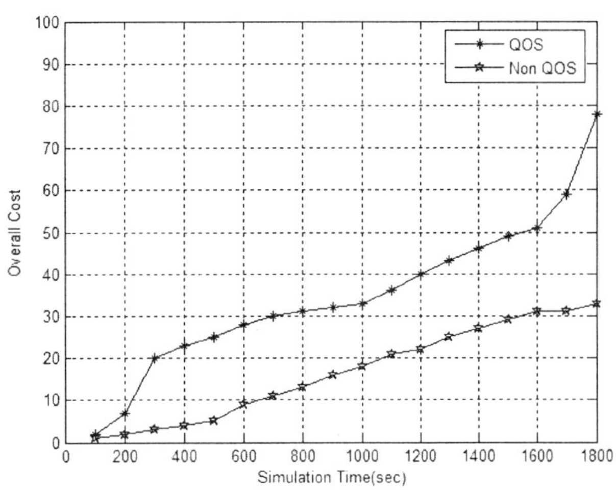

Figure 6. Simulation Time Vs Overall Cost

Fig. 6 shows the overall cost for the nonQos route and QoS route as the simulation time increases. The simulation time is kept as 1800 sec. The data packets are transmitted through the non QoS route and the cost at different time stages are noted down. Similarly, the data packets are transmitted through the Qos route and the cost at different time stages are noted down. It is found that overall cost of QoS route is higher than that obtained in the non Qos route.

5. Conclusion

In this paper, we propose a novel application called auctions over ad hoc networks. It allows the spontaneous creation of the application that the participant nodes can freely join and leave at any time. From the simulation results it has been known that, irrespective of different scenarios, the cost of the route which requires QoS is always higher than the cost of the route which does not require QoS. The results obtained are used to proceed further. An auction has to be introduced to minimize the cost of the QoS route. The packets are to be routed through that path. The overall profit that can be obtained for various node densities are to be studied. These results are to be compared with the existing fixed schemes to evaluate the success of the new scheme. So, if we implement the proposed auction model for routing the packets which require QoS, the cost of the route could be minimized.

6. Future Work

The work can be extended by considering the security problems in the auctions. The security services may be required for both the initiating node and the participating nodes. The security services such as protection against denial of service attacks and against spurious bids are required for auction system. And bids can be protected by applying some cryptography mechanisms.

References

1. L.Buttyan and J P Hubaux, "EnforcingService Availability in Mobile Ad-Hoc WANs", Proc. Mobi Hoc, August 2000.
2. S Marti, T J Giuli, K Lai, and M Baker, "Mitigating Routing Misbehavior in Mobile Ad Hoc Networks", Proc. of Mobicom, August2000
3. L Aderegg and S Eidenbenz, "Adhoc – VCG: A truthful and cost efficient routing protocol for

mobile ad hoc networks with selfish agents", ACM Mobicom' 03, 2003V. Baran, M. Colonna, M. Di Toro and V. Greco, *Phys. Rev. Lett.* **86**, 4492 (2001).

4. S Zhang, L Li, Y Liu and Y R Yang, "On designing incentive compatible routing and forwarding protocols in wireless ad hoc networks – an integrated approach using game theoretical and cryptographic techniques", Tech. Rep. YALE/DCS/TR-1286, Yale University, 2004.
5. S Eidenbenz, G Resta, and P Santi, "COMMIT: a sender centric truthful and energy-efficient routing protocol for ad hoc networks with selfish nodes", IEEE International Parallel and Distributed Processing Symposium, 2005.
6. Z Li, W Yu and K J R Liu, "An Optimal Dynamic Pricing Framework for Autonomous Mobile Ad Hoc Networks", IEEE INFOCOM, 2006.
7. Z Ji, W Yu, and K J R Liu, "Dynamic Pricing Approach foe Self Organized Mobile Ad Hoc Networks", IEEE Globecom,2005.
8. C Siva Ram Murthy and B S Manoj, "ADHOC WIRELESS NETWORKS: Architecture and Protocols", First Indian Reprint, 2005.
9. Imad Jawhar and Jie Wu, "Quality of Service Routing in Mobile AdHoc Networks", Kluwer Academic Publishers, 2004.
10. Vinh Dein Hoang Shao, Z Fujise M, "A New Solution to Estimate the available Bandwidth in MANETs", IEEE 63rd Vehicular Technology Conference, 2006.
11. McAfee R P and McMillan J (1987), "Auctions and Bidding", Journal of Economic Literature, Vol.25, No.2, June, pp.699-738.
12. Jorge Nuevo, "A Comprehensible GloMoSim Tutorial", 2004.

Linear PIC Receiver for DS CDMA Systems

K. R. Shankar Kumar

(PhD, Indian Institute of Science, Bangalore)
Professor, Department of Electronics and Communication
Sri Ramakrishna Engineering College, Coimbatore 641022

R. Krishna Kumar

Student, Department of Electronics and Communication
Sri Ramakrishna Engineering College, Coimbatore 641022

In this paper, we present a weighted linear parallel interference canceller (LPIC) where the multiple access interference (MAI) estimate in a stage is weighted by a factor before cancellation on Rayleigh fading and diversity channels. We obtain exact expressions for the average signal-to-interference ratio (SIR) at the output of the cancellation stages which we maximize to obtain the optimum weights for different stages. We also obtain closed-form expressions for the optimum weights for the different stages. We show that this SIR-optimized weighted LPIC scheme clearly outperforms both the matched filter (MF) detector as well as the conventional LPIC (where the weight is taken to be unity for all stages), in both near-far as well as non-near-far conditions on Rayleigh fading and diversity channels.

1. Introduction

Parallel interference cancellation (PIC) is a multi-user detection scheme where a desired user's decision statistic is obtained by subtracting an estimate of the multiple access interference (MAI) from the received signal [1]. PIC lends itself to a multistage implementation where the decision statistics of the users from the previous stage are used to estimate and cancel the MAI in the current stage, and a final decision statistic is obtained at the last stage. When an estimate of the MAI is obtained from the hard bit decisions from the previous stage, it is termed as 'hard-decision PIC' (non-linear PIC). The multistage PIC scheme originally proposed by Varanasi and Aazhang in [2] and several other schemes considered in the literature (e.g., [3],[4]) are of this type. On the other hand, MAI estimates can be obtained using the soft values of the decision statistics from the previous stage, in which case the PIC is termed as linear PIC (LPIC) [5],[6]. LPICs have the advantages of implementation simplicity, analytical tractability, and good performance under certain conditions.

In a conventional LPIC, an estimate of the MAI for a desired user in a stage is obtained using all the other users' soft outputs from the previous stage. It is likely that these MAI estimates are inaccurate due to poor channel conditions (e.g., high interference, deep fades, etc.). Under such conditions, the cancellation can become ineffective to an extent that it may be better not to do cancellation. In fact, it has been known that the conventional LPIC performs worse than the MF detector (where no cancellation is done) at low SNRs, due to the poor accuracy of the MAI estimates at low SNRs. This can be alleviated by properly weighing the MAI estimates before cancellation [6]. A key question is how to choose the weights for different cancellation stages. An intuitive approach is to keep the value of the weight low at the early stages and large at the later stages, as done in [6], because the MAI estimates can be more reliable in the later stages since much of the interference would have been cancelled by then. A more formal approach, which we adopt in this letter, is to obtain appropriate functions (e.g., expressions for interference variance or SIR) which when optimized will give the optimum weights.

The issue of the choice of weights in LPIC has been addressed in [7]-[9], but only for AWGN channels. A new contribution in this letter is that we derive closed-form expressions for optimum weights for different stages in an LPIC on Rayleigh fading and diversity channels. Also, our approach to obtain the optimum weights is that we derive exact expressions for the average SIR at the output of the cancellation stages of the weighted LPIC, and maximize these SIR expressions to obtain the optimum weights for the different stages. In fact, we obtain exact closed-form expressions for the optimum weights for each stage of the LPIC. We show that the proposed SIR-optimized weighted LPIC clearly outperforms the MF detector and the conventional LPIC, in both near-far as well as non-near-far scenarios on Rayleigh and diversity channels.

2. System Model

Consider a K-user synchronous CDMA system

where the received signal is given by

$$y(t) = \sum_{k=1}^{k} A_k h_k b_k s_k(t) + n(t), \qquad t \in [0, T], \qquad (1)$$

where $b_k \in \{+1, -1\}$ *is* the bit transmitted by the k_{th} user, T is one bit duration, A_k is the transmit amplitude of the k_{th} user's signal, h_k is the complex channel fade coefficient corresponding to the k_{th} user, $s_k(t)$ is the unit energy spreading waveform of the k_{th} user defined in the interval $[0, T]$, i.e., $\int_0^T s_K^2(t)dt = 1$, and $n(t)$ is the white Gaussian noise with zero mean and variance σ^2. The fade coefficients h_k's are assumed to be i.i.d complex Gaussian r.v's (i.e., fade amplitudes are Rayleigh distributed) with zero mean and $E[h^2_{kI}] = E[h^2_{kQ}] = 1$, where h_{kI} and h_{kQ} are the real and imaginary parts of h_k. The channel fade is assumed to remain constant over one bit interval.

We consider a multistage LPIC at the receiver. The first stage is a conventional MF, which is a bank of K correlators; each matched to a different user's spreading waveform. The received vector $\mathbf{y}^{(1)}$ at the output of the MF stage (the superscript (1) in $\mathbf{y}^{(1)}$ denotes the first stage) is given by

$$y^{(1)} = [y_1^{(1)}, y_2^{(1)}, \ldots\ldots, y_K^{(1)}], \qquad (2)$$

Where $y_k^{(1)}$ is the k_{th} user's MF output, given by

$$y_k^{(1)} = A_k h_k b_k + \sum_{j=1, j\neq k}^{K} \rho_{jk} A_j h_j b_j + n_k, \qquad (3)$$

where ρ_{jk} is the cross-correlation coefficient between the jth and kth users' spreading waveforms, given by $\rho_{jk} = \int_0^T s_j(t) s_k(t)dt, \left|\rho_{jk} \leq 1\right|$, and n_k's are complex Gaussian with zero mean and $E\left[n_j n_k^*\right] = 2\sigma^2$ when $j = k$ and $E\left[n_j n_k^*\right] = 2\sigma^2 \rho_{jk}$ when $j \neq k$. The received vector $y^{(1)}$ (without hard decision) is used for MAI estimation and cancellation in the second stage.

2.1 Conventional LPIC

In a conventional LPIC, an estimate of the MAI for a desired user in the current stage is obtained using all the other users' soft outputs from the previous stage for cancellation in the current stage. More specifically, the MAI estimate for the desired user k in stage m, $m > 1$, is obtained by multiplying $y_j^{(m-1)}$ with ρ_{jk} for all $j \neq k$ and summing them up, i.e., $\sum_{j\neq k} \rho_{jk} y_j^{(m-1)}$ is the MAI estimate for the desired user k in stage m. Accordingly, the bit decision for the k_{th} user after interference cancellation in the m_{th} stage, $\hat{b}_k^{(m)}$, in conventional LPIC is given by

$$\hat{b}_k^{(m)} = \text{sgn}\left(\text{Re}\left(h_k^*\left(y_k^{(1)} - \sum_{j=1, j\neq k}^{K} \rho_{jk} y_j^{(m-1)}\right)\right)\right) \qquad (4)$$

3. Weighted LPIC

In a weighted PIC, the MAI estimate of the desired user k in stage m, $m > 1$, is weighted by a factor $p_k^{(m)}$ before cancellation. In other words, $p_k^{(m)} \sum_{j\neq k} \rho_{jk} y_j^{(m-1)}$ is the weighted MAI estimate for the desired user k in stage m. That is, the m_{th} stage output of the desired user k, $y_k^{(m)}$ is given by

$$y_k^{(m)} = y_k^{(1)} - p_k^{(m)} \sum_{j=1, j\neq k}^{K} \rho_{jk} y_j^{(m-1)} \qquad (5)$$

Note that both the conventional LPIC as well as the MF detector become special cases of the weighted LPIC for $p_k^{(m)} = 1, \forall m$ and $p_k^{(m)} = 0, \forall m$, respectively. The bit decision for the desired user k after weighted interference cancellation in stage m is

$$\hat{b}_k^{(m)} = \text{sgn}\left(\text{Re}\left(h_k^* y_k^{(m)}\right)\right). \qquad (6)$$

In the following, we obtain exact expressions for the average SIRs at the output of the different stages of the weighted LPIC, which are then used to obtain closed-form expressions for the optimum weights for the different stages.

3.1. *Average SIR at 2nd Stage Output*

The weighted interference cancelled output of the 2nd stage for the desired user k is given by

$$y_k^{(2)} = y_k^{(1)} - p_k^{(2)} \sum_{j=1, j\neq k}^{K} \rho_{jk} y_j^{(1)}$$
$$= A_k h_k b_k \left(1 - p_k^{(2)} \sum_{j=1, j\neq k}^{K} \rho_{jk}^2\right) + I_2 + N_2, \qquad (7)$$

Where

$$I_2 = \left(1 - p_k^{(2)}\right) \sum_{j=1, j\neq k}^{K} A_j h_j b_j \rho_{jk} - \sum_{j=1, j\neq k}^{K} p_k^{(2)} \rho_{jk} \sum_{\substack{i=1 \\ i\neq j,k}}^{K} \rho_{ij} A_i h_i b_i , \quad (8)$$

$$N_2 = n_k - p_k^{(2)} \sum_{j=1, j\neq k}^{K} \rho_{jk} n_j . \quad (9)$$

The terms I_2 and N_2 in (7) represent the interference and noise terms introduced due to imperfect cancellation in using the soft output values from the MF stage. Since *h's* are complex Gaussian, both I_2 and *N2* are linear combinations of Gaussian r.v's with zero mean. The variance of $I_2, \sigma_{I_2}^2$ can be obtained as

$$\sigma_{I_2}^2 = \sum_{i=1, i\neq k}^{K} 2A_i^2 \left(\left(1 - p_k^{(2)}\right)\rho_{ik} - p_k^{(2)} \sum_{\substack{j=1 \\ j\neq k,i}}^{K} \rho_{jk}\rho_{ij} \right)^2 , \quad (10)$$

and the variance of N_2, $\sigma_{I_2}^2$ can be obtained as

$$\sigma_{N_2}^2 = 2\sigma^2 \left(1 - 2p_k^{(2)} \sum_{\substack{j=1 \\ j\neq k}}^{K} \rho_{jk}^2 + \left(p_k^{(2)}\right)^2 \sum_{\substack{i=1 \\ i\neq k}}^{K} \sum_{\substack{j=1 \\ j\neq k}}^{K} \rho_{ik}\rho_{jk}\rho_{ji} \right) . (11)$$

The average SIR of the desired user k at the output of the second stage, $\overline{SIR}_k^{(2)}$ is then given by

$$\overline{SIR}_k^{(2)} = \frac{2A_k^2 \left(1 - p_k^{(2)} \sum_{j=1, j\neq k}^{K} \rho_{jk}^2 \right)^2}{\sigma_{I_2}^2 + \sigma_{N_2}^2} . \quad (12)$$

The optimum weight for the second stage $p_{k,opt}^{(2)}$ is chosen to be the value of $p_k^{(2)}$ that maximizes the average SIR in (12).In Sec. IV, we present a closed-form expression for $p_{k,opt}^{(2)}$.

3.2. *Average SIR at 3rd Stage Output*

The soft values of the interference cancelled outputs of all the other users from the second stage are used to reconstruct (Estimate) the MAI for the desired user k in the third stage. The MAI estimate is then weighted by the factor $p_k^{(3)}$ and cancelled. The third stage output of the desired user k, $y_k^{(3)}$ is then given by

$$y_k^{(3)} = y_k^{(1)} - p_k^{(3)} \sum_{j=1, j\neq k}^{K} \rho_{jk} y_j^{(2)} = A_k h_k b_k X + I_3 + N_3 , \quad (13)$$

$$X = 1 - p_k^{(3)} \sum_{\substack{j=1 \\ j\neq k}}^{K} \rho_{jk}^2 \left(1 - p_j^{(2)}\right) + p_k^{(3)} \sum_{\substack{j=1 \\ j\neq k}}^{K} \rho_{jk} p_j^{(2)} \sum_{\substack{i=1 \\ i\neq j,k}}^{K} \rho_{ij}\rho_{ki} , \quad (14)$$

$$I_3 = \sum_{\substack{l=1 \\ l\neq k}}^{K} \rho_{lk} A_l b_l h_l \left(1 - p_k^{(3)} \left(1 - p_l^{(2)} \sum_{\substack{j=1 \\ j\neq l}}^{K} \rho_{jl}^2 \right) \right) + p_k^{(3)} \sum_{\substack{l=1 \\ l\neq k}}^{K} \rho_{lk} p_l^{(2)} \sum_{\substack{i=1 \\ i\neq l}}^{K} \rho_{il} \sum_{\substack{j=1 \\ j\neq l,i,k}}^{K} \rho_{ji} A_j h_j b_j - p_k^{(3)} \sum_{\substack{l=1 \\ l\neq k}}^{K} \left(1 - p_l^{(2)}\right)\rho_{lk} \sum_{\substack{j=1 \\ j\neq l,k}}^{K} \rho_{jl} A_j h_j b_j , \quad (15)$$

$$N_3 = n_k - p_k^{(3)} \sum_{\substack{l=1 \\ l\neq k}}^{K} \rho_{lk} \left(n_l - p_l^{(2)} \sum_{\substack{j=1 \\ j\neq l}}^{K} \rho_{jl} n_j \right) . \quad (16)$$

The terms N_3 and I_3 are linear combinations of Gaussian r.v's with zero mean and variances $\sigma_{N_3}^2$ and $\sigma_{I_3}^2$, given by

$$\sigma_{N_3}^2 = 2\sigma^2 \left(1 + p_k^{(3)} \sum_{\substack{l=1 \\ l\neq k}}^{K} p_l^{(2)} \rho_{lk}^2 \right)^2 + 2 p_k^{(3)} \sigma^2 \sum_{\substack{i=1 \\ i\neq k}}^{K} \rho_{ik} \left(1 + p_k^{(3)} \sum_{\substack{l=1 \\ l\neq k}}^{K} p_l^{(2)} \rho_{lk}^2 \right) \cdot \left(-\rho_{ik} + \sum_{\substack{j=1 \\ j\neq k,i}}^{K} p_j^{(2)} \rho_{jk}\rho_{ij} \right) + \left(p_k^{(3)}\right)^2 \sigma^2 \sum_{\substack{i=1 \\ i\neq k}}^{K} \sum_{\substack{l=1 \\ l\neq k}}^{K} \rho_{il} \left(-\rho_{ik} + \sum_{\substack{j=1 \\ j\neq k,i}}^{K} p_j^{(2)} \rho_{jk}\rho_{ij} \right) \cdot \left(-\rho_{lk} + \sum_{\substack{j=1 \\ j\neq k,l}}^{K} p_j^{(2)} \rho_{jk}\rho_{lj} \right) , \quad (17)$$

$$\sigma_{I_3}^2 = \sum_{\substack{l=1 \\ l\neq k}}^{K} 2A_l^2 \left[p_k^{(3)} \sum_{\substack{j=1 \\ j\neq l,k}}^{K} \rho_{jk} p_j^{(2)} \sum_{\substack{i=1 \\ i\neq l,j}}^{K} \rho_{ij}\rho_{li} - p_k^{(3)} \sum_{\substack{j=1 \\ j\neq k,l}}^{K} \rho_{lj}\rho_{jk} \left(1 - p_j^{(2)}\right) + \rho_{lk} \left(1 - p_k^{(3)} \left(1 - p_l^{(2)} \sum_{\substack{j=1 \\ j\neq l}}^{K} \rho_{jl}^2 \right) \right) \right]^2 . \quad (18)$$

The average SIR of the desired user k at the third stage output, $\overline{SIR}_k^{(3)}$ s then given by

$$\overline{SIR}_k^{(3)} = \frac{2A_k^2 X^2}{\sigma_{I_3}^2 + \sigma_{N_3}^2}. \tag{19}$$

The optimum weight for the third stage $p_{k,opt}^{(3)}$ is chosen to be the value of $p_k^{(3)}$ that maximizes the average SIR in (19).In the next section, we present a closed-form expression for $p_{k,opt}^{(3)}$.

4. Optimum Weights in Closed Form

Expressions for the optimum weights $p_{k,opt}^{(2)}$ and $p_{k,opt}^{(3)}$ can be obtained by differentiating (12) and (19) w.r.t. $p_k^{(2)}$ and $p_k^{(3)}$, respectively, and equating to zero. Accordingly, we obtain the expression for $p_{k,opt}^{(2)}$, in closed-form, as

$$p_{k,opt}^{(2)} = \frac{c_1(1-a_1)+e_1}{-a_1(c_1+e_1)+c_1+d_1+2e_1-\sigma^2(a_1^2-f_1)}, \tag{20}$$

Where,

$$a_1 = \sum_{\substack{j=1\\j\neq k}}^{K} \rho_{jk}^2, \quad c_1 = \sum_{\substack{l=1\\l\neq k}}^{K} A_l^2 \rho_{lk}^2,$$

$$d_1 = \sum_{\substack{l=1\\l\neq k}}^{K} A_l^2 \left(\sum_{\substack{j=1\\j\neq k,l}}^{K} \rho_{jk}\rho_{lj} \right)^2,$$

$$e_1 = \sum_{\substack{l=1\\l\neq k}}^{K} A_l^2 \rho_{lk} \sum_{\substack{j=1\\j\neq k,l}}^{K} \rho_{jk}\rho_{lj}, \quad f_1 = \sum_{\substack{j=1\\j\neq k}}^{K} \rho_{jk} \sum_{\substack{i=1\\i\neq k}}^{K} \rho_{ij}\rho_{ik}.$$

Likewise, the closed-form expression for can $p_{k,opt}^{(3)}$ be obtained as

$$p_{k,opt}^{(3)} = \frac{-2a_2 g_2 - f_2 - \sigma^2 (2a_2 + t_2)}{a_2 f_2 + 2e_2 + \sigma^2 (a_2 t_2 + 2v_2)}, \tag{21}$$

Where,

$$a_2 = \sum_{\substack{j=1\\j\neq k}}^{K} \rho_{jk}^2 \left(1 - p_j^{(2)}\right) - \sum_{\substack{j=1\\j\neq k}}^{K} \rho_{jk} p_j^{(2)} \sum_{\substack{r=1\\r\neq j,k}}^{K} \rho_{rj}\rho_{rk},$$

$$e_2 = \sum_{\substack{l=1\\l\neq k}}^{K} A_l^2 \left(\rho_{lk}^2 w_2^2 + (c_2 - d_2)^2 + 2\rho_{lk} w_2 (c_2 - d_2)\right),$$

$$f_2 = \sum_{\substack{l=1\\l\neq k}}^{K} A_l^2 \left(-2\rho_{lk}^2 w_2 - 2\rho_{lk}(c_2 - d_2)\right), \quad g_2 = \sum_{\substack{l=1\\l\neq k}}^{K} A_l^2 \rho_{lk}^2,$$

$$w_2 = 1 - p_l^{(2)} \sum_{\substack{q=1\\q\neq l}}^{K} \rho_{ql}^2, \quad c_2 = \sum_{\substack{j=1\\j\neq k,l}}^{K} \rho_{jk}\rho_{lj} \left(1 - p_j^{(2)}\right),$$

$$d_2 = \sum_{\substack{j=1\\j\neq k,l}}^{K} \rho_{jk} p_j^{(2)} \sum_{\substack{r=1\\r\neq j,l}}^{K} \rho_{rj}\rho_{rl}, \quad t_2 = 2(u_1 + z_1),$$

$$z_1 = \sum_{\substack{i=1\\i\neq k}}^{K} \rho_{ik} \left(-\rho_{ik} + \sum_{\substack{j=1\\j\neq k,i}}^{K} p_j^{(2)} \rho_{jk}\rho_{ij} \right),$$

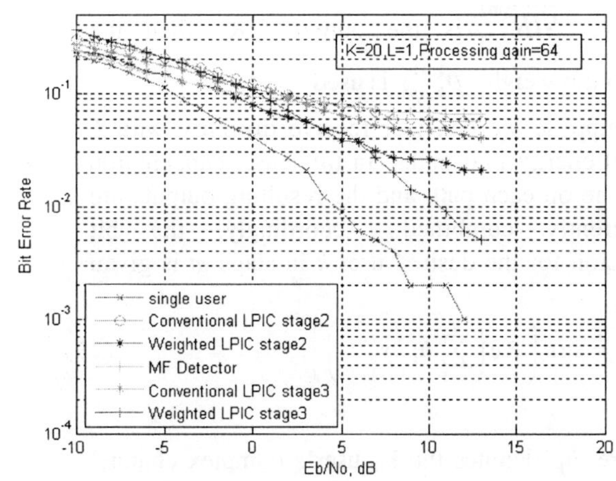

Fig. 1. Comparison of the BER performance of the SIR-optimized weighted LPIC as a function of SNR with that of the MF detector and the conventional LPIC on flat Rayleigh fading channels (L = 1). K = 20. Processing gain = 64. Random spreading sequences. No near-far effect: $A1$ = $A2$ = ⋯ = A_K.

$$u_1 = \sum_{\substack{l=1\\ l\neq k}} p_l^2 \rho_{lk}^2 , \qquad \upsilon_2 = u_1^2 + 2u_1 z_1 + t_1 ,$$

$$t_1 = \sum_{\substack{i=1\\ i\neq k}}^{K} \sum_{\substack{l=1\\ l\neq k}}^{K} \rho_{il} \left(-\rho_{ik} + \sum_{\substack{j=1\\ j\neq k,i}}^{K} p_j^{(2)} \rho_{jk} \rho_{ij} \right) \cdot \left(-\rho_{lk} + \sum_{\substack{j=1\\ j\neq k,l}}^{K} p_j^{(2)} \rho_{jk} \rho_{lj} \right).$$

As can be seen from (20) and (21), the complexity of optimum weights calculation for second and third stages, in terms of number of multiplication/addition operations, is of order K^2 and K^4, respectively.

4.1. *Probability of Bit Error*

The probability of bit error for the desired user k at the output of the m_{th} stage can be obtained in terms of the optimized SIR as

$$P_k^{(m)} = \frac{1}{2}\left(1 - \sqrt{\frac{\overline{SIR}_{k,opt}^{(m)}}{1 + \overline{SIR}_{k,opt}^{(m)}}} \right). \qquad (22)$$

Where $\overline{SIR}_{k,opt}^{(m)}$ is the output SIR when the optimum weight $p_{k,opt}^{(m)}$ is used.

Suppose we consider receive diversity with L equal-energy i.i.d paths. In this case, cancellation is done on each path and the resulting outputs are coherently combined. Accordingly, the bit decision for the desired user k in stage m is given by

$$\hat{b}_k^{(m)} = \operatorname{sgn}\left(\operatorname{Re}\left(\sum_{l=1}^{L} h_k^{l\,*} y_k^{(m)_l} \right) \right), \qquad (23)$$

where h_k^l denotes the k_{th} user's complex channel coefficient on the l_{th} receive antenna path, and $y_k^{m_l}$ denotes the k_{th} user's interference cancelled output of the m_{th} stage on the l_{th} receive antenna path, given by

$$y_k^{(m)_l} = y_k^{(1)_l} - p_k^{(m)_l} \sum_{j=1, j\neq k}^{K} \rho_{jk} y_j^{(m-1)_l} . \qquad (24)$$

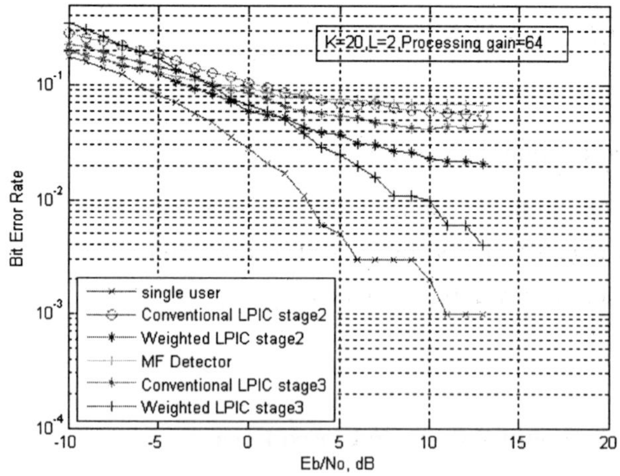

Fig. 2. Comparison of the BER performance of the SIR-optimized weighted LPIC as a function of SNR with that of the MF detector and the conventional LPIC on diversity channels (L = 2). K = 20. Processing gain = 64. Random spreading sequences. No near-far effect: $A1 = A2 = \cdots = AK$.

On each receive antenna path, the expressions for the variances due to interference, $\sigma_{I_m}^2$ and due to noise, $\sigma_{N_m}^2$ remain the same as those for the flat fading case given before. The probability of bit error for the desired user k with L equal energy diversity paths can be obtained as (similar to obtaining Eq. 3.140 in [1])

$$P_k^{(m)} = \frac{1}{2}\left[1 - \sqrt{\frac{\overline{SIR}_{k,opt}^{(m)}}{1 + \overline{SIR}_{k,opt}^{(m)}}} \left(1 + \sum_{n=1}^{L-1} \frac{1.3.5...(2n-1)}{n!2^n \left(1 + \overline{SIR}_{k,opt}^{(m)}\right)^n} \right) \right]. \qquad (25)$$

5. Results and Discussions

In this section, we present the BER performance of the SIR-optimized weighted LPIC scheme on Rayleigh fading and diversity channels. In Fig. 1, we illustrate a BER performance comparison of the SIR-optimized weighted LPIC as a function of average SNR per bit with that of the MF detector as well as the conventional LPIC (where the weight is taken to be unity in all stages) on flat Rayleigh fading channels (L = 1) for K = 20 users with no near-far effect (i.e., $A1 = A2 = ... = AK$). In all the numerical results presented here, we assign different random spreading sequences of processing gain 64 to different users, and the cross-correlation coefficients are computed for these random sequences. User 1 is taken to be the desired user. The BER plots for the SIR-optimized weighted LPIC are computed using (22) with the appropriate optimized SIR values. Figure 2 shows a similar performance comparison for diversity channels for $L = 2$, where the BER for the SIR-optimized weighted LPIC are computed using (25).We have obtained the BER through simulations as well (we found close match between analysis and simulation results, which is expected since the expressions are exact and there is no approximation involved). The decorrelating detector performance as well as the single user performance is also shown for comparison.

From Figs. 1 and 2 the following observations can be made. At high SNRs, the 2nd stage of the conventional LPIC performs better than the MF detector, due to accurate MAI estimates in good channel conditions (i.e., high SNRs). However, at low SNRs, the 2nd stage of the conventional LPIC performs poorer than the MF detector, which happens due to poor accuracy of the MAI estimates in the early stages of the PIC, particularly when channel conditions are poor (i.e., at low SNRs). This performance behavior improves in the 3rd stage of the conventional LPIC which performs better than the MF detector. However, it is noted that the SIR-optimized weighted LPIC clearly outperforms both the MF detector as well as the conventional LPIC. In fact, even the 2nd stage of the SIR optimized weighted LPIC outperforms the 3rd stage of the conventional LPIC, and the performance of the 3rd stage of the SIR-optimized LPIC tends closer to that of the decorrelating detector.

REFERENCES

[1] S. Verdu, *Multiuser Detection.* Cambridge University Press, 1998.

[2] M. Varanasi and B. Aazhang, "Multistage detection in asynchronous code-division multiple-access," *IEEE Trans. Commun.*, vol. 38, pp. 509-519, Apr. 1990.

[3] K. R. Shankar kumar and A. Chockalingam, Parallel Interference Cancellation in Multicarrier DS-CDMA Systems, *Proc. IEEE ICC'04,* Paris, June 2004

[4] R. Chandrasekaran and J. J. Shynk, "Analysis of parallel interference canceller for DS-CDMA signals," in *Proc. 37th Allerton Conf. onCommunication, Control and Computing*, Urbana, IL, Sept. 1999.

[5] D. R. Brown *et al.*, "On the performance of linear parallel interference cancellation," *IEEE Trans. Infor. Theory,* vol. 47, no. 5, pp. 1957-1970,July 2001.

[6] D. Divsalar, M. K. Simon, and D. Raphaeli, "Improved parallel interference cancellation for CDMA," *IEEE Trans. Commun.*, vol. 46, no. 2, pp.258-268, Feb. 1998.

[7] D. Guo *et al.*, "MMSE-based linear parallel interference cancellation in CDMA," in *Proc. IEEE ISSSTA,* pp. 917-921, Sept. 1998.

[8] Y-H. Li, M. Chen, and S-X. Chen, "Determination of cancellation factors for soft decision partial PIC detector in DS-CDMA systems," *Electronics Letters,* pp. 239-241, 3 Feb. 2000.

[9] M. Ghotbi and M. R. Soleymani, "A simple method for computing partial cancellation factors in CDMA using PPIC receiver," in *Proc. IEEE ICASSP,* pp. 973-976, 2004.

NETWORKS FOR NCW: CONCEPTS AND ISSUES

D. K. SUNIL
CHIEF MANGER (DESIGN)
STRATEGIC ELECTRONICS R&D CENTRE,
HINDUSTAN AERONAUTICS LIMITED.

ABSTRACT

Network centric warfare is the latest military doctrine that promises to increase combat power enormously. Network centric operations, as they are called presently, imply sharing of information among all the participants to improve situational awareness. The requirement is to have self synchronization in the network without dependence on fixed infrastructure. This article is an overview of such networks and the performance issues involved.

INTRODUCTION

Network centric warfare enables war fighters to leverage information advantage, an advantage broadly characterized by significantly improved capabilities for sharing and accessing information, to dramatically increase combat power [1].

In this paradigm, mobile devices self organize to create a network by exploiting their wireless network interfaces , without a requirement for pre-deployed infrastructure[2].

The advantages of such self organizing capability are[3] :

1. Adaptability with respect to changes in the system or environment.
2. Robustness against failure. There is no single point of failure and the system can repair or correct damage without external help.
3. A high lcvcl of scalability , which means that the system still works if the number of entities is very large.

This network model is called MANET(**M**obile **A**d hoc **NET**work). The network is composed of nodes which could be heterogeneous in terms of capabilities. These networks can be broadly classified as :

1. Pure MANET
2. Hybrid MANET

Pure MANET

This consists of devices that dynamically configure themselves to set up a temporary ad hoc network. Thus the network nodes must provide the functionality usually provided by fixed network infrastructure (e.g., routers, switches or servers). In this form it is like a peer to peer network on the internet. The data is transferred as packets among the nodes. A Bluetooth piconet is probably the most widespread example of a single hop MANET.

However the source and destination nodes may not always be within reception range. In such a case the packets would have to be routed to the destination via intermediate nodes. Then the network is called a multi hop network.

These networks suffer from the traditional problems of wireless networking such as multipath fading, interference and LOS (Line of Sight) propagation. In addition the multi hop nature, mobility and changing network topology add complexity in terms of routing and link maintenance.

The protocol stack consists of :

- Enabling technologies
  This includes data link , including the MAC (Media Access Control) and the physical layers. The following wireless network standards support the ad hoc network paradigm: IEEE 802.15.4 (Zigbee) for short range low data rate (<250 kbps) networks, Bluetooth (IEEE 802.15.1) for personal area networks, the 802.11 (Wi Fi, Wi Max etc) standards suite for high speed medium range MANET and 802.16 standards suite for high speed wide range networks.
- Networking protocols
  Network protocols do the routing and forwarding functions. They are of two

types : reactive and proactive .Proactive protocols attempt to maintain consistent and updated routing information for every pair of nodes by propagating proactively route updates at fixed time intervals e.g., AODV(Ad hoc On demand Distance Vector) protocol. In, contrast reactive protocols establish a route to a destination only when requested. After a route is established , it is maintained until either the destination becomes inaccessible or until the route is no longer used e.g., OLSR (Optimized Link State Routing) protocol.
On top of the networking protocols , MANET generally assumes the TCP(Transmission Control Protocol) . TCP manages message acknowledgment, retransmission and timeout. Many attempts to reliably deliver the message are made. If it gets lost along the way, the server will re-request the lost part. In TCP, there's either no missing data, or, in case of multiple timeouts, the connection is dropped.

- Applications
  Applications run directly on top of the transport layer by exploiting the services offered by TCP and UDP(User Datagram Protocol) and each protocol must implement other services it requires.

Hybrid MANET

By relaxing one of the main constraints of pure MANET , that is, the network is made of user devices only and no infrastructure exists , we move towards hybrid MANET. These are also known as Mesh Networks. Mesh networks are built upon a mix of fixed and mobile nodes interconnected via wireless links to form a multi hop ad hoc network. Unlike pure MANET , a mesh network introduces a hierarchy in the network architecture by adding dedicated nodes (called mesh routers) that communicate wirelessly to construct a wireless backbone. The wireless backbone has a (limited) number of connections with the wired Internet. Mobile nodes can be connected directly to each other's nodes, or can obtain multi hop connectivity to the Internet by connecting to the closest mesh router. The project RoofNet (MIT) demonstrated that it is possible to provide a city such as Boston, with broadband access with an 802.11b based wireless network backbone infrastructure. RoofNet consists of a limited number of nodes, positioned on roofs operated on a volunteer basis, which dynamically create the backbone and support mesh networking [4] . Other variants of MANET which are attracting a lot of research activity are VANET (Vehicular Ad hoc Networks) and WSN (Wireless Sensor Networks).
In Figure 1 a diagram of a typical mesh network with its three-tier architecture [5].

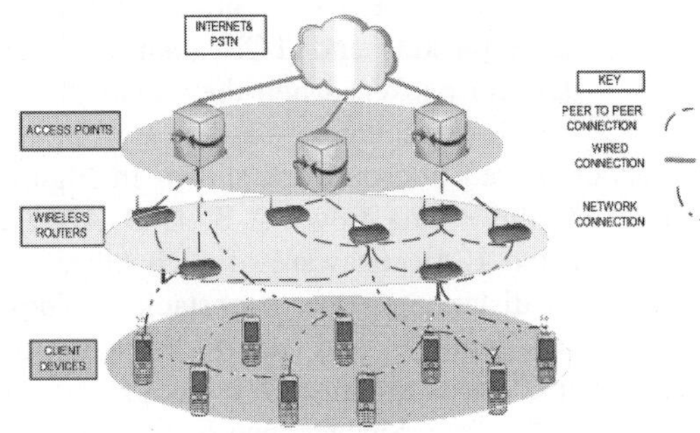

Figure 1

MANET throughput

In [6] it is shown that in a MANET with 'n' nodes, the per node throughput is bounded by **c/√n** where c is a constant. As 'n' increases, the per node throughput decreases. A plot for the case where c=1 is given in Figure 2

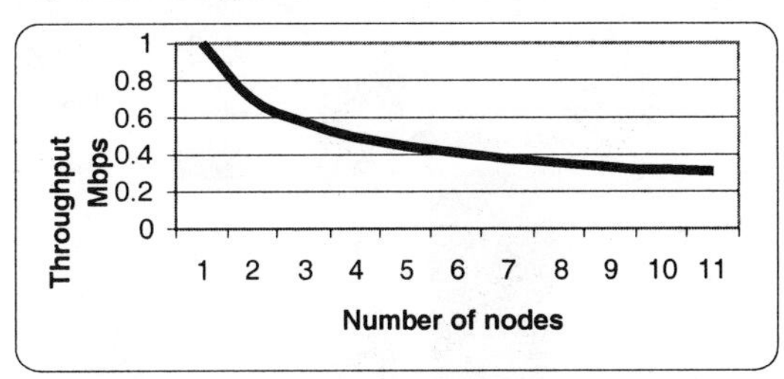

Figure 2

In Figure 3 , a comparison of throughput under wired and wireless multi hop given in [7] is shown.

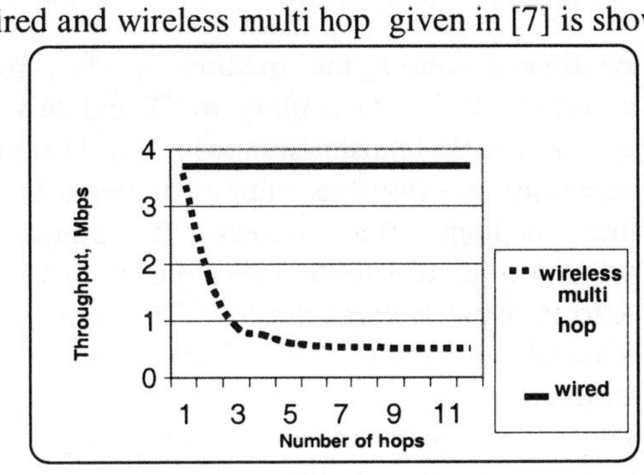

Figure 3

It is obvious that the throughput drops off after few hops are traversed. The throughput comes down due to packet loss caused by one or more of the following reasons[7]:

- Transmission failure due to high bit error rate of the wireless channel
- Channel access contention in the medium access (MAC) scheme used
- Transmission failure due to channel interference , known as *hidden terminal* and *exposed terminal* problems (also known as *fairness problem*)
- Channel access contention between TCP data packets and TCP acknowledgement (ACK) packets when they share the same wireless resources.

Consider the ad hoc network shown in Figure 4 . There are three data flows A-B, C-D AND E-F. Nodes A and E are unaware of each other either because of distance or due to obstacles . They are totally independent and emit asynchronously. Whenever C wants to transmit, it has to wait for the medium to be free. Since A and E are independent their silence periods never coincide. Therefore C sees the medium to be busy more often the others. Therefore its throughput will be less than the other two. This is known as the *exposed terminal* problem.

In the network shown in Figure 5, the line of sight between A and C is blocked by an obstacle.

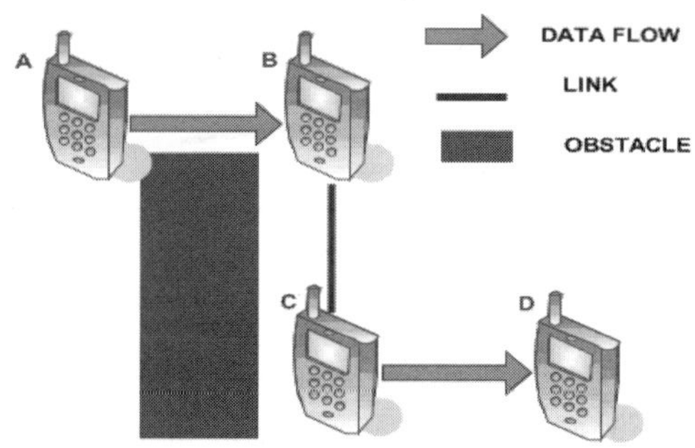

Figure 5

A always senses the medium to be free and transmits. C is transmitting to D and this causes collision at B. Transmission from C to D are always successful as collisions cannot happen at D. C sees the medium free unless B transmits an acknowledgement to A. Therefore the chances for A to transmit a frame are low. This again leads to reduced throughput . This is known as the *hidden terminal* problem.

This fairness problem can be alleviated by using the **RTS** (Request To Send)-**CTS**(Clear To Send) handshake but throughput will reduce. For example , in a chain of five nodes in a straight line A,B,C, D and E , parallel communications between A-B and D-E are possible, but if RTS-CTS is active ,and if D is transmitting to E then B cannot reply to the RTS of A(as it is in the interference range of D). Since spatial reuse is reduced , the throughput decreases. This is shown for a 802.11 network in the Figure 6 [8]:

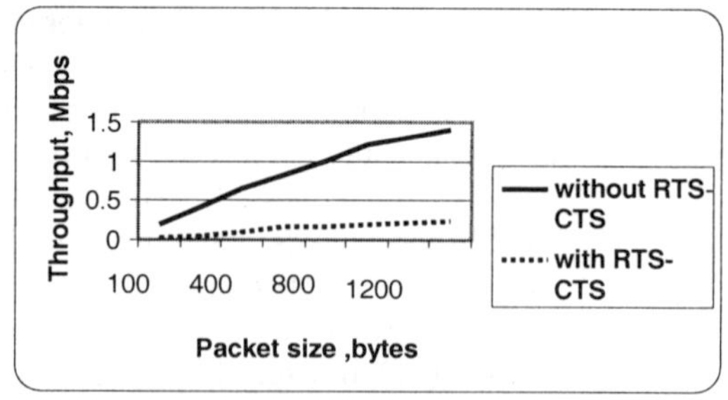

Figure 6

It is shown in [9] that the same inefficiencies of 802.11 apply of regular topologies like mesh and on random topologies with random traffic. The traffic pattern determines whether an ad hoc network's per node capacity will scale to large networks. In particular, for total capacity to scale up with network size the average distance between source and destination nodes must remain small as the network grows. Non-local traffic patterns in which this average distance grows with the network size result in a rapid decrease of per node capacity[9].

In [10] a battlefield scenario was created to demonstrate the network centric concept to DARPA in 2006, shown in Figure 7.

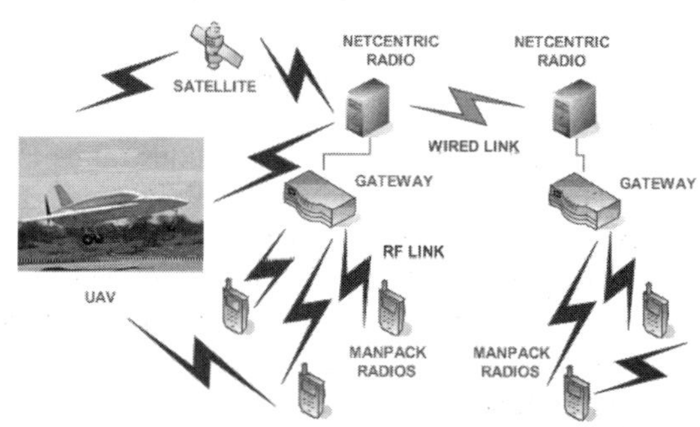

Figure 7

Central to this was a network centric radio system which provided a Broadband Mobile Ad-Hoc Radio backbone . Each NC(Network Centric) node operated as a vehicular or airborne relay mobile ad-hoc router (UAV borne) for the terrestrial backbone tactical network. Routing in each ground vehicle selected between this terrestrial backbone path and an alternate satellite backbone for assured line-of-sight (LoS) and beyond line-of-sight (BLoS) communications

As seen in Figure 8[10], throughput due to multihop transmission and mobility of nodes goes down from a peak of of 5 Mbps to a low of 45 kbps at larger distances. As network topology changes traffic congestion or packet loss trigger a reduction in data rate to assure delivery.

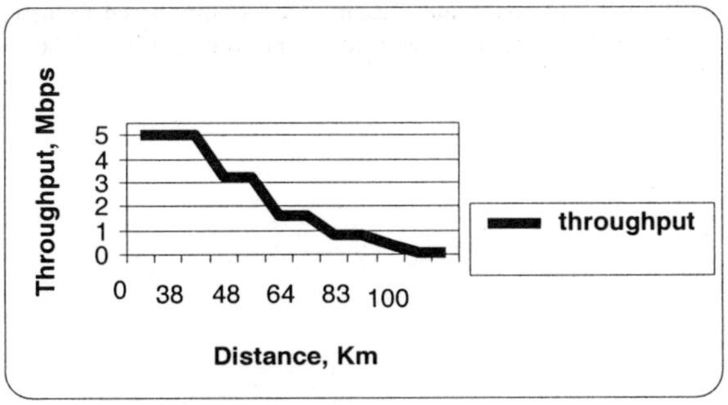

Figure 8

Implementing MANET in the battlefield

So is MANET the solution for the battlefield? Can it provide data intensive battlefield information using this multi hop paradigm? In the network centric paradigm the unit at the fringe "pulls " the required data from the network, as against the current idea of a central command post "pushing" data to the unit.

For example target footage available from a UAV(Unmanned Aerial Vehicle) or a helicopter could be delivered to the fringe unit on the ground , where the data is most required, through an ad hoc multi hop network. The ' fringe' unit would find necessary information on the ad hoc network.

How can these networks be applied to airborne platforms? For example, a pilot would be in a position to view data about a target from different sources. The sources could be a UAV, satellite or an AWACS(Airborne Warning and Control System). As the aircraft need not always be in LOS of the Command centre, it is difficult to push data to the aircraft. Therefore an ad hoc network would give the pilot more information leading to an informed decision.

So what are the requirements of constructing an ad hoc network? The ad hoc network throughput suffers from the following problems as outlined above:

1. As the data traverses through many nodes throughput falls due to collisions.
2. The wireless link is affected by frequency and time selective fade due to physical obstacles or due to mobility of the nodes

The network design would involve implementing the following steps:

1. Implement a hierarchical network of clusters[12] at different topology levels . Each node belongs to one cluster , each cluster has one clusterhead and each node is at most few hops from the clusterhead. The clustering would be effected using Basagni's algorithm[11]. The radios at the lowest level would have one wireless interface, the radios at the next higher level with two wireless interfaces. These nodes can relay messages using a frequency band or MAC protocol that can differ from the one used for communication at the lower level. The third level nodes can represent high capacity airborne nodes with multiple wireless interfaces.
2. Provide alternate direct links through satellite or UAV to guarantee throughput in conditions where the throughput falls dramatically.
3. Reduce collisions by exploiting implicit coordination[3] . This means nodes detect and analyze the communication messages exchanged in the vicinity. The nodes adjust their traffic accordingly. It also has implications in terms of developing 'cognitive radios' with advanced spectrum monitoring capabilities.
4. Design protocols that adapt to changes in the vicinity. There are three levels of adaptation required[3] of the protocol :
   a. **Level 1**: It should cope with node failure and mobility. An example is Basagni's[11] mobility adaptive clustering algorithm.
   b. **Level 2** : It should adapt its own parameters (e.g., value of timers, cluster size) as a reaction to change in order to optimize system performance. An example is McDonald's clustering algorithm[13] which adapts the cluster size as a function of the observed level of mobility in the network.
   c. **Level 3** : It should realize that if the changes are so severe that the currently employed mechanism is no longer suitable. For example, the dynamics of a network may be so high that a clustering algorithm no longer converges, it could then switch from cluster based hierarchical routing to flooding.

CONCLUSIONS

Large scale ad hoc networks require a large number of nodes which are *clustered* so that each node sends only to nodes within a fixed radius, independent of the network size. So a battlefield network would have *clusters* with mesh routers as the backbone with connections to the internet. However the scale of deployment is obviously large. The throughput depends on network topology, node mobility and quality of the radio links. The actual data rate could be surprisingly less than that expected theoretically. The traffic pattern determines whether an ad hoc network's per node capacity will scale to large networks. In particular, for total capacity to scale up with network size the average distance between source and destination nodes must remain small as the network grows. Non-local traffic patterns in which this average distance grows with the network size result in a rapid decrease of per node capacity. The network implementation would have to look at issues like added radio capabilities , protocol adaptation to a hierarchical topology for guaranteed throughput.

REFERENCES

[1] John J. Garstka, Joint Staff Directorate for C4 Systems, " Network Centric Warfare : An Overview of Emerging Theory", http://www.mors.org/publications/phalanx/dec00/feature.htm.

[2] M.Conti, S.Giordano, "Multihop Ad hoc Networking: The Theory ", IEEE Comm. Mag, April 2007, pp.78-86

[3] C.Prehofer, C.Bettsetter, "Self-Organisation in Communication Networks: Principles and Design Paradigms", IEEE Comm. Mag, July 2005, pp.78-85

[4] M.Conti, S.Giordano, "Multihop Ad hoc Networking: The Reality ", IEEE Comm. Mag, April 2007, pp.88-95

[5] "Las Vegas meshes its network", Communications News, October 2004

[6] P.Gupta, P.R.Kumar, "The capacity of Wireless Networks, " IEEE Trans. Info. Theory, vol. IT-46, No2, Mar 2000, pp 388-404.

[7] Li-Ping Tung, *et al,* "TCP throughput enhancement over Wireless Mesh Networks", IEEE Comm. Mag. Nov 2007, pp 64 -70.

[8] C. Chaudet *et al,* "Performance Issues with IEEE802.11 in Ad hoc networking", IEEE Comm. Mag, July 2005, pp.110-116.

[9] J.Li *et al,* "Capacity of Ad hoc Wireless Networks", MIT Laboratory for Computer Science, http://pdos.csail.mit.edu/pubs.html

[10] S.Seidel *et al,* "An Adaptive Broadband Mobile Ad-Hoc Radio Backbone System", www.darpa.mil/STO/Solicitations/WAND/pdf/DARPA_NC_Radio_System.pdf

[11] S.Basagni, "Distributed clustering for ad hoc networks," Proc. Int'l Symp. Parallel Architectures, Algorithms and Nets. , Perth, Australia, June 1999.

[12] L.V.Gonzalez, *et al,* "HOLSR : A Hierarchical Proactive Routing Mechanism for Mobile Ad hoc Networks", IEEE Comm. Mag, July 2005, pp.118-125.

[13] A.B.McDonald and T.Znati, "A Mobility based framework for adaptive clustering in wireless ad hoc networks," IEEE JSAC , vol 17, Aug 1999, pp 1466-87.

Session 8

OPTIMIZING TCP QUALITY OF SERVICE PARAMETER USING LINUX KERNEL BASED TUNING PARAMETERS FOR HIGH PERFORMANCE NETWORKS

S N PRADHAN, PRIYANKA SHARMA

Nirma University of Science and Technology, S G Highway
Ahmedabad, Gujarat, India

HITESH NIMBARK

Nirma University of Science and Technology, S G Highway
Ahmedabad, Gujarat, India

TCP has become the dominant protocol for all network data transport because it presents a simple uniform data delivery service. With the growth of high performance networking, a single host may have simultaneous connections that vary in bandwidth. Consequently, connections on a single host can and will scale in bandwidth by several orders. TCP, now, requires queues proportional in size to a path's bandwidth. Traditional statically fixed mechanisms for allocating and limiting TCP queue space fall short on today's Internet, and often limit throughput only a small fraction of the available bandwidth specially for long- fat network (large bandwidths and high round-trip times). The paper proposes a novel linux kernel based TCP tuning approach to meet the above requirements.

1. Introduction

The congestion control algorithms [1] and large window extensions [2] in TCP permit a host running a single TCP stack to support concurrent connections across the entire range of band-width. In principle, all application programs that use TCP should be able to enjoy the appropriate share of available bandwidth on any path without involving manual configuration by the application, user, or system administrator.

For a given path, TCP requires at least one bandwidth-delay product of buffer space at each end of the connection. An experienced system administrator can tune a system for a particular type of connection, but then performance suffers for connections that exceed the expected bandwidth-delay product, while system resources are wasted for low bandwidth-delay product connections. Since there are often many more "small" connections than "large" ones, system-wide tuning can easily cause buffer memory to be inefficiently utilized by more than an order of magnitude. Expertise in network is not normally available to end users, and it is wrong to require it of applications and users. Further, even an expert cannot predict changes in conditions of the network path over the lifetime of a connection. We proposed a straightforward modification to Linux 2.6.26.5 kernel that automatically and transparently address the above problems while maintaining connection semantics and the ubiquitously deployed feature for TCP.

This paper proposes a system for adaptive tuning of buffer sizes based upon network conditions and system memory availability. It is intended to operate transparently without modifying existing applications. Since it does not change TCP's Congestion Avoidance characteristics, it does not change TCP's basic interactions with the Internet or other Internet application

2. Quality of service

QoS means providing consistent, predictable data delivery service. The service realized by TCP over today's Internet is generally known as "best-effort". The need for service differentiation has lead to develop a number of architectural solutions to satisfy heterogeneous application requests and provide QoS.

There are two main approaches to delivering QoS services. The first is to create for each service request a reservation state and keep it for all the connection. This is the basic idea on which the Integrated Service Architecture (IntServ) [3] has been built. The second is to perform the classification of the traffic at the entering of the network and then to develop a policy administration function to create service outcomes. This is the basic principle of Differentiated Service (DiffServ) [4]. The novel approach provided here by tuning the OS to increase the over all network throughput.

3. TCP Window

A TCP window of data is the amount of data transmitted on a connection during one round-trip time. The concepts regarding various TCP windows used here, is explained below.

Receive window: is the buffer amount as receiving end to store data before process or send it upper layer of TCP stack. Receiving application is not able to process data as quickly as the sending application or the network can transmit it. In this case, it is necessary to have a flow control mechanism to slow the transmission rate of the sender. TCP implements flow control by announcing a receive window (rcWnd) in each segment header. This window announced by the receiver is an upper bound on the sender's window size. A classical TCP implementation in Linux kernel maintains a buffer know as receiving limit window (rclWnd) of a static size. TCP announces it's receive window as the amount of space available in that buffer. If the application reads slower than data arrives, the buffer will start to fill. As the buffer fills, the window size and therefore throughput will fall (eventually reaching zero when the buffer fills entirely). Throughput will quickly match the application's consumption rate.

Retransmit queue: As stated above, the sender must keep all outstanding data in a retransmit queue. If the amount of memory available for this queue is an upper bound on window size.

Congestion window: In many cases, the amount of traffic coming into a router is greater than its outgoing bandwidth. A finite quantity of packets may be queued in the router, but in a steady state a certain percentage must be dropped. In this case, the router is said to be a bottleneck and experiencing congestion. One of TCP's functions is to detect this congestion (usually by observing lost packets) and limit its transmission rate accordingly. A TCP sender maintains a congestion window, an upper bound on window size based on the observed properties of the network.

Sending window: The amount of data the sender produces per round-trip time is yet another bound on window size. If a sender has little or no data to send, the window will be accordingly small. For example, an interactive application such as telnet will likely send between zero and a few segments per round-trip time.

If a connection's throughput is limited only by the network, its window size will be limited by the congestion window (cwnd). In this case, we ideally have: window = cwnd and throughput = bandwidth (BW). Since throughput = window/Round Trip Time (RTT), we have bandwidth = cwnd/RTT. Therefore, we have:

$$cwnd = BW * RTT \qquad (1)$$

This quantity is known as the bandwidth-delay product, or BDP (It should be noted that this cwnd is the ideal congestion window). In practice, bandwidth is not known and may change over time, so the congestion control mechanism grows and shrinks cwnd as it drives the network into congestion. The RTT between two endpoints is fundamentally limited by the distance between them and the speed of light. The highest bandwidths, however, have been growing exponentially with time (similar to the way processors follow Moore's "law"). Consequently, BDPs across the Internet are also increasing over time. Further, connection BDPs may vary by many orders of magnitude on a single host. For example, a host connected with 100 Mbps fast Ethernet may connect to a similar host at the same time as it connects to one with a 56 kbps modem.

Mathis [5] described the relationship between the upper bound of TCP bandwidth, packet round trip time RTT , and packet loss p with the equation 2

$$BW \leq (MSS/RTT) * (C/\sqrt{p}) \qquad (2)$$

To achieve substantial network performance over a wide area network that has a relatively large RTT, the required maximum packet loss rate p must be very low. The relationship derived by Mathis for the maximum packet loss rate required to achieve a target bandwidth.

For example, if the minimum link bandwidth between two hosts is OC-12 (622 Mbps), and the average round trip time is 20 msec, the maximum packet loss rate necessary to achieve 66% of the link speed (411 Mbps) is approximately 0.00018%, which represents only two packets lost out of every 100000 packets. Current loss rates on the commercial Internet backbone [6] are on the order of 0.1%, which puts a hard upper limit on the potential bandwidth available to an application.

We need to ensure our buffers are large enough to “fill the pipe”– That is, they must be able to hold a bandwidth-delay product’s worth of data. Suppose on a 1Gbps link with 100ms delay that’s 1Gbps x 100ms = 12.5 MB, But stock buffers are far too small - only 8KB by default for window and 16KB for Linux so stock flows will use: 16KB/12.5MB ≈ 0.0013which is

1/1000th of available bandwidth. We could see the big size of available bandwidth being west in case of high performance long-fat network.

4. Linux /proc FileSystem

The two primary functions of Linux kernel is to control access to physical devices on the computer and to schedule when and how processes interact with these devices.

The /proc/ directory contains a hierarchy of special files which represent the current state of the kernel allowing applications and users to peer into the kernel's view of the system. The /proc/ directory contains virtual files.

5. Web100

The web100 [7] tool provides a window to access the characteristics of a TCP connection for application developers and systems administrators.

Using web100 we can receive instantaneous value of cWnd through the instrument curr_cWnd (current congestion window). The instruments are collectively referred as a Kernel Instrument Set (KIS). Web100 is part and partial implementation of RFC2578 [8] and RFC1323 [9].

6. Implementation

The web100 kernel has added a number of variables (exposed externally through /proc filesystem) or instruments to the kernel sock structure which tracks a number of critical events on each of the TCP connections on the system.

The kernel API consists of a few essential data structures. An essential overview of these data structures are provided below.

Agent - web100_agent: Agent is the top most object of the library, and any web100 based developed using this library starts off by obtaining a pointer to this object. This object contains a list of "connection" objects and "group" objects. Connection - web100_connection: This is an object identified by a Connection ID (CID) that is set up by the kernel, one for each TCP connection on the host. Group - web100_group: A group is a collection of web100 "variable" descriptors. A group has a name which shows up as file in /proc/web100/<cid> directory. By having access to a group, one can read all the variables in that group. Variable - web100_var: A variable is descriptor that contains the name of the variable and the necessary information to get its value from the kernel. Snapshot - web100_snapshot: A snapshot contains a connection, a group, and all the values for that combination of connection and group at a particular time. Here we are reading per connection, per agent, per group, per snap variables and set accordingly the tune groups. The core part of implemented algorithm is shown below.

```
Create local_type agent 'agnt'
Ceate group 'grp'
Identity address type 'addType'
While 'grp'
Identify connection 'con' , 'snp', 'cid'
Disable kernel default buffer setting facility
Check address type ipv4/v6
Read local address and port 'ladd', 'lport'
Read remote address and 'radd', 'rport'
Define snap 'snp'
If rport is not in reserved
While inst in snap
If inst is rcWnd and con_state is "Established"
enable window scaling
Set rclWnd = 2 * curr_cWnd
If rclWnd >=12000000 then
Disable SACK
Disable spoofin, sy-flood attech if require
Disable ICMP redirect if require
Set ssThrsh
Release memory if con closed
```

When project module starts up, it reads /proc/web100 file and read per connection kernel instruments, convert IP and port address from kernel space to user space. It also converts the instruments value in normal data type for the display and modification. We are setting The rclWnd $\geq 2 *$ curr_cwnd (current congestion window) to fully open the TCP. The twice is for the saving packet in case of retransmission and reordering. We enable the scaling window size opetion for extension for the high-performance. We require to check the size of rclWnd, which not be exceed 12MB. If it is grater then 12MB and selective retransmission event occur then searching for interested packet take long time then RTO (retransmission time out), which force the slow start [10]. Next store the rcvWnd to /proc/web100/cid/tune file. If the local/remote port is on a "Stop or not Selected

Connection" list then leave the connection un-tuned. Upon notification of new TCP connection ended, project algorithm releases the memory.

Slow start threshold (shThrsh) is use when switching from exponential increase to linear increase. The value for ssthresh for a given path is cached in the routine table If there is a retransmission on a connection to a given host, then all connections to that host for the next 10 minute will use a reduced ssthresh or if previous connect to that host is practically good. Then you might stay slow start in long time. We are using following parameter to disable the same.

net.ipv4.web100_no_metrics_save

We disable the parameters like *net.ipv4.conf.eth0.accept_source_route,net.ipv4.conf.lo.accept_source_route,net.ipv4.conf.default.accept_source_route,net.ipv4.conf.all.accept_source_route* to prevent a hacker from using a spoofing attack against the IP address of the server. The *net.ipv4.tcp_syncookies* parameter enables TCP-SYN cookies, which protect the server from syn-flood attacks, both denial-of-service (DoS) or distributed denial-of-service (DDoS).

The parameters like *net.ipv4.conf.eth0.secure_redirect, net.ipv4.conf.lo.secure_redirects,net.ipv4.conf.default.secure_redirects,net.ipv4.conf.all.secure_redirects* were used to configure the server to ignore redirects from machines that are listed as gateways. Redirect can be used to perform attacks, so we only want to allow them from trusted sources. In addition, we could allow the interface to accept or not accept any ICMP redirects. The ICMP redirect is a mechanism for routers to convey routing information to hosts. We disable these redirects also.

For ignoring all kinds of icmp packets or pings we used *net.ipv4.icmp_echo_ignore_all*

Some routers send invalid responses to broadcast frames, and each one generates a warning that is logged by the kernel. These responses can be ignored using *net.ipv4.icmp_ignore_bogus_error_response.* One of the issues found in servers with many simultaneous TCP connections is the large number of connections that are open but unused. TCP's keepalive function can be overwritten to drop the connection after 30 minutes, instead of 7200 seconds (which is a default number).

7. Testing Tools

The network measurement tools to measure physical data-link bandwidth, RTT, loss rate, router buffer sizes at each hop in the network, and measure end-to-end network bandwidth. Tools like Iperf [11], and Xplot[14] was used with Tcpdump[12], Tcptrace[13] for for per-connection throughput measurements

8. Test Bed

The Testbed setup consisted of senders and receivers connected with high speed routers. Large avi files were transferred between the nodes.

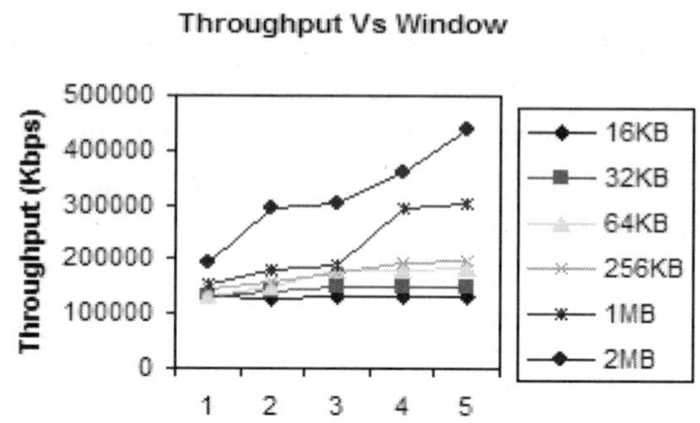

Figure 1. Throughput Vs Window size.

For 16KB of window size we are having throughput of 132Mbps maximum while for 2MB of window size it is 438Mbps as shown in Figure 1. Figure 2 shows the throughput for the connection port 52218. The instantaneous throughput value by yellow dots are at around 150MB.

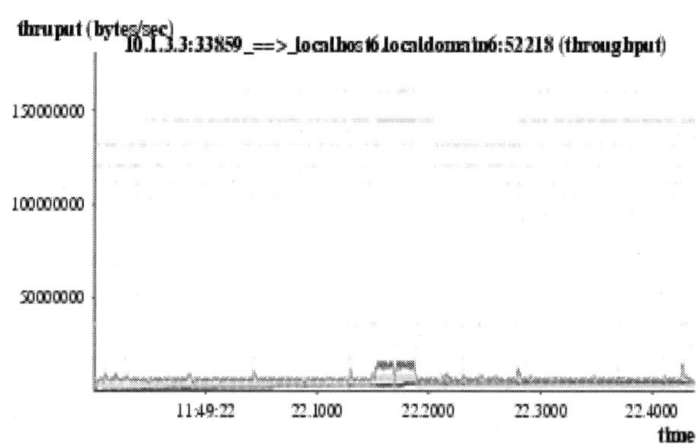

Figure 2. Throughput before window tuning.

The Figure 3, shows that after tuning the window buffer, maximum dots at seen at 550MB. We can conclude that the throughput increase from 150-580Mbps.

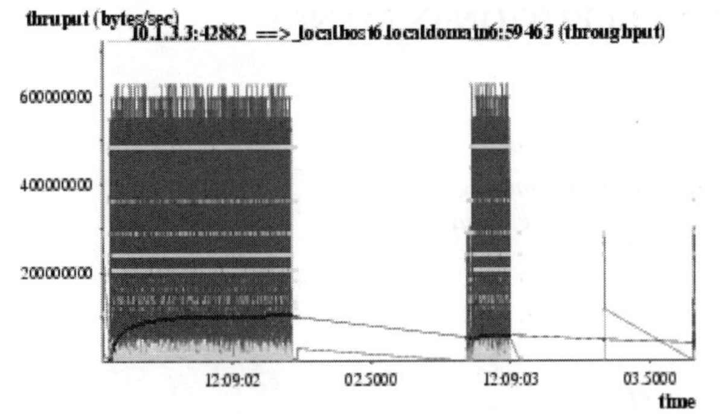

Figure 3. Throughput after window tuning.

The Figure 4 shows the announce window size vary with every transaction. This is because at the receiving end the window size is not fixed.

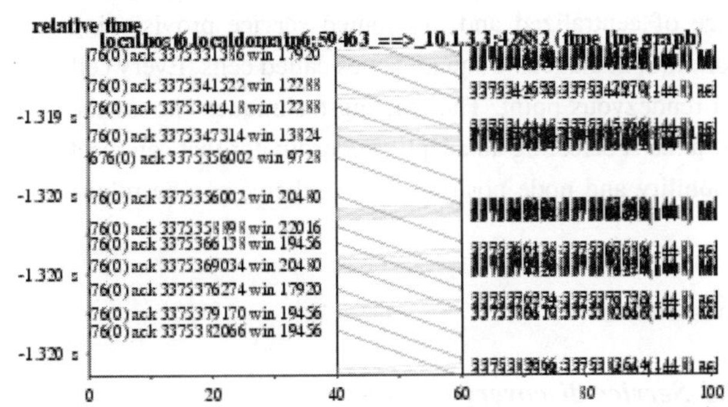

Figure 4. Timeline graph after tuning.

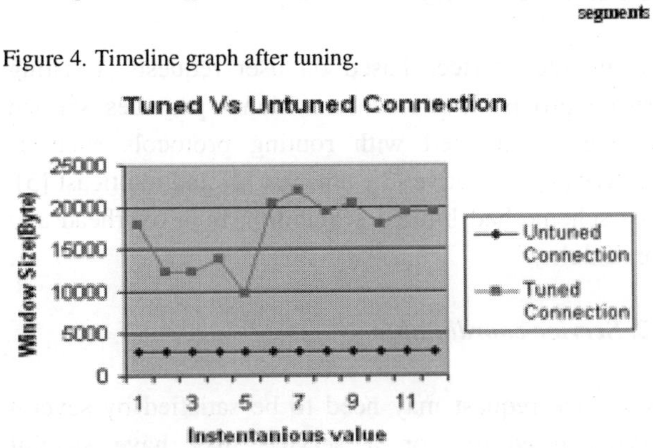

Figure 5. Tuned/Untuned Connection.

The Figure 5 shows the 12 instantaneous window sizes for before and after tuning. For tuned connection, we can get the window with varying sizes like 17920, 12288 etc. in case of long fat network.

9. Conclusion

This paper demonstrates TCP tuning using the /proc file system is a novel approach. We have identified requirements for QoS parameter tuning for TCP as a per connection per destination approach, to achieve maximum throughput across all connections simultaneously within the resource limits of the sender. The technique modifies TCP implementation of Linux kernel 2.6.26.5 to optimize the memory and bandwidth requirements of network connections resulting in greatly improved performance, a decrease in packet loss under bottleneck conditions, and greater control of buffer utilization by the end hosts.

10. References

1. W. Stevens, RFC 2001 TCP Slow Start, Congestion Avoidance, Fast Retransmit, and Fast Recovery Algorithms, (January 1997)
2. V. Jacobson, RFC1323 TCP Extensions for High Performance, (May 1992)
3. A Braden R., Clark D. and Shenker S., Integrated Services in the Internet, (1992)
4. Blake S., Black D., Carlson M., Davies E., WangZ. and Weiss W. Web1 Architecture: an Overview, RFC 1633, (June 1994), An Architecture for Differentiated Services, RFC 2475, December 1998.
5. M Mathism H Senjke, Mahdavi, T. The Macroscopic Behaviour of the TCP Congestion Avoidance Algorithm, Computer Communication Review, volume 27, Number3, (July 1997)
6. H Sivakumar, S. Bailey, R. L. Grossman, PSockets: The Case for Application-level Network Striping for Data Intensive Applications using High Speed Wide Area Networks", Proceedings of Supercomputin, IEEE (2000)
7. Bryan Henderson Linux Loadable Kernel Module HOWTO ww.ibiblio.org/pub/Linux/docs/HOWTO/other-formats/pdf/Module-HOWTO.pdf
8. K McCloghrie, J Case, M Rose, Structure of Management Information Version 2 (SMIv2)" RFC2578
9. V Jacobson, R. Braden, D. Borman, TCP Extensions for High Performance, RFC1323
10. TCP Tuning, http://www-didc.lbl.gov/TCP-tuning/linux.html
11. Iperf tool www.noc.ucf.edu/Tools/Iperf/
12. V Jacobson, C. Leres, S. McCanne, tcpdump available at ftp://ftp.ee.lbl.gOv/tcpdump.tar.Z
13. Tcptrace, Ohio University, available at http://irg.cs.ohiou.edu/software/tcptrace/download.html
14. Xplot project, http://www.xplot.org

ADAPTIVE SERVICE COORDINATOR ELECTION IN MANET

Cynthia. . J

Senior Lecturer, Department Of Information Technology
Kumaraguru College Of Technology, Coimbatore, ndia
Cynthia_clement@rediffmail.com

Sumathy. V

Asst. Professor, Department of ECE
GCT, Coimbatore, Tamil Nadu, India.sumi_gct2001@yahoo.co.in

Abstract

Supporting scalable and efficient routing and service provisioning in MANET has been a big research challenge. Hierarchical service provisioning is flexible and takes advantage of centralized and distributed service provisioning schemes. A hierarchical structure is created by dividing the network into manageable square zones called cells. Every cell in the hierarchy has an access point and the entire region has an rendezvous point. The existing techniques choose the leaders based on Zone ID or geographic hash function. This paper aims at selecting an adaptive coordinator that can meet the QoS requirements such as remaining battery power, node mobility and node position. Such scheme can be robust against the unpredictable faults in MANETs.

Keywords: multicast, service provision, geographic position, coordinator election

1. Introduction

Emerging ad hoc networks are infrastructure-less networks consisting of wireless devices with various power constraints, capabilities and mobility characteristics. An essential capability in future ad hoc network is the ability to provide scalable multicast services. In MANET, service provisioning is done on the existing proactive and reactive routing protocols [1]. Multicast based service provisioning is needed for today's commercial mobile applications. From literature its found that hierarchical position based multicasting [12,13,14] is an efficient and scalable method of delivering a service from a service provider to a service requester.

2. Service Provisioning in MANET

The service-provisioning framework[1] comprise of service discovery, coordination and delivery.

2.1 Service discovery

Locate the services based on user requests. Existing service provision protocol in Manet provides service discovery combined with routing protocols such as reactive [2], proactive [3], uni-cast [4] and multicast [5]. This scheme had limited scalability, high overhead and unreliability.

2.2. Service coordination

A service request may need to be satisfied by several service providers, or a service may have several candidate providers. To enable coordination, the service provision framework should be able to track a group of service providers and their services.

Service coordination was tough to handle in the existing schemes. Centralized directory based scheme, [6] help the communication between the service provider and clients, but is hard to scale and leads to bottlenecks. Local directory based scheme [7] search as request by distribution but is hard to scale for large networks. A generic architecture has been provided in [10], with the role of each layer differing for the client and the service provider.

2.3. Service delivery

Deliver relevant service data and control messages. Multicasting is used to support efficient group communication. Position based routing is, routing to the destination based on a nodes location. Its also known as geocasting. In geographic uni-cast routing [7] mobile nodes are aware of their own positions and source can identify destination by location service [8], but they had high control overhead in dynamic environment. When service delivery is done by geographic multicast routing [9], the routing performance was increased but it needs information in packet header and is also hard to scale in large networks. To improve scalability and improve data encoding various hierarchical geographic multicasting algorithms are proposed in the literature.

3. Hierarchical service provisioning infrastructure

3.1. Virtual zone construction [12]

The network terrain is divided into virtual zones. The length of a side of square zone is defined as zone size. A node can calculate its ZID from its position coordinates (x,y)as a = [(x-$x_{0)}$ / zone_size] and b = a = [(y-$y_{0)}$ / zone_size], where (x0,y0) is the position of the virtual origin. The position of its center (x_c,y_c) is x_c =x_0 +(a+0.5)*zone_size, y_c =y_0 +(b+0.5) * zone_size. The value of decomposition index d can be fixed depending on the scalability requirements. However even a decomposition index of 2 can scale to sufficiently large number of group members. A region can be divided into d^2 cells with one AP each and d^2 AP are managed by one RP [13].

3.2. Membership management

In Hierarchical Geographic multicast routing HGMR[14], a rendezvous point (RP) maintains the membership vector indicating the cells having the group members. A source that has to provide the service gets the membership information from the RP and constructs the overlay minimum spanning tree(With only the group members and no intermediate nodes) using PRIMs algorithm. HGMR uses the geographic forwarding technique of HRPM [13] to deliver the packets from source to AP of each cell with the group member and uses the cost over progress of GMR[12] to deliver the packet from AP to member.

3.3. Geographical Position based Multicast routing

The geographical position based multicast algorithm does group management and multicast forwarding [8]. The group management scheme is responsible for the dissemination of the membership information for the multicast groups, so that the forwarding nodes know in which direction receivers are located.

The multicast forwarding algorithm is executed by a forwarding node to determine the neighbors that should receive a copy of a given multicast packet. This decision is based on the information provided by the group management scheme. Assuming that each node in the network is able to determine its own position, e.g., through the use of GPS.

Position-based multicast requires that the forwarding nodes know the locations of the destinations. Including all destinations explicitly in the data packet header, does not scale well as the size of the multicast group increases. Therefore the proposed schemes in [13, 14], introduces hierarchical group membership management. To deliver multicast packets, from a source to the subscribed group members, the nodes use the information stored in their member tables.

4. Overview of Zone ID and geographic hashing based coordinator selection

4.1. An efficient geographic multicast protocol for mobile ad hoc networks EGMP [15]

EGMP elects a leader through leader election process. Wherein, a node checks its neighbor table to decide its leader. If the neighbor table has no other zone nodes, it announces itself as a leader. If no other node has been elected as leader and if the new node finds itself closer to the zone center it announces itself as the leader. If more than one node is willing to announce it as a leader, the one with the largest node ID is elected as leader and maintains the multicast table. This is accomplished by having each node periodically broadcast beacon messages containing the ID and position of the node. Beacon messages are not forwarded by the receiving nodes.

4.2. Hierarchical Rendezvous point multicasting protocol HRPM[13] :

HRPM uses hierarchical rendezvous point multicast, where each cell is managed by an access point and entire region is managed by an rendezvous point(RP). To avoid keeping track of AP and RP using some external location service HRPM adopts the concept of mobile geographic hashing. The multicast members can make use of an agreed upon hash function to hash the multicast group identifier (GID) and obtain the RP / AP location. Any node can get the position of AP / RP using a well-know hash function and its GID: H(GID) = (x,y) where x,y € MANET region

4.3. Vote Based (VB) Algorithm

Even though the use of hash function minimizes the detours by hashing to a scoped area, it can also cause a hotspot at the center of the network; Fei Li et al have proposed a vote-based clustering (VC) algorithm [11], for election of the cluster head using location and power information. The eligibility factor for selection of a cluster head, is selected depending on parameters like computational ability, battery power, the node transmission power, the node mobility, and position. We use this model for selection of a core node (Rendezvous point \ access point). In the voting process, every node in a zone, calculates its own eligibility factor as follows,

$EF_i(t) = a_1e^{-vi(t)} + a_2B_i(t) + a_3(1-E_i(t))$

Where $v_i(t)$ is the mobile node average speed at time t_i and $B_i(t)$ is the remaining battery power in node i at time t_i. $E_i(t)$ is the Euclidian distance of node i to the Zone center calculated at time I and a1,a2,a3 are weighting factors that reflect the importance of each parameter ($0 \leq a_i \leq 1$), i =1,...,3). The node with highest value of eligibility factor will be elected as core node.

VB Algorithm:

1. When a new node enters a zone, it sends a beacon message to learn about the core node (RP \ AP).
2. If there is no other core node the new node declares itself as the core node.
3. To elect an AP \ RP, initially the nodes in one hop distance to centre of zone, calculates its eligibility factor, to elect one amongst itself as an AP \ RP.
4. When the AP \ RP moves more than 100 meters or for every Intvalmin seconds for AP and Intvalmax seconds for RP, all one hop neighbours of old core node recalculates its eligibility factor to elect a new AP \ RP.

4.4. Service provisioning

Once an AP for a zone is elected all the data are routed through it. It maintains the record of all the nodes and the services present in its network. It also has prior information about the leaders of its neighboring zones. So when a node requests a service present in its own zone or from another zone, the request is made through the leader [5]. If the service is present in the same zone, the leader routes the QUERY MESSAGE to the service provider and the service provider responds to the service requester by means of a HIT MESSAGE. [15].

5. Performance evaluation

5.1 Simulation Environment

The simulator setup uses ns2 simulator. The network field size of 1500m×1500m, containing 40-50 mobile nodes is considered. For the multicast traffic, the source of multicast session generates packets at a constant rate. The performance of Zone Id, Hash function and voting based algorithms that are used to select service coordinator are compared. The experimentation is particularly interested in the scalability of the multicast protocols and service provisioning.

5.2 Effect of Data Loss

The simulation is run at various time intervals. The coordinator is elected using Zone Id, Hash function and voting based algorithms. The data loss using vote based algorithm is less than hash function based selection which is less when compared to Zone Id based selection. This is because as the coordinator stays for longer period within the zone. It continues to route packets without data loss.

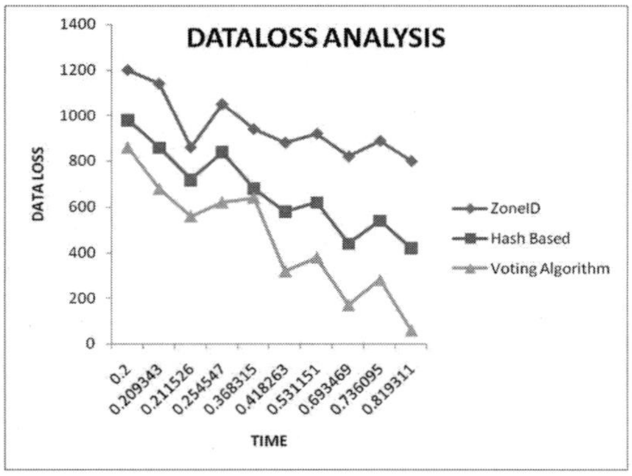

Figure 1. VB algorithm _ Data Loss

5.3 Effect of Throughput :

The simulation is run at various time intervals. The coordinator is elected using Zone Id, Hash function and voting based algorithms. The throughput using vote based algorithm is greater than hash function based selection which is greater when compared to Zone Id based selection. This is because as the coordinator stays for longer period within the zone the throughput is high. The throughput values are calculated by extracting the values of the packet sizes from the trace file. The throughput values of a particular node when packets are routed through the different leaders elected by different algorithms are plotted in a graph wherein the throughput are markd along the Y axis and the time scale is marked along the X axis.

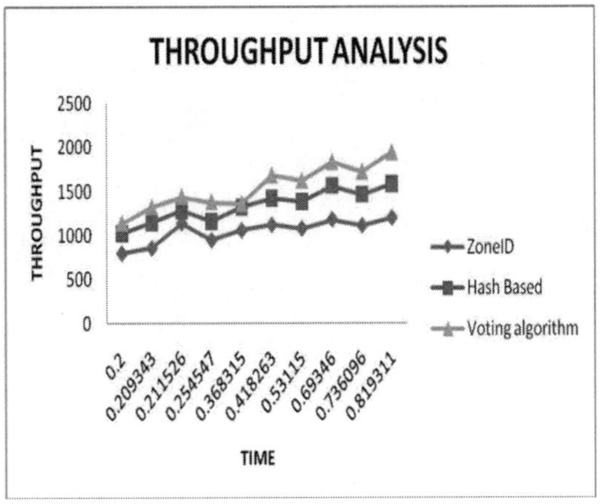

Figure 2. VB Algorithm - Throughput

6. Conclusion

A core node in hierarchical geographic service provisioning framework does Service coordination and membership management. In this paper the performance of selecting a core node, using Node ID, Geographical hashing and vote based election algorithm are evaluated. The vote based service coordinator election proposed, adapts itself to the service and management requirement in the network. The efficiency of the voting algorithm and the proficient routing of data packets through the leader elected by that algorithm is justified by the performance evaluation of the throughput and data loss. The throughput has consistently increased and the data loss has decreased.

References

1. Xiaojing Xiang and Xin Wang, "A scalable Geographic Service provision framework for mobile Ad Hoc Network", IEEE conference on Pervasive Computing and Communication 2007
2. J.Garcia-Macias and D.Torres, "Service discovery in adhoc networks: better at the network layer?" International conference workshops on Parallel processing 2005
3. L.Li and L..amont., "A lightweight service discovery mechanism for mobile adhoc pervasive environment using cross layer design", IEEE PerCom, 2005
4. C.Ververidis and G.Polyzos, "Routing layer support for service discovery in mobile ad hoc networks", IEEE percom, 2005
5. L.Cheng. "Service advertisement and discovery in mobile adhoc networks." Proceeding of CSCW, November 2002
6. F.Sailhan and V,Ussarbtm "Scalable service discovery for MANET".IEEE percom, 2005
7. P.Bose, P.morin, I.Stojmenovic and J.Urrutia, "Routing with guaranteed delivery in adhoc wireless netowrks." Workshop on Discrete Algorithms and Methods for Mobile Computing and Communications August 1999
8. Matthias Transier, Holger Füßler, Jörg Widmer, Martin Mauve, and Wolfgang Effelsberg, "Scalable Position-Based Multicast for Mobile Ad-hoc Networks ",ACM / IEEE mobicom 2004

9. S. Basagni, I. chlamtac, and V.R. Syrotiuk., "Location aware, dependable Multicast for mobile adhoc networks." Computer Networks, August 2001
10. Rohan Sen, Gregory Hackmann, Gruia-Catalin Roman, and Christopher Gill, "Towards Predictable Service Provision in Mobile Ad Hoc Networks", Department of Computer Science and Engineering Washington University in St. Louis, October 2005.
11. Fei Li, Shile Zhang, Xin Wang, Xiangangxue and Hong Shen, "Vote – based clustering algorithm in mobile ad- hoc networks", Fudan University, 2004, Shangai, china.
12. J. Sanchez, P. Ruiz, X. Liu, and I. Stojmenovic, "GMR: Geographic Multicast Routing for Wireless Sensor Networks," in *Proc. of IEEE SECON*, 2006.
13. S. M. Das, H. Pucha, and Y. C. Hu, "Distributed hashing for scalable multicast in wireless ad hoc networks," *IEEE TPDS*, 2007.
14. Dimitrios Koutsonikolas, Saumitra Das1, Y. Charlie Hu, and Ivan Stojmenovic, "Hierarchical Geographic Multicast Routing for Wireless Sensor Networks," 2007 International Conference on Sensor Technologies and Applications
15. Xiaojing Xiang; Xin Wang; Xehua Zhou , "An efficient geographic multicast protocol for mobile ad hoc networks" World of Wireless, Mobile and Multimedia Networks, 2006. WoWMoM 2006.

RESEARCH ON COMPENSATION POLICY SCHEDULING ALGORITHM FOR MULTI-CORE PROCESSORS

BENHAI ZHOU [1], JIANZHONG QIAO[1,2], SHU-KUAN LIN[1,2] , ENZE WANG[1]

1. College of Information Science and Engineering, Northeastern University, Shenyang, Liaoning Province, 110004, China

2. Key Laboratory of Software System and Development Generic Technology, Shenyang, Liaoning Province, 110004, China

With rapid development of processors, multi-core processors occupied the main market due to their superior performance and power characteristics. Threads run concurrently on a multi-core processor and share the processor's the second-level (L2) cache. Cache allocation and sharing is critical to the effective utilization of multi-core processors. Unfair CPU cache allocation can easily delay the critical task and cause serious problems, such as thread starvation, priority inversion, and inadequate CPU accounting. To solve these problems, this paper proposed a compensation policy scheduling algorithm which can decrease system variability and improve system performance effectively. The experiment results show that the system variability adopting compensation policy scheduling algorithm is lower than that using conventional scheduling algorithms. Consequently, compensation policy scheduling algorithm improves the stability of system and applications effectively on multi-core processors.

Key words: *multi-core; compensation policy; cache; performance variability*

1. Introduction

Nowadays, multi-core processors occupied the main market due to their superior performance and power characteristics.[1,2] With an increasing number of processor cores being integrated onto a single chip, multi-core processors require efficient organization and management of the on-chip cache resources to provide fast data accesses for concurrently running threads. [3-6]

This paper focus on a specific shared resource: the second-level (L2) processor cache. Cache allocation on multi-core processors is hidden from the operating system. The shared L2 cache is a performance-critical resource on multi-core processors.[7] Most processors completely mask any information on cache allocation from the operating system. Although some multi-core processors, such as Intel's Core Duo, allow measuring the number of cache lines allocated to each co-runner, they provide no mechanism to enforce fair cache sharing.

When the OS scheduler ignores fair allocation of L2 cache, there are at least three serious problems that can render the OS scheduler ineffective. The first problem is thread starvation,[8] which happens when one thread fails in competing for sufficient cache space necessary to make satisfactory forward progress. The second problem is priority inversion,[9,10] where a higher priority thread achieves a slower forward progress than a lower priority thread, despite the attempt by the OS to provide more timeslices to the higher priority thread. T The third problem is inadequate CPU accounting: the forward progress rate of a thread is highly dependent on the thread mix in a co-schedule. This makes the forward progress rate difficult to characterize or predict, making the high system performance variability.

Therefore, compensation policy operating system scheduling algorithm, which increases the performance stability of system and applications is presented. The algorithm works by reducing effects of unequal CPU cache sharing on threads' performance. The algorithm dynamically determines each thread's CPI (cycles per instruction) achieved under balanced cache sharing, and if the thread's CPI deviates from its fair CPI, the algorithm adjusts the thread's CPU time quantum. As a result, the system performance stability is improved by this algorithm effectively.

The rest of the paper is organized as follows: Section2 analyzes the algorithm; In section3, describes the compensation policy scheduling algorithm in detail; The experiment results can be get and explained in section 4; In last section gives the conclusion of this paper.

2. Algorithm analysis

On conventional processor (Figure 1), each thread is large enough to populate the entire L2 cache. However, when the threads become co-runners on a multi-core processor (Figure 2), the cache is not equally allocated among the threads.

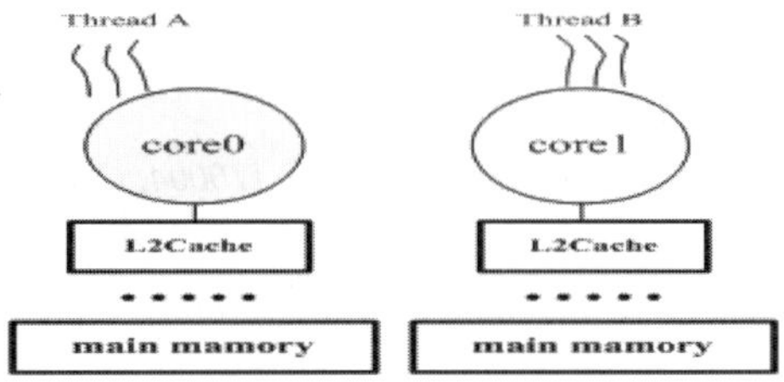

Figure 1. Conventional processor

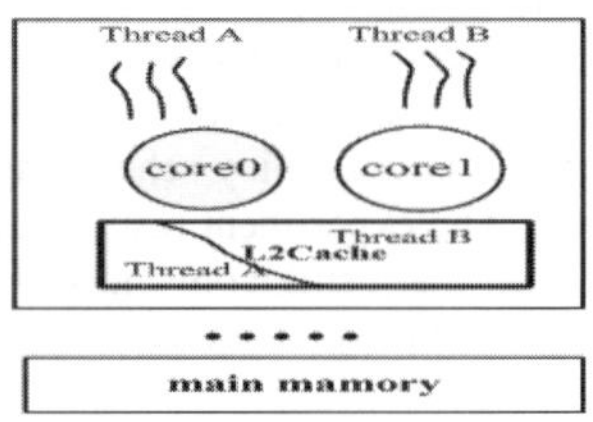

Figure 2. Co-scheduling in multi-core processor

As can be seen from Figure 3, there are three threads sharing L2 cache. First, the ideal situation, L2 cache is shared equally; Second, in conventional situation, L2 cache is shared unfairly; Last, in new compensation policy algorithm scheduling, the L2 cache is shared fairly by adjusting size.

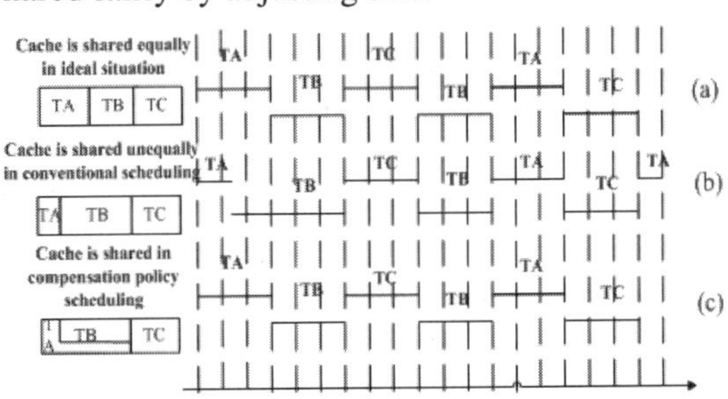

Figure 3. Three scenarios of cache allocation and thread scheduling

The scenario (a) describes the ideal scheduling: the cache is allocated equally, the goal of compensation policy algorithm is to complete the same amount of work in the same time it takes in the ideal scenario. Scenario (b) shows that thread A completes less work per unit of time than in ideal scheduling, because it does not get an equal share of the cache when running with Thread B. As a result, it takes longer to complete the same amount of work; its latency is longer than its latency under equal cache sharing. In scenario (c), by giving Thread A more CPU cycles, it makes Thread A retain the same latency as under equal cache sharing. Note that the adjustment to Thread A's CPU quantum is temporary. Once the thread catches up with its work, its CPU quantum is restored to its initial value.

This paper expects that critical job that value performance predictability, such as servers, will be in the Protected- Thread set, and that other, less critical, jobs will fall into the Service-Thread set. Users decide and communicate to the system the importance of each application, allowing the system to appropriately distinguish between critical and non-critical jobs. The system in turn makes sure that critical jobs achieve performance similar to what they would achieve under balanced cache sharing, while less critical jobs are subject only to mild performance penalties.

3. Description of algorithm

This paper divided the compensation policy operating system scheduling algorithm into four steps. The detail analysis is described as follows:

Table 1. The first step of compensation policy operating system scheduling algorithm

Initialization: the number of cores; Protected- Thread set Tp; Service-Thread set Ts
Step1: Find the running Tpi and compute the protected cache thread's actual *CPI* $CPI = perfectCPI + L2CacheLatencyPI$;

Step 1:

The new operating system scheduler computes the Protected-Cache thread's actual cycles per instruction (CPI)

$$CPI = perfectCPI + L2CacheLatencyPI \qquad (1)$$

where $perfectCPI$ is the CPI when there are no L2 cache misses, and $L2CacheLatencyPI$ is the per-instruction latency cycles of per instruction due to handling L2 cache misses. The expression for $L2CacheLatencyPI$ is:

$$L2CachesLatencyPI = StoreBuffLatencyPI + MemoryLanency \times (L2MissPI + L2CopyBackPI) \qquad (2)$$

L2MissPI denotes the number of cache misses per instruction; *L2CopyBackPI* represents the number of transactions (per instruction) writing dirty cache lines back to memory; *MemoryLatency* equals memory access time required to fetch a cache line and memory-bus delay per memory transaction. *StoreBuffLatencyPI* presents the number of cycles per instruction a processor latency on a store buffer

Now, we can calculate the CPI, where $MemoryLatency$ and $StoreBufferLatencyPI$ can get from performance hardware counters.

Table 2. The second of compensation policy operating system scheduling algorithm

Step2: Determine the cache-protected thread's balanced CPI ($BalaCPI$) $BalaCPI = perfectCPI + BalaL2CacheLatencyPI$;

Step 2:
Scheduler computes the Protected-thread's $BalaCPI$.

$$BalaCPI = perfectCPI + BalaL2CacheLatencyPI \quad (3)$$

Where $BalaCPI$ is the CPI when the thread experiences its miss rate of balanced cache allocation. To estimate $BalaCPI$, we need to determine $perfectCPI$ and $BalaL2CacheLatencyPI$:

From Equation (1), $L2CacheLatencyPI$ can be computed by utilizing hardware performance counters. Subtracting $L2CacheLatencyPI$ from CPI (also measured) gives the $perfectCPI$.

$$BalaL2CachesLatencyPI = StoreBuffLatencyPI + MemoryLantencyX(BalaL2MissPI + L2CopyBackPI) \quad (4)$$

To compute the $BalaL2CacheLatencyPI$, $BalaL2MissCPI$ is the key part. The procedure of getting $BalaL2MissCPI$ as follows:

The paper assumes that a thread's L2 cache accesses are uniformly distributed in the cache. Choose benchmarks from the SPEC CPU2000[11] suite with different cache access patterns and ran them in pairs on our experiment environment. Make each benchmark ran in several pairs. By analyzing the relationship between the miss rate of each benchmark and the miss rates of its co-runners and found that a linear equation approximated these relationships better than other simple functions.

The relationship between the co-runners' miss rates for a processor with *n+1* cores is presented by equation (5)

$$Missrate\ (T) = a * \sum Missrate\ (Ci) + b \quad (5)$$

Where T is a thread for which we compute the balanced miss rate, Ci is the ith co-runner, n is the number of co-runners, and a and b are the linear equation coefficients. Thread T experiences its balanced cache miss rate $Missrate(T)$ when all concurrent threads experience the same miss rate:

$$Missrate(T) = Missrate(Ci) = BalaMissCPI(T) \quad (6)$$

Finally, the $BalaL2MissCPI$ can be describe as follows:

$$BalaL2MissCPI = b/(1 - a*n) \quad (7)$$

Table 3. The third of compensation policy operating system scheduling algorithm

```
Step3:
   Compare Tpi's balanced CPI to its actual CPI and readjust the temporary quantum from Service-Thread set Ts to offset Tpi's CPU quantum
if ( AutualCPI < BalaCPI )
{
Tp[i]_quantum = Tp[i]_quantum + gran ;
/ *gran is the adjusted quantum offseting to thread Tp[i]*/
select the service thread Ts[i] , which has suffered the least performance penalty
Ts[i]_quantum = Ts[i]_quantum - gran ;
The CPU quantum offset of Ts[i] resumes the original value when thread Tp[i] has run with it.
}
else
{
Tp[i]_quantum = Tp[i]_quantum - gran ;
/ *gran is the adjusted quantum offseting to thread Ts[i]*/
select the service thread Ts[i] , which has suffered the largest performance penalty
Ts[i]_quantum = Ts[i]_quantum + gran ;
The offset CPU quantum of Tp[i] resumes the original value when thread Ts[i] has run with it.
}
```

Step 3:

The scheduler compares *T*'s balanced CPI to its actual CPI and estimates the temporary adjustment to *T*'s CPU quantum, so that by the end of the next quantum, *T* completes the number of instructions corresponding to its balanced CPI.

If *T* has been running faster than it would at its balanced CPI, the scheduler decreases is CPU quantum. If *T* has been running slower, the scheduler selects a thread from Service-Thread set, whose CPU quantum is adjusted to offset *T*'s CPU quantum. In this case, we select the service thread that has suffered the least performance penalty. If the scheduler increases *T*'s CPU quantum, it decreases Service-Thread's quantum by the same amount, and vice versa. The offset CPU quantum resumes the original value when thread T has run with it.

4. Experiment and analysis

This paper set evaluation experiments to estimate the accuracy and performance of compensation policy operating system scheduling algorithm. Table 4 shows the main experiment component.

Table 4. Experiment component list

Component	Parameters
Processors	2 cores, each 4-issue, each running at 1.66GHZ
L1 cache (Instuction)	32KB, 4-way,64-B line
L1 cache (Data)	32KB, 4-way,64-B line
L2 cache	512KB, 8-way,64-B line
Memory bus	6.4GB/s peak bandwidth
OS kernel	Linux kernel 2.6.20

Note that, in our experiment, the L1 cache is private, while the L2 cache is shared. Then, we selected the SPEC 2000 benchmark suite. SPEC 2000 benchmark is commonly used for CPU studies and has been recently updated to include programs with large cache working sets, to reflect trends in modern commercial applications. This suite is built of real applications with all CPU-bound. For our experiments, we picked twelve benchmarks that represent a variety of popular workloads.

Table 5 shows the meanings of each benchmark we chose.

Table 5. Meaning of Benchmark

Benchmark	Meaning
crafty	game playing: chess
art	image recognition
bzip	a compression utility
ammp	computational chemistry
vpr	FPGA circuit placement and routing
vortex	object-oriented database
twolf	place and route simulator
parser	word processing
mcf	combinatorial optimization
gzip	a compression utility
gcc	a compiler
gap	group theory, interpreter
eon	computer visualization

In our experiment environment, the compensation policy operating system scheduler runs the test benchmark with three randomly selected identical co-runners in Service-Thread set. Thus, we can be aware of any benefits with the compensation policy scheduler due to our scheduling algorithm, and not to any co-scheduling effects. The scheduling scheme can be divided by two classes. The first, the test benchmark's co-runners consist mainly of high miss rate threads; the other's co-runners are low miss rate threads. For the previous one, we call expensive scheduling scheme, and the other is named by cheap scheduling scheme.

The performance variability is defined as follows:

$$PerformVar = \frac{EpenScheduleTime - ChpScheduleTime}{EpenScheduleTime} \quad (8)$$

Table6 displays the scheduling schemes, the left of table shows the test benchmarks and each of the schedule schemes is in right part. Aiming at each scheduling scheme, the first benchmark belongs to the Protected-Thread set and one of its three co-runners is in Service-Thread set.

Table 6. Scheduling schemes of test benchmarks

Test	Cheap Scheduling scheme	Expensive scheduling scheme
crafty	{crafty, ammp, ammp, ammp}	{crafty, gzip, gzip, gzip }
art	{art ,bzip,bzip,bzip}	{art , gzip, gzip, gzip }
bzip	{bzip, crafty, crafty, crafty}	{bzip, gzip, gzip, gzip }
ammp	{amp, art, art,att}	{amp, gzip, gzip, gzip }
vpr	{vpr, ammp, ammp, ammp}	{vpr, gzip, gzip, gzip }
vortex	{vortex, crafty, crafty, crafty}	{vortex, gzip, gzip, gzip}
twolf	{twolf, ammp, ammp, ammp}	{twolf, gcc, gcc, gcc }
parser	{parser, crafty, crafty, crafty}	{parser, gcc, gcc, gcc }
mcf	{mcf, crafty, crafty, crafty}	{mcf, mcf,mcf,mcf}
gzip	{gzip, gcc, gcc, gcc}	{gzip, gcc, gcc, gcc}
gcc	{gcc, crafty, crafty, crafty}	{gcc, gzip, gzip, gzip }
gap	{gap, crafty, crafty, crafty}	{gap, gzip, gzip, gzip }

Figure 4 shows the result of the normalized execution time of test benchmarks with the conventional scheduler and the compensation policy scheduler. In conventional scheduling, we can get the performance dependency variability by equation (8). Adopting the compensation policy scheduling algorithm, the performance variability is significantly smaller. For crafty, the difference in execution times was 30%, reduced by more than a factor of three. For gcc, the difference was reduced from 25% to 5% – a factor of five. For the remaining test benchmarks, the minimum performance variability of conventional scheduler is 5% higher than that of compensation policy scheduler. At the same time, we also observed that, the execution time of test benchmarks is lower than that adopting conventional scheduler.

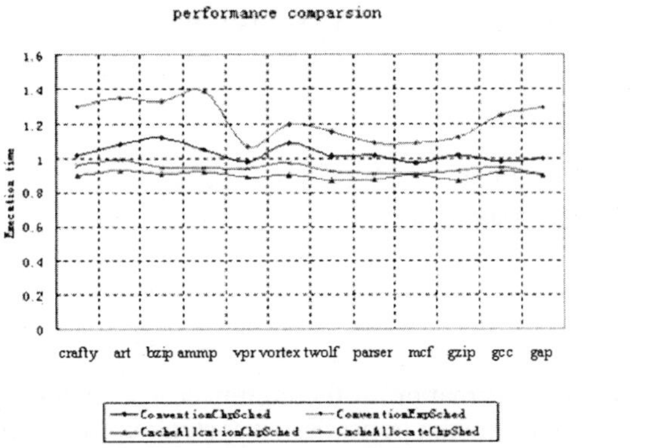

Figure 4. Execution time in conventional and compensation policy scheduler

As can be seen from Figure 5, the curve of the performance variability of compensation policy algorithm is more stable than conventional scheduling method. Meanwhile, we found that the compensation policy scheduler's performance variability is lower than conventional scheduler. Thus, the compensation policy OS scheduling algorithm is helpful to increase system stability and improve system performance effectively.

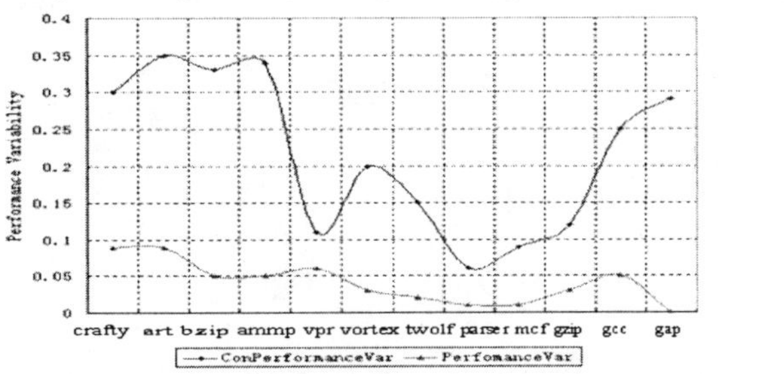

Figure 5. Comparison with two scheduler's performance variability

5. Conclusion

FOR co-runner dependency is a serious problem which affects the stability of applications and operating system. This paper analyzes and designs the thread scheduling algorithm which utilizes compensation policy method on multi-core architecture. This paper compares the performance variability between compensation policy operating system scheduling algorithm and original scheduling policy. The experiment results indicate that the compensation policy scheduler's performance variability is lower than original scheduler. As a result, the compensation policy operating system scheduling algorithm is helpful to increase system stability and improve system performance effectively.

References

1. AMD, "Multi-core Processors – the Next Evolution in Computing",http://multicore.amd.com/WhitePapers/ Multi-Core_Processors_WhitePaper.pdf
2. A.Buttari, J.Langou, and J.Kurzak, "Parallel Tiled QR Factorization for Multicore Architectures", *LECTURE NOTES IN COMPUTER SCIENCE*, University of Tennessee Knoxville, Tennessee USA, 23(2007)
3. L. Hammond, B. A. Hubbert, and M. Siu, "The Stanford Hydra CMP". *IEEE Micro*, California USA,71(2000)
4. L. A. Barroso, K. Gharachorloo, and R. McNamara, "A Scalable Architecture Based on Single-Chip Multiprocessing". In *Proceedings of the 27th Annual International Symposium on Computer Architecture (ISCA-27)*, 145(2000)
5. J. M. Tendler, J. S. Dodson, and B. Sinharoy, "IBM Power4 system microarchitecture". *IBM Journal of Research and Development*, USA, 5(2002)
6. M. Zhang and K. Asanovic. "Victim Replication: Maximizing Capacity while Hiding Wire Delay in Tiled CMPs" *Proceedings of the 32nd Annual International Symposium on Computer Architecture (ISCA-32)*, 336(2005)
7. L. R. Hsu, S. K. Reinhardt, and S. Makineni, "Communist, utilitarian, and capitalist cache policies on CMPs: caches as a shared resource" *Proc. PACT'06*, Washington, USA, 13(2006).
8. D.Chandra, F.Guo, and Y.Solihin "High-Performance Computer Architecture, 2005. HPCA-11. 11th International Symposium on, HPCA-11. 11th International Symposium, 334(2005)
9. K.W.Lam, S.L Hung , "A pre-emptive transaction scheduling protocol for controlling priority inversion" ,*Real-Time Computing Systems and Applications,* 144(1996)
10. K.H.Kim, "Basic program structures for avoiding priority inversions", *Object-Oriented Real-Time Distributed Computing, Sixth IEEE International Symposium*, 26(2003)
11. Standard Performance Evaluation Corporation. *SPEC CPU2000*, http://www.spec.org

Design and Realization of Wireless Real-time Flood Control and Disaster Relief System

Zhang Wumei
Zhejiang Tongji Vocational College of Science and Technology, Hangzhou, 311231
Zhejiang University of Technology, Hangzhou, 311231
Hangzhou, China
zwm83863026@126.com

***Abstract*—Based on the research and design of flood control and disaster relief system in the aspects of networking, system structure and interface, etc, this paper realizes that the system provides as much as 2Mbps ascending and descending wireless data service, real-time multimedia information for flood control and disaster relief and real-time information support for decision-making and command under the condition of occupying 4MHz bandwidth.**

Keywords- flood control; real-time; transmission

I. INTRODUCTION

Since 1949, our country has built a large quantity of water conservancy projects, which have played an important role in the aspects of flood resistance, water source supply and ecological environmental protection, etc, and got enormous social and economic benefits. However, we must face tens of thousands of losses caused by natural disasters every year---typhoon, for example. And therefore, we must adopt a positive attitude towards utilizing modern science and technology to reduce losses caused by natural disasters and serve water conservancy cause and society.

In the flood control and disaster relief system, hydrological data communication mainly adopts wired transmission and large flood control and disaster relief data is transmitted by satellite. When the wired network can not be set up and you cannot bear the rent of a satellite link, how to realize the transmission of mass multimedia data well and provide the real-time and synchronous communication and transmission of image and speech data for flood control and disaster relief is the problem this paper needs to study and solve. And therefore, this paper studies and designs a real-time flood control and disaster relief local area network.

II. NETWORKING TYPE

In flood control and disaster relief, time is money and life, so the real-time requirements for the system are particularly high, according to different geographical environments and network coverage ranges, we adopt different networking modes.

A. Networking scheme of single-center station

When the coverage radius is about 20Km, the whole communication network system can be composed of a center station and a car remote terminal station. Center station is selected at command center. As system terminal, car remote terminal station sends video, audio and data information to the command center through a mobile multimedia transmission system; uploads image, data and speech information through the monitoring system and computer of local area network at large screen terminal respectively; and meanwhile, it receives command orders and database information from command center and finishes two-way information exchange. The concrete networking structure is shown as Fig 1.

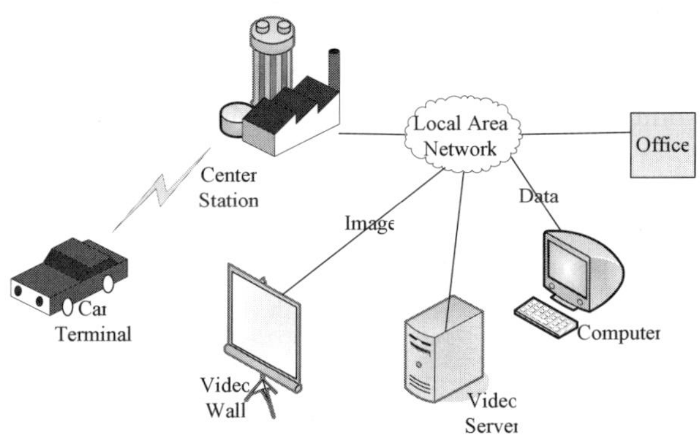

Figure 1. Networking Schematic Diagram of Single-Center Station

Its network topology is a point-to-point structure and its car remote terminal station can move within the network coverage area of the center station of the mobile multimedia command and transmission system.

B. Networking scheme of multi-center station

If the coverage range is much larger than 20Km, starting from the angle of solving maneuverable coverage, we will adopt the networking scheme of multi-center station and the concrete networking structure is shown as Fig 2.

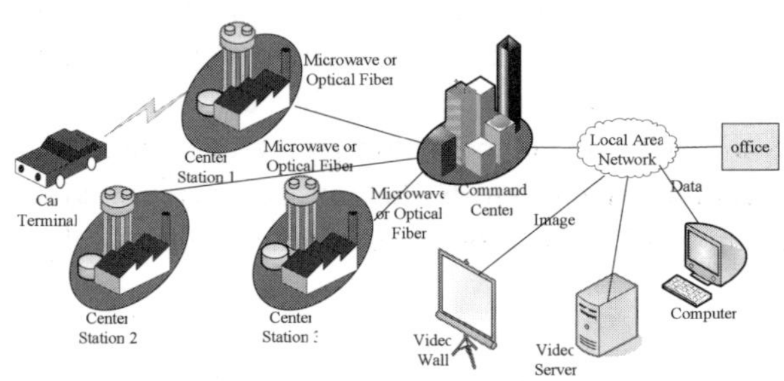

Figure 2. Networking Schematic Diagram of Multi-Center Station

The whole mobile communication network will be composed of several center stations and car remote terminal stations. These center stations will be selected at appointed places or places which have favorable geographical scope respectively. Within the coverage range of each center station, car remote terminal station will finish the wireless multimedia transmission and communication with the center station. The switching of car remote terminal stations between different center stations is finished by hard handover. This kind of networking scheme solves the network coverage problem of mobile monitoring and command transmission system within a large regional range.

The connection modes between various center stations usually includes two wireless and wired modes, namely 5.8G wireless bridge (or spread spectrum microwave) and optical fiber. If there are available ready optical fiber resources, we should give priority to the wired solution. At the places where optical cables cannot be set up, we should adopt the wireless bridge (spread spectrum microwave) solution to provide a reliable and carrier class device connection.

Its network topology is a point-to-point structure within coverage area and its car remote terminal station can move within the network coverage area of the mobile monitoring and command transmission system.

C. Networking scheme of multi-remote terminal station (one point, multiple access)

When the coverage range of center station is between 10Km and 20Km, we can adopt the networking mode of multi-remote terminal station and the concrete networking structure is shown as the following diagram:

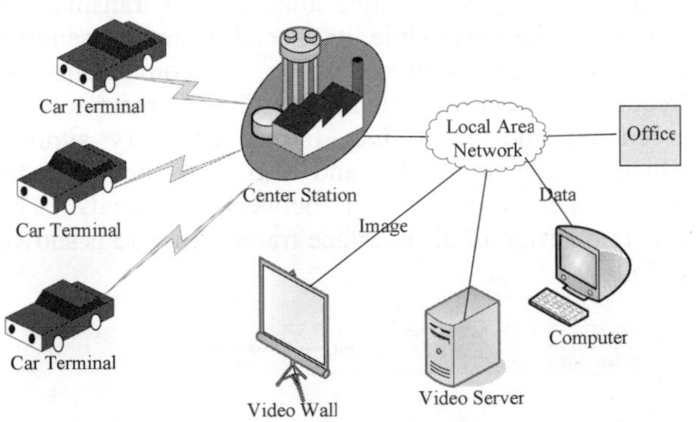

Figure 3. Networking of Multi-Remote Terminal Station

(One Point, Multiple Access)

Adopt the same frequency point switching mode to realize the maneuverable communication need of multiple remote terminal points within a large range. We can configure multiple remote terminal stations in one center station and the number of remote terminal stations can be between 1 and 255. If necessary, it can support more remote terminal stations. The remote terminal station can be car device or piggyback device with the same frequency point and identification code. Each remote terminal station has its independent station number (Station No.1 to No.255) and all remote terminal stations can start up simultaneously, but only one remote terminal station keeps multimedia data transmission with the center station at the same time and other remote terminal stations are in monitoring state. If the center station wants to communicate with that remote terminal station, it can choose through its button menu or computer software.

D. Networking scheme of personal piggyback terminal combining with car remote terminal station

In the regions where communication and command vehicles are inconvenient to arrive, we adopt the networking scheme of personal piggyback remote terminal station combining with car remote terminal station to realize field multimedia information acquisition and solve the blind area of system coverage better and the concrete networking structure is shown as Fig 4.

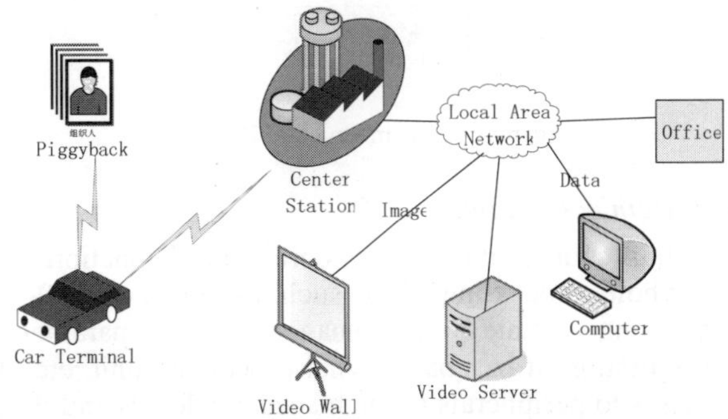

Figure 4. Networking Schematic Diagram of Personal Piggyback Terminal Combining with Car Remote Terminal Station

The coverage radius of application service of personal piggyback remote terminal station is between 1Km and 5Km and the coverage radius of car remote terminal station is 20Km; (If distance needs to be increased, we need to adjust antenna and power), the whole maneuverable communication network will be composed of car remote terminal station, personal piggyback remote terminal station and center station. When personal piggyback remote terminal station works, it transmits field information to car remote terminal station within the coverage range as system terminal and then car remote terminal station transmits information to command center as relay station; and meanwhile, car remote terminal station can also collect field information and transmit the information to center station as communication terminal station. In this way, we can realize the collection and transmission of image, speech and data multimedia information of mobile monitoring and command transmission system through the whole emergency communication network.

Its network topology is a point-to-point structure and the staff with an individual piggyback remote terminal station can move around the car remote terminal station within the range between 1Km and 5Km, and meanwhile car remote terminal station can move within the coverage range of center station---20Km.

III. SYSTEM STRUCTURE

Baseband processing chip is mainly composed of seven parts, namely main control unit (MCU), baseband signal processing unit (BPU), memory unit (MU), timing management unit (TMU), digital front-end processing unit (DFPU), protocol processing unit (PPU) and debugging interface unit (DIU) and the concrete structure is shown as Fig 5.

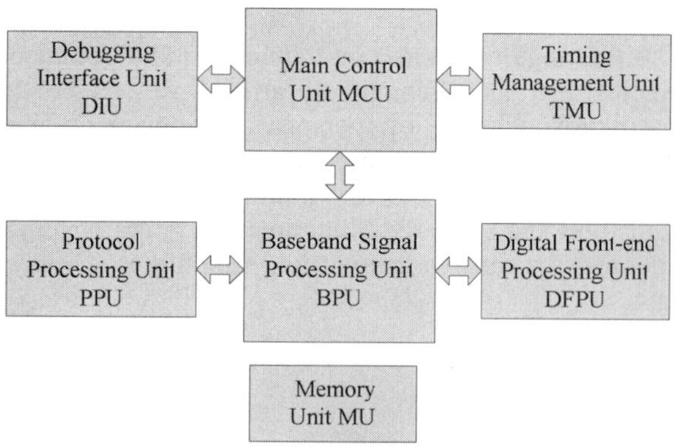

Figure 5. System Structure Diagram

A. *Main control unit*

Main control unit finishes core control functions of the whole processing chip, such as processing flow scheduling, state maintenance and parameter configuration of baseband signal processing unit, etc. It accesses to peripherals through special address and data buses, namely corresponding processing units.

B. *Baseband signal processing unit*

Baseband signal processing unit finishes core algorithm functions of chip, such as modulation, demodulation and channel coding and decoding, etc. Each baseband signal processing unit is connected to the main control unit through control bus to receive the query, configuration and scheduling of main control unit; and meanwhile, it is connected to the memory unit through data bus to realize the input of processing data and the output of processing results. Baseband signal processing unit accesses to the memory unit in DMA mode to reduce the burden of processor.

C. *Memory unit*

Memory unit is the set of all on-chip RAM-organized memories. On-chip memory unit has the advantages of high access speed and large throughput, but its realization conditions restrict its memory capacity. And therefore, we use on-chip RAM to realize the memory requirements for high access speed and small capacity in the system.

D. *Timing management unit*

Timing management unit finishes the timing synchronization on air interface and provides timing references for on-chip processing units.

E. *Digital front-end processing unit*

Digital front-end processing unit is the interface module between baseband processing module and RF module and it realizes the functions, such as digital filtering, sampling rate transformation, digital up and down conversion, AFC and AGC, etc.

F. *Protocol processing unit*

Protocol processing unit realizes the bridge protocol of MAC layer of 802.3.

G. *Debugging interface unit*

Debugging interface unit provides the debugging channel from PC to on-chip main control unit through Ethernet MAC protocol and it can further access to baseband processing unit through the external bus of main control unit. Its debugging environment is compatible with VisualStudio and supports common debugging functions, such as breakpoint, single-step and register query, etc, and its debugging interface is simple and has rich functions. In addition, we can carry out in-system programming for on-chip processor through debugging interface, which greatly improves the flexibility and expansibility of the system.

IV. SYSTEM DESIGN

A. *Two-way time division duplex*

In flood control and disaster relief, we need to carry out two-way communication, but a mass of multimedia information mainly centers on the transmission from acquisition system to command center, so the transmission system is also required adjustable in two directions to make maximum use of bandwidth to improve the transmission rate.

The system adopts the time division duplex mode and the boundaries of ascending and descending frames of time division duplex can be adjusted flexibly, which is favorable to the dynamic allocation of transmission resources, and meanwhile, its ascending and descending frequencies are shared, which is convenient for frequency spectrum planning. The formats of its ascending and descending frames are very similar, which is easy to realize and also convenient for the direct intercommunication between terminals. The concrete design of air interface frame structure is shown as follows:

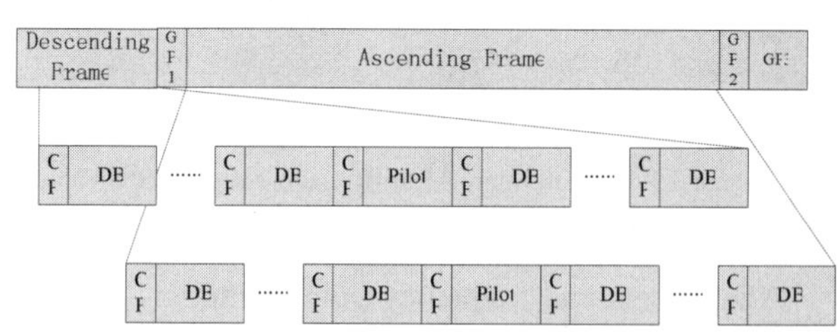

Figure 6. The concrete design of air interface frame structure

Its frame structure is shown as Fig 6. Its ascending and descending frames have similar structures which are convenient for frequency sharing and frequency spectrum allocation, but we can adopt different code modulation modes. One ascending or descending frame is composed of several data blocks and a pilot block, corresponding to FFT unit of a SC-FDE and ascending and descending data blocks have the same length. The lengths of ascending and descending encoding blocks can be different and they can be mapped to the fixed-length transmission block through multiple connections and rate matching. The structure of pilot block is the same as that of data block. The number of ascending and descending data blocks can be allocated flexibly according to ascending and descending traffics. We add a cyclic prefix CP to the front of each data block to fight against the inter-symbol interference caused by multipath time delay spread.

We reserve a proper protection time between ascending frame and descending frame, GP1 and GP2 are used for switching time protection of RF module and GP3 is used for TDD transmission delay protection.

B. *Flexible modulation scheme and advanced scheme fighting against time delay spread*

In the scheme fighting against time delay spread, we adopt SC-FDE which has very good frequency-domain diversity characteristics, simple modulation and low peak-to-average power ratio under low-order modulation (BPSK or QPSK). And therefore, the system can put modules with high complexity and power amplifiers with high linearity in the base station and the terminal only needs to realize modulation/demodulation with lower complexity and can use power amplifiers with low cost and power consumption. In this way, the terminal device becomes very simple, which is favorable for rapid movement of terminal in complex geographical environment.

C. *High-performance and high-efficiency channel coding*

Channel error correction coding is another key technology influencing system transmission performance. A good channel coding can effectively improve the error rate curve of system and increase the anti-noise performance of system. Based on the study of channel coding technology in recent years, people have found coding schemes whose performances are extremely near to Shannon limit, Turbo code and TPC code are two kinds of coding schemes with outstanding performances.

In our system scheme, descending adopts OFDM modulation mode, under this kind of demand, Turbo coding with low code rate is optimal. And ascending adopts SC-FDE modulation mode and its coding is carried out in time domain and therefore the signal-to-noise deterioration caused by frequency selective fading will be equally distributed to every decoding bit and ascending can select TPC coding with high code rate, which is favorable for increasing the frequency spectrum efficiency of the system.

In sum, for the descending data channel adopting OFDM modulation mode, we choose 1/3 Turbo code as channel coding scheme; for the ascending data channel adopting SC-FDE modulation mode, we choose TPC whose efficiency $R=0.8$ as channel coding scheme.

D. *Hybrid ARQ*

In the ascending traffic channel, we adopt the error control mechanism of hybrid ARQ and this mode can make ascending transmission adapt to the current state of transmission channel automatically, ensure the connectivity rate of channel and increase the throughput rate of system.

E. *MAC layer bridge technology*

MAC layer is integrated on the chip, its application interfaces are also very simple, MAC layer bridge protocol and security authorization supporting IEEE802 series can be handled completely by higher layers.

V. CONCLUSION

The wireless real-time flood control and disaster relief transmission system can provide the access service of high-speed wireless data within a large coverage range, in the high speed mobile environment and under the condition of non-line-of-sight propagation; and it can provide as much as 2Mbps ascending and descending wireless data service, real-time multimedia information for flood control and disaster relief and real-time information support for decision-making and command under the condition of occupying 4MHz bandwidth and within the range whose diameter is 30Km and moving rate is in excess of 300km/h.

ACKNOWLEDGEMENT

Fund project: Research on Application of Wireless Mobile Transmission System in Flood Control and Disaster Relief (Zhejiang Water Conservancy Scientific and Technological Project RC0073).

REFERENCES

[1] Song Ying, Research on Integration for the Flood Prevention System Based on Web Services [D], Hohai University, 2006.

[2] Wei Yimei, Wei Wenchu, Application of Special Shortwave Modem in Flood-prevention System [J], Automation in Water Resources and Hydrology, 2003 (4): 16-19.

[3] Sun Dehui, Ma Wenli, Yao Wenjuan, etc, Design and Realization of Wireless Transmission System Based on GPRS [J], 2007 (21): 104-106.

[4] Tang Xiaoyu; Tang Hong; Feng Huijuan; Design on Remote Supervisory Control System Based on ARM and CDMA Network, Communications Technology [J], 2007 (9): 41-43.

[5] Xu Guoxin, Jiyang, Tianhui, Zhangping, Delay-Fair Radio Resources Scheduling Algorithm for OFDMA Systems, 2005 (05): 11-13.

Sawang: Visualizing Criminal Networks of Telephone Records for Tracking Possible Collaborators

Rosmawati Ab. Raub[1], Rozana Raoh[2]

[1]*TM Research & Development (ros@tmrnd.com.my)*
[2]*UiTM Kelantan (rozana630@kelantan.uitm.edu.my)*

Abstract- Locating a telecommunication fraud in masses of call records is more difficult than looking for a needle in a haystack. Callers are not similar, so calls that look like fraud for one account may look like expected behaviour for another, while needles look the same. One of the best data mining technologies available is visualization because graphical display methods often offer superior results compared to other more conventional data mining techniques. This paper presents Sawang, a graphical investigation tool specifically built for recognizing possible fraudster collaborators through call data records.

Keywords: link analysis, visualization, fraud

I. INTRODUCTION

Fraudulent activity is the most significant threat to telecommunication business including mobile communications and has a major impact on service levels and customer confidence. Telecom operators need to heed these warnings and develop more sophisticated ways of identifying fraudulent activity to limit their losses. Recently, fraud levels have significantly increased due to the use of modern technology, resulting losses billions of dollars worldwide [1]. Due to dramatic increase of fraud which results in losses of billions of dollars worldwide each year, several modern techniques in detecting fraud are continually evolved and applied to many business fields.

Fraud Detection System is a system which is normally used for fraud detection in telecommunication. It is based on transaction records together with some rules that abide to it. However, in this paper, we present another approach of tracking fraudulent activity by identifying fraudster himself through a graphical investigation tool called Sawang.

Data is often best comprehended when presented as a network if the connections between the object of interest in the problem domain are of as great an importance. The link chart or also called directed graph as depicted in Figure 1 represents the calling call pattern between a set of people based on their telephone number.

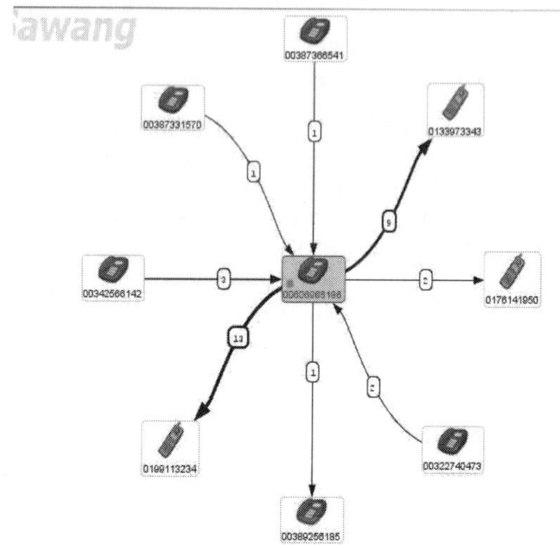

Figure 1: Link Chart based on telephone call

II. CRIMINAL INTELLIGENCE ANALYSIS

One field where visualizing criminal networks is of particular important is in Criminal Intelligence Analysis. To achieve this goal, crime investigators often employ a method called link analysis which can help generate investigative leads and uncover missing information that may be buried in a criminal network. In a narcotic network, for instance, link analysis may reveal that a group of offenders actually belong to the same drug supply chain. In a homicide crime, link analysis may find hidden, intermediate persons connecting the victim with the suspect who denies knowing the victim. In telecommunication networks, fraud investigators have found that fraudsters seldom work alone. Even after an account has been disconnected for fraud, the fraudster will often call the same telephone numbers from another account. Thus, through these telephone calls, networks of fraudsters can be observed [2].

Link analysis was developed in response to a need in fraudster investigation to fully understand the information that has been gathered, as many important facts can be hidden due to the amount of information, as an English proverb says 'A picture is worth a thousand words.' Human pattern recognition skills are remarkable and far exceed the ability of any existing technology to detect interesting patterns and relevant anomalies [3].

The domain of link analysis recently re-ignited interest among researchers due to its applicability to new areas such as intelligence analysis, large scale social network analysis and genomics [4]. Organized crimes such as terrorism, narcotics violations, armed robbery, kidnapping as well as fraud often involve multiple offenders who are connected through various relationships, for instance kinship, friendship, co-workers or business associations [5]. These criminals can be treated as a network in which they interact and play different roles in illegal activities. For instance, a narcotic network may consist of interrelated criminals who are responsible for handling the supply, distribution, sale, drugs smuggling and money laundering [6]. Learning associations between these entities is a critical part of uncovering criminal activities and fighting crimes.

III. AN ILLUSTRATIVE EXAMPLE

Our example will concern on early stages of an investigation. The investigation will start of on getting the call details record (CDR) or telephone records related based on a specific suspected service number, with depth of level two on a selected range of date. By using Sawang, the data required are easily captured as shown in Figure 2.

A link chart as shown in Figure 3 is drawn based on the criteria selected earlier. The links or connection is based on frequency of call from one telephone number to another. However, this condition could be easily changed to total duration of call or total call charges incurred as shown in *Edge Information* feature in Figure 4.

Every incoming and outgoing of each call is differentiated by its color by using feature *Highlight* as shown in Figure 4.

Frequency of each call is also differentiated by the number of call made. The thicker the line, the higher the call frequency is.

The start date and end date of duration of CDR selected can also be adjusted to allow the investigation officer (IO) to focus on a specific data.

We made a definition of collaboration as a form of cooperation activity or coordination of work between two persons/suspects without giving any thought of who initiates it first. In order to support the task of characterizing collaborators, a combination of behavioral measures are used since there is emerging need to discover deep level relationships from user interactions [7]. The behaviour measures include the length of conversation, frequency of call, recency of call and last time call made. These information is available in *View CDR Summary* feature where an IO is able to get a summary of CDR been investigated which consists of total number of call made, total call duration, total call charge, date of first time call, last time call and second last time call made as depicted in Figure 5(i) and 5(ii).

An assumption is made based on a fact that the measures are appropriate measures for the identification of collaborator. The goal/objective is to help IO makes sense of collaboration activities and analyze how their coordination of work (collaboration). By finding these collaborators, IO can narrow down the number of potential suspects to be investigated, therefore expedite their investigation process. These measures are to indicate the degree of relationship between caller and callee. This approach focuses on the relationship between communication behaviors of a caller to a callee, in order to understand their connections to each other and to the entire network.

A collaborator is a person who performs the cooperation. This assumption is made due to the fact that in order to get a fraud activity done, it needs at least a co-operation between two persons or suspects. This assumption is supported by [8] where participants notion of 'who hangs out together' is guided by who works together. In addition, people often seek help from individuals they know socially.

With reference to this assumption, an investigator could make a guess that a collaborator is a person who makes a call more than let say five times and duration of total call is less than 120 minutes. Whatever the rules that the officer might think of, it is easily implemented by using the filtering rules as shown in feature *Filter* in Figure 6.

The depth level of relationship can be selected to a maximum of four. This means that Sawang is able to detect a person who calls a friend of his up to four levels, as shown in Figure 7. The level could also be lowered or increased from its maximum or minimum level to the level desired.

IV. SAWANG ARCHITECTURE

Sawang, a link-analysis architecture based system is made up of data adapter, data aggregator, visualization, search, graphical user interface and report modules as explain below:

Data adapter
Converts data from data source into a common data format used by Sawang. Data can be captured either directly from database server or from flat file.

Data aggregator
Collects and summarizes data.

Visualization
Processes the gathered data and renders it.

Search
Provide a capability to search through the data in visualized form.

Graphical User Interface (GUI)
Provide an interface for dynamic interaction with the chart.

Report
Provide a capability to display data in the form of a report.

Sawang architecture is as shown in Figure 8.

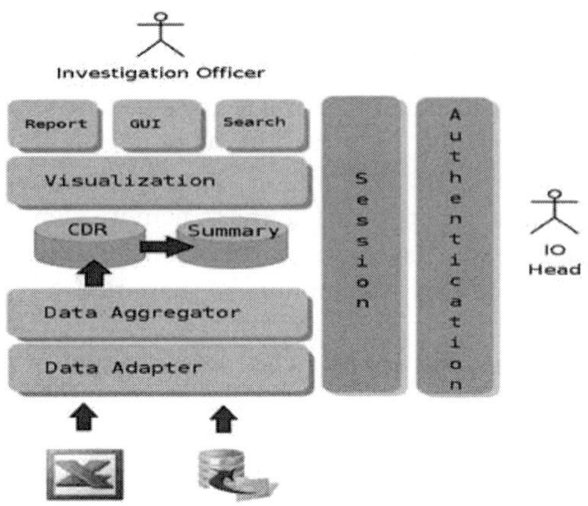

Figure 8: Sawang Architecture

Link analysis usually consists of two major tasks:
i) Extracting information about entity associations from raw data such as call detail records (CDRs)
ii) Constructing a network representation and identifying associations between directly related or indirectly related entities in a network.

V. FUNCTIONALITY OF SAWANG

Both tasks of link analysis can very time-consuming and labor-intensive. Current link analysis practice in law enforcement is mainly an ad-hoc manual process. To solve a crime, investigations may spend a large amount of time performing extensive database searches, reading crime reports and looking for clues of fraudulent associations. Hence, Sawang system is built to overcome the above issues with a number of layout to choose from which include radial, circle, hierarchy and timeline is as shown in Figure 9.

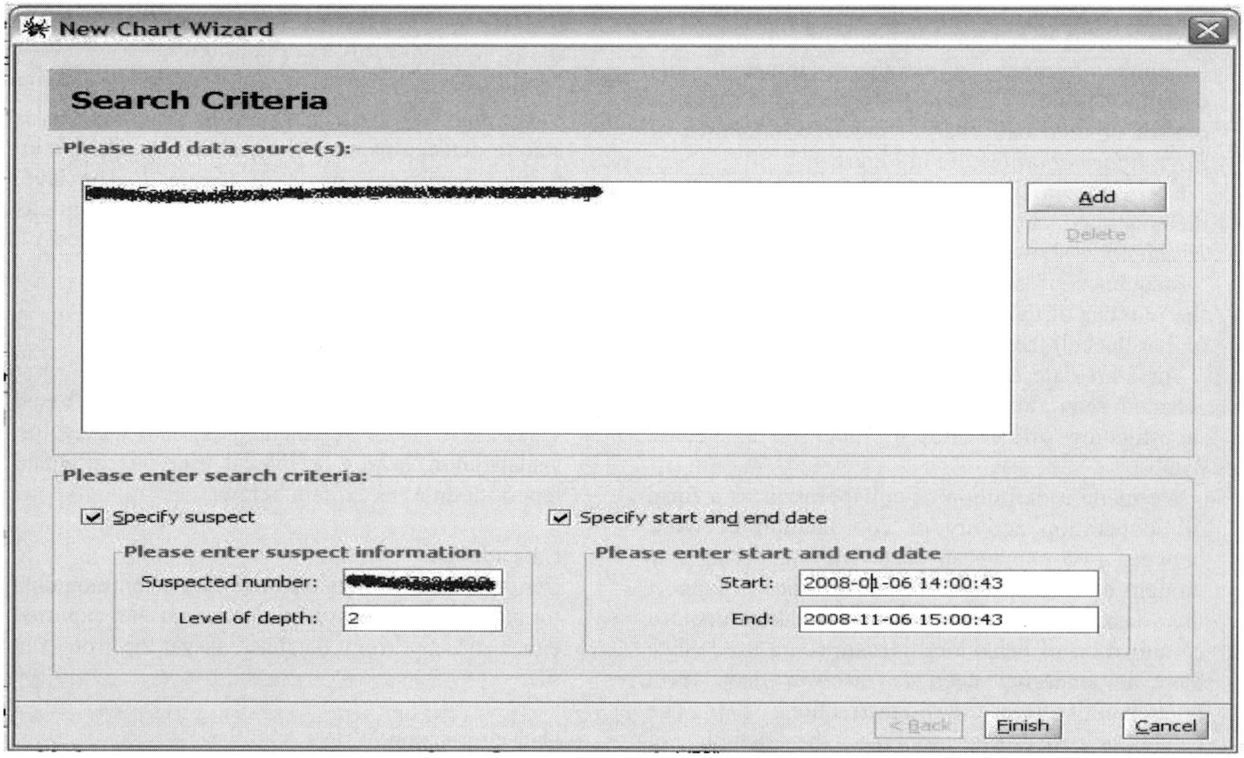

Figure 2: CDRs are selected based on suspected number, level of depth chosen with selected range of date

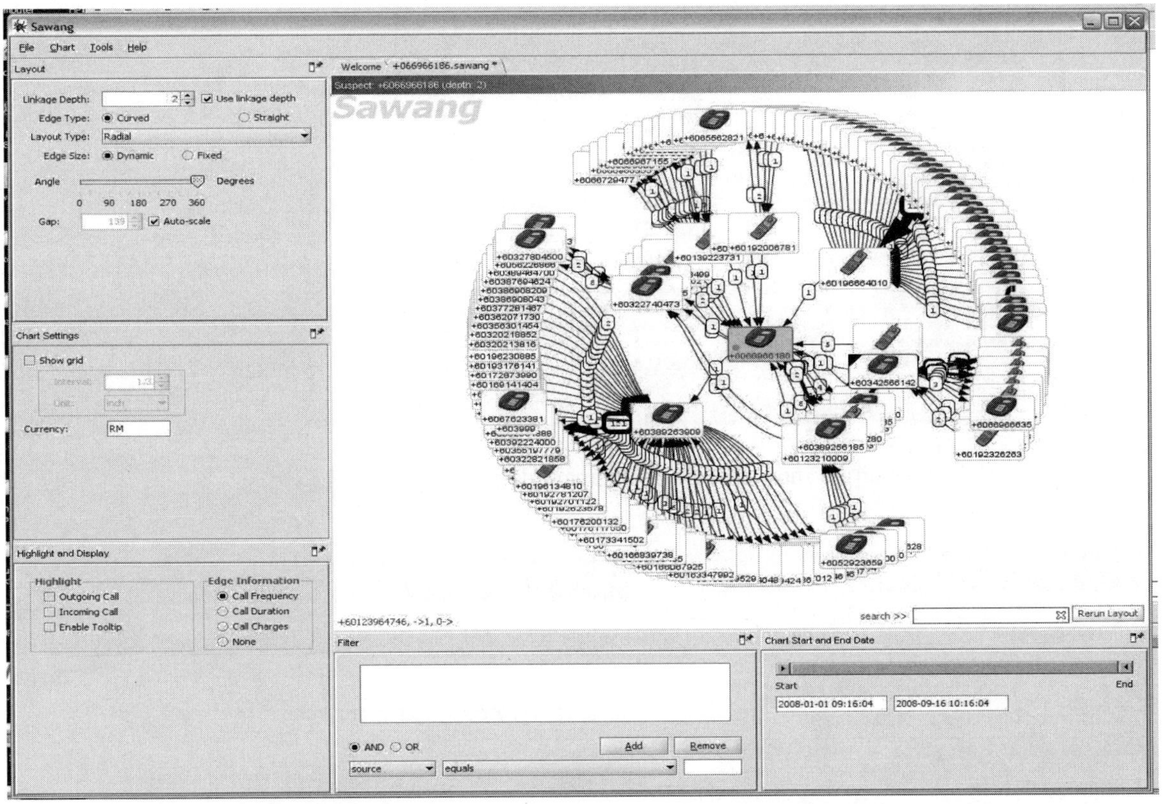

Figure 3: A Link Chart

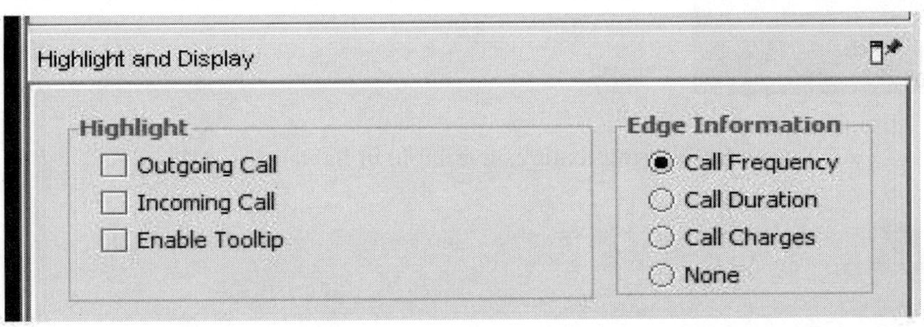

Figure 4: Two Features: Highlight and Edge Information

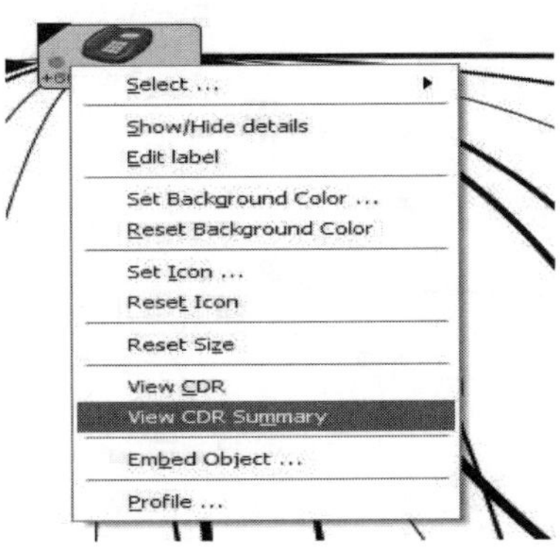

Figure 5(i): Diagram shows option *View CDR Summary* is selected

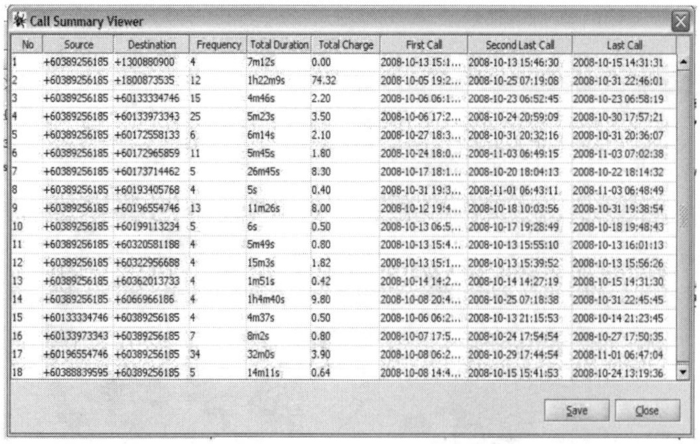

Call Summary Viewer

No	Source	Destination	Frequency	Total Duration	Total Charge	First Call	Second Last Call	Last Call
1	+60389256185	+1300880900	4	7m12s	0.00	2008-10-13 15:1...	2008-10-13 15:46:30	2008-10-15 14:31:31
2	+60389256185	+1800873535	12	1h22m9s	74.32	2008-10-05 19:2...	2008-10-25 07:19:08	2008-10-31 22:46:01
3	+60389256185	+60133334746	15	4m46s	2.20	2008-10-06 06:1...	2008-10-23 06:52:45	2008-10-23 06:58:19
4	+60389256185	+60133973343	25	5m23s	3.50	2008-10-06 17:2...	2008-10-24 20:59:09	2008-10-30 17:57:21
5	+60389256185	+60172558133	6	6m14s	2.10	2008-10-27 18:3...	2008-10-31 20:32:16	2008-10-31 20:36:07
6	+60389256185	+60172965859	11	5m45s	1.80	2008-10-24 18:0...	2008-11-03 06:49:15	2008-11-03 07:02:38
7	+60389256185	+60173714462	5	26m45s	8.30	2008-10-17 18:1...	2008-10-20 18:04:13	2008-10-22 18:14:32
8	+60389256185	+60193405768	4	5s	0.40	2008-10-31 19:3...	2008-11-01 06:43:11	2008-11-03 06:48:49
9	+60389256185	+60196554746	13	11m26s	8.00	2008-10-12 19:4...	2008-10-18 10:03:56	2008-10-31 19:38:54
10	+60389256185	+60199113234	5	6s	0.50	2008-10-13 06:5...	2008-10-17 19:28:49	2008-10-18 19:48:43
11	+60389256185	+60320581188	4	5m49s	0.80	2008-10-13 15:4...	2008-10-13 15:55:10	2008-10-13 16:01:13
12	+60389256185	+60322956688	4	15m3s	1.82	2008-10-13 15:1...	2008-10-13 15:39:52	2008-10-13 15:56:26
13	+60389256185	+60362013733	4	1m51s	0.42	2008-10-14 14:2...	2008-10-14 14:27:19	2008-10-15 14:31:30
14	+60389256185	+6066966186	4	1h4m40s	9.80	2008-10-08 20:4...	2008-10-25 07:18:38	2008-10-31 22:45:45
15	+60133334746	+60389256185	4	4m37s	0.50	2008-10-06 06:2...	2008-10-13 21:15:53	2008-10-14 21:23:45
16	+60133973343	+60389256185	7	8m2s	0.80	2008-10-07 17:5...	2008-10-24 17:54:54	2008-10-27 17:50:35
17	+60196554746	+60389256185	34	32m0s	3.90	2008-10-08 06:2...	2008-10-29 17:44:54	2008-11-01 06:47:04
18	+60388839595	+60389256185	5	14m11s	0.64	2008-10-08 14:4...	2008-10-15 15:41:53	2008-10-24 13:19:36

Save Close

Figure 5(ii): Diagram shows the CDR summary data.

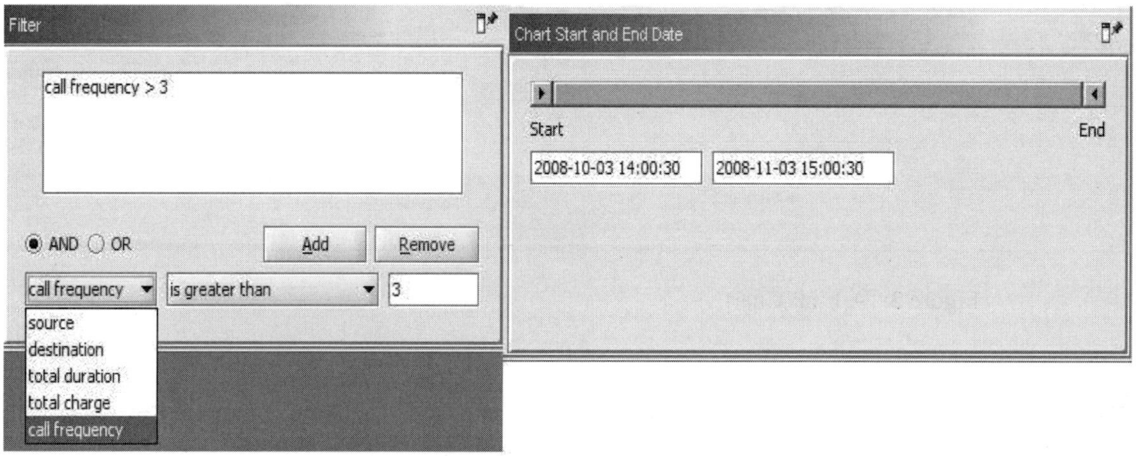

Figure 6: Filtering features available in Sawang.

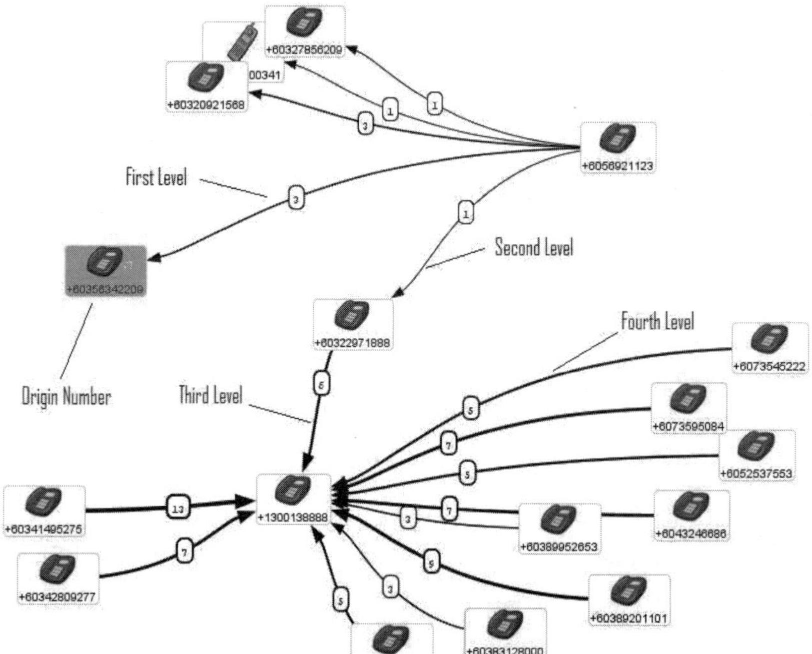

Figure 7: Sawang shows four level of depth based on origin number

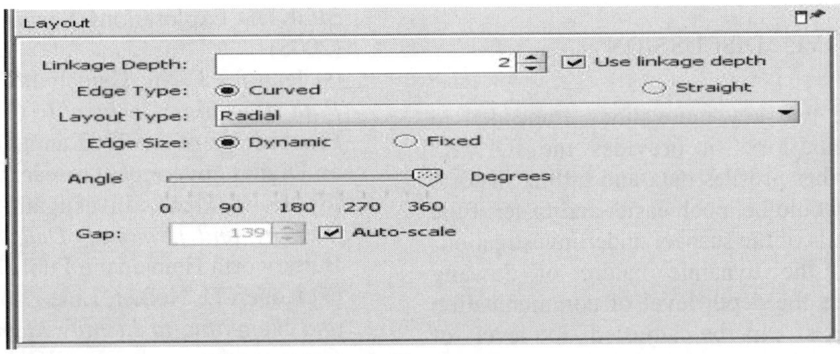

Figure 8: Layout Features

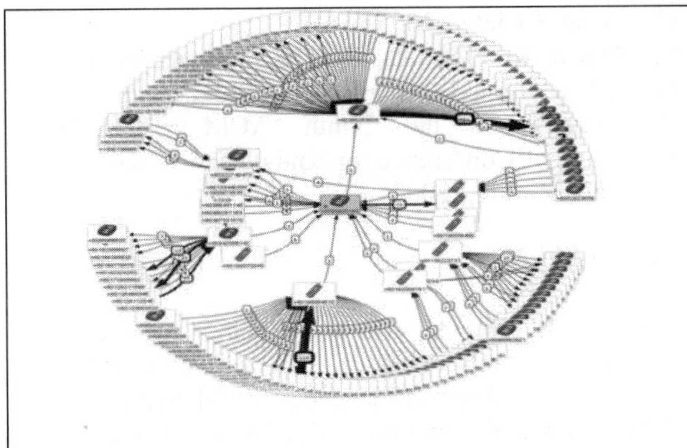

Radial

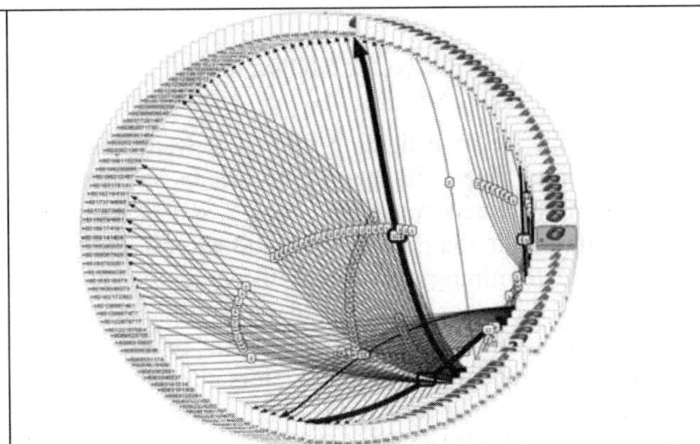

Circle

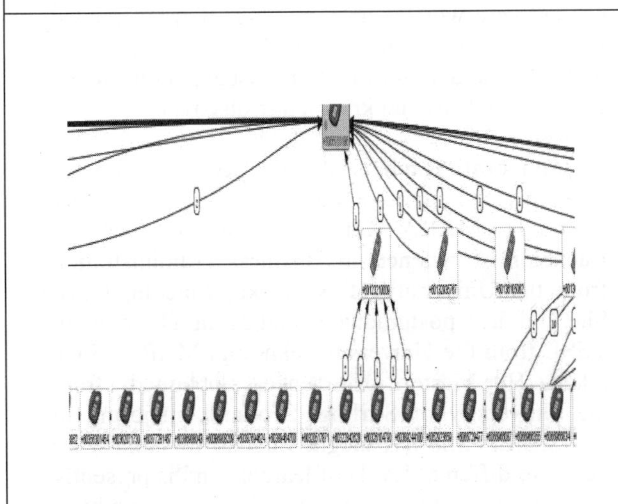

Hierarchy

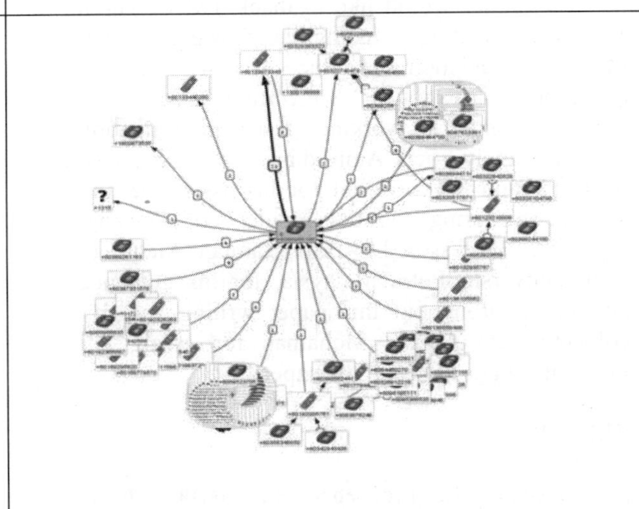

Group

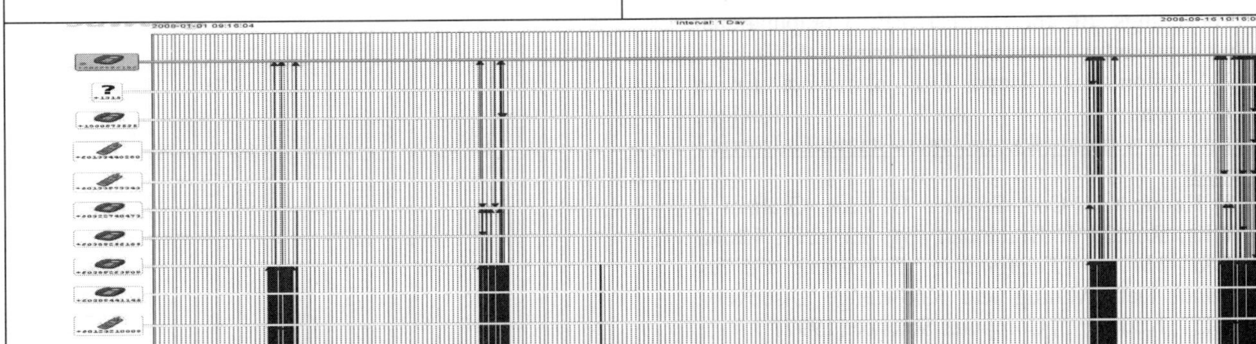

Timeline

Figure 9: Layout Type of Sawang

VI. DISCUSSION

There are two key innovations embedded in Sawang system. First, it provides the IO with current subscriber profiles data and billing history. Investigation would be much easier and faster if the IO knows details of the suspect under investigation.

Secondly, the dynamic nature of Sawang interface where the depth level of communication of the suspects can be adjusted to level of preference, according to the investigation needs.

VII. CONCLUSION

Through the investigation tool of Sawang, an investigation officer will spend less time in finding association between fraudster. Thus, we can see that graph-based diagrammatic visualizations can assist in determining the future direction of an investigation. Further work and research is planned to include social network analysis in order to increase the predictions of collaborators character.

ACKNOWLEDGEMENT

The author would like to thank TM Research & Development for funding the Sawang project. Much appreciation is due to the Sawang development team for converting a research prototype into a working fraud investigation system, namely Encik Amiruddin Hussin, an AGM of TM Fraud Management for his assistance and suggestion during the development of Sawang, Associate Professor Dr Haji Ramlan Mahmod, from Universiti Putra Malaysia, for his guidance and ideas throughout this paper writing and my colleague, Pn Azizan Mohamad for giving her ideas and suggestions of this paper.

REFERENCE

[1] Aleskerov E., Freisleben B., *CARDWATCH: A Neural Network Based Database Mining System for Credit Card Fraud Detection*, pg. 220-226, Proceedings of the IEEE/IAFE, Computational Intelligence for Financial Engineering (1997)

[2] Bolton R.J., Hand D.J. *Statistical Fraud* Detection: A Review, http://www.fraudwiki.org/papers/statmethodsreview.pdf

[3] Kenneth C. Cox, Stephen G. Eick, Graham J. Wills, Ronald J. Brachman, pg. 225-231, *Visual Data Mining: Recognizing Telephone Calling Fraud*, Data Mining and Knowledge Discovery, Vol. 1, Number 2, Computer Science (1997)

[4] Ted E. Senator, pp. 76-83, *Link Mining Applications: Progress and Challenges*, ACM SIGKDD Explorations Newsletter, Vol. 7, Issue 2, (2005)

[5] Jennifer J. Xu, Hsinchun Chen, *Using Shortest Path Algorithms to Identify Criminal Associations*, Proceedings of the 2002 annual national conference on Digital government research dg.o '02, (2002)

[6] Jesus Mena, Investigating *Data Mining for Security and Criminal, Detection*. Burlington,US, Butterworth Heinemann Publisher (2003)

[7] Robert D. Nolker, Lina Zhou. *Social Computing and Weighting to Identify Member Roles in Online Communities*, IEEE/WIC/ACM International Conference on Web Intelligence WI '05, IEEE Computer Society, (2005).

[8] David K., Jon K., Eva T. *Maximizing the Spread of Influence Through a Social Network*, Proceedings of the Ninth ACM SIGKDD International Conference on Knowledge Discovery and Data Mining, (2003).

BIOGRAPHY

Rosmawati binti Ab Raub is a senior researcher of TM Research & Development, received her Bachelor of Applied Science in Mathematical Calculation and Computer Aided Graphic Design (CAGD) from Universiti Sains Malaysia (USM) in 1993. She joined Telekom Malaysia in 1994 and has actively worked on a number of fraud related system projects since year 2000. Her research interests include information visualization, social network analysis and knowledge discovery.

Rozana binti Raoh is a senior lecturer from the Academy of Language Studies from the University Teknologi MARA Kelantan. She received her Bachelor of Science in Business Administration from the University of Nebraska, Lincoln, USA. She did her postgraduate studies in Diploma in TESL from the Universiti Teknologi MARA, Shah Alam. Her Masters Of Science, is obtained from the University of Stirling, Scotland, majoring in T.E.S.O.L. She has taught English for almost 20 years to different levels of learners and is presently the Coordinator Course for the subject Communication in the Workplace.

IMPLEMENTATION OF A SYSTEM DYNAMICS SIMULATION MODEL: PRICING STRATEGY SIMULATOR IN INTERNET-BASED DECISION SUPPORT

Zainuridah Yusof, Rosdalillah Mohamed, Nur Azlin Atikah Husin,Fauzy Che Yayah, Kamarul Bahrim Zainal Abidin

Operation Support System Program, TM R&D Sdn. Bhd., MALAYSIA

zainur@tmrnd.com.my, rosdali@tmrnd.com.my, atikahusin@tmrnd.com.my, Fauzy@tmrnd.com.my; kamarul@tmrnd.com.my

Abstracts

This paper mainly discusses about the Pricing Strategy WebSim, a web-based simulator using system dynamics methodology in decision making process of pricing strategies of voice telephony business. System dynamics methodology is one of the Operation Research (OR) discipline, whereby their conceptual modeling can then be converted into computing models using POWERSIM Studio 2005 software. A mathematical model simulating the growth of subscribers, revenue, traffics, cost and profit of voice telephony business has been made available for use via the Internet. The required input variables are provided by the user and results of multiple simulation runs can be viewed and compared via tables and graphs. The Powersim Software Development Kit (SDK) provides the Application Programmers Interface (API) for bridging the simulation model with the web application. By building a web application for system dynamics simulation model, cost saving is realized by buying a single license and deliver updated versions to multiple users.

***Keywords:* web-based, simulator, system dynamics**

I. NTRODUCTION

The field of system dynamics was created by Jay Forrester in 1956. It is an approach to understanding the behavior of complex systems over time or how things change through time. System dynamics (SD) deals with how the internal feedback-loops within the system and time delay that creating behavior of the entire system. SD is a way of thinking about the future which focuses on 'stock' and 'flow' within processes and the relationship between them. What makes using SD different from other approaches to studying complex system is the use of feedback loops and stock and flows. The existence of these elements enable describes the nonlinearity in the system.

Computer software is used to simulate a system dynamics model of the situation being studied to achieve better understanding of system behavior over time. Running "what if" simulations to test certain policies on such a model can greatly aid in understanding how the system changes over time. The central concept to system dynamics understands how all the objects in a system interact with one another. The objects and people in a system interact through "feedback" loops, where a change in one variable affects other variables over time, which in turn affects the original variable, and so on.

The system dynamics modeling comprise of two types of Operational Research (OR) disciplines, soft OR and hard OR. The soft part is used to yield conceptual modeling or cause and effect diagram. Once the conceptual modeling built, then the hard OR comes into the picture to translate the conceptual modeling to computer modeling using system dynamics software package. In this study, POWERSIM Studio 2005 has been used to build SD simulation model.

II. SIMULATION MODEL OF VOICE TELEPHONY PRICING STRATEGY

The purpose of the simulation model is to be used as a tool for pricing strategy of voice telephony business. The flow of the simulator is depicted in figure 1. Input variables to the simulation model are:-

- Voice telephony rental fee
- Voice telephony publish price
- Voice telephony discount price
- Advertising & promotion (A&P) budget
- Loyalty program budget
- Voice telephony network cost

Outputs from the simulation model are:-

- Voice telephony subscribers
- Usage voice telephony
- Revenue voice telephony
- Cost voice telephony
- Profit voice telephony

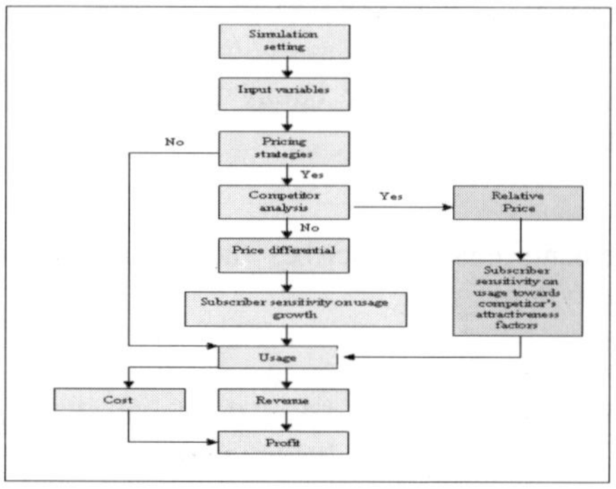

Figure 1: Flow diagram of the pricing strategy simulator

III. INTERNET IMPLEMENTATION OF THE PRICING STRATEGY SIMULATION MODEL

The pricing strategy simulation model is implemented in Powersim Studio 2005 which is a specialized software package of simulation and modeling using system dynamics methodology. The internet interface to the pricing strategy simulation model was implemented in Active Server Pages (ASP) on a Microsoft Internet Information Server with data stored in a Microsoft SQL server. Programming code is in asp.net and VB Scripts. The Powersim studio SDK is a library that can be used by programmers to include simulations in custom-designed software applications. Software developers can use the SDK to develop simulations for the web as well as desktop applications to be run in the Microsoft® Windows environment. Figure 2 provides an overview of the system.

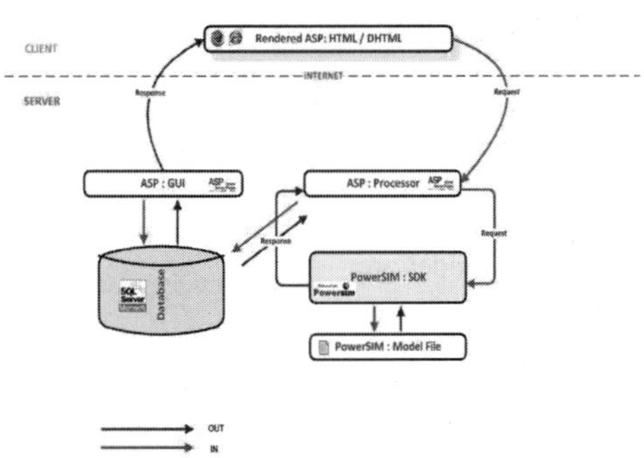

Figure 2: Overview of System

How the Web-based simulator works?

The ASP pages are hosted on a web server. The web server is basically software that serves web pages to clients using the internet layers. A client (typically a browser) requests a page residing on a Web Server like IIS (Internet *Information System*) which support the ASP like language scripting. ASP: Processor sends some functions to the Powersim SDK before starts the simulation. On the simulation process , the Powersim SDK read the model files , define the elements and variables , and generate the results to the ASP : Processor back. ASP: Processor does the business logic and updates the simulation results to the database. ASP : GUI will create some dynamically pages with to the User Interface after fetched the information from the database. Both communication from the server and clients are using HTTP or HTTPS protocol.

Why use Web base Simulator application?

- Easy to publish simulation logics through the web
- Easy to distribute the models via an Intranet or the Internet
- Many user can participate on the same model at the same time
- Reduce the complexity of the clients system requirements – just using the browsers

More info on the Web base PowerSIM application

Web-based application provides a window to manage all the connections. Each connection can be examined, showing the IP address of the connected client, and the average transfer time between the Server and the client. System administrators can often diagnose problems by examining individual connections in more detail. It also can examine the current status of the server. This allows him to monitor how many sessions are active, how many simulation streams are in use, etc. The System Administrator can also examine various historical data about the serving of simulator, through the Event Log. Their capabilities also provides a window for managing sessions. Each session can be examined, showing how many clients are connected, when the last activity happened, how long the simulation model has been run, etc. Furthermore, sessions can also be controlled by the system administrator. For example, the system administrator may want to delete a session that has had no activity for a few hours. Some possibilities that can be provided by web based simulator application are concurrent simulations, simulators with different user roles & historical simulation results.

IV. PRICING STRATEGY SIMULATOR

1. Conceptual Modeling

Causal loop diagrams (CLDs) are a kind of systems thinking tool. CLDs are often used to illustrate cause and effect relationships. The interacting variables involves in pricing strategy simulator were converted into causal loop diagram or conceptual model. Overall presentation of the conceptual model is shown as figure 3 below.

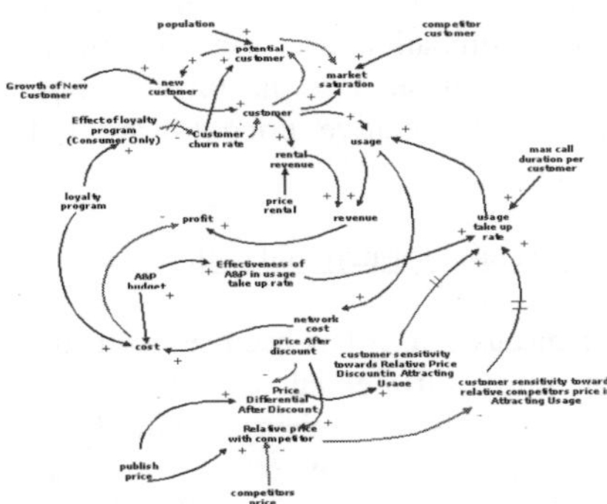

Figure 3: Pricing Strategy Conceptual Model

2. Stock & flow Modeling

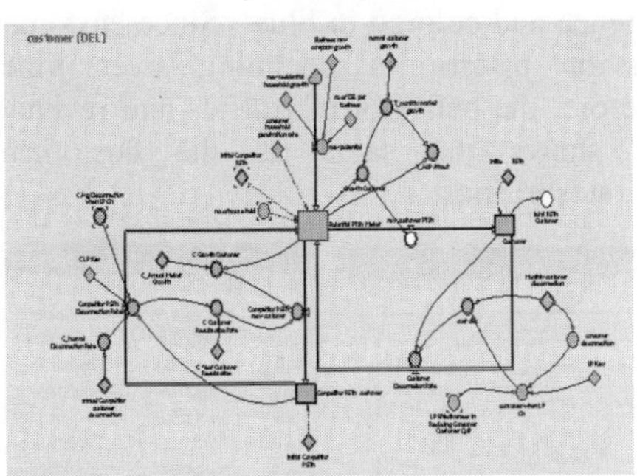

Figure 4: stock and flow diagram for Customer

Figure 4 above shows one of the computer simulations model or stock and flow diagram involves in the pricing strategy simulator. It shows how our company and competitor gained customer from the pool of potential customer. The increases number of potential customer is governed by the factors of population, household growth and business growth as the customer is segmented by two(2) types, Residential and Business customers. The increases number of our company's customer is controlled by the factors of normal customer growth with the effectiveness of Advertising & Promotion. Whilst, the number of customer will be depleted by the factors of normal disconnection rate with the effectiveness of the Loyalty Program. The same environment also is applied to competitor. In other words, the power of attracting customer from potential customer being customer is depends on how strong our company and competitor play a role in advertising and promotion activity and how strong our company and competitor play a role in loyalty program activity to remain their customers.

V. FEATURES IN WEB-BASED PRICING STRATEGY SIMULATOR

The main features of web-based pricing strategy simulator consist of external factors, data input, graphical function of the elasticity's policies changes and result. Figure 5 below shows the overall system involves in developing the pricing strategies simulator.

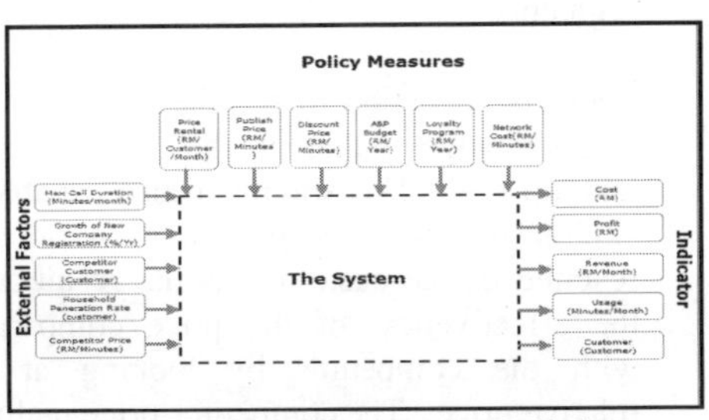

Figure 5: The overall system of Pricing Strategy Simulator

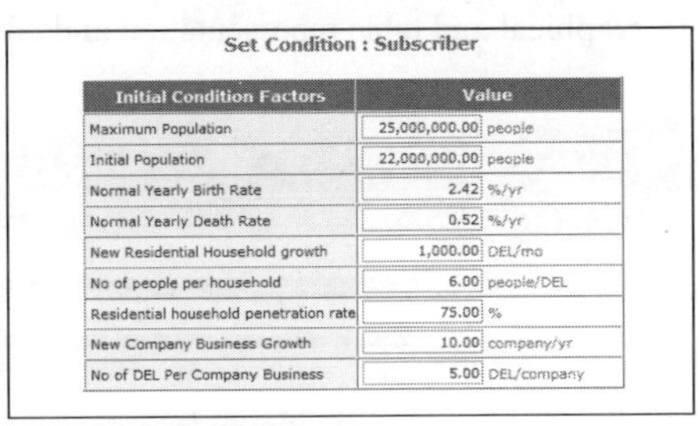

Set Condition : Subscriber

Initial Condition Factors	Value
Maximum Population	25,000,000.00 people
Initial Population	22,000,000.00 people
Normal Yearly Birth Rate	2.42 %/yr
Normal Yearly Death Rate	0.52 %/yr
New Residential Household growth	1,000.00 DEL/mo
No of people per household	6.00 people/DEL
Residential household penetration rate	75.00 %
New Company Business Growth	10.00 company/yr
No of DEL Per Company Business	5.00 DEL/company

Figure 6: Input Data in Web-based Pricing Strategy Simulator

Figure 6 shows an example of input data page in pricing strategy simulator. One of the unique features in pricing strategy simulator is graphical function of the elasticity's policies changes. The displayed graph can be changeable easily based on some study or just accepted the default displayed value. The graphical function shows in the figure 7.

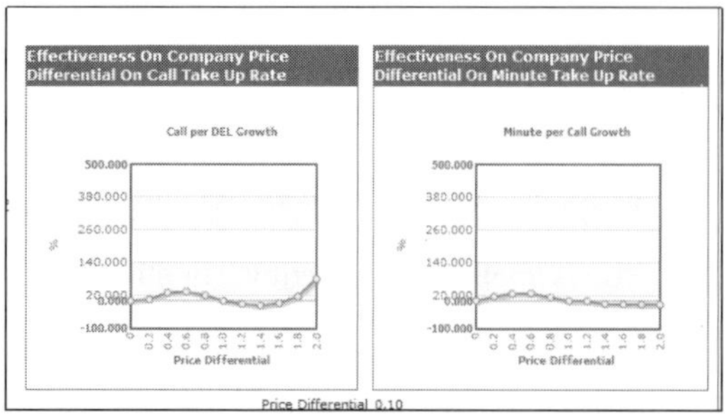

Figure 7: Graphical function in Web-based Pricing Strategy Simulator

There are three (3) types of voice available in our pricing strategies simulator, i.e. local, national, & international as well as strategy for advertisement and promotion (A&P). Figure 8 below shows the national pricing strategy page. The strategy for the pricing was based on two customer segment which are business and residential. Price discount can be given to either for each customer segment or price discount for all customer segments. There are band and tariff type which associated with the customer segments.

There is an option to see the effects of the prices changes either on the call or minute take up rate. This simulator also capable to exhibit the behavior pattern of usage and revenue of the customer as the result from the effectiveness of the price comparable with the competitor by looking at the relative price. The competitor price includes the price of fixed line, mobile and VOIP. The result of simulator is displayed in the graphical and table representation and table.

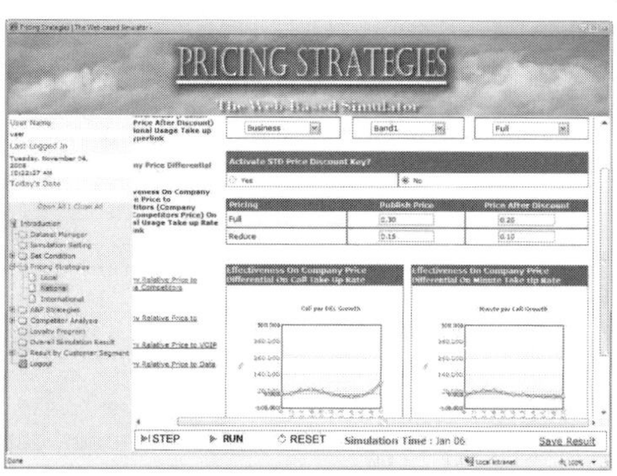

Figure 8: National Pricing Strategy

Strategy for Advertising & Promotion (A&P) is also provided in this simulator which taken into consideration of the A&P medium, Press, Radio, TV and BTL (Below the line). In this part, only the budget of A&P, effectiveness of the A&P activities and time taken by customer to perceive are taken into consideration.

VI. RESULT & DISCUSSION

The attractive pricing will lead the changes of behavior of customer usage take up rate i.e usage in call or minute, thus give advantages to the company in term of revenue and profitability. In other hands, increases of the usage will lead the increment of the network cost, thus will deplete the profit. The effectiveness of the price changes on the usage take up rate will be focuses on two aspects. First, price differential between publish and discounted price and second, relative price between our current price over competitor price. The simulation was run with monthly basis for 3 years to test the impact of price differential and relative price toward traffic and revenue.

Price differential for national call.

For this discussion, It has been set for national call of price differential is 0.1 and it is assumed that this price changes will effect on minute take up rate at 60% from normal average minute per call. Figurc 9 & 10 below shows the scenario analysis of simulation result in graph and table for national traffic and revenue respectively. Do nothing scenario (without price discount) result shows as a reference and colored in blue. Since customer behavior pattern is declining over time, therefore, the behavior of traffics and revenue also shows the same as the customers generates traffics.

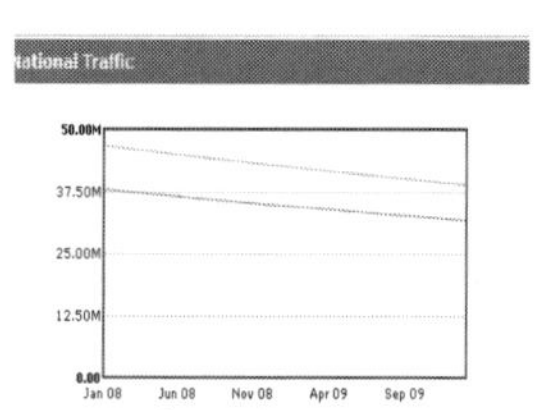

Time	Current	Reference
May 09	41,286,762.16	33,545,494.25
Jun 09	40,974,652.07	33,291,904.81
Jul 09	40,665,481.37	33,040,703.61
Aug 09	40,359,222.28	32,791,868.10
Sep 09	40,055,847.34	32,545,375.96
Oct 09	39,755,329.31	32,301,205.07
Nov 09	39,457,641.24	32,059,333.51
Dec 09	39,162,756.42	31,819,739.59
Jan 10	38,870,648.39	31,582,401.82

Figure 9: Simulation for national traffic

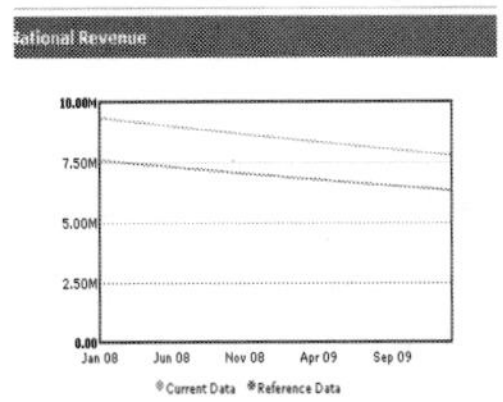

Time	Current	Reference
May 09	8,257,352.43	6,709,098.85
Jun 09	8,194,930.41	6,658,380.96
Jul 09	8,133,096.27	6,608,140.72
Aug 09	8,071,844.46	6,558,373.62
Sep 09	8,011,169.47	6,509,075.19
Oct 09	7,951,065.86	6,460,241.01
Nov 09	7,891,528.25	6,411,866.70
Dec 09	7,832,551.28	6,363,947.92
Jan 10	7,774,129.68	6,316,480.36

Figure 10: Simulation for national revenue

<u>Relative Price for national call.</u>

It is set the relative price with competitor at value 1.33 and assuming that their effects on the minute take up rate at 30% from normal. Figure 12 & 13 below shows the result in graph and table for national traffic and revenue respectively. The time taken by customer to perceive the price changes and anticipate with them is taken into consideration in this simulator. The anticipation of customers could be in both ways, either to stimulate the calls or to switch to competitor.

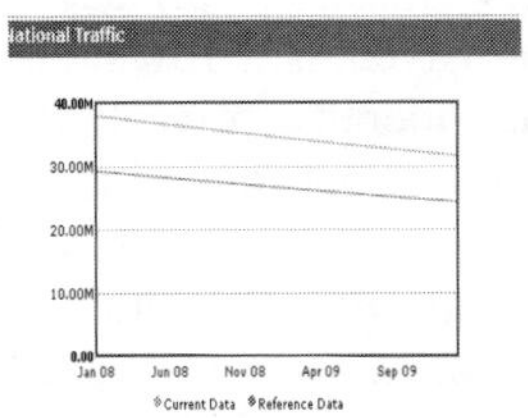

Time	Current	Reference
May 09	33,545,494.25	25,839,254.71
Jun 09	33,291,904.81	25,643,921.11
Jul 09	33,040,703.61	25,450,427.11
Aug 09	32,791,868.10	25,258,755.35
Sep 09	32,545,375.96	25,068,888.62
Oct 09	32,301,205.07	24,880,809.89
Nov 09	32,059,333.51	24,694,502.28
Dec 09	31,819,739.59	24,509,949.08
Jan 10	31,582,401.82	24,327,133.74

Figure 12: Simulation for national traffic

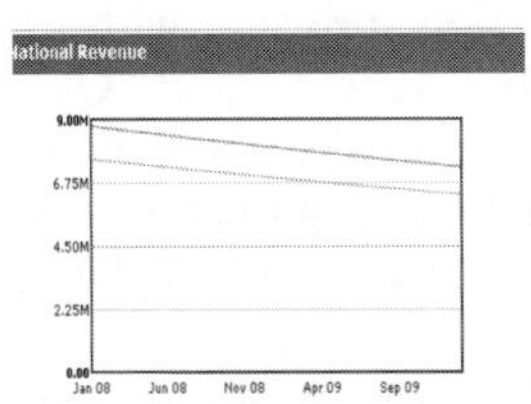

Time	Current	Reference
May 09	6,709,098.85	7,751,776.41
Jun 09	6,658,380.96	7,693,176.33
Jul 09	6,608,140.72	7,635,128.13
Aug 09	6,558,373.62	7,577,626.60
Sep 09	6,509,075.19	7,520,666.59
Oct 09	6,460,241.01	7,464,242.97
Nov 09	6,411,866.70	7,408,350.68
Dec 09	6,363,947.92	7,352,984.72
Jan 10	6,316,480.36	7,298,140.12

Figure 12: Simulation for national revenue

The sensitivity analysis of the selected strategy before real implementation can be implement, thus the policy lever can be obtained. Other scenario analysis can be done in this simulator are on:-

- The voice local call – business & residential customer, company & competitor
- The voice national call – full & reduce rate, business & residential customer, 3 types of national band, company by price differential and competitor by relative price
- The voice international call - full & reduce rate, business & residential customer, 31 top countries, company by price differential and competitor by relative price

REFERENCE

[1] Brown, Gordon S., "Collection Papers of Jay W. Forrestor", Wright-Allen Press, Inc., Cambridge, Massachusetts (1980)

[2] Ernest H.P., Arnold B., Paul A.F. et al, ACM Transactions on Modeling and Computer Simulation, Pages 3-17 (January 2000)

[3] Forrester, J.W., "Industrial Dynamics". John Wiley and Sons ,New York (1961)

[4] Jasna Kuljis, Ray J. P., A review of Web Based Simulation: Whither We Wander?, Proceedings of Winter Simulation Conference (2000)

[5] Nazareth S.B., Jian W.J., Joe M., Jeremy T., ESIM Software for Web-Enabled Distributed Analysis and Simulation, AIAA Modeling and Simulation technology Conference & Exhibit, Canada (2001)

[6] P. Micheal, System Modeling: Theory and Practice, John Wiley & Sons, (April 2004)

[7] Paul A. Fishwick, Web-Based Simulation, Proceedings of the 1997 Winter Simulation Conference (1997)

[8] Peter M. Senge. The Fifth Discipline Fieldbook: Strategies and Tool for Building a Learning Organization, Doubleday, New York (1994)

User-centered Privacy and Trust Model in Cloud Computing Systems

Ali Dehghantanha
Faculty of Computer Science & Information Technology- University Putra Malaysia
Dehqan@gmail.com

Ramlan Mahmod
Cyber Security Lab, MIMOS Berhad
Technology Park Malaysia
Ramlan.mahmod@mimos.my

Nur Izura Udzir
Faculty of Computer Science & Information Technology- University Putra Malaysia
izura@fsktm.upm.edu.my

Zoriati Ahmad Zulkarnain
Faculty of Computer Science & Information Technology- University Putra Malaysia
zuriati@fsktm.upm.edu.my

Abstract— **the fact that cloud computing systems (formally known as pervasive computing systems) are typically embedded or invisible, making it difficult for users to know when these devices are collecting data. So privacy appears as a major issue for this environment. In this paper we propose a User-centered privacy and trust Model which provides user control over data, identity, location, and time privacy with less than 10% of unobtrusiveness.**

Keywords-Privacy, Trust, Cloud Computing.

I. INTRODUCTION

Providing users with enough privacy level is a basic requirement in cloud and pervasive systems which provide services seamlessly everywhere, at any time for all the users.

Privacy and trust have always been an inter-related concepts.

Different evaluation methods proposed for security and privacy in cloud and pervasive computing systems. Ranganathan et al [1] proposed a benchmark which considered three characteristics for privacy models as follow:

1. User control over information: identified with model ability to provide content, identity, and location privacy.

2. Unobtrusiveness of mechanisms which is the percent of time user wastes on interacting with privacy/trust sub-system.

3. Expressiveness of privacy policies which is the policies ability to support mandatory and discretionary rules, context sensitivity, uncertainty handling, and conflict resolution.

The main unobtrusiveness challenge is to provide a balance between usability and privacy [2].

Several projects and models have already addressed some concerns of privacy protection. Privacy Sensitive Information Diluting Mechanism (PSIUM) [3] provides location privacy without any concern about model unobtrusiveness. Mix networks and mix nodes model [4] provides location privacy without looking into model unobtrusiveness. Pseudonyms and mix-zones model [5] provides both location and identity privacy but it doesn't have any concern for model unobtrusiveness. LocServ [6] model just supports location privacy with attention to its unobtrusiveness. Mist model [7] provides location and identity privacy for the user regarding to the model unobtrusiveness. Paws (Privacy Awareness System) [8] supports user identity and location privacy with concern on model unobtrusiveness. Geopriv model [9] provides user location privacy but it was not concerned about model unobtrusiveness. Spirit [10] provides location privacy with concern about model unobtrusiveness. QoP (Quality of Privacy) model [11] provides location, content, and identity privacy and provides a balance between user privacy and services that can be provided for him.

Today enhanced pervasive devices providing real time user information, make researchers to provide user with control over her time privacy.

In this paper we present a User-centered Privacy Model (UPM) which provides user control over content (data), location, identity, and time privacy. Then we evaluate the model and measure its unobtrusiveness.

Section 2 describes the model, its phases and its privacy policies. Section 3 discuses model ability to provide user with control over content, identity, location, and time privacy. This section continues with evaluating model unobtrusiveness. Conclusion and future works presents in section 4.

II. PROPOSED MODEL

Three parties are communicating in proposed model as follow:

1) User: User requests services.

2) Service provider: Provides services for the user using the data that is provided by the owner.

3) Owner: Owner is the content provider.

4) User light houses: Each user has one or more light houses. Light houses are user trusted parties that have user identity information but they never have any information of the user location, content, and time. Light houses providing other parties with user identity information based on user identity privacy policy.

5) Portals: portals are wireless nodes managing user context. Each context consists of one portal which plays two roles:

- All devices of the context - including users' device- sending and receiving data through the portal.
- Portal manages all devices that gather user private information in the context. By default a portal has access just to user location information but it does not have any access to user identity, content, and time information.

These parties are communicating within three layers as follow:

1) User context layer: This layer surrounds user. Context includes one portal and several devices which are capable of gathering user private data. These devices are managed and controlled by the portal. In a specific time, user can be just within one portal covered environment but user might move between several portals experiencing different context.

2) Service layer: User light houses and service providers are in this layer.

3) Owner layer: Information owners are in this layer to provide required contents for service providers. Figure 1 shows the model parties and layers.

In proposed model user sends data to the portal without sending any information of his identity. Portal hides user location and forwards data to the light house. So the user portal just knows user location and the user light house just knows user identity. User light house will be responsible to communicate with the service provider. Service provider receives its needed contents through owners.

A. The Model Privacy Files

The model privacy management method is based on XML files using for describing privacy policies and preferences. Each user, portal, and service provider has two XML privacy files, namely privacy policy file and privacy preferences file. These two files format and tags are similar for each party. The privacy preferences file describes preferred level of privacy to communicate with other parties. Privacy policy file describes each party current and agreed privacy level during communication with other parties.

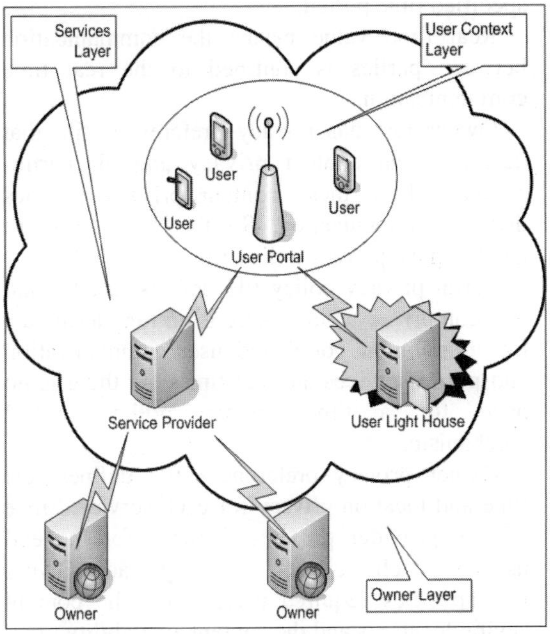

Fig. 1. Model parties and Layers

These XML files define each party identity, location, and time privacy. The identity privacy tag value can be No ID, Confirm ID, or Real ID.

Real ID value means the party will provide or ask the real identity in communication with other parties.

Confirm ID means the party will use a pseudonym ID that its trust ability and access level has been confirmed by a common trusted third party.

NoID means the party will use or ask an anonymous ID in communicating with other parties.

Location privacy tag value can be No Loc, Confirm Loc, or Real Loc.

Real Loc value means the party will provide or ask the exact location information of the other communicating parties.

Confirm Loc value means the party will

confirm its existence in a certain area through a common trusted third party or ask the other parties to confirm their existence in a certain area.

No Loc value means the party will not reveal or ask any location information in communicating with other parties.

The time privacy tag value can be No time, Confirm time, and Real time.

No time value means there is not any time limitation to communicate with other parties.

Confirm time value means the parties are confined to communicate just within a pre-specified time period.

Real time value means the communication between parties is confined to the real time communication.

Owner just has privacy preferences file that describes the content privacy and all parties should follow these content privacy policies during communication. So the owner doesn't need to have privacy policy file.

Portal privacy policy file defines just ID and location privacy. Since there is no long term data transmission in portal and user communication and portal services are real times, so there is no need for a time privacy policy control mechanism.

Owner privacy preferences file defines just time and location privacy for each service. Since service provider presents contents for the end users so it checks user identity privacy. Owner just specifies required privacy for the content saving locations and the content availability time.

All remaining privacy files have time, location, and identity tags.

B. The Model Phases

The proposed model contains five phases. Figure 2 shows proposed model phases and relations with different parties.

In authentication phase users are able to authenticate to the system through various authentication methods. System assigns a number called Authentication Precision Level (APL) in [0,100] to each authentication method. More precise authentication methods get higher APLs (These levels should be set previously by device manufacturer or system administrator).

System works on different automation level based on APL.

With APL in [0, 25), functionality is more important than privacy for the user. In this case in any conflicts or uncertain privacy situation

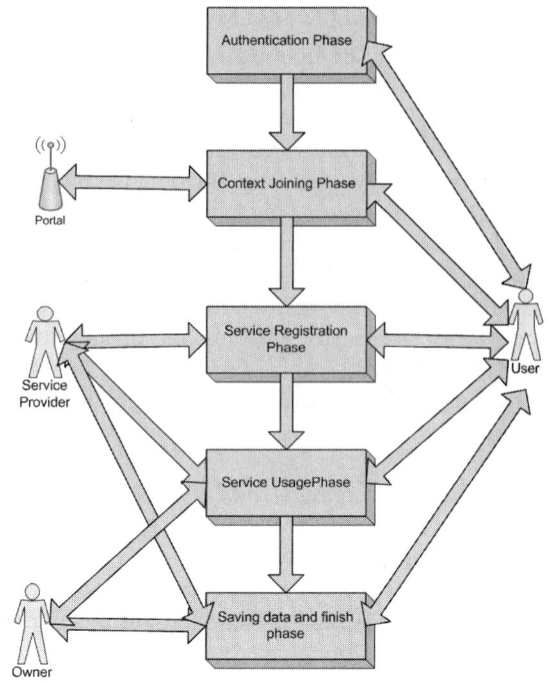

Fig. 2. Model phases

between user and other parties (when the other party cannot provide user required privacy level), user automatically accepts and applies the other party highest provided privacy level and start communication.

With APL in [25, 75], user receives alarms on communication with the parties with lower privacy levels than user requested. In this case user has the ability to accept or deny communication offer. So the model provides user notice and choice in this level.

With APL in (75,100], user does not accept any privacy level less than her required privacy. So if the other party could not provide user required privacy level, the system will not let user to use the other party services.

APL would be saved in <APL> tag of user privacy policy file for later comparisons and decision making during the other phases.

Each context device that gathers user private information has a device privacy policy file. Context privacy policy file will reflect lowest level of each privacy type in the context.

In context joining phase user sends his required privacy level to the context portal. If context is able to provide that privacy level then user will join to the context. The agreed privacy level between user and context will be written in Context Privacy Policy tag of user privacy policy file.

To start using a service, user sends requested service privacy level to the service provider. Service provider has preferred identity, location, and time privacy for each service that it provides in service provider privacy policy file.

In service registration phase if service provider would be able to provide user requested privacy level then it sends service usage key to the user otherwise user will not be able to use that service. The agreed privacy policy would be written in user privacy policy and service provider privacy policy files that consist of the agreed ID, location, and time privacy.

There is an information space tag for each content part of a service on the service provider each of which defines time and location privacy of related content part. In service usage phase service provider should get assure that user provides requested content privacy level before sending content to the user.

When user finishes using a part of the content or tries to save the content, system first applies content privacy policy on the saved content part so in future access to the content user needs to provide required privacy level.

Figure 3 shows a sample of user privacy policy file after service usage phase.

```
<?xml version="1.0" encoding="utf-8"?>

<UserUsagePrivacyPolicy>
<APL Level="50" />

<ContextPrivacyPolicy PortalName="University Portal"
IDPolicy="ConfirmID" LocationPolicy="NoLoc" />

  <ServiceProviderPrivacyPolicy ServiceProvider="University Service
Provider">
    <ServicePrivacyPolicy ServiceName="Smart Board">
      <ServiceRegistrationPrivacyPolicy IDPolicy="ConfirmID"
LocationPolicy="ConfirmLoc"
TimeType="ConfirmTime">
        <TimeDatePrivacyPref FromDay="03" FromMonth="03" FromYear="03"
ToDay="07" ToMonth="05" ToYear="03" />
  <TimeDayPrivacyPref MonFrom="08" MonTo="22" TueFrom="08" TueTo="22"
    WenFrom="08" WenTo="22" ThurFrom="08" ThurTo="22" FriFrom="08"
                          FriTo="22" />
</ServiceRegistrationPrivacyPolicy>

      <ServiceContentPrivacyPolicy>

        <InformationSpace ContentName="Class1.PPT" ContentID="200"
LocationPolicy="ConfirmLoc" TimeType="ConfirmType" Status="InUse">

          <TimeDatePrivacyPref FromDay="07" FromMonth="07"
FromYear="05" ToDay="10" ToMonth="10" ToYear="05">

          </TimeDatePrivacyPref>

        </InformationSpace>

      </ServiceContentPrivacyPolicy>

    </ServicePrivacyPolicy>

  </ServiceProviderPrivacyPolicy>

</UserUsagePrivacyPolicy>
```

Fig. 3. User Privacy Policy File after service usage phase

III. DISCUSSION

In this part we evaluate the proposed model based on its unobtrusiveness and user control over private information.

User control over private information discusses based on user control over content, identity, location, and time privacy.

Model unobtrusiveness measures by the percent of time that user wastes on dealing with privacy alerts.

A. User control over content privacy

The proposed model provides two levels of content privacy namely content privacy in communication, and privacy for the service contents.

The public/private keys with ECC algorithms provide content privacy for transferring information between communicating parties. We Used 160-Bit ECC keys to provide the same security level as a 1024 RSA key whiles the smaller size of key leads to less power consumptions and less memory and bandwidth usage.

Each service provider has a unique symmetric key for each service called service using key. All service contents encrypt with this encryption key in service provider. The related decryption key sends in service registration phase to the user. This mechanism ensures service content privacy.

B. User control over identity privacy

The user light house plays the main role in preserving user identity privacy.

In real ID policy, the user light house sends user real identity to the service provider. So user registers on the service provider with his real identity.

In confirm ID policy, since the service provider does not need user real identity, the user identity would just be confirmed by a third trusted party (between user light house and service provider).

In no ID the service provider will generate a random anonymous identity for each service request.

C. User control over location privacy

The user portal plays the main rôle to preserve user location privacy.

In no location policy, the portal completely hides user location from other parties.

In confirm location policy, the portal confirms user existence in its controlled area without divulging user exact location using a symmetric key calls location confirmation key. Service providers have the encryption key and trusted (by service provider) portals have the correspondence decryption key. Service provider encrypts all information, with confirm location policy, using location confirmation encryption key. At the entrance of the portal, portal decrypts the information, using location confirmation decryption key, and forwards it to the user. So just users in the context of these trusted portals can have access to the information and their existence in a certain area would be confirmed in this way.

In real location policy, portal provides information to the users based on their real geographical location place, using a location dependent encryption/decryption symmetric key pair, called exact location confirmation key. Service provider encrypts real location policy data base on the user provided location information. At the other end, portal feeds current user location information to the decryption key and sends the data to the user. Just if the user geographical information on portal matches with those on service provider the original plain information would be accessible to the user. We used the algorithm proposed by Al-Muhtadi et al [12] for encrypting and decrypting data.

D. User control over time privacy

Control of time privacy is assigned to the party that receives services or data.

In real time policy, the service provider generated username is valid just for one time using of one of the services on the service provider. So the user name would be expired once user disconnects from service provider or finish using of the service.

In confirm time policy, user light house and service provider should make an agreement on a certain amount of time that registered username is valid on the service provider for a service.

In no time, the registered username is valid for unlimited time.

The establishment of all previous conditions control when ever user tries to access to the data in each phase.

E. Model unobtrusiveness

We implemented the model and designed an experiment to measure the model unobtrusiveness.

Using C#.Net 2005 we implemented three different services namely "Buying Ticket" (S1), "Reserving Appointment Time with University Lecturers" (S2), and "Using University Smart Board" (S3). Three portals have been implemented namely, "Home Portal" (P1), "Bank Portal" (P2), and "University Portal" (P3). Two service providers implemented namely "Bus Service Provider" (SP1), and "University Service Provider" (SP2). Three content providers (owners) implemented, namely "Ticket Registration Information" (C1), "Project PPT" (C2), and "Lecturer Time Table Document" (C3). The implemented model is shown in figure 4.

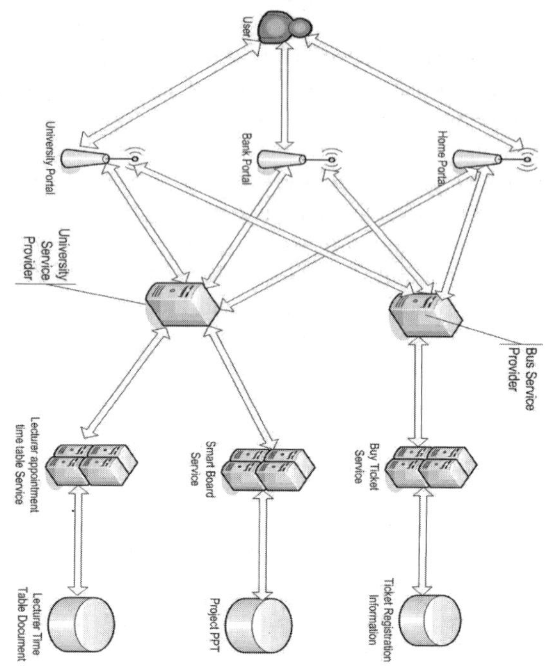

Fig. 4. Implemented model

The experiment follows these steps:

1) Categorize all system situations: The model supports three authentication methods, namely username and password with APL 25, finger print with APL 50, and eye detection with APL 100. The privacy alarms rise when user APL is between 25 and 75. There are three points that might raise privacy alarms (warnings). First at the beginning of joining context phase (I1), second at the beginning of service registration phase (I2), and third at the beginning of authentication phase (I3), because in these points the system checks and compares the user and other parties' privacy policies. Since the scenarios that have privacy alarm at the beginning of authentication phase cannot be continued to the next phases and should be restarted again so users receive at most two privacy alarms in one round of using a service, one at the beginning of context joining phase and another at the beginning of service registration phase. So we can categorize all

system situations into scenarios with zero, one or two privacy alarms.

2) We arrange scenarios into cases in a way that each case consists of one scenario with zero, one with one, and one with two privacy alarms. All possible model scenarios should be covered in the cases while each case has one scenario which is not covered in other cases.

3) We asked each experiment participant to do one case and we measured the whole time of work and the amount of time that user wastes on dealing with privacy alarms in each scenario. The unobtrusiveness of each case computes as follow:
Each case unobtrusiveness = (Sum of all times user wastes on dealing with privacy alarms during the case / Whole time of experimenting the case)* 100.

4) The model average unobtrusiveness computes as follow: Average Model Unobtrusiveness= (Sum of all cases unobtrusiveness / number of cases).

To measure whole time of experiment the implemented software writes an entry into 'windows event viewer' when the user starts working and when he finishes his work.

Whenever user gets a privacy alarm an entry would be written into event viewer and when user makes decision for that alarm another entry registers in event viewer. Sum of all times that user spent to make decision used in above formula.

We distinguished 17 different scenarios in model and 17 postgraduate students participated in our experiment each one experiment one case.

In our experiment we measured:

- Total Time of Work (TTW) which shows the amount of time from the user authentication phase until she finishes using of the service and saves data.
- Total Interruption Time (TIT) which is the total amount of time user wastes on dealing with privacy alerts in each scenario.

Then we calculate Percent of Unobtrusiveness (PU) with following formula:

Percent of Unobtrusiveness (PU) = (TIT/TTW)* 100.

Because each case consists of three scenarios we calculate Average Unobtrusiveness Percent (AUP) using following formula:

Average Unobtrusiveness Percent (AUP) = (PU Scenario 1 + PU Scenario 2 + PU Scenario 3)/3.

Finally we calculate the Average Unobtrusiveness of the Model (AUM) with adding all cases AUP divided by the number of all cases (17).

The experiment result shows that the model AUM (model unobtrusiveness) is 7.49%.

IV. CONCLUSION AND FUTURE WORKS

In this paper we proposed a privacy model which provides user control over content, identity, time, and location privacy with 7.94% of unobtrusiveness. Our future research direction is to evaluate the model scalability and privacy policy expressiveness and analyze model with common privacy attacks.

REFRENCES

[1] Ranganathan,A.,Al-Muhtadi,J.,Biehl,J.,Ziebart,B, Campbell, R. H., & Bailey, B,"Towards a pervasive computing benchmark."*3rd International Conf. on Pervasive Computing and Communications Workshops(PerCom2005Workshops),*2005,pp.*194-198*

[2] P.Bhaskar,S.I.Sheikh,"Privacyin Pervasive Computing and Open Issues", *2nd international conference on Availability, Reliability, and Security (ARES07),*2007

[3] H.S.Cheng, D.Zhang, J.G. Tan, "Protection of Privacy in Pervasive Computing Environments", International Conference on Information Technolog: Coding and Computing, 4-6 April 2005,pp. 242-247

[4] A.R. Beresford, F. Stajano, "Location Privacy in Pervasive Computing", Pervasive Computing, IEEE, Volume 2, Issue 2, April-June 2003, pp. 40-46

[5] A.R. Beresford, F. Stajano, "Mix Zones- User Privacy in Location-aware Services", International Workshop on Pervasive Computing and Communication Security, IEEE, March 2004

[6] G. Myles, A. Friday, N.Davies, "Preserving privacy in environments with location-based applications", Pervasive Computing, IEEE Volume 2, Issue 1, Jan-Mar 2003, pp. 56-64

[7] R. Campbell, J. Al-Muhtadi, P.Naldurg, G. Sampemane, M.D.Mikunas, "Towards Security and Privacy for Pervasive Computing", Proceeding of International Symposium on Software Security, 2002

[8] M. Langheinrich,"A Privacy Awareness System for UbiquitosComputingEnvironments",Ubicomp,Lecture Notes inComputer Science,volume2498,pp.72-74

[9] G Myles, A. Firday, N.Davies, "Preserving privacy in environments with location-based applications", Pervasive Computing, IEEE Volume 2, Issue 1, Jan – Mar 2003,pp. 56-64

[10] A.R. Beresford, F. Stajano, "Location Privacy in Pervasive Computing", Pervasive Computing, IEEE, Volume 2, Issue 1, Jan- Mar 003, pp. 46-55

[11] M. Tentori, J. FavelaM.D. Rodriguez, V.M. Gonzalez,

"Supporting Quality of Privacy (QoP) in Pervasive Computing",Sixth Mexican International Conference on Computer Science,26-30 Sep. 2005,pp. 58-67

[12] Al-Muhtadi, J., Hill, R., Campbell, R., & Mickunas, M. D. (2006). "Context and location-aware encryption for pervasive computing environments".Pervasive ComputingandCommunicationsWorkshops,2006.PerComWorkshops2006.FourthAnnualIEEE International Conference

A CASE STUDY OF BARRIERS TO ERP ADOPTION IN A MALAYSIAN MEDIUM-SIZED ENTERPRISE

MOHD SHUKOR ABD RAHMAN
Fakulti Teknologi Maklumat & Sains Kuantitatif
Universiti Teknologi MARA
Shah Alam, Malaysia
shukor.rahman@gmail.com

NORSHIDAH MOHAMED
Kuliyyah of Information Communication Technology
International Islamic University Malaysia
Gombak, Malaysia
norshidah@iiu.edu.my

RAMLAH HUSSEIN
Kuliyyah of Information Communication Technology
International Islamic University Malaysia
Gombak, Malaysia
ramlah@iiu.edu.my

In order to explore problems facing by local Small Medium Enterprises (SMEs) in adopting Enterprise Resource Planning (ERP) systems, this paper seeks to investigate what are the barriers to ERP system adoption by SMEs? The research was conducted in a Malaysian medium-sized company that planned to adopt ERP systems. Prior researches have identified that high cost; lack of knowledge; highly centralized structure; and issue of misfit to be barriers to ERP adoption by SMEs. From the case study, apart from the previous mentioned factors, the company has to do without a project champion and influenced by the perceived risk associated ERP systems implementation. Limitation of the research is that it was based on a single-case study, imposes care in generalizing the results of the study. This research, however, allows the identification and understanding of barriers to ERP adoption in local setting.
Keywords: Enterprise Resource Planning, Small Medium Enterprises, and Barrier

1. Introduction

An Enterprise Resource Planning (ERP) system is a computer software package that enables a company to manage its business operations, such as sales, manufacturing, inventory, accounting, etc. using a single platform [1]. An ERP system promises seamless integration for all information that flows across business processes (e.g. supply chain, customer relationship etc.) in a company. An ERP system is a highly complex technology. Installing ERP system requires large investment in money, time, and expertise, and involves the coordination of requirements across multi-adopters at different organisational levels [2]. Benefits of ERP systems include reduced inventory and inventory carrying costs; reduced manpower cost, reduced material cost; improved sales and customer service; and effectuated financial management [3]. SAP and Oracle are the samples of common ERP systems in the market.

For many years, software vendors had been focusing on the implementation of ERP systems in large organisations. In line with this, many past researches focused on ERP systems adoption and implementation in large organisations. As the total cost of ownership for ERP decreases, small companies might view that they could afford these systems. Hence, in recent years, we have been seeing the trend in immense enthusiasm among researchers for issues of ERP adoption and implementation in small and medium enterprises [4,5]. Small and medium enterprises (or SMEs) are characterised by their informal, flatter, highly centralized organisational structure [6], and more dynamic organisational culture [1] that accepts incremental change rather than radical change. SMEs have a dominant leader that is often the owner [6]. The leader usually involved in the day-to-day operational decisions [7]. It has been cited that SMEs lack in strategic planning; receive minimal training and development; [8] and have limited human and financial resources. Given such constraints, SMEs often lack a dedicated full-time Information Technology (IT) person [1].

Other characteristics, in particular, external attributes that distinguish SMEs from large organisations are their typical role in the supply chain and their limited ability to influence their market environment [1]. Because of their position in the upstream of the supply chain, SMEs have a higher variation in their customer orders, which have serious cost implications [1]. Besides, SMEs have little control over their market environment [6], which is attributable to SMEs' having large organisations as their primary customers. Hence, SMEs face the pressures that are the results of large organisations moving into their territory.

The literature indicates that many past researches on ERP adoption in SMEs were conducted in western countries [9-12]. To the best of our knowledge, researches on ERP adoption in SMEs in developing countries are limited. Hence, our motivation is to understand the barriers to ERP adoption in a Malaysian medium-sized enterprise. This paper is an attempt to provide insights on barriers to ERP adoption in a Malaysian medium-sized enterprise through a single-case study approach. There are five sections in this paper. Section one is the introduction. In section two, we discuss the barriers to ERP adoption base on our literature review. Next in section three, we present our case study. The analysis and discussion of the results will be in section four. Finally, in section five, we discuss the conclusion and limitation of the research.

2. Literature On Barriers To ERP Systems Adoption

In a period of one year, we conducted a literature search on barriers to ERP adoption in SMEs. In this paper, we discuss the following barriers, although we believe that they may not be exhaustive.

In line with the characteristics of SMEs, past researchers indicated that ERP's high implementation cost influenced SMEs decision to adopt ERP systems [12-15]. Kostopoulos et al. [13] found that financial constraint negatively influenced ERP adoption in Greece SMEs. Everdingen et al. [12] suggested that cost was one of the factors that influenced ERP adoption by European SMEs. In Asia, Liang et al. [16] attributed to cost for the lack of ERP adoption in China. Cost was also identified as the primary barrier to ERP adoption in Sri Lanka [17]. Overall, prior literatures confirmed that cost was one of the barriers to adoption facing by SMEs.

Everdingen et al. [12] found that the fit between ERP systems and the company's business process is one of the most important factors for European mid size companies in adopting ERP. Soh et al. [18] reported misfit between the functionality offered by the western ERP packages and Singapore organizations requirements. Moreover, Liang et al. [16] also reported that misfit was one the reason why western vendors did not dominate China ERP market. From these researches, we have identified that misfit was one of the barriers that inhibited ERP adoption by SMEs.

A successful ERP implementation demands experienced and knowledgeable workers in not only business processes but also ERP system functions. Without them, SMEs would be reluctant to adopt ERP [13]. With limited resources, in particular knowledge workers, SMEs might experience difficulties in gathering user's requirements and aligning ERP's functions to the requirements.

Lastly, SMEs usually managed in highly centralized structure [13]. SMEs usually are family businesses that have highly centralized structure where the owner has absolute power and control over his/her business. Middle and low-level management seldom contributes in decision-making. Employees are waiting to be told, rather than making their own judgments. However, ERP requires decision-makings at all levels of management. Consequently, ERP may clash with the decision making structure of the adopting organisation. Highly centralised organization can negatively affect ERP adoption process in SMEs [13].

3. Case Study

We conducted a case investigation in a medium-sized company located in Shah Alam, Selangor, Malaysia. We interviewed four members of the steering committee who were involved in the selection of an ERP system. They are the Director of the company, the Accountant, the Production Manager, and the IT Executive. We adopted a semi-structured approach for the interviews. Participants explained in great details many issues pertaining to the adoption guided by the researcher. Further information was collected from the company documents, and websites. Data of the interviews were recorded, transcribed and coded. A draft of case study was produced to one of the participants for further confirmation.

Company X is a medium-sized establishment located in Shah Alam, Selangor, Malaysia. The company has an intention to adopt an ERP system. Company X is in the business of metal stamping, electronics components and product assembly. The company has 113 employees. The last annual turnover was RM15 millions. The Chairman is the major shareholder of the company. A management team led by the Chief Operating Officer (COO) manages the day-to-day operation of the company. Although the COO is in-charge in the smooth running of the company, major decisions have to go through the shareholders. Currently, the company has an IT executive who looks after all the company IT services. The company uses mainly Microsoft Excel spreadsheet, Microsoft Word and an accounting system.

The reason for adopting ERP is to replace the accounting system, which having a problem with multiple users entries. The company COO personally started the ERP adoption initiative. The COO formed steering committee and volunteered to chair the steering committee. The members of the committee were the Director, the Accountant, IT Executive, and all heads of departments. The COO instructed the IT Executive to collect information on requirements of each department. A number of consultants were contacted and asked to present to the steering committee. Few discussions took place and few proposals changed hands.

After a few meetings with various ERP vendors, the steering committee cannot decide on whether or not to adopt ERP. The committee was supposed to report and discuss their decision with the shareholders. The stalemate continued for sometime until the COO left the company. From that moment, no more efforts to kick start the initiative. The COO had been instrumental from the beginning of the adoption process. When she left, other members were reluctant to proceed with the initiative. Since the company decided not to hire a new COO, the adoption project was put on hold. As stated by the Accountant:

"Our last COO committed to the ERP project. When she left, the project stopped."

The steering committee members were concerned with few issues pertaining to the adoption. First of all, they discovered that many ERP systems are too expensive for their company, especially those international brands. Local made ERP systems, though are cheaper but fewer functions. They also concerned with other recurring costs when they have implemented the ERP systems. Below is a quote from the company's Accountant:

"We cannot fund the initiatives, not until we have another project or someone funds the system for us."

The committee also concerned with the current knowledge and skills of the company staffs. Currently, only the Production Manager has experienced working with ERP systems. Beside him, nobody in the top management has any idea on how the adoption process would be. As the Production Manager was saying:

"Beside costs, the skills and knowledge about the software are also barriers to ERP adoption. When we implement it, we have to make sure the person who will be using the system understand it."

The company also lacks of technical people and has to hire if they adopt the ERP systems. As for now, the company has only an IT Executive. Moreover, the time for the staffs to be fully adjusted to the new ERP systems is quite long. Being a midsize company, they cannot afford a highly staff turnover. Furthermore, training a staff will require extra cost, and it will be a bigger loss when the staff leaves the company. One of the vendors had said:

"It takes two years for the staffs to be fully adjusted to the new system."

The steering committee also had trouble to find the best-fit system. Although some systems are cheaper, it has limited modules. The more expensive will surely fit their needs. However, it is out of their budget. As mentioned by the Production Manager:

"We order our raw material in tonnes. From a tonne, we don't use everything for production. Some parts, we sell it as scraps. When they (vendors) present the system to us, they still used one tonne as minimum unit for production."

After a few discussions with vendors, the committee members developed negative perceptions towards the implementation of the ERP systems. Their perceptions were shaped by vendor's explanations on few risks associated with ERP adoption such as high recurring costs, longer absorption time and worst of all the possibilities of dumping the project. Quoting from the IT Executive:

"The vendor told me that some companies had to abandon the ERP project."

Up to the present moment, company X is still not adopting ERP systems. ERP adoption is one of the proposals that do not make it through. However, company X still hopes to implement the system as soon as possible.

4. Analyses And Discussion

Now, we will discuss barriers faced by company X to adopt ERP system.

Barrier 1: The company cannot afford ERP high implementation cost.

As revealed in the case study, this SME cannot afford high investment for ERP implementation. Rajapakse and Seddon [19], Liang et al [16] and Kostopoulos et al. [13] also reported the same experience in Sri Lanka, China and Greece. Imported ERP systems are too expensive for some local

SMEs although they may provide better solutions. Nevertheless, local SMEs have to choose between benefits or high costs before making any decision.

Barrier 2: The company lacks of skills and knowledgeable manpower.
This problem has been clearly illustrated in the case study. Nobody has experiences in ERP systems except the Production Manager. Because of their lack of knowledge, company X's top managements do not know the expectation and outcome of ERP systems implementation. It is important for the top managements to support to ERP systems adoption [20].

Barrier 3: Highly Centralised Structure.
From our observations, we conclude that the company has a highly centralized structure. First, the middle management is reluctant to take responsibility to proceed with ERP adoption when the COO left. Secondly, the members are waiting for orders from the top management on the adoption status. From these behaviors, we come to a decision that the company is highly structured. Highly centralized structure can have a negative effect on ERP. In fact, a highly centralized structure can prevent or delay the ERP adoption [13]. From the case study, we can say that the structure of the company becomes a barrier to adoption of ERP for the company.

Barrier 4: The company failed to find best-fit ERP systems.
Everdigen et al. [12] described that there should be a fit between current business procedure and the ERP systems. From several discussions with the vendors, the committee members have identified misfit between the company requirements with all the proposed ERP systems. The misfit mentioned is identical with Soh et al. [18]. They also discussed about 'data misfit' that arises from incompatibilities between organizational requirements and ERP package in terms of data format. To overcome the problem, Soh et al. [18] suggested that the adopting company would have to work around within the ERP systems. However, this will lead to more confusions and possible mistakes. Considering the constraint, the committee members are reluctant to proceed further.

Barrier 5: The Project champion left the company.
Whenever the COO started the ERP adoption endeavor, she had become the project champion. When she left, the project lost its project champion. The role of project champion is critical in the success of any IT and ERP implementation [21]. The project champion has the resources and motivation needed through the adoption process.

Barrier 6: The steering committee members have negative views towards ERP.
It is apparent from the case study that the committees have perceived risks in ERP adoption. From these perceived risks, they have developed a negative outlook towards the ERP adoption. According to Hwang et al. [22], perceived risk is a subjective probability of suffering a loss in the pursuit of a desired outcome or a person's perception of the possibility of having a negative outcome; or suffering harm or losses associated with ERP implementation. Finally, their perceptions turn into a barrier toward ERP adoption because a company must first have a positive attitude towards a technology before the organization will adopt the technology [23].

5. Conclusion

The study confirmed that the company experienced similar barriers reported in the previous researches. High cost; lack of skill and knowledge; highly centralized structure; and issue of misfit became barriers for company X to adopt ERP. Furthermore, when the COO left the company, the project lost its champion. In conclusion, the perceived risks coupled with no best-fit solution, makes the company thinks twice about the adoption.

For company X to adopt ERP systems, more requirement analysis should be done, especially on the project's financial returns. After all, ERP systems implementation is a big investment. Next, company X can adopt a minimum ERP systems package and consider upgrade in the future.

Finally, this research draws few limitations. Firstly, our research is based on a single case study. Future research should use multiple case studies and quantitative survey to further enhance the findings. Secondly, future research should include vendors and consultants for more thorough results.

References:

[1] B. R. Snider, "Enterprise Resource Planning Implementations at Small and Medium Sized Enterprises: Influential Factors," Haskayne School of Business, University of Calgary, Calgary, Alberta, 2004.

[2] T. H. Davenport, "Putting The Enterprise Into The Enterprise System." *Harvard Business Review*, , vol. 76, no. 4, pp. 121 - 131, 1998.

[3] A. Leon, *Enterprise Resource Planning*, New Delhi: Tata McGraw Hill, 2008.

[4] G. Premkumar, "A Meta-Analysis of Research on Information Technology Implementation in Small Business," *Journal of Organizational Computing and Electronic Commerce,* vol. 13, no. 2, pp. 91 - 121, 2003.

[5] S. W. Congden, D. E. Desplaces, and E. B. Kim, "Differences In Drivers Of ERP Adoption Between Large And Small Firms," *Journal of Business and Entrepreneurship,* vol. 17, no. 1, pp. pg. 85, 2005.

[6] R. McAdam, "Large Scale Innovation – Reengineering Methodology in SMEs: Positivistic and Phenomenological approaches," *International Small Business Journal,* vol. 20 no. 1, pp. 33-52, 2002.

[7] S. F. Huin, L. H. S. Luong, and K. Abhary, "Knowledge-Based Tool For Planning of Enterprise Resources in ASEAN SMEs," *Robotics and Computer-Integrated Manufacturing,* vol. 19, no. 5, pp. 409-414, 2003.

[8] L. Raymond, F. Bergeron, and S. Rivard, "Determinants of Business Process Reengineering Success in Small and Large Enterprises: An Empirical Study in the Canadian context," *Journal of Small Business Management,* vol. 36, no. 1, pp. 72-85., 1998.

[9] S. Laukkanen, S. Sarpola, and P. Hallikainen, "Enterprise Size Matters: Objectives and Constraints of ERP Adoption," *Journal of Enterprise Information Management,* vol. 20, no. 3, pp. 319-334, 2007.

[10] L. Raymond, and S. Uwizeyemungu, "A Profile of ERP Adoption In Manufacturing SMEs," *Journal of Enterprise Information Management* 2007.

[11] B. Ramdani, and P. Kawalek, "SME Adoption Of Enterprise Systems In The Northwest Of England: An Environmental, Technological, And Organizational Perspective," *International Federation for Information Processing,* vol. 235, pp. 409-430, 2007.

[12] Y. V. Everdingen, J. V. Hillegersberg, and E. Waarts, "ERP Adoption By European Midsize Companies. Searching for ERP Systems Offering a Perfect Fit. ," *Communication of The ACM* vol. 43, no. 4, 2000.

[13] K. C. Kostopoulos, D. A. Brachos, and G. P. Prastacos, "Determining Factors Of ERP Adoption: An Indicative Study In The Greek Market," in Engineering Management Conference 2004 Proceedings. , 2004, pp. 287-291.

[14] E. Waarts, and Y. V. Everdingen, "The Influence Of National Culture On the Adoption Status Of Innovations: An Empirical Study of Firms Across Europe," *European Management Journal,* vol. 23, no. 6, pp. 601–610, 2005.

[15] H. Liang, and Y. Xue, "Coping with ERP-Related Contextual Issues in SMEs: A Vendor's Perspective," *The Journal of Strategic Information Systems,* vol. 13, no. 4, pp. 399-415, 2004.

[16] H. Liang, Y. Xue, W. Boulton, R. *et al.*, "Why Western Vendors Don't Dominate China's ERP market," *Commun. ACM,* vol. 47, no. 7, pp. 69-72, 2004.

[17] J. Rajapakse, and P. B. Seddon, "ERP Adoption in Developing Countries in Asia: A Cultural Misfit," 2005.

[18] C. Soh, S. S. Kien, and J. Tay-Yap, "Cultural Fits And Misfits: Is ERP A Universal Solution?," *Communications Of The ACM,* vol. 43, no. 4, 2000.

[19] J. Rajapakse, and P. B. Seddon, "Why ERP May Not Be Suitable For Organisations In Developing Countries In Asia," in Pacific Asia Conference on Information Systems, Bangkok, Thailand, 2005.

[20] S. M. Jafari, M. R. Osman, R. M. Yusuff *et al.*, "ERP Systems Implementation In Malaysia: The Importance Of Critical Success Factors," *International Journal of Engineering and Technology,* vol. 3, no. 1, pp. 125-131, 2006.

[21] J. M. Esteves, and J. A. Pastor, "Understanding The ERP Project Champion Role And Its Criticality," in The Xth European Conference on Information Systems, Gdańsk, Poland, 2002.

[22] W. Hwang, J. Jeong, and U. Nandkeolyar, "The Antecedents Of ERP Adoption: Using Secondary Data," in Proceedings of the 39th Annual Meeting of the Decision Sciences Institute Baltimore, Maryland, 2008.

[23] I. Ajzen, "The Theory Of Planned Behavior.," *Organizational Behaviour and Human Decision Processes,* vol. 50, pp. 179-211, 1991.

AI-Based Friction Modeling and Compensation in Motion Control System Using ANFIS

Tijani, I. B.

Department of Mechatronics Engineering, Intelligent Mechatronics System Research Group, International Islamic University Malaysia (IIUM), Kuala Lumpur, MALAYSIA, ismaeelbit@gmail.com

Wahyudi M.

Department of Mechatronics Engineering, Intelligent Mechatronics System Research Group, International Islamic University Malaysia (IIUM), Kuala Lumpur, MALAYSIA, wahyudi@iium.edu.my

Talib H. H.

Department of Science in Engineering International Islamic University Malaysia (IIUM), Kuala Lumpur, MALAYSIA talib@iiu.edu.my

Abstract— The inherent presence of friction in motion control system has been one of the major sources of performance degradation in terms of slow responses, steady state accuracy, poor tracking and or limit cycles near the reference position. Motivated by the need for simple and at the same time effective friction model, an AI-based (non-parametric) friction model using an adaptive Neuro-Fuzzy inference system (ANFIS) is proposed in this work to estimate the non-linear friction in a motion control system. The effectiveness of the developed model in representing and compensating for the frictional effects is evaluated experimentally on a rotary experimental motion system, and the performance benchmarked with a parametric based model. The results show ANFIS as a viable and better alternative to mathematical-based techniques in representing and compensating friction effects.

Keywords- ANFIS, Friction model, Friction compensation, motion control system

1. Introduction

The demand for high precision performance in motion control system, be it point to point (PTP) or continuous path (tracking) has necessitated the search for simple and efficient means of eliminating the effects of nonlinear friction. Friction has been shown to be one of the major nonlinear sources of performance degradation in terms of slow responses, poor tracking accuracy, and steady state error and or limit cycles near the reference position, [1]. Various techniques have been developed to eliminate the effects of the friction such as discussed in [2-4]. Among the successful method is the well-known model-based friction compensation. In this method, the effect of the friction is cancelled by applying additional control signal which generates a torque/force. The generated torque/force has value the same (or approximately the same) with the friction torque/force but opposite direction. This method requires the precise model of the friction to provide a good performance. Therefore, in the context of model-based friction compensation, identification of the friction is one of the important issues to realize high performance motion control.

However, in the literatures there are many types of friction model starting from static to dynamic models such as Classical Coulomb friction model, Tustin model, Karnop model, LuGre model, Leuven model, Seven parameters model and the most recent Generalized Maxwell-Slip model [2,5].All these are either modeled as discontinuous or piecewise continuous functions. Each friction model thus has its own advantages and disadvantages, which has made the choice of the model problem dependent. As the friction model is an important factor in the model-based friction compensation, it is required to find the most appropriate friction model for realizing high precision motion control system. This has been the basis for continuous search for more efficient and simple model for friction identification and compensation in motion control system.

In addition, the recent development in artificial intelligent approaches allows it for system modeling which is based on the data training and expert knowledge. It has been shown that the major AI-paradigms (Neural Network, Fuzzy Logic, Support vector machine etc) have the capability of approximating any nonlinear function to a reasonable degree of accuracy and hence have been identified and proposed as appropriate alternative for friction model and compensation in motion control systems, [6,7]. Therefore, non-mathematical models based on the artificial intelligence approaches can be used as an alternative for friction identification so that the confusion in friction model selection can be avoided. In addition, the use of artificial intelligence based friction model may also reduce the complexity and time consuming of the process in the friction modeling and identification. Therefore, motivated by the need for simple and at the same time effective friction modeling and compensation in motion control system, an AI-based friction model using an adaptive Neuro-fuzzy Inference System (ANFIS) is proposed in this study to estimate and compensate the non-linear friction in motion control system. The choice of ANFIS is based on its unique advantages over other learning paradigm. ANFIS is an hybrid learning technique, it combines the expert knowledge of fuzzy logic with input-output data pair (data mining) of Neural network training [8] in solving the problems of transforming the expert knowledge into fuzzy rules, and tuning of membership functions associated with ordinary fuzzy inference system. In addition, despite its unique advantages the use of an adaptive Neuro-fuzzy inference system (ANFIS) has hardly been attempted in friction modeling. The rest of this paper is organized as follows; Section two gives the brief information on the Experimental plant and system model as used in this study, the concept of ANFIS in system model is explained in Section three. In Section four, the Experimental Friction measurement and ANFIS model development are detailed, and its implementation in friction compensation reported in Section five. Section six gives the results and discussion. The paper is concluded in Section seven.

2. Plant Description and Modeling

Figure 1 shows the experimental set-up of the DC motor driven rotary motion system used in this paper. It consists of servo motor driven by an amplifier and position encoder attached to the shaft as the feedback sensor. The input to the motor is the armature voltage u driven by a voltage source. The measurable variable is the angular position of the shaft, θ in radian using a Scancon incremental shaft encoder with resolution of $2x10^4$ (in quadrature mode), while the angular velocity of the motor shaft ($\dot{\theta}$ in radian/s) is estimated using an appropriate digital filter. Basically, the system comprises of linear and nonlinear parts (here friction), based on this the problem can thus be formulated as follows. Given a dynamic system represented as

$$J_{eq}\ddot{\theta} + u_f(\dot{\theta}) = u_m \qquad (1)$$

where $u_m = K_t i_a$ represents the force due to motor torque, J_{eq} denotes the total inertial due to the motor and external loads, and $u_f(\dot{\theta})$ is the overall nonlinear friction force present.

It is required to find an accurate estimate $\hat{u}_f$ of the friction such that $\hat{u}_f \approx u_f$ as required in model-based friction compensation

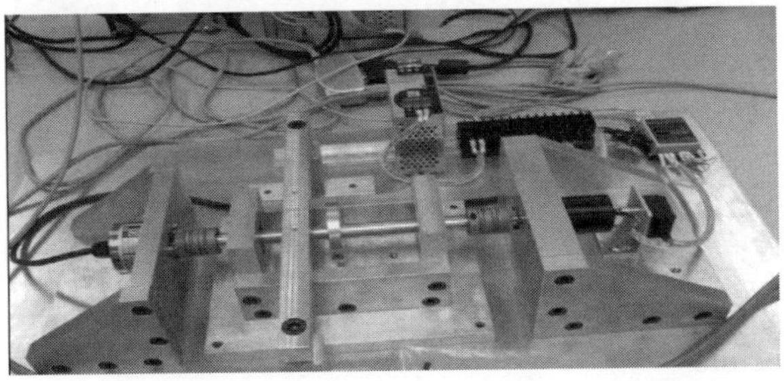

Figure 1: Experimental Set-Up

3. ANFIS as a Modeling tool

Adaptive Neuro-Fuzzy Inference System (ANFIS) is an hybrid AI-paradigm, integrating the best features of Fuzzy System (based on expert knowledge) and Neural Networks (based on data mining) in solving the problems of transforming the expert knowledge into fuzzy rules and tuning of membership functions associated with ordinary fuzzy inference system. It has been shown to be effective in nonlinear system identification,[9],and nonlinear function approximation [8,10].Based on the input space partitioning method, ANFIS is classified into two types namely: grid portioning (ANFIS-GP) and scattering portioning (ANFIS-SC). Grid partition (GP) generates rules by enumerating all possible combinations of membership functions of all input parameters, while scattering partition generates the number of rules equal to the number of clusters.

3.1 ANFIS Architecture

For simplicity, Figure 2 shows two inputs, one output, type III ANFIS structure. As shown in figure 2, square nodes are used as adaptive node with adjustable parameters while the circle nodes represent fixed-node with fixed parameters. Generally,ANFIS consists of five layers minus the input layer O, and its implements Takagi Sugeno Fuzzy Inference System. The two fuzzy rules associated with the system is thus written as:

R1:If X_1 is A_1, and X_2 is B_1, then $Q_1 = p_1X_1 + q_1X_2 + r_1$

R2: If X_1 is A_2, and X_2 is B_2, then $Q_2 = p_2X_1 + q_2X_2 + r_2$

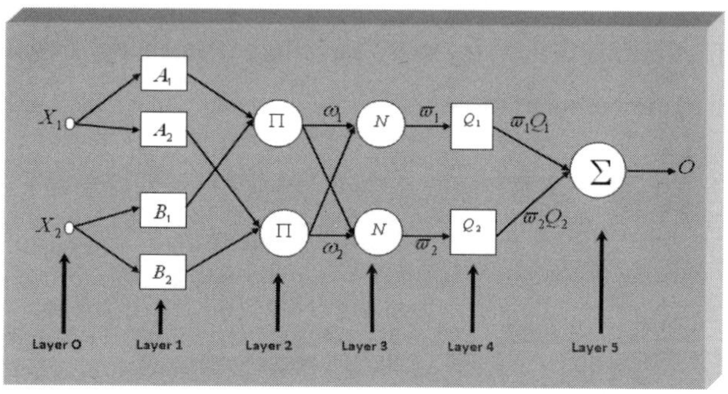

Figure 2: Two Inputs, One output Typical ANFIS Structure

Each layer performs a specific function based on the associated node function as follows:

Layer 1 is responsible for the fuzzification of the input signal with appropriate membership function. It consists of adaptive nodes in which the parameters of membership function are adjusted during learning process. The two common functions in used are bell-shaped (2) and Gaussian (3) membership functions:

$$\mu_{A_i}(X) = \frac{1}{1 + \left[\left(\frac{X - c_i}{\sigma_i}\right)^2\right]^{b_i}} \quad (2)$$

$$\mu_{A_i}(X) = \exp\left[-\left(\frac{X - c_i}{\sigma_i}\right)^2\right] \quad (3)$$

The output of this layer is; $Q_i^1 = \mu_{A_i}(X)$ where vector $[b_i \quad c_i \quad \sigma_i]$ is the set of premise parameters to be determined during training.

Layer 2 compute the firing strength ω_i of each rule using a T-norm (min, product, etc) of the incoming signals. For a product T-norm, $\omega_i = \mu_{A_i}(X) \times \mu_{B_i}(X)$ where for this example $i = 1,2$

The normalized firing strength, ϖ_i of each rule is estimated by Layer 3 by computing the ratio of the ith rule firing strength to the sum of all rule's firing strength:

$$\varpi_i = \frac{\omega_i}{\sum_{i=1}^{k} \omega_i} \quad \text{where} \quad i = 1,2...k, \quad \text{for k=2;}$$

$$\varpi_i = \frac{\omega_i}{\omega_1 + \omega_2} \quad (4)$$

Layer 4 also consists of adaptive nodes for computing the consequence parameters.

So for ith node in this layer, output $Q_i^4 = \varpi_i Q_i = \varpi_i(p_i X_i + q_i X_i + r_i)$ where $[p_i \quad q_i \quad r_i]$ is set of consequence parameters to be optimized during training.

The overall output, O is computed in layer 5 using a linear combination of all the incoming signals from layer 4 :

$$O = \sum_i \varpi_i Q_i = \frac{\sum_i \omega_i Q_i}{\sum_i \omega_i} \quad (5)$$

For $i = 1,2$;

$$O = \frac{\omega_1}{\omega_1 + \omega_2} Q_1 + \frac{\omega_2}{\omega_1 + \omega_2} Q_2$$
$$= \varpi_1(p_1X_1 + q_1X_2 + r_1) + \varpi_2(p_2X_1 + q_2X_2 + r_2)$$
$$= (\varpi_1 X_1)p_1 + (\varpi_1 X_2)q_1 + \varpi_1 r_1 + (\varpi_2 X_1)p_2 + (\varpi_2 X_2)q_2 + \varpi_2 r_2$$

Hence, parametrically, ANFIS can be represented by two sets of parameters: S_1 for set of premise parameters and S_2 for the set of consequence parameters;

$$S_1 = \{([b_1 \quad c_1 \quad \sigma_1]), ([b_2 \quad c_2 \quad \sigma_2]), ...([b_k \quad c_k \quad \sigma_k])\}$$

$$S_2 = \{([p_1 \quad q_1 \quad r_1]), ([p_2 \quad q_2 \quad r_2]), ...([p_k \quad q_k \quad r_k])\}$$

where $i = 1,2...k$ denotes the node in Layer 1 and 4

3.2 ANFIS Hybrid Learning Procedures

Training of ANFIS basically involves determination of optimum values of the parameters S_1 and S_2.Though there are various algorithms that can be employed, the most successful one is hybrid scheme which combine the power of Least Square error(LSE) and gradient descent(usually Back-propagation) for forward and backward pass optimizations respectively. In the forward pass, the premise parameter set S_1 is fixed while the consequent parameter set S_2 is computed by LSE algorithm (off-line learning).While on the other hand for backward pass, the consequence parameter set S_2 is fixed while the premise parameter set S_1 is computed using a gradient descent(Back-propagation) algorithm.

4. Friction Modeling

The first stage in friction modeling, and generally in supervised AI-based modeling is availability of representative data. In this work, two main experiments were conducted in order to acquire the velocity-friction data. The experimental set-up was implemented in MATLAB Xpc-Target environment as shown in figure 3. A 0-5Amp rating current sensor was selected and connected across the motor terminal for measuring the armature current. A simple experiment based on Ohm's Law was carried out to test and model the V-I relationship of the sensor prior to the experimentation. The resulting model is:

$$I_s = 7.8555V_s - 19.6544 \quad (6)$$

where V_s is sensor output in volts

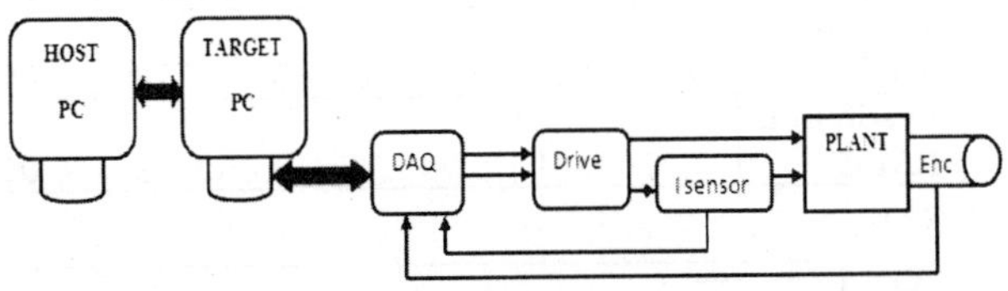

Figure 3: Schematic Diagram of the Experimental Set-Up

The first experiment was designed to yield the break-away friction force,i.e $\tau_f(0)$ in an open-loop mode. The systematic steps followed according to [1] are:

- "Warming-Up" of the Plant at beginning of each run
- Gradual Increase of the motor Current at steps of 0.01volts command signal in Open Loop mode until the shaft moves (or breaks-away), this was taken to be at least 2 encoder counts.
- Repetition of steps 1-2 for several times and averaging of results in order to guarantee repeatability

The procedures were repeated 5 times for both positive and negative direction of motion.

Referring to equation (1), it can be shown that at steady state, the friction torque is approximately equal to the resultant motor torque, i.e.

$J_{eq}\ddot{\theta} + \tau_f(\dot{\theta}) = \tau_m$, for $\dot{\theta} \rightarrow$ constant, $\ddot{\theta} \rightarrow 0$, hence $\tau_f(\dot{\theta}) = \tau_m$

Since, $\tau_m \propto i_a$ it follows that: $\tau_f(\dot{\theta}) \propto i_a$ where i_a is the armature current sustaining the motion.

Hence, the second experiment involves measuring the armature current for several steady state velocities in the range of $0 < \dot{\theta} < 2$ and $-2 < \dot{\theta} < 0$ radian/s for positive and negative direction of motion respectively.

A stiff velocity control scheme was developed using the Pseudo-Derivative Feedback with Feedforward (PDFF) controller [11] in order to achieve the steady state velocity control especially at low velocities. In this study, the PDFF gave better control response compared to its PI counterpart. The gains K_{Vi}, K_{VFR} and K_V are fine tuned according to the procedures described in [11] for high performance stiff velocity control. For each constant velocity, the average of armature current and steady state velocity were computed after the transient period of 0.1s. Five different runs were carried out for each velocity input, and the overall mean computed. Total of 108 data sets were obtained for each direction of motion.

The actual current is computed from the voltage response of the sensor using the relationship given in (16).And the friction torque is then obtained using:

$\tau_f = K_t i_f$ where K_t is the motor torque constant

The complete experimental data set for both directions is shown in figure 4.

4.1 Development of ANFIS Model

The ANFIS-GP model was developed using MATLAB Fuzzy logic toolbox. First the data was partitioned into training (60) and validation (40) sets, and based on prior information about the friction characteristics, two membership function was assigned to the input while the value of the premise parameters were initially set to satisfy ε-completeness [12] with $\varepsilon = 0.5$ .As earlier mentioned, two types of membership functions: Gaussian (gaussmf) and bell-shaped (gbellmf) were used in search of optimum model. The performance of both membership functions were compared in terms of RMSE. The training was carried out using Hybrid training with 0.0001 error target and 100epochs. The initial and final membership functions and performance comparisons of the two membership functions employed are shown in figure 5 and table 1 respectively. The result as shown in table 1 shows gaussmf model as better choice over gbellmf in this study, and hence was selected in representing the friction model.

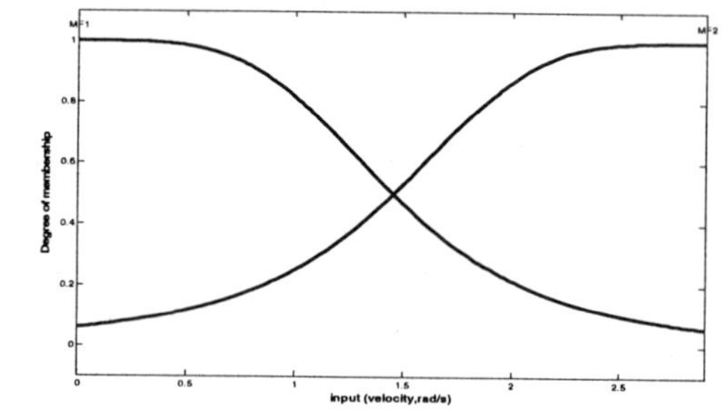

(a)

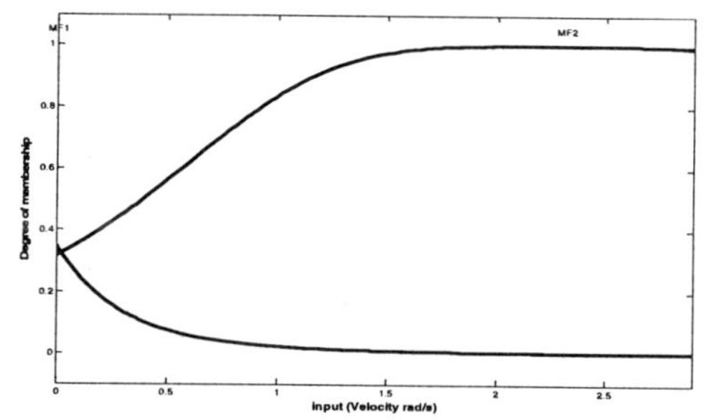

(b)

Figure 5: (a) Initial (b) Final (After Training) 'gaussmf' (Before Training) Membership Function

Table 1: Performance Comparison of gaussmf and gbellmf ANFIS Models

	gaussmf		gbellmf	
		Negative	Positive	Negative
Training RMSE	0.0004582	0.0007249	0.0005610	0.0007924
Prediction RMSE	0.0004431	0.0007437	0.0005539	0.0008135

4.2 Tustin Friction Model

In order to benchmark the performance of the ANFIS model with a known parametric model. Tustin [13] was selected based on the fact that it was the first model that explains the nonlinear negative viscous friction in the analysis of feedback control. The data set was fit into Tustin model represented by:

$$F_f(\dot{\theta}) = F_c + (F_s - F_c)e^{\left(-\frac{\dot{\theta}}{\dot{\theta}_s}\right)} + F_\omega \dot{\theta} \quad (7)$$

where F_c is the minimum level of Coulomb friction, F_s is the level of static friction, $\dot{\theta}_s$ is the stribeck velocity, and F_ω is linear viscous friction parameter. It is assumed here that the viscous path has been modeled with the linear part of the plant, hence it was not included in the model parameter search. The model parameter set $\begin{bmatrix} F_c & F_s & \dot{\theta}_s \end{bmatrix}$ were estimated using MATLAB optimization tool by minimizing the mean square error of the friction force prediction with nonlinear least square optimization algorithm. The estimated parameters for both directions are shown in table 2.The performance comparison of both ANFIS and Tustin models on training and validation data in terms of RMSE is given in table 3 while figure 6 shows comparison of the two models with validation data.

Table 2: Tustin Model Parameters

Parameters	Fc	Fs	$\dot{\theta}_s$	Cost Function
Positive Direction	0.0036	0.0089	0.09	0.00024
Negative Direction	-0.0032	-0.009	-0.09	0.00031

Table 3: Performance Comparison of ANFIS and Tustin Friction Models

	POSITIVE		NEGATIVE	
	ANFIS	Tustin	ANFIS	Tustin
Training RMSE	0.0004582	0.000684	0.0007249	0.00075
Prediction RMSE	0.0004431	0.000563	0.0007437	0.00078

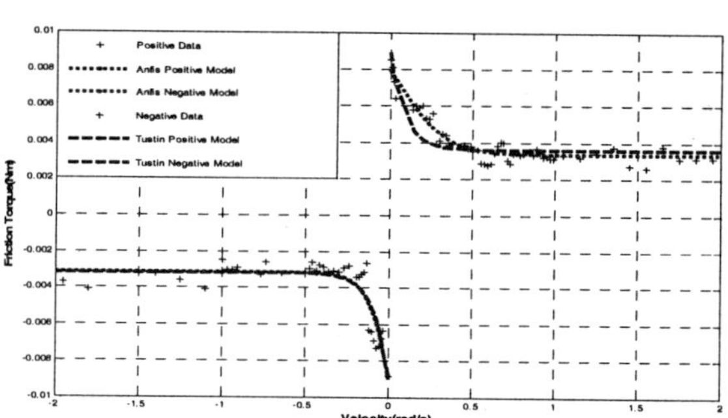

Figure 6: Comparison of ANFIS and Tustin Friction Models with Validation Data set; 'dotted-line' for ANFIS, 'dash-line' for Tustin and '+' for Experimental Data Set

5. Friction Compensation

In order to evaluate the effectiveness of the models developed, compensation scheme comprising of a PD controller with and without the friction compensator in feedback loop were implemented for both point-to-point and tracking positioning control of the motion control system. The control architecture is shown in figure 7.The PD controller was designed based on the linear plant model obtained and fine tuned for real time application to obtain $K_p = 20$ and $K_D = 0.002$. From figure 7, the control law with friction compensation is given as:

$$u_c = u_{in} + \hat{u}_f$$

$\hat{u}_f$ is obtained using the relationship $\hat{u}_f = K\tau_f$, K represents the inverse model of the plant voltage to torque conversion; $K = f\,(R_m, K_t\ K_{amp})$ where R_m, K_t, K_{amp} are motor resistance, torque constant and drive gain respectively.

The system dynamic equation becomes:

$$J\ddot{\theta} + u_f(\dot{\theta}) = u_m + \hat{u}_f(\dot{\theta}) \qquad (8)$$

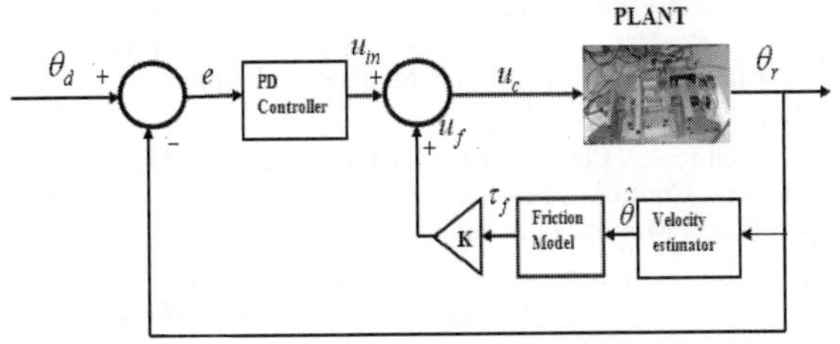

Figure 7: Control Scheme for Friction Compensation

Hence it can be seen that if $\hat{u}_f(\dot{\theta}) \approx u_f(\dot{\theta})$ and the modeling error is approximately zero, the effect of friction force is effectively compensated and the position accuracy improved.

Figure 8 (a & b) shows the response comparison of the plant with both ANFIS and Tustin friction compensator and without either compensator for 1 degree step and sine inputs for PTP and tracking control respectively. This is repeated for 0.5 degree, and the results are shown in tables 4 and 5 for PTP and tracking control respectively in terms of response time, steady state accuracy and root mean square error (RMSE) accordingly.

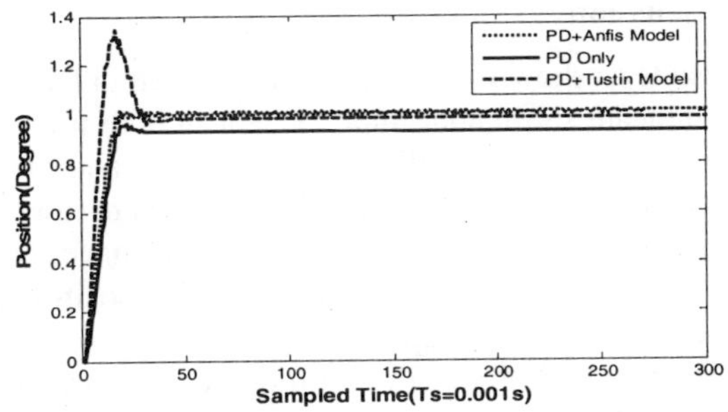

(a)

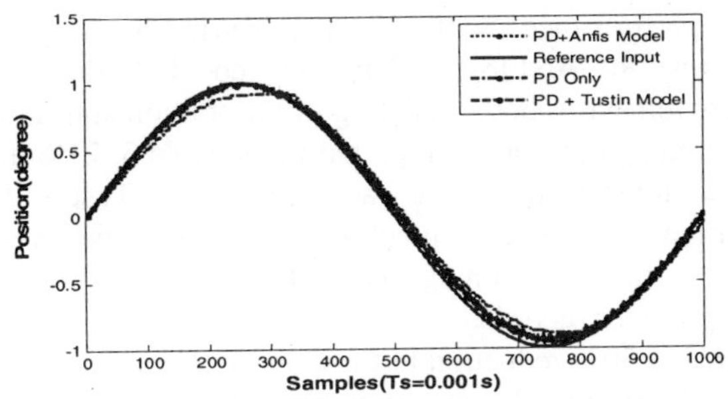

(b)

Figure 8: (a) 1 degree Step input (b) 1 degree 1Hz sine input responses for PTP and Position Tracking respectively with and without Friction Compensators

Table 4: Performance Results for Point-to-Point Positioning control with and without Friction Compensators

	0.5 Deg. Step Input				1 Deg. Step Input			
	Positive		Negative		Positive		Negative	
	Tr	ess (%)	Tr	ess (%)	Tr	ess (%)	Tr	ess (%)
PD Only	0.015	44		30	0.017	7.1		21
PD+ANFIS Model	0.009	0.15	0.008	0.8	0.015	0.8	0.012	0.4
PD+ Tustin Model	0.016	1.6	0.015	1.6	0.016	1.6	0.014	0.8

Table 5: Performance Results for Tracking Positioning control with and without Friction Compensators

	0.5 Deg. Sine Input RMSE	1 Deg. Sine Input RMSE
PD Only	0.0656	0.0874
PD+ANFIS Model	0.0348	0.0489
PD+ Tustin Model	0.0525	0.0533

6. Discussion

The results as shown in figure 8, and reported in tables 4 and 5 indicate substantial improvement in both tracking and point-to-point positioning accuracy and time response with the developed friction compensator. At low velocity range where friction effects have been highly deteriorating, greater reduction in the positioning accuracy was recorded up to 90% reduction in steady state error and 40% reduction in root mean square error for PTP and tracking respectively when compared with the use of only linear (PD) controller. Also comparing the performance with its parametric based-model (Tustin), the ANFIS-based friction model shows better improvement in both modeling of the friction and in the positioning control. As reported in the table 3, 21% and 4.6% improvement was achieved over Tustin for positive and negative direction of motion respectively. While for positioning control, the ANFIS-based compensator recorded

90% and 50% reduction to the error obtained compared with Tustin-based compensator for PTP and tracking control respectively. Similar improvement was evident in other reference inputs used as shown in the tables.

However, the non-smoothness in the tracking responses especially at low reference input was attributed to the effect of velocity estimation used in the compensation scheme. This could be improved upon with the used of observer based estimation or other more sophisticated velocity estimation scheme.

7. Conclusion

This work has explored and documented the suitability of ANFIS in friction modeling and compensation in motion control system. Hence a simple and non-parametric approach, ANFIS was proposed and demonstrated for improved positioning controlled of system with friction.

The results obtained for modeling and compensation show ANFIS as a viable and efficient alternative to mathematical-based techniques in representing and compensating friction effects.

Acknowledgment

This research is financially supported by Ministry of Higher Education under Fundamental Research Grant Scheme (FRGS) Research Project FRGS0106-18.

References

[1] Armstrong-Helouvry B., Control of Machines with Friction, Boston, MA, Kluwer, 1991

[2] Armstrong-Helouvry B., Dupont P. and De Wit C., 1994. "A survey of models, analysis tools and compensation method for the control of machines with friction", Automatica, Vol. 30, No. 7 (1994) pp. 1083-1138.

[3] Wahyudi, "Friction Identification and Compensation for High Precision Motion Control System - Part 1: Friction Identification", Proc. of Industrial Electronics Seminar (IES), 2003.

[4] Canudas de Wit, K.J. Astrom and K. Braun, "Adaptive friction compensation in DC motor drives," Proceeding of IEEE International Conference on Robotics and Automation, San Francisco, Vol. 3, pp. 1556-1561,1986.

[5] Makkar C.,W.E.Dixon,W.G.Sawyer,and G.Hu, "A New Continously Differentiable Friction Model for Control Ssystems Design", Proceedings of the 2005 IEEE/ASME International Conference on Advaanced Intelligent Mechatronics Monterey,California,USA,24-26 July,2005.

[6] Gomes S.C.P., D.Gomes and C.M.Diniz, "Neuro-Fuzzy Friction Compensation to Robotic Actuators", Proceedings of the 2005 IEEE Industrial Conference on Mechatronics, July 10-12, 2005, Taipei, Taiwan.

[7] Wahyudi and Ismaila B.T "Artificial Intelligent Based Friction Identification using Multilayer Feedforward Network", *Proc. of 4th International Colloquium on Signal Processing and Its Applications (CSPA)*, 2008.

[8] Jang J.S.R. "ANFIS: Adaptive-Network-Based Fuzzy Inference System", *IEEE Trans. Systems, Man, Cybernetics*,

[9] ZhixiangHou,QuntaiShen and HeqingLi, "Nonlinear System Identification Based on ANFIS", IEEE Int. Conf. Neural Networks &Signal Processing,Nanjing,China,December 14-17,2003.

[10] Wen-Chen Lih, Satish T. S. Bukkapatnam, Prahalad Rao, Naga Chandrasekharan, and Ranga Komanduri, "Adaptive Neuro-Fuzzy Inference System Modeling of MRR and WIWNU in CMP Process With Sparse Experimental Data", IEEE Transactions on Automation Science and Engineering, vol. 5, no. 1, january 2008 71

[11] D.Y. Ohm, "A **PDFF** Controller for Tracking and Regulation in Motion Control," Proceedings of 18th PCIM. Conference, Intelligent Motion, Philadelphia,1990.

[12] Lee C.C., "Fuzzy logic in control systems: Fuzzy logic controller-Part I," ***IEEE Trans. Syst., Man, Cybern.***, vol. 20, pp. 404418, 1990.

[13] Tustin A. 1947, "The effects of Backlash and of Speed-Dependent Friction on the Stability of Closed-Cycle Control Systems," IEEE Journal,vol. 94,part 2A,p.143-51.

TURN-ON TIME DELAY OF DEGRADED BULK UNCOOLED SEMICONDUCTOR LASER DIODES

MOHAMMAD SYUHAIMI AB-RAHMAN
syuhaimi@vlsi.eng.ukm.my

MAZEN R. HASSAN
mrhassan@vlsi.eng.ukm.my

Computer & Network Security Research Group
Faculty of Engineering & Built Environment
Department of Electrical, Electronic and Systems Engineering,
University Kebangsaan Malaysia (UKM)
43600 Bangi, Selangor, Malaysia.

In this paper, a full analytical and exact expression form of turn-on time delay, t_{on}, of degraded bulk uncooled semiconductor laser diode (DBUSLD) has been presented in terms of nonradiative, A_{nr} , radiative, B_r , Auger recombination coefficients, C_{auger}, cavity dimensions, threshold carrier density, N_{th},, injection current, I_{inj}, number of "0" bits preceding the considered bit, N_{bit}, bit-rate, Brate and temperature of operation, T. Also we included, in addition to the mentioned parameters, dark defect (DD) parameters, i. e. number of DD, n_{DD} and width of DD, w_{DD}. In addition, an exact and full analytical expression form of carrier density, N, corresponding to the current flowing through laser active region, I, and in term of all the above mentioned parameters has been derived which can be used to determine any value of N corresponding to I exactly, therefore, the temperature dependence (TD) of threshold carrier density of DBUSLD (which is used in ton calculation) is calculated corresponding TD of threshold current of the device. Simulation results show that worst case of DBUSLD is when operates with large n_{DD} and at high temperature degree.

1. Introduction

Semiconductor laser diodes (SLD's) are most important for various applications such as material processing, medical surgery, photodynamic therapy, pumping of solid-state lasers and fiber lasers, and for space applications. Latter include communication terminals, light detection and ranging (LIDAR) and the laser interferometer space antenna (LISA), for example [1]. In such systems, the reliability of the SLD is a crucial factor. Device failure can lead to serious system downtime and high repair costs, so the reliability of the SLD's weights heavily in the system specifications. [1-5]. A rapid decrease in optical power was very often observed within a few hundred of hours after the LD is starting to operate under a constant output power [3]. This is due to dark defect (dark line defects (DLD's) growth from dark spot defect (DSD) in the active layer of LD)) as shown in Fig. 1 [1] where it shows the images of three laser stripes, (a) after gradual degradation, (b) after freak failure and (c) sudden failure after gradual degradation.

The images indicate dark spots in case of gradually degraded devices (a and c). A dark line loop along the laser stripe is observed in the freak device (b), but there are no dark spots. The suddenly failed device (c)

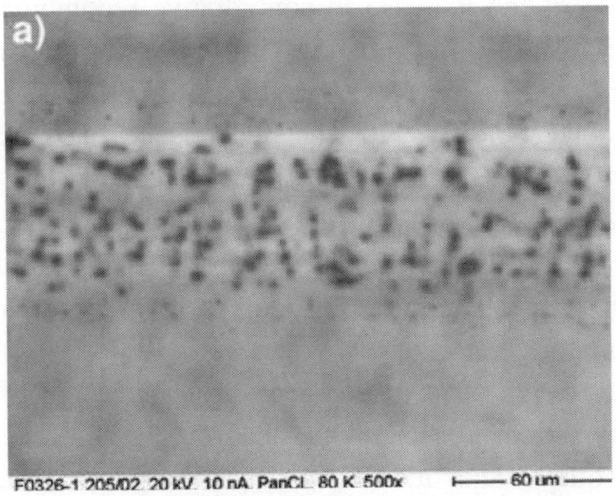

(a) After gradual degradation

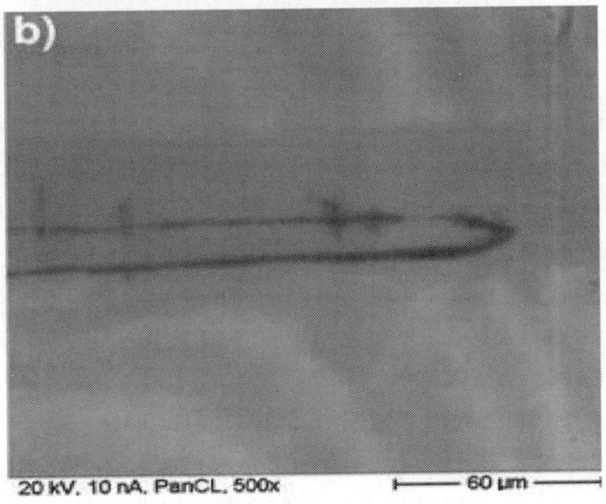

(b) After freak failure

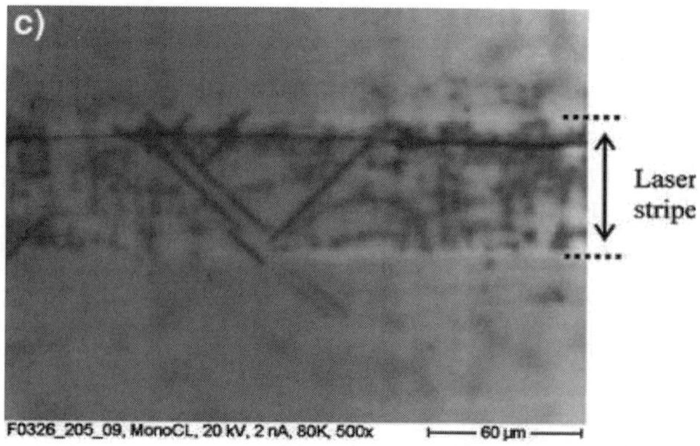

(c) Sudden failure after gradual degradation

Fig. 1 Top view CL images of (a) gradual degradation, (b) freak failure, and (c) sudden failure after gradual degradation [1].

indicates dark lines along the laser stripe. The dark spots are known to originate from dislocation loops [1, 2]. The DLD causes the internal absorption losses to increase and the injected carrier lifetime to be shortened because of the increase in nonradiative recombination. These result in an increase in the lasing threshold current and a decrease in the external differential quantum efficiency [4]. The dependence of threshold current, I_{th}, increase on the number of DD's is explained in terms of a model which includes effects due to the DD's, as well as changes in the regions outside the DD's [2]. The latter is found to be responsible for the major part of I_{th} increase [2]. From the measurements of I_{th} of degraded SLD, threshold carrier density, Nth can be calculated accordingly.

From other hand, it is known that the performance of high-speed, intensity modulated, direct detection systems is critically dependent on the characteristics of SLD [7]. The turn–on time delay, t_{on}, and its jitter plays a significant role in determining the system performance of SLD and has been studied both experimentally and theoretically. To our best knowledge, all the previous studied depended on either experimental or approximated calculations of ton [7-12]. However, In [13], we derived for the first time a full analytical and exact expression form of ton in terms of nonradiative, A , radiative, B , Auger, C_{auger}, recombination coefficients, cavity dimensions, threshold carrier density, N_{th}, (and in turn threshold current density, I_{th}), the device injection current, I_{inj}, and temperature of operation, T. In this paper, we will include, in addition to the mentioned parameters, the main DD parameters, i. e. n_{DD} and w_{DD}. We think that it is the first time of which the influence of DD's of DBUSLD on t_{on} is determined exactly and analytically corresponding to exact and analytical value of N_{th}. In addition, the improvements in laser manufacture allow today operating uncooled direct modulated SLD over abroad temperature range. Given that, a strong cost reduction in optical systems can be achieved by eliminating costly laser temperature control. Uncooled SLD's have been considered as a key technology for future optical network systems [14-15]. The aim of this paper is to study the influence of DD's on ton of DBUSLD in the presence of temperature of operation. The influence of DD on ton will be studied corresponding to its influence on N_{th}, which is calculated analytically and exactly from known value of I_{th}. This will give the designer the chance to determine the exact value of N_{th} from any experimental measurements or proposed model of I_{th} and then determine ton accordingly. It should be noted that we assumed that (1) temperature of operation does not affect DD's themselves and (2) $I_{inj} = u.\ I_{th}(To)$, To=25°C and u =2, in all results corresponding to SLD without degradation, i.e. I_{inj} is independent of temperature and DD. This assumption is made according to the normal operation of laser source. In other words, the current source supplies a fixed value of injection current.

2. Mathematical description

2.1. *Threshold carrier density*

In [2], the authors proposed analytical model of total threshold current, I_{th}^{total}, of DBSLD. In this section we aim to obtain an analytical model of total threshold carrier density, N_{th}^{total}, of DBUSLD in the presence of temperature of operation, $N_{th}^{total}(T)$. To realize that, we will consider Nth (of normal "good region") in [2] as function of T in order to obtain an expression of I_{th}^{total} as function of T, $I_{th}^{total}(T)$ correspondingly. Then in order to obtain the corresponding threshold carrier density we will derive full and exact analytical expression form of carrier density in term of laser cavity parameters and current flowing through the SLD active region.

In the time period ($0<t<t_{on}$), the stimulated emission rate can be neglected and the carrier density rate equation of single mode semiconductor laser can written as [11]

$$\frac{dN}{dt}=\frac{I}{qV}-N(AN+BN^2+C_{auger}N^3) \quad (1)$$

Where q is the electron charge and V is the volume of active region. The steady state solution can be obtained by setting $\frac{dN}{dt}=0$, so Eq. (1) can be re-written as

$$N^3+\frac{B}{C_{auger}}N^2+\frac{A}{C_{auger}}N-\frac{I}{qVC_{auger}}=0 \quad (2)$$

The three root solutions of the above Eq. can be written as

$$N_1=\frac{1}{6}N_{r1}-6\frac{N_{r2}}{N_{r1}}-\frac{1}{3}B_c \quad (3a)$$

$$N_2=\left[\frac{-1}{12}N_{r1}+3\frac{N_{r2}}{N_{r1}}-\frac{1}{3}B_c\right]+j\left[\frac{\sqrt{3}}{2}\left(\frac{1}{6}N_{r1}+6\frac{N_{r2}}{N_{r1}}\right)\right] \quad (3b)$$

$$N_3=\left[\frac{-1}{12}N_{r1}+3\frac{N_{r2}}{N_{r1}}-\frac{1}{3}B_c\right]-j\left[\frac{\sqrt{3}}{2}\left(\frac{1}{6}N_{r1}+6\frac{N_{r2}}{N_{r1}}\right)\right] \quad (3c)$$

where

$$N_{r1}=\left[36A_cB_c+108I_{qv}-8B_c^3+12\left(12A_c^3-3A_c^2B_c^2+54A_cB_cI_{qv}+81I_{qv}^2-12I_{qv}B_c^3\right)^{\frac{1}{2}}\right]^{\frac{1}{3}} \quad (4a)$$

$$N_{r2}=\frac{1}{3}A_c-\frac{1}{9}B_c^2 \quad (4b)$$

and

$$A_c=\frac{A}{C_{auger}},\ B_c=\frac{A}{C_{auger}} \text{ and } I_{qv}=\frac{I}{qVC_{auger}}.$$

Interesting only with real root solution , i. e. Eq. (3a), a full analytical and exact expression form of N in term of all appeared parameters will be obtained i. e. $N=N_1$. The value of N corresponding to any value of I can be obtained from Eq. (3a), therefore, we can obtain the expression of N_{th}^{total}(T) by substituting $I_{th}^{total}(T)$. In [2] the authors presented analytical model of I_{th}^{total} and we modified it by considering it as function of temperature corresponding to TD of N_{th}

$$I_{th}^{total}(T)=\frac{qVN_{th}(T)}{\tau_e(T)}\left[1+(C-1)\frac{w_{DD}}{L}n_{DD}\right] \quad (5)$$

where $C\approx 2$ [2], $\tau_e(T)$ is TD of carrier lifetime, τ_e, corresponding to the TD of threshold carrier density in good region, $N_{th}(T)$, and may be written as

$$\tau_e(T)=\frac{1}{A_{nr}+B_{nr}N_{th}(T)+C_{auger}\left(N_{th}(T)\right)^2} \quad (6a)$$

and $N_{th}(T)$ can be written after modifying [10, 11] as

$$N_{th}(T)=N_t(T)+\frac{1}{\Gamma v_g\, g_o(T)\tau_p(T)} \quad (6b)$$

where Γ is the optical confinement factor of laser cavity , $N_t(T)$, $g_o(T)$ and $\tau_p(T)$ are the TD's of carrier density at transparency, N_t, differential gain, g_o, and photon lifetime, τ_p, and they can be expressed respectively as [13, 14]

$$N_t(T)=\frac{T}{T_o}N_t(T_o) \quad (7a)$$

$$g_o(T)=\frac{T_o}{T}g_o(T_o) \quad (7b)$$

$$\tau_p^f(T)=\frac{1}{v_g\alpha_{total}(T)} \quad (7c)$$

where $\alpha_{total}(T)$ is the TD of total cavity losses of SLD, v_g (= $Clight/n_g$)) is the group velocity and ng is the group refractive index. $\alpha_{total}(T)$ of distributed feedback (DFB) laser can be written, with assumption that the mirror loss is dominate, as [14]

$$\alpha_{total}(T)=\alpha_{int}(T)+\frac{1}{2L}ln\frac{1}{r_1 r_2} \quad (7d)$$

Where L is the cavity length and $r1$ and $r2$ are field reflectiveties of the laser facets and $\alpha_{int}(T)$ is the TD of internal cavity losses, α_{int}, which can be written as [13, 14]

$$\alpha_{int}(T)=\alpha_{int\,o}\frac{T}{T_o} \quad (7e)$$

where $\alpha_{int\,o}$ is internal cavity losses at room temperature, To. By substituting Eq. (5) in (3a) we will obtain a very flexible expression which describes threshold carrier density of DBUSLD in the presence of temperature of operation i. e. $N_{th}^{total}(T)=N_1\big|_{I=I_{th}^{total}(T)}$.

Notes:

1. At room temperate, To = 25oC, $N_{th}^{total}(T)\big|_{T=T_o}=N_1\big|_{I=I_{th}^{total}(T_o)}=N_{th}(T_o)$ and the resulted expression of $Nth(To)$ is as given in [2].

2. When n_{DD}=0, then

$N_{th}^{total}(T) = N_1\big|_{I=I_{th}^{total}(T)}\Big|_{n_{DD}=0} = N_{th}(T)$ and the resulted expression of $N_{th}(T)$ as given in [13] and $N_{th}(To) = 1.837\times10^{18}\,cm^{-3}$ (according to the typical values)

2.2. *Turn-on time delay*

In [13], we derived a full analytical and exact expression form of t_{on} which can be written as

$$t_{on} = \left[f(R,N)\big|_{R=R_1} + f(R,N)\big|_{R=R_2} + f(R,N)\big|_{R=R_3} \right]\Big|_{N=N_{th}} - \left[f(R,N)\big|_{R=R_1} + f(R,N)\big|_{R=R_2} + f(R,N)\big|_{R=R_3} \right]\Big|_{N=N_i} \quad (8)$$

where

$$f(R,N) = \frac{-R}{C_{auger}} \cdot ln\Big[\left(6A_{nr}C_{auger}Q - 2B_r{}^2Q\right)R + 3QC_{auger}{}^2\Big]N + \left(-QA_{nr}B_r - 9IC_{auger}\right)R + QB_rC_{auger}\Big] \quad (9)$$

where R_i is the ith (i =1, 2, 3) root of $G(Z)$ which can be written as

$$G(Z) = \Big[\left(4Q^2A_{nr}^3C_{auger}\right) - \left(Q^2B_r^2A_{nr}^2\right) + \left(18QI_{inj}A_{nr}B_rC_{auger}\right) - \left(4QI_{inj}B_r^2\right) + \left(27I_{inj}{}^2C_{auger}^2\right)\Big]Z^3 + \Big[\left(-3Q^2A_{nr}C_{auger}^3\right) + \left(Q^2B_r{}^2C_{auger}{}^2\right)\Big]Z - \left[C_{auger}^4Q^2\right] \quad (10)$$

The roots of $G(Z)$ can be written as

$$R_1 = G_1 + G_2 \quad (11a)$$

$$R_2 = \frac{-G_1 - G_2}{2} + j\frac{\sqrt{3}}{2}(G_1 - G_2) \quad (11b)$$

$$R_3 = \frac{-G_1 - G_2}{2} - j\frac{\sqrt{3}}{2}(G_1 - G_2) \quad (11c)$$

where

$$G_1 = \frac{\left(\sqrt[3]{12}\right)C_{auger}}{6}\frac{F_1}{D_1} \quad (11a)$$

$$G_2 = \frac{1}{6}Q^2\left(3A_{nr}C_{auger} - B_r{}^2\right)\frac{\left(\sqrt[3]{12}\right)^2C_{auger}}{F_1} \quad (11b)$$

and

$$F_1 = Q^2\left[9C_{auger} + \sqrt{3}\left(\frac{D_2}{D_1}\right)^{\frac{1}{2}}D_1{}^2\right]^{\frac{1}{3}} \quad (12a)$$

$$D_1 = 27C_{auger}^2I_{inj}^2 + 4C_{auger}A_{nr}^3Q^2 + 18I_{inj}QA_{nr}B_rC_{auger} - A_{nr}^2B_r^2Q - 4I_{inj}QB_r^3 \quad (12b)$$

$$D_2 = \left(9A_{nr}B_rC_{auger}Q\right)^2 - 36Q^2A_{nr}B_r^4C_{auger} + 4Q^2B_r^6 + 729C_{auger}^4I_{inj}^2 + 486C_{auger}^3I_{inj}QA_{nr}B_r - 108I_{inj}QB_r^3C_{auger}^2 \quad (12c)$$

where N_i is the initial carrier density. In our work we modified the expression of N_i given by [12] by considering τ_e as a function of $N_{th}(T)$ and may be written as

$$N_i^{total}(T) = N_{th}^{total}(T)\cdot e^{-\frac{N_{bit}/B_{rate}}{\tau_e(T)}} \quad (13)$$

where N_{bit} is the number of "0" bits preceding the considered bit and $\tau_e(T)$ is already given in Eq. (6a). Substituting $N_{th}^{total}(T)$ and $N_i^{total}(T)$ instead of N_{th} and N_i respectively in Eq. (8), we obtain a full analytical and exact expression form of t_{on} in terms of laser cavity parameters, temperature of operation, *T*, and corresponding degradation's parameters (i.e. w_{DD} and n_{DD}).

Note: we used N_{th} rather I_{th} in order to give more physical form and that will be useful to complete the analysis further to include the next two stages (not indicated here). However, one simply can substitute $N_{th}^{total}(T) = \frac{I_{th}^{total}(T).\tau_e(T)}{qV}$ in order to calculate t_{on} in term of $I_{th}^{total}(T)$.

3. Results and discussion

Parameter values of SLD at room temperature can be found in Table 1. The effect of temperature of operation, T, and the number of dark defects, n_{DD}, on the $I_{th}^{total}(T)$ and $N_{th}^{total}(T)$ is shown in Fig. 2a and Fig. 2b respectively. According to the mathematical model of I_{th}^{total} presented in [2] and after the modification (considering the TD of I_{th}^{total}, i. e. $I_{th}^{totald}(T)$, we note at

Table 1. Parameter values used in calculations

Parameter	Description	Value	Unit
d	Active region thickness	0.2	μm
W	Active region width	5	μm
L	Cavity length	500	μm
A	Nonradiative recombination coefficient	5.10^{8}	sec^{-1}
B	Radiative recombination coefficient	1.10^{-16}	m^3/sec
C	Auger recombination coefficient	3.10^{-41}	m^6/sec
g_o	Differential gain	$2.5.10^{-20}$	m^2
Γ	Confinement factor	0.3	
α_{int}	Internal loss	40	cm^{-1}
v_g	Group velocity	$7.5.10^{9}$	cm/sec
C_{light}	Speed of light	3.10^{10}	cm/sec
q	Charge of electron	$1.6.10^{-19}$	C
N_o	Carrier density at transparency	$1.\ 10^{18}$	cm^{-3}
n_g	Group refractive index	4	
r1, = r2	Field reflectiveties of the laser facets	0.566	
I_{inj}	Injection current	2 $I_{th}(T_o)$	A

Fig. 2a the increasing of $I_{th}^{total}(T)$ with T and n_{DD} due to increasing of $N_{th}(T)$ and I_{th}^{total} respectively. In Fig. 2b, $N_{th}^{total}(T)$ increases with T due to increasing of carrier density at transparency, N_t, decreasing of gain coefficient, g_o, and increasing of cavity internal loss, α_i.. and also, $N_{th}^{total}(T)$ increases with the increasing of n_{DD} according to Eq. (5) [2]. Here we combined the influence of both T and n_{DD} by considering, the TD of N_{th} of the normal "good" SLD active region, in the I_{th}^{total} model given by [2]. The worst case of N_{th} is when the DBUSLD operates at higher temperature degrees and with large n_{DD}, for instance (as a comparison), at T = 25°C (room temperature) and n_{DD} =0 (no degradation), N_{th} = $1.837\times10^{18}cm^{-3}$ while it increases

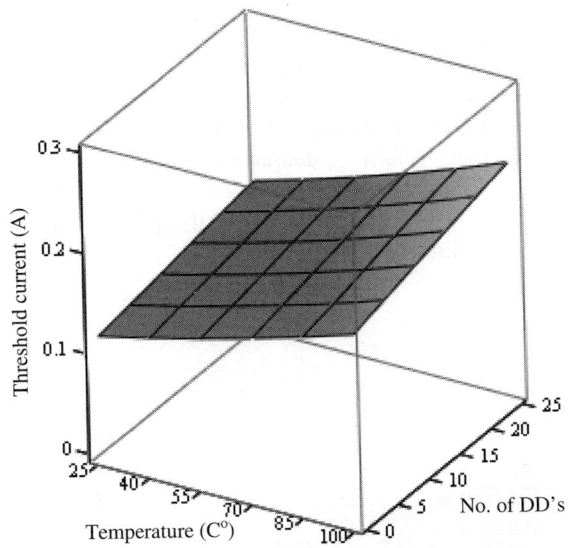

Fig. 2a Threshold current vs. the temperature of operation and number of DD's for DBUSLD.

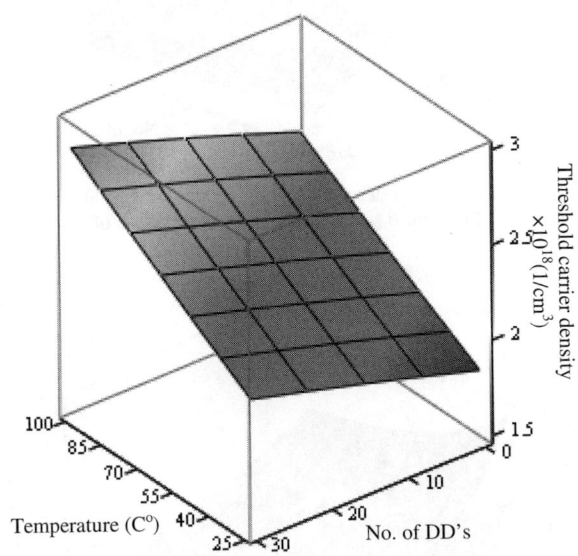

Fig. 2b Threshold carrier density vs. the temperature of operation and number of DD's for DBUSLD.

To $2.814\times10^{18}cm^{-3}$ at T = 100 °C and n_{DD} = 25.
Fig. 3 shows the calculated t_{on} as a function of T and n_{DD} for bit-rate, B_{rate}=4 Gb/s, and different values of N_{bit}. It is noted that t_{on} increases with the increasing of T and n_{DD} due to increasing of N_{th} and N_i. In addition, when N_{bit} increases the whole graphs moves up, i. e. t_{on} increases, because physically, N_{th} (which will be as N_i

for the next "one" pulse) has enough time between the pulses to decrease (diminish) to low level values before the next "one" bit. Also we note that t_{on} takes higher values when n_{DD} is large especially at high temperature degrees. Finally, Fig. 4 is the same of Fig. 3 but for N_{bit} = 1 and different values of bit-rates (B_{rate} = 1, 4 and 7 Gb/s). We note that when B_{rate}, i. e. bit time decreases, N_i increases then in turn t_{on} decreases correspondingly. Physically, N_{th} which will be as N_i for the next "one" pulse has no enough time to decrease; therefore, it still has a relatively high significant value.

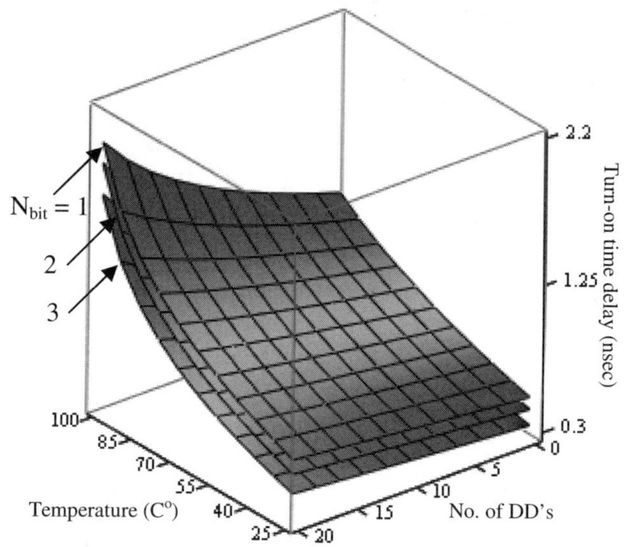

Fig. 3 Turn-on time delay vs. the temperature of operation and number of DD's for B_{rate}= 4 Gb/s and different values of N_{bit}.

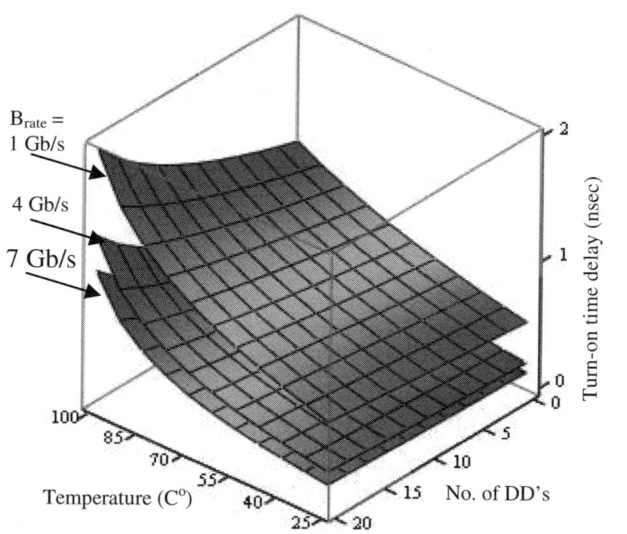

Fig. 4 Turn-on time delay vs. the temperature of operation and number of DD's for N_{bit}=1 and different values of bit-rates.

In this paper we studied the influence of temperature of operation of degraded bulk semiconductor laser and the number of dark defects by considering the threshold carrier density as function of temperature then inserted it in a total threshold current model of degraded bulk SLD presented in [2] to obtain the TD one. In order to obtain the corresponding threshold carrier density we derived full and exact analytical expression form of carrier density in term of laser cavity parameters and current flowed through the SLD active region.. In addition, the effect of dark defects on the turn-on time delay is calculated in the presence of temperature of operation using a full and exact analytical expression form. It is noted that t_{on} increases with the increasing of n_{DD} and T. The analysis can be extended further to include the transient response of degraded bulk uncooled SLD.

Reference

1. K. Hausler, U. Zeimer, B. Sumpf, G. Erbert, G. Trankle, J. Mater Sci: Mater Electron, ©Springer Science + Business Media, **LLC** (2008).
2. T. Kallstenius, J. Backstrom, U. Smith, and B. Stoltz, J. of Lightwave Technol., **17**, 12, (1999).
3. M. Fukudas. Norwood, MA: Artech House (1991).
4. M. Fukuda, Elsevier Science Ltd., Microelectronics Reliability, **42**, 679 (2002).
5. M. Fukuda, Elsevier Science Ltd., Microelectronics Reliability, **46**, 263 (2006).
6. M. Fukuda, Elsevier Science Ltd., Microelectronics, Reliability, **47**, 1619 (2007).
7. T. Stephens, K. Hinton, T. Anderson, and B. Clarke, J. of Lightwave Technol., **13**,4 (1995).
8. P. Pepeljugoski, D. Kuchta and j. Crow, IEEE Photon. Technol. Lett. **8**, 461 (1996).
9. K. Obermann, S. Kindt and k. Petermann, IEEE Photon. Technol. Lett. , **8**, 31 (1996).
10. M. Ming and K. Liu, McGraw-Hill companies, Inc (1996).
11. G. P. Agrawal and N. K. Dutta, New York: Van Nostrand Reinhold (1986).
12. D. M. Curter and K Y. Lau, IEEE Photon. Technol. Lett. **7**,4 (1995).
13. M. R. Hassan, European Phys. J. Appl. Phys, **41**, 41 (2008).
14. J. P. Morgado and A. T. Cartaxo, IEEE J. Select. Topic Quantum Electron., **9**, 1315 (2003).
15. T. Peng, Y. Huang, C. Yang, K. Huang, F. Lee, C. Hu, M. Wu, and C. Ho, IEEE Photon. Technol. Lett., **18**, 12 (2006).

Oops I saw somethin! Ease of access to online adult material by minors

Suku Sinnappan
IT Systems and Multimedia Dept,
Swinburne University of Technology
Victoria, Australia
ssinnappan@swin.edu.au

Peter Vigilante[1], Eileen Robinson[2], Marcus Hughes[3], Ibraam Mansour[4]
Faculty of Higher Education Lilydale
Swinburne University of Technology
Victoria, Australia
Email: 4157001@swin.edu.au[1], 5694957@swin.edu.au[2], 5678293@swin.edu.au[3], 5407249@swin.edu.au[4]

Abstract - This research discusses a pressing issue involving minors and adult materials online. In specific, researchers proposed a framework based on user created content (UCC), technology availability, parental monitoring and internet literacy in an Australian context. The effects of exposure to adult material at a young age are damaging and the increase of internet literacy amongst minors coupled with the spread of UCC based applications is even more concerning.

Adult material, minors, parent monitoring, user created content, internet access

I. Introduction

With increased use of the internet, greater amounts of minors (persons under the legal age) are intentionally or unintentionally exposed to adult material online. Increased internet literacy, lack of parental control, poor internet filters and the increase of UCC sites have immensely contributed to this issue. In today's generation, minors' online activity covers sites such as YouTube, MySpace, Flickr, Bebo, Del.ici.ous, BoingBoing, etc. These sites facilitate self publishing and file sharing where users can write about themselves, upload videos and share it over the internet. Many sites have followed suit to emulate the business model and have found the same reception from the online community which highlights user empowerment [1]. It has been noted that UCC is one of the key subjects in "participative web" [2]. The spread of UCC activities have been a great concern and have been widely discussed even though they are not motivated by economical reasons.

Given the drift, the adult industry has also redefined itself to embrace UCC. Reportedly many forums, blogs, and website have been inundated with adult related topics and exchange of files. Notably, several commercial sites have directly emulated YouTube and leveraged of its popularity and parts of its name "You" and "Tube" separately. Sites such as YouPorn, Sex2ube, Xtube, Redtube and others which will later be reviewed as part of this paper has used UCC as the main thrust of their business model. This approach is central to the argument of this paper which links adult UCC sites and the popularity of UCC activi

amongst young internet users as noted by the [3]. These adult sites operate on the same idea as YouTube except explicit adult material is displayed here. Videos are uploaded by the users and rated on a five star scale. Other features on these sites allowed users to share and create a network of friends. The problems arising from exposure to adult material in a young age has been much discussed in various literatures [4]. Most problems are related to unplanned pregnancies, imitation of behaviours, biased attitude towards a particular gender, distorted mental development, deformed perception towards sex and anatomy. It was cited in Monitor on Psychology that according to a study in February Paediatrics Journal 2007, that 42 per cent of children from age 10 to 17 have been exposed to adult materials online [5]. Similar alarming figures were found in an Australian study where three quarters of 16 to 17 year olds were exposed accidentally to adult materials online [6]. This is only the tip of the iceberg for the Australian scene. According to 'Builder Au' a report by Secure Computing found that the .com.au domain name space had 5.6 million separate pages of adult material [7]. Only two other countries were raked higher than Australia. These were Germany with over 10 million pages and the United Kingdom with 8.5 million. The report excluded the .com domain name space as their location is difficult to be identified. This highlights the severity of the problem and signals the need for government intervention. Even leading search engine – Google, has noted difficulty in curbing this problem with even its safest filters. This is due to the reason that filters work on text rather than the semantic meaning derived from an image or video. This limitation and the aforementioned issues form the main discussions within this paper, which draws on a framework build on Australian context. The paper has five sections and is organised as follows. The second section will focus on online adult materials and its effects on minors and the popularity and drivers of UCC. Issues related to government laws, ... nalysis. monitoring and internet filters will ... will be thereafter. The next section ... framework, rese... Finally

II. Online Adult Materials, UCC and Its Effect on Minors

The growth of the adult industry online is overwhelming. BBC UK recently reported that the porn industry is worth 30 billion pounds quoting a report from Forbes.com [8]. This multi million dollar industry is growing by the minute, and owes much of its success to the ease of accessing adult material and current technology facilitating UCC. The amount of blogs, wikis, forums and website catering adult materials is overwhelming. A simple Google search on "porn" or "adult material" returns millions of hits in a split of a second. This demonstrates the ease of access to adult material and answers why there are so many internet filters around. This worrying development is backed by empirical research highlighting the effects of adult material exposure on minors. The word minor is best described by [9] as individuals who are under full legal age by the law governing the particular country. In Australia a minor is considered being a person under the age of 18 where they are not allowed to vote legally at elections, drink alcohol nor drive a motor vehicle. It is accepted at this age they are still in a development stage both physiologically and emotionally. This leaves them vulnerable to Internet predators but also to age-inappropriate materials. Studies done by [4, 6] conclusively prove that exposure to adult material is harmful. It has been noted that children exposed to these materials misjudge message by mentally accepting that taking part in sex without responsibility is acceptable and fun. They further emulate the same actions either willingly against other children [10], which then leads to childhood sexual abuse or premature sex. Other more common effects of age-inappropriate exposure leads to deformed moral values and lifestyles. The efforts of parents to mould and inculcate virtues values with regards to relationships, love and affection can have a discouraging outcome. Minors are not neurologically ready for an overt exposure to sexually explicit materials; however selected and staggered exposure of sexual norms can lead to a child's healthy sexual orientation. However, the uptake of UCC and communication gadgets such as 3G mobile phones (connected to high speed internet access) paints a dim future in curbing this issue. This combination allows minors with mobile phones that are 3G internet capable to be able to surf the internet without supervision giving them plenty of opportunities to access and share objectionable materials. A recent article in the Independent.ie reported that children as young as 10 years of age are sharing explicit pictures of themselves online [11]. [illegible] further raises the question of how should parents, [illegible] society at large monitor children in their [illegible] what extent should ICANN be [illegible] should government take in [illegible]ing which promotes

The rise of UCC is well documented in a report produced by the Organisation for Economic Co-operation and Development (OECD) in April 2007 and further discussed by [14]. Report discusses how UCC has moved initially from a grassroots movement towards a monetisation with the backing from establish media and internet players. Somehow UCC is a great appeal to the younger generation compared to the other age groups. It was noted that more than half of all 12 to 17 year old Americans use online social networking sites [13]. This seems to be a trend overall the world. The drivers of UCC could be narrowed down to four factors [see 14]; technological drivers – The availability of broadband [12], social drives, economic drivers and Creative Commons licences. The types of UCC and its distribution platforms are discussed in [14], alongside business and revenue models. It seems to be evolving at a rate requiring intervention especially when there are minors involved.

III. Government Laws, Parent Monitoring and Internet Filters

Numerous policies and directives have been initiated by various governments to curb unwanted exposure of adult materials in recent years [15]. Australia has made a number of progresses alongside this global effort. The government has introduced laws to deter would be adult material hosts from setting up locally in Australia. There are criminal penalties in place that prohibit 'X' rated material or material that has been refused classification from being hosted from within Australia. The laws also prohibit the 'R' classified material from being hosted in Australia unless it is subject to adult verification systems [16, 17]. Given the rapid diffusion of internet and the lag in policing, many countries' policies are found outdated and outpaced. Much of the attempts are hampered by the citizen's constitutional right to exercise freedom of speech. It has been suggested that by having an international censorship of the internet would alleviate these issues. However, having the international censorship is demonstrated as being ineffective due to the fact that what is illegal in one country is not illegal in others, and what is deemed unsuitable for minors in one country is not in others. For example films classified R18 in Australia are often classified suitable for persons under 18 years in other countries. e.g. Intimacy (sex scenes) and Hannibal (violence) are classified 18+ in Australia, but are classified 12+ in France. However, France prohibits the display of Nazi related material, including on web pages, which is not prohibited by Australian laws [15]. To this end there isn't a globally accepted solution. The suggestion of the XXX domain in 2006 was probably the closest to addressing this globally. However, the organization that governs Internet domain names (Internet Corporation for Assigned Names and Numbers - ICANN) voted against this proposal [18]. However, the revived discussion about the rule changes to domain names might bring new leads to this [19].

Internet filters are seen as the other solution to address this issue. Filters are normally used to assist parents to block adult material from minors under the age of 18 in Australia. This includes the use of various commercial available filters as well as filters provided by Internet Service Providers. Governments are also morally obligated to test and make recommendation on filters and their performances [20]. To this end, there have been many complaints lodged by concerned parties against the government citing less support and direction with regards to which is the ultimate filter. However, most fail to realise that filters are intended to be used as a precautionary tool on top of parental supervision rather than a single method of protection. Most internet filters work on keywords within Meta tags [21]. If one particular word was found in a Meta tag of a particular site then access to that site will be blocked. Different level settings of adult filters can have different keywords to search for. Unfortunately a downside with this method of filtering is that it can only filter out text based keywords. In effect this means that if a host was to label an adult website or section of a site as something completely different to any adult material then it would bypass the filter. Current technology does not filter images and videos, only text [21]. Other smarter solutions rely on colour clustering. These filters can be set to weed out images which have skin looking like colour pixels. Again, this is fruitless if the images are greyscale.

The Australian Government has certain regulations listed on the Net Alert website, which apply towards Internet Service Providers (ISPs) and their responsibility concerning adult material and minors. Under Australian laws, legislation and codes of practices ISPs need to ensure that logical methods are undertaken to make sure that Internet accounts are not issued to minors under the legal age of 18 in Australia without parental control [20]. In addition to this Internet Service Providers need to supply filtering software for end users or a filtered service direct from the service provider. The Australian Government has also lists several different recommended applications to be used as filters on their Net Alert website (http://www.netalert.gov.au) allowing parents to have individual settings for children of different ages in the family, which can be a great tool to stop younger children from accessing the likes of chat rooms. These softwares use dynamic page analysis and a constant updated database of listed website to filter adult material [20].

IV. CONCEPTUAL FRAMEWORK, RESEARCH METHODOLOGY AND ANALYSIS

From the aforementioned issues we constructed a conceptual framework to address the issue of ease of access of adult material by minors. Central to this framework is minors' internet and technological device literacy and availability, parent monitoring, internet filters, government laws, and adult UCC sites' usability features and popularity. It could be said that, minors that have good internet literacy and knowledge of how to operate technological devices can participate in UCC sites. This is also dependent on parental monitoring, the type of internet filters used and the local government laws. The choice of UCC site would be heavily influenced by how user friendly it is and how widely has it been popular (accepted) among peers. We foresee that even unintentional access is possible given that not many minors would have the ability to read and digest each website's disclaimers with words such as jurisdiction, legal, perjury, etc. The proposed framework (Figure 1) was designed to capture these issues via these hypotheses.

H1 Minors' internet literacy and availability of technological device will increase adult internet access via popular UCC websites and confusing legal and disclaimers.

H2. Minors' internet literacy and availability of technological device will increase adult internet access with poor parental monitoring, weak internet filter and inadequate government laws.

H3. Popular UCC websites and confusing legal and disclaimers will increase online adult material access.

H4. Poor parental monitoring, weak internet filter and inadequate government laws will increase online adult material access.

In order to explore some of the issues and understand the severity of the problem researchers adopted action research method and broke the research into two phases (i.e. survey and online web content analysis). To qualify respondents will have to be aged eighteen years and over. Convenient sampling method will be adopted, whereby questionnaires will be placed at university communal places such as café, bar, gym and sports centre. Researchers also came up with a simple set of questions as shown in Table 1 to address the sensitivity of the topic. It is anticipated that the first phase of the research will be carried out soon while the second phase of the research was to review UCC based adult websites to get a clearer picture of how the websites were designed. Reportedly the adult industry

Table 1: The six questions and responses that are planned for the survey

No	Question/Attribute
1	Respondent's gender
2	Have the participants ever accessed online adult material as a minor
3	How easy it was to access the adult material when they were a minor
4	Do the participants need to confirm their age before entering the adult site
5	Was participants' internet usage was ever monitored as a minor
6	Whether as minors, participants felt that adult site disclaimers discouraged them from accessing the site

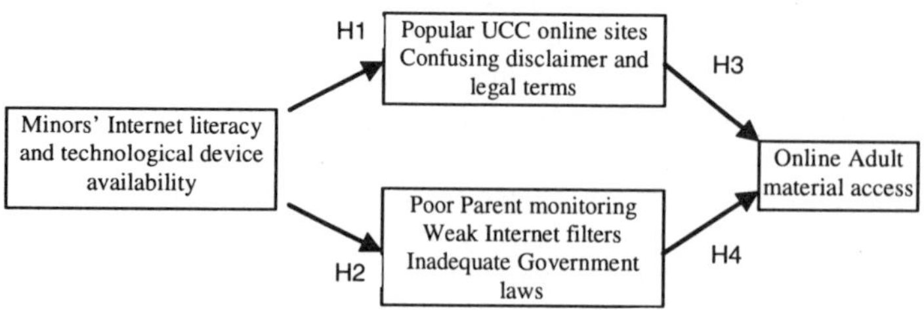

Fig 1: Conceptual framework depicting factors leading to ease of access of adult material by minors

has emulated Web 2.0, which is UCC based to create Porn 2.0 [24]. We wanted to observe the usability and sharing features, popularity and the terms that were used as part of their disclaimer to deter age-inappropriate access. Utilising Wikipedia and Google in combination we reviewed 20 adult sites (*www.vho.com, www.yuvutu.com, www.shufuni.com, www.xxxtube.net, www.pornhub.com, www.fantasti.cc, www.pornkolt.com, www.megarotic.com, www.tube8.com, www.spankwire.com, xhamster.com, www.pornhorneo.com, www.slutload.com, www.xtube.com, www.redtube.com, www.youporn.com, www.sex2ube.com, www.pornotube.com, www.hardcoretube.net, www.yoyovid.com*). The review highlighted the existing problem and was very concerning. Out of the 20 UCC based websites only two required verification of birth date. This means that younger age group children can easily access these. Other issue that caught our attention was the absence of the disclaimer on 55 per cent of the websites when the page was loaded. This meant that anyone typing the *url* would be directly exposed to adult materials. Most websites had good usability features including file sharing, search tools, language options, and click to view and categorized videos. Given the current internet literacy and computer usage in school, it is our belief that even average Australian students will be able to access the websites. It is also quite obvious that 40 per cent of the website sites have used the word "You" or "Tube" as part of their domain name to share the same popularity with YouTube. Further, the terms used on the disclaimer page was not helping either. Our analysis brought up words such *jurisdictions*, *onus*, *perjury*, *law 28 U.S.C 1746* and *objectionable*, which understandably would make no sense to a minor or deter any access. Finally, the domain names of these adult sites resemble nothing of its contents. For example *redtube, fantasti, vho, yuvutu, spankwire and xhamster*. Given the filter limitation due to 'text', these sites could be accessed with ease. This means that hypothesis H3 will most probably hold true, which presents a growing problem in today's digital age.

V. Conclusion and Future Research

In our review it was found that most commercially available internet filters come with the default setting of being low so in effect it seems that it is a smarter idea if it was set at a high filtering setting so that minors do not access adult material from initial start-up and that if setting need to be lowered they can without any mishaps initially. Even though most ISPs have some sort of filter in place for minors at the end user level, it appears to be a better idea if there were more filters in place at the server level to ensure that nothing gets through the network initially. When parents or customers in general are signing up to a new internet connection ISPs could ask whether or not they would be interested in filtering for the server level. If customers were to answer 'yes' then the filter is applied so that no adult material at all will be sent to the end user. Notifying the ISP can obviously turn this off. The downside to this is that it may slow down the users network as it is passing through a filter, in this case customers may need to be notified prior to the filter about this slight degradation in performance [25]. Filters provided from the ISPs some times come at a price, which is a bit of a letdown [22]. Even though it is the ISPs role to ensure that filtering software is provided under Australian law, they are still charging customers to have it in the first place, which causes a problem amongst families. ISPs need to provide parental control filters free of charge [26]. The Government has a major responsibility in ensuring that parents are well aware of the content on the Internet and that there can be inappropriate material can be accessed with real ease. There should be more done so that parents are taken into the equation when considering protecting minors from adult material. Parents should have more supervision over children and keep a much more watchful eye over children. It is practically impossible to prevent minors from viewing adult material online when only relying on Internet Filtering either from ISPs or from Filtering software. A recent initiative that aimed to promote learning by providing one laptop per child in Nigeria has resulted in a negative outcome. The educational equipment was found to be used to view online adult material. This shows that this can happened to minors from any part of the world. Other radical approaches are illustrated by the Saudi Arabian government for example; they blanket control the internet from one centre. They decide based on a set of rules of what is blocked. This technique makes it practically impossible for minors to access adult material. However, this blanket rule has its down side as not only minors are exempted but also the adults themselves. For disclaimers to have any effect in stopping minors from accessing adult material online they need to be clearer, easier to use and have a higher security level. [27] looks at the issues surrounding access to adult material and how easy it is for minors to access these sites as there is no way to actually verify the age of the user. Users are often faced with a "click here if you are 18 years or older" message. It is very easy for anyone to "click here" even if they are not of legal age according to their jurisdiction. These websites need a disclaimer that stops anyone from being able to "click here' and access adult material. To help ensure that minors cannot access adult material, disclaimers need to be much more prominent. Further, the security levels need to be higher to ensure the users are of legal age such as usage of credit card verification. Strong parental supervision of internet usage is also recommended to protect minors from adult material. Parents need to consider different methods of monitoring minors' internet use. This can include checking internet history logs, examining the cookie list, and placing computers in public location instead of in a study or a bedroom [28]. It would seem that the most effective way to stop minors from viewing adult material online is so make sure that their internet usage is supervised and monitored.

As a result of the exploratory nature of this proposed study, a number of directions for future research arise from this paper. First and foremost, the survey needs to be actioned with a large randomised sample size made up of the general minor population to avoid bias and to provide statistical rigor. Future research should also explore parents, teachers and other relevant parties to hear their concerns when it comes to monitoring internet usage. Finally, a study should be done on the direction the government and ISPs are taking with regards to UCC based adult website in order to minimise inappropriate-age exposure.

REFERENCES

[1] Sharp, D. 2006. "Digital Lifestyles Monitor." Retrieved 10 February 2008, From http://smartinternet.com.au/default.aspx?ArticleID=198#2006, Smart Internet CRC Pty Ltd.

[2] O'Reilly, T. 2005. "What Is Web 2.0 Design Patterns and Business Models for the Next Generation of Software", 30 September, from www.oreillynet.com/pub/a/oreilly/tim/news/2005/09/30/what-is-web-20.html.

[3] European Commission. 2006. "Interactive content and convergence: Implications for the information society", Study for the European Commission (DG Information Society and Media), October 2006, http://ec.europa.eu/information_society/eeurope/i2010/docs/studies/interactive_content_ec2006_final_report.pdf

[4] Chetty, I., and Basson, A. 2006. "Report of Internet Usage and The Exposure of Pornography to Learners in South African Schools". Retrieved on May 2008. From http://www.info.gov.za/view/DownloadFileAction?id=81355.

[5] DeAngelis, T. 2008. "Web pornography's effect on children" Retrieved 10 Aril 2008, From http://www.apa.org/monitor/nov07/webporn.html

[6] Flood, M. 2007. "Exposure to pornography among youth in Australia" Journal of Sociology, Vol. 43, No. 1, 45-60 (2007)

[7] Builder.au. 2004. Porn stats make mockery of AU censorship laws, Retrieved on 15/05/08 From http://www.builderau.com.au/news/soa/Porn-stats-make-mockery-of-AU-censorship-laws/0,339028227,339129723,00.htm

[8] BBC UK.com. 2005. "An acceptable career?". Retrieved on April 2008. From http://news.bbc.co.uk/2/hi/uk_news/magazine/4305257.stm

[9] Moore, B 1998, The Australian pocket oxford dictionary, 4th edn, Oxford University Press, Oxford.

[10] Kavanagh, S. 1997. "Protecting Children in Cyberspace" Springfield, VA: Behavioral Psychotherapy Center 58-59.

[11] Horan, N. 2008. "Children producing their own porn" Retrieved June 2008, From http://www.independent.ie/national-news/children-producing-their-own-web-porn-1410447.html

[12] Sharp, D., and Salomon, M. 2008. "User-led Innovation: A New Framework for Co-creating Business & Social Value" Retrieved 27 February 2008, From http://www.smartinternet.com.au/ArticleDocuments /121/ User_Led_Innovation_A_ New_Framework_ for_Co-creating_Business_and_Social_Value.pdf.aspx, Smart Internet CRC Pty Ltd

[13] Lenhart, A. and M. Madden (2007), .Social Networking Websites and Teens: An Overview., Pew Internet and American Life Project, 7 January, www.pewinternet.org/PPF/r/198/report_display.asp.

[14] OECD 2007. "Participative Web: User-Created Content" Retrieved 12 February 2008; From http://www.oecd.org/dataoecd/57/14/38393115.pdf

[15] Internet Censorship, Electronic Frontiers Australia, Retrieved on 14/05/2008 From http://www.efa.org.au/Issues/Censor/cens3.html

[16] Forbes, 1999.'Porn Sites Head Offshore To Beat Law' The Sydney Morning Herald, Retrieved on 14/05/2008

[17] ZDNet, 2003. 'New AU laws to target online porn, e-crime', ZDNet Australia, viewed 14/05/08

[18] CNNMoney. 2006. "Regulators votes against XXX domain", Retrieved January 2008, From http://money.cnn.com/2006/05/10/technology/icann_xxx/index.htm

[19] TheAge.com. 2008. "Rule changes to spark domain name goldrush", Retrieved June 2008, From http://www.theage.com.au/articles/2008/06/27/1214472719636.html

[20] Net Alert 2008, Australian Government, Retrieved on 13/5/2008
From http://www.netalert.gov.au

[21] The Meta Description Tag 2004, High Rankings, Retrieved on 26/5/2008, From http://www.highrankings.com/metadescription

[22] Bigpond Security Solution 2008, Telstra Corporation Limited, Retrieved on 14/5/2008
From http://www.bigpond.com/internet/security/default.asp

[23] Sekaran, U. (2004) Research methods For Managers: A Skill-building Approach, John Wiley and Sons, New York.

[24] Wikipedia,· 2008. "Porn 2.0" Retrieved June 2008, From http://en.wikipedia.org/wiki/Porn_2.0

[25] Moses, A. 2007, "ISP-level filter 'unworkable", The Age, Retrieved 14/5/2008
From http://www.theage.com.au/news/web/isplevel-filters-unworkable/2007/08/10/1186530595566.html

[26] N2H2 Incorporated 2002, Primus Telecommunications Pty Ltd, Retrieved 14/5/2008
From
http://www.iprimus.com.au/PrimusWeb/HomeSolutions/AdditionalServices/WebFilter/

[27] Freeman, L. 2000, 'Children, Teens, and Sex on the Internet', *Sexual Addiction & Compulsivity*, vol 7, no. 1-2, pg 75-90, Retrieved on 20th April 2008, PsycINFO database, AN 2000-03333-004

[28] Dombrowski, Gischlar, Durst, 2007, 'Safeguarding Young People from Cyber Pornography and Cyber Sexual Predation: A Major Dilemma of the Internet', *Child Abuse Review,* vol 16, no. 3, pg 153-170, Retrieved on 20th April 2008, PsycINFO database, AN 2007-10462-003.